# A History of
# Personal Workstations

# A History of Personal Workstations

*Edited by*
**Adele Goldberg**
ParcPlace Systems

ACM PRESS
New York, New York

ADDISON-WESLEY PUBLISHING COMPANY

Reading, Massachusetts ▪ Menlo Park, California
New York ▪ Don Mills, Ontario ▪ Wokingham, England
Amsterdam ▪ Bonn ▪ Sydney ▪ Singapore
Tokyo ▪ Madrid ▪ San Juan

This book is in the **ACM Press History Series**

**Library of Congress Cataloging-in-Publication Data**

A History of personal workstations / Adele Goldberg, editor.
    p.    cm. — (ACM Press history series)
  Revised versions of papers presented at ACM Conference on the
History of Personal Workstations, Jan. 9–10, 1986, Palo Alto,
Calif.; sponsored by Association for Computing Machinery.
  Includes index.
  ISBN 0–201–11259–0
  1. Computers—History—Congresses.  2. Microcomputer workstations—
History—Congresses.  3. Computer networks—History—Congresses.
I. Goldberg, Adele.  II. ACM Conference on the History of Personal
Workstations (1966: Palo Alto, Calif.)  III. Association for
Computing Machinery.  IV. Series.
QA76.17.H57  1988
004.16—dc19                                          87–35911
                                                     CIP

BCDEFGHIJ—HA—898

# Series Foreword

With *A History of Personal Workstations*, the ACM Press inaugurates its History Series, aimed at the preservation, recovery, and interpretation of the historical record of computers and computing. In addition to proceedings of ACM Conferences on the History of Computing and of similar conferences sponsored by other organizations, the series will encompass autobiographies and biographies, general historical surveys, and monographs on special topics. In conjunction with the Anthology Series, it will also include annotated collections of classic papers documenting the development of various areas of computing.

It is particularly fitting that the series should begin with *A History of Personal Workstations*. In supporting the conference on which it is based and in editing its proceedings, Adele Goldberg provided a firm organizational footing for continuing the gatherings that began so auspiciously with the Conference on the History of Programming Languages in 1978. As she noted in the planning document for the Conference series:

> ACM, as the premier scientific and technical society for information processing professionals, has the unique ability to bring together scientists, developers, and users to exchange information about specific areas of the computing field. Many areas have existed long enough to warrant a focused effort to bring together, likely for the first time, those pioneers whose vision and research have made major contributions to these areas. . . . The intent of the conferences is to promote a better understanding of the visions that led to some of the most compelling past research efforts, the impact of this work on the current state of the art, and the potential for impact on the future.

Over the past year two further conferences have taken place, the History of Scientific and Numerical Computation and the History of Medical Informatics. Others are being planned.

Both the conferences and the publications of the History Series are aimed not only at honoring the pioneers whose achievements constitute the history of computing but also at encouraging collaboration between computer professionals and the growing number of professional historians who are seeking to discern the developmental patterns that link those achievements with one another and with the wider technical and social contexts and thereby give them their historical meaning. As Editor of the Series, I invite proposals and inquiries from both communities.

Michael S. Mahoney
*Series Editor*

# Book Foreword

Twenty-five years ago computing was stationary, ponderous, and centralized. Its dominant role was to serve the critical needs and purposes of organizations and the sciences. Today matters are very different. Computation is personal, ubiquitous, and expansive. Power is being supplied at and to the fingertips of the individual. Computation is an amplifier of imagination and labor. The personal workstation is the gateway through which this power is supplied, harnessed, diversified, and distributed.

The transformation was not trivial, nor even inevitable. It was accomplished by people with energy, ambition, and purpose whose visions were supported by great technical expertise and insight. Their difficulties and triumphs are the stuff of which history is made. Thus it is important that we hear from them before the personal workstation becomes so packaged, so much a featureless part of our environment, that its nature and value become invisible, a mere part of the overhead of daily living.

Yale University                                                    Alan Perlis

Xerox Palo Alto Research Center                      John R. White

# Preface

History is made by people; it is made up of the events and inventions of people. The history of computing is especially affected by the visions of a few people. These people believe strongly in the significant technological changes that are possible. They strive to understand how computational and communications power can be made accessible to people in scientific laboratories, professional offices, hospitals, schools, and homes.

This book about a history is dedicated to the people who invented the personal workstation. In January 1986, many of the people who made the history of personal workstations met together in Palo Alto, California. At this meeting, they told their personal stories of how they, as individuals and as members of research teams, contributed to this history. The participants discussed results and trends in computer hardware technologies, software systems, communication networks, and applications for personal use. As representatives of significant centers of research, such as MIT, CMU, Stanford, and Xerox PARC, they also provided a sense of the culture that supported the pursuit of their visions of technology.

The meeting was the ACM Conference on the History of Personal Workstations, chaired by Professor Alan Perlis of Yale University and organized by Dr. John White of the Xerox Palo Alto Research Center. Alan and John brought together an exceptional group of people to tell their personal stories and to answer questions about who participated in which events, and to ponder why some events took place and why other events did not.

This book contains revised versions of the papers presented at the conference and transcripts of key introductions and question and answer sessions. Several referenced papers are included, dating as far back as 1945 with the Vannevar Bush proposal on the Memex machine. Where a conference paper was not available, transcribed speeches or reprints of previously published papers attempt to fill the gap.

Parts of the conference could not be captured in a hardcopy book, namely the films of systems designed by Sutherland, Kay, Engelbart, Schultz, and others. These films are collected together as two videotapes available from the ACM Publications Department. One is a two hour personality tape showing films and excerpts from each speaker's presentation. The other is an edited depiction of Alan Kay's dynamic banquet talk. These tapes are exciting companions to the book.

In reviewing the material, especially the question-answer sessions, two ideas among many stand out. Allan Newell tried to trace the existence of *determinism* in the history of the personal workstation, as he said, ''of the sort that historically makes things go down one path rather than another.'' He pointed out the role of ARPA in *not* funding personal workstation development specifically, and stimulated us to consider how the combinations of funded research, information transferred in site visits as well as conferences, and decisions not to fund a project ultimately affected the path of history.

Second, there is a sense of intellectual *idealism* throughout the personal histories recorded here. There is nothing explicit in the records that says that the research and development pursuits, whether driven from technological vision or business interests, were the by products of such idealism. But each person's efforts depict a search for some ideal, typically stated in terms of understanding how to empower human work efforts, that was rarely usurped by opportunities unexpected or uninvited. Listening to the tapes or reading the papers, one gets the feeling that the personal workstation was not the goal at all, and that the history is about some as yet unknown artifact or alternative to the way things are.

The individuals who organized the History of Personal Workstations Conference are acknowledged later in this book. I would like to express my appreciation to two other groups: the authors who responded to my editorial prodding, and the publications staff at ACM headquarters led by Janet Benton. Most importantly though, I wish to acknowledge Vicki Burich's assistance in bringing this book to final completion, having followed in the path of Jill Maleson who valiantly transcribed hours of audio tape. Initial preparation of the book was supported by Janet Romero. This is also my chance to say how much I enjoyed working with Ken Beckman on editing the videotapes, with Tim O'Shea who attended the conference through the editing process, and with Gloria Warner who proved as always to be the backbone of support needed in such a large project.

ParcPlace Systems                                    Adele Goldberg
Palo Alto, California

# Contents

# Program

**OPENING SESSION:**               *9:00–10:15 (Camino A & B)*

**Welcome**
William J. Spencer, Xerox Palo Alto Research Center

**Keynote Address: Toward a History of (Personal) Workstations**
Gordon Bell, National Science Foundation
(Discussant: Allen Newell, Carnegie-Mellon University)

Coffee Break:               *10:15–10:45 (Camino Foyer)*

**SESSION 2:**               *10:45–11:45 (Camino A & B)*

**A Personal View of the Personal Workstation:**
**Some Firsts in the Fifties**
Douglas Ross, SofTech/MIT
(Discussant: Severo Ornstein, CPSR)

**LUNCHEON:**               *11:45–1:00 (Camino C & D)*

**SESSION 3:**               *1:00–3:00 (Camino A & B)*

**Some Reflections on Early History**
J. C. R. Licklider, MIT Laboratory for Computer Science
(Discussant: Alan Perlis, Yale University)

**The ARPANET and Computer Networks**
Larry Roberts, Net Express West
(Discussant: Frank Kuo, SRI International)

Coffee Break:               *3:00–3:30 (Camino Foyer)*

**SESSION 4:**               *3:30–5:30 (Camino A & B)*

**Mathematical Laboratories:**
**A New Power for the Physical and Social Sciences**
Glen J. Culler, Culler Scientific Systems Corporation
(Discussant: Charles Irby, Metaphor)

**The Augmented Knowledge Workshop**
Doug Engelbart, McDonnell Douglas
(Discussant: Charles Irby, Metaphor)

**RECEPTION:**                6:00–7:30 *(Rose Room)*

**BANQUET:**                 7:30–10:00 *(Camino A & B)*

**BANQUET PRESENTATION:**

**The Dynabook—Past, Present, and Future**
Alan Kay, Apple Computer, Inc.
(Discussant: John Shoch, Asset Management)

---

*Friday, January 10, 1986*

---

**SESSION 5:**               8:30–10:30 *(Camino A & B)*

**Personal Distributed Computing:**
**The Alto and Ethernet Hardware**
Chuck Thacker, Digital Equipment Corporation Systems Research Center
(Discussant: Ed McCreight, Xerox Palo Alto Research Center)

**Personal Distributed Computing:**
**The Alto and Ethernet Software**
Butler Lampson, Digital Equipment Corporation Systems Research Center
(Discussant: Ed McCreight, Xerox Palo Alto Research Center)

Coffee Break:              10:30–11:00 *(Camino Foyer)*

**SESSION 6:**               11:00–12:00 *(Camino A & B)*

**The LINC Was Early and Small**
Wesley Clark, Clark, Rockoff, and Associates
(Discussant: Bert Sutherland, Sutherland, Sproull, and Associates, Inc.)

**LUNCHEON:**               12:00–1:00 *(Camino C & D)*

**SESSION 7:**               1:00–2:00 *(Camino A & B)*

**Hewlett-Packard and Personal Computing Systems**
Chuck House, Hewlett-Packard
(Discussant: Warren Teitelman, Sun Microsystems, Inc.)

Coffee Break:              2:00–2:30 *(Camino Foyer)*

**SESSION 8:**                          *2:30–4:30 (Camino A & B)*

**A History of the Promis Technology:**
**An Effective Human Interface**
Jan Schultz, Promis Information Systems
(Discussant: Peter Denning, RIACS-NASA Ames Research Center)

**User Technology From Pointing to Pondering**
Stuart Card and Thomas Moran, Xerox Palo Alto Research Center
(Discussant: Allen Newell, Carnegie-Mellon University)

# Conference Committee

**General Chairman and Program Chairman**
*Alan Perlis*
*Yale University*

**Conference Organization and Local Arrangements**
*John R. White*
*Xerox Palo Alto Research Center*

**Conference Support**
*Gloria Warner*
*Xerox Palo Alto Research Center*

**Proceedings**
*John R. White and Kathi Anderson*
*Xerox Palo Alto Research Center*

**Registration**
*Susan Mulhern*
*Xerox Palo Alto Research Center*

**Videotaping**
*Ken Beckman and Mark Chow*
*Xerox Palo Alto Research Center*

**ACM Headquarters Coordination**
*Helene S. Tannor*
*Association for Computing Machinery*

Standing (from left to right): Gordon Bell, Butler Lampson, John Shoch, Ed McCreight, Frank Kuo, Jan Schultz, Bert Sutherland, Allen Newell, Larry Roberts, Wes Clark, Doug Ross, Doug Engelbart, Stu Card, John Licklider, William Spencer, Chuck Thacker. Kneeling (from left to right): Charles Irby, Severo Ornstein, Alan Perlis, Bob Taylor, Glenn Culler, Tom Moran, Alan Kay, Peter Denning (behind Alan Kay).

John R. White received a B.A. degree in mathematics and M.S. and Ph.D. degrees in computer science from the University of California, Santa Barbara, in 1967, 1968, and 1974, respectively.

From 1967 to 1971 he was a member of the technical staff of the Computer Research Laboratory at UC Santa Barbara, where he worked on the development of the Culler-Fried On-Line System. In 1973 he joined the Faculty of the Department of Electrical Engineering and Computer Science at the University of Connecticut, where he served as an Assistant and then Associate Professor of Computer Science. From 1979 to 1981 he served as Chairman of the Computer Science Division. In 1982 Dr. White joined the Xerox Palo Alto Research Center and is currently Manager of the Computer Science Laboratory's Software Systems Area.

Dr. White is currently Chairman of ACM's SIG Board and a member of ACM Council. From 1984 to 1986 he served as the Pacific Region Representative to ACM Council and was a member of the Board of Directors and Executive Committee of the newly-formed Computing Sciences Accreditation Board. As a member of the ACM SIGPLAN Executive Committee, he served as Secretary-Treasurer, Vice Chairman, and Chairman.

# Introduction to the Conference

The papers and discussions contained in this book were originally presented at the ACM Conference on the History of Personal Workstations held January 9–10, 1986, in Palo Alto California. The Conference was sponsored by the Pacific Region of ACM and hosted by the Xerox Palo Alto Research Center (PARC).

The idea for a conference on the history of personal workstations evolved from discussions between Al Perlis of Yale University and Bill Spencer, Manager of Xerox PARC. PARC was celebrating its 15 year anniversary, and the idea of a meeting focused on personal workstations seemed like an excellent way to initiate the celebration. Al Perlis agreed to contact potential speakers and try to convince them that a History of Personal Workstations Conference would be a unique opportunity—something not to be missed. In addition, Al had been involved with the 1978 ACM SIGPLAN Conference on the History of Programming Languages, so he knew what perspective to convey in the invitation. The quality of the conference program is a credit to Al Perlis's persuasive personality.

Adele Goldberg suggested that ACM sponsor the Conference to give it an appropriate home and help provide the infrastructure needed to pull off the meeting. Since I both worked at PARC and was active in the ACM, I agreed to organize the meeting and edit the conference proceedings. Kathi Anderson of the Computer Science Laboratory helped immensely with the proceedings and in maintaining contact with authors. Gloria Warner and Susie Mulhern of Xerox provided excellent advice on local arrangements and handled conference registration. Ken Beckman and Mark Chow, also from Xerox PARC, were responsible for videotaping the entire meeting.

There were 13 presentations spread over two days. Each presentation was an hour in length except for Alan Kay's two-hour banquet talk. In addition, each speaker was introduced by an individual that was a part of the history being reported. These "discussants" helped stimulate and lead the discussion that followed each talk.

Without a doubt, the Conference was an unqualified technical success. We all owe a debt of appreciation to the authors for having taken time from current pursuits to rummage through ancient files and resurrect the facts, data, and memories surrounding the early events that have led to modern personal workstations.

Computer Science Laboratory                                    John R. White
Xerox Palo Alto Research Center

# KEYNOTE ADDRESS: TOWARD A HISTORY OF (PERSONAL) WORKSTATIONS

## Gordon Bell
Introduction by Allen Newell

**Allen Newell (left)**
**Bill Spencer (right)**

The simplest way to introduce Gordon is to say he's one of the world's leading computer designers. However, that doesn't necessarily recommend him to be the keynote speaker at a conference on the history of the workstation. There are a couple of other things to be said about him that make it quite relevant that he give the keynote speech.

First of all, of course, Gordon is a product of that whole MIT-related environment up in the northeast corner of the United States from which so much of the development of workstations has come. He did his master's degree at MIT, working with Ken Stevens on speech recognition. He went from there to Digital Equipment Corporation, where he was a principal in Digital's PDP efforts over many years: the PDP-4, the PDP-5, the PDP-8, the PDP-6, the PDP-10, the PDP-11, the PDP-16, (nobody remembers the '16 except Gordon and myself, and perhaps Wes Clark, but there was something called the PDP-16), the VAX, not the PDP-12 (which was related to the LINC and Wes Clark). All of these machines played important enabling roles with respect to our topic here.

Gordon did come to Carnegie-Mellon University in the mid-1960s, which is when I first met him. He has this love-hate relationship with Digital—he went through a hate phase and showed up at Carnegie for about six or seven years, before going back. He never really left Digital,

1

Gordon Bell is currently Vice President of Engineering, Ardent Computer Corporation. He was educated at the Massachusetts Institute of Technology, where he received a S.B. (1956) and S.M. (1957). After a year in Australia as a Fulbright scholar (1958), Gordon continued at MIT in the Division of Sponsored Research Speech laboratory until joining Digital Equipment Corporation in 1960.

At Digital, Gordon was the designer of the PDP-1 Message Switch for ITT (1960–1961). He was architect/designer of the PDP-4 (1962–1963), PDP-5 (1964), PDP-6 (1963–1966), and PDP-11 (1969) hardware and software. From 1966 until 1972, Gordon Bell served as Professor at the Carnegie-Mellon University, returning to Digital in 1972 as Vice-President of Engineering. He held this position until 1983 when he became a founder and Vice-Chairman of Encore Computers. In 1986, Gordon expanded his entrepreneurial activities as a founder and Chief Scientist of Dana Computers, manufacturers of single user supercomputers.

Gordon is coauthor of many books and papers on computer structures and design, especially related to multiprocessor design. He is the recipient of the ACM/IEEE Eckert–Mauchley Award and the McDowell Award. In addition, he is a Member of the National Academy of Engineering.

of course, because things like the PDP-11 and the beginnings of the VAX all happened while he was at Carnegie.

There are other things that you need to know about Gordon. One of them is that he was a key member in founding the Computer Museum in Boston, directed by Gwen Bell. As a matter of fact, Gwen is out here and she has a big inverse Santa Claus bag. If anyone has any great workstation artifacts, you are supposed to just dump them in this bag as you leave the room, and she will take them back to the Computer Museum. So, that's another connection with the history of computers.

Back in the early 1970s, Gordon and I wrote a book called *Computer Structures*. To be more precise, because that's the way it always is with Gordon, I helped Gordon to write this book. I cleaned up the prose and did a few things like that on it. That book really reveals Gordon's interest in developing the frameworks within which things happen. As some of you know, our first and preferred title for that book was *Computer Botany*, not *Computer Structures*. We viewed our goal as laying out the whole structure of the collection of the artifacts we call computers. They were proliferating and needed to be understood, studied, and classified. That same attitude has been with Gordon throughout his career, as I am sure you will see in his talk today. In fact, I could have predicted that Gordon would take the view, which I share, that you can't really write history about things until you have the space laid out in which that history can occur. I think that Gordon's role for us today is to lay out some of the dimensions of the space of workstations so that we can then proceed to deal with the history.

# Toward a History of (Personal) Workstations

*C. Gordon Bell*
Computer and Information Science and Engineering Director
National Science Foundation

I originally accepted this keynote honor for several reasons. First, of course, was to respond to Alan Perlis's request because, ever since he headed the Computer Science Department at Carnegie-Mellon University where he was my boss, I have really had a hard time saying no to Alan. Second, was one to which Allen Newell alluded—to identify the important artifacts that should be preserved in the Computer Museum and, as one of the curators of the museum, to tune up my view of history. The third was to posit a taxonomy of the history of workstations in an evolutionary framework, both in product and in process. How does the technology across all the components drive this evolution? I always insist on knowing the whole picture, going back to the beginning and seeing if I can trace it since 1949 or so. Then, certainly, I feel compelled to write the history into the future, which is no good unless you can get it up to the year 2000. I stop in this history at about 1990. I think it is important when you are doing history to be able to look into the history of the future as well.

It turns out that there were three other reasons to write this paper, all of which were selfish. One was that this might be an interesting way of putting such an evolutionary book together. So I took this as a challenge; this is a breadboard for an outline (I think in terms of breadboards and prototypes and production machines and, ultimately, obsolesence). Then there was some work that I spent six years on, up until 1982, that's now clearly bearing fruit. This is work on VAX and the VAX Strategy, which is the notion of building a hierarchy of compatible machines. I had to put that into an appendix to record this work since I'm not at Digital now. I couldn't help but write that piece of history into the paper in order to clean up that piece of my life. So you may find that this paper is a patchwork quilt, and this is my apology for that patch of the quilt. I believe it is important in the history of workstations since VAX has about 10 percent of the workstation market.

Finally, an idea that has been in my head for many years is that, as an historian, what we really need is an historian's workstation. I hope coming out of this conference will be somebody that will take on the role of building historian's workstations so that, in fact, histories are much easier to do. It's obviously a very important segment of artificial intelligence, because artificial intelligence has a whole discipline that deals with truth maintenance.

## Introduction to the Conference

In June 1976, an international conference was held resulting in a collection of views published in *A History of Computing in the Twentieth Century* (Metropolis, Howlett, and Gian-Carlo, 1980). The participants presented work up to the early 1950s and thus had the benefit of 30 years of hindsight. The late mathematics historian, Kenneth May, outlined the pitfalls of participant-written histories, commenting: ''Historical description requires a time-lagged approach and means getting into understanding things as people understood them then, not as we understand them now.'' He also urged everyone to be open. Most autobiographies rewrite the past from the present perspective. Good diarists and notetakers have reference points. The best we can do is provide grist for the mill of the historian.

The History of Programming Languages Conference held in May 1977 (Wexelblat, 1981) provided a timeline to 1970 as context with detailed coverage of: Algol 60, APL, APT, BASIC, COBOL, FORTRAN, GPSS, JOSS, JOVIAL, LISP, PL/1, SIMULA, and SNOBOL. This covered a period of initial developments from 1954 (FORTRAN) to 1967 (APL) with evolutions up to the present. Ten to twenty years of hindsight gave them the ability to select topics.

If this conference were limited to a 15-year rule, applied by the *Annals of Computing History,* no one would be describing personal workstations. Only a few experiments existed, but people were building systems with multiple graphics terminals and a workstation industry on a profession-by-profession basis started to form. Twenty years ago, most of us were trying to make our newly designed interactive, timesharing system work reliably and economically. In my own case, having also worked on small machines that ultimately became the minicomputer, I saw two independent threads for economical computing, including interactive computing: large shared systems and dedicated small computers.

Personal workstations, like other man-made objects, appear strictly evolutionary, going through the following stages:

1950s   idea (documented article, proposal, movie) stimulated through early stand-alone use of small computers (e.g., LGP-30, G-15)

1960s   breadboards to demonstrate the idea and selected use of large computers with graphic displays (e.g., DEC PDP-1, IBM 7090, LINC, TX-2)

1970s  (early) limited use of interactive shared workstations using graphic display terminals connected to mini-computers; establishment of an industry to supply terminals and professional applications software

1970s  (late) working prototypes of personal workstations with concept testing through use in a complete environment (Xerox PARC)

1981  introduction of personal workstations by Apollo, SUN, Xerox, and first use by early adopters

1983  full-scale use for selected professionals; many companies formed; JAWS (just another workstation) term coined

1985  healthy industry with evolutionary product cycle and beginning shake out of suppliers

?  steady state supply to captive users

?  decline through replacement or superposition of functions in some other form of information processing appliance (e.g., conventional personal computers)

?  extinction

Hence just as we should concentrate on tracing various workstations through these stages, we may also treat this as a conference about the first phases of development. More hindsight will be needed to write history.

Waiting longer, which gives a future view, has the risk that extinction will come through agglomeration with conventional computing. Alan Perlis urged me to come to this conference because he feared this extinction. Conventional personal computers, that is the evolving IBM PC, will become the de facto workstations for virtually all applications by 2005. The latest chip introduction by Intel strongly permits and supports this to occur, if history is any indicator.

The real workstation phenomena and industry are not well described or recorded at all because most of the products have come from industry, where individuals are not rewarded for writing papers but for producing and selling machines. Examples are, Doug Drane and the ATEX system produced law and typesetting offices, doing essentially what a STAR does, only five years earlier and less expensively; GE's genigraphic system for the graphic artist; Bill Poduska and the Apollo workstations; or Applicon, Calma, Computervision, DEC, Evans and Sutherland, IBM, REDAC, Wang, Datapoint's ARCnet, and so on. No university (other than Utah and Brown) really participated until 1980. Noticeably absent are Dave Evans, whose direct contributions or indirect contributions through products at Evans and Sutherland, and graduate students who went on to create much of the science behind workstations. Ivan Sutherland's work was recorded. Xerox PARC was a notable exception, which published its work in a delayed fashion and was marginally successful at taking the research into products in a commercially viable fashion.

We now need to focus and agree on some definitions and dimensions, making sure the various threads of personal workstation development are explored so the historical facts can be recorded properly and eventually interpreted by real historians. We need to find the first use of the name. For example, the second edition of the *Encyclopedia of Computer Science and Engineering,* 1983, uses the word three times, but in a somewhat different context. By the summer of 1983, the phrase JAWS (just another workstation company) could be heard in the venture capital community when they realized they had funded too many companies to build personal workstations.

## What a (Personal) Workstation Is

Terminals connected to large computers (supercomputers, mainframes, and minicomputers) and utilizing interactive professional-applications programs are the clearest antecedents. These had, as direct descendants, terminals connected to shared, but dedicated, minicomputer systems in the mid-1970s to deliver cost-effective computing. An overview of the classic machines and the classes they formed is given in Fig. 1.

Fig. 2 shows several paths leading to the personal workstation. Large machines (with large memories) provide the major impetus. Large shared systems allow the price per terminal to fall in line with the salaries of the professionals using the station. Four lines, corrected for inflation, depict the LINC price, the cost of a supported professional (e.g., an engineer or scientist), the starting professional's salary, and a clerk's salary. The price of facilities such as a computer are ''pegged'' to these constants. The justification of equipment is usually based either on productivity or achieving some new level of performance or capability. While salaries of clerks are greater than $10,000, the workstation industry believes $10,000 to be a magic, highly elastic price barrier that will increase sales. In the later part of the 1980s, large personal computers will easily have enough memory and capability to take over all functions provided by nearly any of today's personal computers or personal workstations. Constant price, very powerful, large workstations will continue to be built, but the mass market will be served by the rapid price decline inherent in the IBM PC evolution.

A *personal workstation* is a relatively large (greater than 50 pounds) and expensive ($10,000 to over $100,000 in 1985) personal computer, with the appropriate transducers, used by a professional to carry out

**FIGURE 1**
Computer system
prices at introduction
and classes versus
time.

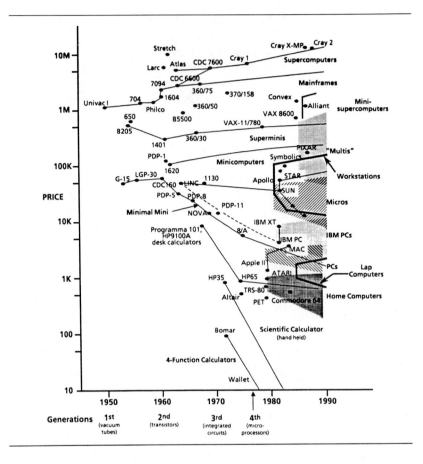

generic (e.g., calculation, mail, and communication) and profession-related activities such as music composition, financial modeling, or computer-aided design of integrated circuits.

Personal workstations are necessarily distributed with the person and interconnected to one another forming a single, *shared* (work and files) but *distributed computing environment*—the *workstation environment*. A workstation's location is either with an individual on a dedicated basis or in an area shared by several members of a group. This choice is dictated by the cost and size of the workstation, relative to the cost and value of the work.

Personal workstations appeared *by name* about 1981 with the concurrent appearance of:

□ microprocessors with at least one-half megabyte of physical memory virtual memory addressing

□ memory chips of at least 64K bits providing primary memories

**FIGURE 2**
Workstation price
versus time for
various workstation
introductions.

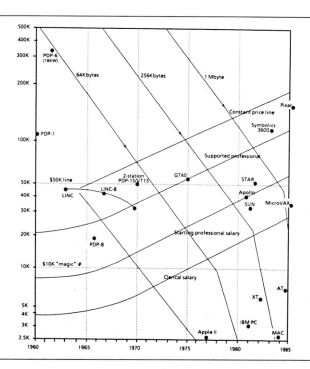

of ¼ to 1 megabyte, permitting the use of large programs and construction of high resolution bit-mapped terminals

□ disks of greater than 10 megabytes

□ local area networks for interconnecting the stations

Future descendants are likely to evolve from extended, lower-priced personal computers, interconnected via LANs. They would include appropriate transducers and corresponding professional applications programs.

A *profession* is any vocation, occupation or business, associated with work, including: secretarial, commercial, science, engineering, mathematics, and the arts.

A *personal computer* or pc is a self-contained computer with secondary file memory and appropriate transducers to interface with people. A personal computer is used interactively by one person at a time, at a location convenient to the user, and may "belong" either to the person or to a group. A personal computer, for a given use, is self-contained (i.e., requiring no external program or data preparation units) permitting a user to go through various stages without external intervention.

The microprocessor, memory, and mass-storage technology appearing in 1975 lead directly to the personal computer industry. Early computers utilized the simple, single process, stand-alone operating systems developed for both interactive, timeshared computers and stand-alone minicomputers. Nevertheless the first personal computer, the LINC (Clark and Molnar, 1964) was built in 1962, long before its predicted technological time.

Personal computers can be used either in a

□ *personal or private environment* encouraging separation of files, resources, and work, with personal security, whereby the only communication with other computers is via secondary memory (floppy) sharing, or transmission of messages via standard communications lines, or

□ *shared, workstation environment* encouraging communication among the pc's, sharing of resources (e.g., files, printers), and working on a single large work assignment or goal.

An *IBM Personal Computer* or PC is a particular personal computer utilizing the Intel 8086 . . . 80386 architectures and the evolving MS-DOS operating systems. A PC may be extended and used in a workstation environment when interconnected via LANs, permitting access and sharing of facilities and work. Hence constant-cost PCs are likely to evolve into the de facto personal workstations.

## Bell Model of Memory Price Decline, Forming New Computer Classes

Hardware technology improvements, specifically in silicon and magnetic storage, have been the sole enabling determinants of progress in computing; they are the "technological devils" that drive the formation of our industries. This is the economic basis that forms all computing classes, including all forms of workstations. Since personal workstations evolve from other computer classes, the entire hierarchy of computers must be understood. In effect, we get no product before its (technological) time!

In 1975, I observed that memory price was falling at a rate of 20 percent per year. Since it was a constant fraction of system prices, they also declined at the same rate. This 20 percent decline was based on the learning curves for manufacturing core memory. Thus a computer would drop by a factor of 10 in price, per decade.

In 1972, with the introduction of semiconductor memories by Intel, price began to decline by a factor of four every three years, the cycle for new memory chip introductions. (The Four Phase company produced the first 1K MOS memory chips before 1970.) Table 1 shows the introduction of semiconductor memories and other devices and the

**TABLE 1**
**Memory chip and microprocessor introductions**
**with resulting personal computer and workstations**

| Year | Memory | Micro | Width | Memory | Examples |
|------|--------|-------|-------|--------|----------|
| 1972 | 1K | 4004 | 4 | | |
| 1973 | | 8008 | 8 | | |
| 1974 | | 8080/6800 | 8 | | |
| 1975 | 4K | 6502 | 8 | 4K–8K | Altair, IBM 5100 |
| 1976 | | Z-80 | 8 | | |
| 1977 | | | | | Apple II, TRS-80, PET |
| 1978 | 16K | 8086 | 16 | 16K–32K | |
| 1979 | | 68,000 | 16 | 16K–64K | Atari |
| 1980 | | 8088 | 8 | | |
| 1981 | 64K | | | 64K–256K | PC, Apollo, SUN 1 |
| 1982 | | 186/286 | 16 | | Commodore 64 |
| 1983 | | | | | Lisa |
| 1984 | 256K | 68020 | 32 | 512K–1M | MAC, AT |
| 1985 | | 386 | 32 | | SUN 3 |
| 1986 | | | | | ? |
| 1987 | 1M | | 32 | 4M | ? |

development of specific personal computers and personal workstations. The reduction in the price per bit of semiconductor memories amounts to a 36 percent price decline each year or a factor of ten every five years, twice as fast as the original core memory (and discrete logic) based model.

In 1975, I also observed that memory size is the determinant of computer use and hence computer classes. That is, computer power is proportional to memory size, or memory size squared when a proportionally faster processor is used. Looking at the declining prices for various sized systems, one can see each computer class taking on the attributes and power of its higher order neighbor. Table 2 classifies what I then thought were the capabilities of various computers versus their memory sizes. I felt then, and still feel, that a one-megabyte address space for a process is the minimum size, and OK at least in terms of what we actually use. Anything smaller (e.g., 64K bytes) is sheer hell to use!

My goal in 1975 was to be able to use the past to project the evolution of simple computer classes to 1980 as the basis for the VAX evolution. Figure 3 shows the price of various systems versus their memory size. Note that a new computer class emerges when the price drops an order of magnitude. This evolutionary model was also described for DEC's hardware development (Bell, Mudge, and McNamara, 1978) shown in Fig. 4. This evolutionary model turned out to be quite accurate, predicting the Apple II (just 3 years away), low-cost shared

**TABLE 2**
**System structure, memory size, and resultant use (G. Bell 1975)**

| Structure | Memory range | Function (use) | |
|---|---|---|---|
| Dedicated (fixed—1 use) | 4KB–8KB | Interactive—e.g., POS cash register Real time—e.g., scope, traffic control, automobile | Special purpose, Fixed |
| Programmable (1 user) | 16KB–65KB | Interactive—RT11 (CP/M) Real time—RSX11S, M | Small scale, generality |
| Dedicated (multiprogrammed *n* users) | 65KB–256KB | Interactive—MUMPS, RSTS, Trans. Proc. Real time—RSX-11M, D | Special purpose |
| Programmable (multiprogrammed *n* users) | 128KB–1024KB | Interactive—LAS, TOPS 10, RSTS Real time—RSX-11D | Generality |

**FIGURE 3**
System price versus time for various memory sizes and system types (Bell 1975).

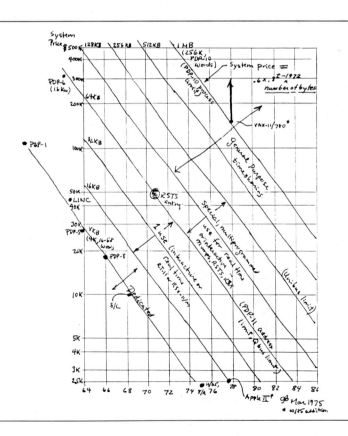

**FIGURE 4**
Price versus time for
each machine class.

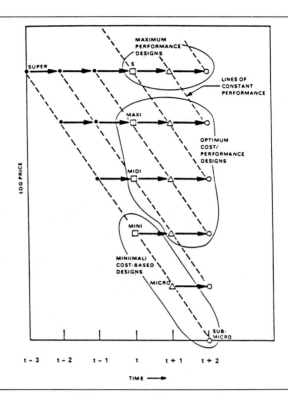

micros, and the new class of mini-supercomputers that are beginning to emerge this year.

The chart labeled Fig. 3 has just the one variable, memory price. The first thing about prediction is to be able to predict the past. This chart allowed me to predict the past; I was able to predict things back to the PDP-1, the LINC, the PDP-5, and the PDP-8. I observed that the only thing that really matters is memory price and that memory size is a single variable. Allen Newell and I played this game in the *Computer Structure* book, that is, if you only had one number to talk about a computer, what would you say about it? And I think it's like any animal: How big is its brain size? This is simply the brain size of the computer, from which you determine all the computer classes. If you want to explain computers in one graph, this is the basic graph. It stopped working as well as I wanted it to in 1980.

The lines in the chart are the 20 percent cost reduction lines that I derived from fundamentals based on DEC markups and what it cost to string core memories. So we were able to show how one went through dedicated machines up through very general purpose machines. What that phenomenon does, what the parallel lines show is that, as you go down in price for a given function, what tends to happen is that the same computer gets reinvented by different people. This then forms a new market for a new computer class, such as a workstation or a personal computer or a pocket calculator or a pocket computer or what have you. The other thing that happens is the people who built that computer then conspire with all their market friends, as engineers, because it's a different problem to solve—namely, how do you build a lower priced computer? By this time you've got a market established and you don't want to build a low-priced computer because you don't know the customers; you know the old customers because they are constant budget customers. The large computer center people always have money. Originally they used to have 3 to 4 million dollars to spend, now they've got about 15 million dollars to spend on a computer and they buy one every five years. You don't know what the computer does, but you know how much you're going to pay for it.

I have plotted what I think are the seminal machines here; these are the production machines or the machine of first use, where a number of people can use them for experimental work. You have to go back a number of years to identify various people that were involved in that experimental use. There is a line of computers that people used as personal computers, starting with the G15 and then the PDP-1; that line of $100,000 seems to be always a reasonable amount, independent of the fact that $100,000 then bought quite a lot more than it does now. It is a kind of a magic number of how much one would spend now to let it be used by an individual before you felt compelled to share it and put it in a batch mode and have to have an organization.

Since computer price determines the performance and therefore the economics and style of use, I began to observe at about the same time that there were roughly three levels of computer use: central (mainframe), departmental (minicomputer), and personal. Dave Nelson, formerly at DEC, Prime, and now at Apollo, extended this view to several other computer classes and introduced a model for price and weight (Table 3).

You buy computers by the pound. You say how much it weighs, you know what its price is, you know the technology at the time, and you know roughly what it's going to do or could do. If you look at the evolution of personal workstations, the ideas were really done on small computers in the 1950s. We saw the Whirlwind being used that way. In fact, a recent book on graphics said that EDSAC was the first personal computer. It was probably the first useful machine, and it was operating in 1949 at Cambridge University. It was a one-of-a-kind the university had built, but the claim was its CRT memory could display bits. It had bit-mapped graphics, and you could photograph the memory bits, and people did and got out functions; it was often used as a personal computer. A lot of the experiments were done there in the 1960s.

**TABLE 3**
Nelson⁺/Bell computer classes

| Tier | Location | Names | Price ($) | Weight (#s) |
|------|----------|-------|-----------|-------------|
| 0 | wallet | calculator | 10 | .05 |
| 1 | pocket | calculator, special function unit | 100 | .5 |
| 2 | briefcase | kneetop, small personal | 1,000 | 5 |
| 3* | office | personal, large personal, "workstation" | 10,000 | 50 |
| 4* | department | shared micro, minicomputer, super-minicomputer, mini-supercomputer | 100,000 | 500 |
| 5* | center | mainframe | 1,000,000 | 5,000 |
| 6* | region | supercomputer | 10,000,000 | 50,000** |

⁺Founder and Vice-President, Research, Apollo Computer Corporation

\* Based on Bell's Distributed Processing Computing Model (circa 1975)

\*\*Perhaps, if heat exchanger is included

People used large computers as though they were personal computers. Out of the work on the TX-2, came a real personal computer, the LINC. When people ask me what was the first personal computer, I have to say, it's LINC, even though individuals used LGP30s and G15s.

These emerging smaller classes put significant pressure on interconnecting all the computers and forced the need for local area networks (LANs). Figure 5 shows the style of use and environment for various computer classes. Note that personal workstations provide roughly the same capability as larger shared computers and are large personal computers interconnected via LANs. IBM appears to have recently adopted this hierarchical view of computing and assigning meaningful work to all the levels, so it must be right (at least for a few years).

## Networks and the Shared and Personal Workstations Evolution

Although technology is a major variable that creates computer classes, the development of networks and changing patterns of use also influenced the evolution of personal workstations. The impact of the network and local area network on workstations is based on my perspective as chief architect of the ensemble of DEC products until 1983.

**FIGURE 5**
Computer use style
versus user
environment for
various computer
classes.

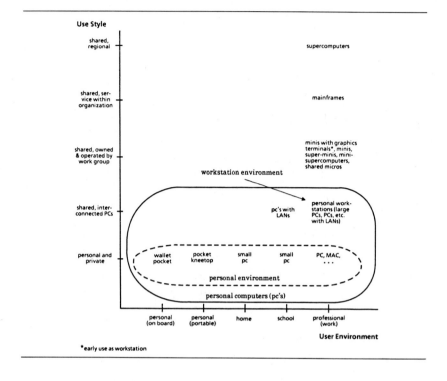

DECNET AND THE INFLUENCE OF ARPANET

The various DECNET architectures were initially created in 1974 by Stu
Wecker while a member of DEC's research group. They were based on
the notion of hierarchical computing according to use, concurrent with
Digital's work on distributed processing. The imperative was to interconnect the hierarchy of DEC's minis and mainframes as tightly as
possible, forming a single computing environment.

The need for DECNET occurred because Digital was proliferating
timeshared and real-time minicomputers that had to have a way to
communicate with one another and with their own and other central
mainframes. DECNET was introduced in the following phases:

I    1975   task-task, file transfer, file access; point-to-point; 8-bit
            net address; operating systems: RSX-11 D, M, IAS

II   1977   improved system generation; used for first DEC engi-
            neering network (now several thousand machines)
            at tens of sites; operating systems: rt-11, rsts

III  1980   routing, virtual terminal, full network management;
            operating systems: DECsystem 20, vms

IV  1983  large routing address, full remote rms files; c-terms;
          ethernet support

1985  portable DECNET (by Wecker's company)

The basic model for DECNET was ARPANET (Roberts, 1970), with the important difference that a network need not have specific IMPs or TIPs to do the packet switching for the worker computers. That is, the worker computers could do the packet switching for the network, and when the packet switching load became too high, one inserted packet-switching computers.

## XEROX PARC ETHERNET/ALTO ENVIRONMENT, CARNEGIE-MELLON SPICE PROPOSAL

In 1979, Carnegie-Mellon published a proposal soliciting vendors for a personal workstation environment. Their statement, which had the effect of stimulating the design of various workstations was:

> The era of time-sharing is ended. Time-sharing evolved as a way to provide users with the power of a large interactive computer system at a time when such systems were too expensive to dedicate to a single individual . . . Recent advances in hardware open up new possibilities . . . high resolution color graphics, 1 mip, 16 K word micro-programmed memory, 1 megabyte primary memory, 100 megabyte secondary memory, special transducers, . . . We would expect that by the mid-1980's such systems could be priced around $10,000.

Although the concept was correct, the details of the machine were wrong because evolving technology was not considered. This led to selecting the wrong vendor, the late Three Rivers or PERQ Systems. Three Rivers's founder, Brian Rosen, a CMU grad who had worked at Xerox Palo Alto Research Center (PARC), designed PERQ as his version of the Xerox ALTO and D-series machines. Carnegie-Mellon may have taken on a leadership role in personal workstation environments by building its SPICE (Scientific Personal Integrated Computing Environment) on the PERQ and then contracting to build a similar environment for IBM, provided the SPICE derivative product is marketed.

The prototype for SPICE, and virtually all other distributed personal workstations environments (e.g., MIT's Chaosnet and the personal LISP workstations that were the basis of LISP Machines Incorporated and Symbolics), was PARC's first 3-megabit-per-second Ethernet interconnecting Altos, operational as an environment in 1975 (Perry and Wallich, 1985; Pake, 1985). Datapoint's ARCnet with personal computers using the Intel 8080 was clearly the first commercial workstation environment. The Alto processor was a near derivative to the Data General Nova with an integrated bit-mapped display. It is important to note that the PARC environment also included a time-shared computer based on the PDP-10 architecture, MAXC, which could be used for shared files and significant computation. In April 1981, Xerox introduced a product version of Alto, the STAR workstation, and various file and print servers utilizing a 10 megabit per second Ethernet, but without a real central computer. The PARC Ethernet was the forerunner of today's 10 megabit per second IEEE 802.3 standard (as originally drafted by Digital, Intel, and Xerox).

## THE DIGITAL VAX, HOMOGENEOUS COMPUTING ENVIRONMENT

The idea of a complete, distributed computing environment, based primarily on the VAX architecture (but including the PDP-11 and DECsystem 10/20 computers) was presented to DEC's Board of Directors in December 1978 and approved as the strategy for guiding future product development.

The goals and constraints of this strategy is outlined in Appendix 1. The impetus was based on the early success of VAX, including plans to make a wide range of products to fill each of the three classes from MOS micros for personal computers to clusters of high-performance ECL VAXen. Furthermore, it was desirable to limit future evolution of the 10/20 and 11 lines, since both were providing essentially the same capability. The need for interconnection and the availability of LANs were critical as described above. Finally, computing was evolving from a centralized computing style to a more distributed computing environment as demonstrated by the Alto environment (but including high-performance and departmental level computers).

The environment, shown in Fig. 6, provided a wide range and hierarchy of compatible computers and ways of interconnecting them to provide users with generic (e.g., word processing, mail) program development, and profession-specific computing using timeshared minicomputers or personal workstations. The goal was to provide the widest range of choices by having complete compatibility for where and how computing was to be performed without having to make a priori commitments either statically (purchase or installation) or even run-time to a particular computer system class (i.e., mainframe, minicomputer, team, or personal workstation). By 1981, the original structure evolved to require the local area network (Ethernet) for connecting all computers, initially called NI for Network Interconnect, as part of the hierarchy of interconnects, as shown in Fig. 7 (CI = Computer Interconnect, NI = Network Interconnect, BI = Backplane Interconnect, and II = Interchip Interconnect; II did not materialize).

The design of the environment is substantially more than the design of a single range of compatible computers because different styles of user are required depending on the machine class, and all the com-

**FIGURE 6**
Digital distributed
computing
environment (Bell,
12–78).

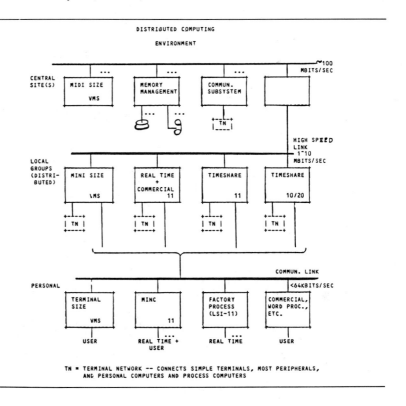

TN = TERMINAL NETWORK -- CONNECTS SIMPLE TERMINALS, MOST PERIPHERALS,
AND PERSONAL COMPUTERS AND PROCESS COMPUTERS

puters must be interconnected and work together in a multi-level hierarchy.

## ETHERNET

While DEC had prototype LANs and proposals for LANs internally, I felt it was essential to have a standard. We hired Bob Metcalfe as a consultant, and his missionary role was to make Ethernet the standard, using Intel's chip design capacity and Xerox's patent and LAN experience. The IEEE got involved once they heard the idea of the LAN. They went on to facilitate the design of many other "standards," which, of course, had the effect of diminishing the notion of a standard. Fortunately the development of Ethernet crept into existence slightly more rapidly than the IBM Token Ring LAN, which was introduced in October 1985, otherwise I doubt if there would be any significant use of LANs today. I understand about 30,000 Ethernets exist today.

In January 1981, when Ethernet was being introduced by various vendors and being completed as an international standard, several of

**FIGURE 7**
Digital homogeneous computing environment 1984.

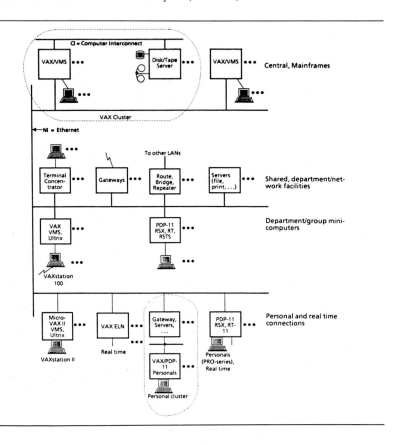

us from the developer companies (myself from Digital, Noyce from Intel, and Liddle from Xerox) made a broad appeal to the U.S. and European press and manufacturers on the importance of the standard. My theme was: ''Ethernet is the Unibus of the Fifth Generation.'' We all argued that the standard was essential

- to interconnect department-level minicomputers and mainframe computers to one another, permitting file-to-file transfers, remote-terminal emulation, and distributed processing among the shared computers;
- as a switch for interconnecting terminals to the higher level computers within the environment;
- to centralize the gateway function in one place, versus requiring every computer to have protocol conversions to communicate outside the Ethernet environment;
- as a bus for building computer systems; and
- for building fully distributed computing environments. The

PARC model of a computing system was to decompose computing into a series of functional servers such as printing, filing, and with individual workstations. The analogy with Unibus (circa 1970) as a computer versus Ethernet (circa 1981) as a computing environment is clear when comparing the two structures (see Fig. 8).

## THE ENCORE CONTINUUM

With the formation of Encore Computer Corporation in 1983, our goal was to provide a complete environment, the "Continuum" (Fig. 9), like the VAX environment, but based on a single microprocessor (Bell et al., 1985). The Continuum provided both the distributed personal workstation style (described in the evolution, Appendix 1) and shared central computing using a multiple, microprocessor architecture that I have named the Multi (Bell, 1985). Ethernet provides the switch for interconnecting terminals to the Multimax using concentrators that preprocess terminal requests for communicating with other environments and for distributed-workstation environments. There are no terminal connections to the shared computers (something I have been trying to eliminate for years).

**FIGURE 8**
Unibus (c. 1970) and Ethernet (c. 1982) computer structures comparison.

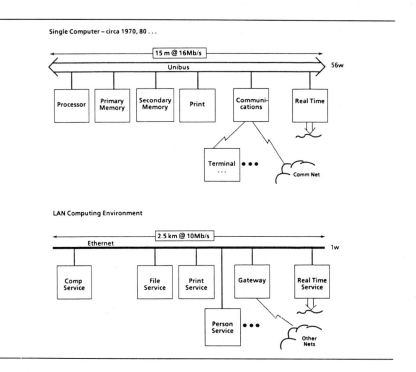

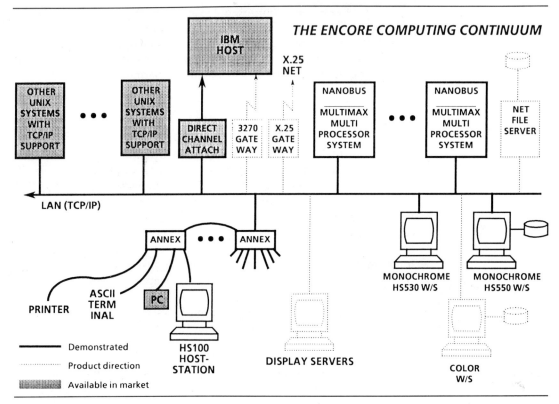

**FIGURE 9**
The Encore computing continuum.

### APOLLO DOMAIN

Dave Nelson, founder of Apollo and Domain architect (May 1980), was in the research group at DEC during the formation of DECNET and VAX. In the late 1970s, he went to Prime to work on the Prime token local area network and then left to develop the Apollo Domain architecture. Domain, introduced in March 1981, most typifies today's personal workstation because it provides a single addressing scheme for accessing all the memory (files) of a system. Dave credits me with stimulating this unifying architecture, which is like the Unibus in terms of addressing.

## Workstation Events, Dimensions, and Timeline Evolution

This section serves as a model for future historical research because it outlines, albeit incompletely, some critical events in workstation evolution.

The evolution of the physical workstation hardware is almost indistinguishable from the computer, and hence the evolution of personal workstations parallels, and is directly coupled to, the development of mainframes, minicomputers, and microprocessors. The principal difference is that workstations include a significant set of transducers to interface with humans and communication links and additional user interface (software) advances.

## PROCESSOR AND MEMORY COMPUTING ENVIRONMENT

The reinvention of the wheel and features within each of the computer classes has been nicely depicted by Burger, Caving, Holton, and Sumney (1984) as a timeline of the critical processor features (see Fig. 10). The single most critical dimension of processing power is virtual mem-

**FIGURE 10**
Computer architectural innovations for mainframes, minicomputers, and microcomputers from 1960 to 1990 (a) and the descriptive legend (b). (Taken with permission from Burger, Cavin, Holton, and Sumney, 1984.)

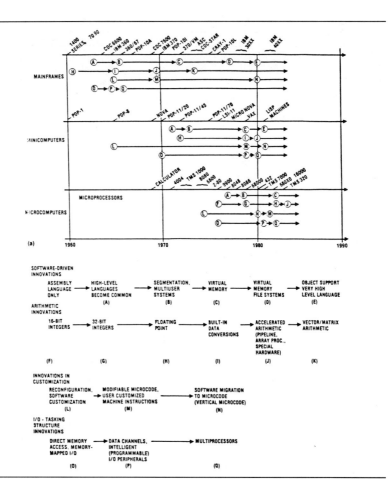

ory size. The reinvention of the wheel of virtual memory size is shown in Fig. 11 from Siewiorek, Bell, and Newell (1982) as each architecture reinvents and evolves the concepts of virtual memory.

### VIDEO ENVIRONMENT

The evolution of displays has occurred along a set of dimensions that are relatively closely correlated with evolutionary time as follows:

□ performance as measured in ability to display objects, including the ability to transform the objects;

□ hardware generation of the picture process (Myers and Sutherland's Wheel of Reincarnation shows the evolution of how pictures are controlled [Fig. 12 reproduced from Bell, Mudge, and McNamara, 1978.] Note the evolution: direct control of the dis-

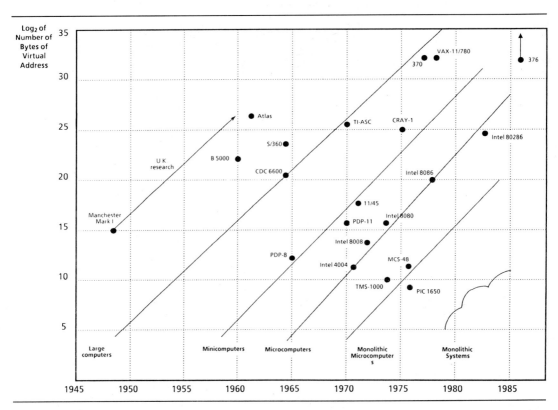

**FIGURE 11**
Virtual address space evolution for various computers and computer classes.
(From Siewiorek, Bell, and Newell, 1982.)

**FIGURE 12**
Myer and Sutherland
wheel of
reincarnation for
display processor
evolution. (From
Bell, Mudge, and
McNamara, 1978.)

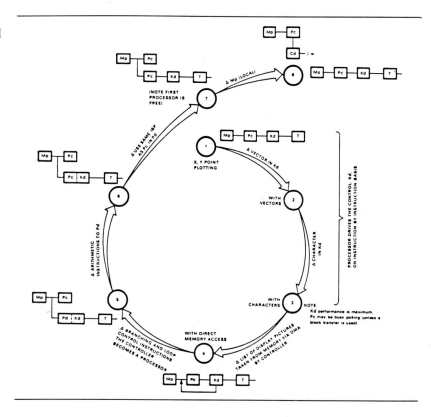

play object by the central processor; display list issued to a DMA controller or external controller; separate processor with loops, subroutines, and the like; arithmetic instructions added to aid dynamic displaying; use of virtual memory [beginning to occur to manage large pictures]; and removing the display processor to form a separate computer.);

□ resolution (in pixels or analog vector resolution);

□ number of bits per pixel including use for monochrome/color;

□ display datatypes
    □ points, characters, lines, curves
    □ 3D line drawing
    □ wireframe meshes, 2D surfaces, 3D surfaces
    □ shading, sculptured surfaces, constructive geometry

□ translation of datatypes
    □ fixed
    □ translation, scaling, rotation
    □ 2D clipping, 3D perspective, 3D clipping

- standard interface evolution: direct control, SIGGRAPH CORE Library, VDI, CGI, NAPLPS, and the like;
- windowing of output images; and
- character, line, picture, and 3D image input.

### TACTILE AND MANUAL POSITION OR LINE INPUT

This category includes keyboard, 2D and 3D light pens, direct touch screen, tablet, digitizing tablet, knob, joystick, track ball, and mouse.

### PAPER OUTPUT

This section must include the evolution of conventional printing and plotting along with early film recorders to capture images, extending to modern dot matrix printers of all kinds for monochrome and color.

### VOICE I/O

While today's personal workstations do not permit substantial voice communication, voice input such as the Kurzweil voicewriter promises to add a significant dimension for human communication. The critical voice "firsts" for use with personal workstations are relatively sparse at this time.

### LINKS, SWITCHES, AND NETWORKS

Links, switches, and communications networks have influenced the formation of computer networks and computing environments. The previous section described their influence on the formation of the DEC computing environment. Others should be traced.

### SPECIAL PURPOSE I/O AND ROBOTS

The ability to handle arbitrary signals from other environments is crucial to the formation of various profession-specific environments (e.g., music and scientific experiments).

### OPERATING SYSTEM, DATABASE, LANGUAGE, AND GENERIC ENVIRONMENTS

Traditional computer science history has laid claim on operating systems, databases, and languages, including their application to personal workstations. For example, the History of Programming Languages conference constructed an excellent timeline of the various languages, including those for specialized environments such as interactive computing and specific application domains such as statistics, science, and engineering.

Generic environments that users of traditional, timesharing computers have required include:

- □ Timesharing oriented with text and graphics terminals (slow links)
  - □ text editing, mail, and network mail
  - □ drawing and graph plotting
  - □ shared work processing
  - □ database access
  - □ transaction processing
- □ Shared workstation and personal workstation oriented (fast links)
  - □ multiprocess control including control and windows
  - □ spreadsheets
  - □ drawing and painting

**PROFESSION SPECIFIC WORKSTATIONS**

In addition to generic applications programs (e.g., word processing and mail), each profession requires an environment to support and "understand" the work of the professional. This may take the form of special hardware (e.g., high-resolution mega-color scopes for the graphic artist, high precision analog output for the musician, or fast simulation processors for the VLSI designer) in addition to specific programs that understand and have knowledge or expertise of the work being carried out. The following taxonomy provides an outline of the environments that have developed quite independently and that historians should research.

- □ Scientific, medical, and mathematics workstations
  - □ life science with transducers appropriate to the measurement task
  - □ medical (e.g., radiologist, cardiologist, bone surgeon)
  - □ geologist and petroleum engineer
  - □ physics experiment control and analysis
  - □ statistician and mathematician
  - □ signal analysis and encryption/decryption
- □ Engineering workstations
  - □ electrical or electronic schematic (2D line drawings)
  - □ VLSI physical design (2-½ D)
  - □ mechanical drafting
  - □ design of sheet metals or piping (2-½ D)

       □ architectural and structural engineering
       □ general mechanical design of arbitrary surfaces for analysis and fabrication
   □ Software and knowledge-engineering workstations
   □ Arts (typesetting, graphics arts, and music) workstations
       □ publisher of newspaper, magazine, or book
       □ scholars including historians, linguists, and literary scholars
       □ graphic artist, illustrator, cartoonist, or choreographer
       □ composer
       □ artistic film production
   □ Commercial workstations
       □ general clerical and transaction processing, office word processing, executive
       □ financial personal workstations for banking, insurance broker
   □ Special control-oriented workstations
       □ air traffic control
       □ process and plant control
   □ Training workstations (and are these workstations?)
       □ simulation of industrial plants and aircraft
       □ computer aided instruction such as Plato

## Some Displays, Personal Computers, and Workstations I Have Known

This section describes various displays connected to computers, which were used as either personal computers or workstations. The MIT and Lincoln Laboratory displays embedded in Whirlwind, TX-O, TX-2, and LINC were among the earliest personal computers. Since these computers (except LINC) were one of a kind, their impact was as prototypes for subsequent developments. One direct impact was in the formation of the DEC computers, many of which were used as personal computers.

The first DEC display, Type 30 for the PDP-1 introduced in 1961, had instructions that permitted direct plotting of points and, optionally, characters and vectors. As DEC evolved and built timesharing computers with operating systems that protected the user from accessing input/output equipment directly, the ability to have highly interactive terminals and workstations decreased.

Nearly all of the DEC computers were used as components for building interactive, "workstation-style" systems. DEC and Original Equipment Suppliers (OEMs) built and sold workstation-style systems for use in the sciences, printed circuit layout, mechanical and architectural drawing, typesetting, and office automation. These pioneering applications (circa 1970), operating on dedicated timesharing systems, served as the basis for much of today's evolving workstations.

## MIT WHIRLWIND, LINCOLN LABORATORY TX-0, TX-2, AND IBM AN/FSQ7 (SAGE)

During Whirlwind's first year of operation, 1950, Bob Everett published a paper that showed a picture of its display (with an attached camera) and listed some actual problems carried out on the machine.

1. An industrial production problem for the Harvard Economic's School
2. Magnetic flux study for Whirlwind's magnetic storage work
3. Oil reservoir depletion studies
4. Ultra-high frequency television channel allocation for Dumont
5. Optical constants of thin metal films
6. Computation of autocorrelation coefficients
7. Tape generation for a digitally controlled milling machine

Whirlwind was initially established as a large specialized simulator to the Airplane Stability and Control Analyzer (ASCA). The actual use turned out to be a prototype for the semi automatic ground environment (SAGE) system for air defense and SAGE, in turn, was the basis for air traffic control. The first successful use of Whirlwind for air defense occurred on April 20, 1951.

MIT's Lincoln Laboratory, established in 1951, moved into its quarters in Bedford, Massachusetts, in the summer of 1953. Lincoln built the TX-0 computer to test the use of transistor circuitry and a large core memory and then the TX-2 for large-scale computing experiments. Both had a point-plotting display with 10″ × 10″ area and 1K point resolution, light pen, camera, switch input, and abilities to interconnect arbitrary I/O devices. Hardware innovations of the TX-2 include addressable magnetic tape for a filing system; the Lincoln Writer, a typewriter for engineering/scientific use; and the TX-2 multiple sequence operation for rapid context switching. While the TX-2 was initially a personal computer, it operated under control of a timesharing operating system by the mid-1960s. The TX computer circuitry was virtually identical to the logic and laboratory modules that DEC sold in its first four years, prior to the introduction of the PDP-1 in 1961.

These machines, used as personal computers, pioneered numerous applications, the most famous being Sutherland's Sketchpad.

I spent a brief but wonderful period (January 1959 to June 1960) using TX-0 for speech research and writing the program to do

''Analysis-by-Synthesis'' (Bell, et al. 1961), which took as input speech spectra directly from a filter bank connected to TX-0. I also spent six months designing an IBM-compatible tape TX-0 and exploring hybrid computation (an analog computer used with TX-0). Peter Deutsch, then age 12, acted as a relatively patient user consultant and helped me debug my macros. Gwen Bell entered data on land use in the Boston area, and I wrote a program to display and explore this data. The program was demonstrated to the city-planning faculties at MIT and Harvard. Ten years later, Harvard was able to turn the clock back over 30 years when they established their computer graphics laboratory to do a simpler version of computer mapping, using punched cards and line printers.

### DEC PDP-1 DISPLAYS: TYPE 30, 31, AND THE FIRST COLOR DISPLAY

The PDP-1 continued in the tradition of the ''MIT personal computers.'' The PDP-1 had three displays. The Type 30 point plotting display took 50 microseconds to display a point on the 10″ × 10″ tube with 1K resolution. This was one of the first displays connected to a commercial computer, converting it into a personal computer for various scientific data analysis applications. Type 30 was extended to include a character generator controlled by loading a 36-bit, 5 × 7 bit raster specifying the character. The circuitry, designed by Ben Gurley, formed the basis of the 3XX displays. The DEC Special Systems Group designed an elaborate display, PEPR, for bubble chamber photograph analysis for MIT using the basic display circuits.

Type 31 designed by Gurley with a 5″ high precision display with 4K point resolution. Only one was delivered to Lawrence Livermore Laboratory (LLL, now LLNL—the ''N'' for National) for use on their PDP-1. The Livermore PDP-1 had every option that DEC had proposed to build including Remington Rand tapes, and was used as a front end and exploratory PC for the large computers including Stretch and LARC. Ben Gurley left DEC and with Ed Fredkin established Information International Inc. (III). The first III product included a high-resolution display for various image input/output applications. The basic high resolution display is still in existence.

One PDP-1 Color Display was delivered to the Air Force Cambridge Research Laboratory (the military counterpart to Lincoln Laboratory). The color display was built by modifying a standard RCA color television for point plotting.

At the Fall Joint Computer Conference in 1961, Ed Jacks, from General Motors, spent almost the entire conference watching people use the PDP-1/Type 30 to draw and doodle using a program I had written. The display influenced Ed to tackle Computer Aided Design, later using the IBM 7090 with a connected display. The classic program

SPACEWAR! was written on the PDP-1 in 1962, by Steve Russell. Today SPACEWAR! continues to be the center to settle litigations about the design of computer games.

### LABORATORY PERSONAL COMPUTERS: LINCOLN LABORATORY LINC, DEC PDP-12, AND MINC

Wes Clark and Charles Molnar continued the MIT tradition of building personal computers, and LINC was designed for wider scale use for the life sciences, by being lower cost (about $40K in 1962). The LINC was designed using mostly DEC modules. The original LINC had two 5″ displays, a keyboard, 1 or 2 Kw, 12-bit memory, and two LINC-tapes. Each unit had approximately 256 Kbytes of addressable tape memory. I believe LINC was the first production personal computer for scientific use (about 50 were produced, 21 by DEC). Its significance was its completeness at the low cost, yet being open-ended.

DEC went on to build 140 LINC-8s beginning in 1967 (designed by Wes Clark and Dick Clayton) and around 1000 PDP-12s beginning in 1970 (Bell, Mudge, and McNamara, 1978).

### DEC 338, 339, AND 340 DISPLAYS

The 338/PDP-8 display/personal computer, introduced in 1967, was used as a front-end computing terminal. The 338 and 339 (for the 18-bit computers) were, I believe, the first display processors (Bell, Mudge, and McNamara, 1978). They took a display program in the PDP-8's primary memory, which specified points, character strings, vectors, subroutines and other program-control instructions and permitted completely autonomous operation of the display, independent of the central processor. The 339 was used with the 18-bit computers, especially PDP-9. Both systems were used for stand-alone data analysis and for display terminal front ends to large computers.

A special version of the 340 was designed on a Saturday morning with Ivan Sutherland for his use within the government just prior to joining ARPA. This PDP-7/340 had every conceivable keyboard and input device we could think of, including switches, trackballs, joysticks, and lighted buttons.

### DEC PDP-15/VT15, AND GT4X "WORKSTATIONS"

The PDP-15/VT15, introduced in 1970, costing about $90K was used as a standalone for one or two users (to reduce the cost to $50,000 per terminal using a $15,000 graphics terminal). About 30 percent of the systems had two terminals. It took about 100 microseconds to draw a vector using the DDA technique. The PDP-15 had from 8 Kw to 32 Kw of memory. Computer Aided Design system for Printed Circuit layout written and marketed by REDAC (U.K.) was a key application, although it was used extensively for scientific-research applications.

In January 1973, the GT40 was introduced at a price of $25,000 with 16 Kw of memory based on the lower cost PDP-11/05. The well-known program, Lunar Lander, was written by Jack Burness for the product introduction. The relatively slow speed of the display, coupled with a limited memory and configuration of the 11/05 limited the application to a preprocessor for time-shared systems doing CAD.

The GT44 was introduced in June 1973 at a price of $38,000, using the same display processor as the GT40, but with an 11/34 computer and RK05, 5 Megabyte disk. The GT44 was used as a complete, stand-alone computer.

The GT48, introduced in October 1975, selling for $55,000, was a high performance personal computer, using the 11/34, with memory up to 128 Kw. Vectors were generated using analog circuitry at a rate of 100,000 vectors per second.

### THE PDP-8 WORD PROCESSING PERSONAL COMPUTERS

In addition to the early use of the PDP-8, with the 338 and various storage tube displays, the PDP-8 began to be used extensively 10 years after its birth for the DECmate series of word processing terminals. The PDP-8 was based on the PDP-5 (1963) 12-bit architecture, and influenced by the CDC 160 and LINC, addressed up to 32 Kw (later expanded to 128 Kw). The following word processing personal computers used the PDP-8:

| Year | Model | Price | Comments |
|---|---|---|---|
| 1975 | DS310 | $16,000 | 8/A, desk, 8″ floppy and VT52 terminal |
| 1976 | WS200 | $40,000 | 8/A, cabinet, 1–8 users, 5 Mbyte disks |
| 1977 | VT78 | $15,000 | Intersil 6100 PDP-8 chip, embedded in VT52, 8″ floppies |
| 1981 | DECmate I | $12,000 | 6120 chip, embedded in VT100, 8″ floppies |
| 1983 | DECmate II | $3,500 | integrated unit, 5″ floppies, bit mapped |
| 1984 | DECmate III | $2,400 | Z80/8086 and 5″ winchester disk options |

By 1984, the twenty-first birthday of the basic architecture, over 100,000 PDP-8 connected terminals or personal computers were used for word processing. More PDP-8s were built in 1984 than in any other year. In a very large fraction of the use, the personal computers connected with larger departmental-level VAX computers for electronic mail, filing, and auxiliary word processing for a true, shared workstation environment.

### LSI-11 BASED PERSONAL COMPUTERS: TERAK, PDT 11/150, AND VT103

The LSI-11 (11/03), introduced in 1976, with a smaller printed circuit board form factor (approximately 10″ square) and using the Qbus proved to be an important building block for Digital's subsequent personal computers.

Terak was founded in 1975 to exploit the notion of a bit-mapped graphics computer and used the LSI-11 (11/03) and subsequently the 11/23. The 8510, first delivered in 1976 to Ken Bowles at the University of California, San Diego, for the development of UCSD Pascal, was developed independent of the Xerox Alto. The system operated with up to 28 Kw of memory, used 256 Kbyte floppies, and the bit-map display's resolution was 320 × 240. About 3000 were built and sold at a price of $5000 to the education market.

DEC introduced the PDT 150 as a small computer with two 8″ floppies and 32 Kw at a price of less than $10,000. While all the DEC marketing groups debated the price and their role in distribution, the personal computer industry formed. DEC was able to discourage Dan Bricklin from using PDT to build Visicalc. (He went on to use the newly introduced Apple II.) The VT103, introduced in 1981, was based on the VT 100, which had been introduced to accept the Qbus, LSI-11/23 modules.

### DEC TYPESETTING TERMINALS: VT20 AND VT71

The PDP-11, introduced in 1974 and 1977, was used as a base for the VT20 and VT71 typesetting terminals. These had a programmable character set of 256 characters, used 15″ portrait-oriented tubes, and communicated with the host via 9600 baud asynchronous communication. The VT20 was based on the 11/05 and could handle two CRTs, while the VT71 used the 11/03 and sold for $8000. These terminals connected to host PDP-11s that carried out the main typesetting editing functions.

### DEC VAXSTATIONS: 100, I, II, AND 500 SERIES

The introduction of high resolution, bit-mapped terminals connected to VAX occurred quite late in VAX's life. A number of attempts were made, including SUVAX (for single user VAX) providing both mono-chrome and color, operating in 1980.

The VAXstation 100, introduced in May 1983, was a high resolu-tion 19″ terminal with bit-mapped graphics that connected to any of the VAX computers by a high speed fiber optic link connected to the VAX's I/O bus (the Unibus).

VAXstation I and II, based on the MicroVAX I and II, were intro-duced in October 1984 and June 1985, respectively. Both units sold for approximately $20,000, with 19″ bit-mapped CRT, using the Qbus for interconnecting I/O equipment.

The VAXstation 500 family was introduced in October 1985 with 1280 × 1024 pixel resolution color permitting 2D and 3D wire frame and 3D shaded solid images.

## Conclusions

If you've ever used paper tape, you know you had to do off-line prepa-ration. Have you ever used cards? (I hope some of you are old enough to know people who used cards.) I used cards one year when I was a Fulbright scholar in 1958. I went to Carnegie and found key punches, and that's why I wrote a book—I didn't want to compute. The 360/67 had just arrived, but the people were using those machines as bread-boards for timesharing. And then, in the 1960s, a lot of these ideas created a whole set of industries using minicomputers and putting one or two high-performance graphics terminals on them, such as the Adage and the Raster Graphics. There are about a hundred companies doing that now, some of which formed in the early 1960s. The goal was to get the cost per workstation seat to on the order of $50,000. You could do that with a $50,000 computer and a couple of $25,000 graphics terminals. The other thing that happened in the early 1970s was that we had the prototypes of the distributed workstations forming at PARC. Datapoint built a distributed workstations environment using an 8080, or an 8008, on a local area network, which may have preceded most everything else. In 1981, with the devil providing technology, namely the right memory sizes and powerful microprocessor, worksta-tions were formed, including those from Apollo, Sun, and Xerox. And then, by 1983, everybody realized there were too many of these com-panies and there were one hundred that built workstations. So the word "JAWS" was coined for "just another workstation company."

By 1985, large companies like IBM and DEC began to embrace the concept. In a few years, a bunch of these companies will begin to shake out and you'll get a steady state supply. Alan Perlis said "we've got to hold this conference because workstations are going to disappear," and I think, to a large extent, they are going to, a large number of them, at least the evolutionary form of what we think of as workstations will disappear because by then the personal computer, as I defined it, will be the workstation.

Figure 1 shows the memory size of a workstation of given capability. These were the lines I drew in 1975 that I said would predict the past, but I found out they were starting to fail. These lines are all 20 percent per year decline lines. That's every ten years you have a decade drop in price. So, if you look at those computer class models, they identify what was a computer in one class ten years ago. Now, can we build an order of magnitude cheaper and form a new machine class? In 1980 we saw a factor of ten decline in five years, and this is 36 percent per year. And that's, of course, because the memory density increases and you build a factor of four bigger chips every three years.

The other phenomenon is how much do you pay for a workstation? That's a function of who uses them. For a few people, a Cray supercomputer is a reasonable personal workstation, if you get that kind of use. In fact, some Crays are used virtually in a personal workstation form. It's a little bit expensive, and off these scales. The thing that I've observed over time is never to judge exactly how much people are willing to spend as single users for a computer; it's what benefit you get that is the important thing. So, starting with the LINC, one could argue, that it was a little bit expensive at below $50,000. But, in fact, if you take the constant price line, LINC today would be about three times the price of that, or $150,000 today. And we do find a personal workstation in that range, the Pixar for example. Other lines show the cost of various professionals per year, and you ask: Would you provide the same amount of computing for that person as you pay for the individual?

So this tries to show what Alan was worried about, that, in fact, you have a machine here today and suddenly that machine is going to drop by a factor of 10 in five years. So workstations will disappear, and the PCs will cause their demise unless software exploits larger machines. To avoid annihilation, the trick is to increase the power, at high price levels, and make it possible for the individual to get more done. Then you run into the problem that since this is the synergy between a system of a human and a computer, if you can't get enough or the right software there, you may just be person-limited rather than computer-limited.

I believe we need a definition of what a personal workstation is now, but I think the definition will change over time. First, there is a professional personal computer. What's a profession? Any vocation, occupation, or business that is associated with work. So playing doesn't count here. Maybe searching for the workstation doesn't count either. That rules out the PARC work, for example. Let me not do that. I just want to raise questions. Second, what is a personal computer? It is a self-contained computer with its own file memory and appropriate transducers, used by one person at a time, at a convenient location. It's self-contained. And then what people say is the personal computer (that's big PC not little pc) is an IBM compatible PC, so this was the definition. Today we think of it as first a personal computer, but it's in a distributed interconnected environment, because work had the nature of being interconnected versus being in a private environment. It's large, about 50 pounds; it's more expensive than a PC; and it has a bunch of generic applications. Also it understands the profession; it has all of the tools that the professional uses and needs.

The reason I take this holistic view is that I look at the interactive systems we built from 1965 to 1985, either as single-user or shared systems, as similar. The important thing is what systems do, not how they are built. For some of the graphics, there's no way you can do some of those functions unless you put them in a single personal computer.

## ACKNOWLEDGMENTS

Dave Fanger, Encore Computer, did the figures on a Xerox Star. Designers of DEC products supplied product information: John Clarke and John Kirk (PDP-8), Herve Lavoie (VT15 and GT4x), Jim Milton (typesetting), and Stu Weckar (DECnet). Dave Nelson, Apollo, contributed a table and much to my understanding of workstations. Gwen Bell helped clarify my thoughts well enough to get a first draft, which she then edited. Mary Jane Forbes prepared the final manuscript.

# APPENDIX 1.
# The Digital VAX, Homogeneous Computing Environment—Technological and Market Background

[Author's Note: This Appendix is solely the view of the author and is not necessarily the view of Digital Equipment Corporation or its engineers.]

## Batch Mainframes for Central Services

In the first two computer generations, 1950–1970, computers were used in batch processing under the name of mainframe computing. During the 1970s the mainframe began to be used almost interactively from remote job entry terminals as "glass key punches." The general direction is to have larger mainframes and larger terminal networks that interconnect to a single computer by an array of front-end computers. When more power is required, more switching computers are connected to several mainframes, each of which performs a particular function. Attached dual processors are used to provide increased power for what is fundamentally a single system. Over time the evolution will be to small-scale multiprocessors for incremental performance and higher availability.

## Minicomputers and Timesharing for a Group

In the mid-1960s, both minicomputers and timesharing were developed at Digital around the PDP-8 and PDP-10 computers, respectively, to lower the cost of computing. Minicomputers were initially used as components of real-time systems and for personal computing. The LINC minicomputer, developed at MIT's Lincoln Laboratory, was the first personal computer, providing a personal filing system and the ability to write and run programs completely on line.

Timesharing started out as a centralized mainframe facility for a large group with the early demonstration at MIT with CTSS, followed by the introduction of products by DEC (PDP-6), GE (using Dartmouth's BASIC), and Scientific Data Systems 940 (based on the Berkeley Timesharing System). Access was via individual teletypes which were eventually replaced by cathode ray tube terminals, or "glass teletypes." By the mid-1970s, low cost PDP-11 timeshared computers began to be used by separate groups and departments to provide "personal computing." By the mid-1970s, a number of minis used high performance graphics terminals for CAD/CAM, typesetting, and other applications requiring graphical output or fast response. These minis were the forerunner of today's distributed, personal workstation environment.

In the early 1980s, low cost disks and large memories permitted two evolved computer structures: the 32-bit supermini, and the microprocessor based "team computer." The supermini had all the power of its mainframe ancestors, especially the critical 32 bits to access memory. The "team computer," based on modern, powerful microprocessors, is simply much lower priced (e.g., $15,000) providing "personal computing" at a price below personal computers.

## Workstations

The fourth generation appeared in 1972 with the microprocessor. With the second 8-bit generation microprocessor, floppy disks and 16 Kilobit semiconductor memories (circa 1976), personal computers were practical and began to be manufactured by Apple, Commodore, Radio Shack, and others. With 16-bit microprocessors (measured by datapath) and 64 Kbit rams, the second generation of PCs that appeared in the early 1980s were suitable for building personal workstation environments. Table 4 summarizes the characteristics of these styles of computing.

**TABLE 4**
**Computing style characteristics (circa 1978, G. Bell)**

| Style* | Central | Departmental Group/Team | Personal |
|---|---|---|---|
| machine | mainframe | mini | micro |
| price range | $500,000–$5,000,000 | $10,000–$500,000 | $1,000–$10,000 $10,000–$50,000 |
| communications | coupled to terminal network | to mainframes, peers and PCs | terminal emulation |
| database | organization's archives as service | organization, project function | personal files |
| terminal access | "glass keypunch" | "glass teletype" | direct CRT |
| typical uses | corporate accounting, electronic mail | project CAD, order entry, small business "mainframe" | word processing, financial analysis, CAD** |
| caretaker | a staff providing service | distributed with user group | the user |

Comments (1985):
* Not including regional-styles supercomputers.

** Workstations used on a one at a time basis.

In 1979, Carnegie-Mellon University wrote a proposal for personal computer research to implement a workstation environment, and declared: ''The era of timesharing was ending.'' Today's powerful personal workstations, such as the Apollo or SUN workstation, provide a large virtual address, connected with shared facilities on a local area network and characterize this type of machine and computing environment.

### PERSONAL COMPUTERS CLUSTERS (I.E., THE WORKSTATION ENVIRONMENT) AS AN ALTERNATIVE TO SHARED COMPUTERS

In the mid-1970s, Xerox PARC researchers developed and provided themselves with a personal computing environment consisting of powerful personal computers all linked together via the first Ethernet cable (3 Mbits), and created the notion of the local area network. Their network had various specialized function servers, including a shared central computer that was compatible with the DECsystem 10, for archival memory and large scale computation.

Figure 13(a) shows the hardware and software of a multipro-

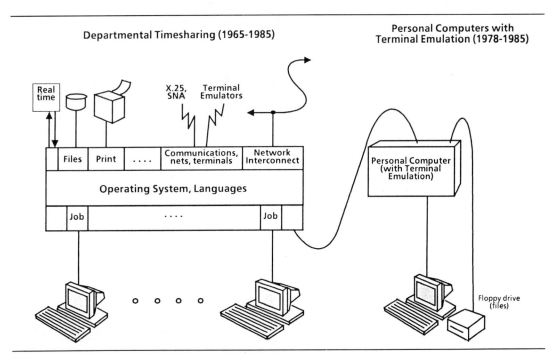

**FIGURE 13(a)**
Departmental timesharing (1965–1985) and personal computers with terminal emulation (1978–1985).

grammed computer used for timesharing, and the corresponding structure of a personal computer cluster consisting of functional services and interconnected by a common interconnect that provides basically the same capability. The timeshared system has a central memory containing various jobs connected to terminals and an operating system that attends to the users and handles the particular functions (e.g., real time, files, printing, and communication). Personal computers are connected to timesharing systems as terminals. By comparing the shared system with the systems formed from functionally independent modules, one would expect two design approaches:

1. decomposing systems to provide shared LAN services, and
2. aggregating personal computer to form PC networks and clusters.

### Decomposing Systems to Provide Shared LAN Services

As shared computers become more complex and more centralized, it's desirable to decompose the functions for execution on smaller computers that can be distributed to be nearer the use. Thus, the decomposition of a shared system into various boxes, each of which perform a unique function permits the evolution of the parts independent of the whole, the physical distribution of a function and the ability of several computers to share a function (see Fig. 13b). While we have described the evolution of local area networks (LANs) as a decomposition of a single system, LANs are generally an aggregate of heterogeneous systems that access a shared service of some kind as described below.

LANs differ from wide area networks (WANs) in that they assume a low latency, high bandwidth interconnect. This permits file access as well as file transfer applications. With file access, it is possible to remotely locate part or all of a system's mass storage to a file-serving computer. File access requires bandwidth and latency that are roughly equal to that of a disk (i.e., 10 Mhz rates); file transfer can be done at substantially slower rates (56 Khz to 1 Mhz).

Using the reasoning that allowed the formation of the file server, we continue the decomposition of a large central system into servers or stations and then combine these servers into a LAN. The major servers include:

1. *Person server* (the personal computer used as a workstation)—local computation and human interface, possibly private storage of files
2. *File server*—mass storage
3. *Compute server*—batch computation or existence of particular programs
4. *Print server*—printing and plotting of graphics images

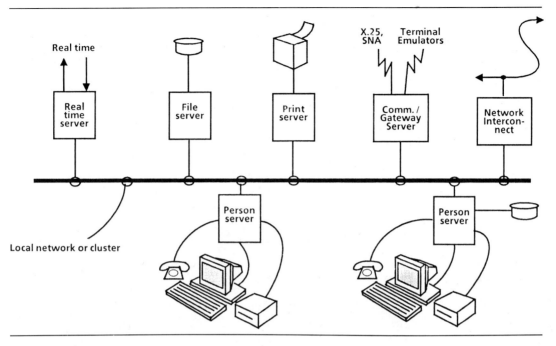

**FIGURE 13(b)**
Personal workstation computing environment using LAN clusters (1980s).

5. *Communication server*—terminal, telephone and PABX, wide area network access including interface to international standards, other companies (e.g., SNA)

6. *Name/authentication/directory server*—naming the network's resources and controlling access to them

A LAN formed as a complete decomposition of a single system and containing no other incompatible servers would be defined as a homogeneous cluster of personal computers or workstations.

### Aggregating Personal Computers to Form PC Networks and Clusters

As personal computers require more facilities (e.g., printing, communication, and files), and the number and type of PCs grow, the need to directly communicate for sending messages and sharing files grows. Furthermore, as a collection of computers in one place forms, economy is gained by sharing common facilities such as printers, phone lines, and disks. Applenet and Corvus Omninet are relatively short and low data-rate local area networks used to permit the construction of what might best be called a network of personal computers because of the heterogeneity of type. The 3Com system for interconnecting IBM PCs is more characteristic of the homogeneous network, or cluster.

For a personal computer cluster, one would expect to have a single File Server that can supply records at random to any of its constituency. Table 5 summarizes what timesharing, PCs, and PC clusters provide.

## DISTRIBUTED PROCESSING USING CAMPUS AND WIDE AREA NETWORKS

The proliferation of timeshared computers required the development of networking in order for various systems to communicate with one another and with mainframes. Thus dispersed computing became dis-

**TABLE 5**
**Timeshared, PC, PC cluster, and PC network characteristics (circa 1981, G. Bell)**

| What | Timeshared system | Personal computer | PC cluster* networks |
|---|---|---|---|
| processing | highest peak | lo–med, guaranteed | = PC |
| programs size | very high peak | small to medium | = PC |
| filing | large | small, guaranteed (+ off line) | = PC and TSS |
| communication | network | term, emulation | = PC and TSS |
| CRT | slow response "glass teletype" | fast response, screen oriented | = PC = PC |
| cost | fixed, can go to lowest $/terminal | lowest entry | f(no. of PCs) |
| secure | shared, public access | totally private | contained/TSS |
| pros | explicit costs, shared programs, large jobs | low entry cost, "owned" by indiv., security, SW publishing = low cost | ability to expand, shared facilities, better match to org. structure |
| cons | shared, poor response for terminals, higher entry cost, security | limited capability, but increasing most rapidly | limited proc./ prog., shared facilities |
| heterogeneity | one homogeneous system | micro computers | one system/can be heterogenous |

*Personal workstation environment

tributed computing. Store and forward wide area networks evolved from the ARPAnet, which was used to interconnect timeshared mainframe computers (mostly PDP-10s).

### Campus Area Networks

When a collection of local area networks are connected together in a single area that extends beyond a typical LAN, we call this a campus. Universities clearly typify the campus as does a collection of buildings. Gateways are used to interconnect LANs of different types (e.g., Omninet, Ethernet [802.3], IBM Rings [802.4], Applenet, Arcnet, Broadband token bus [802.2] PCnet), whereas bridges or repeaters are used to interconnect networks of the same type to form one larger network. Bridge technology is necessary in connecting multiple LANs together on a wide-area basis using high-speed links (e.g., satellites).

### Wide Area Networks

WANs are characterized by low bandwidth (up to 56 Kbits), high latency, errorful transmission, and autonomous operation of the nodes. The applications typically include: mail, file transfer, database query, and low interaction remote terminal access. Wide area networks can be constructed in several ways: direct dial up using conventional circuit switching with voice-grade circuits, an intermediate store and forward network such as Telenet, or a hybrid approach where various worker computers do store and forward switching.

## The VAX, Homogeneous Environment or ''E''

Although the specific design of the VAX Environment began in December 1978 with the approval of the corporation, its origins include:

- □ the original VAX-11 goals for a 1000:1 range of computers;
- □ evolution of distributed processing minicomputer networks, in wide areas, ''campuses,'' and local areas;
- □ the appearance of powerful personal computers and local area networks, permitting the aggregation of tightly coupled ''PC networks and clusters'' that provide some of the benefits of timeshared minicomputers and mainframes; and
- □ the ability to aggregate minicomputers and mainframes into multiprocessors (the 78.2) and multicomputer clusters (VAX clusters) that appear to be a ''single'' system in order to provide higher reliability, higher performance, and incremental performance.

The December 1978 statement about the distributed computing environment (Fig. 6) and subsequent evolution [shown in brackets] was:

Provide a set of homogeneous, distributed-computing-system products based on VAX-11 so a user can interface, store information and compute without re-programming or extra work from the following computer's system sizes and styles:

- □ via [a cluster of] large, central (mainframe) computers or network;

- □ at a local, shared departmental/group/team (mini) computers [and evolving to a minicomputer with shared network servers];

- □ as a single user personal (micro) computer within a terminal [and evolving to PC clusters];

- □ with interfacing to other manufacturer and industry standard information processing systems; and

- □ all interconnected via the local area Network Interconnect, NI [i.e., Ethernet] in a single area, and the ability of interconnecting the Local Area Networks (LANs) to form Campus Area and Wide Area Networks.

Figure 7 shows the origin of the "E" shape that characterizes the VAX Homogeneous Computing Environment. The three horizontal segments of the "E" provide the different computing classes that roughly correspond to different-priced computers; the functions are described in Table 4. In order to implement the environment, many requirements were initially posited, and several developments evolved from necessity:

- □ a range of VAX-11 and 11-compatible computers to meet the requirements of the various computing styles based on different classes of computers; and

- □ interconnection schemes and the corresponding protocols for building multiprocessors, tightly coupled centralized VAX clusters, LAN-based PC clusters, LANs, campus area networks and wide area networks.

### GOALS OF THE ENVIRONMENT

#### Product Range

The important goals and constraints of the environment are contained in the original statement about what the environment should do, which is simply "to provide a very wide range of interconnectable VAX-11 computers." The original goal of VAX was to be able to implement the range (for what appears to be a single system) of a factor of 1000 price range . . . with no time limit given. Since a given implementation tends to provide, at a maximum, a range of 2–4 in price and 10 in performance if performance is measured as the product of processor speed times memory size, then many models and ways of interconnection were required.

At the time the 780 was introduced, the total range of products for both the VAX-11 and 11 family was almost 500, beginning with $1000, LSI-11 boards and going to a $500,000 VAX-11/780. The VAX 8600 increased the performance range by another factor of four. If the LSI-11 is included as a personal computer, the price range is reduced to only a factor of 50. While the two ends of the system were "compatible" and could be interconnected via DECNET, they lacked the coherency necessary for a fully homogeneous computing environment.

By introducing "VAX Clusters" (Fig. 7), the range can be extended by a factor of up to the number in the cluster, or about a factor of 10 more. For VAX, Digital now provides a price range of from about $20,000 for a MicroVAX II to about $7.5 million for a cluster of twelve 8600s and a corresponding performance range of several hundred. The VAX cluster, shown at the highest level of the hierarchy appears to the user as a single, high availability system.

The VAX cluster work was initiated concurrent with the VAX strategy to address the fault-tolerant, and incremental expansion needs for shared computing including a common disk and file system for the cluster. The interconnection of the clusters, using the computer interconnect (CI), was the beginning of a standard's activity for interconnecting computers on a standard basis.

### Static and Dynamic Assignment of Programs to Nodes

Ideally, a user can decide on how to compute on a completely variable basis at the following times:

- At system purchase or rent time ranging from outside facilities reached via gateways, to a central facility, to a shared department or team computer, to a user's own personal computer.

- At system-use time, ranging from access via a terminal, or personal computer interconnected to the system LAN, or a particular shared computer. Here work is bound statically to a particular set of system resources. Most likely, particular nodes would execute special programs on data located at the node.

- At task time on the basis of reliability. VAX clusters provide for dynamic allocation of work among the computers in the cluster to effect load balancing since files are centralized.

- At task-use time on a completely dynamic basis, ranging from computing on his own local system to being able to collect any resources and move work dynamically while programs are in execution. With this ability, as a program goes through its various stages of development, it might be moved from small system to large system to take advantage of increased computational power at higher level nodes.

- At task time on a dynamic basis with the ability to acquire arbitrary resources to engage in parallel computation.

## CONCLUSIONS

The VAX Homogeneous Computing Environment is an important computer structure for providing a computing environment. This environment encompasses all styles, sizes, and computing classes from the traditional mainframe and the high availability cluster (utilizing a fault tolerant architecture) to distributed minicomputers, and now the distributed personal workstations. It was stimulated by a number of factors including the distributed-workstation-environment idea. In terms of architectural scope, it is much broader than simply a range of computers as typified by the evolving IBM 360 − > 370 − > 43xx − > 30xx series because it provides full compatibility through homogeniety for a complete range of computing styles and does not require separate architectures for shared-minicomputer systems (System 36, System 38, and Series 1), personal computing (IBM, PC, word processor), or terminal switching and gateways (e.g., IBM 8100).

## REFERENCES

Bell, C. G., "The Multi: A New Class of Multiprocessor Computers," *Science* Vol. 228, No. 4698, 26 April 1985, 462–467.

Bell, C. G., H. Burkhardt, S. Emmerich, A. Anzelmo, R. Moore, D. Schanin, I. Nassi, and C. Rupp, "The Encore Continuum: A Complete Distributed Workstation-Multiprocessor Computing Environment," *AFIPS Conference Proceeding,* 1985, Vol. 54, 147–155.

Bell, C. G., G. Fujisaki, J. M. Heinz, A. S. Stevens, and A. S. House, "Reduction of Speech Spectra by Analysis-by-Synthesis Techniques," *The Journal of the Acoustical Society of America,* Vol. 33, No. 12, 1961, 1725–1736.

Bell, C. G., J. C. Mudge, and J. E. McNamara, *Computer Engineering,* Digital Press, Bedford, Mass., 1978.

Bell, C. G., and A. Newell, *Computer Structures: Readings and Examples,* McGraw-Hill, New York, 1971.

Burger, R. M., R. K. Caving, W. C. Holton, and L. W. Sumney, "The Impact of ICs on Computer Technology," *Computer,* Vol. 10, No. 10. October 1984, 88–96.

Clark, W. A., and C. E. Molnar, "The LINC: A Description of the Laboratory Instrument Computer," *Annals of the New York Academy of Sciences,* Vol. 115, July 1964, 653–668.

Metropolis, N., J. Howlett, and R. Gian-Carlo (Editors), *A History of Computing in the Twentieth Century,* Academic Press, New York, 1980.

Pake, G. E., "Research at Xerox PARC: A Founder's Assessment," *IEEE Spectrum,* Vol. 22, No. 10, October 1985, 54–61.

Perry, T. S., and P. Wallich, "Inside the PARC: The Information Architects," *IEEE Spectrum,* Vol. 22, No. 10, October 1985, 62–76.

Ralston, A. (Editor) and E. D. Reilly (Assoc. Editor), *Encyclopedia of Computer Science and Engineering,* Second Edition, Van Nostrand Reinhold Company, 1983, New York.

Redmond, K. C., and T. M. Smith, *Project Whirlwind: A History of a Pioneer Computer,* Digital Press, Bedford, Mass., 1980.

Roberts, L. G., ''Computer Network Development to Achieve Resource Sharing,'' *AFIPS Conference Proceedings, SJCC,* Vol. 36, 1970, 543–549.

Siewiorek, D. S., C. G. Bell, and A. Newell, *Computer Structures,* McGraw-Hill, New York, 1982.

Wexelblat, R. L. (Editor), *History of Programming Languages,* Academic Press, New York, 1981.

# Participants Discussion

**Allen Newell**

Let me make just one remark before opening up the discussion. Gordon, right at the beginning, said we all have to be aware of the danger of participant history. In fact, there are a number of biases that come from being participants, even though as Alan Perlis remarked, it's important to get this all out on the table before this whole movement disappears a few years from now. There are a couple of other worries in history that one might note. One of them is called ''whig'' history. I don't know how many of you are familiar with that term. This is the tendency to write history by going back into the past and re-creating it only as it relates to the future. This turns out not to be a very big danger for us since our problem is that we are participants. There is yet a third difficulty in history for scientists—the writing of internal history. We believe that everything flows out of our own internal work and that science or technology proceeds only on the basis of previous science or technology.

One of the nice things about Gordon's talk, it seemed to me, is that he helped us to recognize that we are driven fairly strongly by the commercial interests and also by the technology driver that is outside of us. Consequently, we are not likely to forget, and Gordon certainly hasn't, how much of our history is not internally generated, but is generated by outside boundary conditions. Although the work still has to be done to get from those technologies and interests to the actual workstations.

There is yet one more difficulty about history that I think is peculiar to the workstation and graphics. It is that we will substitute pictures for history. The pictures are only the very top highlights. The question of the human efforts, and where the ideas came from, and the other events that allowed those to happen—the real web of causality—lies below those pictures. One needs to be a little careful about this. And Gordon finally switched from pictures and gave the second half of his talk on the ideas and events. I'm glad he did complete the framework.

**Doug Ross**

Gordon invited comments on his early slides and I have just two. I'm really glad that you had that picture of the Whirlwind test control area (Fig. 14), because I have a later one. Yours, I believe, is from 1951 or 1952—very early. You can figure that out from the MITRE company's cassettes, but that is earlier than the inclusion of the SAGE Cape Cod material. The other comment is with respect to the start of Ed Jack's interest in computer-aided design at General Motors. I'm not sure, be-

**FIGURE 14**
Whirlwind around 1955, because the breadboard for the Cape Cod System, which was the breadboard of SAGE, is shown. This is the console room where you can see a CRT for air traffic control work. Whirlwind also spawned another interactive computer that ran for a few months called MTC, which was used to test the core's memory but was never seriously used.

cause I haven't checked my records, whether it was before or after he became enamored with the PDP-1. But at one point, he and Don Hart visited me at MIT. We had done some of the light cannon work on the 704. Ed had at his plant one of the real-time packages that IBM supplied. He also had a very clever technician who knew about how the on-line printer worked, and so, in order to make his first tracking program there at the beginning of the DEC project, they used the echo check circuitry that was built into the on-line-connected line printer. That was the only way this technician could figure out how to get a signal back into the computer. They hooked that up to the photo multiplier tube and, sure enough, were tracking shadow similar to what I'll be talking about, so I thought that was an interesting comment on your DEC thing. It must have been either 1960 or 1961.

*John Brackett*    I would hope that when the history actually gets written, some of the key software events, rather than just hardware events, that made personal workstations possible will be, perhaps, more identified. Let me just point out a couple about which other speakers might comment. Clearly it was somewhat of a milestone when computers in an interactive mode started to be used by professionals that were not familiar with programming. Glen Culler was the person who got me into this field, although he probably doesn't know it, when I first saw, as a chemist, his system in 1961 or early 1962. But I also believe that in the period of 1964 to 1965, on the MIT time sharing system, there became a critical mass of software that began to bring people from the sciences and engineering, who had never written a program, to use what I will call "program-oriented language systems" that required no real knowledge of how the system worked. And really, if we talk about professional workstations, clearly many of the people from the professions had not the slightest idea how to write a FORTRAN program or a LISP program. It was also an event, one that perhaps Dr. Licklider will come back to, when a person who knew nothing about the internal storage of information in the MIT time-sharing system was able to share other people's information. I remember when that happened. A significant idea was that you could use other people's programs, without knowing anything about where they were, to build even larger pieces of software. I believe that was in early 1965—a very interesting step forward in software. So, hopefully, the software side of key events in this industry will get into the history.

*Thelma Estrin*      I think another part of the history is the pull of the application or the pull of the professionals, how strong the need is, and when the technology is ready to help. I was at the Brain Research Institute all through the 1960s, and we also had a Culler-Fried personal workstation. We used it for graphics and a whole bunch of things; it is not in any history because it's tied up with grants to NIH to try to get funding for brain research. I think that there are probably other examples when the history comes from different application areas, which, very often, are known only internally; it never made it to the market place or was described except in small papers and specialized conferences.

# A PERSONAL VIEW OF THE PERSONAL WORK STATION—SOME FIRSTS IN THE FIFTIES

## Doug Ross
Introduction by Severo Ornstein

**Severo Ornstein**

**M**y name is Severo Ornstein. I've fooled with computers for a little over 30 years and, in fact, I was at Lincoln Laboratory at about the same time as our next speaker. So I've been asked to be the discussant for him.

Hindsight is supposed to be easier than foresight, but it occurs to me that in my experience, hindsight is the hard thing. You get a bunch of computer people together arguing about which way things ought to go, and the arguments can be pretty fierce, but they don't ever seem to be as fierce as the arguments about how things went. I suspect there is going to be more of this as time goes on.

We tend to think of the history of a field as commencing more or less when we got into it ourselves. Everything before was somehow a given when we came along, and so we're really only interested in history from the point where we got into the field. But, of course, it's not really that way. Everything's got an antecedent.

Last night I read through Doug's paper. Although Doug and I were at Lincoln Laboratory at about the same time and must have passed one another a thousand times in the hall, we never actually met until this morning. I was, of course, aware of his work. Reading his paper took me back in a number of ways. First of all, it was lovely to run into familiar names of people and places, conjuring up all sorts of memories. One of the reasons we're here is that we like that a lot; it

51

Douglas T. Ross is Chairman of the Board of SofTech, Inc., in Waltham, Massachusetts. Doug has been with SofTech since its inception, serving as President from 1969 to 1975 when he was appointed Board Chairman. From 1979 to 1981 he was also Chairman of the Board of SofTech Micro-systems, Inc., in San Diego, California. Previously, he held various posts at the Massachusetts Institute of Technology, first as teaching assistant (1951–1952), then head of the Computer Applications Group (1952–1969) as well as lecturer in the Electrical Engineering Department (1960–1969). He continues as a lecturer in the MIT Electrical Engineering and Computer Science departments, where he is a Member of the Life-long Continuing Education Committee.

Educated in mathematics (A.B., Oberlin College 1951) and pure math, and electrical engineering (1951–1956, with M.S., MIT 1954), Doug has published extensively on aspects of automatic programming of numerically controlled machine tools, symbolic manipulation and numerical calculation, CAD systems, software engineering, high-level programming languages, and structured analysis. He served as an editor of the *IEEE Transactions on Software Engineering,* and is currently editor of *SOFTWARE: Practice and Experience* and on the Editorial Board for *Computers in Industry.* He has won many awards, including the 1980 Society of Manufacturing Engineers (SME) Distinguished Contributions Award and the 1975 Joseph Marie Jacquard Memorial Award of the Numerical Control Society, and he authored the book, *Introduction to Software Engineering with the AED-O Language* (Waltham, Mass.: SofTech, Inc., 1969).

locates us, in some sense, in history. In the 1950s, a lot of the ideas that underlay the work that has followed since were brewing in people's heads. As I read Doug's paper last night, I realized how much of that there actually had to be. We tend to think in terms of artifacts as we look back, but what happens is some strange mixture of artifacts and ideas—ways of thinking. It appears that Doug was very influential in seeing what was available in the 1950s and recognizing possibilities growing out of that into the future. The hardware that he had available at that time looks very primitive, but the ideas were very, very far-reaching. It seems to me that the impact on what has happened is just enormous. In reading his paper I suddenly realized how revolutionary the thinking was that was going on at that time. We take it all for granted now, but it was really revolutionary then.

Did you ever notice when you look at pictures of the old computers (ENIAC or something of that era) that people are standing up in front of them? One of the notions that Doug had was that of a partnership between a person and a computer. If you're going to enter into a partnership with somebody, you can't just stand there all day long, you eventually have to spend a lot of time together. It used to be that people sat down only when they wrote programs, off somewhere else while they were thinking through the problem. When they actually got to the computer they stood up and someone took a picture so that we could all sit here today and look at those pictures. But Doug envisioned this idea of a partnership in which you actually sit down and work at the machine. So I like to think that what Doug has done is to make it possible for the rest of us to sit down. True to form, he's going to do that for me right now.

# A Personal View of the Personal Work Station
# Some Firsts in the Fifties

*Douglas T. Ross*
SofTech/MIT

## Introduction

"What the h--- kind of program do you *have* there?" the intercom
blasted forth, the sound distorted by the intensity of the shout. It was
the chief computer operator in Test Control (as the standard control
area for the Whirlwind I Computer was called) calling me in great agi-
tation. I couldn't reply at once, for I was some twelve feet away from
the loudspeaker of the E31 console—in the far back corner of the secret
and darkened room 222 of the Barta Building at MIT. I was hunched
over a 16-inch oscilloscope called the area discriminator. It was
mounted vertically in a box on the floor, so its face made a horizontal
flat surface. Adhered to the tip of my moving finger was a bright,
glowing displayed spot of blue-white light, about 1/4 inch square. I
was in the process of writing my name into the computer with that
spot—freehand. It was sometime in the fall of 1954.

It was one of the few programs I ever wrote that worked the first
time. I remember that I dreamed it up on a long flight back from Texas,
which must have been at most a few days earlier. Fewer than 200 instructions were required, and the hardest part was understanding the
octal constants that calibrated the scope display coordinates.

### MY SOURCES

This is my second foray into the tribulations of writing (rather than
making) history. In 1977 I worked for months on my paper "Origins
of the APT Language for Automatically Programmed Tools" for presentation at the History of Programming Languages Conference, June
1–3, 1978, in Los Angeles (Ross 1977). As was the case for that paper,
I have taken as my primary source my extensive personal collection of
archival working papers, reports, and records, which I have retained
over the years, and I have attempted to include only observations I can
directly support from these records. Unfortunately, I am less sure than
was the case for APT whether or not my current story is complete,
however, for the early portions hinge on older material that is less organized and perhaps less complete. I say "perhaps," because I cannot
determine whether certain materials I remember seeing are missing, or
merely are misplaced. At one point in SofTech's impecunious past,

rather than buying needed file cabinets, all of my historic files were without my knowledge summarily crammed into a large number of storage boxes whose length dimension was more than one file drawer. I still have not been able to retrace what was where, as useful chinks in the boxes were filled here and there by segments of unrelated files! In later years I may be able to fill in more details, as relevant portions come to light, but even so, what I have found already yields an engrossing trail.

As in the APT history paper, to provide concise reference to the materials in my files (which ultimately will reside in the MIT Archives) without spelling out each item I have used the following condensed notation: [C540123] means "correspondence 1954 January 23''; [R56123] means "daily resume (a form of personal professional diary) 1956 December 3''; and [WW2Q55p10] means "Whirlwind I Quarterly Report Second Quarter, 1955, page 10'' (see Project Whirlwind 1952–1957).

### THE THEME

I am not an historian at all, and can't bring myself to write a straightforward (dull) recounting of events. For these stories from the past I feel I must have a theme to provide some perspective. Also, by writing in the first person, I can try to give some of the feel of the times in ways that I hope add interest. But also I think such a style allows a more accurate interpretation of what actually was in the air as the documented events took place, even though surely all that is written is biased by recollections, as well.

I take the unique event of the first hand-drawn input to a computer as the starting point of my theme for this paper—that *The Personal Work Station as a working reality (rather than a speculative idea) did have a recognizable era of beginning more than 30 years ago.* Like the present era, where the physical and performance characteristics of the *work station* aspect of the PWS are so essential, the fact that Whirlwind *had* the Area Discriminator scope was an essential ingredient of my successful program. But my theme is much sharper than that, and in a sense even contradicts the natural emphasis on the *work station* characteristics which dominates most writing on the topic. My real theme is that *it is the revolution in personal work* (i.e., explicitly the PW, rather than the WS, of the PWS) *that was, and is even more so today, what is important.* (This also is why, throughout this paper I purposely spell PWS with three words rather than the accepted (correct) two, to stress my view.)

I hope to show that from the very beginning, the changes in personal working style, made possible by the idea that man and machine can *share* in the problem-solving process, is what makes the personal work station idea a unique and valuable departure from the customary view of using computers. With the PWS idea, the computer becomes a partner not a mere tool. And to integrate and actually realize this PW and WS idea, requires a *systematized treatment* of the software that links man to machine. That is the third component of my theme.

## OVERVIEW

In the time available to me, I can trace only the beginnings of this theme. As was the case with the APT story, I find that my records show that this PWS story breaks "naturally into a number of overlapping but nonetheless distinct *periods* during which the focus of attention highlighted first one and then another and then another aspect of the overall subject" (Ross 1977, p. 282).

The *first period* covers my introduction to Whirlwind and programming, in the summer of 1952, and brings out that even with all its rooms full of equipment in its own building at MIT, Whirlwind was a miniscule microcomputer by today's standards for personal work station capacity. And to start with, Whirlwind lacked some needed features, as well.

The *second period,* from August 1952 through August 1953, saw the flexibility and capacity of Whirlwind expanded, as facilities geared up for the focus on the development of the Cape Cod System—the R&D base that led to the full-scale development of the SAGE Air Defense System by Lincoln Laboratory (Redmond and Smith, pp. 201–213). Most of the environmental equipment for PWS evolution now was present, but my available records don't indicate whether or not I yet had discovered the wonders of the mysterious room 222.

In any case, well before the summer of 1954, during the *third period* when I completed my master's thesis (Ross 1954b) and our work on large-scale data reduction programs (Ross 1953b) actually got under way (which was the driving force for my own insights and endeavors), I did gain access to the classified areas of the Barta Building and knew that we simply *had* to incorporate the marvels of *manual intervention* (or MIV as it was then called) into our system capability. The problem was that I didn't know how to program for all that equipment.

The problem was solved in the *fourth period* (June 1954 through early 1955) by hiring Bill Wolf from Lincoln Lab. Bill had done some of the early MIV programming for Lincoln. His early departure forced me to learn what I needed to know as I completely rewrote his code to conform to my plans, which were more general than Lincoln's use of the same WS equipment. This also, of course, was the period when I wrote the *Scope Input Program* (Ross 1954d). Another innovation triggered by my needs was the creation of the Director Tape utility program [WW3Q54p7], the first real *operating system* command language system (to use present-day terms) to eliminate the computer operator function for my elaborate, multi-tape runs. By the third quarter of 1954 my plans for MIV use were quite general and well developed.

The *fifth period* focuses on the preparations for and delivery of two Servo Lab symposia at MIT. The first, held on March 8 and 9, 1955 on "Design and Evaluation of Bomber Fire-Control Systems" (MIT Servo Lab 1955) covered our project's entire hardware and software system for complex system testing. The second, on June 1 and 2, 1955, covered just the MIV-controlled data reduction methods (Ward and Ross 1955). Both symposia demonstrated the new techniques to large groups from outside MIT. My PWS ideas were now a working reality, in this particular setting.

The *sixth period* concerns my first professional paper, "*Gestalt Programming: A New Concept in Automatic Programming*" (Ross 1956b), which I presented as the opening paper at the Western Joint Computer Conference in Los Angeles, February 7, 1956 (WJCC 1956). I actually had proposed the paper in November 1955 [C551117, to B.J. Bennett, Prog. Chrm.] and had presented a preliminary version at MIT on January 11, 1956 [C56015], but as I recount here, it was a long process to arrive at a reasonable formulation of the ideas in acceptable form, at the beginning. I consider that paper to be my own definitive statement of the PW theme of this current PWS paper, but written at that earlier time.

The *seventh period* actually overlaps periods two through six, in time, for it concerns the long period when, with John Ward and others on the Fire-Control System Evaluation Project, we formulated, proposed, designed, and then assisted in the installation of a full-scale *Charactron-based MIV Console for the Univac 1103* computer at Eglin Field Air Force Base in Florida for the evaluation of the B-58 "Hustler" supersonic bomber tail turret (Ward and Ross 1956). That the actual testing would be done at Eglin had been known since at least early 1954. I had done a special Charactron demo for the June 1955 symposium, and the MIV console itself finally was installed in 1957 [C571024, J. E. Ward to J. L. Moser, Stromberg Carlson]. The Whirlwind facilities were duplicated, and their actual circuit drawings were used in the design, thanks to Lincoln Lab cooperation.

Even the Whirlwind setup was not complete as yet, however, and the *eighth period* mentions briefly my proposal (March 1956) (Ross 1956d) for direct Flexowriter *keyboard input* to Whirlwind to complete our MIV facilities. Until that time, the Whirlwind Flexowriters had been hooked up and used only for printed (or punched) *output* and only punched *tape input*. Barriers to the gestalt programming concept, both conceptual and physical, were very high in those days, and even when the flexo input was available, its use was a far cry from the central role that keyboards play in today's PWS and word processing practice. We lacked the computing capacity for full on-line keyboard use.

The flexo input was just one part of the facilities incorporated into the *SLURP System* (Servo Lab Utility Routine Programs) for large-scale, experimental program development (Ross 1958), which is what the gestalt programming concept then had evolved into. It was made possible by the luxury of the expansion of Whirlwind's magnetic core memory to 6K 16-bit words (yes, that's 12K *bytes*, in today's terminology!) with the *cf*, change fields, instruction to select any two 1K banks of words at one time [WW3Q56p44]. SLURP was the first complete interactive software development environment, with many programming, language development, debugging, and display tools all integrated into an interpretive environment with *group control* for core versus drum storage management, and automatic logging and log playback of all MIV actions. Reminiscent of today's debate regarding menu control and how many buttons to put on a mouse, a universal "MIV Box" subroutine gave complete control over these hierarchic facilities with only *major and minor exit buttons* and one *wait switch* for stepping and selecting from one control level to another. From today's vantage point, I can't imagine how we did all that in just 12K bytes with only a few (two or three?) times that much magnetic drum backup. But we did. I take SLURP to be the systematized solution, third component of my PWS theme in this paper. Development continued until the demise of Whirlwind in 1958.

The *ninth period* artificially cuts off abruptly at the start of 1960, to match my title and put a stop to burgeoning growth of what might be covered. Its beginning overlaps the other periods of focus, with the plans and actions to carry on MIV work on the IBM 704, 709, 7090, and 7094 computers at MIT, after Whirlwind's demise. Although artificial, this actually is a good stopping place, because other, broader themes spring from this period. Timesharing, computer graphics (both hardware and software), computer-aided design, software engineering (both language and practice), and software technology tools and methods all blossomed and flourished at MIT in the 1960s, and have direct ties to the story I present here. But those are tales for another time.

## Preparation

Significant events always are the rearrangement into new forms of otherwise ordinary and insignificant, routine happenings. The ordinariness allows the significance to be recognized. What was the environment, and what was going on at Whirlwind that triggered a new and more intimate kind of computer use? What were the pieces from which the PWS idea began in this story? The preparation for my theme also is the preparation stage of my story.

## PROGRAMMING BACKGROUND

I came to MIT in the Fall of 1951 as a teaching assistant in the mathematics department, having received an A.B. Cum Laude in math from Oberlin College in June. Pat and I had been married the previous January, and she was the first of a group of "computers" hired by Lincoln Laboratory (Badge No. 161), which was just getting under way, performing calculation and graphing assignments for the engineers, using Marchant desk calculators. One of her assignments involved using a mechanical correlation computer, designed by Norbert Weiner, which was in use in the Servomechanisms Laboratory at MIT (Ward 1954). When I needed a summer job for 1952, I applied to the Servo Lab, and was hired also as a "computer." One of my first jobs involved checking some anomalous points that had been obtained on that mechanical correlator, and someone suggested that I see if Whirlwind could be used, for they knew that Jack Arnow had written such a program. Jack later founded Interactive Data Corporation (now part of Chase Manhattan Bank) as one of the early timesharing service companies.

I, of course, had never heard of Whirlwind or of *real* computers, so I was fascinated. I still have Jack's little program, plus the Digital Computer Lab application form for Problem #87 (July 2, 1952) to get computer time, some scribbled yellow papers where John Frankovich (still working at Lincoln Lab) gave me my first programming pointers, and the "Tape 1414 Mod O" July 11 printout of my autocorrelation program. My earliest run request (July 18) shows that I was already up to Mod 3 one week later (Ross 1952).

Before I could complete the debugging of my rather elaborate program (which later was used in many projects and theses by others) Whirlwind was completely shutdown from August 11 through August 30, 1952! [WW3Q52p6] I used the time to write a matching Fourier transform program so that power density spectra could be computed (which also was widely used, and formed the basis for an improved program for my own master's thesis in 1954). The reason for the shutdown is the real starting point for my PWS theme—for in that period the entire input/output system for Whirlwind was drastically modified to provide the elaborate hardware facilities needed for Whirlwind's new and primary Lincoln Lab mission: high priority development of an air defense system for the United States and North America.

The Whirlwind order code (of 32 instruction types, maximum) was revised so that *si, so, rd, rc, bi,* and *bo* for "select input", "select output", "read", "record", "block in", and "block out" could be used for any one of a large number of input/output lines to which analog scopes, mechanical switches, "activate" (one-shot) pushbuttons, indicator lights, and magnetic drums could be attached. The mechanisms for general *manual intervention* in the running of programs were at hand.

Only the barest essentials trickled out to the programmers of the user problems. Most of the subsequent construction took place behind the locked, green, double doors of Room 222, which was strictly off limits. With the end of the summer at hand, and with my important programs in limbo and my enthusiasm for programming running at white heat, my supervisor, John Ward (still at MIT) asked me whether I really wanted to go back to teaching freshman calculus, or would I rather make a career for myself in Servo Lab, full time, taking courses as a special student. I felt obligated to fulfill my 1952 fall teaching assignment, so we arranged for me to do that in addition to working full time programming and taking graduate math courses for that semester. The math department wasn't happy to lose me. I had been so serious and successful about my teaching assistant role that I had been appointed as the only graduate student member of the Dean's group of freshman advisors. But I remained with the lab until August 1969, when my colleagues and I left to found SofTech.

### PROJECT BACKGROUND

The Air Force-sponsored project headed by John Ward was concerned with the test and evaluation of the accuracy and performance of airborne fire-control systems—specifically servo-controlled tail turrets in bombers. The autocorrelation and Fourier transform programs were part of the study of radar noise analysis. I was the only mathematician in the laboratory, and one reason for hiring me was that a new form of air-mass ballistic tables had just been developed (Nielsen and Heyda 1951, p. 9), more accurate than the old tables that had been developed for ground artillery and required extensive compensation to account for rapid movement through rarified air. My first major assignment (November 1952) was to see how these new tables could be used for the evaluation problem.

By January 12, 1953, I had a complete data flow diagram (Ross 1953a) for hit probability density calculation, based on fourteen measured inputs, and using vector calculations well suited to the three-dimensional problem and digital computing. With further elaboration and refinement over the next five years, the complexity of actually programming and operating this solution for production data reduction

(Ross 1953b) was the stimulus for all my MIV developments until the advent of the Computer-Aided Design Project in 1959.

The main part of the project was directed toward the development of airborne flight test instrumentation that could measure the many variables during mock attacks by a fighter aircraft pursuing a bomber. With the feasibility of the digital computer data reduction established, attention focused on digital instrumentation (primarily shaft encoders to convert selsyn-repeated analog quantities into Gray-coded binary) for recording on a flyable magnetic tape that then could automatically be read into the data reduction computer on the ground. (Telemetry was too unreliable in those days to risk on such an expensive program.) By 1954 our efforts were targeted toward meeting the needs for evaluation of the XMD-7 Fire Control System being built by Emerson Electric for the secret supersonic B-58 "Hustler" bomber. The B-58 was not yet ready, so the program was called "Pre-B-58," and tests were run with the B-47 in the beginning (MIT Servo Lab 1958). It was the most sophisticated test program of its time, and cost over $10,000 per flight hour, just for the aircraft, I believe.

By the spring of 1953, programming was complete for the autocorrelation functions and work had begun on a polynomial fit program (Ross 1954c) to place the ballistics tables in computable form. By the summer, an elaborate *mistake diagnosis routine* (MDR) (Ross 1953c) which allowed breakpoints to be set in an arbitrary program, with intermediate results saved for printout or displayed on the camera scope, was written and disclosed that the interpretive floating point arithmetic routines of the Whirlwind comprehensive system (CS) were inaccurate, so they were repaired, to everybody's benefit [WW4Q53-p25andp11]. The MDR played a continuing role in our experimental programming environment, especially when it later was placed under MIV control. In the summer of 1953 the first programming for the evaluation equations also got underway [WW3Q53p25], but most of my time in early 1954 was focussed on my master's thesis on minimizing Gibbs' phenomenon oscillations in the computation of Fourier transforms. But by the summer of 1954 the programming stage was set for our first serious use of manual intervention techniques in our work.

## HARDWARE BACKGROUND

To complete the stage-setting for the Scope Input coup, I will give the following synopsis of Whirlwind hardware developments during the corresponding period. In the summer of 1952, when I started to program on Whirlwind, it had only 1024 words of *electrostatic storage* (ES) of 16 bits each, and operated at the then-blinding speed of 20,000 operations per second (hence its name) [WW3Q52p4]. In those days we used both audio and visual aids in the debugging of programs. Originally, a scope in Test Control duplicated the $X$-$Y$ deflections of the ES tubes' storage matrix so that the loop structure of programs could be seen, in action. The more often a loop body was executed, the brighter its trace. The audio aid consisted of a loudspeaker attached to a digit (I believe was digit 13 of the accumulator) so that every time its binary state changed from a 1 to a 0 or back, a beep was heard. The execution rate of program instructions was such that loops of different lengths made tweedly tones up and down the scale, so that you could hear the various phases of the program taking place.

After the shutdown and changeover to the new I/O system in August 1952, things remained stable for a time, but in the second quarter of 1953 ES was doubled to 2048 words by the addition of another bank of 17 tubes (one was a parity digit) [WW2Q53p30]. Then suddenly and smoothly, in the third quarter of 1953, both ES banks were permanently replaced by the first two banks of *magnetic core memory* (on-line August 8 and September 5, respectively) [WW3Q53p32-34]. The magnetic memory cycled at 9 microseconds versus 23 microseconds for ES, so Whirlwind now could do over 40,000 instructions per second [WW4Q54p4]. But still most loop structures remained in audio range, so the loudspeaker retained its usefulness.

The ES scope trace had been abandoned in the fourth quarter of 1952 when my first-ever program for computing the autocorrelation function couldn't be run without causing Whirlwind to break down. Other programs sometimes gave trouble, too, but mine showed the problem to be that its tightest calculating loop fell in a group of registers that happened to fall in one corner of the square matrix of storage locations. The spherical pattern of the ES tube's holding gun (which uniformly, but with inverse square law fall-off, sprayed the entire storage surface with electrons to compensate for leakage) couldn't be adjusted for the corners without upsetting the center of the matrix, when adjacent bits were accessed so rapidly. The engineers solved the problem by changing the diode pattern of the $X$-$Y$ decoders so that consecutive words were randomly scattered around the square matrix, so that even tight loops were geographically dispersed [WW4Q52p6]. My program, with a short data tape, was added to the regular maintenance test suite used for ES adjustment and checkout, and the ES memory trace scope was no longer useful for debugging, since loops didn't show clearly.

In the meantime, however, many Whirlwind programs made use of the 16-inch display scopes, and Test Control had two of them mounted high up on a rack. The lower one had a 35mm camera under computer control, for making photographic records, and the upper one could have all 16 analog display lines ganged together to serve as a monitor check on whatever program was running. Thus the normal operational milieu for the computer operators still had the full audio-visual complex of lights, scope, and loudspeaker. When a strange sound pattern occurred, the reflex action was to glance at the monitor scope, and then start to examine the indicator lights to gauge roughly by brightness where the program was operating in memory or was the accumulator stuck in some repeating pattern, etc. That's what the operators had done, when I got that loud, panic call over the intercom.

There were more than a dozen other scopes in the cavernous black-painted, shrouded room 222, eerily lit by dark red light (Fig. 1). All except the area discriminator scope were mounted at a slant, surrounded by banks of push buttons and indicator lights in several styles of interactive consoles for the various personnel needed to perform the many functions of airplane tracking and control of the air defense mission. The most elaborate was the *E31 console* of the combat data

**FIGURE 1**
**Room 222 of Cape Cod System.** Closest two airmen with backs to camera are at E31 console (right) and adjacent console (left) used for gestalt programming. Directly beyond them is tripod and box of the area discriminator light cannon. Originally walls were black. Indirect ceiling lamps had red bulbs for system operation. (2/19/54)

director, which in addition to its elaborate set of buttons and lights, duplicated the essential master controls for Whirlwind, so that the entire complex could be controlled from that station, bypassing the normal operations of the master Test Control in the main computer room. But I, of course, had no knowledge of any of this, yet—it was all very hush hush, and you needed special security clearance and a need to know to even take a peek.

My records don't show when it happened, but sometime in 1953 or early 1954 arrangements finally were made with Lincoln Lab to allow John Ward and me to be introduced to the enticing room 222. I can still remember that first walk through the black-cloth-draped entryway into the red-lit, darkened room just *filled* with green-glowing scopes and orange-red neon indicator lights. Neat! Just what we could use to obtain mastery over the behemoth evaluation program, for whose complexity I already had a growing respect. The functioning of the various parts of the Cape Cod system were explained to us (although it was only later that we saw an actual test run with planes being tracked by the operators, etc.). It was clear that the E31 console (Fig. 2), with part of an adjacent console (Fig. 3), would be the best control station (PWS!) for general purposes, since the full complex of capabilities (including light gun and more buttons on an adjacent console) was available there along with the duplicated computer controls and the intercom.

The area discriminator almost got lost in the shuffle. I now will give a complete description of it. All the other scopes were mounted in consoles with switches, buttons, and light gun for manual intervention. The Whirlwind *light gun* (Fig. 4) was shaped like a backward pistol, with a sight close to your trigger finger knuckle and a wire coming out of a barrel that extended back over your hand. The barrel con-

**FIGURE 2**
**E31 console in room 222.** Note intervention register octal keyboard banks and intervention switches, activate pushbuttons and lights, functionally arranged. Intercom and computer restart button on right.

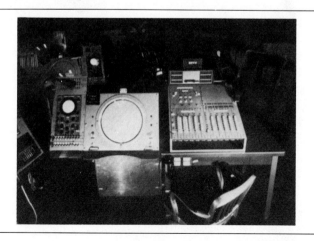

**FIGURE 3**
Cape Cod Console
with light gun and
manual intervention
(MIV) equipment.

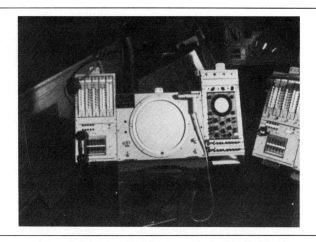

tained a photo-multipler tube, and the wire connected to an ''si'' line of the computer. If a displayed spot was in the sight when the trigger was pulled, that would set an *activate bit* (one-time, read-only) so that a suitable ''si, rd'' sequence following the ''si, rc'' that displayed the spot (but before any other spot was displayed) said that the operator had selected that spot from all the others in the display. This was used to assign tracking functions to radar blips which were returns from airplanes.

**FIGURE 4**
Final design of Cape
Cod light gun, with
sight (10/2/53).

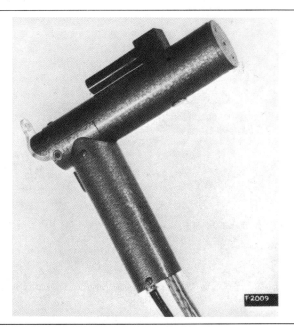

The Area Discriminator had no buttons, lights, or anything for human intervention. It simply sat in a large box in the back corner of the room. Mounted on the box was a tripod that supported a smaller box with no bottom, so that it was suspended about 18 inches over the horizontal scope face surface. This was the light *cannon*—a photomultiplier tube mounted so that it viewed the whole scope face and could be "si, rd" read for any spot in the display. When we saw it in the Cape Cod system use, a large circular piece of dark yellow plexiglass had been laid down, centered over the scope face so that only a narrow annular ring around the edge of the scope was open to the light cannon's view. The yellow filtered out of the blue phosphor flash of any displayed points, so the cannon was blind to all central display activity, but any fresh radar tracks crossing the perimeter could be seen and could be brought to the attention of the track initiator/monitor operator for light gun tracking. This is why it was called "the area discriminator," and with the plexiglass disk in place, it actually was an analog computing element component of the Cape Cod system.

### SOFTWARE BACKGROUND

My guess is that our tour of room 222 probably was sometime in the spring of 1954, for the three 16-inch scopes mentioned in the fourth quarter 1952 Whirlwind Quarterly Report (at the time of the I/O shutdown) had grown to more than twenty, and I think all the Cape Cod consoles were complete at the time. In any case, I had my thesis to finish, Dick Turyn who had been programming on the evaluation program was leaving so I needed a replacement, and we needed to learn the ins and outs of room 222 programming. Therefore we hired Bill Wolf from Lincoln Lab, solving several problems at once. He came in June 1954, but stayed only about six months, (MIT Servo Lab 1952–1958) when he left to go into consulting for himself. Later he formed Wolf Research and Development Corp., which acquired Whirlwind itself under Navy sponsorship, when Lincoln and MIT had no further use for it (Redmond and Smith 1980, p. 224). Wolf R&D also had the first facilities contract to run NASA Houston computers, I believe.

I guess I'd have to say that Bill was a better businessman than programmer. He did a fine job for me, writing a basic set of programs to use all the functions of the E31 console and a program to display large, fat letters on the scope, big enough to be directly read from the 35 mm film so that we could frame our classified results with "CONFIDENTIAL—SERVO LAB—CONFIDENTIAL" before and after our plots and displays (Wolf 1954). But the programming style was very tangled and hard to follow (and I suppose not atypical of the code of other Lincoln people who were learning to master the tricks of this new manual intervention trade, for that was a major reason I hired him). Bill's code was far from debugged when he got the wanderlust. I hadn't been working closely enough with him to know what I was getting into, but I said I'd finish the debugging because that would give me the education I'd wanted anyhow. So off he went to make his fortune.

Almost immediately I saw that I would have to completely rewrite and replace Bill's work, and proceeded to do so. Many features of modularity, flexibility, robustness, and generality were needed in order to match my growing vision of what general MIV (i.e., the PW functionality of PWS) was to be all about. Without Bill's efforts to critique, many of these aspects (which I certainly had not articulated beforehand as specifications) would not have occurred to me until much later. Also some basic principles of MIV programming (that I have seen violated repeatedly in the 1970s and 1980s as the microcomputer age programmers have re-encountered and reinvented those 30-year old phenomena) showed up in my critique of Bill's code. For example, he had the "si, rd" to read a switch directly at the point-of-use in the program flow, throughout. I structured separate read cycles and stored the switch settings in program variables. Not only did this make the overall program better structured, but it also meant that anything that could be done manually also could be done automatically, because actual program control came from the stored variables, not from the switches themselves. This feature made possible our log and playback of manual actions as well as test simulations.

## DIRECTOR TAPES

It was while I was first reading, with some understanding, about the complete set of "si" capabilities of Whirlwind (including the Lincoln Lab-only portions, previously unknown to me) that I discovered that the mechanical tape reader of the Test Control Flexowriter was still operable, even though there always had been a photoelectric tape reader (PETR) since I had been around. Although the print mechanism of the Flexowriter had been in daily use all along, for operator communication, and the direct tape punch recorded some logging information, the tape reader had no current use. The number of separate tapes and the complexity of operator instructions for our evaluation program runs was getting so bad that I suggested to John Frankovich and Frank Helwig (on the Digital Computer Lab staff) that the Whirlwind utilities should be expanded to put all these instructions on a tape that the mechanical reader could read, while the main tapes were read in by the much faster PETR. It was worth the wait for that idea to get worked into their schedule [WW3Q54p7], for the *Director Tape* program, as it was called, included not only the terse control language basics, but also conventions for labelling punched tape headers as to type (binary, program, post mortem request, etc.). When director tapes were further upgraded in the summer of 1956, they still were not used by many programmers (the tape room didn't like to splice all the tapes together) [WW3Q56p23]. But they were essential to our room 222 runs, for they allowed us to completely eliminate the operators. I believe the director tape capability was the first true operating system in the modern sense of the word, especially when combined with our beginning versions of group control (based on the earlier MDR needs) [WW4Q54p15] for manipulating drum storage. Director tapes and group control are parts of the systematized solution third component of my PWS theme.

### THE SCOPE INPUT PROGRAM

My records don't show exactly, but I do remember dreaming up the scope input program on a long flight back to Boston, and my records show that I did attend an early Pre-B-58 meeting with John Brean (the lead engineer on the project's instrumentation work) in Dallas, on August 9, 1954, so I'd guess it was about that time (Convair 1954 and [C54817 to S.C. Marcus, Emerson Electric]). Bill Wolf still was trying to really get his programming under way, but various test runs were being made by both him and me in room 222. So I knew just enough to write the program. Perhaps triggered by the Dallas discussion about all the things that could go wrong with getting flight data from the plane into the computer via a crude tape system, I envisioned patching up bad spots in a plot of the input data, free hand. We already had had enough experience with the polynomial fit and a Lagrange interpolation programs that had been written in preparation for the evaluation program, that I didn't trust any analytic methods. As the earliest written reference I have found so far (Fourth Quarter 1954) says:

> A "scope input" routine has been written which gives a type of two-dimensional analog input to the Whirlwind computer. The principle of the program is similar to the "flying spot scanners" used on analog computers. The equipment used is a 16-inch oscilloscope under the control of the computer with a photocell mounted so that its field of view is the entire scope face. Then by programming a flying spot and asking whether or not the photocell "saw" the spot, the program can be made to follow an opaque pointer as it is moved in a random fashion over the face of the scope. Since the program displays the spot by digital coordinates, the tracking of the pointer constitutes analog input to the computer. [WW4Q54p15]

The scope input program is quite simple and direct. The tracking function itself consists of a tight loop that displays a $5 \times 5$ square array of close-spaced dots, left to right, top to bottom, interrogating the light cannon after the display of each dot (see Fig. 5). If a dot is *not* seen, the array is recentered on that location and the cycle is restarted from

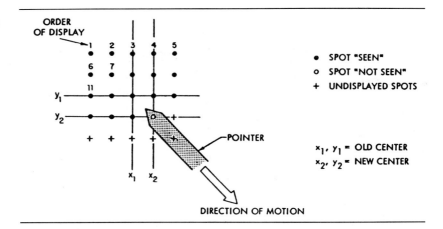

**FIGURE 5**
Tracking principle of first scope input program August, 1954. Shadow was tracked using area discriminator light cannon.

the top left corner again. Otherwise the next dot in sequence is displayed and tested. The cycle is so fast that the array can track even quite fast motions of an opaque pointer—catching up to a new position before it can get very far.

Modified parameters of the same logic allow the pointer position to be located initially. A wide-spaced 32 × 32 array covering the entire scope face zeros in by successive half-spacing until the tracking array can take over. Since the pointer is hand held, at least the hand will be caught by the initial spacing. This two-mode program was the full extent of the initial Scope Input program, for the intent was merely to demonstrate the tracking principle.

On that fateful afternoon, I set up the scope input tape in the PETR, bid the operators adieu without saying anything special, and went off to room 222 by myself. As I approached the E31 console in the middle of the room, about to lay down my papers on its narrow desk I gasped. The restart button was there on the console, but the area discriminator was 12 feet away in the corner! Would I have to call for operator help after all? Suddenly it dawned on me! The top-to-bottom, left-to-right logic of the scan meant that my tracking cycle actually was a maximum-seeker-from-the-left! In other words, whatever shape made the shadow, my spot would rush up its left edge as fast as possible—and then (by the logic) would get stuck at the very top, because it couldn't track downhill! I saw that that was *why* I expected it to track at all.

With that insight, my problem was solved. All of our work was done on pads of yellow paper (opaque to the Ozalid copying process). I merely tore off a blank sheet as I went over to the area discriminator to remove the plexiglass disk. In its place, I laid down my sheet of paper, roughly at a 45 degree angle. I went back to the E31 console and pressed the restart button. The lights indicated that Whirlwind was running. Was my program in a loop? You bet it was. As I approached the area discriminator I could see something was happening. There on the top corner of that piece of paper was a bright spot. The loop was my display loop. So far so good.

Very cautiously I snuck the index finger of my right hand up the yellow page, staying in its shadow. Then very gently I used my left hand to slip the paper out from underneath—and sure enough, the spot remained—but now stuck on my finger. I started to write. *That's* what got the operator's attention in the control room. The almost-random tracking recycling made a rasping sound on the loudspeaker, and that's what first got their attention. The rest is history.

I haven't found the original scope input program in my papers, but I do have the version used in the symposia the following year (Ross 1954d). (I now realize that I could have simplified the program still further, by using the left-edge-following feature to switch into tracking immediately from the first start-up dot, not seen. Then both the half-spacing logic and the initialization for full 32 × 32 spacing could have been eliminated.) Later I had our model shop make an automatic remote button-pusher, since I wasn't allowed to tamper with any of the Whirlwind wiring. A hand-held pushbutton on a long cord activated a solenoid mounted on a bracket held in place by a loosened framing screw of the E31 console frame, so that the restart button could be pushed remotely from the area discriminator area. A wheeled dolly held a power supply for the solenoid, and plugged into a 110 volt outlet. It worked, and our delicate and unique relationship with Lincoln Lab regarding use of the equipment was undisturbed. All I had to negotiate was a place to park the dolly between runs!

We never got around to actually *using* the scope input program for anything, however. I didn't need it for patching our Whirlwind test data for the evaluation program, and for some unknown reason we didn't specify a light cannon for the Eglin Field 1103 Charactron console. We did make a light cannon for the IBM 704 and 709 computers at MIT, but again it only was used for a study of various light pen and other tracking studies in 1960, for the Computer-Aided Design Project (Ross and Ward 1961). I never was successful in interesting anyone to make a generalized shape reader, which could easily be constructed just by changing the sequencing of the 5 × 5 tracking array (to seek minimum from the right, etc.). So in its historical setting, my scope input program was merely an interesting demonstration piece that the crowds loved, but was a bit before its time.

## Practice

The pieces all now were in place. I could actually practice the new MIV techniques in conjunction with the evaluation program. I also could practice talking about what was new and exciting about this intimate coupling of man and machine.

## THE FIRST SYMPOSIUM (MARCH 1955)

In any project, a point is reached when it is necessary and appropriate to demonstrate some initial results to the outside world. This point was reached for the Fire Control System Evaluation Project in the spring of 1955. Even though my part of the project, on data reduction, could have used a bit more time to digest the integration of my reworking of the MIV programming with the parts of the evaluation program, a symposium on the *Design and Evaluation of Bomber Fire-Control Systems* was scheduled for March 8 and 9, 1955 (MIT Servo Lab 1955). The first day covered various engineering matters, mostly concerned with the servo dynamics of a new hydraulic antenna drive, and ended with demonstration of the drive, and (for added interest) the numerically controlled milling machine in Servo Lab. The second day covered evaluation. John Ward presented our philosophy of evaluation, John Brean the concept of digital instrumentation, and I presented the air-mass-based evaluation analysis and MIV-based data reduction programming. In the afternoon, buses shuttled two groups of about 75 people between Servo Lab and Barta Building for digital instrumentation and room 222 demonstrations, respectively. The visitors list shows over 170 names from 48 government, industry, and MIT organizations. It was an impressive show.

Other than an agenda and the visitor's list, there seems to have been no handouts for the symposium. I have a draft copy for some glass slides, an outline of my talk, and a cardboard cutout of a fighter aircraft profile which was placed on the area discriminator scope, so the light cannon could talley hits on the target according to the calculated projectile position. (We used actual test data from Project Hornet, an earlier test program carried out by Emerson Electric for the B-52.)

The complexity of the Data Reduction show is indicated by my detailed instructions (dated 3/8/55 for the demo the next day!) for preparing the ROSS DEMO Director Tape (see Fig. 6) (Ross 1955a). Although I no longer can decipher the director tape language, there are well over 100 operations encoded—loading tape segments onto the drum, executing initialization sections, calling up individual programs and executing them—all of which would have had to be carried out flawlessly by the operator, without the director tape feature. (As a matter of fact, I had pre-loaded my paper tapes onto one of Whirlwind's magnetic tape units, for director-tape-controlled loading. The first time it worked fine, but for the second group of people the magnetic tape unit broke down! I handed the microphone to John Ward to fill the gap as best as he could, ran downstairs to the tape room files, rushed back with an armful of disjointed tapes in boxes, and with the help of

**FIGURE 6
Printout of ROSS
DEMO Director Tape
for March 1955
Symposium.**
Eliminated computer
operator actions and
presaged operating
systems of today.

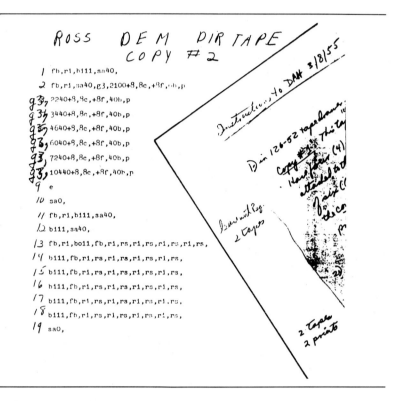

the operator [probably Joe Thompson, who was the best!] managed to complete the second demo, breathlessly but in full. So we did it both ways!)

Every scope in every console in room 222 duplicated the displays I was demonstrating at the E31 console, so everybody had a good view. On request, pertinent variables could be monitored in numerical form; the geometry of the encounter could be shown (including firing pattern, measured through the airplane cutout for the light cannon), and elaborate, calibrated and labelled plots of all functions could be selected. I also showed the scope input capability, as well. The actual demo lasted about half an hour.

Another interesting tidbit about the demonstration is the following quote from the First Quarter 1955 Whirlwind Progress Report: "With the present logic the program demonstrated at the symposium had only five registers unused out of a total of about 3,500 actual program instructions. The new logic will be limited only by the drum capacity of the computer and will be more efficient as well" [WW1Q55p56]. This documents what I remember as a previous panic point in the preparations. The final assignment of group control drum and core addresses came out to be almost 40 registers too big! Only by changing the words labelling the scope plots to abbreviations ("AZ" for "AZIMUTH", etc.) was I able to achieve that tight fit in the nick of time!

### THE MTC CHARACTRON DEMO

On April 14–15, 1955, I attended an *Instrumentation Symposium* at Patrick Air Force Base, Cocoa (Cape Canaveral), Florida, put on by the American Ordinance Association (AOA 1955). The most memorable thing about that meeting was the unauthorized detour the on-base shuttle bus took to drive past a large, flat, open area with some raw concrete in the ground, with reinforcing rods jutting skyward—all with no comment. It was the then-very-secret first launching pad for the Atlas missile, just being built.

The response to the MIV-controlled data reduction in our own March symposium had been so great that we were requested to put on another show on just that topic. On May 2, 1955, John Ward issued an invitation to a *Symposium on Data Reduction* to be held at MIT, June 1 and 2, 1955 (Ward 1955). Inspired by my Cape Canaveral trip, and to provide, in addition to the Room 222 demonstrations, a demonstration of the Charactron display tube capabilities, I quickly learned how to program the *memory test computer* (MTC) (Fig. 7) at Lincoln Lab (Redmond and Smith 1980, p. 206). This was a general purpose vacuum

**FIGURE 7**
**Memory Test Computer (MTC) with magnetic core stack (4/6/53).** Used for Charactron demo in March and June 1955 Symposia on MIV.

tube computer that had been built specially to test the original Forrester magnetic core memory stacks. When the tests were successful and the core stacks were suddenly moved to Whirlwind, another stack was made for MTC, and it was then being used to shake down the Charactron display for use in the SAGE system.

I still have my MTC working papers for my *Missile Launch Simulator* program, along with the original CS Tape Preparation Requisition for "Tape O," submitted at "4:25 PM, May 24" (Ross 1954a). In addition to showing examples of how the MIV monitoring displays of intermediate results would look in Charactron character display format (rather than Whirlwind's elements of a 7-stick figure eight character display [WW2Q53p31]), the program used the vector plotting capabilities of the Charactron to draw a map of the Florida coast plus some islands, and then cycled through a moving display of a missile launch, showing where the pieces would fall if the test director had to abort the mission and blow up the missile in flight. The islanders would have appreciated such thoughtfulness, I reasoned.

### THE SECOND SYMPOSIUM (JUNE 1955)

Three days later (and only one week before the symposium—things moved fast, in those days), John Ward invited Pat Youtz (who had led all the Whirlwind work on the ES memory tubes, and now was in charge of SAGE display work) to "describe to the people at our data reduction symposium just what can be done in the near future in the way of input-output." His letter goes on:

> As you may know we are doing data reduction studies for the Air Force and have developed techniques on Whirlwind using the scope and intervention that are a great improvement over any other techniques in use at present. We are building digital instrumentation for a forth-coming field test which will be evaluated on the ERA 1103 at Eglin Field, Florida, and the primary purpose of this meeting is to get the Eglin Field people and the ERA people together and show them what we have accomplished with Bob Weiser's attachments to Whirlwind, with the hope that they will get inspired to obtain similar equipment. We would therefore like to put on as good a show as possible and that is why we would like to show the charactron tubes in operation. We have permission to use the MTC and Doug Ross has written a special display program to put the charactron through its paces.
>
> It seems to us that if any equipment design is undertaken by ERA that the charactron should be used as the basis for design, and we would greatly appreciate any help you or your group could give us in showing our visitors what the charactron looks like and perhaps your manufacturing and test operation. We have taken the liberty of tentatively scheduling this material on Thursday, June second, as an adjunct to the MTC demonstration at 2:00 p.m. I am sending this to you

so that you can think about the business a little and I will call you Tuesday to see if we can make some final arrangements. We would be most grateful for any assistance you could give us in convincing our visitors of the current feasibility of charactron type displays. I am enclosing a brief list of the organizations who will be present at the symposium. [C55527 JEW to Youtz]

Pat did indeed pitch in, and both the Charactron and the Memotron (a smaller storage tube version) were included in the June 2, Lincoln Lab visit.

On July 29, 1955, John Ward issued "Minutes of M.I.T. Data Reduction Symposium, June 1 and 2, 1955," Report No. 7138-S-1 (Ward and Ross 1955), which includes my 7138-M-112 memorandum "Special In-Out Equipment for Human Participation in High-Speed Computer Operation," July 25, 1955 (Ross 1955c), in which I summarized the "Program Operation" and gave a "Description of Equipment" for activate buttons, intervention switches, indicator lights, and audible alarms, each with a diagram, description of operation, and "Things to Notice" about how they would be used with the EF (external function) instruction of the ERA 1103.

For the record, John Ward's letter to Youtz shows that the following organizations were invited to the symposium, and the minutes show how many people actually attended:

Military Physics Research Laboratory, University of Texas (2)
Emerson Electric Company, St. Louis (3)
Air Force Armament Center, Eglin Field, Florida (4)
Armament Laboratory, Wright Air Development Center (4)
Engineering Research Associates, Remington Rand, Inc., St. Paul (2)
Patrick Air Force Base, Air Force Missile Test Center, FL (3)
Holloman Air Force Base, Alamogorda, New Mexico (0)
Air Force Flight Test Center, Edwards AFB, California (1)
NOTS, Inyokern (0)
Bell Telephone Labs (1)
Convair (3)
Davies (0) [manufacturer of the airborne mag tape unit]
National Security Agency (2)
Watertown Arsenal (0)
White Sands Proving Ground (1)
WCRRU, Aero. Res. Lab. WADC (2)
M.I.T., Instrumentation Lab (2)
M.I.T., Air Force Field Rep (1)
M.I.T., Digital Computer Lab (3)
M.I.T., Lincoln Lab (2)
M.I.T., Servo Lab (12)
M.I.T., Statistical Services (1)

We never had further contact with the Patrick Air Force Base people, but some years later the Sputnik era and NASA TV coverage showed elaborate Mission Control facilities in full bloom. I like to think our earlier efforts at least had some influence on those crucial developments.

## Gestalt Programming

The response to the two MIT symposia and the clarification in my own mind that what we were building was indeed a new way to use computers prompted me to make this the topic of what would be my first professional paper. Even though all of Whirlwind may seem too huge to be a PWS, my view was and is that the PW aspect dominated the WS reality then available, so the theme of that paper and this paper is valid.

### EARLY VIEWS

My records don't indicate when I decided to submit a paper for the 1956 Western Joint Computer Conference (precursor to the Spring and Fall, and now the National Computer Conference series). I was chairman of the printing committee for the November 1955 Eastern Joint Computer Conference (EJCC 1955), held in Boston (we designed the conference logo, combining the logos of the IRE, AIEE, and ACM joint sponsors, which was used for several years thereafter) so I knew how the conferences ran. The earliest dated item I have (the date stamp is October 13, 1955 [Ross 1955d]) is a handwritten, yellow-page draft reading "*[The] Gestalt [System of] Programming*—A New Concept in Automatic Programming," with the bracketed words crossed out, along with an aborted opening sentence. Notice how that subtle and impulsive act makes the title say that this is a paper about a generic concept of a *type* of programming. If the words were not crossed out, the paper could be about a systematic *way to* program, a school of style, or (even more specifically) the paper could be about my particular collection of programs constituting a system with that *name*. In the first two drafts I *do* use the name "Gestalt System I" in a couple of places. But when I see the cross-outs now, I see it as evidence (matching the slant of the words of all drafts of the text) that I always had the generic concept in mind as the subject of the paper.

I remember that from the first rush of insight that so entranced me in that first exciting visit to room 222 I knew that things would be profoundly different when man and machine were intimately coupled. I always had a broader view than just our data reduction application in mind. The earliest record I find on our use of MIV is in the Third Quarter 1954 Whirlwind report, which is suitably subdued, but also clearly is targeted to experimental programming:

Work is progressing on another phase of this problem, using auxiliary in-out equipment both as an integral part of the data-reduction programs for monitoring purposes and as an aid to experimenting with improved computational techniques. Intervention registers and scopes will constitute the working parts of this system with efforts being made to provide the flexibility normally associated with analog computers. Present work is concerned with the development of routines to decode intervention-register inputs and to utilize various specialized scope outputs. After merging these routines with the data-reduction programs, an elaborate logging scheme, using magnetic-tape output, will be written for permanent records of all operations and interventions during an experimental run. [WW3Q54p14]

But in an August 11, 1955 letter to my Oberlin classmate, Ben Scheff, urging him to come and work with me at MIT following his navy tour at the National Security Agency, more of my real feelings show:

The work on fire-control system evaluation has been extremely interesting and has grown continually in scope and capabilities. Now we are really on the forefront of a whole new way of using large digital computers. We are in the fortunate position of being purely a research group and never have to get our hands dirty with actual data reduction. Once we get a new technique developed and proved, we drop it or expand it to new, more comprehensive work.

A large part of our efforts go [sic] into developing new techniques and programs to achieve more flexibility in devision [sic] and testing new programs. The MDR report, which is enclosed, is one such program, and is a pretty good example of the kind of programming and philosophy we like to follow. The other special report on our Symposium gives some idea of the techniques we're now exploring. Both reports are now out of date but give the ideas.

It is really amazing the complexity which arises in making the computer act in these ways, but will be a really nice system when it's done. We have an intermediate version running now which we demonstrated at the Symposium, but the newest version (almost complete) will run rings around it. The new system is really much more general than we now require but it will essentially allow us to program with programs while the computer is running instead of coding for weeks before a run.

In a nutshell, what we're doing is fixing up Whirlwind so that we can manipulate its operation while it's running, turning on and off programs, examining and modifying so that we can use the computer as a research tool on an idea or concept level, rather than on the grungy coding level. Frankly, it's pretty exciting work . . . I can honestly say that I don't know of any other work in computers and their use which is more interesting than what's going on here. [C55811]

## INITIAL DRAFTS

I have several distinct drafts of my attempts to write the gestalt paper. The November 17 version actually submitted to Byron Bennett (SRI), WJCC Program Chairman [C551117] is completely different from the October 13 draft, and that paper, in turn, was completely reworked several more times before the final submission of our Project Technical Memorandum version (Ross 1956c) on February 1, 1956, for publication in the Proceedings. I think it is historically important to dwell briefly on the evolution of my expression of my then year-old, but still elusive ideas, because such an analysis will show my present PW versus WS theme in the struggles of its original context.

The original (October 13) draft jumps right in with the dictionary definition of gestalt psychology: "The theory that . . . events do not occur through the summation of separate elements, . . . but through formed patterns of these, integrated units which function singly or in interrelation," and proceeds to say that standard programming practice is to be replaced "by simple and unambiguous expression of the desired characteristics of behavior, the expression itself in effect tying together integrated units of computer behavior . . . " (presaging today's declarative languages, functional programming, and the reusable components of software engineering). And still in the opening paragraph, "automatic coding systems are aimed at easy *communication* between the human and the computer [see Figs. 8 and 9], whereas a Gestalt system of automatic programming is aimed at easy *conversation* [see Fig. 10] . . . " (a phrasing with which I was particularly pleased, and which I retained in all further drafts) (Ross 1955d). These are indeed the pertinent ideas, but the later drafts are much more roundabout in approach. At the time, even ordinary programming was still immature, and there was a complete lack of the common, shared cul-

**FIGURE 8**
Communication from human to computer.

HUMAN → GESTALT LANGUAGE → GESTALT SYSTEM → COMPUTER

**FIGURE 9**
Communication from
computer to human.

HUMAN ←GESTALT←GESTALT←COMPUTER
         LANGUAGE  SYSTEM

ture we know today. The ideas were very hard to formulate and very hard to assimilate.

The second (November 17) draft, the basis for acceptance of the paper, begins with the following introduction:

> In any human endeavor there are three major phases: conception, expression, and execution. Gestalt programming is an attempt to make these three phases as nearly identical to each other as possible with respect to computer programming. In this paper the word *Gestalt* is used to mean *a concept of a task* to be performed by a computer. In a Gestalt system of programming the Gestalt, or idea, is expressed simply and un-

**FIGURE 10**
Solution by
conversation.

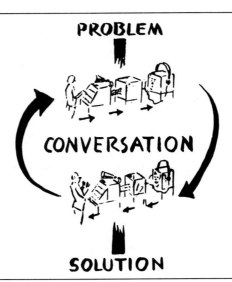

PROBLEM

CONVERSATION

SOLUTION

ambiguously in a special language, rather than through the laborious assembling of machine-codes, pseudo-codes, subroutines, etc. Using a Gestalt system, the expression itself in effect ties together integrated units of computer behavior, which function singly or in interrelation, to achieve the desired effect. The purpose of a Gestalt System is to facilitate the transmission of general ideas as in a conversation, between a human and a computer, so that the maximum use of their respective capabilities can be made.

After presenting the abstract theory of Gestalt Programming this paper discusses several Gestalt Systems in use today at the Massachusetts Institute of Technology and describes briefly the types of computer hardware which are best suited to this application. (Ross 1955f)

This was retained as the *synopsis* for the final paper, but the body was reworked many times. The referenced MIT systems were the Whirlwind comprehensive system (CS) itself (including mention of director tapes), the Whirlwind marginal checking facility (which required a technician to classify oscilloscope traces, etc., through MIV, and then isolated faulty tubes and components), and our own Data Reduction and Experimental Programming System.

In addition to various attempts to describe problems in which MIV was desirable (not an easy task in the hands-off, standard mode of submitting runs to a computer operator) I needed to have an example to illustrate the actual design and programming steps. My draft pages show one attempt using the LIP and RIP (left insertion panel and right insertion panel) and various buttons for CS computer operations, but that was not used. Another complete development says "Consider the launching of the man-made satellite schedule for the coming Geophysical Year," including the suggestion that a "part of the Gestalt Language might be a kind of joy-stick, so that the human could steer the rocket remotely" (Ross 1955e). But I decided that this example would seem too flashy, and instead worked out an example of automatic factory control (Fig. 11) for the final paper (perhaps a prescient choice, since my soon-to-arrive role in APT was unknown to me then).

### ORAL PRESENTATION (FEBRUARY 1956)

Then there follow endless yellow pages of my attempts to work out an oral presentation of the paper (Ross 1956a) ("The title of this paper has probably raised questions in your minds both about what I am going to say and why I have chosen to introduce a new word-usage into the already crowded computer terminology"—scrubbed, fortunately!). I presented an interdepartmental colloquium version at MIT entitled "Talking with Whirlwind—An Introduction to Gestalt Programming" on January 11, 1956 (rescheduled from December 14) [C56016 to Bennett, and (Ross 1955f Addendum)], and finally managed to do a decent

**FIGURE 11**
Gestalt language for automatic factory control.

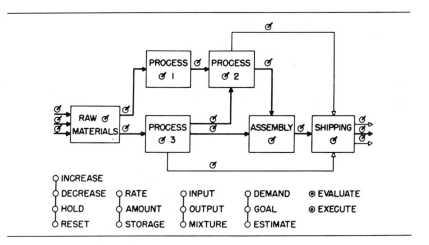

job as the opening paper at the San Francisco WJCC on February 7. *Electronic Design* magazine enthused:

> Programming and coding sessions at the Western Joint Computer Conference, San Francisco, February 7, 1956, were attended by overflow crowds. Highly significant papers were read. Here is a verbatim report of the impressions on [sic] the session chairman, Francis V. Wagner, group leader, engineering computing, North American Aviation, Inc.
>
> The paper on "Gestalt Programming" by Ross, which opened the session, was a milestone of forward thinking. It refused to accept the common fallacy that human beings can contribute little when teamed directly with automatic digital computers, and took the position that only the more versatile human mind can, at present, handle some parts of some problems. In the past, many people have noted that, to exploit such a partnership, there is required not merely a satisfactory language for communication from the human to the computer but a language which allows fluent conversation between the human and the computer. Mr. Ross went beyond merely stating this, [I thought it was original with me, at the time!—D.T.R.] and presented evidence of some serious thinking towards analyzing how such a language ought to be designed. The principles which he stated and the illustrations which he gave of ways to design such a language, and of the hardware which might form the medium for the conversation should go far towards clarifying the problem for future implementation of these ideas. . . .
>
> Audience participation was distinguished more by quality than quantity. No more than three or four questions were asked of each speaker. [Wagner's overall impression of audience was that on the average they probably were not prepared to comprehend the concepts presented.—E.D. Editor] Although these were put by highly competent people, and indicated careful evaluation of the paper, they were aimed more at underlining or amplifying certain points. In no case did

they take violent issue with any of the statements or implications of the speaker, nor did they open up any controversial issues. (*Electronic Design* 1956)

Even the *Scientific American* expressed an interest in the paper. A suitable summary of my thinking at the time is the following quote from my January 12, 1956 reply to Dennis Flannagan, editor, enclosing a copy of the paper. Actually I sent the final, TM version, but I still was concerned about its adequacy in expressing my ideas. This probably was my own dissatisfaction with my MIT talk the day before, even though it was very well received. A few Lincoln people let me know by body-english that they thought I was plagiarizing other people's ideas, however. It was clear that they thought the ideas were important—important enough to let me know their feelings—but I, in turn, saw their upset as evidence that they really didn't see the differences between the specific Cape Cod incorporation of the man in the loop as an engineering necessity and my generic gestalt programming idea. Somehow I wasn't expressing myself clearly enough, or they wouldn't feel that way, I thought. Hence I wrote to Flannagan:

> Since it is not stated too clearly in the present draft, let me try to summarize for you here, what Gestalt Programming is and where it fits into the established computer technology. As computer techniques have developed over the last few years, there has been a growing trend toward more sophisticated methods for connecting the human, who states the problem, to the computer, which is to solve the problem. Out of this trend has come, as a natural consequence of the maturing technology, a desire to use computers for solving problems which cannot be completely specified in terms which the computer can handle. These major trends are united into the general problem of using humans and computers together to solve problems. An analysis of this problem shows that more efficient and natural languages are required to bridge between human and computer, and that these languages must operate at the idea or concept level. In particular, a statement in the language must lead directly to the solution, in the same way that a Gestalt (in the psychological sense) unites at once, basic units into a single entity or pattern. The theory of Gestalt Programming is an attempt to set the initial outlines of the structure of these languages, and to indicate how to construct and use them. The physical content of Gestalt Programming is not new, but the emphasis and point of view is new, and is intended to clarify the directions in which these fascinating developments can go. [C560112]

But nothing further came from the *Scientific American* interest, which is too bad, because unbeknownst to me, at about the same time (and completely independently) George Price was in communication with the editors of *Fortune* magazine, preparing his landmark article on *The Design Machine*, which appeared in the November 1956 issue. Francis Bello, Science editor for *Fortune* wrote to me on March 27, 1957 that

Price wrote us in November, 1955, suggesting his article and we had a rough draft in our office on January 15, 1956, which outlined the major features of his Design Machine. I mention this because it may surprise you that the article was so long in preparation before appearing in Fortune. (And certainly you would be entitled to wonder if Price had heard of your February paper.)

What surprises me still more is that computer experts at I.B.M., Sperry Rand, and Lockheed, who read Price's paper for us, and checked his computations, had not heard of—or at least gave no indication that they had heard of—your work in this area.

From the beginning our concern was that Price's ideas were too blue skyish for serious presentation. The world keeps moving faster than Fortune can keep up. [C57327]

To which the only comment (valid today, as it was then) is—it does indeed. Before I address Price's article, there are more items from our own work to be covered.

## Console Developments

With the PW component established, next comes the WS component of my PWS theme. I can cover here only the earliest developments of what was to be a long term evolution of computer graphics and keyboard language techniques, both hardware and software, well into the 1960s, at MIT.

### DIRECT KEYBOARD INPUTS

It's funny how memory plays tricks on us. For years I have known that it was at my instigation that direct keyboard input to Whirlwind was installed (beginning the chain of events that eventually led to the Compatible Time Sharing System (CTSS) and Project MAC at MIT in the 1960s). But at the same time, I thought that all of our MIV and Charactron console design and installation for the Eglin Field 1103 had come after and had been based upon what we already had going on Whirlwind. The records show that I was mistaken. The Whirlwind keyboard proposal actually *followed* my proposal for the 1103 keyboard. That came as a surprise to me, when writing this paper.

The earliest date I find in my own files regarding the ERA 1103 is a collection of general information (brochure description and installation instructions—where to install the motor generators and air conditioning, etc.) bearing date stamps of John Ward and myself of November 8, 1954 (ERA 1954a and 1954B). Two yellow pages of notes about the order code indicate that this was my first introduction to what was in store. The earliest Charactron information is a collection of Convair Charactron Project documents on the Model 70B Charactron Display Console, the Model 100 Computer Readout System, and the Rapromatic Camera and projection system, all with my date stamp of October 18, 1955 (Charactron Project 1955).

By December 14, 1955, I had written a memo on "Proposed Equipment Modifications for the Pre-B-58 Data Reduction Programs" (Ross 1955g). It recommends that AFAC should procure an additional 4096 registers of magnetic core memory beyond the 1024 electrostatic storage registers that were standard for the 1103, and "that the photoelectric tape reader and the Flexowriter connections be modified," in addition to installation of the "Type 70-A Charactron with photographic facilities under computer control, reported already on order," as well as "the Intervention Switch facilities, reported already on order."

Engineering Research Associates (ERA) definitely was a company of (outstanding) engineers—not programmers. I believe the AFAC 1103 was one of two "Serial One" first models of the ERA 1103 (Cohen 1985), and I encountered several features that were good engineering ideas, executed in such a fashion as to make programming and use most awkward. The 1103 had a 36 bit word length, and an "arithmetic section" with accumulator (A of 72 bits), shifting register (Q of 36 bits), exchange register (X of 36 bits), and two input-output registers (IOA of 8 bits and IOB of 36 bits). The binary form of 7-channel punched paper tape, called "bi-octal," was prepared off-line using a box full of relays with a 10 character per second mechanical tape reader on one side and a mechanical tape punch on the other. A number of empty sockets into which jumper-wired plugs could be inserted allowed the user to control the tape transformation between the two. Absolute address assembly language tapes punched on an off-line Flexowriter (Fig. 12) could be converted to bi-octal with one set of plugs.

We contracted with the MIT Digital Computer Lab to have a *WWI-1103 Input Translation* program, based on CS, built so that we could write 1103 programs with "flads" (floating addresses) etc., translate them on Whirlwind, fly them to Florida, and debug and use them there [WW1Q55p56and79-81]. The 1103 itself had no such software. I wrote a companion 1103 program, handling only absolute addresses, to support our on-site debugging efforts (Ross 1955b).

For this early machine, things were pretty awkward. The ERA photoelectric tape reader (PETR) could only be started manually, the PETR was connected directly to the Q register, thus entangling the Arithmetic Section unnecessarily, and worst of all, as my memo says:

> The bi-octal tape format now in use does not allow the use of programmed checks to insure that the information was read from the tape correctly. Since the read-in program for reading bi-octal tapes is now wired into the computer, the increased flexibility required to change tape format is not presently available.

There are two major approaches to the problem of placing the photo-

**FIGURE 12**
**Flexowriter with**
**10cps reader (front)**
**and punch (back).**
Keyboard was not
used for Whirlwind
direct input until
summer of 1956,
which led to later
timesharing projects
at MIT.

electric reader under computer control. A Ferranti tape reader could
be purchased and installed exactly as in other 1103 computers. This is
the best, but most expensive solution. The other possibility is to put
the drive motor of the present ERA tape reader under computer control,
and to have the photocells read into IOA (or IOB) rather than into the
Q register. The only disadvantage to this inexpensive method is that a
few inches of extra tape feed-out must be placed in the tape wherever
it is to be stopped, since the ERA reader is not a fast start-stop device
like the Ferranti reader. However, this method was used successfully with
a similar ERA reader for several years on the Whirlwind computer at
MIT, before the Ferranti readers were obtained. [p. 2]

(The inexpensive method was chosen, and the WWI-1103 Input Translation program was forced to ensure the proper blank tape sections
were present.)

The memo then continues with similar observations regarding the
keyboard:

6. *Flexowriter Input*

To augment the Manual Intervention facilities mentioned above, it is
suggested that the Flexowriter presently attached to the AFAC 1103
computer be connected to act as both a keyboard input and mechanical
tape reader input device. This method is considered preferable to the
purchase of special keyboard input devices at this time because, again,
it should be very inexpensive, and will give considerably more flexibility than any commercially available keyboard of another type.

An essential part of Manual Intervention Programming is that decimal (or octal, or English) information can be communicated directly
to the computer. In use, this system would use intervention switch settings to tell the program how to interpret the Flexowriter keyboard
input at any given time.

The mechanical tape reader probably could use the same circuitry as the keyboard and would be used to read control tapes (while data or program tapes are in the photoelectric tape reader) so that manual control will not be required for routine operation of the computer system, which will result in greater reliability.

A comment contained in 1103 Newflash No. 15, December 7, 1955, seems to imply that the keyboard of the Flexowriter on the Ramo-Woolridge 1103 is already connected in this way, so that the required engineering may be already available. The comment does seem to imply, however, that the "directly connected typewriter" uses the Q register. It is much better to use IOA (or IOB) for this purpose so that normal operation of the arithmetic element is not impaired. It is very possible that both the keyboard and mechanical reader could share a major portion, at least, of the circuitry connecting the photoelectric tape reader to IOA (or IOB), with resulting savings in engineering and hardware. [p. 3]

It is interesting to me that even though I chide the engineers for their lack of vision, I suffered similar myopia regarding how to establish controls. I'm sure that it would not have taken significantly more programming to have an opening character or so to specify what type of information was on the tape, instead of using MIV switch settings. This had, in fact, already been done for the logging of CS tapes on Whirlwind, after all, when Director Tapes were introduced. Our "modern" views take time to evolve and develop, I guess.

In any case, this December 1955 memo shows that the AFAC 1103 keyboard suggestion formally came before the Whirlwind keyboard suggestion, and in a fashion that surprised me a second time, in my researches for this paper. I had found in my files my memo 7138-M-144 "Suggestions for Manual Intervention Facilities on the Air Force Armament Center ERA 1103 Computer," dated March 1, 1956 (Ross 1956c), and my memo 7138-M-148 "Flexowriter Keyboard Input to WWI, Preliminary Specification," dated March 14, 1956 (Ross 1956d). But digging still deeper I found that my memo 7138-M-160 "A Proposed Flexowriter Input for the Whirlwind I Computer," dated April 30, 1956 (Ross 1956f), was the formal proposal finally sent on to Lincoln Labs for formal consideration, with the concurrence of the Scientific and Engineering Computations Group and "several groups in Lincoln." So at this point in my sleuthing, I was convinced that the actual sequence for my on-line keyboard suggestion definitely was first 1103, then Whirlwind.

The second surprise came from a detailed reading of collected draft papers for a May 8, 1956 revision (to "144A") of my 7138-M-144 March 1 memo, this time done by John Ward (Ward and Ross 1956), for formal forwarding to AFAC and our WADC sponsors. In that revision, which includes John's redesigns of Whirlwind drawings for intervention, activate, and audible alarm circuits, is a large fold-out drawing entitled "Keyboard Read In System, WWI," showing Lou Norcott, "Eng." and Larry Holmes, "Appd." both dated "2-27-56"—with the hand-scribbled notation "see him [Norcott] or Doug R. O.K." The interesting surprise to me is that this shows that I already had been active during February, and probably before, working behind the scenes with the Whirlwind engineers to confirm feasibility and costs before sticking my neck out with formal suggestions. Therefore the actual fact is that I can't sort out which came first, my thoughts regarding the 1103 or Whirlwind. My guess is that they surfaced almost together. That is, I knew general keyboard input was needed for gestalt programming, but the fact that the ERA 1103 already *had* an on-line keyboard of some sort triggered me into action. I first worked the idea out on the basis of Whirlwind, working with Larry Holmes, but the first actual writing was about the 1103.

Larry and I played the game to the hilt, for I also have a short interoffice memo from him to me, dated April 3, 1956 (Holmes 1956), which begins:

> I received a copy of your Memorandum 7138-M-148. The attached chart illustrates the five different plans that you might consider in the determination of a decision as to which installation you will request.

And then goes on to conclude:

> I sense that it would probably be the middle of June before the chosen facility would be operational.
>
> If any additional information is required for your subsequent memorandum to management, I will be pleased to procure same.

## MICROPROGRAMMING FOR WHIRLWIND

It was not all that unusual that I was in close touch with the Whirlwind engineers, for another one of my on-the-side, recreational projects at that time concerned a plan I had to modify the internal logic of Whirlwind I to allow experimentation with microprogramming. This idea had come to me in the same spurt of inspiration when I studied the Lincoln-only, "si"-based input-output lines that led to the original director tape proposal. I discovered that not only was the mechanical tape reader still available (as I have already covered), but much more importantly that there was a whole additional flip-flop register, called PR—the *program register*—just sitting there, completely unused! The PR had temporarily held the memory address for electrostatic storage operating and was no longer required for magnetic core memory. It still had all the wiring that connected it to the WWI Bus, and had three outgates per digit! What a treasure trove! In those days of discrete components and tubes, flip-flops and gates were *very* expensive (several hundred dollars per bit), and here was all that gear, cut out of use by the modifications to the main machine, but all ready to be fixed up if I could find a use for it.

Of the papers I still have, the earliest date stamp I find is that of "Engineering File #2, August 18, 1955" on copies of large drawings of "Timing Diagrams, WWI," Digital Computer Lab drawing E-51744, and "Control Pulse Output Connections, WWI," DCL drawing D-531?? (torn off), which were made for my use. My own vellum master drawing of "Proposed $\mu$-Operation Schematic for *mi* Instruction, WWI" is dated April 5, 1956, and numerous copies show my steps of refining my design after that date (Ross 1956e).

On March 1 and 2, 1956, a seminar on microprogramming, sponsored by the MIT Digital Computer Laboratory was held with papers listed by H. R. J. Grosch (GE), D. J. Wheeler (Cambridge U.), N. R. Scott (U. of Mich.), L. C. Hubbard (IBM), B. D. Smith (ERA), J. J. Eachus (Datamatic), H. P. Donahue (NSA), G. M. Hopper (Remington Rand), J. W. Wegstein (NBS), and J. W. Carr (U. of Mich.) (MIT Dig. Comp. Lab. 1956). I was not even on the list, because the Digital Computer Lab organizers didn't know about the hobby project I'd been doing only by myself, with a few interactions with the Lincoln Lab Whirlwind engineers. I hadn't even gotten an invitation to the seminar, but when I heard about it, I was welcomed, and went.

With a June 6, 1956, date stamp, I got pages of a typed transcript of the seminar from Frank Helwig that shows that at the last minute I had been squeezed into the program before Wheeler's second talk. As is usual for my oral speaking, the transcript is almost incomprehensible, but so is the extended ensuing discussion by others.

I did manage to complete the design of the proposed *mi* microprogramming instruction and my papers do include a complete outline of the report I intended to write, but never completed. (A "to-do" list, buried in these papers starts with "Flexo keyboard memo—Fri; AFAC int sw. diagram; Pre-B-58 MIT meeting; Gestalt Paper to AFAC, etc.; mi-WWI memo" and a slew of other items, including "Numerical Control Personnel," so I'd guess the date was around May 1956 when the outline was done.)

The idea of the proposal was as follows: When you walked inside the bowels of Whirlwind, down one aisle was a mass of bare copper wires and boards of components, neatly arranged in a matrix. First came five bare vertical wires, and then 32 long, horizontal, bare wires going down the length of the aisle. These, in turn, overlaid 120 vertical bare copper wires, each of which terminated in circuitry boards arranged along the bottom, by the floor. There also were eight coaxial cables running horizontally, with one or another feeding each of the lower circuitry boards. These cables carried one of eight *time pulses*, and the original five vertical wires supplied the 5-bit instruction code of the instruction now being executed. This was the control matrix of

Whirlwind (Fig. 13). The neat thing was that soldered right there in front of you, at the various crossing points of the 5 vertical wires and the 32 horizontal wires, was a collection of germanium crystal diodes that spelled out the binary number system, so that each of the horizontal bare wires represented one of the 32 instructions of Whirlwind. To understand what each instruction did, you had merely to similarly read the pattern of diodes soldered between its horizontal wire and the 120 vertical wires. The 120 vertical wires each selected one of the *120 CPO units* (command pulse output gates) of Whirlwind, each of which could do some micro operation (such as clear the I/O register, read from memory into the A register, etc.) when its corresponding time pulse arrived. In a nutshell, my plan was to use the flip-flops and gate connections of the PR to dynamically compose instruction steps from a selection of the existing CPOs—as though a new horizontal line had variable diode connections to the CPOs.

The report outline indicates that I found a subset of 39 CPO micro

**FIGURE 13**
**Control matrix of Whirlwind.** Wires, diodes, and gate boards laid out translation of 5–bit instruction code into 120 command pulse output (CPO) micro operations.

operations that would be useful in various combinations. My design allowed any number of them to be chained together on time pulses 6, 7, 8, and 1, interspersed with memory addresses and I/O operations. Thus microcoded instructions of any length and complexity could be composed and executed, interspersed with standard Whirlwind instructions. As the outline says, ''Very fertile field for problems which can use micro-program in MIV Gestalt Programming.'' The report was never written, however, and the change to Whirlwind was never actually proposed (I had in mind a big gang switch that would include or exclude the *mi* instruction in Whirlwind's repertoire) because when I programmed various test cases with microprogramming and then with ordinary Whirlwind programming, there was very little to be gained. The trouble was that Whirlwind was so closely designed (to save expensive gates, etc.) that the A register formed an insurmountable bottleneck. As the outline says (''md'' is ''multiply digits''—a masking operation):

> Fundamental difficulty with present WW construction for this type of application since only entry to AC is thru AR so that usually AR is not indep. of AC. Also this necessitates use of more steps than really required since first must load AR before can work on AC. Also would be good to have a working operation built into circuitry to give effect of md's since in logical ops this is often fundamental but is lengthy $\mu$-op-wise or md-wise since another mi is necessary to get back to $\mu$-mode.

*Conclusion*

> Study of this report and independent investigation of this kind of approach to $\mu$-prog is very instructive on problems involved. If more major changes in WW structure were acceptable might be able to obtain a useful gadget. Best bet, however, is to contrive basic idea of investigating $\mu$-computers by sim_lation without changing WW.

So my grand scheme for microprogrammed MIV and Gestalt programming came to naught.

## KEYBOARD INPUT FOR WHIRLWIND

The direct Flexowriter input for Whirlwind was built, however, and could be operated from either the E31 console or from Test control, as I had suggested. The Second Quarter 1956 Whirlwind Progress Report says:

> Since 1954, the MIT Servomechanisms Laboratory has been using the WWI manual intervention and display equipment in the development of high-speed data reduction techniques. In order for them to expand their research into computer applications, it was essential that more

versatile manual inputs be made available on the WWI computer. Besides requiring additional on-off switches, many of the new programs will be so complex and will require so many parameters that the only reliable way to instruct them will be to use specially designed mnemonic languages and translation programs. In order to have this general language structure available on a manual intervention basis, it is necessary to have a keyboard such as a Flexowriter for direct input to the computer.

The MIT Scientific and Engineering Computations Group have contemplated the following applications for the new facility:

1. Demonstration programs would be a great deal more effective if this form of input were available for control purposes.

2. Typewriter input for Comprehensive System Flexowriter and post-mortem request tapes. Short program modifications and post-mortem requests can presently be inserted in the insertion registers. However, errors are easily made because the required vocabulary is awkward. A typewriter input facility would make available a normal mnemonic vocabulary for such purposes.

3. Experimental use of a typewriter facility for direct operator control of the computer. Here we would consider using the typewriter to replace the button-pushings required of the operator during normal operations. Vocabulary similar to that of director tapes and performance requests would be devised for these purposes. This could easily prove to be an extremely convenient and efficient method of computer operation.

The new input installation will be available for use by 4 July 1956. Much of the information to be inserted via the keyboard will be the same as is now introduced via a free running photoelectric tape reader using punched paper tapes. The keyboard input will also be treated as a free running device, i.e., selection of the facility by the computer may be followed by an arbitrary number of read instructions, each of which reads the next character which has been struck on the keyboard. The total equipment requirements amount to 15 relays and 20 tubes. [WW2Q56p63]

My original M-148 proposal specified that

since much of the information to be inserted via keyboard will be the same as is now on paper tape, it would be best to have the keyboard operate in a free running mode, i.e. an si selecting the keyboard may be followed by an arbitrary number of rd's, each of which reads the next character which has been struck on the keyboard. In this way, programs such as the entire CS system can be modified to accept keyboard rather than tape input merely by changing one or two si instructions. (Ross 1956d, p. 2)

The existing Test console Flexowriter (Fig. 14) was selected by one si, and another Flexowriter on a wheeled table plugged into the room 222 E31 console and was selected by a different si. We used it some with

**FIGURE 14**
Whirlwind Test Control console (1/2/57) showing MIV panels for computer
operation behind photoelectric tape reader (PETR) and Flexowriter. Monitor
(above) and camera (below) output scopes are on right.

our SLURP developments, but Lincoln people didn't take advantage
of it, to my knowledge.

While digging through my papers, much to my surprise I ran
across a Division 2 Lincoln Lab memorandum dated February 2, 1959
(three years later) on ''The Direct Flexowriter Keyboard Input System
at Whirlwind I (Barta)'' by C.F. Brackett in which I discovered that

> A pushbutton on the direct output Flexo table [in Test Control?—
> D.T.R.] allows the Flexo keyboard to be used as a direct input device.
> If this pushbutton is held depressed and the Flexo keyboard operated,
> the Flexo code for that character will be set up in the keyboard Input Relay
> Register where it will be available for later transfer to the In Out
> Register. . . . Since the keyboard Relay Register is cleared of old infor-
> mation during the read in of new information, the operator should nor-
> mally wait until the indicators are extinguished before typing the next
> character.

I never knew it had such a button. Maybe it was only on the Test
console Flexowriter. If the Lincoln memo indicates what actually happened when my idea was passed through the Lincoln approval cycle
(I never had occasion to use it myself, as I remember), no wonder that

first installation was little used. The button would force pick and peck typing! This equipment did, however, serve as the basis for later direct keyboard inputs to the IBM 704, 709, and then 7090 computers at MIT, which led to the initiation of time sharing.

### THE CHARACTRON/MIV CONSOLE FOR THE AFAC 1103

The Charactron/MIV console for the Eglin Field AFAC 1103 as finally proposed had two 36 bit intervention registers, one 8 bit activate register, one 36 bit indicator light register, a 7 bit MIV flexo register, and two alarm buzzers (Ward and Ross 1956). John Ward and I supplied reworked Whirlwind drawings for all these items plus the Whirlwind drawings for the Ferranti PETR and manual tape winder at various times (Fig. 15). All of these were forwarded to Stromberg Carlson, San

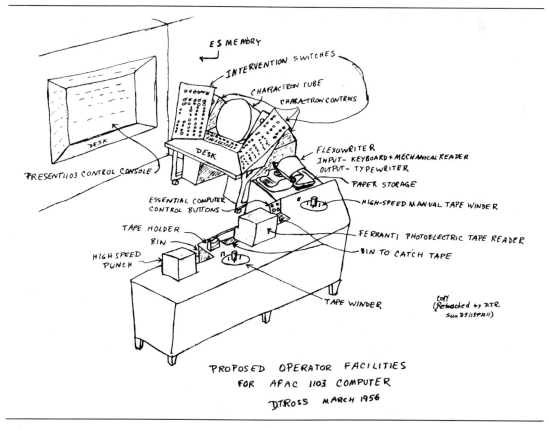

### FIGURE 15
Sketch for Charactron/MIV console for ERA 1103 at AFAC, Eglin Air Force Base. Built by Stromberg Carlson based on Whirlwind experiences of Servo Lab Data Reduction Project.

Diego who reworked the designs further and incorporated them with a 19 inch Charactron for viewing and a 7 inch Charactron with camera, in the final, delivered installation.

My *daily resumes* began at about this point, and various phone calls, letters, and visits to MIT by Ed Allmon and various people from Stromberg Carlson are recorded from October 31, 1956, on. Topics included the vector generator and tape winder [R561031]; Ferranti PETR [R56116]; PETR again, plus the fact that they got the contract from AFAC [R561115]; visit regarding Flexowriter, tape reader, and 1103 MIV system [R561126-27]; connectors and pushbuttons [R561210-11, -12]; calls from their psychologist regarding switch types and layouts (considering a black background for the lights, etc.) [R561218-19]. They finally sent a design study document to us on January 1, 1956 (which I don't have), but still there were more Flexowriter questions a week later [R570118]; the Ferranti automatic turn-off to save motor wear [R57314]; a press release [R57417]; request for a San Diego training program for use of the MIV equipment [R57429]; and finally ''the Charactron and MIV equipment turned up at AFAC today,'' on August 14, 1957 [R57814]. But I have no photos or descriptions of what finally was delivered.

A letter from John Ward to John Moser (Stromberg Carlson) on October 24, 1957, congratulates him ''for a very fine job'' and says we ''hope to be making good use of it within a month's time'' [C571024].

John Walsh (one of my programmers, and still with SofTech) labored many months on an elaborate 1103 program for extendable, labelled plots of functions for the Charactron as a major part of the AFAC system (Ross and Ward 1957). But AFAC programmers always were too short of time to do much elaborate MIV programming. The system was indeed used for the Pre-B-58 and B-58 tests, but I don't know any more about it than that. It's claim to fame really is that it was the first working work station explicitly designed for general purpose use.

### MIT MIV FOR IBM COMPUTERS

In the summer of 1956 preparations were well under way for the installation of the IBM 704 computer in the MIT Computation Center. This also was the time that my Computer Applications Group was officially christened, as we acquired responsibility for the (then unnamed) APT project in addition to our other projects. My first and second memorandum for the group (Ross 1956g and 1956i) concerned an assessment of the impact of the 704 on our work. The second memo begins:

> This memorandum is a supplement to Memorandum CA-M-1, ''Servo mechanisms Laboratory Requirements for Computing Facilities 1956–1957''. That memorandum stated that Project DSR 6873, on the devel-

opment of automatic programming techniques for numerically controlled machine tools, would be transferred to the IBM 704 computer as soon as it became available, but that the work of Project DSR 7138, on the application of digital techniques to airborne weapon systems, would continue to need the facilities of the Whirlwind Computer System because of its dependence on manual intervention techniques. This memorandum considers in more detail the reasons why it is felt that the Whirlwind I Computer must continue to be used, by describing the system of Whirlwind programs which are now being developed for this work, and then considering the modifications to the proposed IBM 704 system which would be required to make this type of system possible using that computer. [p. 1]

Then, after a description of SLURP, it goes on:

*The IBM 704 Computer*

Aside from the large amount of programming which has already been completed, it is apparent that SLURP is independent of the particular computer used, provided it has the appropriate input-output devices. The manual intervention features of the system are central to the philosophy of the system, since without them it becomes merely another elaborate computer programming system. The true significance of the system is that it allows a programmer to conceive of a new method of solution and maintain his momentum and initiative on the problem, unencumbered by the restrictions of the coding system of the computer. In other words, the programmer is permitted to program with programs, and ''program with ideas.''

It would be extremely desirable to have the larger storage capacity and longer word length of the 704 computer for use in SLURP. It already appears that the capacities of the Whirlwind Computer are being taxed by the size and complexity of SLURP. The present incomplete version contains approximately 10,000 instructions in addition to the 20,000 or so in the comprehensive system, and to this figure must be added several thousand registers required for the storage of a satisfactory amount of data for the problem. Since a large portion of the programming for SLURP consists of generating and interpreting coded information, the short word length of the Whirlwind Computer becomes awkward on occasion, and slows down the operating speed of the system due to increased complexities. Since the Share assembly program and the algebraic coding system being developed for the 704 installation by Computation Center personnel [never carried out] will be more modern and flexible than [p. 4] the Comprehensive System in some respects, and may be expected to expand to include those features of the Comprehensive System which are unique and desirable, it is felt that SLURP efficiency could be greatly improved by the use of those systems. Except for the fact that the IBM 704 will not have manual intervention and oscilloscope-type input-output devices, it would be very desirable, and probably worth the additional programming effort, to transfer SLURP from the Whirlwind Computer to the 704 Computer.

There appears to be some indication that there is some interest in applying this type of equipment to the 704. The Servomechanisms Laboratory should be active in support of this thinking. Systems such as SLURP seem to be the next logical step in development of improved programming systems for modern computers. The fact that work for Project DSR 6873 for the automatic programming for numerically controlled machine tools is being formulated and solved within the SLURP structure demonstrates that the philosophy of problem formulation and programming which is embodies [sic] in SLURP is by no means restricted to the type of military problems which have fostered its development and for which it is primarily at present intended. The possibility of detailed research into automatic process control and managerial business decisions should provide ample justification for the active consideration of these techniques as an integral part of the MIT Computation Center facility.

*Conclusions*

It is felt that the problems presently being considered in the Servomechanisms Laboratory cannot be successfully solved without the use of SLURP so that until an equal facility becomes available elsewhere this work is committed to the Whirlwind Computer. It is felt also, however, that the concept of systems such as SLURP is a significant advance in the use of computers as data processing devices, and that active consideration should be given to this type of system as an addition to the facilities of the MIT Computation Center in the near future. It would be necessary to expand the equipment planned for that facility to include manual intervention input devices and oscilloscope-type output devices in order to realize this type of system. The experience gained from the use of this type of equipment in this application in the Servo Lab SLURP system, as well as the experience of the Sage system development, should provide an adequate foundation for the planning of a Computation Center facility of this type. The potentialities of this type of a system as a research tool for experimentation in the newly unfolding area of general data processing are very great. It is felt that it would be in the interests of the Institute as a whole to pursue this line of thought. [p. 5]

My resumes show that on November 1, 1956, F.J. Corbato (still a professor at MIT) ''called to inquire about Servo Lab people giving talks in Digital Computer Center [sic] seminars. He is now on their staff and is in charge of these seminars. I said that we might talk about SLURP and our general problem solving system'' [R56111]. On November 6 ''should possibly consider obtaining support from Mission Director Project [a new component of John Ward's Bomber Defense project] for attaching MIV equipment to the 704. . . . Will IBM let such equipment be attached to the computer and also how do we get enough computer time to make the investment useable?'' [R56116] This was a problem we later solved by joining as a cosponsor of the

MIT Cooperative Computer Lab's IBM 709 in Building 10 in the early 1960s.

On November 27 I gave my Comp Center talk on "SLURP: An Experimental Human-Computer System for Problem Analysis and Solution" [R561114], and the interesting note is that Wes Clark (then doing TX-0 at Lincoln) suggested, in the discussion, "that the switches be programmed on the tube and thrown by means of a light pencil [sic]. In this way a programmer can do all of his own human engineering of switch layouts as well. [We later called this "light buttons" (Ross and Ward 1961, p. 80).] Slurp is already set up so it could do this operation merely by writing an appropriate Slurp program. Wes Clark would like to have several copies of the Gestalt paper and I will plan to take them out when we visit TX-0 tomorrow." Also at the talk, Frank Verzuh (Director of the MIT Comp Center) "said he was interested in talking with me about getting this kind of facility for the Computation Center" [R561126-27]. And the next day "Gave a stack of Gestalt papers to Wes Clark. He seems to be quite interested in what we are doing and there may be a possibility of pooling our interests if not our efforts in making TX-2 specifically designed for Slurp type of problem solving. Should plan to discuss this with him and his group in the near future." [R561128] We did collaborate on light pen design and improvement, under John Ward, after TX-0 was moved to MIT (I heard it was scheduled to move on June 27, 1957 [R57627]), but actual collaboration never took place.

Not much happened during 1957 on these ideas. TX-0 moved from Lincoln to ESL, with Earl Pugh in charge. In September, Whirlwind "passed into Lincoln's hands" [R5794-9] and we continued our developments there and on the AFAC 1103, while doing APT work also on the 704. By year end "A summary-progress report for the mission director is scheduled . . . [writing about SLURP will serve to] explain the whole problem-solving philosophy which I have been evolving over the last several years. [This will serve] as powerful ammunition for battling to keep Whirlwind going for a long time" [R57124-58019]. I cover the gestalt programming to SLURP transition in the next section, briefly.

In January 1958, Peter Elias (then EE Department Head) suggested to John Ward that I should get together with John McCarthy, Marvin Minsky, and Richard Marcus (all then at MIT's Research Lab for Electronics, RLE) about my use of MIV Techniques [R58019-28], and John Ward wrote me a memo to that effect (Ward 1958). John's memo says Dick "is working actively on function display under Manual Intervention Control." Later Dick came to work in my group and still is at MIT. By January 30, I finally arranged to have a lunch with McCarthy, which then transferred to Minsky's home in mid-afternoon, "and we talked some more until around 2:30 in the morning. Oliver Selfridge's group at Lincoln with whom Minsky works has $25,000 a month which must be spent on equipment, not manpower. . . . They are presently thinking of getting the [standard IBM] real time package for the Lincoln 704 and are interested in investigating whether the Convair MIV package that we worked out for AFAC would be within their budget" [R580131]. I don't know whether Oliver contacted Convair directly or what he ended up doing, but this session did begin a long, sporadic interaction on equipment matters with John and Marvin. A week after our long session I loaned John McCarthy "our information on the Stromberg Carlson [Convair] MIV equipment . . . informed him of our present investigations and said . . . perhaps he would be a good one to work on the automatic programming features since he has been working quite a lot on a super compiler with all sorts of logical statements, possible in it which may fit in well with the system we have been working on. We shall see" [R5827]. LISP was in the wind, and I was in the midst of APT, of course.

Again nothing happened regarding MIV equipment for months, although a talk I gave (on APT) at IBM Kingston Labs evoked brief interest on their part in scope input and MIV for their IBM 704 [R58815-20]. In September, Dick Bennett (who then had a consultant company) was under contract to Lincoln to upgrade the Whirlwind utility system, and he thought Frank Heart's group "also should be interested in being able to operate everything from the Room 222 console. . . . We also discussed. . .putting things under direct typewriter control" [R58924]. But most of Dick's plans were not carried out.

Even though the preparations for the APT press conference were pressing, I was concerned about the facilities for follow-on work, so in early January 1959 I said:

> Whirlwind definitely is going to close on June 30 and since it is poor politics to fight it at this time, we are going to go along with it, so that we have to find a substitute. My thought is that by combining TX-0 and 704 we could have a really fancy facility since TX-0 with its newly expanded memory, which is not in yet, of 8,000 words should be able to do [display and light pen support]. . . . We are having a meeting . . . between [Dean] Arden, Jack Gilmore, John McCarthy, myself, Arnie Siegel, and [?] who will be in charge of the Lincoln 709 programming to consider using the real time package [IBM's terminology] on the 709 to simultaneously service about 20 Flexowriters in TX-0 fashion. . . . We are going to start off with one Flexowriter on the 704 real time package. [R581229-59019]

This was the start of MIT's time sharing developments.

In January 1959, "Attended a meeting in Dean Arden's office concerning 704 Flexowriter input . . . I didn't feel that the group accomplished very much" [R590112-21].

In early March, "John McCarthy is calling a series of meetings to consider operator and compiler programs for the 7090 computer which will be the transistorized version of the 709 which will replace the 704. We had a meeting yesterday [March 3]." I spoke about MIV and Group Control. "I am hoping that in later sessions [we can show that MIV] should be an integral part of the programmer's bag of tricks applicable to any problem" [R59219-34]. But by the end of the month "The meeting to discuss 7090 problems seems to have lost momentum, so it is unlikely we will have another one very soon" [R59323-331].

In April,

> With the imminent breakup of Whirlwind, we have started to consider putting a good manual intervention console on the 704. I have now decided to soft pedal the connection of TX-0 to 704 until we have a definite use. We got together with John McCarthy and Herb Teager who is now putting the Flexowriter on the 704. [I believe Arnie Siegel, who knew Whirlwind well, had done some early preparations to adapt our earlier work.] John Ward and Don Clements are going to assist in this and it looks like our first move will be to get a light pen hooked up to the 704 to use the present scope. . . . In the long term, however, we are thinking of developing a self maintaining display system, [Later the ESL Display Console (Ross and Ward 1961, pp. 79–92), which was Rob Stotz's Masters thesis, came from this idea.] possibly built out of Whirlwind components. There is quite a bit of engineering involved there, however. McCarthy and Teager are going over to see the Whirlwind equipment with us at 11 a.m. [R59416-511]

On April 16–18, 1959, a select conference on Symbolic Manipulation (organized by McCarthy, Perlis, and Newell [R59219-34]) was held at MIT (McCarthy 1959). This was the first public presentation of LISP by McCarthy, COMIT by Yngve, and "I talked for a short time on multimode control as applied to list searches, group control, and proposed a modified list structure which seems more appropriate to our design machine application" [R59416-511]. This was my "reversed index registers" (as I later called it) method of general pointers and "n-component elements" of Plex Programming (Ross 1961), which began what now is the field of abstract data types. Evidently Al Newell made no presentation at MIT, but "On May 4, 5 and 6 I attended a conference on self organizing systems . . . in Chicago. [Some papers] were quite good, . . . [especially] one by Allen Newell on the GPS system general problem solver that he is working on with Simon and Shaw. . . . will plan to get together with him" [R59416-511].

On May 12, I took McCarthy, Teager, and Don Clements (then project engineer for the APT Project) "to look over the Whirlwind equipment. They seemed satisfied enough but our present thoughts are to find out what is going on at Lincoln, too" [R59512 & 13]. A memo from me (Ross 1959) shows that Arden, Clements, McCarthy, Minsky, Teager, Ward, and Ross visited Lincoln (re 709, charm, TX-2, and SAGE) on May 19, but "Our meeting out at Lincoln . . . was pretty much of a farce. People were late or missing or not very sympathetic . . . so not much was accomplished" [R59518-20].

## THE DESIGN MACHINE

So as 1960 rolled around, various seminal equipment developments at MIT had been initiated, but they are better treated as components of the history of time sharing, computer graphics (hardware and software), computer-aided design (CAD), software engineering, and software technology, rather than merely as extensions of the personal work station theme of this paper. I hope to be invited sometime in the future (though not too soon, for these papers are excruciating torture to write!) to contribute to the chronicling of those developments, as well.

Any such future consideration of CAD work stations would have to begin with a mention of George Price's prescient article in the November 1956 issue of *Fortune* Magazine, (Price 1956) and since it, too, was a "first in the fifties," I must reference it here.

Going back again in time, in January 1957 I said

Bill Webster [Air Force contract monitor for APT] also had a copy of the article on a design machine which I had been told about in New York. It's amazing the similarity between what is in that article and what was in my Gestalt paper and what we have been working on the past year or so. He even has pushbutton language with sentences of the form that we are planning for our milling machine, and the computer drawing pictures of the part being designed on the scope just like our scope plot, etc. I plan to write him a letter describing our work and enclose a copy of my paper and send a copy of this correspondence to the editor of Fortune and see what results. I think it is quite interesting that we have been actually carrying out what in his article is merely a proposal which everybody feels very strongly isn't as wild as it seems. Webster wanted to check with me that his impression that we were doing just what the article called for was correct, and I assured him that it was. [R57017-8]

I finally got a library copy to read by January 25 [R570125], and on February 6 wrote to Price, enclosing a Gestalt paper reprint, and describing our APT progress, then being issued as the first APT Interim Report. I then go on:

These routines provide the necessary mathematical structure around which a convenient human language can be built to make a complete automatic programming system. The detailed specification of this human language has not been attacked yet, but it will be the major focus point for the efforts of the group. The language will have specially designed features for description of surfaces and their interrelation, as well as for the instruction of the machine tool itself. The form of the language will probably be similar to that which you propose for the design machine, and as outlined in my paper, although it will be a written language and not use push buttons initially [—used in the Gestalt paper and in Price's article]. . . .

Another important part of the language problem is the computer-to-human language, which we envision in two forms. First there will be the ability of the computer to "talk back" to the human in the same type of language which the human uses, probably in a written form. The computer's language also will be of a pictorial form in which the computer will draw pictures for the human to check and work from in a way almost identical with your proposals in the FORTUNE article. A rudimentary routine of this sort has been in operation on the Whirlwind I Computer for several months now, which draws on the output oscilloscope of that computer arbitrarily positioned and scaled axonometric projections of the part being made. True perspective will be programmed later if it seems warranted. At present the picture consists of the sequence of "cut vectors" which are used to program the machine tool, but more elaborate schemes are planned. At the present time the pictorial displays are photographed and no effort has been made to increase the speed of the program so that a cycled display can be viewed easily on the display tube itself. Memotron-type tubes are not presently installed on the Whirlwind Computer although they would be very desirable for this and other applications. [The ARDS Display of Rob Stotz was the first such memory tube display (Ross and Ward 1961, pp. 100–113).]

The striking similarity between our work and the proposals of your FORTUNE article indicate that we have a number of very strong mutual interests and a similar approach to these problems. Mr. William Webster of the Air Materiel Command, who is our project monitor, brought your article to my attention and showed me a letter which you had written to him. In that letter you mentioned a study which you made concerning a design machine using the IBM 704 computer as a major component. I would very much appreciate a copy of this report if you have any available in order that we may know in more detail your ideas on this subject. We plan to transfer our work to the IBM 704 in the very near future.

I look forward with anticipation to further correspondence with you on this most interesting subject. [C5726]

A February 25 reply from Price enclosed a reprint of the *Fortune* article and his retyped "supplementary memo," but said he was changing jobs and moving, so he hadn't "been able to find the time to do more than take a quick glance at your two papers" [C57225]. On May 13 he visited my home and we "talked for an hour or so . . . but we never did get around to talking the same language or really discussing anything. . . . He has no technical training in this field" [R57513]. But he certainly wrote an interesting article, and his Design Machine proposal surely was a first, including many features that later were used in actual CAD work stations. As a side box [p. 153] about "The Author and His Machine" said:

> Price began thinking about his Design Machine some ten years ago. Could the Machine be built today? One leading computer expert shown the proposal was skeptical. Price thereupon prepared a detailed supplementary memorandum demonstrating how an IBM 704 computer could be incorporated into a Design Machine, how a complex part could be described to the Machine, and how with the aid of certain auxiliary devices the Machine would display the part—in 3-D. Computer experts at IBM pronounced the memorandum eminently sound. The first skeptic conceded that Price had shown how the job might be done.

The main thrust of the article was "eight recipes for modernizing R. and D.," one of which was the Design Machine, and another to mechanize "reading" of technical literature for mechanized filing (with a reference to V. Bush and the Patent Office). Besides describing the pushbutton and joy stick preparation of stereoscopic pictures of parts and "invisible models—recorded in a magnetic memory," with "preparation of control tapes for guiding automatized machine tools," the article says "a single Machine might be shared among several companies scattered around the country, for a number of control stations can be in use simultaneously, with keyboard signals being briefly stored on magnetic tape, and the central computer switching from one station to another every few seconds." [p. 228] (An idea also promoted by Jay Forrester for Whirlwind, in 1948 [Redmond and Smith 1980, pp. 233, 234].) Price's article was well ahead of its time.

## System Software

As I said at the beginning, a final essential ingredient for a viable, general, PWS scheme is a systematized way to link the work station capabilities to the class of problems to be solved through some form of software framework. As I have indicated, the earliest such framework, when Whirlwind had only 2K words of memory, took the form of several programming principles, such as "store switch values in variables," the language design principles of the Gestalt programming paper, and the rudiments of drum/ES storage management prompted by the mistake diagnosis routine (MDR). But with the advent of core memory, and its expansion to 6K words, and with the growing sophistication of approach engendered by early efforts at MIV in the evaluation program, a truly systematized solution was the natural evolutionary step.

## THE SERVO LAB UTILITY ROUTINE PROGRAM

The first coherent expression of these ideas appeared in (Ross 1956h) (note—when APT work was just getting under way, as well), which said:

> After some experience with the integration of the manual intervention facilities into the previously fully automatic evaluation programs, by the Servomechanisms Laboratory, it was realized that the manual intervention features could be used as a direct aid to programming by incorporating a number of general-purpose utility routines into the system. Shortly thereafter, the new task concerning the investigation of the techniques and problems for an airborne mission director was undertaken. Since detailed specifications on the mission director problem were not then available, and also since the committment of the evaluation studies to the B-58 program made progress in that direction imperative, it was decided that a worthwhile merging of these two interests could be achieved. This was done by commencing the elaboration of the evaluation program on the Whirlwind computer into a general purpose problem-solving system combining the talents of the human programmer and the electronic computer for the solution of general computer problems. The result is a human-computer system which may be viewed either as an elaborate evaluation program, or as a prototype problem-solving program with the problem of evaluation of airborne fire-control systems as the motivating core. This memorandum stresses the latter viewpoint. [p. 1] . . .
>
> The combined evaluation and problem-solving system which is the subject of this memorandum has been given the name, the Servo Lab Manual Intervention System (MIV System). The main feature which distinguishes this system from other computer programming systems is that all of the major facilities of the system are instantaneously available under manual intervention control. [p. 3] . . .
>
> The facilities of the MIV System may be grouped into three categories according to their primary function and motivation. Some of the features are concerned with the problem itself (in the present case the evaluation program). Other features are strictly of a utility nature having to do with input and output of data in various tabulated and graphical forms. The third category concerns features which arise almost entirely from the fact that a manual intervention system is being used and have primarily to do with reliability and ease of operation of the overall system. The main features of each of these categories will be described in turn. [p. 3]

Five more pages then detail the plans for what came to be called "SLURP," just nine days later, in the second Computer Applications Group memo, mentioned earlier (Ross 1956i). The one-page summary of features, some of which were implemented only in later years, was:

> The Servo Lab utility routine program (SLURP) is a system of Whirlwind Computer programs which combine the manual intervention

features of that computer, with modern programming techniques, into a unique problem-solving system. SLURP includes all of the facilities of the Comprehensive System developed for the Whirlwind Computer by the Digital Computer Laboratory staff, plus a large number of general purpose routines for extracting and analyzing information about arbitrary computer programs. The governing philosophy of the system is to allow the programmer to work on one small part of a very large and complicated problem, virtually independent of the computer which is being used and those aspects of the overall problem which are not of immediate concern. The major features of the system which make this possible are as follows:

1. A group control program which allows the automatic incorporation of new sections of programming into the system.
2. A manual intervention (MIV) system of programs which allow the programmer to interrogate and instruct the computer with respect to the overall problem in terms of a specially designed and easy-to-use language represented by: switches, buttons, lights, and visual displays.
3. A logging program which records all of the MIV actions taken by the programmer.
4. An editing program which edits the logged information into an easy-to-read record of the manual actions taken, and generates a log playback tape.
5. A log playback program which automatically simulates manual actions in response to the instructions on the log playback tape.
6. An elaborate set of plotting and tabulating programs for data presentation and record keeping.
7. A mistake diagnosis routine (MDR) which may be used to abstract arbitrary intermediate computed quantities from any program and present these quantities in any of the above forms [including scope].
8. The SLURP program proper which is a simulated, generalized, special-purpose computer which allows the incorporation of all of these routines into a smoothly functioning system, along with the capacity for continued expansion of these facilities. [p. 3]

### THE SLURP SIMULATED COMPUTER

The SLURP computer had many features that independently were discovered and incorporated into the Burroughs B5000 computer (I was astounded to see the similarities when I first read their manuals in the early 1960s). SLURP included built-in group control (memory paging), the memory table (virtual addresses for re-entrant program segments), alarm conditions (exception conditions with optional MIV and MDR facilities), and the ZIP Interpretive Program (which "serves the important function of establishing the MIV language which is appropriate for a particular program'' and integrated all of the other features, including I/O in a powerful, very condensed macro-command-like language).

A unique feature of SLURP was its ''multimode control element'' (Ross 1958). As the definitive report on SLURP says:

> The instruction repertoire of the SLURP computer contains no mathematical instructions but instead concentrates on a wide variety of a) jump instructions for transferring control from one sequence of instructions to another, and b) instructions which control selection and adjustment of input-output equipment. Individual flexowriter typewriter characters are included in the instruction repertoire and the execution of this type of instruction involves the reproduction of these characters on a selected output device. A SLURP instruction may occupy an arbitrary number of Whirlwind registers. There are two binary digits called the A and C bits which are set aside in each instruction and are used to label individual instructions for execution in the various modes of the control element. . . .
>
> If the A bit is ONE and the C bit ZERO, the instruction will be executed when the control element is set to the A mode but will not be executed if the control element is set to the C mode [etc.]. All SLURP instructions (with the exception of a few jump instructions) are executed when the control element is set to the B mode, independent of the settings of the A and C bits. Since the mode of the control element may be set by jump instructions, the setting of the control element may be changed as often as necessary to accomplish a desired result. . . .
>
> In addition to the return jump instruction for termination of a remember jump sequence, it is also possible to remember jump to a flexo phrase (any sequence of characters or words), and the occurrence of a stop character in that flexo phrase will act as a return jump under certain circumstances. However, if that same flexo phrase is executed by encountering it in the normal sequence of operations (instead of by an entry via a remember jump), the stop character is ignored. In this way a lengthy flexo phrase which contains useful subphrases or words may be extracted from the entire sequence by means of remember jump instructions. (pp. 3–82 to 3–84)

This feature was used to have abbreviated labels for display and long labels for printouts, and the same technique gave complex behavior if the ''words'' were other instructions. Our favorite test case

> THE SKUNK SAT ON THE STUMP
> THE SKUNK THUNK THE STUMP STUNK
> THE STUMP THUNK THE SKUNK STUNK

took only 13 SLURP instructions including output device selection [p. 3–85]. SLURP packed a tremendous punch in very little space.

### THE MIV BOX

One of the most powerful features of MIV language design with SLURP was the *MIV Box* (Figs. 16 and 17), a re-entrant subroutine that could be used in many places [pp. 3–127 to 3–137]. The basic language idea was that

> if the human does not like what is presently going on, he merely needs to remember to depress an appropriate exit button. The appropriateness of the two exit buttons can be given a universal meaning by referring to one as a *major* exit, and the other as a *minor* exit. Then no matter what program is operating, if the human is unsure which of the two exit buttons to press, he may first try the minor exit and if that does not give the desired action, then pressing the major exit is guaranteed to work. . . . It is not necessary to know beforehand all the possible actions which may be controlled by exit buttons if it can be established that those programs will operate on a hierarchy of actions. The major and minor exits can then be associated merely with a change in level within whatever hierarchy exists for a particular program. This uniformity of meaning of language is achieved by combining the MIV Dispatcher, the wait switch, the major and minor exit buttons, and one new switch, the ''cycle'' switch.

The example shows how only two more switches allowed many choices of control for selecting and plotting successive frames of a sequence of functions, as in the evaluation program. One more switch

**FIGURE 16**
Definition of MIV Box re-entrant subroutine of Servo Lab Utility Routine Program (SLURP) simulated computer—basis for systematized MIV languages.

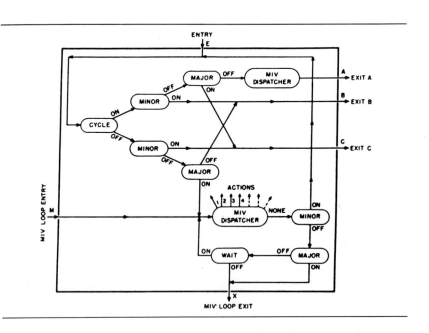

**FIGURE 17**
Hierarchic control of complex program action with generic MIV Box controls. Precursor to current mouse/menu control scheme.

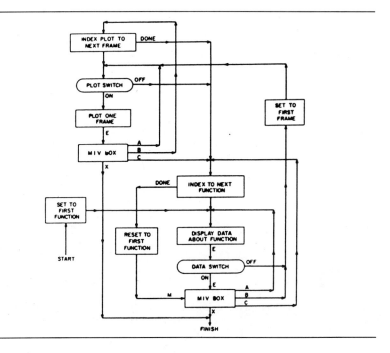

could similarly specify console display only or off-line camera, as well, and the SLURP system would efficiently see to the details.

## Conclusion

I hope that I have succeeded in defending my thesis that there were indeed some significant PWS "firsts in the fifties," even though only a tiny fraction of the computer resources that today are thought to be essential were then available. The revolutionary evolution since those early days has indeed brought much greater sophistication and broader capabilities, including the all-important hardware, software, and systematized approach improvements that allow ubiquitous spread to all types of users. But don't sell the old days short. Big ideas can come in small packages. Maybe that's an idea we've lost track of in today's technology where we *shrink* things mechanically to make them smaller. Maybe we need a sharper return to those earlier days when the only recourse was to *think* big things into their distilled essence—and make them work.

### ACKNOWLEDGMENTS

Thanks to the MITRE Corporation Archives and the MIT Museum for the Whirlwind photos. Thanks also to MIT and my many colleagues for making it all possible.

## REFERENCES

American Ordnance Association (1955) April 14–15. *Symposium on Proving Ground Instrumentation Problems,* Air Force Missile Test Center, Patrick Air Force Base, Cocoa, Fla. (program and papers).

Brackett, C. F. (1959) February 2. *The Direct Flexowriter Keyboard Input System at Whirlwind I (Barta).* Lexington, Mass.: Division 2—Lincoln Lab. Interoffice Memo (no number), 3 pp.

Charactron Project (1955). *Charactron Display Console Model 70B* (January 24, 1955, 14 pp.); *Charactron Computer Readout System, Model 100* (June 3, 1954, 22 pp.); *The Charactron Rapromatic* (no date, 11 pp.). San Diego, Calif. Convair division of General Dynamics Corp.

Cohen, Arnold (1985) October 4. Oral comments to D. T. Ross at Annual Meeting of the Charles Babbage Foundation.

Convair (1954) August 9. *Agenda for Flight Test Program Meeting* see also Ross (1954).

EJCC (1955) November 7–9. *Program of the Eastern Joint Computer Conference and Exhibition,* Statler Hotel, Boston, 27 pp.

Electronic Design Magazine (1956) May 1. New York, N.Y.: Hayden Publishing Co. *Computer Developments: Design Trends from Meetings,* pp. 36 & 37.

ERA (1954a). *ERA 1103 General Purpose Computer System* (brochure). New York, N.Y.: Engineering Research Associates Division of Remington Rand, Inc., 4 pp.

ERA (1954b) January 5. *ERA 1103 Installation Requirements.* St. Paul, Minn.: Engineering Research Associates Division of Remington Rand, Inc., 16 pp.

Forrester, J. W. (1948) July 29. *Whirlwind High Speed Computing.* Cambridge, Mass.: MIT Servo Lab. Rep. No. R-142. Appendix A in Redmond and Smith (1980), pp. 225–236.

Hamilton, D. A. (1955) August 4. *Conventions for Presentation of Results from Whirlwind I Polynomial Fit Program.* Cambridge, Mass.: MIT Servo Lab. Memo 7138-M-116, 4 pp. See also Ross (1954) and Ross, Thompson, and Cundiff (1956).

Holmes, L. L. (1956) April 3. *Flexowriter Input to WWI.* Lexington, Mass.: Division 6—Lincoln Lab. interoffice memo, 2 pp.

McCarthy, J. (1959) February 27. *Invitation to Conference on Symbol Manipulation Systems, April 16–18, MIT.*

MIT Digital Computer Lab. (1956) March 1 and 2. *Seminar on Microprogramming* (Announcement and agenda). Cambridge, Mass. 2 pp. plus map. June 6, 1956: Partial transcript of D. T. Ross presentation pp. 152–161, via F. W. Helwig.

MIT Servo Lab. (1952–1958). Certain Lists of laboratory personnel.

MIT Servo Lab. (1955) March 8, 9. Symposium on *Design and Evaluation of Bomber Fire-Control Systems.*

MIT Servo Lab. (1958) December. *Data Reduction Programming for Pre-B-58 Tests of the XMD-7 Fire-Control System* (3 Volumes). Cambridge, Mass.: MIT Servo Lab. Reports: Ross, D. T. Functional Description of the Data Reduction System (7886-R-1), 44 pp; Scheff, B. H. Initial Data Processing (7886-R-2), 149 pp.; Ross, D. T., and McAvinn, D. F. Evaluation of Fire-Control System Accuracy, (7886-R-3), 177 pp.

Nielsen, K. L., and Heyda, J. F. (1951) July 20. *Mathematical Theory of Airborne Fire Control.* Washington, D.C.: U.S. Government Printing Office, NAVORD Report 1493, 208 pp.

Price, G. R. (1956) November. How to Speed Up Invention. New York, N.Y.: *Fortune* magazine, p. 150 ff.

Price, G. R. (1957) February. *Technical Details Concerning the Design Machine.* Kingston, N.Y.: personal memo, 72 pp.

Project Whirlwind (1952–1957) Quarterly Summary Reports No. 31–No. 50. Cambridge, Mass.: MIT Digital Computer Lab.

Redmond, K. C. and Smith, T. M. (1980). *Project Whirlwind: The History of a Pioneer Computer.* Bedford, Mass.: Digital Press, 280 pp. Index.

Ross, D. T. (1952) July. *Autocorrelation Program* working papers.

Ross, D. T. (1953a). First *Evaluation Program Flow Diagram.* Computation Notebook pp. 26 & 27.

Ross, D. T. (1953b) June 27. *An Introduction to the Use of Air-Mass Ballistic Tables in Airborne Fire-Control System Evaluation* (CONFIDENTIAL, Title Unclassified—declassified November 1958). Cambridge, Mass.: MIT Servo Lab. Rep. No. 6506-ER-46, 25 pp.

Ross, D. T. (1953c) November 24. *A Mistake Diagnosis Routine for Whirlwind I Programs.* Cambridge, Mass.: MIT Servo Lab. Rep. No. 7138-R-1, 26 pp.

Ross, D. T. (1954a) May 24. *Missile Launch Simulator* program for Memory Test Computer working papers.

Ross, D. T. (1954b) June 24. *Improved Computational Techniques for Fourier Transformation.* (M.S. thesis). Cambridge, Mass.: MIT Servo Lab. Rep. No. 7138-R-5, 84 pp.

Ross, D. T. (1954c) July 16. Letter to W. J. Moe of Engineering Research Associates (ERA) regarding 1953 Polynomial Fit Program, 2 pp. See also Hamilton (1955).

Ross, D. T. (1954d) August. *Scope Input Program* (no original; revised copy fc Tape 126-50-505, 2/15/55).

Ross, D. T. (1955a) March 8. Handwritten instructions to DAH for ROSS DEMO. Director Tape, plus printout of same.

Ross, D. T. (1955b) June. *A Basic Input Translation Program for the ERA 1103* (program, runs, and working papers).

Ross, D. T. (1955c) July 25. *Special In-Out Equipment for Human Participation in High-Speed Computer Operation.* Cambridge, Mass.: MIT Servo Lab. Memo 7138-M-112, 8 pp.

Ross, D. T. (1955d) October 13. *[The] Gestalt [System of] Programming—A New Concept in Automatic Programming,* handwritten draft, 15 pp.

Ross, D. T. (1955e) November–December. Handwritten draft pages.

Ross, D. T. (1955f) November 17. *Gestalt Programming: A New Concept in Automatic Programming* (second draft, typed) 12 pp. plus addendum: "Proposed Changes for Final Draft," 2 pp.

Ross, D. T. (1955g) December 14. *Proposed Equipment Modifications for the Pre-B-58 Data Reduction Programs.* Cambridge, Mass.: MIT Servo Lab. memo 7138-M-128, 7 pp.

Ross, D. T. (1956a) January. Handwritten oral presentation drafts and notes.

Ross, D. T. (1956b) February 7. Gestalt Programming: A New Concept in Automatic Programming. New York: *Proceedings of the Western Joint Computer Conference.* AIEE for the JCC (now AFIPS), pp. 5–10. Also Cambridge, Mass.: MIT Servo Lab. Rep. No. 7138-TM-7, 14 pp.

Ross, D. T. (1956c) March 1. *Suggestions for Manual Intervention Facilities on the Air Force Armament Center ERA 1103 Computer.* Cambridge, Mass.: MIT Servo Lab. Memo 7138-M-144, 6 pp.

Ross, D. T. (1956d) March 14. *Flexowriter Keyboard Input to WWI, Preliminary Specifications.* Cambridge, Mass.: MIT Servo Lab. Memo 7138-M-148, 3 pp.

Ross, D. T. (1956e) April 5–Summer 1956. *Proposed Microprogramming Instruction for Whirlwind I Computer.* Working papers, drawings, and memo outline.

Ross, D. T. (1956f) April 30. *A Proposed Flexowriter Input for the Whirlwind I Computer.* Cambridge, Mass.: MIT Servo Lab. Memo 7138-M-160, 4 pp.

Ross, D. T. (1956g) September 26. *Servomechanisms Laboratory Requirements for Computing Facilities, 1956–1957.* Cambridge, Mass.: MIT Servo Lab. memo CA-M-1, 4 pp.

Ross, D. T. (1956h) November 14. *Programming Progress for Mission Director Task.* Cambridge, Mass.: MIT Servo Lab. memo 7138-M-200, 8 pp.

Ross, D. T. (1956i) November 23. *Whirlwind Versus 704 for Servo Lab Problems.* Cambridge, Mass.: MIT Servo Lab. memo CA-M-2, 5 pp.

Ross, D. T. (1958) April. A Multi-Mode Control Element; A Philosophy of Problem Solving; The SLURP System for Experimental Programming. Cambridge, Mass.: *Research in Defense Techniques for Airborne Weapons: 1957 Annual Report, Volume 2.* MIT Servo Lab. Rep. No. 7668-R-5(2), pp. 3–81 through 3-163.

Ross, D. T. (1959) May 13. *Visit to Lincoln Lab., Tuesday, May 19.* Cambridge, Mass.: MIT Servo Lab. memo (no number).

Ross, D. T. (1961) March. A Generalized Technique for Symbol Manipulation and Numerical Calculation. *Communications of the ACM* 4 (3): 147–150.

Ross, D. T. (1977). Origins of the APT Language for Automatically Programmed Tools. *History of Programming Languages* (R. L. Wexelblat, Ed.) (1981) New York: Academic Press, pp. 279–367.

Ross, D. T., Thompson, D. A. (Hamilton), and Cundiff, T. (1956) December 17. *Polynomial Fit Program.* Cambridge, Mass.: MIT Servo Lab. Memo 7138-M-202, 18 pp. See also Hamilton (1955).

Ross, D. T., and Ward, J. E. (1956) May. *Investigations in Computer-Aided Design for Numerically Controlled Production* (Final Report for 1 December 1959 to 3 May 1967). Cambridge, Mass.: MIT Electronic Systems Lab. for Air Force Materials Lab., WPAFB, Ohio. Rep. No. AFML-TR-68-206. MIT Rep. No. ESL-FR-351, 229 pp.

Ross, D. T., and Ward, J. E. (1957) October 22. *Charactron Plot Program for Pre-B-58 Data Reduction.* Cambridge, Mass.: MIT Servo Lab. memo 7668-M-251, 4 pp.

Ross, D. T., and Ward, J. E. (1961) January. Picture and Pushbutton Languages (Chapter VIII), and Ward, J. E., A Manual Intervention Facility (Chapter IX), in *Investigations in Computer-Aided Design,* Interim Report for December, 1959 to May 30, 1960. Cambridge, Mass.: MIT Electronic Systems Lab. Rep. No. 8436-IR-1, 156 pp.

Ward, J. E. (1954) July 23. *Disposal of Mechanical Correlation Computer (MCC).* Cambridge, Mass.: MIT Servo Lab. Memo 7138-M-49, 2 pp.

Ward, J. E. (1955) May 2. *Symposium on Data Reduction* (Announcement). MIT Servolab (no number).

Ward, J. E. (1958) January 27. *Manual Intervention.* (Memo to D. T. Ross.) Cambridge, Mass.: MIT Servo Lab. (no number).

Ward, J. E. (1960) January 15. *Automatic Programming of Numerically Controlled Machine Tools* (Final Report). Cambridge, Mass.: MIT Electronic Systems Lab. Rep. No. 6873-FR-3, for June 26, 1956 to November 30, 1959. Reprints 6873-FR-1 (July 30, 1952) for July 1949 to July 1954, [sic] and reprints 6873-FR-2 (March 15, 1956) for July 1949 to March 15, 1956.

Ward, J. E. (1970) June. *Computer-Aided Design for Numerically Controlled Production* (Final Report for 1 May 1967 to 30 January 1979). Cambridge, Mass.: MIT Electronic Systems Lab. for Air Force Materials Lab., WPAFB, Ohio. Rep. No. AFML-TR-70-78. MIT Rep. No. ESL-FR-420, 121 pp.

Ward, J. E., and Ross, D. T. (1955) July 29. *Minutes of M.I.T. Data Reduction Symposium: June 1 and 2, 1955.* Cambridge, Mass.: MIT Servo Lab Rep. No. 7138-S-1, 20 pp.

Ward, J. E., and Ross, D. T. (1956) March 1. *Suggestions for Manual Intervention Facilities on the Air Force Armament Center ERA 1103 Computer.* Cambridge, Mass.: MIT Servo Lab. Memo 7138-M-144A, 30+ pp.

Ward, J. E., and Ross, D. T. (1956) May 8. Draft paper of Revision of (Ross 1956c), incorporating MIT Digital Computer Lab. memo and drawings. Cambridge, Mass.: MIT Servo Lab. memo 7138-M-144A.

WJCC (1956) February 7–9. *Program of the Western Joint Computer Conference and Exhibit.* Fairmont Hotel, San Francisco, 23 pp.

Wolf, W. M. (1954) September–November. Worksheets and photos for Large Letter program. Flow diagram and WWI code for Manual Intervention tests.

# Participants Discussion

**Severo Ornstein**     What I get out of all of this is the feeling that in order to understand fully the thinking that went on you actually had to be there, and you had to be familiar with the kind of equipment that people had at the time. One K of memory and 20 thousand operations per second were really awesome in those days. When I was working on the communications between subsectors in the SAGE system, we had 1 kilobit lines interconnecting them. It seemed like just an enormous amount of communications capacity at that point.

I have two questions. We were standing talking to Allen Newell in the break here a few minutes ago, and we were wondering what it is that makes new ideas come forth. I think we all are really curious about that. We were talking about the connection between existing hardware, technology, and new insights, and you made some comments that I think others here would find interesting. I'd like to ask you to repeat them. My second question is as follows: Of the array of novel ideas presented here, which do you think are the three most influential ones? I heard you mention a number of things that were new at the time and I wonder what you think are the three most original ones, or most important ones.

**Ross**     I'm really not very programmable, so I'm not sure how I can reproduce what we were talking about with Allen. But the idea that I have about where creative insights come from is that they come from somebody who actually is there, in an environment that's built in terms of whatever is that day's technology. What you do is that that individual penetrates into the technology and has his ideas reflected back to see what is really implied by what's there. I don't think that there are very many things that are really dreamed up completely out of the blue. Some artists do, maybe, but I think that's more that they have a slightly demented mind and are doing just the same thing with a warped set of filters. You need to have a reality in which you are a participant. What creates the innovation is this deeper insight, literally seeing into, but reflected back to you—what is your current total environment. It's always not what's on the surface. There's inherently a built-in level of abstraction that has to go along with it. This is why you do get ideas that are portable—they carry around and can apply to many things. This comes across when you formalize it, when you talk about it: Wow, it's a brilliant idea, it's a great generalization. But it really is just this

112

little-bit-deeper version of the same kind of seeing and interacting and participating that we do all the time for everything else.

As for the top three novel ideas that I would pick from what I was talking about, I think I'd rather leave that to you all or later historians because, again, I've never been able to track down who actually saw or was influenced by my activities. All I know is, I was there, I did them, I remember them vaguely, I found them in my materials, and I've documented them here for you. How they then permeated and influenced other people, I don't know. I do know that all during the years of my having very creative people working with me, there was mutual stimulation—this thing of "it's the environment you're in, the problems you're given, the challenges." We always had to have problems that needed solving yesterday. We had to have real people asking for real solutions in problems that were beyond the state of the art, so we had to do that penetrating and getting further. When you get a creative bunch of people in such an environment, and get the right general way of doing it, you come out with a Whirlwind. You come out with Wes Clark's paper (I just loved to read that last night). You'll just love him; he does a much better job of showing what it was like to be there and to have the people involved.

I think that the main thing is that I was aware, because of this insightful look, from the very beginning after I first walked into room 222 and had that: "wow, whee, look at all those green scopes, and red lights." If they only had laser light shows. That was the version in those days; it really turned me on. I knew that's what I had to have, because I already had building up in me this vast set of needs for what I thought was a very, very complicated set of data reduction programs to do on that little bit of memory.

*Sig Treu*

I wonder whether you could characterize to what extent the history of personal workstations is necessarily overlapping with the history of what one might consider to be computing or computers in general. Or, if I may rephrase the question, Can you identify criteria by which you might separate out those historical aspects that are peculiar to personal workstations? One might argue that some of the things that have been presented this morning could just as well have been included in the history of computer hardware, computer software, and so on.

*Ross*

I think that probably goes along with the comment that you must have that reality in which you're participating to have any of these things happen. Of course, one of the earliest personal workstations is the cobbler's workbench—you sit there and all the things are right there to work with. Again, it's the technology and the problems, the needs of that day, that make that workstation. If you follow through what Gordon Bell was saying, the key thing in this historic development period is the stages of how you bring the cost down so that you can get the power up to match a broader and broader class of individuals, in terms of their problem needs and in terms of their economic needs.

Again, the point that John Brackett was making in the comment on Gordon's talk and the line that Severo was bringing out, is the main one that I'd like to stress: How do you bring those together? How do you bring the PW (personal work) and the WS (work station) together with an architecture and a systematic treatment? It is more than just how to put variables, instead of programs, directly on line; it is more than just having a gestalt language idea with switches and so forth; and it is more than having just a SLURP system that has the software framework and the building blocks. It is also more than just having software engineering tool kits and languages, more than having modular software building blocks, the OCCAM system that takes it right out to the hardware building blocks that you hook together (which is another one of Wes Clark's old pet peeves). These are just stages of development. What they do is reform this reality with which we interact at each stage. As we understand more about it, you find that the man and the machine do in fact become more and more coupled, and their view of what problems are and how to go about solving them becomes more and more sophisticated, more and more coupled. I think it's really exciting stuff to do.

# SOME REFLECTIONS ON EARLY HISTORY

## J. C. R. Licklider
Introduction by Alan Perlis

**Alan Perlis**

In the 1950s we were aware of the magical world of MIT. But MIT was a very singular point on the American landscape; it was a very lush and rich environment, in both people and material. Something in computing was unfolding there that very badly needed to be distributed across the United States. That was not something that could be accomplished trivially; it required not only a ripening of the computer field, but also money and an imagination with the control and access to support, in order for the diffusion to take place. Our next speaker, J. C. R. Licklider, found himself invited to participate in an activity dedicated to force this diffusion and, indeed, to direct it. Prior to the beginning of the ARPA program, computation in the United States, except for a few isolated places, was devoted to machines and people to provide application programs and support for the sciences, technology, and industry. That was the role of the computer. For such purposes batch processing, for example, was quite adequate; indeed, interactive computing was not seen as terribly important, as being crucial to the natural development of computation. What our next speaker did was to galvanize into action, in more and more places, the imagination and energy of people who saw the computer as much more than a stationary numerical engine—people who saw that the computer itself invoked a dynamism that was quite independent of, and really had to flower independently of, the applications with which it had been saddled. To give these people the freedom to operate, to train students, to do research, what was required was a galvanizer. I now introduce that galvanizer, J. C. R. Licklider.

115

J. C. R. Licklider started his career as an experimental psychologist. After receiving a Ph.D. in psychology from the University of Rochester in 1942, Lick held positions as a research associate at Swarthmore and as a researcher in the Psycho-Acoustic Laboratory at Harvard. He continued at Harvard as a lecturer until 1951, when he left to start a research program in speech and hearing at the Massachusetts Institute of Technology. In 1957 Lick decided that it was time to switch from analog devices to digital computing. To get into the computer field, he joined Bolt, Beranek, and Newman (BBN), where his research group is believed to have acquired the very first computer made by DEC.

Lick is widely known for his interest in and support of research on understanding how to improve the interface between human and machine, actually on the nature of the "inner medium" whereby a human is able to obtain depth of use from the computer and the computer is able to lend the human optimal support. In 1962 he took a two-year leave from BBN to start two ARPA funding offices, one on information processing techniques (IPTO) and the other on behavioral science; he later returned to ARPA (1974) to direct IPTO. In 1967, J. C. R. Licklider became the director of MIT Project MAC. He remained at MIT until retirement in 1986.

During his years of service as researcher, teacher, director, and funder, J. C. R. Licklider also served as the President of the Acoustical Society of America and received the society's biennial award. As an outcome of his work at BBN, Lick published a book entitled *Libraries of the Future* (1965, MIT Press).

# Some Reflections on Early History

*J. C. R. Licklider*

MIT Laboratory for Computer Science

[*Editor's Note:* The following is the edited transcript of J. C. R. Licklider's presentation.]

Well, thank you Alan for being more kind than honest. First, it's a great pleasure, and a privilege and an honor, to be here with you and discuss this topic. I had another privilege a few years back to attend a meeting on the history of computing at Los Alamos, where incidently, I was the second youngest participant. Fernando Corbato was there, and he is just a little younger. But mainly it was just the old boys of the field, and it quickly appeared that the main purpose was for each to establish that he was the inventor of the general purpose computer. So I'm going to start this talk by telling you how I invented the workstation.

My family and I lived, at that time, about a mile out of Mt. Kisco, New York. We were having a few people over for cocktails, and my wife discovered we were out of gin and dispatched me to the village. I guess there was plenty of time, because I remember thinking I could walk (I needed the exercise), but I'd have to take the shortcut. It was just then getting a little dark, and I made my shortcut through the cemetery and, to make a longish story short, I stepped into an open grave. It was pretty deep, and I started scrambling, causing dirt to come down on me, and I realized, *I'll never get out of here this way. I'd better sit down and think.* So I went over to the end of the grave and sat there and contemplated a little bit and this idea came into my mind that, well, I get lots of ideas, so that wouldn't really have done it. But there was a clincher. Very shortly there was a thud, and then another guy fell into this same grave. He was facing the other way. He didn't see me; he was much more excitable than I. He was jumping around screaming, and I said, "Better watch out, you'll have heart failure." So he leapt out of the grave and his heel caught me in the jaw—broke my jaw, but cemented this idea for the workstation.

I'm going to try to formulate a few issues that seem to me quite important. Maybe these aren't the germinal issues of workstations, but they're issues. And then I'll fill in with some recollections of how it used to be.

The first general issue I want to deal with is the *delimitation* issue. How are we defining what we are talking about? Do the workstations have to be digital, for instance? Do they have to be really personal, or can they be shared with others on a time-sharing basis, somewhat like a time-share condo? Do we focus only on individual tasks, or are individual tasks that are embedded in group tasks all right? There's a lot of reason for adopting a broad delimitation rather than a narrow one because, if you're trying to find out where ideas came from, you don't want to isolate yourself from the areas that they came from. Thus we have the rich history even prior to, well maybe contemporary with, the first digital computers—the rich history of analog computers, simulations of aircraft cockpits and so on, and the whole movement during World War II in the design and development of combat information centers, which were electronic work places for groups of people dealing with military problems. I remember aircraft cockpit simulations very early at the University of Illinois. Alex Williams had a laboratory devoted to aviation. Stanley Roscoe was there. And they knew a lot of things and understood a lot of problems that are important in the workstation area.

I spent a couple of summers working at Hughes Aircraft Company, and I remember on the lunch hour getting to fly an airplane simulator that was pretty abstract. I had trouble with the rudders, which seemed to me to work the wrong way, but all you had to do was turn the airplane upside down, and then it flew the way I thought was right. There was a beautiful simulator based on the analog equipment of interceptions, where you'd have a bomber and an interceptor airplane, and the vector controller would vector the interceptor to the bomber, and all that sort of thing. I heard this morning about something that took 30 days just to shut down (Whirlwind); I think that turned out to be shut down, fix, and bring back up, but I was visualizing 30 days just to shut it down. But the Hughes thing really did take 30 days to shut down and 30 days to bring up because, instead of being programmed, it took little patch cords to be connected to patch cord sockets, and there were thousands or tens of thousands of them, and it was believed that nobody ever got the thing set up right.

At Beavertail Island, off of Newport, Rhode Island, there was, during World War II, a big, high-priority crash project to develop combat information centers with displays. I think there were also guns at Beavertail Island, but I'm not sure. Anyway, you've got to be very careful about deciding you invented something like that because there's a lot of backlog deserving of credit—the SAGE system, the L systems, Wimix, SAC, NORAD, NATO Systems, for example. In Norfolk there's a Navy system with two-story high displays, where the whole ocean situation is depicted; this system is probably outside the limits with which we are dealing.

One of the issues is whether we're dealing with *general purpose workstations* or *special purpose workstations*. For general purpose ones, we seem to have some restriction to generic software. It seemed not to be economic to have really widespread systems that are used for everybody's workstations that go much beyond word processing, database, graphics, communications, and a few other like functions. How the average individual is going to get the special purpose stuff that he requires, I'm not sure. At any rate, there's a lot of problems associated with delimiting our attention, and I'm for taking a broad view. I think, in fact, we've already started to do that today.

Now about *input*. The workstation, it seems to me, has input, has output; it has some coordination of input and output, it has users, and then it has a set of general problems about coherent standards and the like. On the input side, a lot of the treatment is going to be treatment of input devices, analyzing which one is better than some other one. In particular, there's a long-standing debate about the qualities of keyboards. I think that one of the great inventions was Doug Engelbart's invention of the one-handed keyboard. But there's an awful lot of human factors and ergonomics wrapped up in that. In fact, very few people—maybe Doug is the only one—very few people use one-handed keyboards. It has to be based on a stenotype-like keyboard scheme with multiple finger pressings. It takes a good bit of learning. It's very valuable after you've learned it, but I sort of conclude that people who are buying computers, especially personal computers, just aren't going to take a long time to learn something. They're going to insist on using it awfully quick—easy to use, easy and quick to learn.

Another thing that I think Doug invented is the mouse. A mouse works with a hand offset from the target, from the work. Herb Jenkins at the Lincoln Laboratory back in the early 1950s did studies to determine how various data-take-off arrangements depended upon how much offset there was between the hand and the work and plotted function. The studies showed it was bad, by a factor of two, to have an offset of eight or ten inches. And yet, that seems not to have affected the popularity of the mouse device. I know 20 people who use mice for every person who uses a light pen; I can't understand that, but it seems to be true. We have seen light guns and light cannons, track balls, joy sticks, the RAND tablet—I think I should mention the tiger tablet that was competitive with the RAND tablet. Often these devices differ in a little engineering detail in implementation. I think the RAND tablet was a capacitive device, and the tiger tablet an inductive device, but both used a flat, supine surface on which to move a stylus.

I remember back in my first years in ARPA, which was 1962 to 1964, there were touch sensitive screens up in Ottawa at some Canadian government laboratory. Probably they go back earlier than that, but, if I hadn't seen that, I would have thought Hewlett-Packard had invented them.

One of the areas that we probably need to concern ourselves with is the workstation for the school. There are about 40 million students out there? There's a market potential for 40 million workstations. I think that's a very interesting thing to think about.

There's the idea of instrumenting the body of the user. It hasn't gone anywhere so far really. I remember Craig Fields had an instrumented cushion on the chair, and the computer knew something about how much the user was fidgeting around. There have been various efforts to get data taken directly from the skull, electroencephalographic light. And someone at Stanford Research Institute was claiming to be able to distinguish among 15 different words that the user merely thought of by analyzing the signals from the brain. If that could be brought up to a few thousand, that would be very useful indeed. If we're talking about input, a thing that I want is instrumented fingers. I have this terrible problem of having the keyboard in the middle of my work space, and yet the keyboard is pretty clearly on its way out in favor of graphics instead of the keyboard. I want a stylus pad to write on. I want that, incidentally, to be the display too, but I'll come back to that. When I want to reach and point to something with a light pen, then I really want a detachable fingernail that's got the light pen function in it, so I can continue to type. And now I wonder why I'd have to have keys of any kind to type on, because if there are selectors on my fingers, then you don't need the keys. Incidentally, I've never heard anybody discuss this from an informational point of view, but it's obvious, if you just think of it, that typing is capable of transferring more information than is actually used because there's information in which finger touches the key as well as in which key is touched. And if you could learn to type in such a way that you touched the same key with different fingers, that could be very useful.

On the subject of color, Bert Green at Lincoln Labs back in the early 1950s did an analysis of how color should be used in displays. He found, for instance, that if you have a display screen full of words printed in different colors, the length of time it takes you to find a word is directly affected by the color scheme. For example, suppose you're to find the red word "alpha," and all the words are red but in different orientations on the screen. Discovery time is the same as if "alpha" had been presented in black and white, and there hadn't been anything but the ones that were represented in red. That is to say, the color essentially rules out all of the other stimuli. This seems like a very worthwhile thing to know in the design of displays. Nowadays you get a workstation that is almost surely monochrome, because you want very high resolution rather than increased discrimination. Sutherland's PDP-1 at Harvard had interesting input. He had a helmet that connected through a lever to something up in the ceiling, so that the computer could tell what you were looking at. And then the computer generated what you ought to see if you're looking in that direction.

That was a marvelous display situation. The cathode ray tube was mounted on the same head rig so its output went directly into your eyes. You could move your head around and see different parts of the situation. It was nice for the computer because it didn't have to display what you weren't looking at.

Let us consider the *output* side. All workstation output is heavily visual, although it could be auditory. I think that's coming with the increasing capacity of the computer to deal with speech. The skin is interesting too. Frank Geldard, at Virginia, set up an arrangement of a big matrix of vibrators on the back of the user and, after a certain amount of training, the user could read stuff typed into his back. With cathode ray tubes, we have the problem: Should they be deep or flat? Pretty obviously you want them flat. The Japanese have recently reinvented the flat display, but indeed Willy's West Coast Electronics back in the late 1940s or early 1950s was making displays that were only one inch deep and regular cathode ray screen size. They were making them transparent hoping to use them as windscreens in fighter aircraft. The whole windscreen would be a cathode ray tube and you could draw on the cathode ray tube schematic pictures of airplanes and the like. If a pilot were intent on those images, by changing the depth of focus, one could look out and see the real airplane that was depicted on the cathode ray tube.

Sutherland's PDP-1 seemed to me to indicate something about resolution. There were four of these DEC-element displays that Gordon Bell mentioned, and the four had big boxes around them so you couldn't put the tubes nicely side-by-side without unpackaging everything. You really had to turn around too far to see the side ones. Nevertheless it was marvelous for programming, and I'm sure for many other purposes, to have a big display area.

While we're at it, we might as well get around to this horizontal versus nearly horizontal versus nearly vertical orientation. I just can't for the life of me understand why we continue to put up with vertical screens. You want a display area that you, as well as the computer, can write upon so that you can write notes to each other. And so I go back to a recollection of Mort Bernstein at SDC. He had a display in which text was projected up on the underside of a counter, on a translucent sheet. The user could write proofreader's marks on this sheet. It was pretty early in display technology development, so the brightness was not very good; you had to turn off the lights in the room in order to use it. But you could, in fact, edit and watch your proofreader's marks control the text. As the text changed, the controlling proofreader's marks disappeared. I'm sure that is the way editing needs to be done. It's just a matter of engineering, and now we can do all of those things. The Japanese work on flat displays based on liquid crystal and electroluminescence is leading to wall-sized television displays, in color, of several feet by several feet. If you can have it on the wall, you can have it on your desk. The plasma display remains a pretty neat idea; getting them out is a manufacturing problem, although we ought to wonder why they've stayed expensive over the years.

One of the really fundamental curves in our industry is the curve that shows how the cost-effectiveness of computer hardware increases with time. Gordon Bell addressed that and came up with 20 percent per year, or 36 percent over two years. That seems to me so important an issue that we should get it absolutely straight. Larry Roberts wrote a paper on that back in 1970, but Larry's conclusion was more like double every two years. In fact, it was a little better than that; 1.56 was the exponent of the increase. So I was wondering, since the increment refers to computer hardware, does it also relate to displays? Recently I was sitting in front of VAXStation II looking at the pixels, of which there are 1024 by 896, and I remembered sitting in front of a display years ago of a PDP-1, a vectored display. It was a little unstable, so that a point that's supposed to be in one place would move a little bit in the course of a minute or two; but, it did give you resolution of two points that were only one thousandth of the width or height away from each other. Considering cost, it's clear that there can't have been a factor of more than about ten or twenty in improvement in cathode ray display, while the factor of improvement in the processor and the rest of the computer is well over a thousand in the same time. In fact, I think the TRS80 Model 100, for about $399.00 at Radio Shack, is almost exactly a PDP-1, except it is ten times as fast!

Consider the size of displays. Over 25 years ago Dumont came to the Lincoln Laboratory and almost garnered a contract to build a 20-foot cathode ray tube. Of course, for a personal workstation, you don't really need such a thing, but I find it helpful to have a projector in the lab, projecting on the wall, so I can look up from the console screen and see some big array of information. Nick Negroponte and his people in the media technology lab at MIT have done a lot of studies on spatial data management. It is nice to have this big display to supplement the little ones. Speaking of projectors takes me back to a talk with John Gould, later at IBM Research in Yorktown, who was using the projector in connection with some educational software. He had a display, but he also had a projector that was an Eastman Kodak carrousel (with the label still on it), in a box with an IBM label on the outside. John explained to me that this was the ideal arrangement; as long as it works, they'll think that IBM made it.

On the subject of horizontal displays, in World War II, there were planned position indicators called PPIs, which were cathode ray tubes—big ones that were oriented horizontally with a horizontal face. The people did what was necessary to keep the phosphor from falling off the screen down into the electron gun and shorting it out. Those were very useful displays. I would like to see some of those show up in the computer world. In fact, I was in on the purchase of the very first Digital Equipment PDP-1 when I worked at Bolt, Beranek, and Newman. Ed Fredkin was the go-between with DEC, and I told Ed that we really wanted a scope that swivels. I think I explained, so that you could put it down and write on it or put it up and use it in the regular way. I went off on a trip and when I came back I asked Ed how the PDP-1 was coming and he said, "Oh great. I think you'll really like the swiveling thing—we've even hired a design consultant." I went to look at it, and, indeed, it swiveled, but as you may have seen in the pictures this morning, it swiveled the wrong way. And so I am still a little frustrated about writing on the cathode ray tube.

We ought to deal with the *parameters of processing,* but it's very hard to tell when you stop talking about workstations and when you're just talking about computers in general. Processors have been getting better very, very rapidly—getting smaller, getting less expensive for a given amount of power, or more powerful for a given cost. I remember the LGP30, which was the first computer at whose console I sat for many hours. The LGP30 was made by Royal McBee, and Fredkin took me to see one. I was worried about the ease of use of the thing. It sounded a little difficult because it had 20, or 30, or 40 vacuum tubes. Since they needed more amplification in it, they used what was then a standard technique of taking the signal that comes out of a row of amplifiers, increasing frequency, and putting it back through the same amplifiers. I don't know how many times the train of pulses went through the amplifier before it finally got big enough to grab the display. That worried me. We got the instruction book, and I said, "Ed, can you make it multiply 3 by 4?" He said, "You're not going to like this, but we can." First, you have to know there are 31 bits in the accumulator and only 29 in the memory registers. Everything must go through the accumulator. So we have to multiply by four, so that when you knock two bits off going into the memory it's the right size. And so we multiplied the three by the four and got twelve; put in the twelve, multiply the four by four got sixteen, put that in; multiply those two and got whatever you get with that. Then came the argument. Do we shift back by dividing by four or do we shift back by dividing by sixteen? Four won out and indeed the answer came out twelve!

That was my first experience with personal workstations. My second experience was in the use of a program that I knew full well. I'd been running on an analog computer, a Phillbrick analog computer for those of you who remember them. This thing solved the problem thirty times a second and displayed it so that you could see the output on the scope, turn the knobs, and see what affected what. That's what you're really trying to do with a digital computer most of the time anyway, I think—work your way into an understanding of the problem. I thought, *why don't I program that to run on the LGP30,* and I wrote the program. With Ed's help, we got it debugged. But it took two and a half days to run, and the LGP30 wouldn't run two and a half days; it was down about every three hours. Eventually you invent check pointing. I'll claim that too. The trouble was the only thing to check point on was the paper tape, and the reliability of the paper tape was such that . . . well, you understand the problem.

We can't ignore *software.* In fact, John Brackett said we really ought to deal exclusively with software. I can't do it adequately now since my time is almost gone. Let's note, however, that somebody along the line has invented "closed software." Back in the early days, software was pretty much a public commodity. If somebody had some that you wanted, you wrote a letter and maybe you sent a tape or maybe IBM cards and you got back the needed software. But then, interest in software mushroomed, and it turned out to be lucrative. Mainframe software turned out to be very expensive. You know you can pay $50,000 or $100,000 for it. But little programs were still free, until this wave of personal computing made them valuable. I would observe that putting commercial value on programs is a very bad thing for the user. The user wants open software, software that can be modified and that can participate in a progressive improvement process. It's never right at first, and if the conditions are such that it will be modified in response to user requirements, as in a kind of free academic arrangement, then all goes well. Indeed, if it's very popular software like Lotus 1-2-3, then people at the software companies spend a lot of time and energy making it better, and it gets better. But if it's appealing to a segment of the market, but not to a very rich segment, it can sit around for two or three years without being improved at all, and that is bad.

*Coherence*—much has been said at this meeting about the need for the coherence of the software and the services it renders, in workstations. Originally this talk was to be about the Washington, D.C., view of things, of how things look from ARPA's point of view. But I found I really couldn't say much about that, except that the struggle between two sets of values is very clear to the federal government. They would like to see standards, stable situations, maximal coherence, software, so that everything has maximal value. They would like to see technology transfer lead to actual improvement of user software. At the same time, they would like to see continual improvement. They would like to maintain the diversity, the competitive situation that motivates people to improve process and product. Competitive motivation leads people to keep things a bit close to the vest. Thus the two are in conflict. As it has turned out in our field, the people interested in diversity as the way to gain improvement have won out. How much longer that will continue, I don't know, but I personally hope that that continues a long time.

From the user's point of view, learnability is very important. I remember Klehrer from Columbia University, Hudson Lab, who made a breakthrough in the documentation world, back in the 1960s, with a system that was adequately documented on one page. You could use the system on the basis of the one page. It seems to me that we ought to consider documentation to be one of the parts of the personal workstation. If the documentation isn't good, maybe the workstation isn't really very helpful.

One of the great software ideas that's so old now that it is accepted as commonplace, except it isn't commonplace, is software with the *group property*—the output of any program is suitable input for other programs.

*Convenience*—just commonsense convenience of use. The first time I saw that convenience was really important was at NORAD, in Colorado Springs. I was taken into some dark mountain vault where there was a huge amount of computer equipment. All of the controllers' stations had light pens and keyboards. Light pens were on the left-hand side of keyboards! Match that with a device I saw at an electronics show, where there were the numbers 0 through 9 and right and left; only trouble was they read "R" on the left side, then "L," then 9, 8, 7, 6. . . . It had been designed by an engineer who was working from the back of the equipment!

The competition of the marketplace seems to get people to build great diversity of software for personal workstations, but where is the system for studying systems? It seems to me very important. Studying technical documents, for instance. Cane, Bobrow, Rafael, and I once wrote a program for that, but that was back in the days when we had 4000 18-bit words to work in, and we didn't exactly succeed. But I would really love to have one, just to use as a study aid, and then a short and stream-lined version of that might just be a reading machine. I think that we'll come to a time pretty soon when people who have workstations will really prefer to read in them because there will be extensive supplementary services like search, assembling personal documentations, and the like.

# Participants Discussion

| | |
|---|---|
| *Alan Perlis* | If there are any questions, I think now is the time to ask them of Lick. I'd like to start off with one, and that is, How circumscribed were you by ARPA when you started the IPT program? |
| *Licklider* | Well, actually very, very little, and I don't want to brag about ARPA. It is in my view, however, a very enlightened place. It was fun to work there. I think I've never encountered brighter, more creative people than the inhabitants of the third floor E-ring of the pentagon. But that, I'll say, was a long time ago, and I simply don't know how bright and likable they are now. But ARPA didn't constrain me much. Possibly it was just the enlightenment; possibly it was that the budget was so small that they didn't have time to think much about it. There were big projects in ARPA that made the computer budget look puny. The people who have followed me have built up the IPT budget, and I assure you it isn't puny any more. |
| *John Brackett* | I think Lick hasn't taken enough credit for something that he deserves, and maybe we should put on the record the quality of funding research he established and the quality of people that he brought in to follow after him—Ivan Sutherland and then Bob Taylor. To some extent, much of what we have in personal workstations is a result of the quality of research that Lick funded. There are many agencies that I've dealt with in the past in the government, where the people funding research knew far less than they should have about what they were funding. I think much of this field is due to what Lick started, how he approached funding research, and the caliber of people he brought after him. |
| *Licklider* | Well, thanks, John. I don't want credit for any of that except one part, and that is having some small thing to say about who followed me. That was important. |
| *Allen Newell* | One of the things that characterized ARPA's history was a selection of foci. Thus it went after graphics fairly seriously for a while; it went after time-sharing. Actually, *you* went after time-sharing. You didn't necessarily go after some of the issues that followed, because you weren't there. ARPA had a choice of focusing during the period of an IPT director on a particular thing, like time-sharing or networking. Some of those we recognize now, certainly the graphics and the networking, as critical components to workstations. But it never did, it seems to me, somehow conceive of and go after something called the |

workstation, per se. Do you have any reflections about why you missed that?

*Licklider*

I would observe that the ARPA office was awfully good about calling together leading lights from the contractor community, and letting them say pretty much what the good ideas were, and I'll bet if you look through those lists that the workstations weren't on them.

*Butler Lampson*

Actually, I can remember. I think workstations were really pretty difficult in the 1960s because the hardware was just too expensive. In the 1970s when it became feasible, I remember when I was at PARC going around and talking to people in the ARPA community about why they weren't out pursuing these ideas. And I remember one of the answers I got loud and clear at the time was that ARPA was putting tremendous emphasis on the proposition that they didn't want to support the development of any software or computer systems that you wouldn't be able to buy from manufacturers after they were developed. And, therefore, the idea that people would build nonstandard hardware was very much looked down on. It's a little bit unclear to me to what extent this was actually the ARPA position, but it's extremely clear to me that that's what the contractors thought. And, therefore, a whole bunch of things were just not considered, because they were judged to be unacceptable.

*Licklider*

Well, during Steve Lucas's tenure as director of ARPA, there was a tremendous emphasis on technology transfer. And the project offices were supposed to come up every week with this week's breakthrough. They got extra points if it were the technology transfer of something farther along the line. Well, even in the face of the defense department's insistence upon ADA, ARPA has managed to be tolerant of a lot of languages. I don't know any ARPA contractors who really do work in ADA.

*Butler Lampson*

That's true enough, but I think in the case of workstations, there's a bigger threshold, because . . .

*Licklider*

. . . or maybe you just can't do it in ADA. I'm not sure.

*Doug Ross*

Actually, in the early Project MAC work, there was real workstation work being done, in that the way in which the ESL display console, the KLUDGE, was hooked up to the IBM 7090 and then the 94, namely, it was first hooked up through either a PDP-7 or a PDP-9. And just to show that it was in fact still following the logic of building the architecture for a workstation like we're talking about here today, for example, we had what we called the minimum executive program that ran on the PDP-9. The minimal executive nowadays would have been built into ROM, you see, but it was a built-in piece of software. The only thing that it could do was receive a message and hook it in to be processed. And it couldn't do any sending of messages, only receiving messages. And the message that you first sent, if you wanted to do more than just have things received and go on the display as a bunch of characters or whatever it was set up for, in fact there was nothing there—gee, I'm sorry, just nothing. The first message you sent it was an extension to the executive that would allow it to also be able to respond and say, "I got the message." But sometimes if you wanted it to behave just as a display itself, you didn't even give it anything so as to say, "I got the message." The reason for this was that it had limited memory for supporting the cycling display. So this was our mechanism for allowing you to change the display, but have a maximum amount of memory available for the display itself. And so, it really did go on, depending on what pieces of further software you sent across the same pipe. That display data would be coming across, and communications from buttons and light pens coming back, depending upon what pieces of the modular system you sent across. That way you got more or less behavioral characteristics out of that ESL display console workstation. So the intriguing thing to me was that there was very little follow-up in the ARPA community in this graphics area, in a generalized way. Although, of course, all of the blossoming that a few years later took place through the Evans and Sutherland Company activities certainly carried the ball much, much further.

*Licklider*   One of the big conflicts over the years has been, it seems to me, between time-shared systems and individually appropriable ones. Time-sharing was kind of a necessary step to get enough people involved in all this and to appreciate what the potential values were, but it certainly did make it difficult to deal with the display and the human interaction aspects. I think you see this everywhere, that the economics push you to give a lot of people minimal support. Whereas, to make real advance in human interaction with computers, you need lavish support. If it is, or was, true that hardware economics doubles every two years, and if it's true that it takes eight or ten years to get something from the ideas stage into use, it says a researcher who begins working on something has got to be a factor of 16 or 32 ahead of the time in his lavish expenditure of computer resources to do his work. And that takes very enlightened sponsors and supporters to make that possible, and usually it isn't. So, time-sharing has held back that kind of thinking. But let me say that KLUDGE work did transfer quickly. Al Leventhal did, I believe, the very first rotations of protein molecules and the same technology went to Princeton, where more good work was done with essentially the same KLUDGE technology.

**James McKenney**   You also started Bitzer at Illinois. Now I'm trying to raise the question, How can this community do technology transfer better because the plasma display screen, with the limitations of the technology of the day, developed some very fine graphics, and it was aimed at students and, in some economy of scale, it was relatively cheap? The development was sort of an orphan for a long time without much external interaction because of its unique software. Now that the technology in the mini and the micro are set, we don't see much of the Plato technology in that commercial development.

**Licklider**   My recollection, Jim, is that ARPA didn't substantially support Bitzer or the plasma display, but the Department of Education as well as IBM did later. Oh, yes, Control Data provided substantial development support. IBM seems to be making plasma displays, and I don't see Control Data pushing them now. How did that happen?

**Bert Sutherland**   One quick comment. It seems to me as we look back in history, just calling it time-sharing gives it a bad connotation. I wish we had called it "time and data sharing" because the shorter name obscures one of the main functions.

**Licklider**   I think people understood that at the time. I remember seeing articles that said that this really ought to be "memory sharing" or something of that sort. Well, it's a fantastic field. I wish it were called something else besides "workstations" because that does seem to limit the software and the interconnection aspect a little bit, but maybe that only seems so in my mind.

**Alan Perlis**   I think that we all should be grateful to ARPA for not focusing on very specific projects such as workstations. There was no order issued that said, "We want a proposal on a workstation." Goodness knows, they would have gotten many of them. Instead, I think that ARPA, through Lick, realized that if you get $n$ good people together to do research on computing, you're going to illuminate some reasonable fraction of the ways of proceeding because the computer is such a general instrument. We owe a great deal to ARPA for not circumscribing directions that people took in those days. I like to believe that the purpose of the military is to support ARPA, and the purpose of ARPA is to support research. Just like I'm absolutely certain that when historians look back on these days they will try to understand how our society could have been so foolish as not to realize that the main purpose of AT&T is to support Bell Labs and that, therefore, any action that weakened Bell Labs was so shortsighted as to have almost the quality of an epitaph.

*Licklider*          Back in the late 1960s there were a lot of people, there probably still are, who didn't like the Defense Department much. And one of them told me that he was writing a proposal to ARPA, and it was going to be a real big one because he was told that an aircraft carrier cost a great deal of money. If he could get some of his friends to propose this research, they could spend one aircraft carrier's worth of the government's money.

REPRINT OF HISTORICALLY SIGNIFICANT DOCUMENT
# Man-Computer Symbiosis*

*J. C. R. Licklider*[†]
From *IRE Transactions on Human Factors in Electronics,* March 1960:4–11.
Reprinted with permission. © 1960 IRE (now IEEE).

## I. Introduction

### A. SYMBIOSIS

The fig tree is pollinated only by the insect *Blastophaga grossorum.* The larva of the insect lives in the ovary of the fig tree, and there it gets its food. The tree and the insect are thus heavily interdependent: the tree cannot reproduce without the insect; the insect cannot eat without the tree; together, they constitute not only a viable but a productive and thriving partnership. This cooperative "living together in intimate association, or even close union, of two dissimilar organisms" is called symbiosis.[1]

"Man-computer symbiosis" is a subclass of "man-machine systems." There are many man-machine systems. At present, however, there are no man-computer symbioses. The purposes of this paper are to present the concept and, hopefully, to foster the development of man-computer symbiosis by analyzing some problems of interaction between men and computing machines, calling attention to applicable principles of man-machine engineering, and pointing out a few questions to which research answers are needed. The hope is that, in not too many years, human brains and computing machines will be coupled together very tightly, and that the resulting partnership will think as no human brain has ever thought and process data in a way not approached by the information-handling machines we know today.

### B. BETWEEN "MECHANICALLY EXTENDED MAN" AND "ARTIFICIAL INTELLIGENCE"

As a concept, man-computer symbiosis is different in an important way from what North[2] has called "mechanically extended man." In the man-machine systems of the past, the human operator supplied the initiative, the direction, the integration, and the criterion. The mechanical parts of the systems were mere extensions, first of the human arm, then of the human eye. These systems certainly did not consist of "dissimilar organisms living together . . . " There was only one kind of organism—man—and the rest was there only to help him.

In one sense of course, any man-made system is intended to help man, to help a man or men outside the system. If we focus upon the human operator(s) within the system, however, we see that, in some areas of technology, a fantastic change has taken place during the last few years. "Mechanical extension" has given way to replacement of men, to automation, and the men who remain are there more to help than to be helped. In some instances, particularly in large computer-centered information and control systems, the human operators are responsible mainly for functions that it proved infeasible to automate. Such systems ("humanly extended machines," North might call them) are not symbiotic systems. They are "semi-automatic" systems, systems that started out to be fully automatic but fell short of the goal.

Man-computer symbiosis is probably not the

*Manuscript received by the PGHFE, January 13, 1960; revised manuscript received, January 18, 1960. The background work on which this paper is based was supported largely by the Behavioral Sciences Division, Air Force Office of Scientific Research, Air Research and Development Command, through Contract No. AF-49(638)-355.

†Bolt Beranek and Newman Inc., Cambridge, Mass.

[1]"Webster's New International Dictionary," 2nd ed., G. and C. Merriam Co., Springfield, Mass., p. 2555; 1958.

[2]J. D. North, "The rational behavior of mechanically extended man," Boulton Paul Aircraft Ltd., Wolverhampton, Eng.; September, 1954.

ultimate paradigm for complex technological systems. It seems entirely possible that, in due course, electronic or chemical ''machines'' will outdo the human brain in most of the functions we now consider exclusively within its province. Even now, Gelernter's IBM-704 program for proving theorems in plane geometry proceeds at about the same pace as Brooklyn high school students, and makes similar errors.[3] There are, in fact, several theorem-proving, problem-solving, chess-playing, and pattern-recognizing programs (too many for complete reference[4-15]) capa-

ble of rivaling human intellectual performance in restricted areas; and Newell, Simon, and Shaw's[16] ''general problem solver'' may remove some of the restrictions. In short, it seems worthwhile to avoid argument with (other) enthusiasts for artificial intelligence by conceding dominance in the distant future of cerebration to machines alone. There will nevertheless be a fairly long interim during which the main intellectual advances will be made by men and computers working together in intimate association. A multidisciplinary study group, examining future research and development problems of the Air Force, estimated that it would by 1980 before developments in artificial intelligence make it possible for machines alone to do much thinking or problem solving of military significance. That would leave, say, five years to develop man-computer symbiosis and 15 years to use it. The 15 may be 10 or 500, but those years should be intellectually the most creative and exciting in the history of mankind.

## II. *Aims of Man-Computer Symbiosis*

Present-day computers are designed primarily to solve preformulated problems or to process data according to predetermined procedures. The course of the computation may be conditional upon results obtained during the computation, but all the alternatives must be foreseen in advance. (If an unforeseen alternative arises, the whole process comes to a halt and awaits the necessary extension of the program.) The requirement for preformulation or predetermination is sometimes no great disadvantage. It is often said that programming for a computing machine forces one to think clearly, that it disciplines the thought process. If the user can think his problem through in advance, symbiotic association with a computing machine is not necessary.

However, many problems that can be thought through in advance are very difficult to

[3]H. Gelernter, ''Realization of a Geometry Theorem Proving Machine,'' Unesco, NS, ICIP, 1.6.6, Internatl. Conf. on Information Processing, Paris, France; June, 1959.

[4]A. Newell and J. C. Shaw, ''Programming the logic theory machine,'' *Proc. WJCC*, pp. 230–240; March, 1957.

[5]P. C. Gilmore, ''A Program for the Production of Proofs for Theorems Derivable Within the First Order Predicate Calculus from Axioms,'' Unesco, NS, ICIP, 1.6.14, Internatl. Conf. on Information Processing, Paris, France; June, 1959.

[6]B. G. Farley and W. A. Clark, ''Simulation of self-organizing systems by digital computers,'' IRE TRANS. ON INFORMATION THEORY, vol. IT-4, pp. 76–84; September, 1954.

[7]R. M. Friedberg, ''A learning machine: Part I,'' *IBM J. Res. & Dev.*, vol. 2, pp. 2–13; January, 1958.

[8]O. G. Selfridge, ''Pandemonium, a paradigm for learning,'' *Proc. Symp. Mechanisation of Thought Processes*, Natl. Physical Lab., Teddington, Eng.; November, 1958.

[9]W. W. Bledsoe and I. Browning, ''Pattern Recognition and Reading by Machine,'' presented at the Eastern Joint Computer Conf., Boston, Mass., December, 1959.

[10]C. E. Shannon, ''Programming a computer for playing chess,'' *Phil. Mag.*, vol. 41, pp. 256–75; March, 1950.

[11]A. Newell, ''The chess machine: an example of dealing with a complex task by adaptation,'' *Proc. WJCC*, pp. 101–108; March, 1955.

[12]A. Bernstein and M. deV. Roberts, ''Computer versus chess-player,'' *Scientific American*, vol. 198, pp. 96–98; June, 1958.

[13]A. Newell, J. C. Shaw, and H. A. Simon, ''Chess-playing programs and the problem of complexity,'' *IBM J. Res. & Dev.*, vol. 2, pp. 320–335; October, 1958.

[14]H. Sherman, ''A Quasi-Topological Method for Recognition of Line Patterns,'' Unesco, NS, ICIP, H.L.5, Internatl. Conf. on Information Processing, Paris, France; June, 1959.

[15]G. P. Dinneen, ''Programming pattern recognition,'' *Proc. WJCC*, pp. 94–100; March, 1955.

[16]A. Newell, H. A. Simon, and J. C. Shaw, ''Report on a general problem-solving program,'' Unesco, NS, ICIP, 1.6.8, Internatl. Conf. on Information Processing, Paris, France; June, 1959.

think through in advance. They would be easier to solve, and they could be solved faster, through an intuitively guided trial-and-error procedure in which the computer cooperated, turning up flaws in the reasoning or revealing unexpected turns in the solution. Other problems simply cannot be formulated without computing-machine aid. Poincaré anticipated the frustration of an important group of would-be computer users when he said, "The question is not, 'What is the answer?' The question is, 'What is the question?'" One of the main aims of man-computer symbiosis is to bring the computing machine effectively into the formulative parts of technical problems.

The other main aim is closely related. It is to bring computing machines effectively into processes of thinking that must go on in "real time," time that moves too fast to permit using computers in conventional ways. Imagine trying, for example, to direct a battle with the aid of a computer on such a schedule as this. You formulate your problem today. Tomorrow you spend with a programmer. Next week the computer devotes 5 minutes to assembling your program and 47 seconds to calculating the answer to your problem. You get a sheet of paper 20 feet long, full of numbers that, instead of providing a final solution, only suggest a tactic that should be explored by simulation. Obviously, the battle would be over before the second step in its planning was begun. To think in interaction with a computer in the same way that you think with a colleague whose competence supplements your own will require much tighter coupling between man and machine than is suggested by the example and than is possible today.

## III. Need for Computer Participation in Formulative and Real-Time Thinking

The preceding paragraphs tacitly made the assumption that, if they could be introduced effectively into the thought process, the functions that can be performed by data-processing machines would improve or facilitate thinking and problem solving in an important way. That assumption may require justification.

### A. A PRELIMINARY AND INFORMAL TIME-AND-MOTION ANALYSIS OF TECHNICAL THINKING

Despite the fact that there is a voluminous literature on thinking and problem solving, including intensive case-history studies of the process of invention, I could find nothing comparable to a time-and-motion-study analysis of the mental work of a person engaged in a scientific or technical enterprise. In the spring and summer of 1957, therefore, I tried to keep track of what one moderately technical person actually did during the hours he regarded as devoted to work. Although I was aware of the inadequacy of the sampling, I served as my own subject.

It soon became apparent that the main thing I did was to keep records, and the project would have become an infinite regress if the keeping of records had been carried through in the detail envisaged in the initial plan. It was not. Nevertheless, I obtained a picture of my activities that gave me pause. Perhaps my spectrum is not typical—I hope it is not, but I fear it is.

About 85 per cent of my "thinking" time was spent getting into a position to think, to make a decision, to learn something I needed to know. Much more time went into finding or obtaining information than into digesting it. Hours went into the plotting of graphs, and other hours into instructing an assistant how to plot. When the graphs were finished, the relations were obvious at once, but the plotting had to be done in order to make them so. At one point, it was necessary to compare six experimental determinations of a function relating speech-intelligibility to speech-to-noise ratio. No two experimenters had used the same definition or measure of speech-to-noise ratio. Several hours of calculating were required to get the data into comparable form. When they were in comparable form, it took only a few seconds to determine what I needed to know.

Throughout the period I examined, in short, my "thinking" time was devoted mainly to activities that were essentially clerical or mechanical: searching, calculating, plotting, transforming, determining the logical or dynamic consequences of a set of assumptions or hypotheses, preparing the way for a decision or an insight. Moreover, my choices of what to attempt and what not to attempt were determined to an embarrassingly great extent by considerations of clerical feasibility, not intellectual capability.

The main suggestion conveyed by the findings just described is that the operations that fill most of the time allegedly devoted to technical thinking are operations that can be performed more effectively by machines than by men. Severe problems are posed by the fact that these operations have to be performed upon diverse variables and in unforeseen and continually changing sequences. If those problems can be solved in such a way as to create a symbiotic relation between a man and a fast information-retrieval and data-processing machine, however, it seems evident that the cooperative interaction would greatly improve the thinking process.

### B. COMPARATIVE CAPABILITIES OF MEN AND COMPUTERS

It may be appropriate to acknowledge, at this point, that we are using the term "computer" to cover a wide class of calculating, data-processing, and information-storage-and-retrieval machines. The capabilities of machines in this class are increasing almost daily. It is therefore hazardous to make general statements about capabilities of the class. Perhaps it is equally hazardous to make general statements about the capabilities of men. Nevertheless, certain genotypic differences in capability between men and computers do stand out, and they have a bearing on the nature of possible man-computer symbiosis and the potential value of achieving it.

As had been said in various ways, men are noisy, narrow-band devices, but their nervous systems have very many parallel and simultaneously active channels. Relative to men, computing machines are very fast and very accurate, but they are constrained to perform only one or a few elementary operations at a time. Men are flexible, capable of "programming themselves contingently" on the basis of newly received information. Computing machines are single-minded, constrained by their "preprogram-

ming." Men naturally speak redundant languages organized around unitary objects and coherent actions and employing 20 to 60 elementary symbols. Computers "naturally" speak non-redundant languages, usually with only two elementary symbols and no inherent appreciation either of unitary objects or of coherent actions.

To be rigorously correct, those characterizations would have to include many qualifiers. Nevertheless, the picture of dissimilarity (and therefore potential supplementation) that they present is essentially valid. Computing machines can do readily, well, and rapidly many things that are difficult or impossible for man, and men can do readily and well, though not rapidly, many things that are difficult or impossible for computers. That suggests that a symbiotic cooperation, if successful in integrating the positive characteristics of men and computers, would be of great value. The differences in speed and in language, of course, pose difficulties that must be overcome.

## IV. Separable Functions of Men and Computers in the Anticipated Symbiotic Association

It seems likely that the contributions of human operators and equipment will blend together so completely in many operations that it will be difficult to separate them neatly in analysis. That would be the case if, in gathering data on which to base a decision, for example, both the man and the computer came up with relevant precedents from experience and if the computer then suggested a course of action that agreed with the man's intuitive judgment. (In theorem-proving programs, computers find precedents in experience, and in the SAGE System, they suggest courses of action. The foregoing is not a far-fetched example.) In other operations, however, the contributions of men and equipment will be to some extent separable.

Men will set the goals and supply the motivations, of course, at least in the early years. They will formulate hypotheses. They will ask questions. They will think of mechanisms, procedures, and models. They will remember that such-and-such a person did some possibly relevant work on a topic of interest back in 1947, or at any rate shortly after World War II, and they will have an idea in what journals it might have been published. In general, they will make approximate and fallible, but leading, contributions, and they will define criteria and serve as evaluators, judging the contributions of the equipment and guiding the general line of thought.

In addition, men will handle the very-low-probability situations when such situations do actually arise. (In current man-machine systems, that is one of the human operator's most important functions. The sum of the probabilities of very-low-probability alternatives is often much too large to neglect.) Men will fill in the gaps, either in the problem solution or in the computer program, when the computer has no mode or routine that is applicable in a particular circumstance.

The information-processing equipment, for its part, will convert hypotheses into testable models and than test the models against data (which the human operator may designate roughly and identify as relevant when the computer presents them for his approval). The equipment will answer questions. It will simulate the mechanisms and models, carry out the procedures, and display the results to the operator. It will transform data, plot graphs ("cutting the cake" in whatever way the human operator specifies, or in several alternative ways if the human operator is not sure what he wants). The equipment will interpolate, extrapolate, and transform. It will convert static equations or logical statements into dynamic models so the human operator can examine their behavior. In general, it will carry out the routinizable, clerical operations that fill the intervals between decisions.

In addition, the computer will serve as a statistical-inference, decision-theory, or game-theory machine to make elementary evaluations of suggested courses of action whenever there is enough basis to support a formal statistical analysis. Finally, it will do as much diagnosis, pattern matching, and relevance recognizing as it profitably can, but it will accept a clearly secondary status in those areas.

## V. Prerequisites for Realization of Man-Computer Symbiosis

The data-processing equipment tacitly postulated in the preceding section is not available. The computer programs have not been written. There are in fact several hurdles that stand between the nonsymbiotic present and the anticipated symbiotic future. Let us examine some of them to see more clearly what is needed and what the chances are of achieving it.

### A. SPEED MISMATCH BETWEEN MEN AND COMPUTERS

Any present-day large-scale computer is too fast and too costly for real-time cooperative thinking with one man. Clearly, for the sake of efficiency and economy, the computer must divide its time among many users. Time-sharing systems are currently under active development. There are even arrangements to keep users from "clobbering" anything but their own personal programs.

It seems reasonable to envision, for a time 10 or 15 years hence, a "thinking center" that will incorporate the functions of present-day libraries together with anticipated advances in information storage and retrieval and the symbiotic functions suggested earlier in this paper. The picture readily enlarges itself into a network of such centers, connected to one another by wideband communication lines and to individual users by leased-wire services. In such a system, the speed of the computers would be balanced, and the cost of the gigantic memories and the sophisticated programs would be divided by the number of users.

### B. MEMORY HARDWARE REQUIREMENTS

When we start to think of storing any appreciable fraction of a technical literature in computer memory, we run into billions of bits and, unless things change markedly, billions of dollars.

The first thing to face is that we shall not store all the technical and scientific papers in computer memory. We may store the parts that can be summarized most succinctly—the quantitative parts and the reference citations—but not the whole. Books are among the most beautifully engineered, and human-engineered, components in existence, and they will continue to be functionally important within the context of man-computer symbiosis. (Hopefully, the computer will expedite the finding, delivering, and returning of books.)

The second point is that a very important section of memory will be permanent: part *indelible memory* and part *published memory*. The computer will be able to write once into indelible memory, and then read back indefinitely, but the computer will not be able to erase indelible memory. (It may also over-write, turning all the 0's into 1's, as though marking over what was written earlier.) Published memory will be "read-only" memory. It will be introduced into the computer already structured. The computer will be able to refer to it repeatedly, but not to change it. These types of memory will become more and more important as computers grow larger. They can be made more compact than core, thin-film, or even tape memory, and they will be much less expensive. The main engineering problems will concern selection circuitry.

In so far as other aspects of memory requirement are concerned, we may count upon the continuing development of ordinary scientific and business computing machines. There is some prospect that memory elements will become as fast as processing (logic) elements. That development would have a revolutionary effect upon the design of computers.

## C. MEMORY ORGANIZATION REQUIREMENTS

Implicit in the idea of man-computer symbiosis are the requirements that information be retrievable both by name and by pattern and that it be accessible through procedure much faster than serial search. At least half of the problem of memory organization appears to reside in the storage procedure. Most of the remainder seems to be wrapped up in the problem of pattern recogni-

tion within the storage mechanism or medium. Detailed discussion of these problems is beyond the present scope. However, a brief outline of one promising idea, "trie memory," may serve to indicate the general nature of anticipated developments.

Trie memory is so called by its originator, Fredkin,[17] because it is designed to facilitate re-*trie*val of information and because the branching storage structure, when developed, resembles a tree. Most common memory systems store functions of arguments at locations designated by the arguments. (In one sense, they do not store the arguments at all. In another and more realistic sense, they store all the possible arguments in the framework structure of the memory.) The trie memory system, on the other hand, stores both the functions and the arguments. The argument is introduced into the memory first, one character at a time, starting at a standard initial register. Each argument register has one cell for each character of the ensemble (*e.g.*, two for information encoded in binary form) and each character cell has within it storage space for the address of the next register. The argument is stored by writing a series of addresses, each one of which tells where to find the next. At the end of the argument is a special "end-of-argument" marker. Then follow directions to the function, which is stored in one or another of several ways, either further trie structure or "list structure" often being most effective.

The trie memory scheme is inefficient for small memories, but it becomes increasingly efficient in using available storage space as memory size increases. The attractive features of the scheme are these: 1) The retrieval process is extremely simple. Given the argument, enter the standard initial register with the first character, and pick up the address of the second. Then go to the second register, and pick up the address of the third, etc. 2) If two arguments have initial characters in common, they use the same storage space for those characters. 3) The lengths of the arguments need not be the same, and need not be specified in advance. 4) No room in storage is reserved for or used by any argument until it

17E. Fredkin, "Trie memory," in preparation.

is actually stored. The trie structure is created as the items are introduced into the memory. 5) A function can be used as an argument for another function, and that function as an argument for the next. Thus, for example, by entering with the argument, ''matrix multiplication,'' one might retrieve the entire program for performing a matrix multiplication on the computer. 6) By examining the storage at a given level, one can determine what thus-far similar items have been stored. For example, if there is no citation for Egan, J. P., it is but a step or two backward to pick up the trail of Egan, James. . . .

The properties just described do not include all the desired ones, but they bring computer storage into resonance with human operators and their predilection to designate things by naming or pointing.

## D. THE LANGUAGE PROBLEM

The basic dissimilarity between human languages and computer languages may be the most serious obstacle to true symbiosis. It is reassuring, however, to note what great strides have already been made, through interpretive programs and particularly through assembly or compiling programs such as FORTRAN, to adapt computers to human language forms. The ''Information Processing Language'' of Shaw, Newell, Simon, and Ellis[18] represents another line of rapprochement. And, in ALGOL and related systems, men are proving their flexibility by adopting standard formulas of representation and expression that are readily translatable into machine language.

For the purposes of real-time cooperation between men and computers, it will be necessary, however, to make use of an additional and rather different principle of communication and control. The idea may be highlighted by comparing instructions ordinarily addressed to intelligent human beings with instructions ordinarily used with computers. The latter specify precisely the individual steps to take and the se-

quence in which to take them. The former present or imply something about incentive or motivation, and they supply a criterion by which the human executor of the instructions will know when he has accomplished his task. In short: instructions directed to computers specify courses; instructions directed to human beings specify goals.

Men appear to think more naturally and easily in terms of goals than in terms of courses. True, they usually know something about directions in which to travel or lines along which to work, but few start out with precisely formulated itineraries. Who, for example, would depart from Boston for Los Angeles with a detailed specification of the route? Instead, to paraphrase Wiener, men bound for Los Angeles try continually to decrease the amount by which they are not yet in the smog.

Computer instruction through specification of goals is being approached along two paths. The first involves problem-solving, hill-climbing, self-organizing programs. The second involves real-time concatenation of preprogrammed segments and closed subroutines which the human operator can designate and call into action simply by name.

Along the first of these paths, there has been promising exploratory work. It is clear that, working within the loose constraints of predetermined strategies, computers will in due course be able to devise and simplify their own procedures for achieving stated goals. Thus far, the achievements have not been substantively important; they have constituted only ''demonstration in principle.'' Nevertheless, the implications are far-reaching.

Although the second path is simpler and apparently capable of earlier realization, it has been relatively neglected. Fredkin's trie memory provides a promising paradigm. We may in due course see a serious effort to develop computer programs that can be connected together like the words and phrases of speech to do whatever computation or control is required at the moment. The consideration that holds back such an effort, apparently, is that the effort would produce nothing that would be of great value in the context of existing computers. It would be unre-

[18]J. C. Shaw, A. Newell, H. A. Simon, and T. O. Ellis, ''A command structure for complex information processing,'' *Proc. WJCC*, pp. 119–128; May, 1958.

warding to develop the language before there are any computing machines capable of responding meaningfully to it.

## E. INPUT AND OUTPUT EQUIPMENT

The department of data processing that seems least advanced, in so far as the requirements of man-computer symbiosis are concerned, is the one that deals with input and output equipment or, as it is seen from the human operator's point of view, displays and controls. Immediately after saying that, it is essential to make qualifying comments, because the engineering of equipment for high-speed introduction and extraction of information has been excellent, and because some very sophisticated display and control techniques have been developed in such research laboratories as the Lincoln Laboratory. By and large, in generally available computers, however, there is almost no provision for any more effective, immediate man-machine communication than can be achieved with an electric typewriter.

Displays seem to be in a somewhat better state than controls. Many computers plot graphs on oscilloscope screens, and a few take advantage of the remarkable capabilities, graphical and symbolic, of the charactron display tube. Nowhere, to my knowledge, however, is there anything approaching the flexibility and convenience of the pencil and doodle pad or the chalk and blackboard used by men in technical discussion.

1) *Desk-Surface Display and Control:* Certainly, for effective man-computer interaction, it will be necessary for the man and the computer to draw graphs and pictures and to write notes and equations to each other on the same display surface. The man should be able to present a function to the computer, in a rough but rapid fashion, by drawing a graph. The computer should read the man's writing, perhaps on the condition that it be in clear block capitals, and it should immediately post, at the location of each hand-drawn symbol, the corresponding character as interpreted and put into precise typeface. With such an input-output device, the operator would quickly learn to write or print in a manner legible to the machine. He could compose instructions and subroutines, set them into proper

format, and check them over before introducing them finally into the computer's main memory. He could even define new symbols, as Gilmore and Savell[19] have done at the Lincoln Laboratory, and present them directly to the computer. He could sketch out the format of a table roughly and let the computer shape it up with precision. He could correct the computer's data, instruct the machine via flow diagrams, and in general interact with it very much as he would with another engineer, except that the "other engineer" would be a precise draftsman, a lightning calculator, a mnemonic wizard, and many other valuable partners all in one.

2) *Computer-Posted Wall Display:* In some technological systems, several men share responsibility for controlling vehicles whose behaviors interact. Some information must be presented simultaneously to all the men, preferably on a common grid, to coordinate their actions. Other information is of relevance only to one or two operators. There would be only a confusion of uninterpretable clutter if all the information were presented on one display to all of them. The information must be posted by a computer, since manual plotting is too slow to keep it up to date.

The problem just outlined is even now a critical one, and it seems certain to become more and more critical as time goes by. Several designers are convinced that displays with the desired characteristics can be constructed with the aid of flashing lights and time-sharing viewing screens based on the light-valve principle.

The large display should be supplemented, according to most of those who have thought about the problem, by individual display-control units. The latter would permit the operators to modify the wall display without leaving their locations. For some purposes, it would be desirable for the operators to be able to communicate with the computer through the supplementary displays and perhaps even through the wall display. At least one scheme for providing such communication seems feasible.

[19]J. T. Gilmore and R. E. Savell, "The Lincoln Writer," Lincoln Laboratory, M.I.T., Lexington, Mass., Rept. 51-8; October, 1959.

The large wall display and its associated system are relevant, of course, to symbiotic cooperation between a computer and a team of men. Laboratory experiments have indicated repeatedly that informal, parallel arrangements of operators, coordinating their activities through reference to a large situation display, have important advantages over the arrangement, more widely used, that locates the operators at individual consoles and attempts to correlate their actions through the agency of a computer. This is one of several operator-team problems in need of careful study.

3) *Automatic Speech Production and Recognition:* How desirable and how feasible is speech communication between human operators and computing machines? That compound question is asked whenever sophisticated data-processing systems are discussed. Engineers who work and live with computers take a conservative attitude toward the desirability. Engineers who have had experience in the field of automatic speech recognition take a conservative attitude toward the feasibility. Yet there is continuing interest in the idea of talking with computing machines. In large part, the interest stems from realization that one can hardly take a military commander or a corporation president away from his work to teach him to type. If computing machines are ever to be used directly by top-level decision makers, it may be worthwhile to provide communication via the most natural means, even at considerable cost.

Preliminary analysis of his problems and time scales suggests that a corporation president would be interested in a symbiotic association with a computer only as an avocation. Business situations usually move slowly enough that there is time for briefings and conferences. It seems reasonable, therefore, for computer specialists to be the ones who interact directly with computers in business offices.

The military commander, on the other hand, faces a greater probability of having to make critical decisions in short intervals of time. It is easy to overdramatize the notion of the ten-minute war, but it would be dangerous to count on having more than ten minutes in which to make a critical decision. As military system ground environments and control centers grow in capability and complexity, therefore, a real requirement for automatic speech production and recognition in computers seems likely to develop. Certainly, if the equipment were already developed, reliable, and available, it would be used.

In so far as feasibility is concerned, speech production poses less severe problems of a technical nature than does automatic recognition of speech sounds. A commercial electronic digital voltmeter now reads aloud its indications, digit by digit. For eight or ten years, at the Bell Telephone Laboratories, the Royal Institute of Technology (Stockholm), the Signals Research and Development Establishment (Christchurch), the Haskins Laboratory, and the Massachusetts Institute of Technology, Dunn,[20] Fant,[21] Lawrence,[22] Cooper,[23] Stevens,[24] and their coworkers, have demonstrated successive generations of intelligible automatic talkers. Recent work at the Haskins Laboratory has led to the development of a digital code, suitable for use by computing machines, that makes an automatic voice utter intelligible connected discourse.[25]

The feasibility of automatic speech recognition depends heavily upon the size of the vocabulary of words to be recognized and upon the diversity of talkers and accents with which it must work. Ninety-eight per cent correct recognition of naturally spoken decimal digits was dem-

[20]H. K. Dunn, ''The calculation of vowel resonances, and an electrical vocal tract,'' *J. Acoust. Soc. Amer.*, vol. 22, pp. 740–753; November, 1950.

[21]G. Fant, ''On the Acoustics of Speech,'' paper presented at the Third Internatl. Congress on Acoustics, Stuttgart, Ger.; September, 1959.

[22]W. Lawrence, *et al.*, ''Methods and Purposes of Speech Synthesis,'' Signals Res. and Dev. Estab., Ministry of Supply, Christchurch, Hants, England, Rept. 56/1457; March, 1956.

[23]F. S. Cooper, *et al.*, ''Some experiments on the perception of synthetic speech sounds,'' *J. Acoust. Soc. Amer.*, vol. 24, pp. 597–606; November, 1952.

[24]K. N. Stevens, S. Kasowski, and C. G. Fant, ''Electric analog of the vocal tract,'' *J. Acoust. Soc. Amer.*, vol. 25, pp. 734–742; July, 1953.

[25]A. M. Liberman, F. Ingemann, L. Lisker, P. Delattre, and F. S. Cooper, ''Minimal rules for synthesizing speech,'' *J. Acoust. Soc. Amer.*, vol. 31, pp. 1490–1499; November, 1959.

onstrated several years ago at the Bell Telephone Laboratories and at the Lincoln Laboratory.[26, 27] To go a step up the scale of vocabulary size, we may say that an automatic recognizer of clearly spoken alpha-numerical characters can almost surely be developed now on the basis of existing knowledge. Since untrained operators can read at least as rapidly as trained ones can type, such a device would be a convenient tool in almost any computer installation.

For real-time interaction on a truly symbiotic level, however, a vocabulary of about 2000 words, *e.g.,* 1000 words of something like basic English and 1000 technical terms, would probably be required. That constitutes a challenging problem. In the consensus of acousticians and linguists, construction of a recognizer of 2000 words cannot be accomplished now. However, there are several organizations that would happily undertake to develop an automatic recognizer for such a vocabulary on a five-year basis.

[26]K. H. Davis, R. Biddulph, and S. Balashek, ''Automatic recognition of spoken digits,'' in W. Jackson, ''Communication Theory,'' Butterworths Scientific Publications, London, Eng., pp. 433–441; 1953.

[27]J. W. Forgie and C. D. Forgie, ''Results obtained from a vowel recognition computer program,'' *J. Acoust. Soc. Amer.,* vol. 31, pp. 1480–1489; November, 1959.

They would stipulate that the speech be clear speech, dictation style, without unusual accent.

Although detailed discussion of techniques of automatic speech recognition is beyond the present scope, it is fitting to note that computing machines are playing a dominant role in the development of automatic speech recognizers. They have contributed the impetus that accounts for the present optimism, or rather for the optimism presently found in some quarters. Two or three years ago, it appeared that automatic recognition of sizeable vocabularies would not be achieved for ten or fifteen years; that it would have to await much further, gradual accumulation of knowledge of acoustic, phonetic, linguistic, and psychological processes in speech communication. Now, however, many see a prospect of accelerating the acquisition of that knowledge with the aid of computer processing of speech signals, and not a few workers have the feeling that sophisticated computer programs will be able to perform well as speech-pattern recognizers even without the aid of much substantive knowledge of speech signals and processes. Putting those two considerations together brings the estimate of the time required to achieve practically significant speech recognition down to perhaps five years, the five years just mentioned.

# THE ARPANET
# AND COMPUTER NETWORKS

## Larry Roberts
Introduction by Frank Kuo

**M**y name is Frank Kuo and I'm with SRI International. It's my honor and privilege to introduce Larry Roberts, who was the fourth director of ARPA IPTO and really the father, although not the inventor, of packet switching. Larry Roberts . . .

**Frank Kuo**

Lawrence G. Roberts is Founder, Chairman, and CEO of NetExpress, Inc., and Director of DHL Corporation. Dr. Roberts has been deeply involved in the development of the data communications industry since the early 1960s and is considered the architect of packet switching technology. Dr. Roberts has B.S., M.S., and Ph.D. degrees in Electrical Engineering from MIT. Formerly the Director of Information Processing Techniques at the Advanced Research Projects Agency (ARPA) of the Department of Defense, Dr. Roberts was responsible for the initiation, planning, and development of ARPANET, the world's first major packet network. He was also responsible for a broad program of computer communication research, including computer security, speech compression and understanding, satellite communications, and computer system design.

In 1973 Dr. Roberts founded Telenet Communications Corporation, the world's first packet switched data communications carrier, serving as President and CEO. In 1982 he left Telenet (now merged with GTE) and joined DHL as President of DHL Corporation, founding NetExpress and initiating the DHL Domestic Overnight Service. Dr. Roberts has received numerous awards, including the Secretary of Defense Meritorious Service Medal, the Harry Goode Memorial Award from the American Federation of Information Processing, the IEEE Computer Pioneer Award, the Interface Conference Award, and in 1982, the L.M. Ericsson prize for research in data communications.

# The ARPANET and Computer Networks

*Lawrence G. Roberts*
NetExpress, Inc.

In 1964 only large mainframe computers existed, each with its own separate set of users. If you were lucky the computer was time-shared, but even then you could not go far away since the terminals were hardwired to it or connected by local phone line. Moreover, if you wanted data from another computer you moved it by tape and you could forget wanting software from a different type of computer. Thus, most users were tied by their computer and terminal to a very restricted environment.

Today, your terminal could well be a microcomputer networked with a very large, worldwide collection of other computers. You can obtain data and software from all these computers relatively easily (with room for improvement) or, where convenient, use the software and data on its home computer by remote access, computer to computer.

This change, which has occurred over the past 20 years, is in part a massive and evolutionary change in computer technology, and in part a modest and revolutionary change in communications technology. The revolution in communications started with an experiment in computer networking, the ARPANET, and grew into a communications revolution called packet switching. Today virtually all the world is linked by packet switched communications service so that any terminal can access almost any computer in the world. This packet switched data network has grown up independent of the telephone network, but over the next 20 years the basic fabric supporting all switched services (data, telephone, and video) appear likely to become converted to packet switching, completing the revolution.

## History of Network Concepts

Going back to examine the history of computer networks, the first event for me took place in November 1964 at the Second Congress on the Information System Sciences in Hot Springs, Virginia. In informal discussions with J. C. R. Licklider, F. Corbato, and A. Perlis, I concluded that the most important problem in the computer field before us at that time was computer networking; the ability to access one computer from another easily and economically to permit resource sharing.

That was a topic in which Licklider was very interested and his enthusiasm infected me. My interest was more toward the networking and communications issues rather than the computer language and compatibility issues that were foremost in Lick's mind. For at least the prior year, Licklider, who was then running the ARPA IPT office (then called Command & Control Research), had been pursuing the concept of the "Intergalactic Computer Network," trying to define the problems and benefits resulting from computer networking. In any case, that Hot Springs discussion convinced me that I should change my career objectives to concentrate on computer networking and the related communications problems.

One year later, in 1965, a second important meeting took place at MIT. Donald Davies from the National Physical Laboratory in the United Kingdom was at MIT to give a seminar on time sharing. Licklider, Davies, and I discussed networking and the inadequacy of data communication facilities for both time-sharing and networking. Davies reports that shortly after this meeting he was struck with the concept that a store and forward system for very short messages (now called packet switching) was the ideal communication system for interactive systems. He wrote about his ideas in a document entitled "Proposal for Development of a National Communication Service for On-Line Data Processing" that envisioned a communications network using trunk lines from 100K bits/sec in speed to 1.5 megabits/sec (T1), message sizes of 128 bytes and a switch that could handle up to 10,000 messages/sec (historical note: this took 20 years to accomplish). Then in June 1966, Davies wrote a second internal paper, "Proposal for a Digital Communication Network" in which he coined the word *packet*, a small subpart of the message the user wants to send, and also introduced the concept of an "interface computer" to sit between the user equipment and the packet network. His design also included the concept of a packet assembler and disassembler (PAD) to interface character terminals, today a common element of most packet networks.

As a result of distributing his 1965 paper, Donald Davies was given a copy of an internal Rand report, "On Distributed Communications" by Paul Baran of the Rand Corporation, which had been written in August 1964 (1). Baran's historical paper also described a short message switching network using T1 trunks and a 128 byte message size, but was oriented toward providing extremely reliable communications for secure voice and data in a military environment. In all, there were 11 reports written for the Air Force in the Rand Memorandum group, of which a couple were classified and unfortunately the others were very sparsely published in the scientific press. Thus their impact on the actual development of packet switching was mainly supportive, not sparking its development—that happened independently at Rand, NPL and ARPA.

## THE FIRST NETWORK EXPERIMENT

Convinced that computer networking was important, the first task was to set up a test environment to determine where the problems were. Thus, in 1966, I set up two computer networks between Lincoln Laboratory's TX-2 computer and System Development Corporation's Q-32 computer using a 1200 bps dial channel (high speed in those days). Each computer was operating in time-sharing mode and permitted any program to dial the other computer, log-in, and run programs much as it would execute a subroutine call. The experiment showed that there was no problem getting the computers to talk to each other and use resources on the other computer; time-sharing operating systems made that easy. The real problem uncovered was that dial communications based on the telephone network were too slow and unreliable to be operationally useful. This work, jointly authored with Tom Marill, was published in the AFIPS *FJCC Proceedings,* November 1966 (2). The lesson learned was that *a new data communications network was needed in order to successfully network computers.*

## ARPANET DEVELOPMENT

The chance to develop and build a major computer network experiment based on radically new communications technology came within a few months. I was asked to take over the responsibility of the ARPA Information Processing Techniques (IPT) office and manage and build its programs.*

ARPA was sponsoring computer research at leading universities and research labs in the United States. These projects and their computers provided an ideal environment for an experimental network project; consequently, the ARPANET was planned during 1967 with

---

*[*Editor's Note:* In his presentation at the conference, Roberts told this anecdote. "We realized at that point that the problem was not so much in the computers—the time-sharing monitors that had been written permitted us to allow computers to be shared just fine—the problem was in the communications service. The Western Union circuit was . . . terribly unreliable. It took forever to make a call and didn't have any throughput when you got going. And the cost was enormous. So that was the next job—to undertake how to organize the communications resources. All of these experiments went on during the mid-1960s. At that point, Ivan Sutherland was finishing his tour at ARPA, and Bob Taylor and he were hoping to start some of this network technology. They wanted me to come down to ARPA to help with that program. They didn't convince me of that, so Bob did what he now says I can call 'blackmailing.' He went to the director of ARPA and said, 'look, you fund 51 percent of Lincoln Lab. Why don't you call them up and tell them to send Larry down here?' Which Charlie Hirshfeld did, while Bob was there in the room. And the director of Lincoln called me in that afternoon and said, 'I think that you really ought to go to ARPA.' I wound up down there the next week or two, and found myself working with Bob to set up this network program, and eventually taking over the whole program. So, in some sense, that was how that activity started. It was not quite what I wanted to do at that point in my career, but I found it to be, of course, extremely valuable."]

the aid of these researchers to link these projects' computers together. One task was to develop a computer interface protocol acceptable to all 16 research groups. A second task was to design a new communications network technology to support 35 computers at 16 sites with 500,000 packets/day traffic. The initial plan for the ARPANET was published in October 1967 at the ACM Symposium on Operating System Principles in Gatlinburg Tennessee (3). The reasons given at that time for establishing a computer network were:

1. *Load sharing:* Send program and data to remote computer to balance load.
2. *Message service:* Electronic mail service (mailbox service).
3. *Data sharing:* Remote access to data bases.
4. *Program sharing:* Send data, program remote (e.g., supercomputer).
5. *Remote service:* Log-in to remote computer, use its programs and data.

The communications network design was that of the now conventional packet network; interface message processors (IMPs) at each node interconnected by leased telecommunication lines providing a store and forward service on very short messages (Fig. 1). The main difference from later packet nets was that the IMPs were located at the computer sites and connected by a short parallel cable rather than a

**FIGURE 1**
Early communications network design with IMPs at each node.

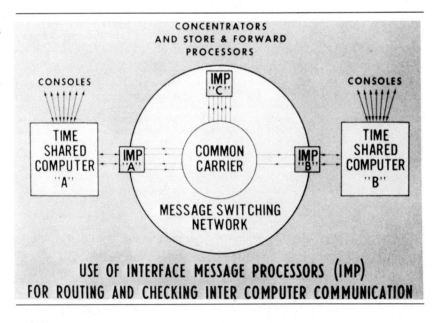

communications line interface. The device that we used, the IMP, was the biggest minicomputer available at that time, 12K of memory. It was a very precious resource. We had to work real hard to get all our stuff done and enough buffers within 12K. That probably had more impact on some of the technological issues of how you did packet switching than anything else that went on because the overall organization was focused on eliminating the necessity for buffers. Buffers were obviously the premium with this size memory.

Also presented at the Gatlinburg Symposium was Donald Davies's first open publication on the NPL packet network concepts presented by Roger Scantlebury, ''A Digital Communication Network for Computers Giving Rapid Response at Remote Terminals'' (4). It detailed the concept of a high-level packet net with high-capacity nodal switches and interface computers in front of mainframe computers. This was the first time that either Davies or I knew anything about each other's work since our 1965 contact. The NPL paper clearly impacted the ARPANET in several ways. The name ''packet'' was adopted, much higher speed was selected (50 Kilobit/sec vs. 2.4 Kilobit/sec) for internode lines to reduce delay and generally the NPL analysis helped confirm the concept of packet switching.

Another confirmation of the basic concepts came from finally being able to read the Rand reports on distributed communications. Paul Baran had done a vast amount of research in 1962 on packet switching. He had designed for the Air Force essentially a telephone system using packet switching back in 1962. Some of the reports were classified as not in the public domain. Therefore, neither Donald Davies nor I had seen anything of the work until we were deep into the design of our respective systems. The Rand work was very detailed, since it covered the whole network including microwave and one valuable analysis on routing. Their hot-potato routing algorithm was a useful starting point for the ARPANET routing design.

In any case, the original published concepts in the Rand reports were done by Paul, although we weren't able to utilize those until later on in this program. The packets we structured at that point were ones that had a header and a content and a check at the end so that they said where they were going and had error checking (Fig. 2). We even designed a network at this point. It was a hypothetical net, which got built exactly as planned. I worked out the network technology structure and the cost effectiveness and the number of hops between all the nodes. Eventually, Network Analysis Corporation wound up doing a huge amount of the computation of this kind of thing to optimize the net for us. It was in 1967 before any net was ever built. Figure 3 shows what we thought it might look like and be organized in terms of a physical map.

During 1968, a request for proposal was let for the ARPANET

**FIGURE 2**
Early network packet
format.

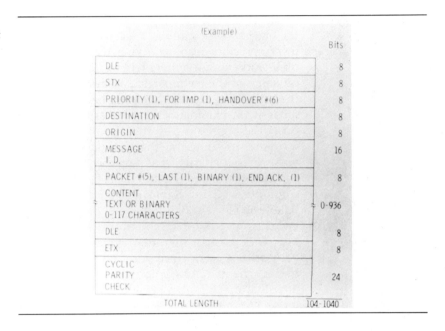

**FIGURE 3**
Physical map
projecting
organization of
ARPANET.

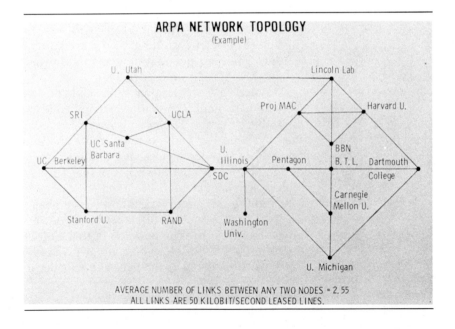

packet switching IMP equipment and the operation of the packet network. The RFP was awarded to Bolt, Beranek, and Newman, Inc., of Cambridge, Massachusetts, in January 1969. The RFP specified the general packet-switching concept, packet size, and interface protocol so that bidders could not totally change the system concept, to circuit or message switching for example. The two largest computer companies to receive the RFP did not bid it because they didn't have minicomputers with which to make an economic bid. BBN bid the Honeywell 516 minicomputer, which was ideal for the task, in 1969. Significant aspects of the network's internal operation, such as routing, flow control, software design, and network control were developed by a BBN team consisting of Frank Heart, Robert Kahn, Severo Ornstein, William Crowther, and David Walden. By December 1969 four nodes of the net had been installed and were operating effectively.

The first set of detailed papers covering the ARPANET were published in May 1970 at the AFIPS SJCC (5–9). These papers reported the motivation and economics (5), the detailed design of the IMP (6), the network delay analysis and experience (7), the topological design programs and results (8), and the host-to-host protocol (9). These papers showed the world for the first time that *packet switching works,* that it is *economic,* and that it is *reliable* and *virtually error free.* They also provided a complete description of how a working network was designed. As such, these papers were the technical and motivational basis for many other network experiments around the world.

The ARPANET utilized minicomputers at every node to be served by the network, interconnected in a fully distributed fashion by 50 KB leased lines. Each minicomputer took blocks of data from the computers and terminals connected to it, subdivided them into 128 byte packets, and added a header specifying destination and source addresses; then, based on a dynamically updated routing table the minicomputer sent the packet over whichever free line was currently the fastest route toward the destination. Upon receiving a packet, the next minicomputer would acknowledge it and repeat the routing process independently. Thus one important characteristic of the ARPANET was its completely distributed, dynamic routing algorithm on a packet-by-packet basis, based on a continuous evaluation within the network of the least delay paths, considering both line availability and queue lengths.

The technical and operational success of the ARPANET quickly demonstrated to a generally skeptical world that packet switching could be organized to provide an efficient and highly responsive interactive data communications facility. Fears that packets would loop forever and that very large buffer pools would be required were quickly allayed. Since the ARPANET was a public project connecting many major universities and research institutions, the implementation and performance details were widely published (10–14). The work of Leonard Kleinrock and his associates at UCLA on the theory and measurement of the ARPANET has been of particular importance in providing a firm theoretical and practical understanding about the performance of packet networks.

The ARPANET was first demonstrated publicly at the first International Conference on Computer Communications (ICCC) in Washington, D.C., in October 1972. Robert Kahn of BBN organized the demonstration installing a complete ARPANET node at the conference hotel, with about 40 active terminals permitting access to dozens of computers all over the United States. This public demonstration was, for many (if not most) of the ICCC attendees, proof that packet switching really worked. At this time, it was difficult for many experienced professionals to accept the fact that a collection of computers, wideband circuits, and minicomputer switching nodes (equipment totaling well over 100 pieces) could all function together reliably. The ARPANET demonstration lasted for three days and clearly displayed its reliable operation in public. The network provided highly reliable service to thousands of attendees during the entire duration of the conference.

## INDUSTRY RECEPTION

From the first time I distributed a description of packet switching outside the computer research community (the 1967 paper) until about 1975, the communication industry's reaction was generally negative since this was such a radically different approach. In some of the initial technical speeches I gave, communications professionals reacted with considerable anger and hostility, usually saying I did not know what I was talking about since I did not know all their jargon vocabulary. The most common technical flaw suggested (before the ARPANET was built) was that the buffers would quickly and catastrophically run out. After the ARPANET was operating successfully, their pitch changed to be that packet switching would never be economic without the government subsidy. Paul Baran reported the same reaction to his papers when he presented them; this reaction was the major reason his proposals never moved the military. Donald Davies reported a somewhat less angry response from the British Post Office, more one of mild interest but no serious consideration.

I learned a major lesson from that experience: People hate to change the basic postulates upon which considerable knowledge has been built. In the case of packet switching, the first postulate to change was the statistical nature of the traffic—data versus voice. The second was that computing was expensive. Some people find it is impossible to consider such a major jolt to their memory organization; they avoid it with putdowns if possible, if not with anger. Other people are more willing to reconsider, but for everyone it requires considerable effort. Those of us proposing packet switching all came from the computing field and did not need to change lots of prior concepts and knowledge. Many of those in the communications field still have not accepted packet switching. (The fight is heating up again as voice packet switching starts to be considered.)

## ARPANET Growth

As soon as the first four nodes were brought up and tested in December 1969 the network grew very rapidly. One year later, in December 1970, the network had grown to 10 nodes and 19 host computers. By April 1971, there were 15 nodes with 23 host computers, as shown in Fig. 4. By this time, it was clear that connecting terminals directly to the network through a PAD-type device was important. Such a device was designed and built in 1970–1971, and the first terminal interface processor (TIP) was added to the network in August, 1971. The TIP permitted users to get on the network directly with their terminals so that they could have direct access to all of the machines rather than having to go through one machine to get anywhere. In many cases, having the user attach his terminal to a TIP and access even his own host(s) through the network was found to be more reliable. This was the start of a trend that today is almost the rule, workstations should attach to a network, not a computer.

By January 1973, the network had grown to 35 nodes of which 15 were TIPs and was connected to 38 host computers. Figure 5 shows a

**FIGURE 4**
The ARPANET in April 1971.

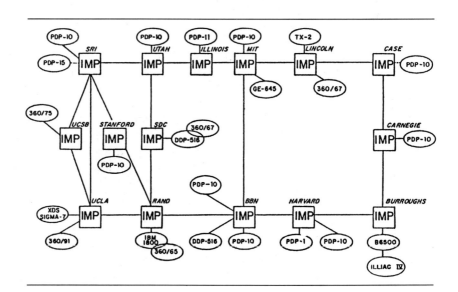

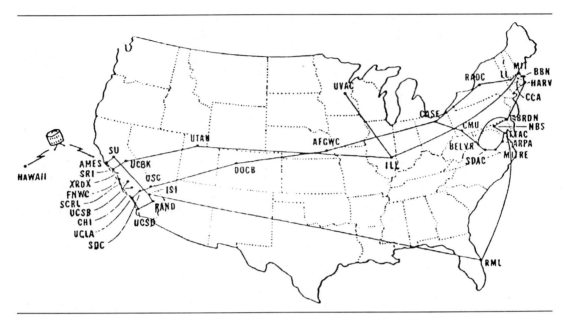

**FIGURE 5**
The ARPA network in January 1973.

map of the network at this point. Network traffic had grown rapidly in 1972, from 100,000 packets/day to 1,000,000 packets/day, exceeding the original estimates I made in 1967. Also in 1973, the first satellite link was added to the network with a TIP in Hawaii; later in the year a pair of TIPs were added in Europe. In September 1973, the network was up to 40 nodes, 45 host computers with internode traffic of 2,900,000 packets/day, had clearly reached a stage of operational stability, heavy usage, and was by any measure a major success. It was at this point that I left ARPA to spread the technology to the commercial world.

The ARPANET has continued to grow since 1973, with 111 host computers in 1977 and more than 400 hosts in all the interconnected networks by 1983. The network has become a utility for both ARPA and the Department of Defense as a whole. Research has continued into internetting and packet radio but little change has occurred in the basic network.

## 1969 CROSSOVER

In 1974, after it was clear that the technology worked, I finally spent time analyzing the economic trends that made packet switching possible (15). These trends could have been analyzed in the mid-1960s if someone were to have asked the right questions, but, as it often turns out, they were examined after the event they could have predicted. Simply, since packet switching requires more computation than circuit switching but saves transmission bandwidth, the trend analysis looked at the cost of computation and the cost of communications and found the situation illustrated in Fig. 6. For packet switching the cost of computation dominated in the early 1960s but in 1969 the cost curves crossed and afterward the cost of communications dominated. The composite cost of packet switching thus fell below the cost of circuit switching also about 1969 and since then the margin of advantage has quickly widened to where it equals the full peak to average transmission ratio for data of about 8 to 1. Subsequently, in a 1982 paper (16) I did a similar analysis for voice and concluded the crossover there was in 1978 and therefore packet voice would have been cheaper. In a somewhat similar fashion to data, the industry may recognize this ten to fifteen years after the event.

**FIGURE 6**
Packet-switching cost performance trends. Incremental cost of moving 1M bits (1 kilopacket) on a nationwide network.

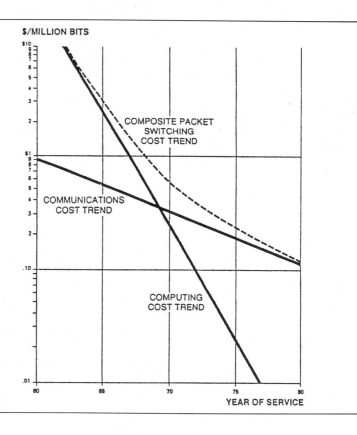

Figure 7 is one of the concept charts that I published of the effective bandwidth of the system versus block size—much higher effective bandwidth than any other technology that we could find for low block size. In other words, to get a kilobit somewhere, you could move it faster than anything else but, of course, by the time you are moving ten million bits, you could move it probably just as well with a number of different technologies, including dial technology. But if you were going to move short blocks a day, this is by far the fastest. And we also looked at costs. Figure 8 shows the cost of different technologies, from telegram at the top at $3300 per million bits, down to mailing a tape at 3 cents per million bits. Of course, today, we have the new option of sending a CD-ROM by courier anywhere in the world and having the lowest possible cost that you can imagine for high speed delivery. In fact, the effective bandwidth is over a hundred kilobits per second.

The costs versus delay was a big issue, as shown in Fig. 9. The cost per megabit was in the 16-cent range in a well-loaded network. The other axis is delay. The higher the delay (where the delay is for dial-up), the worse off your users are in terms of doing the job. But still the cost couldn't get down anywhere near as low.

The actual traffic on the net grew very rapidly in 1973 to where we had a reasonable loading in terms of network activity. The cost versus network size is shown as one upper line of Fig. 10; the lower section, in color, was projected for commercial networks. Actually,

**FIGURE 7**
Concept chart of effective bandwidth versus block size.

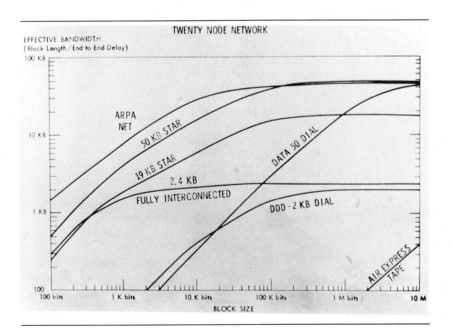

**FIGURE 8**
Costs of different communications technologies.

| Cost per megabit for Various Communication Media 1400 Mile Distance | | |
|---|---|---|
| Media | | |
| Telegram | $3300.00 | For 100 words at 30 bits/wd, daytime |
| Night Letter | 565.00 | For 100 words at 30 bits/wd, overnight delivery |
| Computer Console | 374.00 | 18 baud avg. use[2], 300 baud DDD service line & data sets only |
| TELEX | 204.00 | 50 baud teletype service |
| DDD (103A) | 22.50 | 300 baud data sets, DDD daytime service |
| AUTODIN | 8.30 | 2400 baud message service, full use during working hours |
| DDD (202) | 3.45 | 2000 baud data sets |
| Letter | 3.30 | Airmail, 4 pages, 250 wds/pg, 30 bits/wd |
| W. U. Broadband | 2.03 | 2400 baud service, full duplex |
| WATS | 1.54 | 2000 baud, used 8 hrs/working day |
| Leased Line (201) | .57 | 2000 baud, commercial, full duplex |
| Data 50 | .47 | 50 KB dial service, utilized full duplex |
| Leased Line (303) | .23 | 50 KB, commercial, full duplex |
| Mail DEC Tape | .20 | 2.5 megabit tape, airmail |
| Mail IBM Tape | .034 | 100 megabit tape, airmail |

**FIGURE 9**
Costs versus delay.

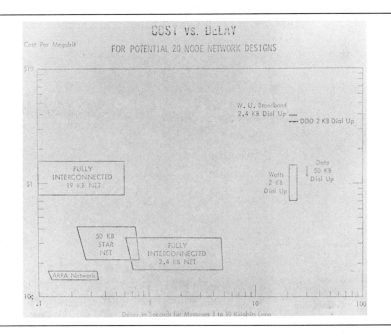

**FIGURE 10**
Cost relative to
network size.

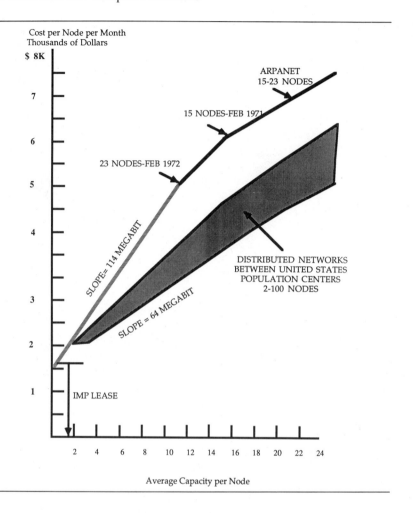

numbers on this chart typically would indicate that the commercial net-works charged more than they needed to, and they did because they had to do so much more work training the users than we allocated in this chart. This is pure cost of communications rather than the cost of running a service. The top of the chart basically says that the vertical column is the cost per million bits, again of moving data; the middle band is between a dollar and ten cents for the cost of communications over the years from 1960 to 1980.

The cost to deliver goes down by a factor of ten every five years. This is a consistent trend that includes the cost of packet switches. The communications trend indicated a sort of flattening out by 1980. What actually happened to communications is that it turned around and started going up again. If you examine communications costs later on, you find that tariff situations and other situations (i.e., primarily the FCC and AT&T fighting) caused that trend to back up again over time. They didn't stay on the downward side, even though the technology trend for installed plant has continued to go down.

**IMPACT ON COMPUTER RESOURCES**

One of the original goals of the ARPANET was resource sharing to optimize computer resources. In 1973 I surveyed the ARPANET users to see what alternative computer facilities they would need if they did not have the network (Tables 1 and 2). In a number of cases there were ARPA projects that did not have a computer at all but utilized computer power from resource centers that had developed. They obtained access through a TIP, typically on site, and used one of a collection of computers often across the country. They were generally happy not to have to run their own computer and had far more reliable service than if they had been limited to one machine. Also, due to the statistics of large groups and the benefit of multiple time zones (from Hawaii to Europe), the number of computers required for these users was far less through consolidation. Another group of users were using the Illiac IV remotely for large numerical problems and would have required their own supercomputer or perhaps had to commute if the network were not there. In other cases individuals needed to use software unique to foreign hardware and thus needed access to other computers besides their own. After finding rational solutions (fiscally sound) to all the

**TABLE 1**

**REMOTE USAGE OF COMPUTER SERVICES WITHIN ARPANET**

Annual Remote Computer Usage Cost Based on March 1973 Data

| Service Resource | Computer | Remote Usage ($ in thousands) |
|---|---|---|
| Univ of Southern Calif, Los Angeles, Calif | PDP-10 | 520 |
| Inst for Adv Computation, NASA-Ames, Calif | ILLIAC IV, PDP-10, B-6700 | 470 |
| Univ of California, Los Angeles, Calif | 360/91 | 340 |
| Bolt Beranek & Newman, Cambridge, Mass | PDP-10 | 179 |
| Stanford Research Institute, Menlo Park, Calif | PDP-10 | 151 |
| Univ of California, San Diego, Calif | B-6700 | 118 |
| Mass Institute of Technology, Cambridge, Mass | Multics-645 | 90 |
| Others | Mainly PDP-10's | 150 |
| Total | | 2018 |

**TABLE 2**

| COMPUTER RESOURCE USAGE WITHIN ARPANET | | | |
|---|---|---|---|
| Annual Remote Computer Usage Cost Based on March 1973 Data | | | |
| User Organisation | Activity | Remote Usage ($ in thousands) | Projected Cost for Local Replacement |
| University of Illinois | Parallel processing research | 360 | 1100 |
| NASA Ames | Air foil design and ILLIAC | 328 | 570 |
| Rand Corporation | Numerical climate modelling | 210 | 660 |
| Applied Data Research | ILLIAC IV compiler development | 151 | 470 |
| Lawrence Livermore Lab | Dev of TENSOR code on ILLIAC | 94 | 370 |
| Stanford University | Artificial intelligence research | 91 | 180 |
| Rome Air Dev Center | Text manipulation and resource evaluation | 81 | 450 |
| ARPA | On-line management | 77 | 370 |
| Seismic Array Analysis Ctr | Seismic data processing | 76 | 300 |
| Mitre Corporation | Distributed file network research | 60 | 240 |
| Natl Bureau of Standards | Network research | 58 | 200 |
| Bolt Beranek & Newman | TENEX system support | 55 | 80 |
| Xerox Parc | Computer science research | 47 | 100 |
| USC-IPL | Picture processing research | 35 | 75 |
| UCLA | Network measurement | 28 | 90 |
| Systems Control, Inc. | Signal processing research | 23 | 70 |
| UCSB | Network research | 22 | 70 |
| Range Measurements Lab | ARPANET management | 17 | 60 |
| Institute for the Future | Teleconferencing research | 13 | 40 |
| Miscellaneous | Computer research | 192 | 880 |
| Total | | 2018 | 6060 |

ARPA user needs assuming no network, the computing cost was compared to the then actual computer cost and found to be *three times as expensive*. Independent of the details of the survey, it is clear that huge savings were possible (in that era of mainframes) by pooling computing demand. Today, when all my computer resources come from microcomputers, I couldn't save anything using remote computers for computing power. Supercomputer users still might save but, in large part, this benefit is mainly historical.

# Other Network Development

### CYCLADES

In France the interest in computer networks grew quickly during the early 1970s. In 1973 the first hosts were connected to a network called CYCLADES that linked several major computing centers throughout France (17). The name CYCLADES refers to both the communications subnet and the host computers. The communications subnet by itself is called CIGALE and is a pure *datagram* network, moving only disconnected packets and delivering them in whatever order they arrive without any knowledge or concept of messages, connections, or flow control. The ARPANET also operates using datagrams but perhaps the most avid supporter of the concept is the designer of CYCLADES,

Louis Pouzin. As with any datagram network, a large part of the communications functions must be implemented in the host computers; the packet ordering, message formation, flow control, and virtual connections support.

### RCP

Another packet network experiment was started in France at about the same time by the French PTT Administration (18). This network, RCP, first became operational in 1974 and was the experimental testbed for the French public network service TRANSPAC. The design of RCP, directed by Remi Despes, differed sharply from that of CIGALE and ARPANET by being organized around the concept of the *virtual circuits* rather than datagrams. RCP's character as a prototype public network may have been a strong factor in this difference since a virtual circuit service is more directly marketable, not requiring substantial modifications to the customers' computer. In any case, RCP pioneered the incorporation of individually flow-controlled virtual circuits into packet switching networks.

### TELENET

The success of the ARPANET led Bolt, Beranek, and Newman (the primary contractor for the ARPANET) to establish a commercial network company, Telenet, in late 1972. In October 1973 I joined Telenet as president, and we filed with the FCC to become a carrier and construct a public packet switching network. The FCC approved the request six months later, and Telenet started the world's first public service in August 1975 with 7 nodes. By April 1978 Telenet's network had grown to 187 nodes providing service to 180 host computers and supporting direct terminal access service in 156 cities and interconnections to 14 other countries. Telenet was designed from the start to appear to the user as a virtual circuit service with the host interface being implemented over a communications line rather than with a box on site. However, for the first several years Telenet operated a core network based on datagrams copied from the ARPANET, but implemented virtual circuits at all interfaces. It used a device that is similar to the IMP in structure but, as a central office device so that the user was over a communication line, rather than having a device at his site (Fig. 11). And the work piled into the site for terminal access. So we had what we called TIPs in all of our central offices and they connected by remote lines to the user site. And then we might have a small device called the TAC to break it out to individual lines for that computer, or an X.25 or similar protocol line to the user. When Telenet started, there wasn't any X.25; we had a similar protocol. Within a year, we had changed to

**FIGURE 11**
Telenet central office
device.

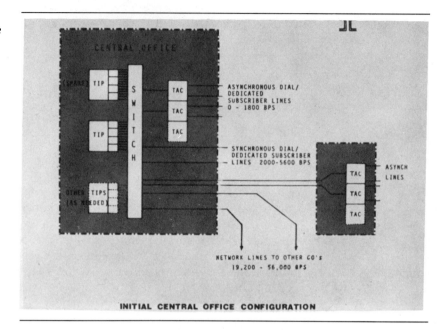

INITIAL CENTRAL OFFICE CONFIGURATION

the now standard X.25. The machines we were using at that time were Prime computers, somewhat better cost effectiveness than the original Honeywell machines, but similar in concept.

It wasn't until the complete shift was made to Telenet's TP-4000 packet switch around 1980 that the savings of virtual circuits in the core net could be realized (about 30 percent for Telenet with a 32 byte average packet size). The communications capability that we were able to offer computing power for at that point was something on the order of $2 an hour for interactive access nationwide, from any place to any place. You dialed into the network and got to another city for $2 an hour, as opposed to what the dial telephone network charges were at that point, something like $25 an hour. So it was cheaper, by about a factor of ten, than what you could do over the telephone network. In the intervening time, packet network charges have gone up to something like $4 to $5 an hour, and the telephone charges have come down somewhat from the $25 range to more like $15 or $20. So you see a flattening of the two with respect to each other.

We also looked at where packet switching was most effective as shown in Fig. 12. It was obviously most effective for interactive terminals where the average utilization of the terminal on the vertical axis was very low (between 5 and 10 percent). The peak transmission rate was relatively low for terminals between 4.8 kilobits, on down; in that range, we could provide very cheap service and have a very cost effec-

**FIGURE 12**
Packet-switching cost versus utilization levels.

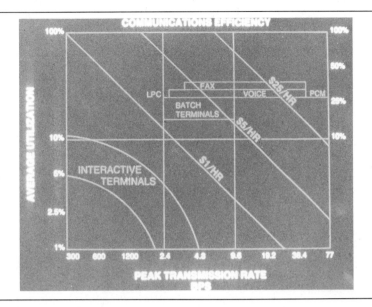

tive situation. When you get the very high percentage utilizations, 100 percent utilization and very high speeds, of course, you virtually need a dedicated line between the two sites. The diagonal lines are what it would cost to provide packet switching at the then tariff prices for packet switching for all these services. You see that batch was quite attractive as compared to dial telephone, which was again still $25, and even voice; most of voice, if compressed at all, was attractive and still is.

The next issue that came up was that the right way to do things was to use datagrams. We had lots of communications capacity, basically because we were using 56 kilobit lines and very few buffers—very little to work with in the computer room. That quickly changed as the cost of computing continued to go down even after 1973, and it has gone down by another few orders of magnitude since then. So now the cost is practically nothing. By the time Telenet was built, there were plenty of buffers available. There is no issue about reassembling and doing all sorts of work to set up to understand the packets at each end of a link. Therefore, the best thing to do is to pre-figure what's going on and store it at both ends, both of the computers and both ends of each link in the network. Just send a very short piece of header on the packets saying this is call #27 and send the data and a sum check. What we originally did in the ARPANET was to send to and from big long addresses that identified everybody and where it was going to and from. That took 31 bytes of overhead, whereas we could get that down to 10 bytes in the upper one. In fact, when you look at a voice packet switch that you'll be seeing in the late 1980s and the 1990s, we're down to maybe 8 bits, 1 byte of overhead on that packet, and everything else is data because you have to have very short packets. So we're progressing to much shorter headers because of the overall capability of the computer site. We can have lots of computer capability to do the best job we can. And there's no sense wasting that huge amount of overhead. When the average data in fact was only 30 bytes, or 20 bytes, in the average call packet, then we were wasting 50 percent of our bandwidth and processing power handling all of that data. And so, as it turns out, that was a major change that took place in the packet networks that we've done commercially from the research networks. There were all sorts of claims that it was less reliable or other things; yet all those problems had been solved. Today the issue remains a debate between the various parties.

Telenet also went to a two-level hierarchy where you have central net, very heavy circuit, and a lot of finer circuits moving into those. And one of the other things that was looked at was, what is the effect of a two-level topology (Fig. 13). The top net shows a single-level network like the ARPANET where every node is equal, every node has four lines connecting to it forming an almost random pattern. The average path length is proportional to the log of the number of nodes, log base three, because you have three additional lines connecting to each

**FIGURE 13**
Single-level versus two-level topology.

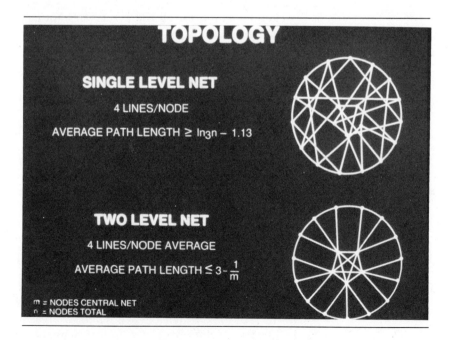

node. In a two-level network, which you see at the bottom of the figure, you have a central network and then a bunch of other nodes on the outer nets, four lines for a node on the average. But every node doesn't have four lines—some have many more, some have less; the average path link was three minus a small amount. The delay and the cost in the network, because every line you traverse costs you money, is proportional to the average path line. So, if you then look at cost of the network, the path link in the network, which is proportional to cost efficiency of the use of the network, you find that the path link and hops for a single-level network keeps going up as the log for the number of nodes. Above a hundred nodes, it's far cheaper to have a two-level network. That was what happened in the commercial environment as well.

The processor we used at that point was called TP. Telenet still uses them, ten years later. We designed a multi-processor device that processed the packets and had a much higher throughput than the original processors.

The international network quickly built up then where Telenet, in particular, was interconnected with a vast number of countries as well as TYMNET in the United States, and any other network that came along in time. There were a number of commercial networks in the United States and a number of overseas networks like those in the United Kingdom and Canada. Soon after this, France and other nations had their own major networks; but many of them just had nodes.

### EIN

Originally known as COST Project II and later as the European Informatics Network, EIN is a multi-nation funded European computer network (19,20). The project director was Derek Barber of NPL, one of the original investigators of packet switching in the United Kingdom. It was organized in 1971 but due to the difficulties of multi-national funding it did not become operational until 1976.

### OTHER PUBLIC DATA NETWORKS

Public packet networks were announced in the United Kingdom, France, Canada, and Japan in the 1973–1974 period. In 1977 the Experimental Packet Switched Service (EPSS) in the United Kingdom and DATAPAC in Canada became operational. Also in 1977 a second public network TYMNET became approved in the United States. In 1978 TRANSPAC in France and DX-2 in Japan became operational as public networks. By the early 1980s public packet network service was available in most countries in the world as an international service and as a domestic service in many of these countries.

## CCITT Standards—X.25

With five, independent, public packet networks under construction in the 1974–1975 period (U.S.—Telenet, Canada, U.K., France, Japan), there was strong incentive for the nations to agree on a standard user interface to the networks so that host computers would not have unique interfacing jobs in each country. Unlike most standards activities, where there is almost no incentive to compromise and agree, carriers in separate countries can only benefit from the adoption of a standard since it facilitates network interconnection and permits easier user attachment. To this end, the parties concerned undertook a major effort to agree on the host-network interface during 1975. The result was an agreed protocol, CCITT Recommendation X.25, adopted in March 1976.

The X.25 protocol provides for the interleaving of data blocks for up to 4095 virtual circuits on a single full-duplex leased line interface to the network, including all procedures for call setup and disconnection. A significant feature of this interface, from the carriers' point of view, is the inclusion of independent flow control on each virtual circuit (VC); the flow control enables the network (and the user) to protect itself from congestion and overflow under all circumstances without having to slow down or stop more than one call at a time. In networks like the ARPANET and CYCLADES, which do not have this capability, the network must depend on the host (or other networks in interconnect cases) to ensure that no user submits more data to the network than the network can handle or deliver. The only defense the network has without individual VC flow control is to shut off the entire host (or internet) interface. This, of course, can be disastrous to the other users communicating with the offending host or network.

Another critical aspect of X.25 is that it defines interface standards for both the host-to-network block transfer and the control of individual VCs. In datagram networks the VC interface is situated in the host computer; there can be, therefore, no network standard for labeling, sequencing, and flow controlling VCs.

The March 1976 agreement on X.25 as the technique for public packet networks marked the beginning of the second phase of packet switching: large interconnected public service networks. In the years since X.25 was adopted, many additional packet standards have been agreed on as well. X.28 was adopted as the standard asynchronous terminal interface and X.29, a protocol used with X.25 to specify the packetizing rules for the terminal handler, was adopted as the host control protocol. Also, a standard protocol for interconnecting international networks, X.75, has been adopted.

## Packet Switched Voice

Packet networks today typically only utilize trunks and lines up to 64 kilobits/sec in speed. As a result, end-to-end delay in these networks remains high—over 100 ms. Network delay would however be vastly reduced given high speed trunks (T1–T3) and high speed packet switches (greater than 100,000 packets/sec). Even with a shift to T1 trunks, the network delay would drop to 10 ms plus propagation. With T2 trunks, the delay would not be practically different than with a circuit switch (1–2 ms plus propagation). For most data applications this is unnecessary but for voice it is critical. The voice network will often return an echo from analog phones and even 20 ms of delay can make such an echo sound bad. Short packets like 32 bytes (4.5 ms of 56 kb voice) are also necessary to reduce delay. But with high speed trunks and short packets, packetized voice is not only toll quality but also saves 67 percent of the transmission and switch bandwidth due to silence suppression. Thus in designing tomorrow's central office switch and toll switches for the telecommunications network, it is clearly extremely desirable to use packet switches for voice of any rate (56kb, 32kb, 16kb, etc.), for data of all speeds and for switched video. Without packet switching the flexibility is vastly reduced and each service must be switched separately. Packet switches of the required speed are both feasible and economic today if restricted to fixed-length, short packets (16 or 32 bytes), all flow control and error checking are done at the network interfaces—not for each link, and a foreshortened virtual circuit header is used (about 1 byte) with only the link number. AT&T has a prototype switch of 2 million packets/sec in test and designs exist for switches up to 35 million packets/sec (21).

The most interesting facet of high speed switch technology is that, for large central office or tandem office switches, the peak switch throughput is limited by the speed of the fastest memory for a time switch and similarly for a packet switch, but the packet switch is able to switch a whole packet not just one byte like the time switch. Thus in general for 32 byte packets, *packet switches can be made about 32 times the maximum throughput of circuit switches.* This becomes very valuable at high level tandem switching offices to switch traffic between many fiber paths.

Based on the importance of coping with variable bitrate demands for data, voice, and video and the cost savings for integrating all services with one switch, it is clear that *the whole telecommunications plant will convert to packet switching in the future.* The date is harder to predict but conversion should occur during the 1990s and be complete by 2000. The basic service will be small packets on virtual circuits, and each application will have its own interface units. Data services will use an X.25 interface that does the flow control and error checking for the VC on an end-to-end basis.

## Future Computer Networks

If we look forward to the year 2000, based on historical trends, computers will be about 500 times cheaper per computation than today. Almost all devices in the home, office, or plant will have complex computers incorporated into them. Simple local area network facilities like shielded twisted pair will connect the majority of these together and a gateway will connect this local network to the public telecommunication system over (hopefully a revised and truly integrated) ISDN facility. Distinctions as to which device is the phone may become difficult because many of the device-computers may use the voice network from time to time for warnings, ordering, and certainly in assisting us to find the party to whom we wish to talk. Phone service today is in great need of automation; we waste large amounts of time nonproductively answering and calling to find people. Thus as the telecommunications network brings data and voice together, home and office automation will integrate them.

**REFERENCES**

(1) P. Baran et al., "On Distributed Communications, Vols. I through XI," *RAND Corporation Memos*, August 1964.

(2) T. Marill and L. G. Roberts, "Toward a Cooperative Network of Time-Shared Computers," *Proceedings FJCC* 1966, pp. 425–431.

(3) L. G. Roberts, "Multiple Computer Networks and Intercomputer Communication," *ACM Symposium on Operating System Principles*, October 1967.

(4) D. W. Davies, K. A. Bartlett, R. A. Scantlebury, and P. T. Wilkinson, "A Digital Communication Network for Computers Giving Rapid Response at Remote Terminals," *ACM Symposium on Operating System Principles*, October 1967.

(5) L. G. Roberts and B. D. Wessler, "Computer Network Development to Achieve Resource Sharing," *Proceedings SJCC* 1970, pp. 543–549.

(6) F. E. Heart, R. E. Kahn, S. M. Ornstein, W. R. Crowther, and D. C. Walden, "The Interface Message Processor for the ARPA Computer Network," *AFIPS Conference Proceedings* 36, June 1970, pp. 551–567.

(7) L. Kleinrock, "Analytic and Simulation Methods in Computer Network Design," *AFIPS Conference Proceedings* May 1970.

(8) H. Frank, I. T. Frisch, and W. Chou, "Topological Considerations in the Design of the ARPA Computer Network," *AFIPS Conference Proceedings*, May 1970.

(9) S. Carr, S. Crocker, and V. Cerf. "HOST-HOST Communication Protocol in the ARPA Network," *AFIPS Conference Proceedings*, May 1970.

(10) S. M. Ornstein, F. E. Heart, W. R. Crowther, S. B. Russell, H. K. Rising, and A. Michel, "The Terminal IMP for the ARPA Computer Network," *AFIPS Conference Proceedings* 40, June 1972, pp. 243–254.

(11) L. Kleinrock, "Performance Models and Measurement of the ARPA Computer Network," *Proceedings of the International Symposium on the Design and Application of Interactive Computer Systems*, Grunel University, Uxbridge, England, May 1972.

(12) L. Kleinrock and W. Naylor, "On Measured Behavior of the ARPA Network," *AFIPS Conference Proceedings* 43, NCC, Chicago, Illinois, May 1974, pp. 767–780.

(13) L. Kleinrock and H. Opderbeck, "Throughput in the ARPANET—Protocols and Measurement," *Fourth Data Communications Symposium*, Quebec City, Canada, October 1975, pp. 6-1 to 6-11.

(14) H. Frank and W. Chou, "Topological Optimization of Computer Networks," *Proceedings of the IEEE* 60, no. 11, November 1972, pp. 1385–1397.

(15) L. Roberts, "Data by the Packet," *IEEE Spectrum* 11, pp. 46–51, February 1974.

(16) L. Roberts, "Packet Switching Economics," presented at L. M. Ericsson Prize Presentation, Stockholm, Sweden, May 1982.

(17) L. Pouzin, "Presentation and Major Design Aspects of the CYCLADES Network," *Third Data Communications Symposium*, Tampa, Florida, November 1973, pp. 80–85.

(18) R. F. Despres, "A Packet Network with Graceful Saturated Operation," *Proceedings ICCC*, Washington, D. C., October 1972, pp. 345–351.

(19) D. L. A. Barber, "The European Computer Network Project," *Proceedings ICCC*, Washington, D.C., October 1972, pp. 192–200.

(20) D. L. A. Barber, "A European Informatics Network: Achievement and Prospects," *Proceedings ICC*, Toronto, Canada, August 1976, pp. 44–50.

(21) A. Thomas, J. P. Coudreuse, and M. Servel, "Asynchronous Time-Division Techniques: An Experimental Packet Network Intergrating Videocommunication," *Proceedings International Switching Symposium*, Florence, Italy, May 1984.

# Participants Discussion

Sig Treu

As an ARPANET user in the early 1970s, I remember seeing some statistical reports concerning the traffic patterns on the network. Specifically, the usage for electronic mail purposes was significantly high, or maybe surprisingly high. I wondered whether you, at that time, were alarmed by that kind of pattern, or whether some people suggested to you that that was not substantive enough use of such a sophisticated technology. Or did you foresee such use as a significant need to be met in the future of person-to-person communication?

Roberts

Well, we were surprised that it happened, although not totally because we had spent a lot of our time developing electronic mail. We thought it was fantastic as a capability. The ARPA office was one of the largest users; the ARPA office converted totally. Steve Lucasick decided it was a great thing, and he made everybody in ARPA use it. So all these managers of ballistic missile technology, who didn't know what a computer was, had to start using electronic mail. I think it went over very well inside and externally; it was probably a larger factor than we had imagined it would be. I remember getting a note back from Paul Baran when we were starting on this (I looked it up the other day when I was running through all this stuff). It said, "These are all fine, what you're talking about for this network. But one thing you ought to watch out for is you can't send out personal message stuff, that's illegal. That's against the postal laws and you'll be in jail in no time." And it happened, but we didn't happen to go to jail.

Allen Newell

If we're looking for the important factors that make these things happen, then, relative to the discussion of ARPA, it is worth re-emphasizing something Larry said: ARPA could remain very cool and easy with respect to the fact that the research community, who it was advertising as its initial customer, was fairly cool about the net. ARPA had the freedom to pursue a development path for quite a long time, without necessarily getting everyone behind it as certified customers before they were able to proceed. That turned out, in retrospect, to be exactly the right strategy to make things work.

To come back to an earlier issue, there is a fairly strong flavor in the meeting so far of "technological determinism." If you simply lay out the physical structure of what happened, then everything else falls into line. Gordon's talk, and Larry's talk to a certain extent (because that's what was on his slides), did not focus simply on the characteristics of discovery, not on the characteristics of who did what when, but just on laying out the major economic and technological factors that seemed to hedge the whole development and make it go in particular ways. One wants to keep looking for the factors that work in the opposite fashion. One was the issue that we brought up earlier, on the workstation. It was the research community that didn't necessarily want to go do the workstation that kept it from happening. Lick said it was the community's fault, and Butler Lampson said that they were not interested in it because the technology was too hard. Yet, in fact, we—ARPA and the community—did a fair number of things in areas where the technology was not available. The network is an example of one area where ARPA forced the technology by several years, and you hung in there. Speech was another example where the technology wasn't really right there, and you took it as your job to force it. Yet, somehow, ARPA never took it upon itself to force the workstation technology as a concept in the long term. I'm not concerned about relatively isolated things like the KLUDGE. For the network, and for several other things that ARPA did, they did it on a scale and for long enough that it actually made the world change. I wonder if you have any reflections on that?

*Roberts*

Workstation development could do quite well on its own. It was quite within the economic capacity of commercial organizations. As you see today, commercial organizations are quite interested in such development. So that was one of the criteria that we built up: Don't fund anything that was obviously going to be done by industry and was straightforward. Rather, fund things that are further out. Butler referred to another example. After the Illiac IV, we decided that we had had enough of this, and we will not undertake another supercomputer project. But, I think the thing that stopped the work on the personal workstation was that we had all seen plenty of the research that would have led to it—the graphics work and everything else that had been done. The issue was that it needed to become a commercial reality, and making a commercial reality wasn't ARPA's job. But, and now I go back to some of the earlier parts of what you said, I think that it's very true that the technology is a forcing factor that brings you there. As you saw in the network research, we could have gone for I think another five years and never had a network if it wasn't for the ARPA office being as free as it was to pursue development. The voice network has not appeared because there hasn't been that kind of undertaking.

*Gordon Bell*

We're using the word ARPA or DARPA very loosely in this. Sometimes it means the collective set of contractors, sometimes it means a little bit of guidance from the top, where a lot of thousand flowers bloom. But, in fact, in this thing we really shouldn't be using ''DARPA''; it was a few people, and namely Larry, who drove it. I wouldn't say it could have been stopped, perhaps because of the ARPA community getting up in arms at not being funded on their own. They took money out of the communal tree and funded this thing. I think Larry's being very generous. Things could have been much worse; it could have been a decade before this happened. I was in this a little bit, too. I had enough dealings with the communications suppliers that it is hard for me to believe that it could ever have happened, left to its own devices. It took an individual and it took the experiment to get it to happen. This is one of the cases where the thing wouldn't have happened by itself. The workstation happened almost *because* of the known technology, but packet switching really wasn't happening. We saw the need for it once we built all those minicomputers. We had to have DEC-net and so, in the 1973 to 1974 timeframe, we said we've got to hook these workstations together, and our model was all of the packet switching that was done in the community. We did it a little bit differently, using the host, but the ARPANET was clearly the model. It was also the model for expanding local area networks (LANs). In fact, there were lots of LANs proposals that were pre–packet switching: loops, pierced loops, and a lot of work at IBM. But this was truly an individual driving it, and it could have been dwarfed, both by the technologists (the communications supplier) and by the other guys who had gotten screwed by it, the ARPA users.

**Doug Ross**

To pick up on Allen's question on why ARPA didn't carry through further with the workstation concept, I think that the thinking and practice was really focused on the workstation, the WS part (to take the point I was trying to make in my paper) and the software architecture. It was less focused on questions about the users' personal work habits. This was very hard to get hold of, especially when the big break took place in going to the PL1/MULTICS root as the primary time-sharing support of ARPA, and then the still different 940 stuff that led to the other packet switching and so forth. There was a break in the underlying software technology that had to be reinvented later in the process by the marketplace.

**Barry Leiner**

I thought I'd add a little bit of perspective; I'm a little more recent than Larry from ARPA. In fact, I can remember a number of discussions at ARPA, while I was there, about the issue of whether we should support the workstation work going on. And the position really was what Larry just described—that it was appropriate for ARPA to support basic research in areas where it could be used to help drive workstation development, but it was inappropriate to go develop workstations because, after all, the commercial world could do that very well and, in fact, did, with ARPA encouragement, but not support.

*Roberts*                    Thank you, I didn't have the perspective of the last years, but I sus-
                             pected that that was certainly the case. Certainly when I was there it
                             would have cost us $100,000 a workstation, and that's a little bit ex-
                             pensive.

*David Wood*                 One of the major impacts of the ARPA networking on workstations
                             today that hasn't been explicitly mentioned is the protocol architecture
                             that came out of the ARPA community ten years ago or so. Much of
                             the networking of workstations has been accomplished using military
                             standard protocols; there are some obvious products in the market-
                             place today that use those. I think that has to be recognized. Yet one
                             of the maybe not-so-successful impacts was selling those protocols to
                             the international standards community. Now we're faced with the sit-
                             uation where DOD is under pressure to abandon those military stan-
                             dards in favor of international standards. What is the impact of that
                             going to be on the marketplace, and on products that have been built
                             up based on those military standards? Do you have any observations
                             on that?

*Roberts*                    My own observation I already gave. I think the military standard is
                             obsolete by this point in time so that the commercial standard is what
                             most people have built commercial products around, as far as I can
                             see. I'm not too concerned with that trend. I think it's just correct.

*Barry Leiner*               I've got to comment on that one. I actually believe the ISO protocols,
                             the international protocols, are one of the sterling successes of ARPA.
                             ARPA's business is to develop technologies not standards and, while
                             the standards that ARPA developed may not be used exactly the way
                             they were developed in the military context of the ARPA research, in
                             fact, if you take a look at the ISO protocols, a good many of them are
                             technologically quite similar, maybe updated for newer technology,
                             but still technologically quite similar to the DOD protocols. The ques-
                             tion is how to transition inside the DOD and how to transition in some
                             of the other communities that are using the DOD protocols to leapfrog
                             into the ISO protocols because, after all, the ISO protocols are still not
                             a usable set of protocols. There's a lot missing in them yet.

# MATHEMATICAL LABORATORIES: A NEW POWER FOR THE PHYSICAL AND SOCIAL SCIENCES

## Glen Culler
Introduction by Charles Irby

**Charles Irby**

**I**n the early 1960s, I was cruising through my college education in Santa Barbara, California. Unlike many of my contemporaries, I had the misfortune of having to support myself through college. So I was in need of employment, and I happened upon a job opportunity in the computer research lab at the university, headed by a man named Glen Culler. It is my privilege today to introduce Glen to you. Working for Glen was a remarkable experience. I was in physics and mathematics at the time, and my experiences with Glen basically completely altered my career and switched me into computer science. Glen put in place in that university a rather remarkable system for mathematical and numerical analysis, moving it from an abstraction into a concrete reality, with visual displays of the effects of the mathematical operations that were being studied. He's going to be talking to you today about some of that experience, and his view of what it was like to be a member of the ARPA community and to be doing this fairly specific workstation work. So, with no further ado, let me introduce you to Glen Culler.

Dr. Glen J. Culler has a B.A. in Mathematics from the University of California at Berkeley and a Ph.D. in Mathematics from the University of California at Los Angeles. He has been involved professionally in scientific computation since 1951 at the Lawrence Radiation Laboratory Berkeley; at UCRL, Livermore; at TRW, Ramo-Woolridge, UCLA, and UCSB.

From 1959 to 1969 he was a faculty member of the University of California at Santa Barbara. While on a leave of absence in 1962, he was Assistant Director of the Computer Research Lab at Ramo-Woolridge. In collaboration with Dr. Burton Fried he designed and directed the installation of the first mathematically oriented on-line computer system. A subsequent version of this system was designed for the Bunker Ramo Corp. and is now known as the "Culler-Fried System."

Dr. Culler founded his own company in 1969 where he developed the patent and the design that became the FPS array processor. In 1985 his company's original name, CHI, was changed to Culler Scientific, and the company again pioneered a revolutionary design for scientific computing. This new machine, designed by Dr. Culler, is the first personal supercomputer and is presently a leader in the market of general purpose scientific machines. Dr. Culler is Chief Architect and Chairman of the Board of Culler Scientific.

# Mathematical Laboratories: A New Power for the Physical and Social Sciences

*Glen J. Culler*
Culler Scientific Systems Corporation

[*Editor's Note:* Dr. Culler's earlier published paper was included in the conference proceedings. What follows is an edited version of his presentation.]

I'll tell you about my experience so far, how far we haven't come, and a little bit about what I'd like to see us do in the future. My background was in mathematics. I became an engineer because we had to use computers. My work training was always in the context of physicists trying to solve problems they couldn't solve and trying to find out how to change them into problems that they could solve, and to do so with the finite budget of money and time. The question I asked was "How can you make what you have in your mind simply *get done* so that you can *see* the consequence?" I wanted to make sure that the mechanics followed by the user to obtain results of an experiment were directly related to the user's ideas or concepts about his problem.

Cut and try. How do you do cut and try scientific problem solving? One way is to write a FORTRAN program. But, wait a minute; you had something in mind, but what you had in mind was not related to the thinking needed to write a FORTRAN program. So we had to have a way to take the things you were able to envision in your mind as simple transformations with consequences, and make it possible for you to cause these things to happen; and the happenings had to happen in the short time you were willing to work on it. If I have an idea and a transformation, and I say "do it," and it starts, and it will be done tomorrow after I get through with breakfast, then that doesn't represent the picture of what I want to do. I want to cause it to happen and see the consequence in a time frame that's useful for me to continue working on the problem.

Back in 1961, there was a gentleman by the name of Burt Fried, who is still a physicist at UCLA. Burt wanted to know nothing about the details of computing; he wanted to know everything to do with conveying thoughts about physics and mathematics and solutions. So, he became director of the Ramo-Woolridge Computer Division Research Lab. I agreed to take a leave of absence from the University of California at Santa Barbara to work as his assistant director. Our goal was to try to make computing useful for physicists. Well, that was 1961, and I don't think we've solved the problem yet.

We had an absolutely wonderful grant from the NSF for a summer study to invite physicists to work with us. We all sat together for the summer to talk about what you could do to make computing useful for physicists. Let me see if I can illustrate the problem we studied. A physicist might say, "Ah hah, I've got a problem that I can't solve analytically, so I'll have it computed. I'll give it to people in the computer center who will do some numerical analysis and put together an algorithm, and then write a program, using batch systems, they'll check it out." And three months later, back comes a great computer listing. The physicist is invited into the place to go look at the listing, and he says, "Well, if I had known that it was going to come out like that, I wouldn't have given it to you in the first place. What I really want to solve is . . . " And the problem got changed. And it got changed in such a way that no known variation of all of the computer work will be useful. So the real problem is, how do you get the practitioner of the art to be able to do some quality assurance before you commit immense funds to the project?

We set out to do that. It began by having that summer meeting. The staff that was put together included young people. One of them was a guy named Bob Shreifer, and he became a Nobel laureate. It was just an unbelievable group of young people who were all going to succeed. Most of them would come in groups for one day a week, until we finally ended up with a description of what we wished we had. Basically it was rather like something J. C. R. Licklider described: Suppose you constrain your problem enough to be able to envision some kind of graph, and you have thought enough about what you wish you could see. And further suppose you have some things you can do to control what's going on. Then, when you see what you thought you wanted to see, you'd like to think of the result as a solution to your problem in some sense. But nothing's nearly that simple. So you want to have a graphical, visual way to pursue the solution to your problem. You want to experimentally try variations within the intellectual framework that defines the problem, and you want to sit there and compute until you're happy with the consequence.

Out of the summer design work came a little on-line computer system. The hardware we had to work with was the RW400 ANFSQ27 Polymorphic computer. I will not say that it was the first workstation, although it may have been the first mathematical workstation. But I might say it was probably the "worst-station." It was many millions of dollars worth of equipment. It was not made for this project, or we never could have afforded it and used it. We used the CPU1, that's the wonderful mainframe that has 1024, 26-bit words of core memory in which we programmed everything. (If you can't do it in that amount of space, then you don't want to use this machine.) It would only do I/O operations. We could program it to do I/O operations, and it included a cross bar switch, with a memory that allowed all of the I/O devices to talk to each other at exactly the same time. So that was neat, but there were a bunch of mag tapes that sometimes would run off and go "whoa," and you'd run quick and pull the plug out of the wall. There was a display drum, and the live data coming off that drum refreshed the display analysis console display. Then we had two 8K drums and a big mass memory, and an 80K drum that would hold what we're going to work on.

That system gave us a one user, on-line interactive system. The next year we added a little gadget we built ourselves that gave us a two-user system. The display analysis console was two 12-inch tubes, standing "this" high and about six feet wide. The aluminum material on it and the corner castings and so forth cost twice as much as any of the user stations we would pay for today. It had thirty-two function keys, 24 additional function keys used for variables, and some number keys. The thing that we did was to assign to each function key a mathematical transformation. We labeled the keys to be the functions we were interested in. What should the labels be? You'd like to add and subtract and multiply and divide for sure, but we're not talking about numbers. We're talking about whatever the mathematical object is. So, if you're dealing in two-dimensional arrays, you want to add all the numbers in the two-dimensional arrays together by simply pressing a button. Sine, cosine, log—you need those. But this is not formal mathematics. We're talking about discrete analysis; so, therefore, we need to have something going on about numerical analysis. Right shift and left shift means you take the array and move all the numbers one coordinate position. It's intellectually the same idea as the shift operator for bits, but it's for vector objects. Load, store, display, erase, enter, halt, list, user, dimension (you need to know how many elements you've used), ID, delete, evolve, repeat, 1,2,3,4. I am not going to try to teach you this language that's some twenty years old, although if you did this work today, you wouldn't do it a whole lot differently because, somehow, these functions are basically what you need to have. They're not an invention, they're just in the woodwork.

We took that big 80K drum, and we said that you can have four banks of real vectors and each bank will have "A" to "Z" minus two, because there are only 24. I think "I" and "O" were left out. Then you can have four banks of complex vectors for each of the two users. That's where the user's data lives. Suppose that within bank 1 there's an "A" from the keyboard and, whatever you say, you're referring to that physical object of storage. Sine A would mean exactly that—get that A into the computer, take the sine of every entry in it, and leave that in your accumulator. Very simple. Incidentally, with 1024 words of memory, we had a vector accumulator. Therefore, it was constrained to a hundred or so coordinates. Then we had another vector auxiliary space. We had all of the elementary operations we described, but sine and cosine, which take a little more programming room. The values came out of a buffer where they were stored whenever they were used; when they weren't used, they were waiting there until other values replaced them. So, you could do something several times in a row without having to transfer values around in memory.

The interpreter took all of the keys you had pushed and figured out what to compute. Therefore, if you ask the questions: Why do you want to have a single character for all of your variables? Wouldn't it be neat if you had six characters for your variable name. The answer is: Sure, if you only had a computer to figure out what it meant. With one character you have a direct association; you just go do what you're told. So you can make a tiny interpreter, because it doesn't have to think very hard.

There were a lot of arguments: Can't you make this kind of system with just one keyboard so that you don't have to have two? Should we use single letter variables; and so forth? You sure can; it's a little more button pushing, but only twice as much. But, the fact is that this way everything is absolutely distinct when it gets into the computer so you don't have to fool with what you've got. You can take that number and add it to the base and go branch off somewhere and you're already working, and that was very necessary. In today's world, naturally, you throw that away, and you use a control key in front of any of the others, and it makes no difference. The world is grandly changed.

ARPA funded a project to set up this kind of facility on the Santa Barbara campus, and there was a classroom that had a Tektronix storage tube, with a bunch of stuff put around it, and a keyboard. There were 16 stations of this type back to the RW400 for a little bit and then the 360 model 50 a little bit later. And then it went on up the line and stayed around for about ten years, until it all got replaced by much more adequate things.

Now, if you go back to the RW400 that we started with, with drums supporting it, 60 rotations per second for the drum so you can bring in a subroutine; you can run through and compute the sine, you can put the data somewhere, and you can do that ten times a second. So you're sitting there and you feel like you own that computer all by yourself. When you use a time-sharing system today, to do virtually the same thing, you don't feel that you're getting that much more computing done because of all that is involved to get your turn. From the user's perspective, until you have something that really uses the internal system power, the situation isn't a whole lot better interactively today than it was way back then. Part of that is due to the system, part of it is intrinsic, but a lot of it is the fact that as we go forward and change from displaying a small number of grid points to displaying a large number of grid points, say 2000 by 2000. I've got a million things I want to compute on. I have to get the data available to compute—do those transformations for all of those points, send them out to the display. I'll bet you don't want to do it even over a multi-bus, if you're trying to see that come back at you within a third of a second or something. What keeps happening is that you cannot do what you cannot fund, what people are not ready to use. We could have wanted to do this kind of display, with this kind of computing, and we did want to as long ago as I can remember, and we can't do it at all quite yet. It looks like there's some neat things to do now for the next few years, to take advantage of supercomputing kind of capability, which is barely more than just adequate for what we wanted—full bandwidth video display, the use of colors for visualization, a plasma simulation, 4000 times steps, two million particles, nine hours of computing time doing it, five gigabytes worth of data, and so on.

How do you know what you're computing? You'd like to study it. You don't want to sit there all night and watch it compute. You'd like to say, "We've somehow put the consequence of that calculation down." We'd like to say, "Take a cut through the physical space, show me a picture as a function of time of what it is I've computed, because I might see something that will give me an idea." It's this interactive, dynamic study that I'm still trying to find a way to do. I think it's fine that I might have been some kind of a modest pioneer in this area, but I think it would be wonderful if we just had something we could really use.

Well, I'm not going to hassle this. Take a definition of a bunch of vector operations, period. And you can do each one of those by pressing a key, that's all, just one key. You can answer the question, "Why can't you do what I'm talking about today in C, with the Unix operating system?" You absolutely can. But the things we did to see results in a matter of a one or two-second experience with the computer will take a talented guy, doing what I tell him, ten minutes to show me a graph of, because the Unix system isn't oriented to handling these kinds of little experiments. It can be, but it's not that way yet.

As an illustration of what I want, take a little bit of speech data. It can have, for example, two different forms of display. One form has dots to create a graph. It may need an axis and scaled to fit into a certain area for publication. In the publication, I do not want to show numbers, just graphical characteristics. Scaling is done automatically by the system. I can experiment with the visual quality—say, be changing the dot size so that overlapping curves might be better distinguished. The system should provide a family of little modifiers to alter the characteristics of the displayed data.

Everywhere in such a system the style is: Remember where you are, and do what you wish to change what you've got. Don't make a system that's going to make sure that you didn't make a programming error by checking everything under the sun you do. The world has all come along this way now; the whole Unix operating system thing has a style that feels just like this in terms of where you can stay and where you can go and how it all works. What we want is a little program so that you can push buttons to generate a graph, and put it on the curves so you can see what it looks like. You can run it through, and then decompose something into a set, and so on. Much of this is common on workstations today.

*Anecdote:* How did we get an on-line system to play with? Well, we didn't have any use of the one in the lab as it was on a real project that was being paid for, but everybody that worked at the lab went home at night, so we could use it at night. So we set up this system for solving the BCS (Barting, Cooper, Sheaper) energy gap parameter equation. We wanted to solve it interactively. So, we set up a system for doing that. In this case, we had some choices with some polynomials and coefficients that you could assign. The user could put in a curve with crosshairs and a joystick and whatever, or he could modify it with a family of transformations for that purpose, or he could specify values for coefficients and polynomials. At any stage he could see just what he constructed. This is his ''guess'' test case. Then this goes into an operator, transforms it, and then you look and you can display that, and say, ''Oh my god, that wasn't what I wanted at all.'' Letting it run, going around, sometimes you'd see something would come back, let's say after seven or eight passes when you were just ready to give up, you'd find that you'd say, ''Oh my goodness, that's an old friend, I've seen him before.'' No way, outside of getting in there and experiencing it, could you possibly know that if you just kept mapping that thing for seven times, that you'd almost go around the ring and come back somewhere. But if it was locally linear, adding all of those together and dividing by seven would nearly give you solutions. But, adding six of them together and dividing them by six wouldn't help you at all. You get into a pattern of the kind of processing where you can perceive things that are happening, and then create a very casual program to incorporate the findings in the process and keep working. Therefore, you want to have means for these transformation controls where you can perceive what you did—that's the on-line interacting mass system stuff.

The main paper reporting our work came out of an ACM meeting in 1968 in Washington (Culler, Glen J. ''Mathematical Laboratories: A New Power for the Physical and Social Sciences.'' *Interactive Systems for Experimental Applied Mathematics, Proceedings of an ACM Symposium,* edited by M. Klerer and J. Reinfelds. New York, Academic Press, 1968, pp. 59–72). As part of that, there was an auxiliary meeting where people could talk about these on-line math kind of things. We were there with a console, tied back to Santa Barbara in over the same 201B data set from Western Union that didn't work any better for us than for you, and the RW400 little guy was sitting there waiting for people to push buttons. We had means to watch the display so the audience could see. You could poke a button to watch the transformation. The APL people were there with a console back into IBM. So we spent a lot of time after the meeting saying: "But can you do . . . Oh yes, I can do . . . But, you don't have displays. Well, we can put in displays." It turns out that the inner structure of the two systems were surprisingly stylistically similar, though none of us knew each other at all, and it's all sort of, what you're doing keeps running back into forcing you to have certain ways to do it, so that structures of systems are really heavily depicted by the requirements that are placed on them. It's a little tough to think that within that domain you did anything but respond to the requirements. I thing we're all in that kind of situation.

When I was invited to think about history, I thought a little about it, and I got out the ACM paper, thinking, *I'm going to look back.* I read the first paragraph, and I thought, *My Lord, this has hardly changed.* I would write almost the same things now, except that I'd like to have one more dimension in my objects than I've got, and that requires a hundred times as much computing power (if you think a hundred is a good granulation, or a thousand times, if you think a thousand is), and all of my adult life we've been solving one-dimensional problems well, some two-dimensional ones, and in a few years, we're going to tackle three-dimensional ones, and that had stayed ever since I was in Livermore in 1953. Still, if you want to do interactive computing where you see the results in mathematical transformations, there isn't a supercomputer in the world that can keep up with you—yet. Technology is still developing. But intelligent ways to get information out— that's what this console stuff is about, what these interactive systems are about—we're always forced to live with what we've got and to try to change it a little. There's no way that we've just about got everything done, you know. This whole thing has just started. So, I think we're very early in history, because we haven't had time to get everything done yet.

# Participants Discussion

**Tom Osbourne**

I'm Tom Osbourne. I think Glen is due some credits that he is too shy to take. One credit is that, unlike recognizing a problem but not inventing its solution, Glen did invent some solutions. I know for a fact that one of the patents that he obtained has been extensively licensed. I think that he invented the user-definable keys that we find on many machines today, and I think that a large number of corporations around the country think that too.

Were I an historian in the future looking for a source of information, I think I would go into the patents. By the time a patent has been issued, it has undergone a surprisingly thorough test. Especially when some company decides to pay another company lots of money for a patent, you know the patent has been heavily examined. Glen's patent has survived. And so I'd like to make sure that he gets a feather where it should be.

**Allen Newell**

I don't know whether Glen wants to talk about this, but I would like to hear a little bit about the whole connection between what Glen described and the kind of computing set-up that existed at the Brain Research Institute (BRI). I don't know much about it, but I gather that the BRI had an off-shoot of Glen's kind of systems. I don't know whether you want to do that, Glen, or whether, since Thelma Estrin's still around, she would want to do that.

**Culler**

I can say a word or two. One of the questions I have been asked for very many years is, Why didn't you go commercial? There never was a commercial system like this available, but there have been a fairly large number of private, individual efforts that were cooperatively done where the concept was taken, but then enhanced and made personal and special. The Brain Research Lab did it basically all by themselves, in their own direction, although there was a lot of commonality. There were other cases where, through ARPA and through NSF, we built some consoles and put them at the end of a telephone line. There were ten chemistry departments scattered around. People in those departments were playing with the Culler-Fried system back there in Santa Barbara. Some knew what they were connected to and others did not. There is even such a system now running at CERN, and has been since the 1960s. So there've been a few places where the physicists involved have caused something to happen for their own uses, but it isn't broadly commercialized. We would like to think that if the computers are good enough and the displays are good enough, there may be something worth doing now. I don't know. It's a system and a style that a special guy really falls in love with, and another guy says: "Don't make me have to use that." If you have somebody that really looks at computing in terms of organization and programming, and thinks of mathematics as something you do because you have to, then you really don't need a good floating point arithmetic part of your system; you just do that when you have to, because no way that this is a meaningful thing for him. But, if he can't get enough of it, and he has difficulty seeing through the veil into his problem, then you give him a little opening with our kind of system. Most of the people that support the kind of thing I do don't feel like they're involved in computing, but are just involved in their own research.

**Dennis Arnon**

Could you comment on the relations between your activity and the field which is known as symbolic mathematical computation, computer algebra?

**Culler**

Nothing that I have done directly relates to symbolic computing. Everything I'd like to do in the future wants to use it as one of the clear tools of our whole system. If you think about mathematics for a medical system, you want to take all of the symbolic stuff that you can and use it as a workhorse to help you go from doing what you can analytically and then to computing. So it should be integrated; but it is not. You have both systems available. You'd like to have a heavy number capability as a consequence for the scientific stuff and for the analytic stuff and for the symbolic stuff, but neither of them can do the whole thing living alone because you keep solving problems that are mixed. But these capabilities have not been integrated anywhere, as far as I know. I think that that's a thing that needs to be done.

**Thelma Estrin**

I'd like to comment on Allen Newell's Brain Research Institute (BRI) question. The BRI System comes directly from Glen's systems. Somebody by the name of Dan Brown, who was at TRW then, came to the BRI and built what we called the SLIP system (the Shared Laboratory Interpretive Processor). This was essentially the Culler-Fried system with different keys that were useful to people who were doing experiments in neurophysiology. We had about four systems. At that time I was interested in getting an EEG, which was an analog signal, into the computer. I did that remotely by using the SLIP console to control digitization of analog data, so that it didn't have to be recorded on tape. It was directly sent into an SDS computer we had.

I was looking at some of the old grant requests for renewals from NIH, and it was interesting to see that about 15 people used the BRI system in different ways, for neurophysiology data that was easier for them to access. It was essentially the same problem that you had with the physicists. The neurophysiologists wanted to do something, and the system had to be easy to use. We used this to control some experiments, to test hypotheses, to get some insight while we were working with the data. The limbs sort of died, and other things took over, but I think it was a little picture in time, invaluable until the minicomputer came on the scene.

*Charles Irby*

Having this particular job opportunity when I did was a pretty interesting thing for me. Here I was, 19 years old, but I had some programming experience. I walked into this job, which was to take care of this RW400 computer. This was a very daunting experience. For one thing, Glen failed to mention to you that there was no assembler for that machine—it was all programmed in octal. You had to figure out where every address was and get it right. When the machine crashed, there was not a "boot" button. You had to key in a boot program in octal and get the whole thing to start up again, and you had to do it right. I also acted as an operator for a lot of the remote users we had at 4 A.M. in the morning; that also was quite an experience. As Glen said, the tape drives periodically went totally bananas, and people could lose their entire morning's work.

Glen also failed to mention that in the fall of 1965 we got permission to start the redesign effort to transport the system onto the IBM 360, which was a major undertaking that took several years. At about that time, Glen contracted hepatitis. He ran the entire project from his hospital bed for over a year, and he managed to pull the whole thing off. He was the only one who really understood how this system had to work, and he was able to pull that off. I think that's quite an achievement.

# THE AUGMENTED
# KNOWLEDGE WORKSHOP

## Doug Engelbart
## Introduction by Charles Irby

**W**hen I left Glen's group, I spent a year working for Lytton Industries on the ground control system supporting a precursor to skylab. Then I went to a conference that was being held up in San Francisco. It was the Fall Joint Computer Conference. This particular conference was very, very special for me and for a lot of people because there was an hour and a half session in which Douglas Engelbart from the Augmentation Research Center at SRI in Menlo Park, California, gave a live video demonstration of a highly interactive computer graphics and computer text manipulation system that had been developed at SRI. I went to that particular session not knowing what to expect, and I was completely blown away. I happened to find afterward the particular person who seemed to be in charge technically; his name was Bill English. I cornered him and said, ''This is really nifty and I think I can help you.'' And he said, ''We're looking for a few good men. Why don't you come by?'' The next week I went by and the personnel department said, ''No, we have no openings.'' I said, ''Wrong. I'm going to sit here until Bill English comes to talk to me.'' (I was fairly bold in those days.) And he did. They hired me, and it was the beginning of a seven-year effort on my part at SRI with Doug Engelbart. A great many of the concepts that people now think of as commonplace, like the mouse and multiple windows, editing across windows, integrated text and graphics—all those things originated, from my point of view, from Doug and his group at SRI.

I'd like to introduce Doug Engelbart and his perspective of the last 20 years or so.

Doug Engelbart is a pioneer in the design of modern interactive computer environments. He holds the patent on the mouse; created the first two-dimensional editing system, and was the first to demonstrate such things as the use of remote procedure protocols, mixed text-graphics, and shared screen viewing.

Doug holds a B.S. in EE from Oregon State University and a Ph.D. in Electrical Engineering from the University of California at Berkeley. His career has led him from the U.S. Navy as an electronics technician to NASA's Ames Research Laboratory and then to Stanford Research Institute (now SRI International) where he led the team that designed and built the NLS "Augmented Knowledge Workshop."

From January 1977 to March 1984 Doug was a Senior Scientist at Tymshare, Inc., Cupertino, California. In 1984, Tymshare was acquired by McDonnell Douglas. Doug continues as a Senior Scientist in the Information Systems Group, promoting the type of integrated-system architecture conceived and implemented by him at SRI International.

# The Augmented Knowledge Workshop

*Doug Engelbart*
McDonnell Douglas

## Introduction

The story of my involvement with on-line workstations begins in early 1951 with a vision and a life-time professional commitment. Over 34 years of pursuit have created a lot of personal history, and the object of this historical exercise, the workstation, occupies a unique place in it.

For me, a workstation is the portal into a person's "augmented knowledge workshop"—the place in which he finds the data and tools with which he does his knowledge work, and through which he collaborates with similarly equipped workers. I consider that the large system of concepts, skills, knowledge, and methods on the human side of the workstation has to be taken into account, in a balanced way, when pursuing increased human effectiveness. So, my workstation-history story embraces a rather large sphere.

The task of writing an historical piece is unfamiliar enough to cause me difficulty by itself, but the associated stirring of old records and old memories has added a nearly overwhelming burden of dreams, events, people, stresses, pleasures, disappointments—the firsts and the failures. Now, what from all of this—and how to organize it—will make an appropriate "history" paper? I could provide a solid measure of objective reporting—events and dates. I have been an involved observer of related computer history since 1951. I watched and experienced how the supportive hardware, languages, and architecture evolved; witnessed the people and efforts that brought time-sharing into being; and was even more closely involved with the emergence of computer networks. Through all of this, I was wholly focused on what these things could do for people at workstations. And then there was office automation and personal computers; you don't have to be an old guy to have watched these emerge, but I'm sure they looked different to me than to most.

I could also provide lots of objective reporting about the events and dates associated with the things I have caused or had a direct hand in. There seems to be a lot there that is quite relevant to this "history of the workstation" theme. It was dusty, laborious work, this process of brainstorming for candidates, culling and ordering and trying to describe them in some reasonable sequence and context. But what I came to realize is that there is one, clearly dominant factor that underlies essentially every cause for any uniqueness that I might list for historical record. It isn't a technology, it isn't a science, and it isn't a marketing or business model. And I am going to give it dominant coverage in this paper. It is what I call my "Framework." My Framework is based upon an intuitive conviction, implanted in my head (apparently permanently) over 30 years ago, that the gains in human knowledge-work capability that we will achieve by properly harnessing this new technology will be very large. Metaphorically, I see the augmented organization or institution of the future as changing, not as an organism merely to be a bigger and faster snail, but to achieve such new levels of sensory capability, speed, power, and coordination as to become a new species—a cat.

Based upon this conviction about huge potential gains for mankind, my Framework explains for me generally where such gains are going to come from, and provides strategic principles that can help guide a conscious pursuit of these gains.

## Genesis

I was several years out of school, possessing a B.S. in electrical engineering and two years' experience during World War II (halfway through college) as an electronics technician. I was doing odd-job electrical engineering work at Ames Research Laboratory in Mountain View, California, with the National Advisory Committee for Aeronautics (NACA, forerunner of NASA). For several months I had been devoting most of my spare time to searching for professional goals; for some reason I wanted to invest the rest of my heretofore aimless career toward making the most difference in improving the lot of the human race.

I had initially dashed off in many fanciful directions, but yet managed enough interludes of reasonably sober thinking to build up some useful, strategic generalizations. Retreading myself professionally, to become proficient and then extraordinarily productive in some new field wasn't worth considering without a significantly attractive scenario, embedded in a reasonably structured strategic framework. The high-payoff scenarios all seemed to involve creating or joining something that, however disguised, would essentially be a crusade. Crusades have many strikes against them at the outset. In particular, they don't connect to a normal source of government or business revenue. They don't have nice organizational frameworks. You can't go out on the streets and expect to find financial, production, or marketing vice-presidents interested in the crusade. Moreover, even if you accomplish the sweeping change that is the ultimate objective, chances are that in this very complex world the side effects might be bad enough to make you wish you hadn't tried.

Suddenly, up through all of this delightful, youthful abstraction bobbed the following clear realization: The complexity of the human situation was steadily increasing; not only that, but its rate of increase was increasing. Along with the increasing complexity had come a general increase in the urgency associated with the more critical problems. If one invented a measure for each of these—complexity and urgency—then for a given problem, the product of its complexity times its urgency would represent a fair measure of the difficulty mankind would find in dealing with that problem.

- □ FLASH-1: The difficulty of mankind's problems was increasing at a greater rate than our ability to cope. (We are in trouble.)
- □ FLASH-2: Boosting mankind's ability to deal with complex, urgent problems would be an attractive candidate as an arena in which a young person might try to ''make the most difference.'' (Yes, but there's that question of what does the young electrical engineer do about it? Retread for a role as educator, research psychologist, legislator, . . . ? Is there any handle there that an electrical engineer could . . . ?)
- □ FLASH-3: Ahah—graphic vision surges forth of me sitting at a large CRT console, working in ways that are rapidly evolving in front of my eyes (beginning from memories of the radar-screen consoles I used to service).

The imagery of FLASH-3 evolved within a few days to a general information environment where the basic concept was a document that would include mixed text and graphic portrayals on the CRT. The imagery carried on to extensions of the symbology and methodology that we humans could employ to do our heavy thinking. There were also images of other people at consoles attached to the same computer complex, simultaneously working in a collaboration mode that would be much closer and more effective than we had ever been able to accomplish.

Within weeks I had committed my career to ''augmenting the human intellect.'' In a few months, I left the NACA and enrolled as a graduate student at UC Berkeley, where Professor Paul Morton had started a computer science activity (although it would be many years before universities began calling it that). He was several years along in developing the California Digital Computer (CALDIC).

Within a few years I had to accept the fact that research on any kind of interactive computer applications would not provide me with a program acceptable to the university community for Ph.D. and later faculty pursuit. So, I settled for something else, got my Ph.D., and went to Stanford Research Institute (SRI) where I hoped ultimately to promote support for an augmentation program.

## FRAMEWORK

That was 1957. By 1959 I was lucky enough to get a small grant from the Air Force Office of Scientific Research (AFOSR, from Harold Wooster and Rowena Swanson) that carried me for several years—not enough for my full-time work, but by 1960 SRI began pitching in the difference.

It was remarkably slow and sweaty work. I first tried to find close relevance within established disciplines. For a while I thought that the emergent AI field might provide me with an overlap of mutual interest. But in each case I found that the people I would talk with would immediately translate my admittedly strange (for the times) statements of purpose and possibility into their own discipline's framework. When rephrased and discussed from those other perceptions, the "augmentation" pictures were remarkably pallid and limited compared to the images that were driving me.

For example, I gave a paper in 1960 at the annual meeting of the American Documentation Institute, outlining the probable effects of future personal-support use of computers. I discussed how a focus on personal support would change the role of their future systems and how such a change would enable more effective roles for the documentation and information specialists.[1] I received no response at all at the meeting. One reviewer gave a very ho-hum description of the paper as the discussion of a (yet another) personal retrieval system. Later, during a visit to a high-caliber research outfit, an information-retrieval researcher got very hot under the collar because I wouldn't accept his perception that all that the personal-use augmentation support I was projecting amounted to, pure and simple, was a matter of information retrieval—and why didn't I just join their forefront problem pursuits and stop setting myself apart?

Then I discovered a great little RAND report written by Kennedy and Putt[2] that described my situation marvelously and recommended a solution. Their thesis was that when launching a project of inter- or new-discipline nature, the researcher would encounter consistent problems in approaching people in established disciplines. They wouldn't perceive your formulations and goals as relevant, and they would become disputative on the apparent basis that your positions were contrary to "accepted" knowledge or methods. The trouble, said these authors, was that each established discipline has its own "conceptual framework." The enculturation of young professionals with their discipline's framework begins in their first year of professional school. Without such a framework, tailored for the goals, values, and general environment of the respective discipline, there could be no effective, collaborative work. Furthermore, if such a conceptual framework did not already exist for a new type of research, then before effective research should be attempted, an appropriate, unique framework needs to be created. They called this framework-creation process the "Search Phase."

So, I realized that I had to develop an appropriate conceptual framework for the augmentation pursuit that I was hooked on. That search phase was not only very sweaty, but very lonely. In 1962, I published an SRI report entitled, "Augmenting Human Intellect: A Conceptual Framework."[3] With the considerable help of Rowena Swanson, this was condensed into a chapter of a book published in 1963.[4] I can appreciate that these framework documents appear to many others as unusably general and vague. But, for me, the concepts, principles, and strategies embodied in that framework look better and better every year. The genesis of most of what was and is unique about the products of the augmentation work can be traced back to this framework, which I'll return to later with a fuller description.

## PROGRAM SUPPORT

I submitted many proposals before getting support to pursue the augmentation program outlined in the Framework report. Among the stream of politely phrased regrets, there was one that, in contrast to today's environment, can provide useful perspective on the environment of 1961. Four high-quality civilian experts had been enlisted by one agency as a site-visit team—a brain researcher, a psychologist, and a computer expert—and for me it was a very enjoyable day's dialog. But the subsequent letter from the agency informed me regretfully that (paraphrased) " . . . since your interesting research would require exceptionally advanced programming support, and since your Palo Alto area is so far from the centers of computer expertise, we don't think that you could staff your project adequately. . . . "

When J. C. R. Licklider ("Lick") came from Cambridge to take over ARPA's newly formed Information Processing Techniques Office (IPTO) in late 1962, I was figuratively standing at the door with the "Conceptual Framework" report and a proposal. There the unlucky fellow was, having advertised that "man-computer symbiosis," computer time-sharing, and man-computer interfaces were the new directions. How could he in reasonable consistency turn this down, even if it was way out there in Menlo Park?

Lick moved very swiftly. By early 1963 we had a funded project. But, whereas I had proposed using a local computer and building an interactive workstation, Lick asked us instead to connect a display to the System Development Corporation's (SDC's) AN/FSQ32 computer, on site in Santa Monica, to do our experimenting under the Q32's projected new time-sharing system. (Converting the Q32 to be a time-shared machine was SDC's IPTO project.)

Later that year, our project was modified to include an online data link from Menlo Park to Santa Monica, with a CDC 160A minicomputer at our end for a communication manager, supporting our small-display workstation. For various reasons, not uncommon in pioneering ventures, that first year was very unproductive relative to the purposes and plan of our project. Lick was willing to put some more support into the direct goal (more or less as originally proposed), but the support level he could offer wasn't enough to pay for both a small research staff and some interactive computer support. Mind you, the CDC 160A, which was the only commercially suitable minicomputer that we knew of, even though having only 8K of 12-bit words, and running at about 6 microseconds per instruction, cost well over $100,000 (1963 dollars). It had paper tape in and out; if the system crashed, you had to load the application program from paper tape, and the most recent dump of your working file (paper tape), before you could continue. A crude, industry-standard Flexowriter (online typewriter) could be driven; otherwise it was paper tape in and out.

What saved my program from extinction then was the arrival of an out-of-the-blue support offer from Bob Taylor, who at that time was a psychologist working at NASA headquarters. I had visited him months before, leaving copies of the Framework report and our proposal. I had been unaware that meanwhile he had been seeking funds and a contracting channel to provide some support. The combined ARPA and NASA support enabled us to equip ourselves and begin developing Version 1 of what evolved into the NLS and AUGMENT systems. Paul Fuhrmeister, and later Eugene Gribble of NASA's Langley Research Center, had to stick out their necks as successive heads of Langley's large computational division to support the direction and supervise NASA's support for our program, which continued several years after Taylor left NASA to join ARPA's IPTO office.

Our ARPA support grew and was fostered by Lick's successors—Ivan Sutherland, Bob Taylor, and Larry Roberts. Meanwhile, the Air Force's Rome Air Development Center, at Rome, New York, began to supply supporting funds. By 1967, it was recognized that the respective contributions from ARPA, NASA, and RADC represented significant parts of a coordinated program. The other agencies began funneling their funds through RADC, which served for many years to both monitor and manage our contracts, as well as provide their own significant share of support funds. John McNamara and Duane Stone provided strong support and contract liaison from RADC.

NASA support ended by 1969, and ARPA and RADC provided

significant support until 1977, although from 1974 the funding became even more for supporting applications and developments for other organizations, for targets formulated by others (e.g., the National Software Works). The continuing pursuit of augmentation along my strategic vector virtually stopped.

## The Augmentation Research Center (ARC)

An historically important organizational cluster emerged at Stanford Research Institute in the 1960s, peaked about 1974, and was scattered in 1977—with a small core carrying forth in a commercial (and then industrial) environment to the present. It grew by ones and twos from 1963, as it collected ''permanent'' members from the SRI technical staff, and recruited new ones from the outside. By 1969 I believe we were about 18 strong; this grew steadily until by 1976 we totalled about 45. In 1973 we made two explicit subgroups, one headed by Dick Watson doing development of software (and some hardware), and one headed by Jim Norton handling operations and applications support.

SRI was organized by divisions, each containing a group of laboratories, the hierarchy being formed according to the associated disciplines. ARC grew to laboratory size and status, but it became something of a problem for SRI. Other laboratories (at least in science and engineering) operated more or less as a ''farmers' market,'' where small and changing clusters of researchers promoted and conducted research projects as a loose federation. The management structure, budgeting, accounting, and financing for the Institute had evolved to support this kind of business. But ARC was driven by a coherent, long-term pursuit. This involved the continuing evolution of an ever-larger and more sophisticated system of hardware and software. It also came to involve delivering solid support service to outside clients to provide meaningful environments for learning about the all-important process of coevolution between the human-system and tool-system components of our organizations (as per my conceptual framework).

It didn't seem unreasonable to me to pursue this course; things similar and on a grander scale are common for other researchers. It is taken for granted, for example, that funding agencies will build and operate accelerators and observatories in support of research in nuclear physics and astronomy, or will outfit ships and airplanes to support research expeditions. But whatever my perception, there were some significant problems and stresses with which our over-all environment didn't have effective ways to cope. In the particular dynamics involved, there were probably seven relevant parties: me, the ARC staff, other SRI researchers, SRI management and administration, ARC's sponsors, ARC's utility-service clients, and other groups of researchers outside of SRI. It would be an interesting historical study to try to understand the diversity of perception that must have existed among this set of players. What did the different parties perceive for the future of workstations, for the range of function and application that would come about, for the systems architectures and standards that must emerge, and for the impact on the organizations that learned how to harness these most successfully?

Even as a central party in what happened, I've not understood the dynamics. But I am pretty sure that disparities among the perceptions of all of the above parties had a major part in what to me was the ''great collapse of SRI-ARC.'' Even if I had done everything right over the years (a laughable hypothesis), it is now fairly clear to me that it isn't the market's fault if someone fails in trying to sell it something that the market isn't ready for. In other words, I can't blame those other groups. (Which of course makes for a personal problem, since during those times of black discouragement when one wants desperately to blame someone, there is only one candidate—that guy at the head of the list.)

In 1977, SRI judged it better to move our large-system development and external-service activities out from the research institute environment and into a suitable commercial environment. They advertised, entertained prospective bidders, made a selection, and negotiated a transfer of the business to Tymshare, Inc., of Cupertino, California. The system was renamed AUGMENT and marketed as part of Tymshare's integrated Office Automation services. In 1984, McDonnell Douglas Corporation acquired Tymshare, and the small AUGMENT business is now operated as the Augmentation Systems Division of the Computer Systems Company within the MDC Information Systems Group.

### SOME OF ARC'S EARLY PRODUCTS—1964 TO 1968

Let's take a look at some of the actual experiments we tried during the years from 1964 to 1968 at SRI. Around 1964 we got off the CDC-160A system, which in fact we were using as a personal system. This was our first, real, stand-alone machine.

### Screen Selection Tests and the Mouse

In those days the cost of getting display systems to work was very high. My strategic plan under the above-mentioned framework was to skip the then-prevalent, interactive typewriters and focus from the outset on displays. My assumption was that there is a great deal to learn about how to harness highly interactive display capability, and by the time we really learned how, the prices would be down considerably.

We wanted to start early experimenting with screen selection. The idea of working and interacting very actively with the display meant that we had to tell the computer what we were looking at, so we needed a screen selection device. There was a lot of argument about light pens and tracking balls in those days, but none of those arguments served our needs very directly. I wanted to find the best thing that would serve us in the context in which we wanted to work—text and structured items and interactive commands.

The context was important. So we set up computer-controlled experiments oriented to our working mode, where we assumed that purposeful knowledge workers would be spending a significant portion of their time writing, studying, analyzing, and even debugging. We collected a set of candidate screen-selection devices to test. We did our experiments with our one workstation of that period, which is shown in Fig. 1, together with one of our test devices. In trying to be complete about the array of test devices, I dug up some old notes of mine describing a possibility that eventually turned into the very first mouse (Fig. 2). The tests were carefully run, and we even integrated selection errors and their correction penalties in evaluating the ''goodness'' of a device. The experiments and their results were fully reported,[5] and later described in a paper.[6] The graph in Fig. 3 is representative of our results.

The mouse consistently beat out the other devices for fast, accurate screen selection in our working context. For some months we left the other devices attached to the workstation so that a user could use the device of his choice, but when it became clear that everyone chose to use the mouse, we abandoned the other devices.

**FIGURE 1**
CDC3100 workstation at which we experimented with selection devices.

**FIGURE 2**
Bottom of wooden
"mouse," one of the
first selection
devices.

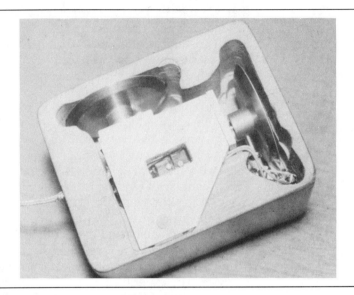

No one is quite sure why it got named a "mouse," or who first started using that name. None of us would have thought that the name would have stayed with it out into the world, but the thing that none of us would have believed either was how long it would take for it to find its way out there.

We also experimented with a way to move your knee up and down or swing it sideways to move the cursor, so you could keep your hands on the keyboard (Fig. 4). I also built something that allowed one to control the cursor movement by rotating your head for sideways cursor control, or nodding your head up or down for vertical cursor control. This "nose-pointing control" of the cursor left both hands free

**FIGURE 3**
Cursor-select test
graph comparing
various selection
devices.

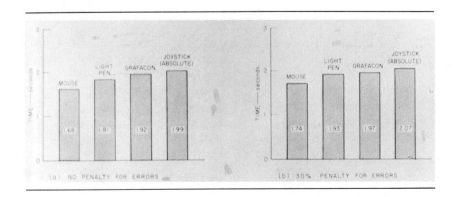

**FIGURE 4**
An experimental
knee control device.

to operate the keyboard. In each case, some muscles would cramp up. Really, in almost any of these cases, you can get used to things like that. I'm sure there are a lot of things to explore in the future about what is going to work best for interfacing, so that you can tell the computer to which objects on the screen you want to direct its attention. However, we had many things to do, so it was a diminishing return for us to pursue these alternative devices—we stayed with the mouse. I have always assumed, though, that something better than the mouse is likely to emerge once the user market becomes more adventurous in exploring the means to higher performance.

## OUR MULTI-USER COMPUTER AND DISPLAY SYSTEM, CIRCA 1968

The first time-sharing system we got was an SDS940. We considered a number of alternative ways to provide ourselves with a flexible, responsive display system, and finally designed our own. The computer and display drivers time-shared their attention among multiple, 5-inch CRTs, which happened to be the most economical size for a given percentage of screen resolution. In front of each CRT we added a commercial, high-quality video camera, mounted with a light shroud over the camera lens and CRT screen (Fig. 5). The resulting video signal, amplified and piped out to our laboratory, drove the video monitors that were our workstation displays. Two display generators, each driving up to eight CRTs, implemented with vacuum-tube technology were both bulky (Fig. 6) and very costly. It took one and a half people to keep those things running all of the time. The stroke-generated characters and vector graphics allowed us to have flexible, mixed text and

FIGURE 5
Our early computer
set up with 5-inch
CRTs.

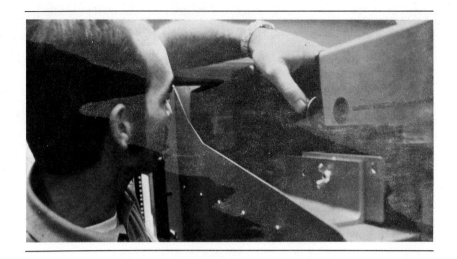

graphic document presentations. The display generators were driven
from a direct-memory-access channel that provided very fast (i.e., one
refresh-cycle time) creation of a new display image. Figure 7 is a picture
of one of our workstations—the TV monitor, with a little wooden table
we made and a keyboard and a mouse and a keyset.

   We explicitly designed for a detached keyboard. My workstation-
design philosophy was to fix it so what you are looking at is positioned
for best viewing, and the devices you use to control the computer
should be located where it is best for you to operate them. Don't get
caught in the anachronism that because we got used to paper and pencil and that technology, we ought to be able to have our controls right

FIGURE 6
The Augmentation
Project display
system.

**FIGURE 7**
Basic workstation:
table with keyset,
detached keyboard,
mouse, and a
separate monitor.

on the surface of the thing that we're working on. It may end up that that way is best, but don't make an a priori assumption. So we didn't.

One way of explaining to somebody why it could make a significant difference if you can do things faster, is to provide a counter example. So, I had them write with a brick taped to their pencil (Fig. 8), because it's only a matter of happenstance that the scale of our body

**FIGURE 8**
Brick ''writing''
device.

and our tools and such lets us write as fast as we can. What if it were slow and tedious to write? A person doesn't have to work that way very long before starting to realize that our academic work, our books—a great deal would change in our world if that's how hard it had been to write.

What if you speed it up? The keyset shown in Fig. 9, in combination with the mouse, provides a two-handed, higher-speed option. When you strike a chord, the computer interprets it as a character— not really distinguishing between characters generated by keyset or keyboard. Our chord-character code (a binary counting scheme mapped to the alphabet) is not really very difficult, my six-year old kids took less than a week to learn it. At SRI, we had a project in the early 1960s to experiment with computer-aided, psycho-motor skill training, and we used this keyset skill for the very first thing to be learned. The experiment blew up because everybody learned it so fast we couldn't differentiate between those who did and those who didn't have special computer aids.

Figure 10 is sort of the picture that I think about when I'm told that we've got to make it easy to learn. Tricycles are "easy to learn and natural to use"—no hard balancing problems. How much is it worth to you to extend your mobility? A few hours of learning to balance on two wheels?

By 1968 I had a workstation like the one in Fig. 11 in my office, and I just started "living" on it. In our lab we had six to ten more, time-shared among our group. The whole feeling was great. It was a very, very interesting sort of activity in those days. Who says we didn't do workstation research? This one, our "Yoga Workstation" (Fig. 12 with Bill Duval), got to be one of the favorites for some reason. This is what you saw all the time—people sitting there in their two-handed working mode, occasionally switching to type on a keyboard.

Figure 13 shows Bill English with a workstation made for us by the Herman Miller office furniture company, who were trying to experiment with us. This little console swivelled on one of the chairs and

**FIGURE 9**
Keyset input device.

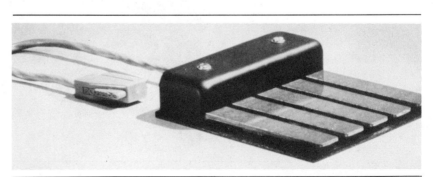

**FIGURE 10**
Trike/Bike.

went where you went; you could lean back and work with it very nicely. I wanted to show this workstation and Bill English, who deserves an immense amount of credit for getting things to work. I waved my hands and pointed, and somehow didn't make much progress. But Bill really made things work in those days, so I owe him a lot.

**FIGURE 11**
Doug's office workstation replicated 6–10 times in the lab.

**FIGURE 12**
Yoga workstation—
Bill Duval is pictured
here.

## OUR "BIG SHOW"—THE 1968 FALL JOINT COMPUTER CONFERENCE

By 1968 we had a marvelous system. We called it "NLS" (later "AUG-MENT"). "NLS" stood for "online system," in contrast to "offline system," which we dubbed "FLS" just to have different acronyms. A few people would come and visit us, but we didn't seem to be getting the type of general interest that I expected. I was looking for a better way to show people, so we took an immense risk and applied for a special session at the ACM/IEEE–CS Fall Joint Computer Conference in San Francisco in December 1968.

We set up to give an online presentation using a video projector pointing at a 20-foot screen. Brooks Hall is a large auditorium, and that

**FIGURE 13**
Bill English at our
Herman Miller
designed
workstation.

video projector could put up our display images so you could read them easily from up in the balcony (Fig. 14). The video projector we rented (built by a Swiss company, Eidophor) used a high-intensity projection lamp whose light was modulated by a thin film of oil, which in turn was modulated by the video signal. On the right side of the stage, I sat at our Herman Miller console. We set up a folding screen as a back drop behind me. I saw the same image on my workstation screen there as was projected for the audience to see.

We built special electronics that picked up the control inputs from my mouse, keyset, and keyboard and piped them down to SRI over a telephone hookup. We leased two microwave lines up from our laboratory in SRI, roughly 30 miles. It took two additional antennas on the roof at SRI, four more on a truck up on Skyline Boulevard, and two on the roof of the conference center. It cost money—running that video projector, and getting people to help us do all of that, cost money; making the special I/O cost money; and leveraging special remote-presentation technology on top of our advanced, developmental laboratory technology created extra risk—and I was using research money. The nice people at ARPA and NASA, who were funding us, effectively had to say, ''Don't tell me!'' because if this had flopped, we would have gotten in trouble. But anyway, it worked, and the main reason was because of Bill English's genius for making things work.

Back in our lab, we dismantled a number of the display units in our display system, so that we could use the cameras in San Francisco and SRI. We borrowed a few tripods and got some extra people to be

**FIGURE 14**
Auditorium of the ACM/IEEE-CS Fall Joint Computer Conference, December 1968.

camera people. One of our friends, Stuart Brand, who was at that time working on his first *Whole Earth Catalog,* helped as well. So it was really a group project; there were about 17 of us.

On my console on the stage, there was a camera mounted that caught my face. Another camera, mounted overhead, looked down on the workstation controls. In the back of the room, Bill English controlled use of these two video signals as well as the two video signals coming up from SRI that could bring either camera or computer video. Bill could select any of these four video images with optional mixing and frame splitting. We had an intercom that allowed him to direct the action of the people in our lab at SRI who were generating computer images or handling the cameras sending the video up from SRI.

We didn't use any specially made system capabilities; we were just using NLS the way it worked at that time. It had mixed text and graphics, so we could use those to display and represent things. We had the agenda in NLS, and we could run different parts and show diagrams; we could do things as examples. So it was a mix of things of: here's the script and stuff to tell you about, and here's the way it runs; we could also bring other display screens or faces, from our SRI lab, in and out on the screen. At that time we firmly imagined that this was the way future conferences would be run.

We could do screen splitting. Figure 15 shows the agenda list with a little marker to show that I'm between two particular items. In Fig. 16, I make a temporary (shopping) list. This was the beginning of our demonstrating ways of structuring ideas. The NLS system supported the user in getting the list organized into categories.

We wanted to show how the mouse works. The projected video showed Don Andrews controlling a cursor from our SRI laboratory by

**FIGURE 15**
Still frame from the FJCC '68. Split screen with Doug on the right and demo agenda on the left.

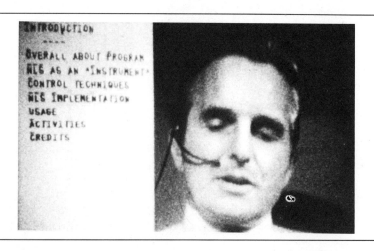

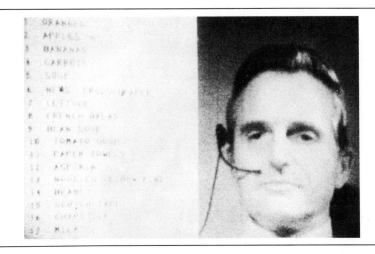

**FIGURE 16**
The text is now an unstructured shopping list.

moving his mouse around. The superimposed video image of the display screen showed that the cursor would follow it exactly to show how the wheels worked. Remember, this was 1968—the first public appearance of a mouse. I could also show how the simultaneous use of mouse and keyset worked in such a way that the audience could watch my hands in the lower window and see the computer action in the upper window.

Then we brought in Jeff Rulifson to tell about how the software works (Fig. 17). At the same time, his face could be brought in and out

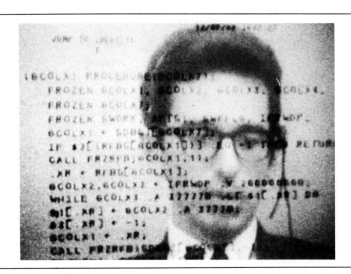

**FIGURE 17**
Jeff Rulifson can be seen on the screen mixed in behind code of a procedure.

behind the display image that he was working with, demonstrating NLS's power for working with very explicitly structured software. He showed graphical diagrams that were embedded in the source-code documentation. During Jeff's presentation, Bill English brought the picture from a laboratory camera that caught the view (Fig. 18) of Jeff's keyset operation as he was manipulating his demonstration images—unconscious and unhurried—a nice way to show the fluid speed offered by combined mouse and keyset use.

Toward the end, we also showed that we could cut a ''hole'' in the screen and see Bill Paxton's face from SRI (Fig. 19). For the computer-display part of the screen, we could switch back and forth between his work and mine; and we could also switch which of us was controlling all of this.

The associated FJCC publication about NLS[7] and other relevant references are listed at the end of this paper.

[*Editor's Note:* Engelbart's colleagues—Bill English, Charles Irby, Jeff Rulifson, Bill Duval, and Bill Paxton—all found themselves at Xerox PARC in the 1970s, creating a personal workstation that embodied these ideas.]

### NLS ENHANCEMENTS—INTO THE MID-1970s

You can't imagine the relief when it worked. It went on for 90 minutes, and afterward we thought for sure that the world would be talking about everybody starting to augment now. Well, it didn't happen, but we went ahead anyway. I want to discuss a few of the things we did

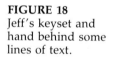

**FIGURE 18**
Jeff's keyset and hand behind some lines of text.

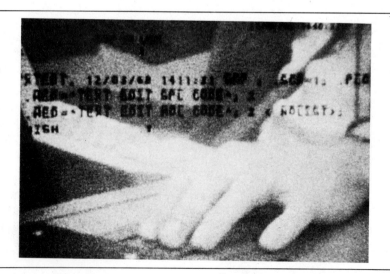

**FIGURE 19**
View of text retrieval
with image of Bill
Paxton in
background.

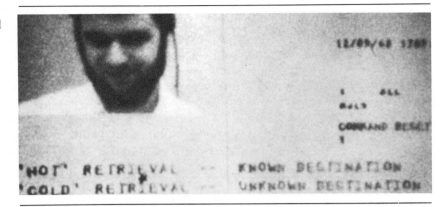

physically to the system after that, and then go into some of the conceptual framework.

### 1969

- □ We began design of windowing capability for NLS.
- □ We developed concept of a user "reaching through" his personal work place (i.e., his familiar online working files and application programs) to access less basic, specialized data and application processes (and other people); that is, the "reach through" should provide access to these, translated by the integrated support system, so as to appear as coherent parts of his familiar, personal work place.
- □ We specified our first mail and "Journal" system as part of an explicit pursuit of a "Dialog Support System," planning for it to be part of our ARPANET-NIC service.
- □ We developed document-outputting capability processing our composite, text-graphic document files to drive a service-bureau, CRT-based, full-page, Stromberg-Carlson photo printer to produce documentation with graphics and text mixed on the same pages.
- □ We became the second host on the ARPANET with our SDS 940. (UCLA was first, UCSB next, then the University of Utah, then. . . .)

### 1970[8]

- □ Detailed use of NLS began for internal management processes of ARC: cost records, working forecasts, purchase requisitions, and so on.

□ We began using the ARPANET to facilitate our reprogramming of NLS for the forthcoming PDP-10 TENEX. The University of Utah had a TENEX on the network, and we used NLS on the 940 to write our new PDP-10 code; using our tree-meta compiler, we developed a cross-compiler for our 940 that produced PDP-10 relocatable binary code. We would ship that over the net for loading and debugging on Utah's TENEX. When the two computers and the intervening network link were all working properly (lots of "flat tires" as in the early days of automobiles), our programmers would do all of this back and forth transitioning "through" the same workstation. I think that it was not only a record-making way of working, but the NLS transport task was accomplished in remarkably short time (we attributed part of the efficiency to the network, and part to the use of NLS).

□ We brought NLS up on the PDP-10 TENEX with improved and new features (including multiple windows). The transfer process, and a detailed description of the design changes and new features for NLS are described in a June 1971 technical report.[9]

□ We began using our Mail/Journal system within our group. Integrated into NLS, this assumed that a mail item was a document—so any part of all of an NLS document could be sent—and provided for a permanent record in explicitly retrievable form (our Journal). As an electronic-mail system, this was quite advanced. It had a directory service (our Ident System) to provide mail-relevant information about registered users; mail distribution was addressed by people's Idents, with no need to know or specify which host they used. Fields were provided for superceding other items, and for attaching keywords. An on-line index was provided for stored items.[10]

### 1972

□ We began developing our first, integrated Help system.

□ We formulated the "AKW Architecture," implemented in stages.[11]

□ We implemented the "shared-screen," televiewing mode of on-line collaboration between two or more NLS users.[12]

### 1973

□ We brought up a table subsystem in NLS.

□ We designed our first, totally modular user interface system, as later described in the *OAC '82 Digest*,[13] and got it running on a PDP-11 that talked to our TENEX through the network, via our procedure call protocol.

- We developed our line processor, as described by Don Andrews.[14] It incorporated Intel's first microprocessor (the 4004) in a special box that was inserted in the communication line between a dumb display terminal and a modem. This made use of our virtual terminal protocols, and managed a multi-window, two-dimensional screen using off-the-shelf, "dumb" display terminals. Our mouse and keyset input devices were plugged into the line processor, which appropriately translated their actions to control cursor position and special communications to the host. A printer port on the line-processor provided local printout service; a special communication protocol allowed the host to send printer packets mixed in with display-support packets.

- We finalized specification for our network virtual terminal, something that has become a key part of our architecture. The objective, on the one hand, was to free the application programmers from worrying about the special features of different workstations, and on the other hand, to enable more flexible evolution by users of workstations they may adopt to fit particular needs. As part of this, there was a terminal-independent display manipulation protocol for communication from application program to terminal, and an application independent input protocol for communicating from terminal to application program.

- We generalized the file structure of our document files to provide for generalized property structures associated with each addressable object, intended to accommodate composite integration of such as graphics, digitized speech, scan-coded images, or any other arbitrary data form.

**1974**

- We gave up our high-performance, local display system for the line-processor supported, remote display system—to make ourselves live with the same remote services as our NIC clients and Utility customers. (On principle, we gave up our integrated, direct-view graphics and the fast response of our direct-memory-access, local display generator.)

- We opened our "Workshop Utility Service." Delivering NLS service over the ARPANET to DOD customers as pilot applications of office information service. We had gone out on bid for commercial time-sharing services, selected Tymshare Inc. of Cupertino, Calif.; their host, named Office-1, provided the computer service. We fielded special trainers and application development staffs and cultivated special customer representatives into a spirited community.

**1975**

□ We implemented our new, integrated graphics system, which could support remote display and manipulation of illustrative graphics on a Tektronix 4014 storage-tube display plugged into the line-processor's printer port. Figure 20 shows the graphic-station setup used for development in our lab. Bob Belleville, to the right in the picture, developed this "new" graphics software. (He subsequently went to Xerox and helped them with the Star hardware, and then was the project manager for the Apple MacIntosh.)

In 1973 we had generalized our file structure with provision for attribute-value property structures associated with each hierarchic node. We could then embed arbitrary data objects in our documents. The first utilization was to reinstate embedded graphics, extending our hierarchical list structure and its pointers to the text objects with, for example, an associated pointer on one of the text objects to a graphic substructure for the associated illustration. The user's concept would be shown in an associated "document-page" image. We assumed that soon we would be using digitized speech strings and executable object code as part of our composite documents. And some day, when storage would be cheaper, we would even be embedding scanned images.

An illustration produced as a plotter-driver file by any other graphics system could be picked up and attached to a specified location in an NLS document, and could be subsequently viewed and modified

**FIGURE 20**
Bob Belleville at Tek graphic workstation.

with the NLS Graphics Subsystem. Figure 21 shows two such "in-gested" illustrations, as viewed in two adjacent NLS graphic win-dows. Our use was oriented toward "illustrative graphics," and we had a reasonably complete set of capabilities for construction and ma-nipulation.[15]

By this time, we had a well-developed Output Processor (our "document compiler"), which acted upon a large vocabulary of embedded-text directives to provide font selection, columnation, run-ning headers and footers, and much more.[16] In conjunction with the Graphics Subsystem, the Output Processor was enhanced so that a user could direct that a properly scaled image of any graphic illustra-tion be located appropriately within a multi-font page layout.

All this was available by 1975–1976. But the problem at the time was that for somebody to use this, they would have to buy a $10,000 or $15,000 storage tube terminal to go with the line processor and text terminal. We couldn't get past this business of "if they don't have it, they don't know they need it; and if they don't know they need it, they don't want to buy it." It was a little difficult at the time, so the graphics sort of atrophied until recently.

The whole approach was that our files were document oriented—documents in a very general sense. These are what contain the descrip-

**FIGURE 21**
Tek view of mixed text-graphic, two-column page, produced with NLS.

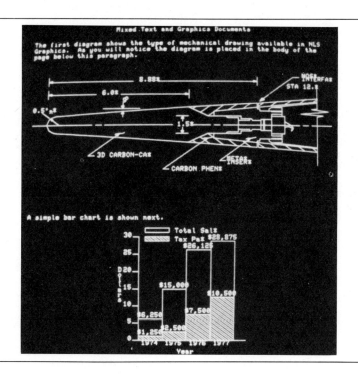

tions, arguments, proposals, whatever, the things you're trying to map your thoughts and arguments into to form a communication.

Another thing we did, though, in 1967, was to help people collaborate in face-to-face meetings. Here again, Bill English whipped it all together very fast—special small narrow tables that you could work around and sit at in a conference meeting, where the monitors were down low enough so you could see over them and see each other well. Each monitor had the same image that was brought from our one-user 3100 at the time, but we had one workstation and some mice. Anybody who wanted to pick up a mouse and push the button could, and this would activate a large, special cursor that could be controlled and moved around, so any participant could point out things on the common display. We had a review meeting among our sponsors at the time. The picture (Fig. 22) shows Bill English, Don Andrews, Dave Hopper, and Barry Wesler, who was Bob Taylor's assistant. Bob was in attendance at the time, too, participating in this conference.

Another thing we did by 1970 was to bring up our electronic mail system as part of our collaboration. There was really a very sophisticated mail system with user identification, catalogs, and all sorts of fields that you could use to send and answer things. One extra feature was that you could send whole documents; it didn't matter whether it was a little one sentence note or a whole document.

A document could go in and be catalogued into a system called the "Journal," which was similar to the idea of pasting it down on a table (Fig. 23). We had linkages and internal addressability, so an embedded link in one document could directly cite an arbitrary pas-

**FIGURE 22**
1967 multi-CRT conference room. Seated are Don Andrews, Dave Hopper, Bill English, Doug, and Barry Wexler.

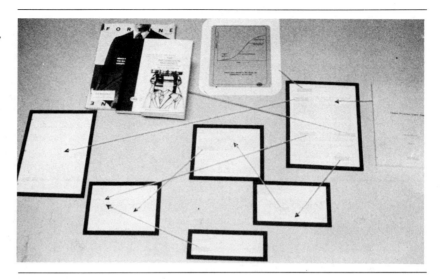

sage in any other. Successive documents could be entered in the system and easily be cross-referenced back to each other. This supported what we called our "recorded dialog"—an important part that we assumed was needed for a community of people to work together effectively. It is an extremely powerful capability.

We originally designed our Mail/Journal system to give the user a choice as to whether to make an entry unrecorded (as in current mail systems), or to be recorded in the Journal. I knew that there would be lots of question, and some quandry, associated with the question "to record or not to record." I assumed that many fewer items would be recorded than "should be"—as might be judged after we someday would learn the value and establish criteria for recording. So, I ordained that *all* entries would be recorded—no option. It put some people under considerable strain. I think that one person actually never could bring himself to enter a memo into the Journal—the idea that it was "forever" stopped him cold. Another person, a very valuable contributor, somehow felt violently opposed to the basic concept, and it possibly hastened his departure. But after a year or so, it was used as a matter of course by essentially everyone. There were interesting and unexpected payoffs.

Up until about 1975, we made a practice of printing out every one of the stored documents—mostly as an alternate analytic process to watch the dynamics of Journal use. The documents are stored by number, in binders as shown in Fig. 24. This indicates how big our Journal collection got in about four or five years. The number now for that particular journal is well over 100,000 items. We have an arbitrary

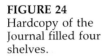

**FIGURE 24**
Hardcopy of the
Journal filled four
shelves.

number of other journal systems that customer groups can install and administer themselves, a very powerful potential archive for collaborative work.

### FRAMEWORK—TO 1968 NLS

Let's now shift back to the conceptual framework, originally documented in a 1962 paper.[17] I had this immensely intuitive feeling that humans were going to be able to derive a great deal of capability from computer systems. I had very real images in my mind of sitting at a display console, interacting with a computer, seeing all sorts of strange symbology coming up that we could invent and develop to facilitate our thinking. We would no longer be limited to working with paper and other such laborious means. Other people could be sitting at similar consoles tied to their machine and we could be collaborating in brand new, exciting ways. We could be doing all sorts of things to control a computer.

At that time, even though I didn't know how the innards of a computer worked, I had enough engineering background to know that if a computer could read a card, it could sense keys and any other action I might want to do. If it could drive a printer or card punch, it could put whatever I wanted onto a display. What I didn't understand at the time was the economics and all that, but I said, "Look, I've got a whole career ahead of me, let's go after all of this."

By 1959 or so, I got a chance to sit down and say, "How would that really work? What are the basics?" As an engineer, I ended up with a simplifying model (Fig. 25). Here's a human wanting to do this

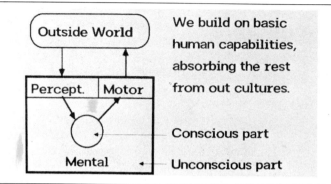

We build on basic human capabilities, absorbing the rest from out cultures.

Conscious part

Unconscious part

knowledge work; he's got capabilities within his skin that we can make use of, a lot of mental capabilities we know of, and some of it he's even conscious of. Those are marvelous machines there—motor machinery to actuate things in the outside world, and sensor and perceptual machinery to get the idea of what's going on. And that's what he has to support his interaction with the outside world.

How can we improve the human's capability (Fig. 26)? Well, it turns out that there have been a lot of people working on this problem for many generations. And we've got a whole "culture-full" of things that we are indoctrinated and trained into, both conscious things and unconscious things. We have lots of skills, motorwise and perception wise, that we're not even aware of. For example, just how long do you think it took to learn to brush your teeth? It takes quite a while; it's a skill. These sensory-motor things all developed in order to help us interact with the layers of other things that our culture provides.

Many such things are available to us, tools and methods that let us live within a social structure and be effective in our interactions.

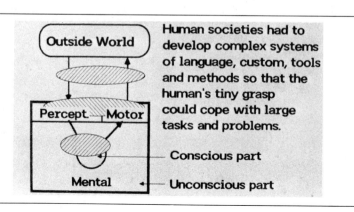

Human societies had to develop complex systems of language, custom, tools and methods so that the human's tiny grasp could cope with large tasks and problems.

Conscious part

Unconscious part

And there's a whole subset of tools and methods that help us be effective in dealing with knowledge work. So take all those things together and call them an "augmentation system" (Fig. 27). That's what augments humans. And for good, practical purposes, let's divide the system into two parts. One part has all the technology in it and the other has all the rest. So I called these the "tool system" and "human system."

The *human system* includes training, knowledge, and skills that have to be installed as well as language, an extremely important invention that transcends, as an invention, anything else we have come up with. The methods, and all that we use to knit together all the little steps that we take during a day, are extremely important. Our customs for working, our procedures, the way our organizations are run, they're all done so that humans can realize effective results. Within this framework, any given capability that a human has is really a composite. The human capability is made up of the use of a lot of things and skills and training and conditioning, in addition to all the customs we just accept and the language that we've learned. It's this composite that we need to find ways to accentuate.

So along comes a lot of new technology for our tool system, which is great. But the technology side, by itself, is not sufficient. Our real capabilities are essentially hierarchical (Fig. 28). We learn a lot of lower-order capabilities, like writing and typing and reading. And we have built up many higher capabilities on top of these. So, if we bring in some new technology, like a longer lasting pen, it's going to make a little bit of effect. But if we bring in the kind of digital technology that was predictable, even in 1960, then potential changes throughout the whole system, affecting significantly the entire capability hierarchy, can begin to take place.

**FIGURE 27**
It is important to treat it as a two-part augmentation system; one part technology, the other the rest.

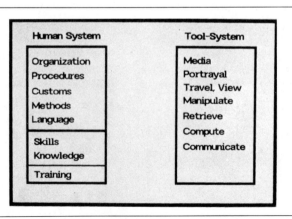

**FIGURE 28**
Capabilities grow
hierarchically.

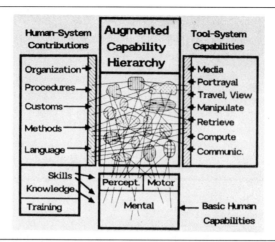

It takes a long time (generations) to discover and implement all of the fruitful changes in the human system made possible by a given, radical improvement in technology. Where, as is the situation now, technology improves by rapid, large steps, it is predictable that the human system will become critically stressed in trying to adapt rapidly in ways that formerly took hundreds of years. There has to be a much-enhanced consciousness about concurrent evolution in the human system.

The technology side, the *tool system*, has inappropriately been driving the whole. What has to be established is a balanced coevolution between both parts. How do we establish an environment that yields this coevolution? Well, that's where the bootstrapping in a laboratory comes in. I said I wanted to do what I knew it was going to be like in our future. So we had to be more conscious of the candidates for change—in both the tool and the human systems. Whenever you hear somebody say it has to be ''easy to learn and natural to use,'' put up a little flag and go question it. What's ''natural''? Is there a natural way to guide a vehicle, as with reins? Well, that lasted a long time.

No! What's natural is what we have grown to accept. And if we look at how much learning it took to drive automobiles, and own and operate them, it would make ridiculous the things people say now regarding what they expect their computer system's learning to cost them. If it's going to be the kind of working companion that it's bound to be, then the learning part of it is relatively trivial. I know it's what sells now, because the market isn't very mature for people to buy things that look like they're going to be hard to learn. But I'm talking about the long-term trends, and the responsibilities of people that are doing the research and downstream planning. I think they should start looking much more seriously for really significant gains in human performance and consider many more candidates for change, with special attention to the much-neglected human system candidates. This will bring up lots of things that might not have been even thought of before, because now there is explicit, active ''prospecting'' for ways to do things differently.

The mouse and the keyset came from trying to do something new in the tool system (similarly for structured files and their viewing and linking). I didn't realize at the time how strange they'd seem and how long it would take for people to start considering them.

So then, how does the change take place? In a large organization (Fig. 29) there are lots of different parties taking part in a change. An idea for change in one place often ''needs'' help from another before the original idea can be implemented—for example, one might ask if the mail room could make one more daily delivery. Then, when such a need is fulfilled by a change in capability of one of the ''lower'' parts, it provides new ''possibilities'' for change among the ''higher'' parts that depend upon it. Evolution proceeds by reverberation: needs propagate downward, and when fulfilled, a new possibility propagates upward. Correspondingly, a possibility propagated by a new capability in a lower-level place can trigger a new idea in a higher place. Continuing the example, we can improve our operation by taking advantage of the extra mail delivery, but we'd need the copy center to change. . . . Possibilities tend to stimulate new needs.

So when we've got a fairly large organization, or large system of things, with specialists working all over the place that are responsible for changes in certain areas, there will have to be some extraordinary

**FIGURE 29**
Coevolution by reverberation—needs propagate downward and a new possibility propagates upward.

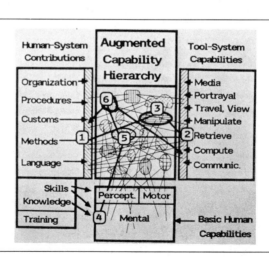

communicating to provide decade-frame evolution on a scale previously requiring centuries. Changes once took place so slowly that we weren't really aware of the evolutionary process. People moved and finally heard about something and tried it. But now, with a catapulting rate of change, and the pressures to become more effective, the changes within our organizations are just going to exceed the rate that we know how to deal with. Unless people start getting conscious and understanding about the evolution, for many, many structures this fast changing rate is going to exceed the elastic limit, and things are going to break.

So I said, "What better place could you start putting to work the new tools and things than in the process that is going to facilitate the evolution you have to go through." That produced a strong push toward computerized documents, and toward collaboration among groups.

One way to look at how to use the computer to help work with documents would be the possibility of a conventional word-processor approach. It's a very straightforward way. The orientation is to simulate paper on a display, targetted solely to produce hard copy. A considerable advantage in many situations, but it is a very anemic example of what the above framework promises.

It didn't even enter my mind to go with that picture. Instead, what my framework produced is shown in Fig. 30. The motor capability of the abstracted human module drives the computer tools and employs the associated methodological and conceptual-linguistic parts of his augmentation system in the special modes indicated. The result is quite a bit different from "word processing" and "office automation."

**FIGURE 30**

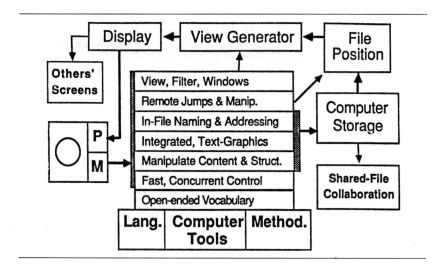

For instance, we should have an open-ended command vocabulary. Once we get hooked up to running in a more flexible environment, the computer tools must provide us with more and more functionality. Since we've got a very powerful beast that can do things, let's really look for fast control means where, for instance, we aren't limited to doing things sequentially, but can do things with both hands, concurrently. This stimulated the chord-keyset option.

I thought we should make it so that both content and structure can be stored and explicitly manipulated. Bring text and graphics together, because they're both important.

Every object in a file should be addressable, because I wanted to do remote jumping and manipulation. So we developed a very flexible addressing scheme that seems to fit well with a user's mental map of his working domain and offers handy addressing options that, in any command, can optionally be used in place of cursor selection. One should be able to move around in existing files rapidly and precisely, and easily jump across any intervening "file or content space" to an explicitly prescribed position. The computer should help navigate throughout the entire working space.

When I am positioned at a desired file object, I want to generate a view that will best serve my purpose of the moment. So, we evolved a flexible set of "view specifications" that can be invoked at any time—and an explicit opportunity is offered the user at any "jump" operation to designate "ViewSpecs." For example, "in this window, show only the first line of each statement, no blank lines between statements, show location addresses (e.g., "3b4") in front of each statement, show only the statements hierarchically "under" the targeted statement, and only those that are in the first two sub-levels." A content filter, of any degree of sophistication, can be invoked within any such ViewSpec so that, among the candidate statements already specified, only those that have a given content will be shown. Simple filters (e.g., to find a given embedded string) can be keyed in at any time and compiled on the fly. More sophisticated filter patterns can be stored as text strings that a user can specify with a "Set Content Pattern" command. Or, a programmer can write and compile very sophisticated filters that a user can easily designate by name to be instituted.

With a comprehensive addressing scheme it is easy to implement citation links, special text strings that both user and computer can interpret as addressing some object and also optionally specifying a particular view to be employed. "Jumping on a link" is a basic command, taking the user directly to the target object. A link can also be employed as part of the addressing in any other command where some file object is to be specified.

If I am moving around in somebody else's stuff, so I can study and analyze it much more effectively, I want to be able to train the displays myself, because a display may not look as I expect it to look when I'm looking at it straight down on paper, and indeed it doesn't. And do I want it also so that I can share that display with others, so that we can collaborate? And share files? So that's the image, and that's why NLS was designed as it was.

## ARCHITECTURE—TO SPECTRUM OF FUNCTION

Now to discuss architecture. I'll use a series of simple illustrations to lead up to the general approach we settled upon. Consider, as in Fig. 31, an application program on top of an operating system in a computer, serving a terminal. For any such application program, there are two facets: an interface process and the actual process that does the substantive work—two different parts. Let's think about them as two distinct but related design issues. For instance, I don't want the smart programmer who knows all about how this program works internally to think that he's the one to tell the world how to interface with it.

By 1968 we had begun evolving the programming language so that it was different for each part, and we could actually think and design for two separate modules (Fig. 32). The next step was to ask, Why, for each different application package, should you have a different front end? Frontends should be universal things, as in Fig. 33, to serve multiple (or all) applications for the user. So our language ideas were evolving to handle this approach. The system that we brought up on the SDS940 in 1968 was organized along these lines, as shown in Fig. 34. All the subroutines that did the application work were written with our special, MOL940 language that we had to develop ourselves. The control processes were specified in a control metalanguage, then compiled with a control-metalanguage translator into the control processor, which interacted with the user. We had a tree-meta translator that let

**FIGURE 31**
An application program has two different tasks: the frontend and the backend.

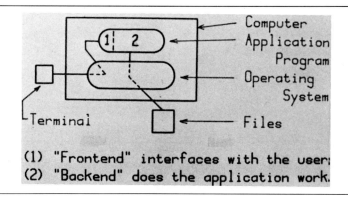

(1) "Frontend" interfaces with the user;
(2) "Backend" does the application work.

**FIGURE 32**
Frontend is actually a specialized application program divided into the interface part and actual process work.

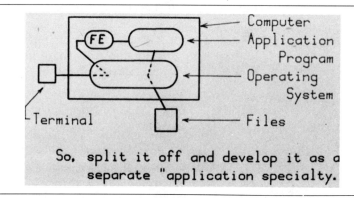

So, split it off and develop it as a separate "application specialty.

us do our compiler compiling. We described a new compiler in a meta-compiler language, then compiled it with the tree-meta translator into the new, running compiler.

Incidentally, in those days I would talk about control language and control metalanguage rather than the command language because I felt that we were doing a lot of things that normally people don't think of as commands. But the pressure of external-world usage pulled us around so now we call it command language.

It was really fortunate for us to be involved in the ARPANET from the beginning. My early ideas of "community" support services could be made explicit in planning for the Network Information Center. One of the papers I wrote[18] pointed out that besides allowing us to share data and process resources, the emergent networks will also provide us with a knowledge marketplace that's wide open for people sitting at their terminals all over the world. Topologically, Fig. 35 depicts what we assumed by the early 1970s would be the future environment for knowledge workers.

**FIGURE 33**
Why not provide a general purpose frontend, an all-application "User Interface System"?

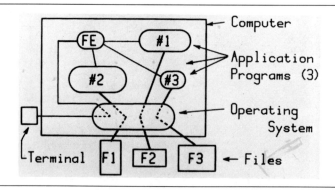

**FIGURE 34**
FJCC'68 system
architecture.

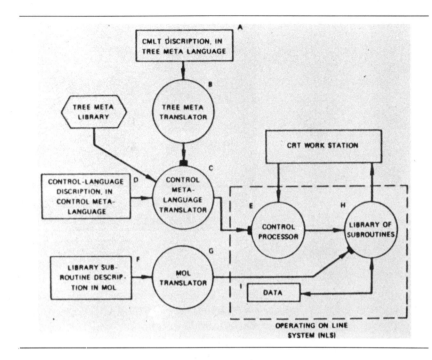

Let's not argue about how much functionality is in any one place. To the user, it doesn't matter whether the workstations are smart or not, as long as they do what he wants them to do. So let's look at topology. The topology that we wanted (Fig. 36), involved a user interface system (UIS) that's between the user's physical interface hardware (display, keyboard, mouse) and all the ''smart'' application

**FIGURE 35**
Our expected Tool
System architecture
(network of
networks).

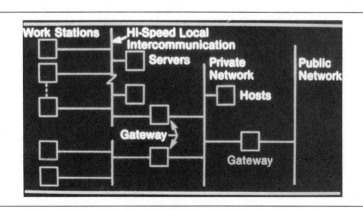

**FIGURE 36**
Desired Tool System
topology.

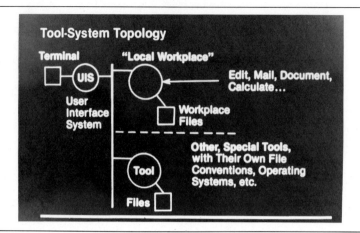

software. I don't care how much of these smarts are in his local work-station, but I'm never going to say that it all has to be there.

Between the user interface system and all of the application systems is a "virtual bus"—some UIS communication will be to applications in the local workstation, some to applications on the local-area network, and some may be far out through gateways to the UIS of a colleague. An important part of what we wanted to provide was a set of functions that the user thinks of as his private or "local" (topologically) workplace where he does his composing, studying, mail management, and calculations. But also he should be able to "reach through" his local workplace to get at all the other services.

The internal architecture of the UIS (Fig. 37) contains a virtual terminal controller (VTC) so all of the applications are programmed to deal with a standard, virtual terminal. The VTC translates to and from particular physical-terminal I/O streams, enabling different classes of terminal equipment for different classes of users—and also, importantly, makes evolution within the whole system easier.

The command language interpreter (CLI) interprets the user actions according to the command-language specification coded into the currently attached grammar file, which was created from a command metalanguage description via the command metalanguage compiler. The CLI also deals with a user-specific, user-profile file that enables individuals and classes of users to have independent control options.

The procedure call interface (PCI) modules translate back and forth between the procedure-call conventions of the various larger modules and the remote procedure call protocol we developed for use between arbitrary modules (including those connected via byte-sequential network circuits).

**FIGURE 37**
AUGMENT Modules
(User Interface
System with VTC,
CLT, PCI, and
grammar).

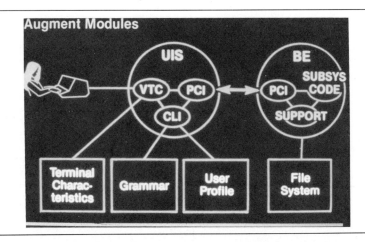

We called this architectural configuration "The Augmented Knowledge Workshop," and figured that all knowledge workers in the future would work in some such environment. The early framework concepts led us to believe that open-ended functionality was inevitable. Also, it emphasized how essential it was to facilitate the coevolution of the human and tool systems. One important objective in this architectural approach was to support this coevolution: Hardware and software could be changed with minimum disturbance to the human system and, conversely, changes in terminology, methodology, and functional dependence upon the tools could evolve with minimum disturbance to the tool system.

One way to illustrate payoff from this architecture is to consider the different profiles of functionality that different classes of users would likely want to employ as they look through their respective classes of terminals into their "knowledge workshops." A high-level project manager, a support clerk, or a skilled, heavy-working professional can each work with grammar and user-profile files that provide the functionality he or she needs, with command terminology and interaction modes suited to skill levels and ways of thinking.

All of this architecture was working by 1976, although it has only been recently that we could interest user organizations in trying to harness it toward an integrated knowledge-work environment. A number of our publications explicate various aspects of this architecture.[19]

## Human Unit, Evolution, and Communities

It is important that the evolution of the user side should go on maximumly; it has been badly neglected. The "basic human unit" is shown in Fig. 38. How are we going to evolve it? The reverberation concept

**FIGURE 38**
The basic human
unit.

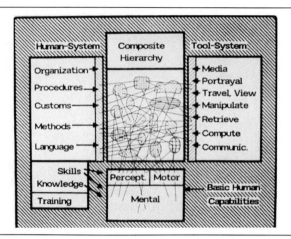

of its evolution is very important in my framework, and I have come
to believe that it is only done by what you'd call "communities." Even
in a large, highly structured organization much of the change process
must involve stakeholders in groupings that are different from the line-
management structure (i.e., like a community).

This is a big, important concept that started in the mid-1960s. If
we depend critically upon a community that must interact in really
effective collaboration, we need to build support systems especially designed for this purpose. Part of the conscious evolutionary process for
our large organizations and institutions must therefore be to provide
effective collaboration support for widely dispersed communities (Fig.
39).

But how was I going to promote an R&D program, with a "pilot
community," to learn how to develop and provide effective "community support" tools and associated new collaborative methods? Well,
in the spring of 1967, at an ARPA principal investigators meeting, Bob
Taylor and Larry Roberts told us that ARPA was going to make computer network R&D a major program thrust, and that our "research
computers" were going to be the ones connected by an experimental
"ARPA Network." Even though many others were disturbed by the
idea (because of perceived interference with their major research
thrusts), I was thrilled. Finally, after listening to the initial interactions,
I volunteered to develop and operate what became the ARPANET Network Information Center (NIC).

What I wanted was for the NIC to become a community support
center that would really go after the development of collaboration-
support tools and methods, and would provide services to encourage
the ARPANET R&D folks to evolve their working ways accordingly.

**FIGURE 39**
An augmented
community needs
active, explicit,
evolutionary
mechanism!

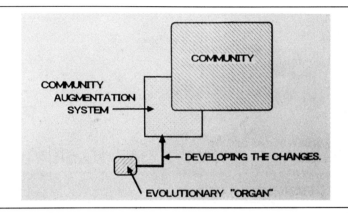

**FIGURE 39**
An augmented
community needs
active, explicit,
evolutionary
mechanism!

Hopefully, there would emerge a subcommunity out there composed of those interested in the various aspects of augmenting (Fig. 40). Just consider the kind of leverage you get this way. So I've talked about a "bootstrap community" in my notes for over 15 years now, and it's something I still very much would like to see established (Fig. 41). Many features and capabilities built into NLS/AUGMENT were directly motivated by these community-support and distributed-collaboration concepts.

Unfortunately, the ARPANET grew so fast that the Network Information Center had to trim down what it could do functionally. We couldn't provide the extensive support services we had planned (discussed at some length in a 1972 paper[20]), such as what we could do to support a community by integrating a lot of its dialog, and getting an intelligence system there; handbooks that evolved to integrate what to

**FIGURE 40**
Needed: A
community for
pursuit of maximum,
whole-system
capability!

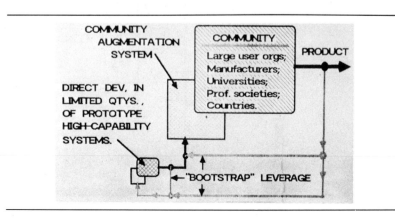

FIGURE 41
Strategy: Early
augmentation
system changes that
also facilitate the
evolution process.

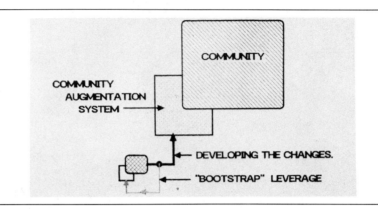

do; and professional facilitation staff, which adds important value. There is a lot that can be embedded in this.

NLS/AUGMENT was built to be able to handle external document (XDOC) control, the community intelligence collection that everyone contributes to and participates in, and indexes to it. When the community has a special mission or disciplinary interest, we also could significantly facilitate the development and maintenance of a ''dynamic community handbook'' that integrates current status (terminology, hypotheses, conventions, plans, expectations, and so forth) in a coherent, self-consistent fashion. Figure 42 portrays all of this community support in a fashion peculiar to the NLS/AUGMENT set of features and capabilities. While each user had his own collection of working files, there would be a large collection of shared information—all of it

**FIGURE 42**
A community's
handbook would be a
periodically updated
on/off-line
publication.

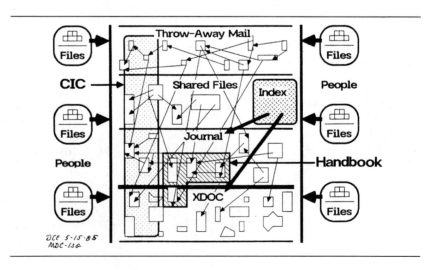

embedded in uniform, composite-document structures. The generalized citation-link capability interconnects passages of any of these documents in meaningful ways as evolved with user conventions and collaborative methods. Ordinary, unrecorded mail and shared files gain significant value thereby. The Journal system provides its own unique value, considerably amplified with linkage use.

A "community intelligence collection" (CIC) can be distributed over all of the document types—embodying useful information and discussion about external activities relevant to the community's interests. Special indexing into this collection is again much enhanced with links. The Community Handbook fits into the picture nicely; any given "edition" is "published" in the Journal (and is probably available also in corresponding hard copy), which is controlled with the XDOC system.

I'm going to terminate at this point, since after 1976 we really had no chance to continue pursuing this "augmentation framework." It seemed no longer to fit in the pattern of the research at ARPA, or with what SRI wanted to do. When we landed out in the commercial world, we found it wasn't what people there wanted to do, either. The AUGMENT system stayed alive in sort of a funny, dumb way, often like taking a bulldozer in to help people work in their back yards. Then, McDonnell-Douglas bought Tymshare, and inside of its aerospace organization it's a very different situation because of the very heavy knowledge work involved. For a year I've been going out and talking with all those people involved in big projects and CAD systems, and finding out that these concepts are directly relevant to the needs and problems now being recognized there.

We're starting this year to build special interest communities. The first one is the AI community; possibly followed by the Ada™ community. Also, explicit consideration of integrated architectures similar to ours is under way, including not only virtual terminals, command interpreters, remote procedure calls, and shared-screen support, but also composite documents with addressable objects and citation links.

So that's a quick pass over my historical record.

## REFERENCES

1. D. C. Engelbart, "Special Considerations of the Individual as a User, Generator, and Retriever of Information," *American Documentation* 12, No. 2, pp. 121–125, April 1961. (Paper presented at the Annual Meeting of the American Documentation Institute, Berkeley, Calif., 23–27 October 1960.)

2. J. L. Kennedy and G. H. Putt, "Administration of Research in a Research Corporation," RAND Corporation Report P-847, 20 April 1956.

3. D. C. Engelbart, "Augmenting Human Intellect: A Conceptual Framework," Summary Report, Stanford Research Institute, on Contract AF 49(638)-1024, October 1962, 134 pp.

4. D. C. Engelbart, "A Conceptual Framework for the Augmentation of Man's Intellect." In *Vistas in Information Handling*, edited by Howerton and Weeks, Washington, D.C.: Spartan Books, 1963, pp. 1–29.

5. W. K. English, D. C. Engelbart, and B. Huddart, "Computer-Aided Display Control," SRI Final Report to NASA Langley Research Center under Contract NAS 1-3988, July 1965, 104 p.

6. W. K. English, D. C. Engelbart, and M. L. Berman, "Display-Selection Techniques for Text Manipulation," *IEEE Transactions on Human Factors in Electronics*, Vol. HFE-8, No. 1, March 1967, pp. 5–15.

7. D. C. Engelbart and W. K. English, "A Research Center for Augmenting Human Intellect," *AFIPS Conference Proceedings*, Vol. 33, Fall Joint Computer Conference, San Francisco, December 1968, pp. 395–410.

8. See also D. C. Engelbart, "Computer-Augmented Management-System Research and Development of Augmentation Facility," Final Report, RADC, 1970; and D. C. Engelbart, "Online Team Environment: Network Information Center and Computer Augmented Team Interaction," Final Report RADC-TR-72-232 to Air Force Rome Air Development Center for SRI work under ARPA Order No. 967., 8 June 1972, 264 p.

9. D. C. Engelbart "Network Information Center and Computer Augmented Team Interaction," Technical Report RADC-TR-71-175, as principal investigator for SRI Contract F30602-70-C-0219 under ARPA Order No. 967. June 1971, 99 p.

10. For descriptions see D. C. Engelbart, "Network Information Center"; and D. C. Engelbart, "NLS Teleconferencing Features: The Journal, and Shared-Screen Telephoning," *CompCon75*, 9–11 Sept. 1975, Digest of papers, pp. 173–176. (IEEE Catalog No. 75CH0988-6C.)

11. Described in D. C. Engelbart, "Toward High-Performance Knowledge Workers," *OAC'82 Digest, Proceedings of the AFIPS Office Automation Conference*, San Francisco, 5–7 April 1982, pp. 279–290.

12. See D. C. Engelbart, W. K. English, and J. F. Rulifson, "Development of a Multidisplay, Time-Shared Computer Facility and Computer-Augmented Management-System Research," SRI Final Report for AF Rome Air Development Center under Contract AF 30(602)-4103, April 1968, Engelbart, "NLS Teleconferencing"; and D. C. Engelbart, "Toward Integrated, Evolutionary Office Automation Systems," *Proceedings of the Joint Engineering Management Conference*, Denver, Colo., 16–18 October 1978, pp. 63–68.

13. Engelbart, "Toward High-Performance Knowledge Workers."

14. English, Engelbart, and Berman, "Display-Selection Techniques."

15. *Experimental Graphics Users' Guide*, SRI-ARC, 11 June 76, 32 pp.

16. *Output Processor Users' Guide*, SRI-ARC, 29 July 75, 97 pp.

17. Engelbart, "Augmenting Human Intellect."

18. D. C. Engelbart, "Coordinated Information Services for a Discipline- or Mission-Oriented Community," *Proceedings of the Second Annual Computer Communications Conference*, San Jose, Calif., 24 January 1972. (Also published in *Computer Communication Networks*, edited by R. L. Grimsdale and F. F. Kuo, Leyden: Noordhoff, 1975.

19. D. C. Engelbart, R. W. Watson, and J. C. Norton. "The Augmented Knowledge Workshop," *AFIPS Conference Proceedings*, Vol. 42, pp. 9–21, National Computer Conference, 4–8 June 1973; J. E. White, "A High-Level

Framework for Network-Based Resource Sharing," *AFIPS Conference Proceedings*, June 1976, NCC, Vol. 45, pp. 561-570; R. W. Watson, "User Interface Design Issues for a Large Interactive System," *AFIPS Conference Proceedings*, Vol. 45, Montvale, N.J.: AFIPS Press, 1976, pp. 357-364; K. E. Victor, "The Design and Implementation of DAD, A Multiprocess, Multimachine, Multilanguage Interactive Debugger," *Proceedings of the Tenth Hawaii International Conference on System Sciences*, University of Hawaii, 1977, pp. 196-199; Engelbart, "Toward Integrated"; and Engelbart, "Toward High-Performance Knowledge Workers."

20. Engelbart, "Coordinated Information Services."

## OTHER IMPORTANT PUBLICATIONS

Andrews, D. I., "Line Processor—A device for amplification of display terminal capabilities for text manipulation," *AFIPS Conference Proceedings*, pp. 257-265, National Computer Conference, 1974.

"Augmenting Your Intellect," editorial interview with D. C. Engelbart, *Research/Development*, August 1968, pp. 22-27.

Bush, V., "As We May Think," *The Atlantic Monthly*, July 1945, pp. 101-108. (See also this volume.)

Culler, G. J., and R. W. Huff, "Solution on Non-Linear Integral Equations Using On-Line Computer Control," paper prepared for Spring Joint Computer Conference, San Francisco, May 1962. (Assumedly published in *Proceedings Spring Joint Computer Conference*, Vol. 21, [Palo Alto, Calif.: National Press, May 1962].)

Engelbart, D. C., "Augmenting Human Intellect: Experiments, Concepts, and Possibilities," Summary Report, Stanford Research Institute, under Contract AF 49(638)-1024 for Directorate of Information Sciences, Air Force Office of Scientific Research, March 1965. SRI Project 3578; 65 p.

———, "Intellectual Implications of Multi-Access Computer Networks," *Proceedings of the Interdisciplinary Conference on Multi-Access Computer Networks*, Austin, Texas, April 1970.

———, "Design Considerations for Knowledge Workshop Terminals," *AFIPS Conference Proceedings*, Vol. 42, pp. 221-227, National Computer Conference, 4-8 June 1973.

———, "Evolving the Organization of the Future: A Point of View." In *"Emerging Office Systems," Proceedings of the Stanford International Symposium on Office Automation*, March 23-25, 1980, edited by R. Landau, J. Bair, and J. Siegman, Norwood, N.J.: Ablex Publications Corporation.

———, "Collaboration Support Provisions in AUGMENT," *OAC '84 Digest, Proceedings of the 1984 AFIPS Office Automation Conference*, Los Angeles, Calif., February 20-22, pp. 51-58.

———, "Authorship Provisions in AUGMENT," *COMPCON '84 Digest, Proceedings of the 1984 COMPCON Conference*, San Francisco, Calif., February 27-March 1, 1984, pp. 465-472.

Engelbart, D. C., and B. Huddart, "Research on Computer-Augmented Information Management," Technical Documentary Report No. ESD-TDR-65-168, under Contract No. AF 19 (628)-4088 from Electronic Systems Division, Air Force Systems Command, USAF, March, 1965. 128 pp.

Foth, T., "The Origin, Anatomy, and Varieties of Mus Computeralis" (It's the Year of the Mouse!), *Softalk*, Vol. 2, April 1984, pp. 88–96.

Levy, S., "Of mice and Men," *Popular Computing*, May 1984, pp. 70, 75–78.

Licklider, J. C. R., "Man-Computer Symbiosis," *IRE Transactions on Human Factors in Electronics*, March 1960.

Licklider, J. C. R., and W. E. Clark, "On-Line Man-Computer Communication," *Proceedings of the Spring Joint Computer Conference*, Vol. 21, pp. 113–128 (Palo Alto, Calif.: National Press, May 1962).

Licklider, J. C. R., and Robert W. Taylor, with Evan Herbert editor, "The Computer as a Communication Device," *Science & Technology*, April 1968, pp. 21–31.

Lindgren, N., "Toward the Decentralized Intellectual," *Innovation*, No. 24, September 1971.

Rheingold, H., "The Loneliness of a Long-Distance Thinker," chapter nine, pp. 174–204, in *Tools for Thought: The People and Ideas behind the Next Computer Revolution*, New York: Simon & Schuster, 1985. 335 pp.

Victor, K. E., "A Software Engineering Environment," *Proceedings of AIAA/NASA/IEEE/ACM Computers In Aerospace Conference*, Los Angeles, Calif., October 31–November 2, 1977, pp. 399–403.

# Participants Discussion

**Hank Strub**

I'd like to hear your feelings on why it took so long for the mouse to be adopted into personal workstation technology, and why that hasn't happened yet with the chord keyset?

*Engelbart*

It's part of a larger story that I think fits in with culture. If you looked at the whole map I drew you would see that on the human system side all the opportunities have changed; the technology side has grown way out of proportion, in my view, just stupendously so. Fifth generation and all the hoopla about it is just all the more pushed in there, so there's got to be a balance. There's a reason that in our culture we grew up and absorbed all of the human system side that we used without even questioning it or thinking of it—they didn't come to us as inventions. We look upon other cultures where there is not the idea of ''progress,'' and we laugh at them. But all we have to do is turn and look at ourselves to realize that our culture has not yet understood that the human side is open for progress and change. We more or less resist the change and say, ''Boy, I'll be damned if I'm going to let that computer make me change; if it's so smart it ought to do it for me.'' We're totally missing the point, in my estimation. Well, people look at the mouse and say, ''Geez, who wants to do all that?'' Or they say the keyset is even worse. It's part of the culture.

The biggest challenge that's ahead for us, if we want to make progress, is to start affecting the perceptions that people have about what potential is there. We need to start looking for change and finding out a rational way to do the evolution so it doesn't break us apart. I just love to get into a dialog with people about the strategies for that evolution. I found people at McDonnell Douglas who were talking about it. There are top level guys who say, ''We're going to remake the corporation.'' That's given people at many of the other levels the courage to go ahead and try. I come and say, strategically, we ought to do this; so they're sticking their necks out and giving me a chance to start.

*Greg Heil*

I'd like to ask you, have you considered combining the mouse and the keyset into a single device, a handwriting recognition system?

*Engelbart*

Yes, I thought I'd have a mouse and a keyset in each hand. There's a lot of potential to that, and people say, ''Hey, what about this number of buttons on a keyset? Why did you pick three buttons on your mouse?'' Why, it was all we could get in at the time. So, yes, I'd go

233

for more. There's a lot to learn. I did a lot of thinking one time about the ways you could get transducers to pick up almost any kind of a signal that your motor system or nerve system could produce and translate that into actions you want; it's a whole new control language you could learn. I was just wondering about the bandwidth and the effect of that, and I could just picture really going through space—it's wide open.

**Greg Heil**  My suggestion was not to increase the number of transducers, but to decrease them to a single one, to a handwriting recognizer, so that you don't have extra buttons; you only use one hand to do it.

**Engelbart**  Well, that's a pretty slow way to enter characters, at least for English. Try it, but I think that if you've got such a marvelous machine there, you don't want to keep driving it with reins. And that's what I think would happen with the handwriting recognizer. I feel similarly about speech recognition. It's very nice in a lot of ways, but you couldn't control a system like we had with speech commands; you couldn't go fast enough unless you got some very sophisticated signals.

**Charles Irby**  I have two questions, one is on the tool system side and the other is on the human system side. Let's take the human system side first: Given the work that you've done in this area, what insights do you have about the changes that are going to be required in the human system, given the changes in technology in the tool side that we are experiencing today?

**Engelbart**  Well, I've got a lot of general ideas and I can tell you some of those. The main need is to find an evolutionary process that starts the exploration. Many people and many things to try. An example is that our organizations can get much flatter. The kind of communication can be so much greater, that if I could just go like this, and be in voice contact with you, same screens, diving around the information we're familiar with, you can be in any place in the country. It can change considerably the kind of roles that we can have, lots of specialty roles that can flip in and out of your work to help you from any place in the country. There isn't any way it would be practical with the kind of time it would take for you to get together and look at your stuff. Administrative and managerial structures can be different, and things like the matrix organizations, which have a lot of appeal in project-oriented environment but are difficult to administer, have a whole new breath of life coming to them because of the kind of coordination communication. Working groups that can be separated geographically. We do it a lot of ways now, but no one has been really focusing on the pursuit of ways to collaborate.

*Charles Irby*

On the tools side, a lot of the technology that was developed at SRI has readily transferred into other commercial products. Yet there are some, such as the structured text and the view controls that you had over the structured text, the linking mechanism from one place in the document to another place in possibly another document, and the notion of a mail system that is supported by a database, automatically cataloging all of the mail that has been sent. These things haven't readily transferred into other products. Why is that?

*Engelbart*

I was hoping the historians would answer that. I don't know, it's puzzled me. I used to take it personally and every once in a while it flashes . . . all I can say is that it just didn't fit cultural perceptions. When the computers first started becoming really available—personal computers or time-sharing—it was enough for people to make the adjustment to start interacting with them. If the marketplace isn't ready for something like that, who's going to invest money in trying to get it out there? Who has to decide to invest the money? It's guys who have been in the business for a while, and they have to depend upon consultants. They're experienced and familiar with things that aren't very often the ones that are in the vanguard. The whole process of who gets it out there and decides they are going to invest the money in it and risks it or goes out there and tries to train the customers. Once you get a system built, then you've got to put a lot of money into PR that tells everybody that's the best. So, you're doing yourself in down the way if, later on, you come back and say, now this is the best. So anyway, a big part of the user organizations have to get in gear and start saying, ''Quit coddling us, we're ready to change. We're looking for what to do better, don't give us this bull about what's easy to learn.''

*Larry Press*

I notice in reading one of your early reports that you paid a lot of respect, I guess, and commented a lot on Vannevar Bush's suggestions. And I just wondered if you could comment on how important you feel he was, his thinking and also his work, to the development of all this interactive computing.

*Engelbart*

I don't know about other people in that respect. For me, it was part of a singular thing, because I was a little navy boy, an electronics technician in World War II out in the Philipines, and getting moved from one place to another. They stuck you on an island to wait to get you assigned to somebody else. Somebody said there was a library there. It was a Red Cross library, up on stilts in a native hut, really neat, nobody there. I was poking around and found this article in *Life* magazine about his memex, and it just thrilled the hell out of me that people were thinking about something like that. So I didn't really act on that, but I'm sure later, as I got into this, that it started to affect me. Later, when we were starting the parts of the way NLS was built, there's a thing called a sequence generator that you could flip in your own user choices of a sequence that goes and picks you this thing and that; the links were a lot coming from Bush's idea of trail generation, through his documents. So it was a very explicit connection in that respect. I wish I could have met him, but by the time I caught on to the work, he was already in a nursing home and wasn't available. History is moving faster nowadays, incidentally, so you can find some of us old fossils that are still alive.

REPRINT OF HISTORICALLY SIGNIFICANT PAPER
# As We May Think

*Vannevar Bush*
From *The Atlantic Monthly*, July 1945: 101–108. Reprinted with permission.

This has not been a scientist's war; it has been a war in which all have had a part. The scientists, burying their old professional competition in the demand of a common cause, have shared greatly and learned much. It has been exhilarating to work in effective partnership. Now, for many, this appears to be approaching an end. What are the scientists to do next?

For the biologists, and particularly for the medical scientists, there can be little indecision, for their war work has hardly required them to leave the old paths. Many indeed have been able to carry on their war research in their familiar peacetime laboratories. Their objectives remain much the same.

It is the physicists who have been thrown most violently off stride, who have left academic pursuits for the making of strange destructive gadgets, who have had to devise new methods for their unanticipated assignments. They have done their part on the devices that made it possible to turn back the enemy. They have worked in combined effort with the physicists of our allies. They have felt within themselves the stir of achievement. They have been part of a great team. Now, as peace approaches, one asks where they will find objectives worthy of their best.

## 1

Of what lasting benefit has been man's use of science and of the new instruments which his research brought into existence? First, they have increased his control of his material environment. They have improved his food, his clothing, his shelter; they have increased his security and released him partly from the bondage of bare existence. They have given him increased knowledge of his own biological processes so that he has had a progressive freedom from disease and an increased span of life. They are illuminating the interactions of his physiological and psychological functions, giving the promise of an improved mental health.

Science has provided the swiftest communication between individuals; it has provided a record of ideas and has enabled man to manipulate and to make extracts from that record so that knowledge evolves and endures throughout the life of a race rather than that of an individual.

There is a growing mountain of research. But there is increased evidence that we are being bogged down today as specialization extends. The investigator is staggered by the findings and conclusions of thousands of other workers—conclusions which he cannot find time to grasp, much less to remember, as they appear. Yet specialization becomes increasingly necessary for progress, and the effort to bridge between disciplines is correspondingly superficial.

Professionally our methods of transmitting and reviewing the results of research are generations old and by now are totally inadequate for their purpose. If the aggregate time spent in writing scholarly works and in reading them could be evaluated, the ratio between these amounts of time might well be startling. Those who conscientiously attempt to keep abreast of current thought, even in restricted fields, by close and continuous reading might well shy away from an examination calculated to show how much of the previous month's efforts could be produced on call. Mendel's concept of the laws of genetics was lost to the world for a generation because his publication did not reach the few who were capable of grasping and extending it; and this sort of catastrophe is undoubtedly being repeated all about us, as truly significant attainments become lost in the mass of the inconsequential.

The difficulty seems to be, not so much that we publish unduly in view of the extent and variety of present-day interests, but rather that publication has been extended far beyond our present ability to make real use of the record. The summation of human experience is being expanded at a prodigious rate, and the means we use for threading through the consequent maze to the momentarily important item is the same as was used in the days of square-rigged ships.

But there are signs of a change as new and powerful instrumentalities come into use. Photocells capable of seeing things in a physical sense, advanced photography which can record what is seen or even what is not, thermionic tubes capable of controlling potent forces under the guidance of less power than a mosquito uses to vibrate his wings, cathode ray tubes rendering visible an occurrence so brief that by comparison a microsecond is a long time, relay combinations which will carry out involved sequences of movements more reliably than any human operator and thousands of times as fast—there are plenty of mechanical aids with which to effect a transformation in scientific records.

Two centuries ago Leibnitz invented a calculating machine which embodied most of the essential features of recent keyboard devices, but it could not then come into use. The economics of the situation were against it: the labor involved in constructing it, before the days of mass production, exceeded the labor to be saved by its use, since all it could accomplish could be duplicated by sufficient use of pencil and paper. Moreover, it would have been subject to frequent breakdown, so that it could not have been depended upon; for at that time and long after, complexity and unreliability were synonymous.

Babbage, even with remarkably generous support for his time, could not produce his great arithmetical machine. His idea was sound enough, but construction and maintenance costs were then too heavy. Had a Pharaoh been given detailed and explicit designs of an automobile, and had he understood them completely, it would have taxed the resources of his kingdom

to have fashioned the thousands of parts for a single car, and that car would have broken down on the first trip to Giza.

Machines with interchangeable parts can now be constructed with great economy of effort. In spite of much complexity, they perform reliably. Witness the humble typewriter, or the movie camera, or the automobile. Electrical contacts have ceased to stick when thoroughly understood. Note the automatic telephone exchange, which has hundreds of thousands of such contacts, and yet is reliable. A spider web of metal, sealed in a thin glass container, a wire heated to brilliant glow, in short, the thermionic tube of radio sets, is made by the hundred million, tossed about in packages, plugged into sockets—and it works! Its gossamer parts, the precise location and alignment involved in its construction, would have occupied a master craftsman of the guild for months; now it is built for thirty cents. The world has arrived at an age of cheap complex devices of great reliability; and something is bound to come of it.

## 2

A record, if it is to be useful to science, must be continuously extended, it must be stored, and above all it must be consulted. Today we make the record conventionally by writing and photography, followed by printing; but we also record on film, on wax disks, and on magnetic wires. Even if utterly new recording procedures do not appear, these present ones are certainly in the process of modification and extension.

Certainly progress in photography is not going to stop. Faster material and lenses, more automatic cameras, finer-grained sensitive compounds to allow an extension of the mini-camera idea, are all imminent. Let us project this trend ahead to a logical, if not inevitable, outcome. The camera hound of the future wears on his forehead a lump a little larger than a walnut. It takes pictures 3 millimeters square, later to be projected or enlarged, which after all involves only a factor of 10 beyond present practice. The lens is of universal focus, down to any distance accommodated by the unaided eye, simply because it is of short focal length. There is a built-in photocell on the walnut such as we now have on at least one camera, which automatically adjusts exposure for a wide range of illumination. There is film in the walnut for a hundred exposures, and the spring for operating its shutter and shifting its film is wound once for all when the film clip is inserted. It produces its result in full color. It may well be stereoscopic, and record with two spaced glass eyes, for striking improvements in stereoscopic technique are just around the corner.

The cord which trips its shutter may reach down a man's sleeve within easy reach of his fingers. A quick squeeze, and the picture is taken. On a pair of ordinary glasses is a square of fine lines near the top of one lens, where it is out of the way of ordinary vision. When an object appears in that square, it is lined up for its picture. As the scientist of the future moves about the laboratory or the field, every time he looks at something worthy of the record, he trips the shutter and in it goes, without even an audible click. Is this all fantastic? The only fantastic thing about it is the idea of making as many pictures as would result from its use.

Will there be dry photography? It is already here in two forms. When Brady made his Civil War pictures, the plate had to be wet at the time of exposure. Now it has to be wet during development instead. In the future perhaps it need not be wetted at all. There have long been films impregnated with diazo dyes which form a picture without development, so that it is already there as soon as the camera has been operated. An exposure to ammonia gas destroys the unexposed dye, and the picture can then be taken out into the light and examined. The process is now slow, but someone may speed it up, and it has no grain difficulties such as now keep photographic researchers busy. Often it would be advantageous to be able to snap the camera and to look at the picture immediately.

Another process now in use is also slow, and more or less clumsy. For fifty years impregnated papers have been used which turn dark at every point where an electrical contact touches them, by reason of the chemical change thus produced in an iodine compound included in the paper. They have been used to make records, for a

pointer moving across them can leave a trail behind. If the electrical potential on the pointer is varied as it moves, the line becomes light or dark in accordance with the potential.

This scheme is now used in facsimile transmission. The pointer draws a set of closely spaced lines across the paper one after another. As it moves, its potential is varied in accordance with a varying current received over wires from a distant station, where these variations are produced by a photocell which is similarly scanning a picture. At every instant the darkness of the line being drawn is made equal to the darkness of the point on the picture being observed by the photocell. Thus, when the whole picture has been covered, a replica appears at the receiving end.

A scene itself can be just as well looked over line by line by the photocell in this way as can a photograph of the scene. This whole apparatus constitutes a camera, with the added feature, which can be dispensed with if desired, of making its picture at a distance. It is slow, and the picture is poor in detail. Still, it does give another process of dry photography, in which the picture is finished as soon as it is taken.

It would be a brave man who would predict that such a process will always remain clumsy, slow, and faulty in detail. Television equipment today transmits sixteen reasonably good pictures a second, and it involves only two essential differences from the process described above. For one, the record is made by a moving beam of electrons rather than a moving pointer, for the reason that an electron beam can sweep across the picture very rapidly indeed. The other difference involves merely the use of a screen which glows momentarily when the electrons hit, rather than a chemically treated paper or film which is permanently altered. This speed is necessary in television, for motion pictures rather than stills are the object.

Use chemically treated film in place of the glowing screen, allow the apparatus to transmit one picture only rather than a succession, and a rapid camera for dry photography results. The treated film needs to be far faster in action than present examples, but it probably could be. More serious is the objection that this scheme would involve putting the film inside a vacuum chamber, for electron beams behave normally only in such a rarefied environment. This difficulty could be avoided by allowing the electron beam to play on one side of a partition, and by pressing the film against the other side, if this partition were such as to allow the electrons to go through perpendicular to its surface, and to prevent them from spreading out sideways. Such partitions, in crude form, could certainly be constructed, and they will hardly hold up the general development.

Like dry photography, microphotography still has a long way to go. The basic scheme of reducing the size of the record, and examining it by projection rather than directly, has possibilities too great to be ignored. The combination of optical projection and photographic reduction is already producing some results in microfilm for scholarly purposes, and the potentialities are highly suggestive. Today, with microfilm, reductions by a linear factor of 20 can be employed and still produce full clarity when the material is re-enlarged for examination. The limits are set by the graininess of the film, the excellence of the optical system, and the efficiency of the light sources employed. All of these are rapidly improving.

Assume a linear ratio of 100 for future use. Consider film of the same thickness as paper, although thinner film will certainly be usable. Even under these conditions there would be a total factor of 10,000 between the bulk of the ordinary record on books, and its microfilm replica. The *Encyclopœdia Britannica* could be reduced to the volume of a matchbox. A library of a million volumes could be compressed into one end of a desk. If the human race has produced since the invention of movable type a total record, in the form of magazines, newspapers, books, tracts, advertising blurbs, correspondence, having a volume corresponding to a billion books, the whole affair, assembled and compressed, could be lugged off in a moving van. Mere compression, of course, is not enough; one needs not only to make and store a record but also be able to consult it, and this aspect of the matter comes later. Even the modern great library is not generally consulted; it is nibbled at by a few.

Compression is important, however, when it comes to costs. The material for the microfilm *Britannica* would cost a nickel, and it could be mailed anywhere for a cent. What would it cost to print a million copies? To print a sheet of newspaper, in a large edition, costs a small fraction of a cent. The entire material of the *Britannica* in reduced microfilm form would go on a sheet eight and one-half by eleven inches. Once it is available, with the photographic reproduction methods of the future, duplicates in large quantities could probably be turned out for a cent apiece beyond the cost of materials. The preparation of the original copy? That introduces the next aspect of the subject.

## 3

To make the record, we now push a pencil or tap a typewriter. Then comes the process of digestion and correction, followed by an intricate process of typesetting, printing, and distribution. To consider the first stage of the procedure, will the author of the future cease writing by hand or typewriter and talk directly to the record? He does so indirectly, by talking to a stenographer or a wax cylinder; but the elements are all present if he wishes to have his talk directly produce a typed record. All he needs to do is to take advantage of existing mechanisms and to alter his language.

At a recent World Fair a machine called a Voder was shown. A girl stroked its keys and it emitted recognizable speech. No human vocal chords entered into the procedure at any point; the keys simply combined some electrically produced vibrations and passed these on to a loud-speaker. In the Bell Laboratories there is the converse of this machine, called a Vocoder. The loud-speaker is replaced by a microphone, which picks up sound. Speak to it, and the corresponding keys move. This may be one element of the postulated system.

The other element is found in the stenotype, that somewhat disconcerting device encountered usually at public meetings. A girl strokes its keys languidly and looks about the room and sometimes at the speaker with a disquieting gaze. From it emerges a typed strip which records in a phonetically simplified language a record of what the speaker is supposed to have said. Later this strip is retyped into ordinary language, for in its nascent form it is intelligible only to the initiated. Combine these two elements, let the Vocoder run the stenotype, and the result is a machine which types when talked to.

Our present languages are not especially adapted to this sort of mechanization, it is true. It is strange that the inventors of universal languages have not seized upon the idea of producing one which better fitted the technique for transmitting and recording speech. Mechanization may yet force the issue, especially in the scientific field; whereupon scientific jargon would become still less intelligible to the layman.

One can now picture a future investigator in his laboratory. His hands are free, and he is not anchored. As he moves about and observes, he photographs and comments. Time is automatically recorded to tie the two records together. If he goes into the field, he may be connected by radio to his recorder. As he ponders over his notes in the evening, he again talks his comments into the record. His typed record, as well as his photographs, may both be in miniature, so that he projects them for examination.

Much needs to occur, however, between the collection of data and observations, the extraction of parallel material from the existing record, and the final insertion of new material into the general body of the common record. For mature thought there is no mechanical substitute. But creative thought and essentially repetitive thought are very different things. For the latter there are, and may be, powerful mechanical aids.

Adding a column of figures is a repetitive thought process, and it was long ago properly relegated to the machine. True, the machine is sometimes controlled by a keyboard, and thought of a sort enters in reading the figures and poking the corresponding keys, but even this is avoidable. Machines have been made which will read typed figures by photocells and then depress the corresponding keys; these are combinations of photocells for scanning the type, electric circuits for sorting the consequent variations, and relay circuits for interpreting the result into the action of solenoids to pull the keys down.

All this complication is needed because of the clumsy way in which we have learned to write figures. If we recorded them positionally, simply by the configuration of a set of dots on a card, the automatic reading mechanism would become comparatively simple. In fact, if the dots are holes, we have the punched-card machine long ago produced by Hollorith for the purposes of the census, and now used throughout business. Some types of complex businesses could hardly operate without these machines.

Adding is only one operation. To perform arithmetical computation involves also subtraction, multiplication, and division, and in addition some method for temporary storage of results, removal from storage for further manipulation, and recording of final results by printing. Machines for these purposes are now of two types: keyboard machines for accounting and the like, manually controlled for the insertion of data, and usually automatically controlled as far as the sequence of operations is concerned; and punched-card machines in which separate operations are usually delegated to a series of machines, and the cards then transferred bodily from one to another. Both forms are very useful; but as far as complex computations are concerned, both are still in embryo.

Rapid electrical counting appeared soon after the physicists found it desirable to count cosmic rays. For their own purposes the physicists promptly constructed thermionic-tube equipment capable of counting electrical impulses at the rate of 100,000 a second. The advanced arithmetical machines of the future will be electrical in nature, and they will perform at 100 times present speeds, or more.

Moreover, they will be far more versatile than present commercial machines, so that they may readily be adapted for a wide variety of operations. They will be controlled by a control card or film, they will select their own data and manipulate it in accordance with the instructions thus inserted, they will perform complex arithmetical computations at exceedingly high speeds, and they will record results in such form as to be readily available for distribution or for later further manipulation. Such machines will have enormous appetites. One of them will take instructions and data from a whole roomful of girls armed with simple keyboard punches, and will deliver sheets of computed results every few minutes. There will always be plenty of things to compute in the detailed affairs of millions of people doing complicated things.

## 4

The repetitive processes of thought are not confined, however, to matters of arithmetic and statistics. In fact, every time one combines and records facts in accordance with established logical processes, the creative aspect of thinking is concerned only with the selection of the data and the process to be employed, and the manipulation thereafter is repetitive in nature and hence a fit matter to be relegated to the machines. Not so much has been done along these lines, beyond the bounds of arithmetic, as might be done, primarily because of the economics of the situation. The needs of business, and the extensive market obviously waiting, assured the advent of mass-produced arithmetical machines just as soon as production methods were sufficiently advanced.

With machines for advanced analysis no such situation existed; for there was and is no extensive market; the users of advanced methods of manipulating data are a very small part of the population. There are, however, machines for solving differential equations—and functional and integral equations, for that matter. There are many special machines, such as the harmonic synthesizer which predicts the tides. There will be many more, appearing certainly first in the hands of the scientist and in small numbers.

If scientific reasoning were limited to the logical processes of arithmetic, we should not get far in our understanding of the physical world. One might as well attempt to grasp the game of poker entirely by the use of the mathematics of probability. The abacus, with its beads strung on parallel wires, led the Arabs to positional numeration and the concept of zero many centuries before the rest of the world; and it was a useful tool—so useful that it still exists.

It is a far cry from the abacus to the modern keyboard accounting machine. It will be an

equal step to the arithmetical machine of the future. But even this new machine will not take the scientist where he needs to go. Relief must be secured from laborious detailed manipulation of higher mathematics as well, if the users of it are to free their brains for something more than repetitive detailed transformations in accordance with established rules. A mathematician is not a man who can readily manipulate figures; often he cannot. He is not even a man who can readily perform the transformations of equations by the use of calculus. He is primarily an individual who is skilled in the use of symbolic logic on a high plane, and especially he is a man of intuitive judgment in the choice of the manipulative processes he employs.

All else he should be able to turn over to his mechanism, just as confidently as he turns over the propelling of his car to the intricate mechanism under the hood. Only then will mathematics be practically effective in bringing the growing knowledge of atomistics to the useful solution of the advanced problems of chemistry, metallurgy, and biology. For this reason there will come more machines to handle advanced mathematics for the scientist. Some of them will be sufficiently bizarre to suit the most fastidious connoisseur of the present artifacts of civilization.

## 5

The scientist, however, is not the only person who manipulates data and examines the world about him by the use of logical processes, although he sometimes preserves this appearance by adopting into the fold anyone who becomes logical, much in the manner in which a British labor leader is elevated to knighthood. Whenever logical processes of thought are employed—that is, whenever thought for a time runs along an accepted groove—there is an opportunity for the machine. Formal logic used to be a keen instrument in the hands of the teacher in his trying of students' souls. It is readily possible to construct a machine which will manipulate premises in accordance with formal logic, simply by the clever use of relay circuits. Put a set of premises into such a device and turn the crank, and it will readily pass out conclusion after conclusion, all in accordance with logical law, and with no more slips than would be expected of a keyboard adding machine.

Logic can become enormously difficult, and it would undoubtedly be well to produce more assurance in its use. The machines for higher analysis have usually been equation solvers. Ideas are beginning to appear for equation transformers, which will rearrange the relationship expressed by an equation in accordance with strict and rather advanced logic. Progress is inhibited by the exceedingly crude way in which mathematicians express their relationships. They employ a symbolism which grew like Topsy and has little consistency; a strange fact in that most logical field.

A new symbolism, probably positional, must apparently precede the reduction of mathematical transformations to machine processes. Then, on beyond the strict logic of the mathematician, lies the application of logic in everyday affairs. We may some day click off arguments on a machine with the same assurance that we now enter sales on a cash register. But the machine of logic will not look like a cash register, even of the streamlined model.

So much for the manipulation of ideas and their insertion into the record. Thus far we seem to be worse off than before—for we can enormously extend the record; yet even in its present bulk we can hardly consult it. This is a much larger matter than merely the extraction of data for the purposes of scientific research; it involves the entire process by which man profits by his inheritance of acquired knowledge. The prime action of use is selection, and here we are halting indeed. There may be millions of fine thoughts, and the account of the experience on which they are based, all encased within stone walls of acceptable architectural form; but if the scholar can get at only one a week by diligent search, his syntheses are not likely to keep up with the current scene.

Selection, in this broad sense, is a stone adze in the hands of a cabinetmaker. Yet, in a narrow sense and in other areas, something has already been done mechanically on selection. The personnel officer of a factory drops a stack of a few thousand employee cards into a selecting machine, sets a code in accordance with an established convention, and produces in a short time a list of all employees who live in Trenton and know Spanish. Even such devices are much too slow when it comes, for example, to matching a set of fingerprints with one of five million on file. Selection devices of this sort will soon be speeded up from their present rate of reviewing data at a few hundred a minute. By the use of photocells and microfilm they will survey items at the rate of a thousand a second, and will print out duplicates of those selected.

This process, however, is simple selection: it proceeds by examining in turn every one of a large set of items, and by picking out those which have certain specified characteristics. There is another form of selection best illustrated by the automatic telephone exchange. You dial a number and the machine selects and connects just one of a million possible stations. It does not run over them all. It pays attention only to a class given by a first digit, then only to a subclass of this given by the second digit, and so on; and thus proceeds rapidly and almost unerringly to the selected station. It requires a few seconds to make the selection, although the process could be speeded up if increased speed were economically warranted. If necessary, it could be made extremely fast by substituting thermionic-tube switching for mechanical switching, so that the full selection could be made in one one-hundredth of a second. No one would wish to spend the money necessary to make this change in the telephone system, but the general idea is applicable elsewhere.

Take the prosaic problem of the great department store. Every time a charge sale is made, there are a number of things to be done. The inventory needs to be revised, the salesman needs to be given credit for the sale, the general accounts need an entry, and, most important, the customer needs to be charged. A central records device has been developed in which much of this work is done conveniently. The salesman places on a stand the customer's identification card, his own card, and the card taken from the article sold—all punched cards. When he pulls a lever, contacts are made through the holes, machinery at a central point makes the necessary computations and entries, and the proper receipt is printed for the salesman to pass to the customer.

But there may be ten thousand charge customers doing business with the store, and before the full operation can be completed someone has to select the right card and insert it at the central office. Now rapid selection can slide just the proper card into position in an instant or two, and return it afterward. Another difficulty occurs, however. Someone must read a total on the card, so that the machine can add its computed item to it. Conceivably the cards might be of the dry photography type I have described. Existing totals could then be read by photocell, and the new total entered by an electron beam.

The cards may be in miniature, so that they occupy little space. They must move quickly. They need not be transferred far, but merely into position so that the photocell and recorder can operate on them. Positional dots can enter the data. At the end of the month a machine can readily be made to read these and to print an ordinary bill. With tube selection, in which no mechanical parts are involved in the switches, little time need be occupied in bringing the correct card into use—a second should suffice for the entire operation. The whole record on the card may be made by magnetic dots on a steel sheet if desired, instead of dots to be observed optically, following the scheme by which Poulsen long ago put speech on a magnetic wire. This method has the advantage of simplicity and ease of erasure. By using photography, however, one can arrange to project the record in enlarged form, and at a distance by using the process common in television equipment.

One can consider rapid selection of this form, and distant projection for other purposes. To be able to key one sheet of a million before an operator in a second or two, with the possibility of then adding notes thereto, is suggestive in many ways. It might even be of use in libraries, but that is another story. At any rate, there are now some interesting combinations possible. One might, for example, speak to a microphone, in the manner described in connection with the speech-controlled typewriter, and thus make his

selections. It would certainly beat the usual file clerk.

## 6

The real heart of the matter of selection, however, goes deeper than a lag in the adoption of mechanisms by libraries, or a lack of development of devices for their use. Our ineptitude in getting at the record is largely caused by the artificiality of systems of indexing. When data of any sort are placed in storage, they are filed alphabetically or numerically, and information is found (when it is) by tracing it down from subclass to subclass. It can be in only one place, unless duplicates are used; one has to have rules as to which path will locate it, and the rules are cumbersome. Having found one item, moreover, one has to emerge from the system and re-enter on a new path.

The human mind does not work that way. It operates by association. With one item in its grasp, it snaps instantly to the next that is suggested by the association of thoughts, in accordance with some intricate web of trails carried by the cells of the brain. It has other characteristics, of course; trails that are not frequently followed are prone to fade, items are not fully permanent, memory is transitory. Yet the speed of action, the intricacy of trails, the detail of mental pictures, is awe-inspiring beyond all else in nature.

Man cannot hope fully to duplicate this mental process artificially, but he certainly ought to be able to learn from it. In minor ways he may even improve, for his records have relative permanency. The first idea, however, to be drawn from the analogy concerns selection. Selection by association, rather than by indexing, may yet be mechanized. One cannot hope thus to equal the speed and flexibility with which the mind follows an associative trail, but it should be possible to beat the mind decisively in regard to the permanence and clarity of the items resurrected from storage.

Consider a future device for individual use, which is a sort of mechanized private file and library. It needs a name, and, to coin one at random, "memex" will do. A memex is a device in which an individual stores all his books, records, and communications, and which is mechanized so that it may be consulted with exceeding speed and flexibility. It is an enlarged intimate supplement to his memory.

It consists of a desk, and while it can presumably be operated from a distance, it is primarily the piece of furniture at which he works. On the top are slanting translucent screens, on which material can be projected for convenient reading. There is a keyboard, and sets of buttons and levers. Otherwise it looks like an ordinary desk.

In one end is the stored material. The matter of bulk is well taken care of by improved microfilm. Only a small part of the interior of the memex is devoted to storage, the rest to mechanism. Yet if the user inserted 5000 pages of material a day it would take him hundreds of years to fill the repository, so he can be profligate and enter material freely.

Most of the memex contents are purchased on microfilm ready for insertion. Books of all sorts, pictures, current periodicals, newspapers, are thus obtained and dropped into place. Business correspondence takes the same path. And there is provision for direct entry. On the top of the memex is a transparent platen. On this are placed longhand notes, photographs, memoranda, all sorts of things. When one is in place, the depression of a lever causes it to be photographed onto the next blank space in a section of the memex film, dry photography being employed.

There is, of course, provision for consultation of the record by the usual scheme of indexing. If the user wishes to consult a certain book, he taps its code on the keyboard, and the title page of the book promptly appears before him, projected onto one of his viewing positions. Frequently-used codes are mnemonic, so that he seldom consults his code book; but when he does, a single tap of a key projects it for his use. Moreover, he has supplemental levers. On deflecting one of these levers to the right he runs through the book before him, each page in turn being projected at a speed which just allows a recognizing glance at each. If he deflects it further to the right, he steps through the book 10

pages at a time; still further at 100 pages at a time. Deflection to the left gives him the same control backwards.

A special button transfers him immediately to the first page of the index. Any given book of his library can thus be called up and consulted with far greater facility than if it were taken from a shelf. As he has several projection positions, he can leave one item in position while he calls up another. He can add marginal notes and comments, taking advantage of one possible type of dry photography, and it could even be arranged so that he can do this by a stylus scheme, such as is now employed in the telautograph seen in railroad waiting rooms, just as though he had the physical page before him.

## 7

All this is conventional, except for the projection forward of present-day mechanisms and gadgetry. It affords an immediate step, however, to associative indexing, the basic idea of which is a provision whereby any item may be caused at will to select immediately and automatically another. This is the essential feature of the memex. The process of tying two items together is the important thing.

When the user is building a trail, he names it, inserts the name in his code book, and taps it out on his keyboard. Before him are the two items to be joined, projected onto adjacent viewing positions. At the bottom of each there are a number of blank code spaces, and a pointer is set to indicate one of these on each item. The user taps a single key, and the items are permanently joined. In each code space appears the code word. Out of view, but also in the code space, is inserted a set of dots for photocell viewing; and on each item these dots by their positions designate the index number of the other item.

Thereafter, at any time, when one of these items is in view, the other can be instantly recalled merely by tapping a button below the corresponding code space. Moreover, when numerous items have been thus joined together to form a trail, they can be reviewed in turn, rapidly or slowly, by deflecting a lever like that used for turning the pages of a book. It is exactly as though the physical items had been gathered together from widely separated sources and bound together to form a new book. It is more than this, for any item can be joined into numerous trails.

The owner of the memex, let us say, is interested in the origin and properties of the bow and arrow. Specifically he is studying why the short Turkish bow was apparently superior to the English long bow in the skirmishes of the Crusades. He has dozens of possibly pertinent books and articles in his memex. First he runs through an encyclopedia, finds an interesting but sketchy article, leaves it projected. Next, in a history, he finds another pertinent item, and ties the two together. Thus he goes, building a trail of many items. Occasionally he inserts a comment of his own, either linking it into the main trail or joining it by a side trail to a particular item. When it becomes evident that the elastic properties of available materials had a great deal to do with the bow, he branches off on a side trail which takes him through textbooks on elasticity and tables of physical constants. He inserts a page of longhand analysis of his own. Thus he builds a trail of his interest through the maze of materials available to him.

And his trails do not fade. Several years later, his talk with a friend turns to the queer ways in which a people resist innovations, even of vital interest. He has an example, in the fact that the outranged Europeans still failed to adopt the Turkish bow. In fact he has a trail on it. A touch brings up the code book. Tapping a few keys projects the head of the trail. A lever runs through it at will, stopping at interesting items, going off on side excursions. It is an interesting trail, pertinent to the discussion. So he sets a reproducer in action, photographs the whole trail out, and passes it to his friend for insertion in his own memex, there to be linked into the more general trail.

## 8

Wholly new forms of encyclopedias will appear, ready-made with a mesh of associative trails running through them, ready to be dropped into the memex and there amplified. The lawyer has at his touch the associated opinions and decisions of his whole experience, and of the experience of friends and authorities. The patent attorney has on call the millions of issued patents, with familiar trails to every point of his client's interest. The physician, puzzled by a patient's reactions, strikes the trail established in studying an earlier similar case, and runs rapidly through analogous case histories, with side references to the classics for the pertinent anatomy and histology. The chemist, struggling with the synthesis of an organic compound, has all the chemical literature before him in his laboratory, with trails following the analogies of compounds, and side trails to their physical and chemical behavior.

The historian, with a vast chronological account of a people, parallels it with a skip trail which stops only on the salient items, and can follow at any time contemporary trails which lead him all over civilization at a particular epoch. There is a new profession of trail blazers, those who find delight in the task of establishing useful trails through the enormous mass of the common record. The inheritance from the master becomes, not only his additions to the world's record, but for his disciples the entire scaffolding by which they were erected.

Thus science may implement the ways in which man produces, stores, and consults the record of the race. It might be striking to outline the instrumentalities of the future more spectacularly, rather than to stick closely to methods and elements now known and undergoing rapid development, as has been done here. Technical difficulties of all sorts have been ignored, certainly, but also ignored are means as yet unknown which may come any day to accelerate technical progress as violently as did the advent of the thermionic tube. In order that the picture may not be too commonplace, by reason of sticking to present-day patterns, it may be well to mention one such possibility, not to prophesy but merely to suggest, for prophecy based on extension of the known has substance, while prophecy founded on the unknown is only a doubly involved guess.

All our steps in creating or absorbing material of the record proceed through one of the senses—the tactile when we touch keys, the oral when we speak or listen, the visual when we read. Is it not possible that some day the path may be established more directly?

We know that when the eye sees, all the consequent information is transmitted to the brain by means of electrical vibrations in the channel of the optic nerve. This is an exact analogy with the electrical vibrations which occur in the cable of a television set: they convey the picture from the photocells which see it to the radio transmitter from which it is broadcast. We know further that if we can approach that cable with the proper instruments, we do not need to touch it; we can pick up those vibrations by electrical induction and thus discover and reproduce the scene which is being transmitted, just as a telephone wire may be tapped for its message.

The impulses which flow in the arm nerves of a typist convey to her fingers the translated information which reaches her eye or ear, in order that the fingers may be caused to strike the proper keys. Might not these currents be intercepted, either in the original form in which information is conveyed to the brain, or in the marvelously metamorphosed form in which they then proceed to the hand?

By bone conduction we already introduce sounds into the nerve channels of the deaf in order that they may hear. Is it not possible that we may learn to introduce them without the present cumbersomeness of first transforming electrical vibrations to mechanical ones, which the human mechanism promptly transforms back to the electrical form? With a couple of electrodes on the skull the encephalograph now produces pen-and-ink traces which bear some relation to the electrical phenomena going on in the brain itself. True, the record is unintelligible, except as it points out certain gross misfunction-

ing of the cerebral mechanism; but who would now place bounds on where such a thing may lead?

In the outside world, all forms of intelligence, whether of sound or sight, have been reduced to the form of varying currents in an electric circuit in order that they may be transmitted. Inside the human frame exactly the same sort of process occurs. Must we always transform to mechanical movements in order to proceed from one electrical phenomenon to another? It is a suggestive thought, but it hardly warrants prediction without losing touch with reality and immediateness.

Presumably man's spirit should be elevated if he can better review his shady past and analyze more completely and objectively his present problems. He has built a civilization so complex that he needs to mechanize his records more fully if he is to push his experiment to its logical conclusion and not merely become bogged down part way there by overtaxing his limited memory. His excursions may be more enjoyable if he can reacquire the privilege of forgetting the manifold things he does not need to have immediately at hand, with some assurance that he can find them again if they prove important.

The applications of science have built man a well-supplied house, and are teaching him to live healthily therein. They have enabled him to throw masses of people against one another with cruel weapons. They may yet allow him truly to encompass the great record and to grow in the wisdom of race experience. He may perish in conflict before he learns to wield that record for his true good. Yet, in the application of science to the needs and desires of man, it would seem to be a singularly unfortunate stage at which to terminate the process, or to lose hope as to the outcome.

# THE DYNABOOK—PAST, PRESENT, AND FUTURE

## Alan Kay
### Introduction by John Shoch

**John Shoch**

**M**y name is John Shoch. I have both the great privilege and the great challenge of introducing Alan Kay, our banquet speaker. Why do I say that it's both a privilege and a challenge? Well, my first reaction when I was invited to introduce Alan was that I was very flattered and appreciated the invitation. Although I'm now in the venture capital business here in Palo Alto, I spent fourteen years at Xerox. I was, in fact, hired by Alan Kay into the Palo Alto Research Center (PARC) shortly after it was formed. It was a wonderful time working for Alan. It was a period where I got to participate in some tremendously challenging research, and we all came away with many wonderful stories to tell.

So, I accepted instantly—and foolishly. As soon as I hung up and thought about it for another thirty milliseconds, the trepidation set in. To use a trite phrase, ''How do you go about introducing someone who needs no introduction?'' I considered lots of war stories and anecdotes, but I concluded that I would just stick to a few of the formalities and a brief observation.

As I said, for many of you who know Alan, he needs no introduction. Yet, conversely, I'd like to think that we have a broader audience tonight and that there are at least some people here who were not participants back in those early days of workstation development. There is much to be relearned from these experiences, and I hope that we're not just talking to ourselves. So with the hope that there might be a few people here who don't know Alan Kay's background: He has

249

a Ph.D. from Utah, he taught at Stanford University, joined Xerox PARC in 1971, went on a sabbatical to USC-ISI, went from there to Atari, and is now at Apple as an Apple Fellow. These credentials are *not* the reasons, of course, why Alan has been invited to come here tonight. Rather, the reason is what I would characterize as almost two decades of commitment to an idea that spans more than the individual contributions. This idea is the notion of *powerful, personal tools* including, but not limited to, computers for children of all ages.

Thomas Kuhn, in his book *The Structure of Scientific Revolutions*, talks about shifts in paradigm that are the important inflection points in the evolution of science. I believe that's what we've seen with personal workstations—that they represented a different kind of paradigm for computing. When you step back and try to integrate over all the individual contributions described in many of the speeches we've heard here, I really think it is that broad shift in paradigm that made the most profound difference.

Having that idea of the ultimate paradigm of personal workstations and powerful tools is necessary, but it's not sufficient in order to succeed. You have to be able to lead others—to exhort them to accomplish more than they thought was possible. You have to be able to establish a vision and then communicate that vision to others. Alan has been able to do that—to create broad and ambitious targets, and to describe those images with powerful words and pictures.

Many of you are familiar with some of his images, such as ''the pursuit of the Holy Grail,'' or the establishment of a target that we can then try to reach, even though it appears to be well beyond our grasp. The ''Dynabook,'' of course, is the most well known of his visions that has helped to motivate people for many years. Those of you who have had a chance to dig through some of the old papers will recognize other visions and symbols that were used to crystallize our thinking, including the Reading Machine, the Kiddy Comp, the Mini-Com, the Flex Machine (also known as the ''Reactive Engine''), and probably many more that I don't know about.

In addition, Alan expressed his ideas in phrases that we will most likely not forget. Many of us have heard the exhortation, ''Software is just like a waffle; you have to be prepared to throw out the first one.'' And we all once took part in an off-site meeting at Pajaro Dunes where he exhorted all of us to break out of what we had done and to go back and ''burn the disk packs.'' On the other hand, not all of his expressions were associated with the computer business. One of the fond memories I have was a day many years ago when Alan and I went out for a drink with Bob Barton, who had come to visit. We went to a local watering hole in Palo Alto. As we walked in, Alan sort of looked around and in his inimitable manner calmly observed, ''Yea, it's a nice place. Sort of a plush sewer.''

In helping to drive the creation and evolution of powerful workstations, Alan has had this tremendous ability to establish a vision, to create images for communicating that vision, and ultimately to motivate us to pursue and implement that vision. Without further ado and without further comment, let me now invite Alan Kay to come up to talk about his view of personal workstations.

Alan Kay grew up in Australia, Massachusetts, and New York, eventually attending Brooklyn Technical High School. He received his bachelor's degree in mathematics and molecular biology from the University of Colorado in 1966. He was a computer programmer during his Air Force years, and then received his Ph.D. in 1969 from the University of Utah. Alan joined the artificial intelligence project at Stanford and in 1970 became a member at the newly formed Xerox Palo Alto Research Center, where he remained for ten years. Since Xerox, Alan has worked at Atari and is presently with Apple Computer where he is an Apple Fellow.

While at Xerox PARC, Alan conceived of Dynabook, the powerful lap-sized personal computer of the 1980s to come that would allow people to draw and write anywhere they might be. Dynabook was the inspiration for Alto, the forerunner of Macintosh. He pioneered the development of object-oriented programming (Smalltalk), and the use of interactive high-resolution graphics as the basis for the computer-to-user interface. Along with Adele Goldberg and Dan Ingalls, Alan won the ACM Software Systems Award in 1987.

# The Dynabook—Past, Present, and Future

*Alan Kay*
Apple Computer, Inc.

[*Editor's Note:* Alan Kay presented his historical perspective at the banquet. A videotape of the complete talk is available from the ACM Publications Department. A paper that contains the basic content of Kay's material has been included.]

# Personal Dynamic Media

*Alan Kay and Adele Goldberg*
*Xerox Palo Alto Research Center*
From *Computer*, March 1977:10; 31–41 (and amended by Adele Goldberg, April 1988, to compensate for missing pictures). © 1977 IEEE. Reprinted with permission.

## Introduction

The Learning Research Group at Xerox Palo Alto Research Center is concerned with all aspects of the communication and manipulation of knowledge. We design, build, and use dynamic media which can be used by human beings of all ages. Several years ago, we crystallized our dreams into a design idea for a personal dynamic medium the size of a notebook (the *Dynabook*) which could be owned by everyone and could have the power to handle virtually all of its owner's information-related needs. Towards this goal we have designed and built a communications system: the Smalltalk language, implemented on small computers we refer to as "interim Dynabooks." We are exploring the use of this system as a programming and problem solving tool; as an interactive memory for the storage and manipulation of data; as a text editor; and as a medium for expression through drawing, painting, animating pictures, and composing and generating music. (Figure 1 is a view of this interim Dynabook.)

We offer this paper as a perspective on our goals and activities during the past years. In it, we explain the Dynabook idea, and describe a variety of systems we have already written in the Smalltalk language in order to give broad images of the kinds of information-related tools that might represent the kernel of a personal computing medium.

## Background

### HUMANS AND MEDIA

"Devices" which variously store, retrieve, or manipulate information in the form of messages embedded in a medium have been in existence for thousands of years. People use them to communicate ideas and feelings both to others and back to themselves. Although thinking goes on in one's head, external media serve to materialize thoughts and, through feedback, to augment the actual paths the thinking follows. Methods discovered in one medium provide metaphors which contribute new ways to think about notions in other media.

For most of recorded history, the interactions of humans with their media have been primarily nonconversational and passive in the sense that marks on paper, paint on walls, even "motion" pictures and television, do not change in response to the viewer's wishes. A mathematical formulation—which may symbolize the essence of an entire universe—once put down

**FIGURE 1**
The Alto—the original vehicle for exploring the interim Dynabook.

*Note:* An expanded version of this paper was produced as Xerox PARC Technical Report SSL-76-1, March, 1976.

on paper, remains static and requires the reader to expand its possibilities.

Every message is, in one sense or another, a *simulation* of some idea. It may be representational or abstract. The essence of a medium is very much dependent on the way messages are embedded, changed, and viewed. Although digital computers were originally designed to do arithmetic computation, the ability to simulate the details of any descriptive model means that the computer, viewed as a medium itself, can be *all other media* if the embedding and viewing methods are sufficiently well provided. Moreover, this new "metamedium" is *active*—it can respond to queries and experiments—so that the messages may involve the learner in a two-way conversation. This property has never been available before except through the medium of an individual teacher. We think the implications are vast and compelling.

## A DYNAMIC MEDIUM FOR CREATIVE THOUGHT: THE DYNABOOK

Imagine having your own self-contained knowledge manipulator in a portable package the size and shape of an ordinary notebook. Suppose it had enough power to outrace your senses of sight and hearing, enough capacity to store for later retrieval thousands of page-equivalents of reference materials, poems, letters, recipes, records, drawings, animations, musical scores, waveforms, dynamic simulations, and anything else you would like to remember and change.

We envision a device as small and portable as possible which could both take in and give out information in quantities approaching that of human sensory systems. Visual output should be, at the least, of higher quality than what can be obtained from newsprint. Audio output should adhere to similar high-fidelity standards.

There should be no discernible pause between cause and effect. One of the metaphors we used when designing such a system was that of a musical instrument, such as a flute, which is owned by its user and responds instantly and consistently to its owner's wishes. Imagine the absurdity of a one-second delay between blowing a note and hearing it!

These "civilized" desires for flexibility, resolution, and response lead to the conclusion that a user of a dynamic personal medium needs several hundred times as much power as the average adult now typically enjoys from timeshared computing. This means that we should either build a new resource several hundred times the capacity of current machines and share it (very difficult and expensive), or we should investigate the possibility of giving each person his own powerful machine. We chose the second approach.

## DESIGN BACKGROUND

The first attempt at designing this metamedium (the FLEX machine[4]) occurred in 1967–69. Much of the hardware and software was successful from the standpoint of computer science state-of-the-art research, but lacked sufficient expressive power to be useful to an ordinary user. At that time we became interested in focusing on children as our "user community." We were greatly encouraged by the Bolt Beranek and Newman/MIT Logo work that uses a robot turtle that draws on paper, a CRT version of the turtle, and a single music generator to get kids to program.

Considering children as the users radiates a compelling excitement when viewed from a number of different perspectives. First, the children really can write programs that do serious things. Their programs use symbols to stand for objects, contain loops and recursions, require a fair amount of visualization of alternative strategies before a tactic is chosen, and involve interactive discovery and removal of "bugs" in their ideas.

Second, the kids love it! The interactive nature of the dialogue, the fact that *they* are in control, the feeling that they are doing *real* things rather than playing with toys or working out "assigned" problems, the pictorial and auditory nature of their results, all contribute to a tremendous sense of accomplishment to their existence. Their attention spans are measured in hours rather than minutes.

Another interesting nugget was that children really needed as much or more computing power than adults were willing to settle for when using a timesharing system. The best that timesharing has to offer is slow control of crude wire-frame green-tinted graphics and square-wave musical tones. The kids, on the other hand, are used to finger-paints, water colors, color television, real musical instruments, and records. If the "medium is the message," then the message of low-bandwidth timesharing is "blah."

## An Interim Dynabook

We have designed an interim version of the Dynabook on which several interesting systems have been written in a new medium for communication, the Smalltalk programming language.[2] We have explored the usefulness of the systems with more than 200 users, most notably setting up a learning resource center in a local junior high school.

The interim Dynabook is a completely self-contained system. To the user, it appears as a small box in which a disk memory can be inserted; each disk contains about 1500 page-equivalents of manipulable storage. The box is connected to a very crisp high-resolution black and white CRT or a lower-resolution high-quality color display. Other input devices include a typewriter keyboard, a "chord" keyboard, a pointing device called a "mouse" which inputs position as it is moved about on the table, and a variety of organ-like keyboards for playing music. New input devices such as these may be easily attached, usually without building a hardware interface for them. Visual output is through the display, auditory output is obtained from a built-in digital-to-analog converter connected to a standard hi-fi amplifier and speakers.

We will attempt to show some of the kinds of things that can be done with a Dynabook; a number of systems developed by various users will be briefly illustrated. All photographs of computer output in this paper are taken from the display screen of the interim system.

### REMEMBERING, SEEING AND HEARING

The Dynabook can be used as an interactive memory or file cabinet. The owner's context can be entered through a keyboard and active editor, retained and modified indefinitely, and displayed on demand in a font of publishing quality.

Drawing and painting can also be done using a pointing device and an iconic editor which allows easy modification of pictures. A picture is thus a manipulable object and can be animated dynamically by the Dynabook's owner.

A book can be read through the Dynabook. It need not be treated as a simulated paper book since this is a new medium with new properties. A dynamic search may be made for a particular context. The non-sequential nature of the file medium and the use of dynamic manipulation allows a story to have many accessible points of view; Durrell's *Alexandria Quartet*, for instance, could be one book in which the reader may pursue many paths through the narrative.

### DIFFERENT FONTS FOR DIFFERENT EFFECTS

One of the goals of the Dynabook's design is *not* to be *worse* than paper in any important way. Computer displays of the past have been superior in matters of dynamic writing and erasure, but have failed in contrast, resolution, or ease of viewing. There is more to the problem than just the display of text in a high-quality font. Different fonts create different moods and cast an aura that influences the subjective style of both writing and reading. The Dynabook is supplied with a number of fonts which are contained on the file storage.

The Dynabook as a personal medium is flexible to the point of allowing an owner to choose his own ways to view information. Any character font can be described as a matrix of black and white dots. The owner can draw in a character font of his own choosing. He can then immediately view font changes within the context of text displayed in a window. With the Dynabook's fine grain of display, the rough edges disappear at normal viewing distance to produce high-quality characters.

The malleability of this approach is illustrated in Figure 2: this owner has decided to embellish some favorite nouns with their iconic referent. Such a facility would be useful in enhancing an early reading curriculum.

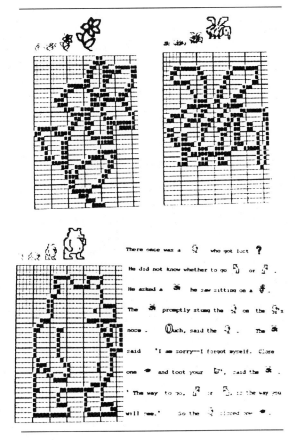

**FIGURE 2**
Fonts for a bear, a flower, and a bee used to tell a
story with pictures.

## EDITING

Every description or object in the Dynabook can
be displayed and edited. Text, both sequential
and structured, can easily be manipulated by
combining pointing and a simple "menu" for
commands, thus allowing deletion, transposi-
tion, and structuring. Multiple windows, allow
a document (composed of text, pictures, musical
notation) to be created and viewed simultaneously at several levels of refinement. Editing operations on other viewable objects (such as
pictures and fonts) are handled in analogous
ways.

## FILING

The multiple-window display capability of Smalltalk has inspired the notion of a dynamic *document*. A document is a collection of objects that
have a sensory display and have something to do
with each other; it is a way to store and retrieve
related information. Each subpart of the document, or *frame,* has its own editor which is automatically invoked when pointed at by the
"mouse." These frames may be related sequentially, as with ordinary paper usage, or *inverted*
with respect to properties, as in cross-indexed file
systems. *Sets* which can automatically map their
contents to secondary storage with the ability to
form unions, negations, and intersections are
part of this system, as is a "modeless" text editor
with automatic right justification.

The current version of the system is able to
automatically cross-file several thousand multi-
field records (with formats chosen by the user),
which include ordinary textual documents in-
dexed by content, the Smalltalk system, personal
files, diagrams, and so on.

## DRAWING/PAINTING

The many small dots required to display high-
quality characters (about 500,000 for an 8-½"
× 11" sized display) also allow sketching-quality
drawing, "halftone painting," and animation.
The subjective effect of gray scale is caused by the
eye fusing an area containing a mixture of small
black and white dots. The pictures in Figures 3
and 4 show a palette of toned patterns with
some brushes. A brush can be grabbed with the
"mouse," dipped into a paint pot, and then the
halftone can be swabbed on as a function of
the size, shape, and velocity of the brush. The
last pair of pictures shows a heart/peace symbol
shaped brush used to give the effect of painting
wallpaper.

Curves are drawn by a *pen* on the display
screen. (Straight lines are curves with zero cur-
vature.) In the Dynabook, *pens* are members of a
class that can selectively draw with black or
white (or colored) ink and change the thickness
of the trace. Each *pen* lives in its own *window*,
careful not to traverse its window boundaries but

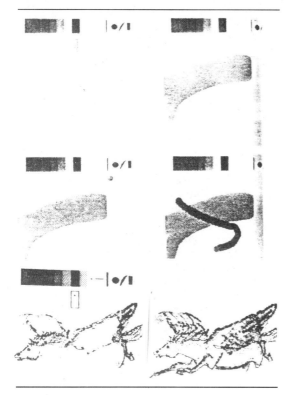

**FIGURE 3**
A sketch of Pegasus is shown being drawn with a
Smalltalk drawing tool. The first two pictures in the
sequence show halftone "paint" being scrubbed on.

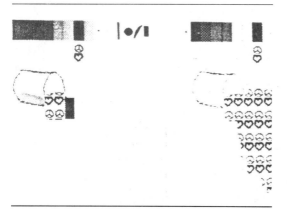

**FIGURE 4**
A sketch of a heart/peace symbol is created and used
as a paint brush.

to adjust as its window changes size and position. This window idea is illustrated in Figure 5; a number of simple and elegant examples are displayed in the windows.

### ANIMATION AND MUSIC

Animation, music, and programming can be thought of as different *sensory views* of dynamic processes. The structural similarities among them are apparent in Smalltalk, which provides a common framework for expressing those ideas.

All of the systems are equally controllable by hand or by program. Thus, drawing and painting can be done using a pointing device or in conjunction with programs which draw curves, fill in areas with tone, show perspectives of three-dimensional models (see Figure 6), and so on. Any graphic expression can be animated, either by reflecting a simulation or by example (giving an "animator" program a sample trace or a route to follow).

Music is controlled in a completely analogous manner. The Dynabook can act as a "super synthesizer" getting direction either from a keyboard or from a "score." The keystrokes can be captured, edited, and played back. Timbres, the "fonts" of musical expression, contain the quality and mood which different instruments bring to an orchestration. They may be captured, edited, and used dynamically.

## Simulation

In a very real sense, simulation is the central notion of the Dynabook. Each of the previous examples has shown a simulation of visual or auditory media. Here are a number of examples of interesting simulations done by a variety of users.

### AN ANIMATION SYSTEM PROGRAMMED BY ANIMATORS

Several professional animators wanted to be able to draw and paint pictures which could then be animated in real time by simply showing the system roughly what was wanted. Desired changes

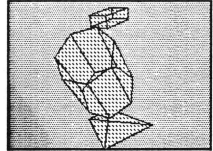

**FIGURE 6**
A model of three-dimensional graphics as
implemented in Smalltalk.

**FIGURE 5**
Curves can be drawn using Smalltalk line-drawing
commands. These curves are constrained to show in
display windows. Black and white can be reversed for
interesting effects.

would be made by iconically editing the animation sequences.

Much of the design of SHAZAM, their animation tool, is an automation of the media with
which animators are familiar: *movies* consisting of
sequences of *frames* which are a composition of
transparent *cels* containing foreground and background drawings. Besides retaining these basic
concepts of conventional animation, SHAZAM

incorporates some creative supplementary capabilities.

     Animators know that the main action of animation is due not to an individual frame, but to the change from one frame to the next. It is therefore much easier to plan an animation if it can be seen moving as it is being created. SHAZAM allows any cel of any frame in an animation to be edited while the animation is in progress. A library of already-created cels is maintained. The animation can be single-stepped; individual cels can be repositioned, reframed, and redrawn; new frames can be inserted; and a frame sequence can be created at any time by attaching the cel to the pointing device, then *showing* the system what kind of movement is desired. The cels can be stacked for background parallax; *holes* and *windows* are made with *transparent* paint. Animation objects can be painted by programs as well as by hand. The control of the animation can also be easily done from a Smalltalk simulation. For example, an animation of objects bouncing in a room is most easily accomplished by a few lines of Smalltalk that express the class of bouncing objects in physical terms. Figure 7 shows some animations created by young children.

*A DRAWING AND PAINTING SYSTEM*
*PROGRAMMED BY A CHILD*

One young girl, who had never programmed before, decided that a pointing device *ought* to let

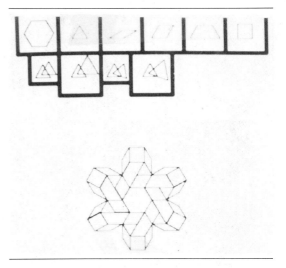

**FIGURE 8**
One of the first painting tools designed and implemented in Smalltalk by a twelve-year-old girl.

her draw on the screen. She then built a sketching tool without ever seeing ours (displayed in Figure 8). She constantly embellished it with new features including a menu for brushes selected by pointing. She later wrote a program for building tangram designs (Figure 9).

     This girl has taught her own Smalltalk class; her students were seventh-graders from her junior high school. One of them designed an even more elaborate system in which pictures are

**FIGURE 7**
An animation of a galloping horse, with and without a rider.

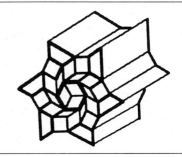

**FIGURE 9**
Tangram designs are created by selecting shapes from a ''menu'' displayed at the top of the screen. This system was implemented in Smalltalk by a fourteen-year-old girl.

constructed out of geometric shapes created by pointing to a menu of commands for creating regular polygons. The polygons can then be relocated, scaled, and copied; their color and line width can change.

## A HOSPITAL SIMULATION PROGRAMMED BY A DECISION-THEORIST

The simulation represents a hospital in which every *department* has resources which are used by *patients* for some *duration of time*. Each patient has a *schedule* of departments to visit; if there are no resources available (doctors, beds), the patient must *wait* in line for service. The Smalltalk description of this situation involves the class of *patients* and the class of *departments*. The generalization to any hospital configuration with any number of patients is part of the simulation. The particular example captured in the pictures shows patients lining up for service in *emergency*. It indicates that there is insufficient staff available in that important area.

## AN AUDIO ANIMATION SYSTEM PROGRAMMED BY MUSICIANS

Animation can be considered to be the coordinated parallel control through time of images conceived by an animator. Likewise, a system for representing and controlling musical images can be imagined which has very strong analogies to the visual world. Music is the design and control of images (pitch and duration changes) which can be *painted* different *colors* (timbre choices); it has synchronization and coordination, and a very close relationship between audio and spatial visualization.

The Smalltalk model created by several musicians, called TWANG, has the notion of a *chorus* which contains the main control directions for an overall piece. A chorus is a kind of *rug* with a warp of parallel sequences of ''pitch, duration, and articulation'' commands, and a woof of synchronizations and global directives. The control and the *player* are separate: in SHAZAM, a given movie sequence can animate many drawings; in TWANG, a given chorus can tell many different kinds of instrumentalists what should

be played. These *voices* can be synthetic timbres or timbres captured from real instruments. Musical effects such as vibrato, portamento, and diminuation are also available.

A chorus can be *drawn* using the pointing device, or it can be *captured* by playing it on a keyboard. It can be played back in real time and dynamically edited in a manner very similar to the animation system.

We use two methods for real-time production of high-quality timbres; both allow arbitrary transients and many independent parallel voices, and are completely produced by programs. One of these allows independent dynamic control of the spectrum, the frequency, the amplitude, and the particular collection of partials which will be heard.

For children, this facility has a number of benefits: the strong similarities between the audio and visual worlds are emphasized because a single vernacular *which actually works* in both worlds is used for description; and second, the arts and skills of composing can be learned at the same time since tunes may be drawn in by hand and played by the system. A line of music may be copied, stretched, and shifted in time and pitch; individual notes may be edited. Imitative counterpoint is thus easily created by the fledgling composer.

## A MUSICAL SCORE CAPTURE SYSTEM PROGRAMMED BY A MUSICIAN

OPUS is a musical score capture system that produces a display of a conventional musical score from data obtained by playing a musical keyboard. OPUS is designed to allow incremental input of an arbitrarily complicated score (full orchestra with chorus, for example), editing pages of the score, and hard copy of the final result with separate parts for individual instruments.

## Conclusion

What would happen in a world in which everyone had a Dynabook? If such a machine were designed in a way that *any* owner could mold and channel its power to his own needs, then a new kind of medium would have been created: a metamedium, whose content would be a wide range of already-existing and not-yet-invented media.

An architect might wish to simulate three-dimensional space in order to peruse and edit his current designs, which could be conveniently stored and cross-referenced.

A doctor could have on file all of his patients, his business records, a drug reaction system, and so on, all of which could travel with him wherever he went.

A composer could hear his composition while it was in progress, particularly if it were more complex than he was able to play. He could also bypass the incredibly tedious chore of redoing the score and producing the parts by hand.

Learning to play music could be aided by being able to capture and hear one's own attempts and compare them against expert renditions. The ability to express music in visual terms which could be filed and played means that the acts of composition and self-evaluation could be learned without having to wait for technical skill in playing.

Home records, accounts, budgets, recipes, reminders, and so forth, could be easily captured and manipulated.

Those in business could have an active briefcase which travelled with them, containing a working simulation of their company, the last several weeks of correspondence in a structured cross-indexed form—a way to instantly calculate profiles for their futures and help make decisions.

For educators, the Dynabook could be a new world limited only by their imagination and ingenuity. They could use it to show complex historical inter-relationships in ways not possible with static linear books. Mathematics could become a living language in which children could cause exciting things to happen. Laboratory experiments and simulations too expensive or difficult to prepare could easily be demonstrated. The production of stylish prose and poetry could be greatly aided by being able to easily edit and file one's own compositions.

These are just a few ways in which we envision using a Dynabook. But if the projected audience is to be "everyone," is it possible to make the Dynabook generally useful, or will it col-

lapse under the weight of trying to be too many different tools for too many people? The total range of possible users is so great that any attempt to specifically anticipate their needs in the design of the Dynabook would end in a disastrous feature-laden hodgepodge which would not be really suitable for anyone.

Some mass items, such as cars and television sets, attempt to anticipate and provide for a variety of applications in a fairly inflexible way; those who wish to do something different will have to put in considerable effort. Other items, such as paper and clay, offer many dimensions of possibility and high resolution; these can be used in an unanticipated way by many, though *tools* need to be made or obtained to stir some of the medium's possibilities while constraining others.

We would like the Dynabook to have the flexibility and generality of this second kind of item, combined with tools which have the power of the first kind. Thus a great deal of effort has been put into providing both endless possibilities and easy tool-making through the Smalltalk programming language.

Our design strategy, then, divides the problem. The burden of system design and specification is transferred to the user. This approach will only work if we do a very careful and comprehensive job of providing a general medium of communication which will allow ordinary users to casually and easily describe their desires for a specific tool. We must also provide enough already-written general tools so that a user need not start from scratch for most things she or he may wish to do.

We have stated several specific goals. In summary, they are:

- to provide coherent, powerful examples of the use of the Dynabook in and across subject areas;

- to study how the Dynabook can be used to help expand a person's visual and auditory skills;

- to provide exceptional freedom of access so kids can spend a lot of time probing for details, searching for a personal key to understanding processes they use daily; and

□ to study the unanticipated use of the Dynabook and Smalltalk by children in all age groups.

## REFERENCES AND BIBLIOGRAPHY

The following is a list of references that provides further details on some of the different systems described in this report.

1. Baeker, Ronald, "A Conversational Extensible System for the Animation of Shaded Images," *Proc. ACM SIGGRAPH Symposium*, Philadelphia, Pennsylvania, June 1976.

2. Goldberg, Adele and Alan Kay (Eds.), *Smalltalk-72 Instruction Manual*, Xerox Palo Alto Research Center, Technical Report No. SSL 76-6, March 1976.

3. Goldeen, Marian, "Learning About Smalltalk," *Creative Computing*, September-October 1975.

4. Kay, Alan, *The Reactive Engine*, Doctoral dissertation, University of Utah, September 1969.

5. Learning Research Group, "Personal Dynamic Media," Xerox Palo Alto Research Center, Technical Report No. SSL 76-1, March 1976.

6. Saunders, S., "Improved FM Audio Synthesis Methods for Realtime Digital Music Generation," *Proc., ACM Computer Science Conference*, Washington, D.C., February 1975.

7. Smith, David C., *PYGMALION: A Creative Programming Environment*, Doctoral dissertation, Stanford University Computer Science Department, June 1975.

8. Snook, Tod, *Three-dimensional Geometric Modelling*, Masters thesis, University of California, Berkeley, September 1976.

# PERSONAL DISTRIBUTED COMPUTING: THE ALTO AND ETHERNET HARDWARE

## Chuck Thacker
### Introduction by Ed McCreight

**Ed McCreight**

**M**y name is Ed McCreight. For the past 15 years, I've had the honor and delight of knowing Chuck Thacker and Butler Lampson. When I first met them, they were working at Berkeley Computer Corporation (BCC) and I was working for Boeing. Berkeley Computer Corporation was the outgrowth of project Genie at Berkeley, an early time-sharing system funded by Bob Taylor at ARPA. When I met them both, Berkeley Computer Corporation and Boeing were in the middle of the 1970–1971 recession. Boeing had larger financial resources and survived, but Berkeley Computer Corporation did not. At that time, the Berkeley Computer Corporation was making the BCC1. It was later renamed, for marketing reasons, the BCC 500, because nobody wants to buy number one of anything, and the number 500 had to do with the number of simultaneous users who could be connected to the Berkeley Computer Corporation 500 time-sharing computer. These would have to be patient users, I suppose.

When BCC fell apart, and my laboratory at Boeing fell apart, we all fell into the tender hands of Bob Taylor, who was setting up a new computer science research laboratory for Xerox. Although all of us were a little perplexed about what Xerox was going to do about computer science, we were happy to start a new lab. One of the first things that we did was to build another computer (MAXC). The story of that is like stories of yesterday, we won't have to go into that. This was a machine that didn't know it wasn't a PDP-10 (it ran the Tenex operating system). The point of that computer was to have a computer with

265

Charles P. Thacker is currently a Senior Consultant Engineer with the Digital Equipment Corporation Systems Research Center in Palo Alto, California. He is responsible for hardware development.

Chuck has a B.A. in Physics from the University of California, Berkeley, 1967. While at Berkeley, he worked for the Berkeley Instruments Corporation as an engineer responsible for the specification and implementation of digital hardware and transducers for meteorological data-gathering equipment. In 1967 he worked at the University on Project Genie as an engineer designing the 6700 time-sharing system and upgrades to the SDS 940 time-sharing system. The Berkeley Computer Corporation (BCC) was the commercial successor of Project Genie; from 1969 to 1971, Chuck was a project leader at BCC, responsible for the design of the CPU for the BCC 500 time-sharing system. From 1971 until 1983 he was a senior engineer/designer in the Computer Science Laboratory of Xerox PARC where he worked on the Alto, mouse device, design automation tools, Dorado and Dolphin. Along with Butler Lampson and Bob Taylor, Chuck won the ACM Software Systems Award in 1984.

which you could design another computer, because if you look at the history of Chuck Thacker's work, the work is either designing a computer or preparing to design the next computer. From that point on, Chuck designed a series of computers. Without further ado, I give you Chuck Thacker, who will tell you about the next computer after MAXC.

# Personal Distributed Computing: The Alto and Ethernet Hardware

*Charles P. Thacker*
Systems Research Center
Digital Equipment Corporation

## Introduction

In the last few years, a new type of computing environment has become available. These *distributed personal computing* systems represent another step in the process, started by time-sharing, of bringing computing power closer to the user. Although many variations are possible, these systems share a number of characteristics:

- They are based on *workstations*—personal machines that are sufficiently powerful to satisfy essentially all the computational needs of a single user. The workstations include high resolution displays, and provide a highly interactive user interface.
- The workstations are interconnected by *local networks* that provide high bandwidth communication throughout a limited area, typically a single building.
- In addition to the workstations, the network contains *servers*—nodes that provide capabilities that need to be shared, either for economic or logical reasons.

Time-sharing systems grew primarily from the vision of man-computer symbiosis presented by J. C. R. Licklider in a landmark 1960 paper [29]. Efforts to realize the possibilities presented in this paper occupied the creative talents of many computer science researchers through the 1960s and beyond. Distributed personal computing systems build on this view of the way computers and people interact by providing a level of responsiveness that time-sharing systems cannot achieve.

The first distributed personal computing system was built at the Xerox Palo Alto Research Center over a period spanning 1972 to 1980. The workstation used in this system was the Alto [36]; the network was Ethernet. This paper describes the hardware that was the foundation of this system. A companion paper by Butler Lampson [24] describes the software that was built on the hardware base described here.

This paper contains seven sections: The first describes the environment in which the work was done. The second traces some of the underlying ideas. The third describes the early implementation period, and the fourth discusses the servers that provide printing and file storage in the system. In the fifth section, the reengineering effort that made the Alto into a successful internal product is described. The sixth section briefly discusses some of the Alto's successors, and the last section contains concluding remarks.

## The Environment

The Xerox Palo Alto Research Center (PARC) was established in 1970, primarily through the efforts of Jacob Goldman, director of corporate research. It was composed of three laboratories: the Computer Science Laboratory, the System Sciences Laboratory, and the General Science Laboratory. To direct the new center, Goldman recruited George Pake, a physicist who was at that time provost of Washington University, St. Louis.

To establish the Computer Science Lab, Pake engaged Robert Taylor, who had directed the Information Processing Techniques Office of ARPA during the late 1960s. Taylor had worked with and funded many of the leading computer science research groups during this period. As a result, he was in a unique position to attract a staff of the highest quality.

During the first year of CSL, Taylor built a group of approximately fifteen researchers, drawn from MIT, the University of Utah, and CMU. Several members of CSL came from Berkeley Computer Corporation, a start-up company composed primarily of individuals from the University of California at Berkeley, who had built one of the first time-sharing systems [25]. From Bolt, Beranek, and Newman, Taylor later brought Jerome Elkind, who was the manager of CSL from 1971 until 1976. Also during this period, Alan Kay, who was to provide much of the vision on which the Alto was based, was recruited into the Systems Sciences Laboratory by Taylor. Kay established the Learning Research Group (LRG), and defined its goal: To produce a programming system in which " . . . simple things would be simple, and complex things would be possible"[20].

The research environment built by Taylor was one of the main reasons for the success of CSL and its projects over the next decade. Unlike other PARC laboratories, CSL was not organized into permanent groups. Instead, researchers were encouraged to move between projects as their talents and the needs of the projects dictated. This flat structure and the mobility it made possible encouraged members of the lab to become familiar with all activities. Additionally, it provided a continuous form of peer review. Projects that were exciting and challenging obtained something much more important than financial or administrative support; they received help and participation from other CSL researchers. As a result, quality work flourished, less interesting work tended to wither.

During 1971 and early 1972, most of the effort in CSL was spent in building a set of hardware and software facilities to support the future work of the laboratory. The MAXC time-sharing system [13] was built and the Tenex [2] operating system was acquired and modified for it. Projects in graphics, computer networking, and language design were started.

The main research theme of CSL—office information systems—was also developed during this period. Most of the research done in CSL and SSL during the next five years was organized around this theme, which reflected the desire of Xerox to expand its traditional copier business to include most of the functions performed in offices. Eventually, this theme was broadened to include what is now known as distributed personal computing, but initially our ambitions were lower.

A strategy for carrying out work in experimental computer science was also adopted at this time. It was based on the idea that demonstrations of "toy" systems are insufficient to determine the worth of a system design. Instead, it is necessary to build *real* systems, and to use them in daily work to assess the validity of the underlying ideas and to understand the consequences of those ideas. When the designers and implementors are themselves the users, as was the case at PARC, and when the system is of general utility, such as an electronic mail system or a text editor, there is a powerful bootstrapping effect. This view of systems research is quite different from that found in most academic environments, since it requires larger groups working over a longer period than a university can usually support.

It was clear that the ability to provide systems with high levels of functionality would be limited by software considerations far more than by the capabilities of the underlying hardware. While it would be necessary for us to build hardware, since the needed capabilities were not commercially available, the characteristics of the devices would be determined primarily by the needs of the software systems for which they were intended. This view is commonplace today, as hardware performance has increased and its cost has declined, while the cost of delivering large, reliable software systems has continued to increase. It was much more radical in 1971.

Although hardware development was an integral part of the work carried out in CSL, it represented a small fraction of the overall activity of the laboratory. At no time did the number of people engaged primarily in hardware work exceed five—roughly 10 percent of the total professional staff. This core group was very effectively augmented during large projects (e.g., the development of the Dorado [27] during 1977–1980) by laboratory members with computer science, rather than electrical engineering backgrounds. However, most things were done by a relatively small group. For this reason, it was necessary to be selective in our choice of projects. Simplicity and utility were the most important criteria. Highly complex designs would have been beyond our capabilities, and the construction of systems without a wide user community would not have justified the expenditure of scarce design and implementation talent.

## Sources of Ideas

By late 1972, most of the laboratory facilities were in place in CSL, and the researchers who had produced them began planning longer-term projects. It was at this time that the main ideas underlying the Alto were discussed and refined into an actual design. Although a number of people in CSL and SSL contributed to the specification of the new system, Butler Lampson, Alan Kay, and Bob Taylor were the individuals who were primarily responsible for shaping the design. To the extent that CSL had project managers, I filled that function. My task was to convert the vision of Lampson, Kay, and Taylor into working hardware.

Taylor had originally proposed that the primary computing facility in CSL should be an interconnected collection of small display-based machines, rather than a central time-sharing system. He thought that a sufficient amount had been learned about the design of interactive systems, and that hardware costs were low enough that it would be feasible to produce such a system in modest quantities. In 1970, this idea contained a number of technical difficulties. Lampson and I argued that a stable set of computing facilities as well as experience in producing hardware in the new laboratory would be required before embarking on such an ambitious project. This conservative view prevailed, but by 1972 sufficient progress had been made in a number of areas, particularly semiconductors, that the difficulties did not seem as overwhelming.

In his 1969 thesis, Alan Kay had described a small computer system, the "reactive engine" [21], that shared many of the characteristics of the new machine. Like Taylor, Kay wanted a system that would provide a complete work environment for its user, including text and graphics manipulation, computing, and communications capability. By 1972, this vision of computing had acquired a name—Dynabook—and for a while, the Alto was called the "interim Dynabook" by its developers. Kay's vision was that the ultimate Dynabook would be portable so that it could provide all the functions provided by books, paper, pencil, and terminals. Although the Alto never achieved this part of his vision, it served for a number of years as the hardware environment for the Smalltalk system [16], in which a number of text and graphics, music, and simulation applications were built.

Lampson's view of the capabilities of the new system and its uses was perhaps the most explicit. In a 1972 guest editorial [23] in *Software—Practice and Experience,* he had predicted that within five years, it would be possible to build a system " . . . comparable to a 360/65 in computing power for a manufacturing cost of perhaps $500." In the same article, he predicted significant advances in programming technology, and foresaw some of the effects that would follow from these developments:

> As a result, millions of people will write nontrivial programs, and hundreds of thousands will try to sell them. . . . Almost everyone who uses a pencil will use a computer, and although most people will not do any serious programming, almost everyone will be a potential customer for serious programs of some kind.

Although it was clear that we could not achieve these goals in 1972, there was a consensus that the new system should have characteristics that were prototypical of this vision. Cost was not a primary consideration in the design, but it could not be outrageous, since the system had to be producible in modest quantities to justify the development of software for it.

By late 1972, the principal features of the new machine had been defined. The major departure from past systems was the machine's display (see Fig. 1). To emulate as many of the characteristics of paper

**FIGURE 1**
**The Alto II workstation.** The Alto I had an identical display, keyboard, and mouse, but a slightly different cabinet.

as possible, we chose to provide a full bitmap, in which each screen pixel was represented by a bit of main storage, and to use raster scanning rather than the lower-cost calligraphic techniques popular at the time. We were encouraged by the earlier experiences of a group in SSL, which had developed a character generator for a similar, but higher resolution display. The display resolution was 606 pixels horizontally by 808 pixels vertically, which allowed display of a full page of text. The display image was refreshed directly from main memory, so arbitrary graphics could also be produced using the machine's load and store instructions. Initially, a specialized instruction was provided to paint characters from a font in memory into the bitmap; this facility was later superseded by the more general BitBlt primitive invented by Dan Ingalls [17]. The Alto contained no support for other graphic primitives, since we were primarily interested in text and engineering drawing applications that could be done with specialized character sets and straight lines.

The decision to provide a high-performance display came directly from our view that the most important purpose of the machine and the software that would be written for it was to provide a high bandwidth interface to the human user. Time-sharing systems had made computing more accessible and decreased its cost, but they had done little to increase the *quality* of man-machine interaction. We viewed improvement of the user interface as extremely important, and were willing to expend a considerable fraction of the machine's resources in providing it.

Another important feature of the user interface provided by the Alto was the use of a mouse as a pointing device. This was not a PARC innovation; it had been used with considerable success in the pioneering NLS system of Engelbart done at SRI in the late 1960s [12,11,10]. When rolled over a work surface adjacent to the keyboard, the mouse provides relative positioning information, usually used by software to control the position of a cursor on the display screen. It also provides additional input through buttons on its top surface. Subsequent research [5] has shown that the mouse is a Fitts's law device, in that it is as efficient for target selection as manual pointing. The practical impact of this is that in the domain for which it was intended, the mouse, like the compact disk in the audio domain, does as well as the limits of the human user allow. This is often overlooked by those attempting to provide better pointing devices. The mouse is not as effective as a pencil or a graphics tablet for freehand drawing, but very few graphic applications made use of a tablet, although an interface for one was provided.

The display's cursor was a small image, 16 pixels square, whose contents and position could be controlled by software. Many programs made considerable use of the programmability of the cursor, using its contents to convey information about the item to which the user was pointing.

The Alto keyboard was similar to that of a typewriter; it was not accidental that it lacked the cursor positioning keys and numeric keypad found on most personal computers today. In addition to the normal typing keys, it provided eight uncommitted keys that could be used by software as option or function keys. A five-finger keyset, which had been used successfully in Engelbart's NLS, was provided as an enhancement to the keyboard, but it required a trained operator for use, and never became popular as an input device.

The original Alto contained 128 thousand bytes of main storage, and a 2.5 million byte cartridge disk. This was similar to contemporary minicomputers and constituted a fairly serious error. If we had understood how rapidly semiconductor technology would advance, and how long the Alto would live, we would have included more convenient means for accessing a larger memory. We failed to do this, and although the main memory was subsequently expanded to 512 thousand bytes, it was difficult for programs to make use of the additional memory. This hampered software development quite a bit in later years.

The processor of the Alto was specified with flexibility and expansion in mind. It was microcoded, which allowed us to experiment with new instruction sets and with new input-output devices. The principal characteristic that served to differentiate it from the minicomputers of its time was that the microprogrammed processor was shared between the emulation of a target instruction set and the servicing of up to fifteen additional fixed-priority *tasks,* most of which were associated with the machine's input-output devices. Task switching occurred rapidly, typically every few microseconds. This mechanism allowed the input-output controllers to be very simple, since they could make use of the processor for much of their work. Since access to the single-ported memory is the bottleneck in a small system, multiplexing the processor in this way did not degrade system performance. This technique had been used before on the Lincoln Laboratory TX-2 [14]; it was very successful in the Alto, and has been used in several of the Alto's successors.

To be an effective replacement for centralized computing facilities, personal workstations require a means for communicating with other nearby workstations and with servers that provide shared facilities such as file storage, printing, and long-haul communication. When the Alto design was started, we realized that such a facility would be needed, but did not understand its requirements well enough to begin a design. During late 1972 and early 1973, a number of alternatives were considered, ranging from star-connected serial links operating at a few hundred thousand bits per second to a parallel bus scheme operating at several million bytes per second. The need for bulk file transfers ruled out the low bandwidth of the first approach, and the complexity of the required cabling made the parallel bus unattractive. Coaxial cable, connected with standard cable television components, was tentatively selected as the transmission medium, since it would meet both the bandwidth and reliability requirements.

Several transmission methods were also considered, and a variant of the packet-based ALOHA [1] radio system was selected. In pure ALOHA, stations needing to transmit packets simply do so, and the resulting interference between stations reduces the channel capacity considerably. We realized that better performance was possible, since our cable ALOHA stations could detect when their own transmissions were being interfered with, and abort them without transmitting a complete packet. We chose a baseband, as opposed to a carrier system because it is considerably simpler, and the extra bandwidth afforded by the latter scheme did not appear to be needed. These tentative decisions about the form that the network would take were made in late 1972, but little progress was made on an actual network design until Bob Metcalfe, who had joined CSL in mid-1972, and David Boggs, who came to SSL in March 1973, began working on what was to become the Ethernet [31].

## Implementation

In November 1972, implementation of the Alto began. The design was completed in approximately two months, including an initial version of the microcode for an instruction set emulator and for the display and disk controllers. Two prototype machines were then built using wirewrap technology, and were in operation in April 1973. One reason for the short schedule was that we had developed a rapid prototyping facility as a part of the construction of the MAXC time-sharing system during 1971 and 1972. We were also able to use the memory boards originally developed for the MAXC system in the Alto, which saved considerable engineering effort. The design of the processor, memory subsystem, and display controller was done by Chuck Thacker, while the disk controller and its microcode were designed and implemented by Ed McCreight. Larry Clark built the early systems and designed the package.

The Alto was a very simple machine by today's standards. The processor (Fig. 2) is composed of three printed circuit boards containing about 200 small- and medium-scale integrated circuits. Each of the input-output controllers occupies a single board containing approximately 60 integrated circuits. The processor is organized around a 16-bit bus connected to the main memory, an arithmetic unit, a number of high speed registers (R and S), and the input-output controllers.

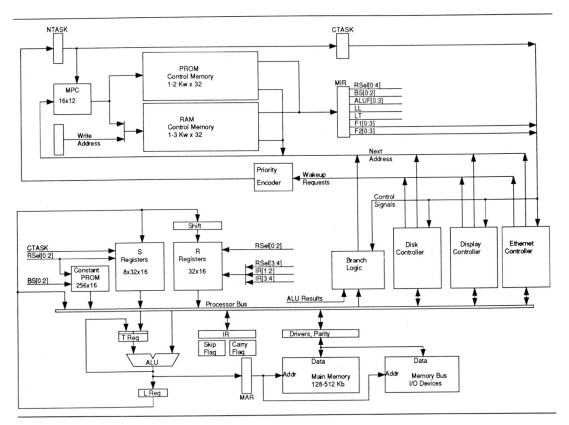

**FIGURE 2**
The Alto microprocessor.

The transfer of data over the bus, the operations to be performed on the data, and the tests to be applied to it are controlled by a 32-bit microinstruction taken from PROM or RAM control store. Microinstructions are executed by a two-stage pipeline that can start a new instruction every 170 nanoseconds. The processor is shared among 16 fixed priority tasks. The NTASK and CTASK registers hold the number of the task currently in control of the processor. NTASK addresses the 16-element MPC RAM, which holds the task program counters. NTASK is loaded with the number of the highest priority wakeup request whenever the running task is willing to relinquish the processor. The only state associated with a task that is saved by the hardware is the task's program counter. Other machine resources are shared among tasks by programming convention. Normally, a task switch takes place with no overhead, unless it is necessary for the task giving up control to save and restore the L or T register.

The Alto main memory is synchronous with the processor, which starts all references by explicitly loading the memory address register (MAR). The memory can read or write a single 16-bit word in five machine cycles, or it can read a 32-bit doubleword in six cycles. The doubleword read was originally provided to support the display, which consumes two-thirds of the memory bandwidth even with this operation; it was also used very effectively by instruction set emulators for instruction fetching and to manipulate 32-bit quantities.

The Alto was not a high-performance machine, even by the standards of its time. Without the performance degradation caused by the input-output devices, it requires between one and three microseconds to execute a single emulated instruction. With the display running, these times are increased by a factor of three. Until software was developed that required a great deal of computation for simple user actions (e.g., the Bravo text editor), the speed of the machine was adequate. Perhaps more important than the absolute speed is the fact that the performance of the Alto is *predictable*. It is very difficult to provide this characteristic in a time-sharing system, and its lack can be very disconcerting to the user. The Alto cannot provide the peak performance of a time-sharing machine, but it has the desirable property, pointed out by Jim Morris, that it doesn't run faster at night.

Once the design was complete, the microprocessor was simple enough that the hardware worked almost immediately. Debugging the microcode was more difficult, but was simplified considerably by an auxiliary writeable microstore built for the purpose. This device was connected to the control logic of the Alto under test. It replaced the PROM control store with RAM, and also added several bits to the microword. These additional bits were used to provide a breakpoint capability that made debugging much easier. The test unit was under control of a dedicated minicomputer that ran a microcode assembler and debugger. Using these tools, microcode debugging could be carried out as easily as debugging an assembly language program on a conventional machine.

The first of several microcoded instruction set emulators developed for the Alto was done for a virtual machine similar to the Data General Nova minicomputer. We had previously purchased a number of these systems, and had developed for them a compiler for BCPL [32], a predecessor of the popular C language. The main differences between the Alto instruction set (Fig. 3) and that of the Nova were that the size of the Alto's address space was twice that of the Nova, and a number of instructions were added to support the Alto's input-output and interrupt system and to optimize BCPL procedure calls.

The resulting instruction set was not compatible with that of the Nova, but it was sufficiently similar that modifying the compiler was straightforward. Most of the early software for the Alto was written in BCPL. Only a small amount of assembly code was ever written for the

**FIGURE 3**
The BCPL instruction set and processor model.

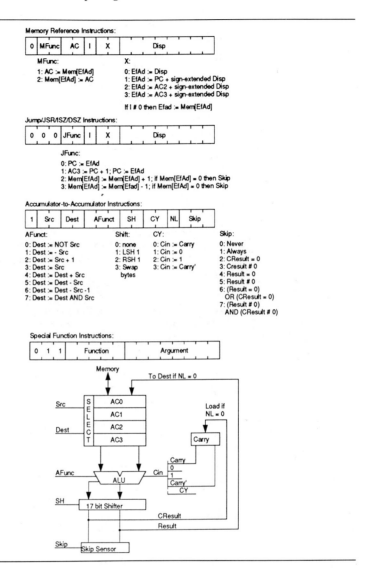

Memory Reference Instructions:

| 0 | MFunc | AC | I | X | Disp |
|---|-------|----|----|----|------|

MFunc:

1: AC := Mem[EfAd]
2: Mem[EfAd] := AC

X:

0: EfAd := Disp
1: EfAd := PC + sign-extended Disp
2: EfAd := AC2 + sign-extended Disp
3: EfAd := AC3 + sign-extended Disp

If I ≠ 0 then Efad := Mem[EfAd]

Jump/JSR/ISZ/DSZ Instructions:

| 0 | 0 | 0 | JFunc | I | X | Disp |
|---|---|---|-------|----|----|------|

JFunc:

0: PC := EfAd
1: AC3 := PC + 1; PC := EfAd
2: Mem[EfAd] := Mem[EfAd] + 1; if Mem[EfAd] = 0 then Skip
3: Mem[EfAd] := Mem[Efad] - 1; if Mem[EfAd] = 0 then Skip

Accumulator-to-Accumulator Instructions:

| 1 | Src | Dest | AFunct | SH | CY | NL | Skip |
|---|-----|------|--------|----|----|----|------|

AFunct:

0: Dest := NOT Src
1: Dest := - Src
2: Dest := Src + 1
3: Dest := Src
4: Dest := Dest + Src
5: Dest := Dest - Src
6: Dest := Dest - Src -1
7: Dest := Dest AND Src

Shift:

0: none
1: LSH 1
2: RSH 1
3: Swap bytes

CY:

0: Cin := Carry
1: Cin := 0
2: Cin := 1
3: Cin := Carry'

Skip:

0: Never
1: Always
2: CResult = 0
3: Cresult ≠ 0
4: Result = 0
5: Result ≠ 0
6: (Result = 0)
   OR (CResult = 0)
7: (Result ≠ 0)
   AND (CResult ≠ 0)

Special Function Instructions:

| 0 | 1 | 1 | Function | Argument |
|---|---|---|----------|----------|

machine. The microprocessor hardware contained a small amount of logic to enhance the performance of the BCPL emulator. This logic included a register to hold the instruction being executed and a method to address the registers used for the emulated machine's accumulators from its fields. This logic was not used by later emulators, and it probably would have been better to have used the same amount of hardware to provide functions with more general utility.

Emulators for several other instruction sets, including Smalltalk [18,16], Lisp [8,7], and Mesa [15] were written for the Alto. All were based on the idea of encoding the instructions as *bytecodes*. This arrangement allows instruction decoding to be done by a single 8-bit dispatch, rather than the several dispatches required to decode a BCPL instruction. The performance gained in this way more than offsets the lack of specialized decoding hardware. Most of the software written for the Alto after 1977 used Mesa, which was the choice in CSL, or Smalltalk (which was the language of choice in LRG). The Alto Lisp system was unsuccessful, primarily due to the lack of sufficient memory.

Input-output devices can be connected to the Alto in several ways. High-performance controllers that make use of the microprocessor or require a high-bandwidth connection to the memory are connected directly to the processor bus. The display, disk, and Ethernet controllers are examples of devices in this class. Lower-performance devices are attached to the memory bus and addressed as locations at the end of memory, as in the PDP-11. The keyboard and keyset are connected in this way. Finally, a parallel port is provided for low performance devices outside the cabinet. This port was used to connect a variety of devices, including impact printers, a PROM programmer, and X-Y digitizing tablet, and a cassette tape deck.

The hardware controllers for the disk, the display, and the Ethernet are similar. They contain data buffering, logic to drive and receive control lines required by the device, and a small amount of device-specific timing and control logic. Most of the complexity associated with a controller is contained in its microcode. The display, for example, makes use of 3 of the Alto's 16 microtasks: one is awakened during the display's vertical synchronization period, one is awakened during horizontal synchronization, and one is responsible for transferring raster data from main memory to the controller data buffer. The controller hardware provides wakeup requests at the appropriate times, but the microcode is responsible for carrying out most of the work required to maintain the display.

This arrangement, in which a device controller has the full computational power of the processor at its disposal, allowed us to provide convenient logical interfaces between devices and the driver software that operated them. The display interprets a chain of control blocks in main memory, each of which defines the contents of a horizontal band on the display screen. Since areas of the screen containing only white space, such as the space between lines and paragraphs, are not required to have any underlying bitmap memory, this technique reduces the display storage required by the standard text editor from the 61 thousand bytes required to represent a full screen to approximately 50 thousand bytes, a substantial saving in a machine with only 128 thousand bytes of memory. Drawing programs that allow the user to manipulate full-screen images cannot take advantage of this economy, but such programs are considerably simpler and smaller than the editor, so efficient use of space is less important in these applications.

The disk controller also makes extensive use of the Alto microprocessor. Like the display, it executes a chain of control blocks from main memory. Each control block specifies a 512 byte page to be read or written. The controller is able to transfer consecutive physical sectors between the disk and memory, which represented unusually high performance for the time. The controller uses two of the Alto's microtasks, one of which is awakened every sector, and one which is responsible for data transfers within a sector.

The disk controller and the file system were designed concurrently by Ed McCreight and Butler Lampson, with reliability as a primary goal. The designers wanted to provide a system in which hardware or software errors would result in a minimum amount of information loss. An important innovation—the use of label blocks—contributed substantially to the system's reliability. Labels add a third record to the header and data records customarily contained in a disk sector. The label record contains a unique integer identifier for the file containing the sector, the sector's position in the file, the addresses of the previous and next pages of the file, and the number of valid bytes in the data record. The controller microcode checks the information in the label block before doing any operation on the data record. This check ensures that the disk is properly positioned, both physically and logically, before any access to the data is done.

The use of label blocks, combined with replication of directory information in the first page of every file, means that the directory, which is an ordinary file, can be reconstructed from the contents of the disk itself if it becomes scrambled. Similarly, if data pages are corrupted, it is possible to determine precisely the extent of the loss, and to preserve the balance of the file system. One of the earliest programs written for the Alto was the Scavenger, which verified the integrity of a file system and corrected inconsistencies. This program, the first version of which was written by Jim Morris, makes the loss of even a small portion of a file system an extremely rare event.

The original Alto prototypes did not contain Ethernet interfaces, but during 1973 substantial progress on both network hardware and protocols was made. The name "Ethernet" was first used in May 1973 by Bob Metcalfe. Metcalfe and David Boggs worked on the network facilities during the summer and fall, and the prototype machines were exchanging packets by the end of 1973. Although the Alto was the first machine equipped with an Ethernet interface, Metcalfe and Boggs went on to design controllers for all the PARC computers, including Data General Novas and DEC PDP-11s. The Ethernet transceiver, an analog device that connects the controller to the coaxial cable, was designed by Tat C. Lam. The original Ethernet was slower than the commercial version available today. Its transmission rate was 2.94 million bits per second, half the rate of the Alto master clock, and it used Manchester encoding for the serial data. For collision detection, it relied on comparison between the actual signal on the coaxial cable and the signal the transmitting station was attempting to send, rather than the level monitoring done by the commercial version. The 3 million bit per second bandwidth of the network was of some concern initially, in that we were not sure that it would be sufficient for a large system. Subsequent measurements [33] of a large network revealed that loads in excess of 10 percent of full capacity were rare. There might have been less excess capacity if diskless workstations that paged over the network had been employed, but the use of local disks made this unnecessary.

In April 1973, the first Alto prototype was completed. It was able to run simple programs to exercise the disk and display. The first image to be displayed was the Sesame Street "Cookie Monster," which had been carefully digitized by a member of Kay's group.

During the balance of 1973, nine more prototype machines were built at PARC. During the summer, the prototypes had been tested sufficiently that we were willing to commit the design to printed circuit boards. At the same time, we realized that the lack of writable control store would be a serious limitation in a machine intended for experimentation and added one thousand words of instruction RAM to the original PROM control store. The original microcode was improved substantially, and a number of test programs for the hardware were written. Software development had begun, but there was not enough software available by the end of 1973 for the Alto to replace our time-sharing system as the main computing facility for users.

One of the major strengths of the Alto in a research environment was that it could provide very high performance if the user were willing to accept the unpleasantness of microprogramming the processor directly. The first demonstration of such an application took place in the summer of 1973. Alan Kay, who was an accomplished organist, wanted a synthetic instrument with natural sound quality. He believed that this could be accomplished by recording and digitizing a real organ, and doing table lookup to provide a completely faithful replica of the waveshape. We decided to give him his wish, and purchased a two-manual organ keyboard (with pedals), a precision digital-to-analog converter, and a high fidelity amplifier and loudspeaker system. The keyboard and DAC were interfaced so that a task-specific function could read the keyboard as a bit vector and load a value into the DAC. The organ simulator kept in main memory a table, consisting of the amplitudes at 256 points along a single cycle of the desired waveshape. Samples were generated for the DAC at a 25 kHz rate by taking points from this table at offsets that were inversely related to the frequency to be generated. The microprogram computed up to ten such samples every 40 microseconds, one for each key that was depressed. Samples were summed and the result was transmitted to the DAC. A variety of different effects could be generated by using different variations of the "canonical cycle." Although this application was fairly frivolous, it was an impressive demonstration of the real-time capability of the machine. Later, a serial line concentrator that connected up to 64 serial 300 baud lines to the Ethernet was built using similar techniques. The only extra hardware used in this device was a group of level converters and latches to allow the microprogram to read the value of the received data and store the data to be transmitted. All other processing was done by specialized microcode.

By late 1973, we were ready to produce a quantity of the machines for CSL and SSL. Although we had been able to build a small number of prototypes, the manufacture of the 30 systems we needed was beyond our capabilities. Fortunately, the company had established a custom systems manufacturing group in Los Angeles, and this group agreed to manufacture the Alto for us. The first machines were delivered between May and September 1974. This was only slightly later than the first release of the basic Alto software, which took place in March 1974. This early software consisted of the operating system [28], the BCPL compiler, and a primitive text editor. It allowed many of the researchers in CSL and SSL to begin doing a substantial amount of their work on the Alto, although the MAXC time-sharing system was still used for electronic mail, file storage, and printing.

## Servers

The most important components of a distributed computing system, after the workstations and the network that interconnects them, are the servers that provide shared facilities. We initially underestimated the importance of servers, assuming that the facilities provided by a set of workstations would be sufficient. We soon discovered that this was incorrect. Some functions, such as high-quality printing, are very expensive and must be shared for economic reasons, while in other cases, sharing is used to provide communication between the users of the system. File storage is an example of the latter situation, although the low cost per byte of large disk files also provides economy of scale.

The first PARC server was EARS, a printing server named after its components: Ethernet, Alto, RCG (research character generator), and SLOT (scanning laser output terminal). This system was quite successful, in spite of the considerable obstacle to its acceptance presented by its bizarre name. It was the forerunner of the Xerox 9700 printer, which has been an extremely successful product.

The printing portion of EARS had been under development even before PARC was founded. Gary Starkweather, an optical engineer at the Xerox Webster Research Center, joined SSL in 1971. He brought with him a prototype printing engine consisting of a laser scanner attached to a standard Xerox copier. This device used a rotating polygon to scan an intensity-modulated laser beam across a standard xerographic drum, building up a raster image of the page being printed. During 1972, Ron Rider of SSL and Butler Lampson designed and implemented a character generator capable of printing high quality text in several fonts on Starkweather's engine, at a speed of one page per second.

A printer based on these components, driven by a Data General Nova minicomputer, was demonstrated in late 1973, but was never placed in service. Instead, Rider decided to build an Ethernet-based print server. He modified the character generator to allow it to be driven from an Alto and wrote the necessary software to control the printer. The network-related portions of the server were written by Bob Metcalfe. EARS was the first major application for the Ethernet, and during its development, several experimental communications protocols [30] were tested and refined. EARS was placed in service in the fall of 1974 and provided printing service to CSL and SSL until it was replaced by the Dover printer in 1977.

The final component needed for a complete distributed computing system was a file server. The hardware basis for several experimental file servers was a high-performance disk controller designed by Roger Bates in 1975. Like earlier Alto device controllers, it made use of the Alto's microprogrammed tasking for many of its functions, but it was considerably more complex than the earlier controllers because of the high bandwidth of the attached disks. Using this device, it was possible to connect as many as seven 300 million byte disks to a single Alto.

The first file server, Juniper, was to have provided page-level access to files, as well as atomic transactions. Planning for Juniper began in 1974, but actual programming did not begin until 1976. It was completed in 1977, but was never used extensively because of its poor performance.

The file server that was used most widely was the "Interim File Server," or IFS. This software was written in 1976 by Ed Taft and David Boggs, when it became clear that Juniper would not be ready as early as originally anticipated. It was an extension of the simple Alto file system, combined with the PUP (PARC Universal Packet) file transfer protocol [3]. It provided only bulk file storage, but it was completed rapidly and was reliable and efficient. However, as an "interim" system, it was a failure, since the IFS still provides the majority of the file storage in the Xerox internetwork.

The most complex server built using the Alto was the Dover printer, designed in 1976. Dover used a raster printing engine that was a descendant of the SLOT used in the EARS server, driven by a controller that relied heavily on the input-output processing capability of the Alto. Dover was a large project, involving several groups within the company. The design of the printing engine was done by the Special Projects Group (SPG) in Los Angeles, the group that manufactured the Alto. John Ellenby of CSL was responsible for management of the engine development. Software for the Dover was written by Dan Swinehart of SSL and Bob Sproull of CSL. The development of the controller was done by Severo Ornstein of CSL, Bob Sproull, and Jim Leung of SPG from a design by Butler Lampson.

The controller was considerably simpler than the earlier EARS character generator. Instead of using hardware to generate the bit stream for the printer in real time, the controller built up the image to be printed incrementally. Two buffer memories were used, each capable of holding 16 of the printer's scan lines. While one of these buffers was being serialized and sent to the printer under hardware control, the other was being loaded with video information. The text to be printed and the bitmap representations for the fonts to be used were kept in Alto main memory, and written into the buffer by a high-priority microcoded task. This process was then repeated for each of the roughly 250 bands that made up each page. Spooling of files received from the network was done by a BCPL program, which also sorted the contents of each page into bands in preparation for transmission to the controller. The resolution of the Dover was 384 pixels per inch, lower than the 500 pixels per inch of EARS, but still adequate for text and line graphics. The bandwidth requirements of the printer were high enough that the machine could not receive and spool files while printing, but its printing speed of one page per second was high enough that this was not a problem, since it could stop between pages to receive files. Incremental image generation also placed a limit on the complexity of pages that could be printed. For the few images that exceeded the limit, another server that composed an entire page on disk and transmitted it to a slower printing engine was available.

The controller contained approximately 300 integrated circuits, making it about one-eighth as complex as the character generator used in EARS. This simplification was made possible by the extensive use of the Alto's microprocessor to provide the low-level control functions for the interface. Several dozen Dovers were built, and a number are still in operation.

## Expansion

During 1975, the Alto was redesigned to improve its reliability and reduce its cost. The work was done by the Special Projects Group in Los Angeles that had been producing Altos for PARC and was planned and supervised by John Ellenby of CSL. As part of this effort, all the boards and the package were redesigned. The memory system was reimplemented using 4 thousand bit RAM chips, and error correction was added. The resulting machine was much easier to build and service than the earlier system, and its cost was much lower—approximately $12,000, rather than $18,000. The Los Angeles group had built a total of 60 of the original systems over a period of two years, most of which had been purchased by CSL and SSL. They were now able to produce the system in high volume. Over the next four years, approximately fifteen hundred Altos were built, of which approximately a thousand are still in use today. Most are used by individual engineers and scientists in a number of Xerox facilities, although many were configured as servers, and a few were used for marketing probes or donated to university computer science groups.

A final redesign done in 1979 replaced the memory with 16 thousand bit RAM chips, and increased the amount of memory that could be attached to 512 thousand bytes. At the same time, the microcode store was changed from 1 thousand words of RAM and 2 thousand words of PROM to 1 thousand words of PROM plus 3 thousand words of RAM. By this time, other language emulators had almost totally superseded the original BCPL emulator. These emulators were usually loaded at bootstrap time or as part of starting a program that used a particular language. The additional RAM control store made it possible to spend less time minimizing the space required by the microcode and concentrate instead on its functionality and performance. The microcode was improved somewhat after the final redesign, but by 1980 most new development had shifted to the Alto's successors, described in the next section.

Although most of the software developed in CSL and SSL was distributed with the Alto, three application programs were primarily responsible for the machine's popularity with technical professionals in Xerox. The Bravo editor [22], designed by Charles Simonyi and Butler Lampson, and implemented and improved by Simonyi and others from 1974 through 1978, was the first and most important of these. Bravo was the first WYSIWYG (what you see is what you get) editor. It supported multiple fonts, and its high-quality output could be printed on one of the many Dover printers that were available throughout the company.

The second important application program was the Laurel mail system [4], written by Doug Brotz, Roy Levin, and Mike Schroeder in 1978. Electronic mail has a profound effect on communication within an organization, since it combines the permanence and precision of memos with the speed of the telephone. By 1980, the Xerox internetwork, composed of local Ethernets connected by telephone lines, had been expanded to most of the engineering and research sites within the company. Laurel was rapidly adopted by a large fraction of this community, and by 1983 there were over four thousand regular electronic mail users in Xerox.

The third popular application was a group of tools for digital logic design, including the SIL illustrator [35], written by Chuck Thacker in 1975, and a routing program for prototypes written by Ed McCreight. These programs also produced high quality documentation on the Dover printers. They increased the productivity of designers significantly and are used by most of the electronic engineers in the company.

## Successors

The Alto was only the first of several personal workstations built at Xerox. The Dorado [26,6,27] and the Dicentra were developed at PARC, and the Dolphin and the Dandelion were commercial systems designed in the Electronics Division and the System Development Division.

Dorado is the largest hardware engineering project ever undertaken by the Computer Science Laboratory. It was difficult to think of the Dorado as a personal machine, since it consumed 2500 watts of power, was the size of a refrigerator, and required 2000 cubic feet of cooling air per minute (while producing a noise level that has been compared to that of a 747 taking off).

It was *used* as a personal machine, however, and supplied computing power comparable to three VAX-11/780s. This may seem profligate, but it was consistent with the view that the CSL hardware base should be equivalent to that which would be commercially available and affordable in five to ten years. With hardware that is not limiting, it is possible to explore ways of using computers that are considerably ahead of current practice.

The Dorado project was started in CSL during 1975. It was moved to the System Development Division in 1976, but returned to CSL in 1977 when it became clear that the machine's high cost would not meet SDD's needs. The initial design was completed in late 1978, and two prototypes were built. A redesign, completed in 1979, was then done to simplify the machine. Manufacture of the machine started in 1980 in a small production facility that had been established for the purpose. By 1982, approximately 30 systems had been built, and the Dorado had replaced the Alto as the principal computing vehicle in CSL and SSL.

The Dorado achieved its high performance through its aggressive technology and a great deal of attention to detail on the part of its designers. It uses emitter-coupled logic (MECL 10K) with two to four nanosecond gate delays. The processor is microprogrammed and, like the Alto, employs multitasking at the microcode level to operate input-output controllers. Unlike the Alto, it has virtual memory, an eight thousand byte cache, and a separate instruction fetch unit associated with the CPU. Up to 16 million bytes of main memory may be attached to the Dorado. The memory bandwidth available for input-output devices and to service cache misses is 66 million bytes per second. The processor executes microinstructions in a three-stage pipeline that can start a new instruction every 60 nanoseconds. The separate instruction fetch unit allows many instructions in the common emulators to execute in a single microinstruction.

In terms of man-years expended on a single project in CSL, the Dorado is second only to the Cedar programming environment [9,34], which its high performance made possible. The initial design was done by Butler Lampson and Chuck Thacker; the design was continued in SDD by Thacker, Brian Rosen, Don Charnley, and Tom Chang. When the project returned to PARC, it was partitioned into a number of subsystems: Ed McCreight and Severo Ornstein were the project managers; Butler Lampson was the technical leader of the project. The microprocessor was designed by Ken Pier, Roger Bates, and Ed Fiala. The instruction fetch unit was designed and implemented by Severo Ornstein, Gene McDaniel, and Will Crowther. The storage system was done by Doug Clark, Ed McCreight, and Ken Pier. A number of individuals produced the microcode for the machine, including Ed Taft, Peter Deutsch, Willie-Sue Haugeland, and Nori Suzuki.

The Dolphin was a much less ambitious successor to the Alto, designed in the Electronics Division of Xerox in 1977–1979. In a sense, it was the successor of the Dorado, rather than the Alto, since it was done by the same group (Thacker, Charnley, Rosen, and Chang) that had worked on the Dorado in SDD as well as a group in Los Angeles that included Jack Cameron, Howard Kakita, and Malcolm Thomson. Dolphin employed a number of ideas that had been incorporated into the Dorado, including virtual memory and a high-bandwidth input-output system. Its technology was not as aggressive as that of the Dorado—Schottky TTL, rather than ECL—and it was smaller and much less expensive. The Dolphin was used as the processor in the Xerox 5700 Electronic Printing System, and a version configured as a Lisp workstation became the 1100 Scientific Information Processor. Although PARC built approximately 50 Dolphins for internal use and provided emulators for the Alto instruction set, Mesa, and Lisp the machine was not popular. It had a higher-resolution display, more memory, and a larger disk than the Alto, but it was only about twice as fast. Dolphin became available slightly before the Dorado, but the performance of the latter machine made it much more attractive, particularly for a research environment.

The Dandelion [19], known commercially as the Star 8010 workstation, was implemented in 1979 and 1980 by a group in SDD consisting of Bob Belleville, Robert Garner, and Ron Crane. Dandelion was based on a paper design called Wildflower done by Butler Lampson and Roy Levin of CSL. It was intended to have high performance and extremely low cost but limited configuration flexibility. The Dandelion CPU used 2901 bit-slice processors and employed a fixed time-slice form of multitasking that was quite different from that of the Alto. Dandelion was the first of the Alto's descendants that did not provide an emulation mode in which Alto software could be run. It was programmed exclusively in Mesa and the extended Mesa developed for the Cedar system. Dicentra, built by David Boggs and Hal Murray in 1982, was a variant of the Dandelion that included a Multibus rather than a proprietary bus for the attachment of input-output devices and memory. It provided a low-cost way to obtain a Mesa-compatible processor to which industry standard peripheral controllers and devices could be attached.

In addition to its direct descendants at Xerox, the Alto has inspired a number of similar systems from other commercial vendors. The Apple Lisa and Macintosh are perhaps the most familiar of these; Table 2 in Lampson [24] lists several others.

## Conclusion

The Alto is small and slow by today's standards. The four generations of memory and microprocessor development that have passed since 1972 have made it straightforward to build low-cost personal workstations with a hundred times the memory capacity and ten times the speed of the Alto. It seems likely that progress in semiconductors will continue at its present rate for perhaps another decade before fundamental physical limits are reached, so much more powerful systems are inevitable.

Higher-bandwidth networks have also become much easier to engineer with the advent of fiber optics. However, experience with the Ethernet indicates that even with very high performance machines such as the Dorado, network bandwidth is not the limiting factor in overall system performance.

A surprising fact that has emerged from the work on the Alto and its successors is that the amount of software required to support interactive user interfaces is much greater than originally anticipated. Invariably, the complexity of the software is much greater than that of the hardware on which it runs. Except in a few applications in which the users are experts (e.g., programmers using programming environments), it has not yet become possible to provide the kind of symbiotic relationship between computer and human envisioned by Licklider in 1960. Advances in programming technology, as well as better hardware, will be required to achieve the kind of system he described. Distributed personal computing systems will help bring about these advances by providing more productive and efficient computing environments for developers.

## REFERENCES

[1] N. Abramson. The ALOHA System. In *Proc. AFIPS FJCC*, pages 281–285, 1970.

[2] D. G. Bobrow et al. Tenex: A paged time-sharing system for the PDP-10. *Communications of the ACM*, 15(3):135–143, March 1972.

[3] D. R. Boggs et al. Pup: An internetwork architecture. *IEEE Trans. Comm.*, 28(4):612–624, April 1980.

[4] D. K. Brotz. *Laurel Manual*. Technical Report CSL-81-6, Xerox Palo Alto Research Center, 1981.

[5] S. Card et al. Evaluation of mouse, rate-controlled isometric joystick, step keys and text keys for text selection on a CRT. *Ergonomics*, 21(8):601–613, August 1978.

[6] D. W. Clark, B. W. Lampson, and K. A. Pier. The memory system of a high-performance personal computer. In *The Dorado: A High-Performance Personal Computer—Three Papers, CSL-81-1*, pages 51–80, Xerox Palo Alto Research Center, 1981.

[7] L. P. Deutsch. Experience with a microprogrammed Interlisp system. *IEEE Transactions on Computers*, C-28(10), October 1979.

[8] L. P. Deutsch. A Lisp machine with very compact programs. In *Proc. 3rd IJCAI*, Stanford, 1973.

[9] L. P. Deutsch and E. A. Taft. *Requirements for an experimental programming environment*. Technical Report CSL-80-10, Xerox Palo Alto Research Center, June 1980.

[10] D. C. Engelbart. The augmented knowledge workshop. In this volume.

[11] D. C. Engelbart. A conceptual framework for the augmentation of man's intellect. In Howerton and Weeks, editors, *Vistas in Information Handling, Volume 1*, pages 1–29, Spartan Books, Washington, 1963.

[12] D. C. Engelbart and W. K. English. A research center for augmenting human intellect. In *Proc. AFIPS Conf.*, pages 395–410, 1968.

[13] E. R. Fiala. The MAXC systems. *IEEE Computer*, 11(5):57–67, May 1978.

[14] J. W. Forgie. The Lincoln TX-2 input-output system. In *Proc. Western Joint Computer Conf.*, pages 156–160, February 1957.

[15] C. M. Geschke et al. Early experience with Mesa. *Communications of the ACM*, 20(8):540–553, August 1977.

[16] A. Goldberg and D. Robson. *Smalltalk-80: The Language and its Implementation*. Addison-Wesley, 1983.

[17] D. Ingalls. The Smalltalk graphics kernel. *Byte*, 6(8):168–194, August 1981.

[18] D. H. Ingalls. The Smalltalk-76 programming system: Design and implementation. In *Proc. 5th ACM Symp. Principles of Prog. Lang.*, pages 9–16, January 1978.

[19] R. K. Johnsson and J. D. Wick. An overview of the Mesa processor architecture. *ACM SIGPLAN Notices,* 17(4):20–29, April 1982.

[20] A. C. Kay. Microelectronics and the personal computer. *Scientific American,* 237(3):236–245, September 1977.

[21] A. C. Kay. *The Reactive Engine.* Ph.D. thesis, University of Utah, 1969.

[22] B. W. Lampson, editor. *Alto User's Handbook.* Xerox Palo Alto Research Center, 1976.

[23] B. W. Lampson. Guest editorial. *Software—Practice and Experience,* 2:195–196, 1972.

[24] B. W. Lampson. Personal distributed computing: The Alto and Ethernet software. In this volume.

[25] B. W. Lampson et al. A user machine in a time-sharing system. *Proc. IEEE,* 54(12): 1744–1766, December 1966.

[26] B. W. Lampson, G. A. McDaniel, and S. M. Ornstein. An instruction fetch unit for a high-performance personal computer. In *The Dorado: A High-Performance Personal Computer—Three Papers, CSL-81-1,* pages 21–50, Xerox Palo Alto Research Center, 1981.

[27] B. W. Lampson and K. A. Pier. A processor for a high-performance personal computer. In *Proc. 7th Symp. Computer Arch.,* pages 146–160, ACM Sigarch/*IEEE,* May 1980.

[28] B. W. Lampson and R. F. Sproull. An open operating system for a single-user machine. *ACM Operating Sys. Rev.,* 13(5), November 1979.

[29] J. Licklider. Man-computer symbiosis. *IRE Trans. Human Factors in Electronics,* HFE-1:4–11, March 1960.

[30] R. M. Metcalfe and D. R. Boggs. Ethernet: Distributed packet switching for local computer networks. *Communications of the ACM,* 19(7):395–404, July 1976.

[31] R. M. Metcalfe, D. R. Boggs, C. P. Thacker, and B. W. Lampson. U.S. Patent 4,063,220: Multipoint Data Communication System With Collision Detection. December 1977.

[32] M. Richards. BCPL: A tool for compiler writing and system programming. In *AFIPS Conf. Proc.,* pages 557–566, 1969.

[33] J. F. Shoch and J. A. Hupp. Measured performance of an Ethernet local network. *Communications of the ACM,* 23(12):711–721, December 1980.

[34] W. Teitelman. A tour through Cedar. *IEEE Software,* 1(4), April 1984.

[35] C. P. Thacker. SIL—a simple illustrator for cad. In S. Chang, editor, *Fundamentals Handbook of Electrical Computer Engineering, Volume 3,* pages 477–489, Wiley, 1983.

[36] C. P. Thacker et al. Alto: A personal computer. In Siewiorek et al., editors, *Computer Structures: Principles and Examples,* chapter 33, McGraw-Hill, 1982. Also CSL-79-11, Xerox Palo Alto Research Center (1979).

# PERSONAL DISTRIBUTED COMPUTING: THE ALTO AND ETHERNET SOFTWARE

## Butler Lampson
Introduction by Ed McCreight

The next speaker is Butler Lampson. Butler was one of the founders of the 940 project at Berkeley, and has a history that parallels that of Chuck. Butler, as you've heard from everyone who's come before, I think, has been into everything. Chuck will tell you mostly about the hardware, although I can point to several charming pieces of software that he's written. But Butler has been just all over the map, including Philadelphia. Butler has had a hand in everything. It would be hard for me to point to anything that was developed at PARC in the computing area that Butler hadn't at least kibitzed on.

Butler Lampson has his B.A. in Physics (1964) from Harvard and a Ph.D. in Electrical Engineering and Computer Science (1967) from the University of California, Berkeley. He was an Assistant and Associate Professor of Computer Science at UC, Berkeley from 1969 to 1971. At that time, he helped form the Berkeley Computer Corporation (BCC). In 1971, he joined the Xerox Palo Alto Research Center, where he remained until 1983. Butler is currently a Senior Scientist at the Digital Equipment Corporation Systems Research Center.

Butler is interested in designing and building computers, such as the MAXC, Alto, Dorado, and Dandelion, all developed while he was at Xerox. He is a designer of several operating systems, including those for the SDS 940 and the Alto as well as Cal TSS. His work on distributed systems has created the BCC terminal system, network transactions, remote procedure call techniques, and a network name server. While working at Xerox, he participated in the design and development of several printers, such as EARS, Dover, and Interpress, and several significant approaches to applications (Bravo text editor and Telesil network based graphics editor).

Along with Chuck Thacker and Bob Taylor, Butler won the ACM Software Systems Award in 1984.

# Personal Distributed Computing: The Alto and Ethernet Software

*Butler W. Lampson*
Systems Research Center
Digital Equipment Corporation

## Introduction

A substantial computing system based on the Alto [58] was developed at the Xerox Palo Alto Research Center between 1973 and 1978, and was considerably extended between 1978 and 1983. The hardware base for this system is simple and uniform, if somewhat unconventional. The software, which gives the system its visible form and knits together its many parts, is by contrast complex, variegated, even ramified. It is convenient to call the whole complex of hardware and software "the Alto system." This paper describes the major software components of the Alto system. It also tries to explain why the system came out as it did, by tracing the ideas that influenced it, the way these ideas evolved into the concept of personal distributed computing, and the nature of the organization that built the Alto. A companion paper by Chuck Thacker [56] describes the hardware.

### THEMES

But a man's reach should exceed his grasp, or what's a heaven for?
*—Browning*

The Alto system grew from a vision of the possibilities inherent in computing: that computers can be used as tools to help people think and communicate [39]. This vision began with Licklider's dream of man-computer symbiosis [32]. When he became head of the Information Processing Techniques Office at ARPA, Licklider pursued the dream by funding the development of computer time-sharing. His successors, Ivan Sutherland, Robert Taylor, and Larry Roberts, continued this work throughout the 1960s and extended it to computer networks. Taylor went on to manage the laboratory in which most of the Alto system was built, and people who worked on these ARPA projects formed its core. Their collective experience of time-sharing and networks became a major influence on the Alto design.

Another important influence, also funded by ARPA, was Doug Engelbart. He built a revolutionary system called NLS, a prototype of the electronic office. In NLS all the written material handled by a group of people is held in the computer and instantly accessible on a display that looks something like an ordinary sheet of paper. He demonstrated this system at the 1968 Fall Joint Computer Conference in San Francisco [12,13]. NLS was too expensive to be practical then, but it made a profound impression on many of the people who later developed the Alto.

Yet another ARPA project that had a strong influence on the Alto was Alan Kay's Flex machine, also called the Reactive Engine [21]. Kay was pursuing a different path to Licklider's man-computer symbiosis: the computer's ability to simulate or model any system, any possible world, whose behavior can be precisely defined. And he wanted his machine to be small, cheap, and easy for nonprofessionals to use. Like Engelbart, he attached great importance to a high-quality, rapidly-changing display. He later coined the name "Dynabook" for the tool he envisioned, to capture its dynamic quality, its ubiquity, and its comfortable fit with people [22].

The needs of the Xerox Corporation also influenced the Alto, since Xerox provided the money that paid for it. In 1970 Xerox started a research center in Palo Alto called PARC to develop the "architecture of information" and establish the technical foundation for electronic office systems that could become products in the 1980s. It seemed likely that copiers would no longer be a high-growth business by that time, and that electronics would begin to have a major effect on office systems, the firm's major business. Xerox was a large and prosperous company with a strong commitment to basic research and a clear need for new technology in this area. To the computer people at PARC, this looked like a favorable environment in which to take the next step toward making computers into effective tools for thinking.

The electronic office and the Dynabook, then, were the two threads that led to the Alto system. The idea of the electronic office is to do all the work of an office using electronic media:

- capturing information,
- viewing it,
- storing and retrieving it,
- communicating it to others, and
- processing it.

The idea of the Dynabook is to make the computer a personal and dynamic medium for handling information, which can model the world and make the model visible.

Of course the Alto system is not an electronic office, or a Dynabook; these were ideals to draw us on, not milestones to be achieved (or millstones either). In the course of developing the Alto we evolved from these ideals to a new style of computing, which is the preferred style in the 1980s just as time-sharing was the preferred style of the 1970s; witness the conference for which this paper was prepared. For this style there is no generally accepted name, but we shall call it "personal distributed computing." Why these words?

The Alto system is *personal* because it is under the control of a person and serves his needs. Its performance is predictable. It is reliable and available. It is not too hard to use.

And it is fast enough. In 1975 it was hard for people to believe that an entire computer is required to meet the needs of one person. The prevailing attitude was that machines are fast and people are slow; hence the merits of time-sharing, which allows one fast machine to serve many of the slow people. And indeed time-sharing, with response times measured in seconds, is an advance over a system that responds in hours. But this relationship holds only when the people are required to play on the machine's terms, seeing information presented slowly and inconveniently, with only the clumsiest control over its form or content. When the machine is required to play the game on the human's terms, presenting a pageful of attractively (or even legibly) formatted text, graphs, or pictures in the fraction of a second in which the human can pick out a significant pattern, it is the other way around: People are fast, and machines are slow. Indeed, it is beyond the current state of the art for a machine to keep up with a person. But the Alto system is a step in this direction.

So a personal system should present and accept information in a form convenient for a person. People are accustomed to dealing with ink on paper; the computer should simulate this as well as possible. It should also produce and accept voice and other sounds. Of these requirements, we judged most important the ability for the machine to present images, and for its user to point at places in the image. The Alto can do this quite well for a single 8.5" × 11" sheet of paper with black ink; it puts no restrictions on the form of the images. It cannot read images, nor can it handle sound; other people's experience suggests that these abilities, while valuable, are much less important.

The Alto system is *distributed* because everything in the real world is distributed, unless it is quite small. Also, it is implicit in our goals that the computer is quintessentially a communication device. If it is also to be personal, then it must be part of a distributed system, exchanging information with other personal computers. Finally, many things need to be shared, not just information but expensive physical objects like printers and tape drives.

Finally, the Alto system is a *computing* system, adaptable by programming to a wide and unpredictable variety of tasks. It is big and fast enough that fitting the programs into the machine is not too hard (though the Alto's address space and memory size limitations were its most serious deficiency). And programming is possible at every level from the microcode to the user of an application. It is interesting, though, that user programming plays a much smaller role in the Alto system than in Unix [23] or EMACS [46]. Users *interact* with the system, nearly to the exclusion of *programming* it. In retrospect it seems that we adopted this style because interacting with the Alto was so new and enthralling, and that we went too far in excluding systematic programming facilities like the Unix shell or M-Lisp in EMACS. The same mistake was made in early time-sharing systems such as CTSS [8] and the SDS 940 [26], whose builders were enthralled by a cruder kind of interaction, so we should have known better.

### SCHEMES

> Systems resemble the organizations that produce them.
>
> *—Conway*

The Alto system was affected not only by the ideas its builders had about what kind of system to build, but also by their ideas about how to do computer systems research. In particular, we thought that it is important to predict the evolution of hardware technology, and start working with a new kind of system five to ten years before it becomes feasible as a commercial product. If the Alto had been an article of commerce in 1974, it would have cost $40,000 and would have had few buyers. In 1984 a personal computer with four times the memory and disk storage, and a display half the size, could be bought for about $3500. But there is still very little software for that computer that truly exploits the potential of personal distributed computing, and much of what does exist is derived from the Alto system. So we built the most capable system we could afford within our generous research budget, confident that it could be sold at an affordable price before we could figure out what to do with it. This policy was continued in the late 1970s, when we built the Dorado, a machine with about ten times the computing power of an Alto. Affordable Dorados are not yet available, but they surely will be by the late 1980s. Our insistence on working with tomorrow's hardware accounts for many of the differences between the Alto system and the early personal computers that were coming into existence at the same time.

Another important idea was that effective computer system design is much more likely if the designers use their own systems. This rule imposes some constraints on what can be built. For instance, we had little success with database research, because it was hard to find significant applications for databases in our laboratory. The System R project [17] shows that excellent work can be done by ignoring this rule, but we followed it fairly religiously.

A third principle was that there should not be a grand plan for the system. For the most part, the various parts of the Alto system were developed independently, albeit by people who worked together every day. There is no uniform design of user interfaces or of system-wide data abstractions such as structured documents or images. Most programs take over the whole machine, leaving no room for doing anything else at the same time, or indeed for communicating with any other program except through the file system. Several different language environments are available, and programs written in one language cannot call programs in another. This lack of integration is the result of two considerations. First, many of the Alto's capabilities were new, and we felt that unfettered experimentation was the best way to explore their uses. Second, the Alto has strictly limited memory and address space. Many applications are hard enough to squeeze into the whole machine and could not have been written if they had to share the hardware resources. Nor is swapping a solution to the shortage of memory: The Alto's disk is slow, and even fast swapping is inconsistent with the goal of fast and highly predictable interaction between the user and the machine.

There was some effort to plan the development of the Alto system sufficiently to ensure that the basic facilities needed for daily work would be available. Also, there was a library of packages for performing basic functions like command line parsing. Documentation for the various programs and subroutine packages was maintained in a uniform way and collected into a manual of several hundred pages. But the main force for consistency in the Alto system was the informal interaction of its builders.

The outstanding exception to these observations is the Smalltalk system, which was built by a tightly knit group that spent a lot of effort developing a consistent style, both for programming and for the user interface. Smalltalk also has a software-implemented virtual memory scheme that considerably relaxes the storage limitations of the Alto. The result is a far more coherent and well-integrated world than can be found in the rest of the Alto system, to the point that several of the Alto's successors modelled their user interfaces on Smalltalk. The price paid for this success was that many Smalltalk applications are too slow for daily use. Most Smalltalk users wrote their papers and read their mail using other Alto software.

There was much greater consistency and integration of components in later systems that evolved from the Alto, such as Star and Cedar. This was possible because their designers had a lot of experience to draw on and 4 to 16 times as much main storage in which to keep programs and data.

The Alto system was built by two groups at PARC: the Computer Science Laboratory (CSL), run by Robert Taylor and Jerome Elkind, and the Learning Research Group (LRG), run by Alan Kay. LRG built Smalltalk, and CSL built the hardware and the rest of the system, often in collaboration with individuals from the other computer-related laboratory at PARC, the Systems Science Laboratory. George Pake, as manager first of PARC and then of all Xerox research, left the researchers free to pursue their ideas without interference from the rest of Xerox.

The Star system, a Xerox product based on the Alto [43], was built by the System Development Division (SDD), run by David Liddle. The Dorado, a second-generation personal computer [27] and Cedar, a second-generation research system based on the Alto [53], were built in CSL. Table 1 is a chronology of these systems.

**TABLE 1**
**Systems and chronology**

```
1973    1974    1975    1976    1977    1978    1979    1980    1981    1982

HARDWARE

  Alto ---            Alto 2        Dolphin -----------
                      Dorado ----------------------          Dicentra ---
                                             Wildflower Dandelion ----
mouse     mouse
Ethernet  Ears ----         Dover -------              8044 -------
                            Orbit ----
                                     Puffin ---


OPERATING SYSTEMS

Alto OS ---                 Pilot -------------------------------- Cedar exec ----
          Scavenger
          Alto exec


LANGUAGES

BCPL -- Swat    Mesa --------------------------------- Cedar ---------
                Mesa debugger -------------------------------
                                     Copilot --------------------------------

Smalltalk 72 ---        Smalltalk 76            Smalltalk 80 -------
Alto Lisp ----------            Interlisp D ---------


COMMUNICATIONS

          Pup -----    worm            RPC ----------------
                Chat          Grapevine ----------
                FTP


Servers:

Ears ------     Press         Spruce              Interpress

    Juniper ---------------------------- Alpine ----------------
                WFS IFS -----


APPLICATIONS

            Gypsy    Officetalk  Star ---------------------------
Smalltalk windows    Tajo ----------------          Viewers

            Bravo ------------ Laurel --- BravoX --------- Tioga ------------
        Sil    Markup    Sil
        Fred ---- AIS ------
            Draw
```

## WHAT WAS LEFT OUT

A number of ideas that might have been incorporated into the Alto system did not find a place there. In some cases we made deliberate decisions not to pursue them, usually because we couldn't see how to implement them on the Alto within an interactive application. Classical computer graphics, with viewports, transformations, clipping, 3-D projection and display lists, falls in this category; one implementation of a computer graphics package was done, but it didn't get used because it took up too much of the machine. High-quality typesetting (as in TeX [24]) is another; doing this interactively is still an unsolved problem. Linking together a large collection of documents so that the cross-references can be quickly and easily followed, as Engelbart did in NLS [13] is a third. Most of these ideas were incorporated into Cedar.

We also did very little with tightly linked distributed computing. The 150 Altos at PARC could have been used as a multi-processor, with several of them working on parts of the same problem. But except for the Worm programs described in the third section, this was never tried. And, as we have already seen, the Alto system gave little attention to high-level programming by users.

Other things were tried, but without much success. We built two file servers that supported transactions, one low-level database system, and several applications that used databases. In spite of this work, by 1984 databases still did not play an important role in the Alto system or its successors. This appears to be because the data in our applications is not sufficiently well-structured to exploit the capabilities of a database system. Most Unix users apparently have had similar experiences.

We also tried to apply ideas from AI to office systems, with work on natural language understanding and on expert systems. But ten years of work did not yield systems based on these ideas that were useful enough to make up for their large size and slow speed. A full-scale Lisp system was built for the Alto, but the machine proved too small for it in spite of much effort; this system was later successful on larger machines.

One important idea that would have been a natural application for the Alto was simply overlooked: spreadsheets. Probably this happened because except for the annual budget planning and keeping track of purchase orders, there were no applications for spreadsheets in the research laboratory.

## OVERVIEW

The Alto system software was begun in the middle of 1973. In October 1976 the *Alto User's Handbook* was published [25]. It describes a system that includes an operating system, a display-oriented editor, three illustrators, high-quality printing facilities, and shared file storage and electronic mail provided by local network communication with a time-sharing machine. There were also two programming languages and their associated environments. This was a complete personal distributed computing system; it met nearly all of the computing and information-handling needs of CSL and LRG.

The rest of this paper tells the story of the Alto system from the bottom up, except for the hardware, which is described elsewhere [56]. The second section covers *programming:* operating systems, programming languages, and environments. The third section presents the basic *communication* facilities: internet protocols, remote procedure calls, file transfer, and remote terminals. The fourth section discusses the *servers* that provide shared resources: long-term storage, printing, naming and mail transport.

The last two sections deal with the parts of the system that interact with users, which after all is the purpose of the whole enterprise. The fifth section considers the *user interfaces:* how the screen is organized into windows, how images are made, and how user input is handled. The sixth section describes the major *applications,* programs the user invokes to do some job with results that are useful outside the computer system. In the Alto system these are text editors, illustrators, electronic mail, and computer-aided design programs.

The conclusion reflects on the future of personal distributed computing and the nature of computer systems research.

Throughout I describe the Alto system in some detail, especially the parts of it that have not been described elsewhere. I also sketch its evolution into the Dorado system and the Xerox 8000 products (usually called Star). The "Dorado system" actually runs on three machines: Dolphin, Dorado, and Dandelion. These have different microengines, but the same virtual memory structure, and all the major programming environments run on all three systems. They differ in performance and availability: the Dolphin, with about twice the power of the Alto and ten times the memory, first ran in 1978; the Dorado, ten times an Alto, in 1979; the Dandelion, three times an Alto, in 1980. Star runs on the Dandelion and was announced in 1981. A fourth member of the family, the Dicentra, was designed as a server and runs only the Mesa environment.

Readers may be surprised that so much of this paper deals with software that has little or nothing to do with the display, since "screen flash" is the most obvious and most immediately attractive property of the Alto system. They should remember that the Alto system put equal emphasis on *personal* and on *distributed* computing, on *interacting* with the computer and on *communicating* through it. It also seems important to explain the programming environment that made it possible to develop the large quantity of software in the Alto system.

# Programming Environments

The Alto system is programmed in a variety of languages: BCPL, Mesa, and Smalltalk (see the section entitled Languages and Environments). Each language has its own instruction set and its own operating system. The entire system has in common only the file system format on the disk and the network protocols. These were established by the BCPL operating system and did not change after 1976; they constitute the interface between the various programming environments.

### OPERATING SYSTEMS

The first Alto operating system [29], usually called the OS, is derived from Stoy and Strachey's OS6 [47]. It provides a disk file and directory system, a keyboard handler, a teletype simulator for the screen, a standard stream abstraction for input-output, a program loader, and a free storage allocator. There is no provision for multiple processes, virtual memory, or protection, although the first two were provided (several times, in fact) by software or microcode packages. The OS is written entirely in BCPL [40]. It was designed by Butler Lampson, and implemented by him, Gene McDaniel, Bob Sproull, and David Boggs.

The distinctive features of the Alto OS are:

- its open design, which allows any part of the system to be replaced by client program;
- the world-swap facility, which exchanges control between two programs, each of which uses essentially all of the machine; and
- the file system, which can run the disk at full speed and uses distributed redundancy to obtain high reliability.

The OS is organized as a set of standard packages, one providing each of the functions mentioned (except for the stream abstraction, which is entirely a matter of programming convention). When it is initialized, all the packages are present and can be called by any program that is loaded. However, there is a *junta* procedure that can be used to remove any number of the preloaded packages and recover the space they occupy. Thus a program can take over nearly the whole machine. BCPL programs can include any subset of the standard packages to replace the ones removed by the junta. Alternatively, they can provide their own implementation of a function that has been removed by a junta, or do without it altogether. Thus the system is entirely *open*, offering services to its client programs but preempting none of the machine's resources. Other packages not normally loaded as part of the system, but available to be included in any user program, provide nonpreemptive concurrent processes, internet datagrams and byte streams, program overlays, and other facilities that might have been part of the standard system.

At the base of the OS is a *world-swap* function that saves the entire state of the machine on a disk file and restores it from another file; this allows an arbitrary program to take control of the machine. The new program communicates with the old one only through the file system and a few bytes of state that are saved in memory across the world-swap. The world-swap takes about two seconds; it is used for bootstrapping, checkpointing, debugging (to switch between the program and the debugger), and switching back and forth between two major activities of a program.

The file system represents a file as a sequence of disk blocks linked by forward and backward pointers. By careful integration with the disk controller, it is able to transfer consecutive file blocks that are contiguous on the disk at the full disk speed of 1 Mbit/second, while leaving time for nontrivial client computing; this performance allows world-swapping, program overlaying, and other sequential file transfers to be fast. In addition, each disk block contains the file identifier and block number in a *label* field of its header; this information is checked whenever the block is read or written. As a result, the disk addresses of file blocks can be treated as *hints* by the system, rather than being critical to its correct functioning and to the integrity of other files. If a disk address is wrong, the label check will detect the error, and various recovery mechanisms can be invoked. A Scavenger program, written by Jim Morris, takes about a minute to check or restore the consistency of an Alto file system; it can be routinely run by nonprofessional users. As a result of this conservative design, the file system has proved to be very reliable; loss of any information other than bits physically damaged on the disk is essentially unheard of. This reliability is achieved in spite of the fact that many programs besides the standard operating system have access to the disk.

The file system also runs on the 80 and 300 MByte disks that are interfaced to some Altos, and in this form is the basis of a successful file server (see the section entitled Storage).

The Alto has a conventional hierarchical directory system that allows multiple versions of each file, with provisions for keeping a pre-specified number of versions. The subdirectory and version facilities were added late, however, and did not enjoy widespread use. A directory is stored as an ordinary file that is processed by a variety of programs in addition to the file system.

A program called the Executive processes command lines and invokes other programs; it is much like the Unix Shell, but with far more primitive facilities for programming at the command level. From the point of view of the OS it is just another program, the one normally invoked when the machine is booted. From the point of view of a user it is the visible form of the OS.

Some of the design choices of the Alto OS would not be made in an operating system for a 1985 workstation; its much greater computing power and especially memory capacity make them unattractive. Separate address spaces simplify program development and concurrent execution of separate applications; virtual memory simplifies programming; a clean virtual machine makes it easier to port client programs to a new machine. But these comforts have a significant cost in machine resources: memory and response time. The open and unprotected character of the Alto OS were essential to the success of many Alto applications, both interactive programs like editors and illustrators, and real-time programs like the file, print, and gateway servers.

Distinct operating systems evolved for other programming environments. The Alto Lisp and Smalltalk operating systems were built using many of the Alto OS packages. Over time, these packages were replaced by new code native to the Lisp and Smalltalk environments. Mesa had its own operating system on the Alto from the start, but it was modelled closely on the OS.

For the Xerox 8000 products, the Alto OS was replaced by a considerably bigger system called Pilot, which supports virtual memory, multiple processes, and a more elaborate file system [38]. Pilot was also used in the Cedar system, but was eventually supplanted by the Cedar nucleus, a much simpler system quite similar in spirit to the Alto OS. Cedar also has CFS, the Cedar File System [41], which provides a network-wide file system to Cedar programs by caching files from a server on the workstation. In CFS modified files are written back only by explicit request. This arrangement supports about 20 Dorados from a single Alto-based file server, using about 30 MBytes of local disk on each Dorado for the cache. Almost any file server will do, since it need only support full file transfers.

## LANGUAGES AND ENVIRONMENTS

One of the distinctive features of the Alto as a programmer's system is the wide variety of programming environments it supports: BCPL, Smalltalk, Mesa, and Lisp. Each of these has its own language, which gives the environment its name, and its own instruction set, implemented by its own microcode *emulator*; the BCPL instruction set is always present, and there is a RAM with room for a thousand microinstructions, enough for one other emulator. Each also has its own compiler, loader, runtime system, debugger, and library of useful subroutine packages. The ensuing subsections describe these parts for each of the Alto environments.

Distinct environments communicate only by world-swap or through the file system. This isolation is not a good thing in itself, but it allows each system to stretch the resources of the machine in a different way, and thus to support effectively a particular programming style that would be impractical on such a small machine if all of the systems had to share a common instruction set and operating system.

### BCPL

BCPL [40] is an implementation language quite similar to C (indeed, it is C's immediate ancestor). BCPL has a fairly portable compiler which Jim Curry ported to the Data General Nova, and thence to the Alto. Curry also wrote a loader for compiled code. It can produce an executable image or an overlay file that can be loaded and unloaded during execution; overlays are used in several large programs to make up for the limited address space. The Swat debugger, built by Jim Morris, is the other component of the BCPL programming environment; it understands BCPL's symbols, but is basically a machine-language debugger. The entire BCPL environment is very much like the C environment in Unix. Most Alto software was programmed in BCPL until 1977. By 1978 new programs were being written almost entirely in the other languages.

### Mesa

Mesa [15] is an implementation language descended from Pascal. Its distinguishing features are:

- Strong type-checking, which applies even across separate compilation units.
- Modules, with the interface to a module defined separately from its implementation. Intermodule type-checking is based on the interface definitions; an implementation can be changed without affecting any clients [30].
- Cheap facilities for concurrent programming, well integrated into the language [28].
- A very efficient implementation, which uses an instruction set highly tuned to the characteristics of the client programs [20]. Compiled Mesa programs are typically half the size of similar C programs for the VAX, for example. The instructions are called byte-codes; many are a single byte long, and none are longer than three bytes. The byte-codes are interpreted by a microcoded emulator.
- A symbolic debugger well integrated with the source language and the type system, which allows breakpoints to be placed

by pointing at the source code, and values to be printed in a form based on their type.

Mesa was begun in 1971 on a time-sharing computer by Jim Mitchell, Chuck Geschke, and Ed Satterthwaite; ported to the Alto in 1975 with the assistance of Rich Johnsson and John Wick; and adopted by SDD in 1976 as the programming language for all SDD products. It continued to evolve there into a complete integrated programming environment [49]. A separate path of evolution in CSL led to the Cedar system described below.

The main goal of the Mesa research and development was to support the construction of large software systems and to execute them efficiently. This was accomplished very successfully: by 1982 there were several systems programmed in Mesa that contain more than a quarter of a million lines of code each, and many more that are 20 to 50 thousand lines long.

## Smalltalk

The Smalltalk system is an integrated programming environment for the Alto, the first one to be built. It consists of a programming language, a debugger, an object-oriented virtual memory, an editor, screen management, and user interface facilities [22]. The latter are discussed in the fifth section.

The Smalltalk language is based on *objects* and *classes*; each object has a class, which is a collection of procedures that operate on the object. A *subclass* inherits the procedures of an existing class, and generally adds new ones. The class of an object acts as its type, which is determined at runtime; when a procedure is applied to an object, the name of the procedure is looked up in the object's class to find the proper code to execute. Smalltalk source code is compiled into bytecodes similar to the ones used for Mesa, although much more powerful (and hence slower). The bytecodes are quite close to the source, so the compiler is small and fast; a typical procedure can be compiled and installed in a few seconds on an Alto, without disturbing the rest of the running system.

Objects are allocated and garbage-collected automatically. A class is itself an object, as are the source and compiled code for each procedure, and the stack frame for an executing procedure. So everything in the system can be accessed as an object and manipulated by Smalltalk programs within the system [19]. The entire system contains 100 to 200 classes, ranging from streams and collections to processes and files, rectangles and splines [16].

The dynamic typing, garbage collection, accessibility of every part of the system, and ease with which a procedure can be added or changed without any loss of state make Smalltalk similar to Lisp as a programming environment. The object-oriented programming style and the subclass structure, along with the careful design of the hierarchy of standard classes, give Smalltalk its unique character. The system is fairly easy to learn, and very easy to use for building prototypes. Its limitations are relatively slow execution and (in the Alto implementations) modest memory capacity; these factors have prevented production systems from being built in Smalltalk.

There have been three generations of the Smalltalk language and system: Smalltalk-72, Smalltalk-76, and Smalltalk-80; the description above refers to the latter two. The first two run on the Alto, the last on the Dorado and also on several VAX, 68000, and 80286 implementations.

### Lisp

Several researchers in CSL used PDP-10 Interlisp [54,55] for their programming in the 1970s. Interlisp became part of the Alto system through software that allows the Alto to be used as a very capable graphics terminal [45] that supports multiple fonts and windows, along with the standard Alto raster graphics primitives (see the fifth section). The resulting Interlisp-D system [52] was the first to integrate graphics into a Lisp system.

A complete Interlisp system was built for the Alto by Peter Deutsch and Willie-Sue Haugeland [9,10]. It uses many of the BCPL OS packages for operating system functions, and the Lisp runtime is also written in BCPL. Lisp programs are compiled into byte-codes much like those used for Mesa and Smalltalk; they fall about half-way between those in the amount of work done by a single instruction. As with Mesa, programs are about twice as compact as when compiled for a conventional instruction set. The system uses an encoded form for list cells, which allows a cell to be represented in 32 bits most of the time, even though addresses are 24 bits.

Alto Lisp worked, and was able to run most of PDP-10 Interlisp, but it was too slow to be useful, mainly because of insufficient memory. It therefore did not play a role in the Alto system. The implementation was moved to the Dorado, however, where after considerable tuning it has been very successful [7].

### Cedar

With the advent of the Dorado in 1979, we saw an opportunity to improve substantially on all of our existing programming systems. After considerable reflection on the desirable properties of a programming environment for personal computing [11], CSL decided in 1979 to build a new environment, based on Mesa, to exploit the capabilities of the Dorado. The goals were significantly better tools for program development, and a collection of high-quality packages implementing the major abstractions needed to write applications.

Cedar added several things to the program development system: garbage-collected storage, dynamic types, complete program access to the representation of the running program, a version control system, and uniform access to local and remote files. It also had a large assortment of generally useful packages: an integrated editor for structured documents, a powerful graphics package, a relational database system, remote procedure calls, user-programmable interpretation of the keyboard and mouse, and a screen manager based on icons and nonoverlapping windows [51,53].

By early 1982 the Cedar system was usable; by mid-1984 it had grown to about 400,000 lines of code, ranging from the compiler and runtime support to an electronic mail system based on the Cedar editor and database system. It was possible to implement realtime servers such as a voice data storage system and a transactional file system, using the full facilities of Cedar.

Cedar was quite successful in overcoming the major limitations of the Alto programming environment. It also succeeded in providing good implementations for a number of widely used high-level abstractions. However, an additional goal was to equal Lisp and Smalltalk in supporting rapid program changes and late binding, and here it was less successful. In spite of this limitation, it probably represents the state of the art in programming environments for workstations in 1984.

## Communication

In order not to lose the ability of time-sharing systems to support sharing of information and physical resources in moving to personal computing, it was necessary to develop communication facilities far beyond the state of the art in 1973. The Ethernet provided the hardware base for this development. A great deal of work also went into the software.

The first generation of Alto communication software, called Pup for PARC Universal Packet [4], is based on ideas developed for the ARPANET in the late 1960s [33], with changes to correct known problems. Pup was originally designed by Bob Metcalfe, and implemented by him together with David Boggs and Ed Taft.

The model for communication was structured in four levels:

1. *Level 0:* Transport—various mechanisms for transporting a datagram from one machine to another: Ethernet, ARPANET, leased telephone lines, etc.

2. *Level 1:* Internet datagrams

3. *Level 2:* Interprocess communication primitives—byte system protocol (BSP), rendezvous/termination protocol, routing table protocol, etc.

4. *Level 3:* Data structuring conventions—file transfer protocol (FTP), remote terminal protocol (Telnet), mail transfer protocol (MTP), etc.

Internet datagrams are the common coin, decoupling higher levels from the details of the packet transport mechanism. Unlike other systems based on local networks, such as the Cambridge ring [36] or the Apollo domain system [31], the Alto system takes no advantage of the special properties of the Ethernet. Instead, all clients of the communication facilities use internet datagrams, which present the same interface whether the data travels over the Ethernet, over a telephone line, or through a dozen different transport mechanisms. Pup thus treats a transport mechanism just as the ARPANET treats an IMP-to-IMP telephone line; the role of the IMP is played by a *gateway* that routes each datagram onto a transport mechanism that is expected to take it closer to its destination.

A major difference from the ARPANET is that Pup offers no guarantee that a datagram accepted by the network will be delivered. When congestion occurs, it is relieved by discarding datagrams. This design reflects the expectation that most datagrams will travel over lightly loaded local networks; when links become congested, clients of the network may get disproportionately degraded service.

The main level 2 mechanism is the byte stream protocol, which provides a reliable full-duplex byte stream connection between two processes. It turns out to be fairly hard to use this kind of connection, since it is complicated to set up and take down, and has problems when unusual conditions occur. As in the ARPANET, however, this was of little concern, since the main customers for it are the level 3 file transfer and remote terminal services. These are normally provided by programs called FTP and Chat, invoked by users or their command scripts from the Executive command line processor [25]. FTP was written by David Boggs, Chat by Bob Sproull. There is also an FTP library package that programs can call directly to transfer files; this is used by the Laurel mail-reading program, and (in an abbreviated version) by many applications that send files to the printer.

Pup byte streams have fairly good performance. They are capable of transferring about 0.3 MBits/second between two Altos, using datagrams with 512 data bytes plus a few dozen bytes of overhead. This is an order of magnitude better than the performance exhibited by a typical byte stream implementation on a comparable machine. The difference is due to the simplicity of the Pup protocols and the efficient implementation.

Other important network services in the Alto system were booting a machine and collecting reports from diagnostic programs. These used internet datagrams directly rather than a level 2 protocol, as did one rather successful application, the Woodstock File System [50] described in the fourth section. But with these few exceptions, users and applications relied on FTP and Chat for communication services.

The only truly distributed program built in the Alto system other than the Pup internet router is the Worm [42], which searches for idle machines into which it can replicate itself. It isn't entirely clear why more attempts were not made to take advantage of the 150 Altos or 50 Dorados available at PARC. Part of the reason is probably the difficulty of building distributed programs; this was not alleviated by RPC until 1982 (see following material). The lack of a true network-wide file system before 1984 was probably another factor.

The Xerox 8000 network products use an outgrowth of Pup called Xerox Network System or XNS [60]. XNS adds one important level 3 protocol, the Courier remote procedure call protocol designed by Jim White. Courier defines a standard way of representing a procedure call, with its argument passing and result returning, between two machines. In other words, it includes conventions for identifying the procedure to be called, encoding various types of argument (integers, strings, arrays, records, etc.), and reporting successful completion or an exceptional result. Courier uses XNS byte streams to transport its data.

At about the same time, as part of the development of Cedar, Andrew Birrell and Bruce Nelson in CSL developed a remote procedure call mechanism that uses internet datagrams directly [2]. They also built a *stub generator* that automatically constructs the necessary program to convert a local procedure call into a remote one, and a location mechanism based on Grapevine (see the section entitled Naming and Mail Transport) to link a caller to a remote procedure. Like Courier, Cedar RPC uses a Mesa interface as the basic building block for defining remote procedures. Unlike Courier, Cedar RPC is fast: Two Dorados using Cedar RPC can execute a null remote procedure call in about a millisecond. Earlier work by Nelson indicates that further optimization can probably reduce this to about 200 microseconds; currently Cedar RPC has no clients that are limited by the performance.

The goal of Cedar RPC was to make it possible to build distributed programs without being a communications wizard. A number of successful weekend projects have demonstrated that the goal was reached. An unexpected byproduct was independent implementations of the same RPC mechanism in Lisp, Smalltalk, and C for the 8088; all these clients found it easier to implement the Cedar RPC than to design a more specialized mechanism for their own needs.

## Servers

The main use of distributed computing in the Alto system is to provide various shared services to the personal computers. This is done by means of *servers*, machines often equipped with special input-output devices and programmed to supply a particular service such as printing or file storage. Although there is no reason why a single machine could not provide several services, in fact nearly all the servers are Altos, and have no room for more than one server program.

**PRINTING**

Printing is the most complex and most interesting service in the Alto system. A considerable amount of research had to be done to build practical printers that can make high-quality hard copies of the arbitrary images the Alto screen can display. The end product of this work at PARC was a printing system that stores many thousands of typeset pages, and can print them at about 40 pages per minute. The quality is fairly close to a xerographic copy of a professionally typeset version. All the documentation of the Alto system and all the technical papers, reports and memos written in the computer research laboratories were stored in the system and printed on demand.

There are several aspects of a printing service. First, there must be a printing *interface*, a way to describe the sequence of pages to be printed by specifying the image desired on each page as well as the number of copies and other details. Second, there must be a *spooler* that accepts documents to be printed and queues them. Third, there must be an *imager* that converts the image descriptions into the raster of bits on the page and sends the bits to the printing hardware at the right speed.

The spooler is fairly straightforward: Nearly all the printers include a disk, accept files using a standard file transfer protocol, and save them in the OS file system on the disk for printing. Since imaging consumes the entire machine, it is necessary to interrupt printing to accept a new file, but file transfers are fast, so this is not a problem. The interfaces and the imagers are worth describing in more detail.

The main point of a printing interface is to decouple creators of documents from printers, so that they can develop independently. Four printing interfaces were developed for the Alto and Dorado systems, each providing more powerful image description and greater independence from the details of printer and fonts. The first, devised for the XGP printer by Peter Deutsch, is rather similar to the interfaces used to control plotters and dot-matrix printers nearly 15 years later: it consists of the ASCII characters to be printed, interspersed with control character sequences to change the font, start a new line or a new page, justify a line, set the margins, draw a vector, and the like. The graphics capabilities are quite limited, and the printer is responsible for some of the formatting (e.g., keeping text within margins).

This interface, with its lack of distinction between formatting a text document and printing, proved quite unsatisfactory; there was constant demand to extend the formatting capability. All the later interfaces take no responsibility for formatting, but require everything to be specified completely in the document. Thus line and page breaks, the position of each line on the page, and all other details are determined before the document is sent to the printer. This clear separation of responsibilities proved to be crucial in building both good printers and good document formatters.

The second printing interface was designed by Ron Rider for use with the EARS printer, the first raster printer capable of high-quality printing. The graphics capability of the EARS printer is limited, and as a consequence the EARS interface can only specify the printing of rectangles; usually these are horizontal or vertical lines. It does, however, allow and indeed require the document to include the bitmaps for all the fonts to be used in printing it. Thus font management is entirely decoupled from printing in EARS, and made the responsibility of the document creator. The great strength of this interface is the complete control it provides over the positioning of every character on the page, and the absence of restrictions on the size or form of characters; arbitrary bitmap images can be used to define characters. Font libraries were developed for logic symbols so that logic drawings could be printed, and other programs generate new fonts automatically for drawing curves.

After several years of experience with EARS, the advent of two new printers stimulated the development of a new, printer-independent interface called Press, designed by William Newman and Bob Sproull. Its main features are a systematic imaging model, arbitrary graphics, and a systematic scheme for naming fonts rather than including them in the document, since font management proved to be too hard for document creators. Thus the printer is responsible for storing fonts, and for drawing lines and spline curves specified in the document. The device-independence of Press makes it possible to display Press documents as well as print them.

Press served well for about six years. In 1980, however, the development of general-purpose raster printing products motivated yet another interface design, this time called Interpress; it was done by Bob Sproull and Butler Lampson, with assistance from John Warnock [44]. The biggest innovation is the introduction of a stack-based programming language, which contains commands to draw a line or curve, show a character, and the like, as well as to manipulate the stack and call procedures. The document is a program in this language, which is executed to generate the image. This design provides great power for describing complex images, without complicating the interface. Interpress also has extensive provisions to improve device-independence, based on experience in implementing Press for a variety of printers. It handles textures and color systematically.

Imagers evolved roughly in parallel with interfaces. The task of generating the 10–25 million bits required to define a full-page raster at 300–500 bits/inch is not simple, especially when the printer can generate a page a second, as most of those in the Alto system can. Furthermore, the fonts pose a significant data-management problem, since a single typeface requires about 30 KBytes of bitmap, and every size and style is a different typeface. Thus one serif, one sans-serif and one fixed-pitch font, in roman, italic, bold, and bold italic, and in 6, 7, 8, 9, 10, 12, 14, 18 and 24 point sizes, results in 108 typefaces; actually the system uses many more.

The first imager, written by Peter Deutsch, drove the Xerox Graphics Printer. This machine is slow (five pages/minute) and low resolution (200 dots/inch); it is also asynchronous, so the imager can take as long as it likes to generate each line of the raster. Only crude imaging software was developed for it, together with a few fonts. Raster fonts were unheard of at the time, except in $5 \times 7$ and $7 \times 9$ resolution for terminals, or at very high resolution for expensive photo-typesetters. The XGP fonts were developed entirely manually, using an editor that allows the operator to turn individual dots in the roughly $20 \times 20$ matrix on and off. They had to be new designs, since it is impractical to faithfully copy a printer's font at such low resolution. These XGP fonts were later widely used in universities.

The second imager drives EARS, a 500 dot/inch, 1 page/second xerographic printer based on a Xerox 3600 copier engine and a raster output scanner developed at PARC by Gary Starkweather. EARS is controlled by an Alto, but there is a substantial amount of special-purpose hardware, about three times the size of the Alto itself, to store font bitmaps and generate a 25 MHz video signal to control the printer. Both the imager and the hardware were developed by Ron Rider, with design assistance from Butler Lampson. This machine revolutionized our attitude to printing. The image quality is as good as a xerographic copy of a book, and it can print 80 pages an hour for each member of a 40-person laboratory (of course we never used more than a fraction of its capacity). A second copy of EARS served as the prototype for the Xerox 9700 computer printer, a very successful product. Fonts for EARS were produced using the Fred spline font editor described in the sixth section.

As Alto systems spread, there was demand for a cheaper and more easily reproduced printing server. This required a new printing engine, new imaging hardware, and a new imager. The engine was the Dover, also based on the 3600 copier, but at 384 dots/inch; its development was managed by John Ellenby. Bob Sproull and Severo Ornstein developed the Orbit imaging hardware based on a design by Butler Lampson; this is about half the size of the Alto that drove it, a better balance. Sproull and Dan Swinehart wrote the Spruce imager to accept Press files and drive the Dover and Orbit. About 50 copies of this system were made and distributed widely within Xerox and elsewhere. It was cheap enough that every group could have its own printer. Spruce includes the font management required by Press, and is normally configured with an 80 MByte disk for font storage and spooling. Although Press can specify arbitrary graphics, Spruce handles only lines, and it can be overloaded by a page with too many lines or small characters. These limitations are the result of the fact that Orbit has no full-page image buffer; hence Spruce must keep up with the printer, and may be unable to do so if the image is too complex.

Another Press imager, confusingly also called Press, was built by Bob Sproull and Patrick Baudelaire to drive two slower printing engines, both at 384 dots/inch, and one able to print four colors. This imager constructs the entire 15 MBit raster on a disk, and then plays it out to the printer; this is possible because the engines are so much slower. It was the first Press imager, and the only one able to handle arbitrary images, by virtue of its complete raster store. Among other things, Press produced some spectacular color halftones.

The first Interpress imager was developed by Bob Ayers of SDD for the 8044 printer, part of the Xerox 8000 network product family. Subsequently Interpress imagers have been built for several other engines.

## STORAGE

Although not quite as exciting as printing, shared storage services are even more necessary to a community of computer users, since they enable members of the community to share information. No less than five file servers were developed for the Alto and Dorado systems.

For its first three years, the Alto system used CSL's mainframe [14], running the Tenex operating system [3], as its file server. A Pup version of the ARPANET file transfer program, written by Ed Taft, provides access to the Tenex file system. Both Alto and Tenex have user and server ends of this program, so either machine can take the active role, and files can also be transferred between two Altos.

The second file server, called WFS and written by David Boggs [50], is near the opposite extreme of possible designs. It uses a connectionless single-datagram request-response protocol, transfers one page of 512 bytes at a time, and implements only files; directories are the responsibility of the client. There is a very simple locking mechanism. This extreme simplicity allowed WFS to be implemented in two months on a Data General Nova; it was later ported to the Alto. Of course, only clients that provided their own naming for data were possible, since WFS had none. These included an experimental office system called Woodstock, the Officetalk forms-handling system, Smalltalk, and a telephone directory system.

As the Alto system grew, the file service load on Tenex became too great. Since the Alto has a disk controller for 300 MByte disks, it is possible to configure an Alto with several GBytes of storage. David Boggs and Ed Taft assembled existing Alto packages for files (from the OS), file transfer (from FTP), and directories (a B-Tree package written by Ed McCreight) to form the Interim File System (IFS). A considerable amount of tuning was needed to fit the whole thing into a 128 KByte Alto memory, and a new Scavenger had to be written to handle large disks, as well as an incremental backup system. IFS served as the main file server throughout the Alto system for at least seven years and dozens of IFS servers were installed.

IFS supports multiple versions of files, write locking, and a clumsy form of subdirectories. Over time it acquired single-packet protocols to report the existence of a file to support CFS (see the section entitled Operating Systems), a WFS-style file server, an interim mail server, and access to Grapevine (see the next section) for access control.

Concurrent with the development of WFS and IFS was a research project to build a random-access multi-machine file server that supports transactions and fine-grained locking. This became the Juniper system, designed and developed by Howard Sturgis, Jim Mitchell, Jim Morris, Jay Israel, and others [34]. It was the first server written in Mesa, the first to use an RPC-like protocol (see the Communications section), and the first to attempt multi-machine computation. Juniper was put into service in 1977, but performance on the Alto was marginal. Later it was moved to the Dorado. The goals proved to be too ambitious for this initial design, however, and it was never widely used.

Cedar includes a second-generation file server supporting transactions. Called Alpine, it was built by Mark Brown, Ed Taft, and Karen Kolling [6]. Alpine uses Cedar RPC and garbage-collected storage; it also supports multi-machine transactions and fine-grained locks, using newer algorithms that benefit from the experience of Juniper and System R [17]. It is widely used in Cedar, especially to store databases.

## NAMING AND MAIL TRANSPORT

The Alto system initially relied on Pup host names to locate machines, and on the Tenex mail system for electronic mail. These worked well until the system grew to hundreds of machines, when it began to break down. It was replaced by Grapevine, designed and implemented by Andrew Birrell, Roy Levin, Roger Needham, and Mike Schroeder.

Grapevine provides naming and mail transport services in a highly available way [1]. It also handles distribution lists and access control lists, both essential for a widespread community.

Grapevine was the second Mesa server. It was put into service in 1980 and has been highly successful; dozens of servers support a community of about two thousand machines and seven thousand registered users. All the machines in the Alto and Dorado systems use it for password checking and access control, as well as for resource location and mail transport. It is also used to register exporters of RPC interfaces such as Alpine file service. The database is replicated; in other words, each item is stored on several servers; as a result it is so reliable that it can be depended on by all the other components of the distributed system.

# User Interfaces

Perhaps the most influential aspects of the Alto system have been its user interfaces. These of course depend critically on the fact that the screen can display a complex image, and the machine is fast enough to change the image rapidly in response to user actions. Exploiting these capabilities turned out to be a complex and subtle matter; more than ten years later there is still a lot to be learned. The ensuing description is organized around four problems, and the Alto system's various solutions to them:

- organizing the screen,
- handling user input,
- viewing a complex data structure, and
- integrating many applications.

A final subsection describes the facilities for making images.

### WINDOWS

As soon as the limited display area of the screen is used to show more than one image, some scheme is needed for multiplexing it among competing demands. There are two basic methods:

- *switching,* or time-multiplexing—show one image at a time, and switch quickly among the images; and
- *splitting,* or space-multiplexing—give each image some screen space of its own.

Various approaches were tried, usually combining the two methods. All of them organize the major images competing for space, typically text documents or pictures of some kind, into rectangular regions called *windows*. All allow the user some control over the position and size of the windows. The windows either *overlap* or they *tile* the screen, arranged in one or two columns and taking up the available space without overlapping. Thus overlapping is a combination of splitting and switching; when two windows overlap, some of the screen space is switched between them, since only the one on top can be seen at any instant. Where windows don't overlap, the screen is split. Tiling, by contrast, is a pure splitting scheme.

With overlapping, the size of one window can be chosen independently of the size or position of others, either by the system or by the user. With tiling, this is obviously not the case, since when one window grows, its neighbor must shrink. As a practical matter, this means that a tiled system does more of the screen layout automatically.

An overlapped system can have any number of windows on the screen and still show the topmost ones completely, perhaps at the cost of completely obscuring some others so that the user loses track of them. In a tiled system, as more windows appear, the average size must become smaller. In practice, four or five windows in each of one or two columns is the limit. Either system can handle more windows by providing a tiny representation, or *icon*, as an alternative to the full-sized window. This is another form of switching.

A minor image, usually a menu of some kind, either occupies a subregion of a window (splitting), or is shown in a *pop-up* window that appears under the cursor (switching). The pop-up temporarily obscures whatever is underneath, but only for a short time, while a mouse button is down or while the user fills in a blank. Thus it has an entirely different feeling from a more static overlapped window.

Figures 1–3 are typical screen arrangements from three systems. Smalltalk (Fig. 1) uses overlapping windows without icons, and the position of a window is independent of its function (unless the user manually arranges the windows according to some rule). Smalltalk was the first system to use overlapping windows and pop-up menus. The Bravo editor (Fig. 2) uses one column of tiled windows, with a control window at the top, a message window at the bottom, and a main window for each document being edited, which may be subdivided to look at different parts. Cedar (Fig. 3) uses two tiled columns and rows of icons at the bottom (which can be covered up). This window system is called Viewers; much of its design was derived from Star. The top line or two of a window is a menu. Cedar also allows the entire screen image, called a *desktop*, to be saved away and replaced by another one; this is switching on a large scale. Markup has a pop-up menu scheme like Smalltalk's, but considerably more elaborate (Fig. 4).

**FIGURE 1**
A Smalltalk screen;
note the overlapping
windows and the
browser.

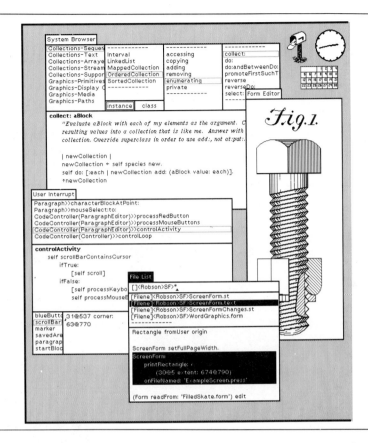

## INPUT

User input comes from the keyboard, the mouse buttons, or the cursor position, which is controlled by the mouse. The crucial notion is *clicking* at an object on the screen, by putting the cursor near it and pushing a button. There are three mouse buttons, so three kinds of click are possible; sometimes multiple clicks within a short interval have different meanings; sometimes the meaning of a click is modified by shift keys on the keyboard; sometimes moving the mouse with a button held down has a different meaning. An interface for novices will draw sparingly from this variety of mouse inputs, but one designed for experts may use all the variations.

If the screen object clicked is a *menu button*, this gives a *command* that makes something happen; otherwise the object is *selected*, in other words, designated as an operand for a command, or some point near the object is designated, such as an insertion point for text. The selec-

**FIGURE 2**
A Bravo screen; note
the formatted
document.

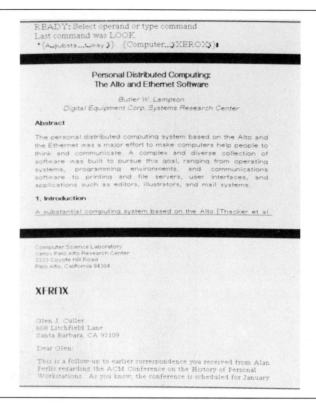

tion is made visible by underlining or reversing black and white; the insertion point is made visible as a blinking caret, I-beam, or whatever.

Many interfaces also have *scroll bars,* thin rectangles along one side of a window; clicking here scrolls the document being viewed in the window so that another part of it can be viewed. Often a portion of the scroll bar is highlighted, to indicate the position and size of the region being viewed relative to the whole document. A *thumbing* option scrolls the view so that the highlight is where the mouse is; thus thumbing a quarter of the way down the bar scrolls a quarter of the way into the document.

Frequently commands are given by keystrokes as well as, or instead of, menu clicking. Nearly always the commands work on the current selection, so the selection can be changed any number of times before a command is given without any effect on the state. An expert interface often has mouse actions that simultaneously make a selection and invoke a command, for instance to open an icon into a window by double-clicking on it, or to delete an object by selecting with a shift key depressed.

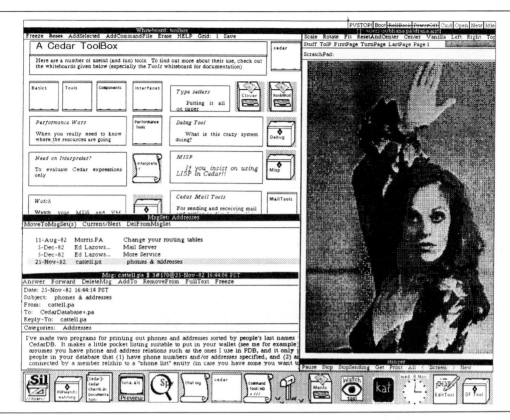

**FIGURE 3**
A Cedar screen; note the two-column tiling, the icons, and the whiteboard.

Most Alto system interfaces are *modeless,* or nearly so: Any keystroke or mouse click has the same general meaning in any state, rather than radically different meanings in different states. For example, an editor is modeless if typing the ''A'' key always inserts an ''A'' at the current insertion point; an editor is not modeless if typing ''A'' sometimes does this, and sometimes appends a file. A modeless interface usually has postfix commands, in which the operands are specified by selections or by filling in blanks in a form before each command is given.

Many of the user input ideas described here were first tried in the Gypsy editor (see the Applications section); others originated in Smalltalk, yet others in the Markup or Sil drawing programs (also described in the Applications section). One of the main lessons learned from these and other experiments is the importance of subtle factors in the handling of user input. Apparently minor variations can make

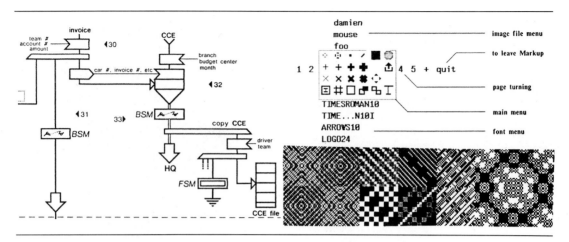

**FIGURE 4**
Typical Markup pictures.

a system much easier or much more difficult to use. In Bravo and Cedar this observation led to schemes that allowed the expert to rearrange the interpretation of user input, attaching different meanings to the possible mouse actions and keystrokes, and redesigning the menus. This decoupling of input handling from the actions of an application has also been successful in EMACS [46].

## VIEWS

More subtle than windows, menus, and double-click selections, but more significant, is the variety of methods in the Alto system for presenting on the screen a meaningful view of an abstract structure, whether it is a formatted document, a logic drawing, the tree structure of classes in Smalltalk, a hierarchical file system, or the records in a database. Such a view represents visually the structure and content of the data, or at least an important aspect of it. Equally important, it allows the user to designate part of the data and change it by pointing at the view and giving commands. And these commands have immediate visual feedback, allowing the user to verify that the command had the intended effect and reinforcing a sense of direct contact with the data stored in the machine.

There are many ways to get this effect; all the methods that have been developed over the centuries for presenting information visually can be applied, along with others that depend on the interactiveness of the computer. A few examples must suffice here.

Perhaps the most familiar is the "what you see is what you get" editor. The formatted document appears on the screen, complete with fonts, subscripts, correct line breaks, and paragraph leading; page lay-out should appear as well, but this was too hard for the Alto. The formatted text can be selected, and the format as well as the content changed by commands which show their effect immediately. Figure 2 is an example from Bravo.

The Smalltalk browser shown in Fig. 1 is a visual representation of part of the tree of Smalltalk classes and procedures. The panels show successive levels of the tree from left to right; the highlighted node is the parent of all the nodes in the panel immediately to its right. Under-neath the panels is the text content of the last highlighted node, which is a leaf of the tree. Again, subtrees can be selected and manipulated, and the effect is displayed at once.

The list of message headers in Fig. 3 is another example. Each line shows essential properties of a message, but it also stands for the mes-sage; it can be selected, and the message can be deleted, moved or copied to another file, read, or answered. The same methods are used in Gypsy and Star to represent a hierarchical file system, using the visual metaphor of files in a folder and folders in a file drawer. The icons on the screen in Star, Cedar, and more recent systems like the Apple Macintosh repeat the theme again.

The idea of views was first used in Sketchpad, which provides a graphical representation of an underlying structure of constraints [48], but it was obscured by the fact that Sketchpad was intended as a draw-ing system. In the Alto system it appeared first in Gypsy and Bravo (for formatted text and files), then in the Smalltalk browser, and later in nearly every user interface. It is still a challenge, however, to devise a good visual representation for an abstraction, and to make the point-ing and editing operations natural and fast.

## INTEGRATION

An integrated system has a consistent user interface, consistent data representations, and coresident applications. What does this mean?

A consistent user interface is one in which, for example, there is a single "delete" command that deletes the selected object, whether the object is a text string, a curve, a file, or a logic element. Every kind of object has a visual representation, and operations common to sev-eral objects are specified in the same way and have the same results on all the objects. Most computer systems are constructed by amalga-mating several applications and lack any consistency between the ap-plications.

A consistent data representation is one that allows two applica-tions handling the same kind of data to accept each other's output. Thus a document editor can handle the drawing produced by an illus-trater or a graph plotting program, and a compiler can read the output of a structured document editor, ignoring the structuring information that isn't relevant to the syntax of the programming language.

Two applications are coresident if control can pass from one to the other quickly and smoothly, without loss of the program state or the display state. If a text document editor allows pictures in the document, can pass control to the picture editor, and the picture can be edited while it appears on the screen along with the text, then the text and picture editors are coresident. In the same way a spreadsheet, a database query system, or a filing system might be coresident with editors or with each other.

Integration is difficult for several reasons. Designing consistent interfaces is difficult, both technically and organizationally. Consistent data representations require compromises between the different needs of different applications; most Alto programmers were uninterested in compromise. Coresidency requires common screen-handling facilities that meet the needs of both applications, and enough machine resources to keep the code and data for more than one program readily available.

In spite of these problems, integration was always a goal of many Alto system applications, but success was limited. Gypsy has excellent integration of text editing and filing. The window system of Smalltalk provides some integration, the later Star and Cedar systems continue this, and all three have some consistency in user interfaces. All three also have a common data representation for simple text, and make it easy to copy text from one application to another as pipes do in Unix. Star goes furthest in consistency of interfaces and representations, and also has coresidency of all its applications. A great deal of effort was devoted to the user interface design [43] to achieve these results. Unfortunately, it pays a considerable penalty in complexity and performance. In Cedar some applications, notably the Tioga structured document editor, can be easily called as subroutines from other applications.

## MAKING IMAGES

The Alto user interface depends heavily on displaying images to the user. These are of two main kinds: text and pictures. The application programs that allow users to make different kinds of images are described in the next section. They all, however, use a few basic imaging facilities that are discussed here.

The basic primitive for making images is BitBlt, designed by Dan Ingalls [18,37]. It operates on rectangular subregions of two *bitmaps* or two-dimensional arrays of pixels, setting each pixel of the target rectangle to some function of its old value and the value of the corresponding source pixel. Useful functions are

- □ constant black or white, which sets the target black or white;
- □ source, which copies the source to the target;
- □ merge, which adds black ink from the source to the target; and
- □ xor, which reverses the target color where the source is black.

There is also provision for a *texture* source that is an infinite repetition of a 4 × 4 array of pixels; this provides various shades of gray, striping, and the like. The Alto has a microcoded implementation of BitBlt that is quite fast.

BitBlt is used for rearranging windows and for scrolling images in a window. In addition, a single BitBlt can draw an arbitrary rectangle, and in particular a horizontal or vertical line, or it can copy or merge the image of a character from a source image called a *font* that contains all the characters of a typeface. Arbitrary lines and curves are drawn by procedures that manipulate the target image directly, since the rectangles involved are too small for BitBlt to be useful. In many cases, however, the resulting images are saved away as templates, and BitBlt copies them to the screen image.

In the Alto system applications make images by using BitBlt directly, or by using procedures to paint a character string in a given font or to draw a line or spline curve. Curves, once computed, are stored in a chain encoding that uses four bits to specify the direction of the curve at each pixel. There is also a package that handles arrays of intensity samples, built by Bob Sproull, Patrick Baudelaire and Jay Israel; it is used to process scanned images. Cedar has a complete graphics package that handles transformations, clipping, and halftoned representations of sampled images within a uniform framework [59].

# Applications

Most people who look at the Alto system see the applications that allow users to do many of the major tasks that people do with paper: preparing and reading documents with text and pictures, filing information, and handling electronic mail. This section describes the major Alto system applications that are not programming systems: editors, illustrators, and filing and mail systems.

### EDITORS

The Bravo editor was probably the most widely used Alto application [25]. It was designed by Butler Lampson and Charles Simonyi, and implemented by Simonyi, Tom Malloy, and a number of others. Bravo's salient features are rapid screen updating, editing speed independent of the size of the document, what-you-see-is-what-you-get formatting (with italics, Greek letters, and justified text displayed on the screen), and semi-automatic error recovery. Figure 2 shows a Bravo screen, illustrating the appearance of formatted documents. Later versions also have style sheets, which introduce a level of indirection between the document and its layout, so that the layout can be changed systematically by editing the style sheet; the document specifies "emphasis" and the style sheet maps it to "italic" or to "underlined" as desired.

Bravo is a rather large program, since it includes a software-implemented virtual memory for text and fonts; layout of lines and paragraphs in a variety of fonts with adjustable margins, tab stops, and leading; mapping from a point in the displayed text back to the document; incremental screen update; a screen display identical to the final printed copy; hard-copy generation for EARS and Press printers as well as daisy-wheel devices; and page layout. Later versions have a document directory, style sheets, screen display of laid-out pages, hyphenation, a remote terminal service, an abbreviation dictionary, form letter generation, and assorted other features.

Good performance in a small machine comes from the representation of edits to the text and of formatting information, and from the method for updating the screen. The text is stored as a table of *pieces*, each of which is a descriptor for a substring of an immutable string stored in a file. Initially the entire document is a single piece, pointing to the entire file from which it was read. After a word is replaced, there are three pieces: one for the text before the word; one for the new characters, which are written on a scratch file as they are typed; and one for the text after the word. Since binary search is used to access the piece array, the speed is logarithmic in the number of edits. This scheme was independently invented by Jay Moore [35].

Formatting information is represented as a property record of 32 bits for each character (font, bold, italic, offset, etc.); since consecutive characters usually have the same properties, they are stored in run-coded form in a table much like the piece table. Changes in formatting are represented by a sequence of *formatting operators* attached to each piece. Thus to find the font for a character it is necessary first to find its entry in the run-coded table, and then to apply all the formatting operators in its piece. But it takes only a few instructions per piece to make a 60,000 character document italic. When an editing session is complete, the document is written to a file in a clean form, so that the piece table doesn't keep growing.

To make screen updating fast, the screen image is maintained as a table of lines, each containing its bitmap and pointers to the characters used to compute it. This table is treated as a cache: When an edit is done, any entries that depend on characters changed by the edit are invalidated. Then the entire screen is recomputed, but the cache is first checked for each line, so that recomputation is done only if the line is actually different.

Bravo has a clumsy user interface. The Gypsy editor, built by Larry Tesler and Tim Mott, uses much of the Bravo implementation but refines the user interface greatly. Gypsy introduced a modeless user interface, editable screen display of bold and italics, and an integrated file directory that is modified by the same commands used for editing. All these ideas were later used in many parts of the Alto system. The parallel development of Bravo and Gypsy is an illustration of the many elements required in a good application. Both the refined implementation methods of Bravo and the refined user interface of Gypsy are important; each required several years of work by talented people.

The Star editor evolved from Bravo and Gypsy, with further refinement of the user interface [43] and the integration of graphics (see the next section). The Star interface design in turn had considerable influence on later versions of Bravo, from which Microsoft Word was then derived. It also influenced the Cedar document editor, Tioga, which is distinguished by its support of tree-structured documents (derived from Engelbart's system [13]), and by a fully programmable stylesheet facility that can do arbitrary computations to determine the format of a piece of text.

There are also simple text editors embedded in the Smalltalk and Mesa programming environments. These allow plain text files to be created, read, and modified. They are used for editing programs and for viewing *typescripts*, the output of programs that produce a sequence of unformatted lines.

## ILLUSTRATORS

The Alto system has a number of different illustrators for different kinds of pictures: pure bit-maps (Markup), spline curves (Draw), logic diagrams and other images involving only straight lines (SIL), and font characters (Fred). They all handle multi-font text as well, and all produce Press output for printing; most can show a screen image that exactly matches the printed image. Usually they work on only one picture at a time. None is integrated with a text editor; however, there is a separate batch program called PressEdit (written by William Newman), that can combine images from several Press files into a single file. PressEdit is used to assemble complete documents with text and figures; it has the drawback that the assembled document cannot be edited interactively. Several designs for integrated text and graphics editors stumbled over the limited size of the Alto.

William Newman's Markup was the first illustrator for the Alto [25]. It edits multipage Press files, one page at a time, but it can only handle text and bitmap images, not lines or curves. Markup provides an assortment of brushes for painting into the bitmap, as well as operations for erasing and for moving or copying a rectangular region of the image. There are separate facilities for text strings, so that these can be printed at full resolution, since screen-resolution text looks terrible in hard-copy. Figure 4 is an example of the kind of picture that can be made. The Apple Macintosh's MacPaint is quite similar to Markup.

There are two very different illustrators that deal with synthetic graphics, in which the picture is derived from a set of mathematically defined curves. Draw, written by Patrick Baudelaire, builds up the picture from arbitrary lines and spline curves [25]. It has facilities for copying parts of the image and for applying arbitrary linear transformations. Curves can be of various widths, dashed, and fitted with various arrowheads. Thus very pretty results can be obtained; Fig. 5

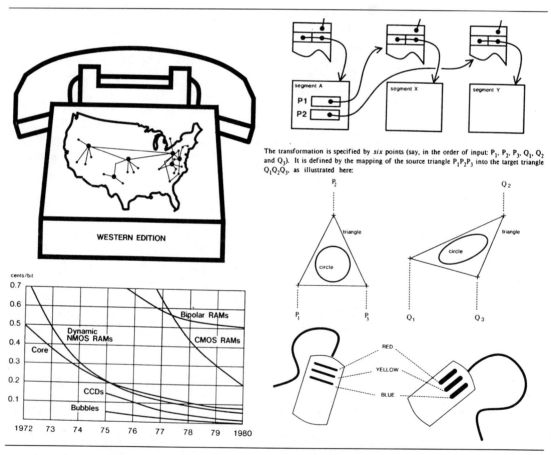

**FIGURE 5**
Typical Draw pictures.

shows some examples. The great variety of possible curves makes it difficult to use Draw for simple pictures, however, and it runs out of space fairly quickly, since it needs a full-screen bitmap (60 KBytes) and code for real arithmetic and spline curves, as well as the usual font-handling code, space for the fonts, the user interface, and so on. All of this must fit in the 128 KBytes of the Alto. Draw does not use the software virtual memory or overlaying techniques that allow Bravo to fit; these would have made the program quite a bit more complicated.

SIL was built by Chuck Thacker for making logic drawings [57]. Thus the main requirements were capacity for a complex drawing, a user interface well suited to experts who spend tens or hundreds of hours with the program, and a library facility for handling the images of logic components. SIL allows only characters and horizontal and vertical lines, which are easily handled by all the raster printers. There is a special font of bitmaps that represent and-gates, or-gates, resistors, and a few other specialized shapes, and a macro facility allows drawings of complex components to be built up from these. Since SIL drawings can be rather complex (see Fig. 6 for an example), redrawing the picture must be avoided. Instead, SIL draws a picture element with white ink to erase it, and in background redraws every element that intersects the bounding box of the erased element. This simple heuristic works very well. Somewhat to everyone's surprise, SIL is the illustrator of choice when curves are not absolutely required, because of its speed, capacity, and convenience.

For designing font characters with spline outlines Patrick Baudelaire built Fred. An Alto interfaced to a television camera captures an image of the character, and the user then fits splines around it. The resulting shapes can be scan-converted at various resolutions to produce different sizes and orientations of the character for printing.

SIL and Fred are illustrators associated with batch-processing programs: a design-rule checker and wire-list generator for logic drawings made in SIL, and a battery of scan-conversion, font-editing, and management software for Fred.


**FILING**

From its earliest days the Alto system has had the usual operating system facilities for managing stored information: Directories can be listed and files renamed or deleted. This is quite clumsy, however, and many attempts have been made to provide a better interface. Most of these involve listing the contents of a directory as a text document. Lines of the listing can be selected and edited; deletion means deleting the file, changing the name renames the file, and so forth. Gypsy was the first system to use this scheme; it was followed by the Descriptive Directory System (DDS) built by Peter Deutsch [25], by Neptune built by Keith

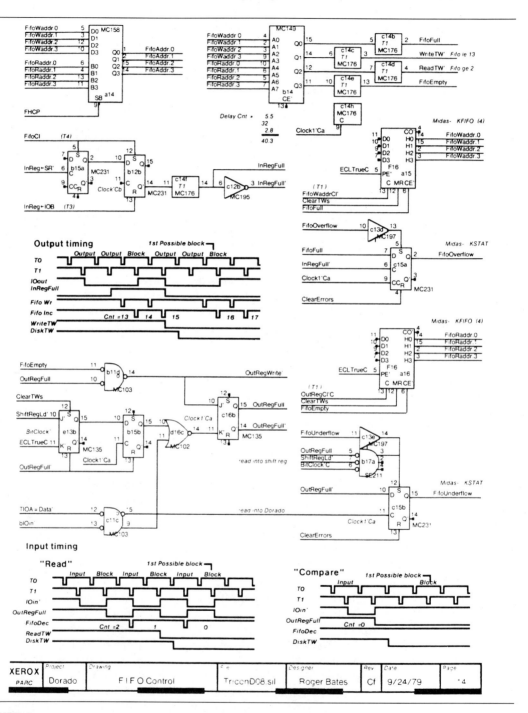

**FIGURE 6**
A logic drawing done in SIL.

Knox, and later by Star's file folders. DDS and Neptune allow the user to control what is displayed by writing filters such as ''memo *and not* report,'' which are applied to the file names. Star has a standard hierarchical directory system, which it manifests by allowing folders to appear in other folders.

Some other experiments with filing were more interesting. The Smalltalk browser is described in the section on Views and illustrated in Fig. 1; it has been very successful. Cedar has a facility called Whiteboards, illustrated in Fig. 3, which deals with a collection of pages, each containing text and simple figures. A picture on one page can be a reference to another page; when the reference picture is clicked with the mouse, the page it points to is displayed. This is a convenient way to organize a modest amount of information. Finally, the electronic mail systems are heavily used for filing.

## ELECTRONIC MAIL

The Alto system certainly did not introduce electronic mail, and in its early days the mail service was provided by Tenex. One of the most successful applications, however, was the Laurel user mail system built by Doug Brotz, Roy Levin, Mike Schroeder, and Ben Wegbreit [5]. Laurel provides facilities for reading, filing, and composing electronic messages; actual transport and delivery is handled by Grapevine or some other transport mechanism.

Laurel uses a fixed arrangement of three windows in a single column (see Fig. 7). The top window is a message directory, with one line for each message in the current folder. The other two windows hold the text of a message being read and the text of a message being composed; the latter can be edited, and text can be copied from the middle window to the bottom. Above each window is a line of menu buttons relevant to that window; some of them have associated blanks that can be filled in with text when that button is clicked. A set of messages can be selected in the directory by clicking, and deleted, moved, or copied as a unit. Deleted messages are marked by being struck out in the directory; the actual deletion is only done when exiting Laurel, and can be undone until then.

Laurel can handle any number of message folders, and allows a message to be moved or copied from one folder to another. It also provides commands to forward or answer a message; these set up the composition window in a plausible way, but it is easy for the user to edit it appropriately. Message bodies are copied to the user's Alto from a mail server when the message is first retrieved. A message folder is represented as two Alto files, a text file for the messages and a table-of-contents file; there is a scavenger that reconstructs the latter from the former in case of trouble.

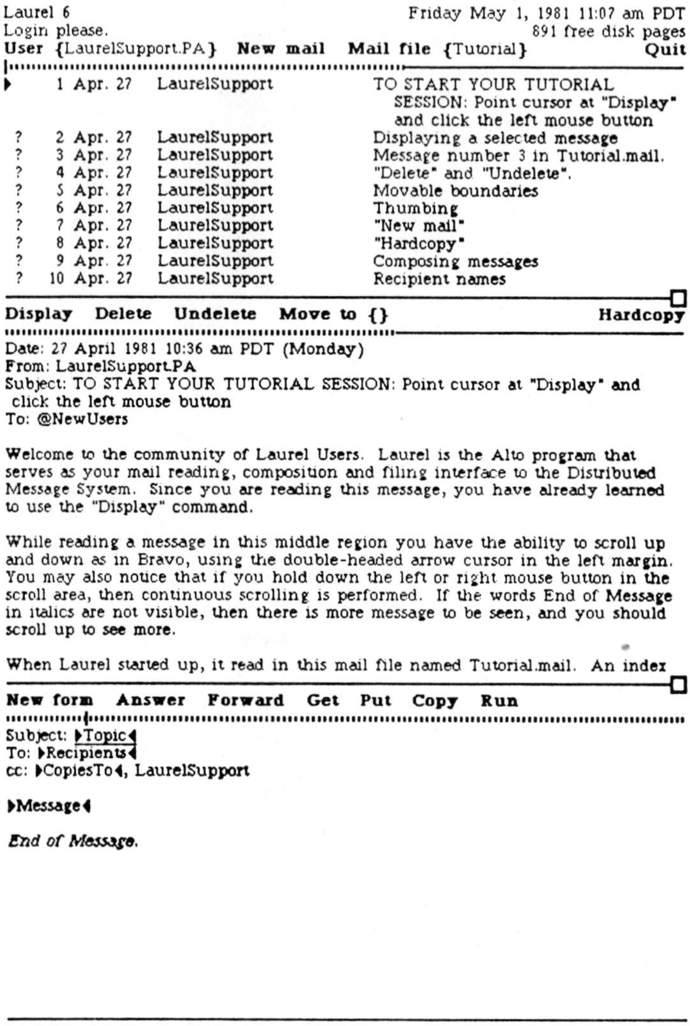

**FIGURE 7**
A Laurel screen.

```
Laurel 6                                    Friday May 1, 1981 11:07 am PDT
Login please.                                          891 free disk pages
User {LaurelSupport.PA}  New mail   Mail file {Tutorial}            Quit
|...............................................................................

▶      1 Apr. 27   LaurelSupport          TO START YOUR TUTORIAL
                                          SESSION: Point cursor at "Display"
                                          and click the left mouse button
   ?   2 Apr. 27   LaurelSupport          Displaying a selected message
   ?   3 Apr. 27   LaurelSupport          Message number 3 in Tutorial.mail.
   ?   4 Apr. 27   LaurelSupport          "Delete" and "Undelete".
   ?   5 Apr. 27   LaurelSupport          Movable boundaries
   ?   6 Apr. 27   LaurelSupport          Thumbing
   ?   7 Apr. 27   LaurelSupport          "New mail"
   ?   8 Apr. 27   LaurelSupport          "Hardcopy"
   ?   9 Apr. 27   LaurelSupport          Composing messages
   ?  10 Apr. 27   LaurelSupport          Recipient names
                                                                         □
Display   Delete   Undelete   Move to {}                          Hardcopy
|...............................................................................
Date: 27 April 1981 10:36 am PDT (Monday)
From: LaurelSupport.PA
Subject: TO START YOUR TUTORIAL SESSION: Point cursor at "Display" and
   click the left mouse button
To: @NewUsers

Welcome to the community of Laurel Users. Laurel is the Alto program that
serves as your mail reading, composition and filing interface to the Distributed
Message System. Since you are reading this message, you have already learned
to use the "Display" command.

While reading a message in this middle region you have the ability to scroll up
and down as in Bravo, using the double-headed arrow cursor in the left margin.
You may also notice that if you hold down the left or right mouse button in the
scroll area, then continuous scrolling is performed. If the words End of Message
in italics are not visible, then there is more message to be seen, and you should
scroll up to see more.

When Laurel started up, it read in this mail file named Tutorial.mail. An index
                                                                         □
New form   Answer   Forward   Get   Put   Copy   Run
|...............................................................................
Subject: ▶Topic◀
To: ▶Recipients◀
cc: ▶CopiesTo◀, LaurelSupport

▶Message◀

End of Message.
```

This apparently simple user interface is the result of about a man-year of design, and shows its value in the fact that most users never refer to the manual. This friendliness, together with the transparent view of the state provided by the message directory and the high reliability of message retrieval and storage, made Laurel very popular. A variant of Laurel called Cholla is used as the backbone of a control system for an integrated circuit fabrication line; special messages called recipes contain instructions for the operator and the computer-controlled equipment, and messages are sent to the next station and to administrators and logging files as a job progresses through the system. The beauty of this system is that everything is immediately accessible to a person trying to determine the state or track down an error and that the high reliability of the Grapevine transport mechanism makes lost data extremely unlikely.

Cedar has a mail facility called Walnut, patterned on Laurel, but using the standard Viewers windows and menus; it was built by Willie-Sue Haugeland and Jim Donahue. Walnut uses the Cedar entity-relationship database built by Rick Cattell to store messages; this turned out to be relatively unsuccessful, much to our surprise. It seems that a database system does not have much to contribute to a mail system.

# Conclusion

During the 1970s the Computer Science Laboratory and Learning Research Group at Xerox PARC built a complete personal distributed computing system: computers, display, local network, operating systems, programming environments, communication software, printing, servers, windows, user interfaces, raster graphics, editors, illustrators, mail systems, and a host of other elements. This Alto system did not have a detailed plan, but it was built in pursuit of a clear goal: to make computers better tools for people to think and communicate.

The Alto system has spawned a great variety of offspring. The Dorado system and the Xerox Star are the most direct line. Table 2 lists

**TABLE 2**
**Commercial systems descended from the Alto**

| | |
|---|---|
| Engineering worksta-tions | Perq; Apollo; Sun; Tektronix; DEC |
| AI workstations | MIT Lisp machine; Xerox 1100/1108/1132; Symbolics; LMI |
| Personal computers | Apple Lisa, Macintosh; Xerox 8065 |
| Office workstations | Convergent NGen; Xerox 8010; Apple Macintosh; Grid |
| Graphics terminals | BBN Bitgraph; Bell Labs Blit |
| Local area networks | Ethernet/IEEE 802.3 |
| Networks protocols | ARPA IP/TCP; Xerox Network Services, Clearinghouse |
| Laser printers | Xerox 9700, 5700, 8044; Imagen; Apple Laserwriter |
| Printing interfaces | Xerox Interpress; Adobe Postscript |
| Servers | 3Com file server, Xerox 8044 and Apple Laserwriter print servers |
| User interfaces | Xerox 8010; Apple Macintosh; Microsoft Windows |
| Editors | Apple MacWrite; Microsoft Word |
| Illustrations | Xerox 8010; Apple MacPaint, MacDraw |

a number of commercial systems derived from the Alto. There have also been many in universities and research laboratories.

A dozen years of work have made it clear that these systems only begin to exploit the possibilities of personal distributed computing. Continuing progress in devices ensures that processors and networks will get faster, storage devices larger, displays clearer and more colorful, and prices lower. Compact discs, for example, allow half a gigabyte to be reproduced for a few dollars and to be on-line for a few hundred dollars; the impact will surely be profound.

These improvements and, even more important, a better understanding of the problems will lead to systems that are easier to program and use, provide access to far more information, present that information much more clearly, and compute effectively with it.

## ACKNOWLEDGMENTS

I am grateful to Bob Sproull, Peter Deutsch, David Boggs, Carol Peters and Cynthia Hibbard for comments on earlier versions of this paper, and to Ed McCreight and Adele Goldberg for supplying some of the figures.

## REFERENCES

[1] A. D. Birrell et al. Grapevine: An exercise in distributed computing. *Communications of the ACM,* 25(4):260–274, April 1982.

[2] A. D. Birrell and B. J. Nelson. Implementing remote procedure calls. *ACM Transactions on Computer Systems,* 2(1):39–59, February 1984.

[3] D. G. Bobrow et al. Tenex: A paged time-sharing system for the PDP-10. *Communications of the ACM,* 15(3):135–143, March 1972.

[4] D. R. Boggs et al. Pup: An internetwork architecture. *IEEE Transactions on Communications,* 28(4):612–624, April 1980.

[5] D. K. Brotz. *Laurel Manual.* Technical Report CSL-81-6, Xerox Palo Alto Research Center, 1981.

[6] M. R. Brown et al. The Alpine file system. *ACM Transactions on Computer Systems,* 3(2), November 1985.

[7] R. R. Burton et al. Interlisp-D: Overview and status. In *Proc. Lisp Conference,* Stanford, 1980.

[8] P. A. Crisman, editor. *The Compatible Time-Sharing System: A Programmer's Guide.* MIT Press, 2nd edition, 1965.

[9] L. P. Deutsch. Experience with a microprogrammed Interlisp system. *IEEE Transactions on Computers,* C-28(10), October 1979.

[10] L. P. Deutsch. A Lisp machine with very compact programs. In *Proc. 3rd International Joint Conference on Artificial Intelligence,* Stanford, 1973.

[11] L. P. Deutsch and E. A. Taft. *Requirements for an experimental programming environment.* Technical Report CSL-80-10, Xerox Palo Alto Research Center, June 1980.

[12] D. C. Engelbart. The augmented knowledge workshop. In *Proc. ACM Conference on the History of Personal Workstations*, January 1986.

[13] D. C. Engelbart and W. K. English. A research center for augmenting human intellect. In *Proc. AFIPS Conference*, pages 395–410, 1968.

[14] E. R. Fiala. The MAXC systems. *IEEE Computer*, 11(5):57–67, May 1978.

[15] C. M. Geschke et al. Early experience with Mesa. *Communications of the ACM*, 20(8):540–553, August 1977.

[16] A. Goldberg and D. Robson. *Smalltalk-80: The Language and its Implementation*. Addison-Wesley, 1983.

[17] J. Gray et al. The recovery manager of the System R database manager. *ACM Computing Surveys*, 13(2):223–242, June 1981.

[18] D. Ingalls. The Smalltalk graphics kernel. *Byte*, 6(8):168–194, August 1981.

[19] D. H. Ingalls. The Smalltalk-76 programming system: Design and implementation. In *Proc. 5th ACM Symposium on Principles of Programming Languages*, pages 9–16, January 1978.

[20] R. K. Johnsson and J. D. Wick. An overview of the Mesa processor architecture. *ACM Sigplan Notices*, 17(4):20–29, April 1982.

[21] A. C. Kay. *The Reactive Engine*. Ph.D. thesis, University of Utah, 1969.

[22] A. C. Kay and A. Goldberg. Personal dynamic media. *IEEE Computer*, 10(3), March 1977.

[23] B. W. Kernighan and R. Pike. *The Unix Programming Environment*. Prentice-Hall, 1983.

[24] D. E. Knuth. *TeX and Metafont: New Directions in Typesetting*. Digital Press and American Mathematical Society, 1979.

[25] B. W. Lampson, editor. *Alto User's Handbook*. Xerox Palo Alto Research Center, 1976.

[26] B. W. Lampson et al. A user machine in a time-sharing system. *Proc. IEEE*, 54(12):1744–1766, December 1966.

[27] B. W. Lampson and K. A. Pier. A processor for a high-performance personal computer. In *Proc. 7th Symposium on Computer Architecture*, pages 146–160, ACM Sigarch/IEEE, May 1980.

[28] B. W. Lampson and D. D. Redell. Experience with processes and monitors in Mesa. *Communications of the ACM*, 23(2):105–117, February 1980.

[29] B. W. Lampson and R. F. Sproull. An open operating system for a single-user machine. *ACM Operating Systems Review*, 13(5), November 1979.

[30] H. C. Lauer and E. H. Satterthwaite. The impact of Mesa on system design. In *Proc. 4th International Conference on Software Engineering*, pages 174–182, September 1979.

[31] P. J. Leach et al. The architecture of an integrated local network. *IEEE Journal on Selected Areas of Communication*, SAC-1(5):842–856, November 1983.

[32] J. Licklider. Man-computer symbiosis. *IRE Trans. Human Factors in Electronics*, HFE-1:4–11, March 1960.

[33] J. M. McQuillan and D. C. Walden. The Arpanet design decisions. *Computer Networks*, 1(5):243–289, September 1977.

[34] J. G. Mitchell and J. Dion. A comparison of two network-based file servers. *Communications of the ACM*, 25(4):233–245, April 1982.

[35] J. S. Moore. *The TXDT Package-Interlisp Text Editing Primitives*. Technical Report CSL-81-2, Xerox Palo Alto Research Center, January 1981.

[36] R. M. Needham and A. J. Herbert. *The Cambridge Distributed Computing System*. Addison-Wesley, 1982.

[37] W. M. Newman and R. F. Sproull. *Principles of Interactive Computer Graphics*. McGraw-Hill, 2nd edition, 1979.

[38] D. D. Redell et al. Pilot: An operating system for a personal computer. *Communications of the ACM*, 23(2):81–92, February 1980.

[39] H. Rheingold. *Tools for Thought*. Simon and Schuster, 1985.

[40] M. Richards. BCPL: A tool for compiler writing and system programming. In *Proc. AFIPS Conference*, pages 557–566, 1969.

[41] M. D. Schroeder et al. A caching file system for a programmer's workstation. *ACM Operating Systems Review*, 19(5), December 1985.

[42] J. F. Shoch and J. A. Hupp. Notes on the "worm" programs—some early experiences with a distributed computation. *Communications of the ACM*, 25(3):172–180, March 1982.

[43] D. C. Smith et al. The Star user interface: An overview. In *Proc. AFIPS Conf.*, pages 515–528, 1982.

[44] R. F. Sproull. *Introduction to Interpress*. Xerox Printing Systems Division, 1984.

[45] R. F. Sproull. Raster graphics for interactive programming environments. *Computer Graphics*, 3(3), July 1979.

[46] R. M. Stallman. EMACS: the extensible, customizable self-documenting display editor. In *ACM SIGPLAN Notices*, pages 147–156, June 1981.

[47] J. E. Stoy and C. Strachey. OS6—an experimental operating system for a small computer. *Computer Journal*, 15(2 and 3), May and August 1972.

[48] I. Sutherland. Sketchpad, a man-machine graphical communication system. In *Proc. AFIPS Conf.*, pages 329–346, 1963.

[49] R. E. Sweet. The Mesa programming environment. *SIGPLAN Notices*, 20(7):216–229, July 1985.

[50] D. Swinehart et al. WFS: A simple shared file system for a distributed environment. *ACM Operating Systems Review*, 13(5), November 1979.

[51] D. C. Swinehart et al. The structure of Cedar. *SIGPLAN Notices*, 20(7):230–244, July 1985.

[52] W. Teitelman. A display-oriented programmer's assistant. In *Proc. 5th International Joint Conference on Artificial Intelligence*, pages 905–917, 1977.

[53] W. Teitelman. A tour through Cedar. *IEEE Software*, 1(4), April 1984.

[54] W. Teitelman et al. *Interlisp Reference Manual*. Technical Report, Xerox Palo Alto Research Center, 1978.

[55] W. Teitelman and L. Masinter. The Interlisp programming environment. *IEEE Computer*, 14(4):25–34, April 1981.

[56] C. P. Thacker. Personal distributed computing: The Alto and Ethernet hardware. In *ACM Conference on the History of Personal Workstations*, January 1986.

[57] C. P. Thacker. SIL—a simple illustrator for CAD. In S. Chang, editor, *Fundamentals Handbook of Electrical and Computer Engineering, Volume 3*, pages 477–489, Wiley, 1983.

[58] C. P. Thacker et al. Alto: A personal computer. In Siewiorek et al., editors, *Computer Structures: Principles and Examples*, chapter 33, McGraw-Hill, 1982. Also CSL-79-11, Xerox Palo Alto Research Center (1979).

[59] J. Warnock and D. K. Wyatt. A device independent graphics imaging model for use with raster devices. *Computer Graphics*, 6(3), July 1982.

[60] J. E. White and Y. K. Dalal. Higher-level protocols enhance Ethernet. *Electronic Design*, 30(8):31–41, April 1982.

# Participants Discussion for Thacker and Lampson

**Mark Richer**   In the first talk, Chuck said that in a few years we may have user interfaces that would be good enough that a broader audience of people would be able to use computers more effectively. I was wondering if either of you could point out some specific things that you think could be done to make that happen—things that we could work on, major problems.

**Thacker**   Well, I think that one of the things that happens now is that interaction of the computer, although it is very fast, particularly with modern machines, still means *typing* and *looking*. Looking is a high bandwidth activity, but typing is not, particularly if you do not know how to type. It would be very reasonable if you could talk to your machine, for instance; that's still a completely unsolved problem, although there's a lot of work going on about it. I think that we're probably close to the limit of what you can do with things like pointing. I think we'll hear later this afternoon that we're doing about as well as a person can do, just nervous system limitations will keep improvements down. But I'm sure there are other ways.

**Lampson**   Most of the game really is to be had at a higher level, one notch up. There's a tremendous amount of gain to be had just by making the machines faster. There are a lot of things, for instance, that are in the Macintosh user interface that are quite nice, but that are almost completely crippled by the fact that the screen changes too slowly. You can really see that when you compare the things that are nice, but that are unusable because the screen changes too slowly. There's just a lot of room for improvement in that area. I mentioned one or two examples of that in my talk.

   The other thing that I think is even more important, in that it makes the current systems difficult to use, is that they are still very poorly integrated. We have pretty good systems for word processing but, for all the work that you need to do in a day, we're still in fairly bad shape. You have to make these gigantic lurches from one place to another, and there's a lot of inconsistency and funny breaks and boundaries and so forth. I believe that's a very difficult problem. It seems clear to me that in the course of time it can be overcome. It's going to require a lot more computing resources, a lot more storage resources, and a lot of hard work, but it's clearly possible to make things much, much better.

*Gordon Bell*

Since this is an historical conference, I have seven questions that I would like to get into the record, but I do not think there is time to address them all. So I can either present them orally in order to put them in the record, and then have their response prepared later, or ask them one at a time for immediate response. Which do you prefer?

[*Editor's Note:* The general agreement was that Gordon would state all of his questions. Butler and Chuck would compose written responses to be included in the conference record. The responses so obtained are provided after each question.]

1. Given what I have read and heard, both at PARC and at this conference, I understand that your work was influenced by the ALOHA network project at the University of Hawaii, by hardware efforts at Data General, and by the BCPL programming language design. Were you also influenced by the work at CMU on the LDX? The hardware work on the LDX was done at CMU, although a lot of software came from the University of Rochester. In 1972, I recall printing a book with neat fonts using CMU's LDX.

*Response:* The LDX (for Long Distance Xerography) was a facsimile machine developed by Xerox during the late 1960s. There were two LDX machines at PARC shortly after the Center was founded, one of which was subsequently donated to Stanford. I believe that several more of these machines (which were obsolete by that time) eventually found their way into universities. Perhaps this is where the CMU system came from. In any case, the LDX was a very slow device, since the image was formed by a CRT, not a laser. It was used as a printer at PARC for perhaps two years, but had little influence on the development of EARS.

2. Also, there were publications preceding 1972 about token bus structures. Did these influence you?

*Response:* Token busses (and rings, of which at least one existed at the time), were rejected because it was believed they would require either very reliable stations or an electromechanical relay as a fail-over device. Both solutions seemed unattractive, although they were considered. The design of the Ethernet cable tap, which has very few components whose failure can cause the entire network to fail, made further consideration of these solutions unnecessary.

3. In your presentations, you indicate that the Apollo workstation, the Bell Labs BLIT machine, and the BBN Jericho are direct descendents of your work at PARC. Could you support this claim?

*Response for Apollo:* Apollo based their user interface directly on the RIG system done on Altos at the University of Rochester by Keith Lantz.

*Response for the BLIT:* In "The BLIT: A Multiplexed Graphics Terminal," *AT&T Bell Labs Tech J.* 63(8), part 2, pp 1607–1631, R. Pike says: "The original idea behind the development of the BLIT hardware was to provide a graphics machine with about the power of the Xerox Alto [cited], but using 1981 technology. . . ."

*Response for BBN:* I don't know. . . .

4. Given your claim for influencing work on the workstations listed in question 2, why were the Apple II and IBM PC not included?

*Response:* The Apple II and the IBM PC were not included because there is no evidence that the Alto had any influence on them. These systems were reactions to the availability of single chip microcomputers (in the case of Apple, the 8-bit 6502, and in the case of the PC, the 16-bit 8086), while the processor of the Alto was based on a minicomputer. In addition, the provisions for graphics were entirely different.

5. You made a good statement about the need for a small number of interface standards. I agree. Could you state which standards you consider to be important?

*Response:* Files (Alto file system), communications (Pup and RPC), imaging and printing (Press), manning (Grapevine), mail, and formatted text.

6. In your paper, you mention a computer named MAXC [*Editor's Note:* Multi-Access Xerox Computer], a central time-shared computer. In my paper, I refer to a VAXC Environment. In this Environment, a workstation is a small part of a total computing environment. Given my experiences as a Star and VAXC user, I believe that we cannot accomplish all of our work requirements in a single workstation. A workstation environment is useful for only a limited set of applications. I believe that a major part of the success of your environment at PARC is that you did have this central machine. What role did MAXC play in your environment? Did it, for example, extend the kinds of applications you were able to do?

*Response:* Even after Altos had proliferated, MAXC was used for electronic mail handling and as an interface to the ARPA network, for file storage (until the file servers became operational), and for Lisp programming. It was also used less heavily for a wide variety of other applications, but I think it is fair to say that use of MAXC decreased over time. This was deliberate, since CSL was experimenting with distributed personal computing, and it was considered important to see the extent to which the Alto could provide all the needs of a single user. Also, the main advantage of MAXC was space, not speed, since a few time-sharing users could reduce the performance delivered to a single user to less than that of an Alto. MAXC had more than a mega-byte of memory, while the early Altos had 128K. Since most programs that were heavily used fit within this limit, MAXC was not as critical a resource as one might initially think.

7. In your presentation, you showed a movie of the OfficeTalk application in which office procedures were carried out using forms displayed on the bitmap screen. Computing environments for the last 15 years or so have made good use of such forms-oriented interfaces. How did the OfficeTalk forms differ?

*Response:* Office talk is much more like familiar paper forms than any computer-based system of the 1970s that I know about. It also had user-level programming facilities!

*Hank Strub*

In the last three very interesting talks, what I see is a sort of Camelot at PARC in the early 1970s. I haven't heard any talk about how the work was influenced by marketing concerns and how much time was spent with hardware and software and methods. I'm thinking of things like: How might we package this to sell someday? Who might buy it? And how much might it cost? I'm also interested in hearing people's perspectives, looking back over ten years, on these questions.

*Lampson*

We did back of the envelope calculations on how much we thought these things would cost as a function of time, if they were product engineered. But the artifacts we built were intended for researchers, they were never intended to be used as products. Xerox started a development organization in 1976 that, in fact, was charged with the task of turning the research into products. They produced the Xerox 8000 series network systems. They obviously worried about the questions you stated a great deal, and there was a tremendous amount of interaction between that organization and PARC. In general, PARC was run on the principle that the things we built were functional prototypes. We were trying to explore what you could do with hardware that was outrageously expensive at the time we built it, knowing that the march of technology would make that hardware much cheaper. So we worried about these matters only in trying to get a good enough prediction of where the hardware was going so that we could come in five or ten years ahead of it.

*Allen Newell*

This is really a comment. I keep worrying about this question about determinism of the sort that historically makes things go down one path rather than another. It seems to me that there were two very interesting examples in the two PARC talks. One of them was from Butler Lampson, when he was trying to decide why they hadn't done spreadsheets. Spreadsheets were certainly one of the technological possibilities that, even in retrospect, was available right there on the surface. The issue seems to be that there is a kind of general philosophical equality of whole groups with respect to what problems they find interesting.

The other example, quite in contrast, was the one from Chuck Thacker when he remarked that they, too, made the mistake of not putting enough memory in the machine. That problem is something that every designer has known for 20 years; every designer says to himself, ''I will not make that error.'' I remember back in the Air Force, the AFSQ machines in which they had 8k to 16k of memory. (I guess they jumped over 32 and 64k.) Each one of those created a major boundary of capabilities in those systems. Everybody understood that, and yet we keep making that error. So it's a question of being driven by the boundaries and convincing yourself that it's all right to do it, even though you know it's not all right for past generations of designers. We will probably still go on and make that error another dozen or two dozen times.

**Ed McCreight**

Maybe Chuck can tell the story of how it was that we found out how the TX2 worked. Do you want to tell that story Chuck, or shall I?

[Chuck tells Ed to go ahead.]

Well, the next speaker, Wes Clark, stopped by one day after having read some of the Alto documentation. I was in the office. Wes said, ''Say this Alto stuff is pretty interesting. I wonder if you could, in a few words, say what the relationship is to the TX2 and, in particular, to the task structure of the TX2?'' Chuck and I looked at each other and said, ''Well, ah, well, ah, not really very well.''

Wes said, ''Well, as it happens, the TX2 papers were in the WJCC—Western Joint Computer Conference. I have some copies here I can leave with you, and I could ask the question later.'' So Chuck and I avidly read these things and compared notes and, as I said to Wes the next day when he came back for our answer, my only excuse is that I was in the eighth grade at the time. We were all of a group of people of about the same age. People at the age we were then have a feeling that it's all coming as a given, that somehow the world just arrived that way; and there was no need to explain it, and not much to really understand about what had happened before. I think one answer to Allen's question is that there are newer and newer generations of computer designers who don't know what the old problems are.

**Thacker**

I think that incident that Ed just mentioned, and the thing that Allen mentioned, were the two most embarrassing things about the Alto. I, of course, had the same problem. I think I was in the ninth grade at the time. It is interesting, because we've seen at the conference today a lot of people who were sort of first- or second-generation machine designers, and PARC was a third-generation place. When the Western Joint Computer Conference was held, it was going to be three years before I sat down at an LGP30 and tried to program it.

*Alan Kay*          I have one slight comment. I remember just a little bit about that story I didn't tell last night, but I have to tell it, because it was pretty funny. After I had gotten turned down by XE [reference to a Xerox Executive] to build the MiniCom machines, I was going to put together a bunch of old character generators, get more built, and cobble them to Novas. I managed to convince my funders to give me $230,000.00. I was in the process of piecing together a machine when Butler and Chuck came up to me one day and said, "Have you got any money?" I said, "Yes I do, I've got about $230,000.00." They said, "How would you like us to build your machine?" I said, "I'd like it fine, but what about XE?" They said, "Well, XE is away on a Xerox task force for a few months, so we have to get it done before he comes back." And so, part of the urgency that went on there was that this thing had to be done very quickly. One of the classic memos of all times is one Butler wrote when XE came back inadvertently, right in the middle while Chuck was busy throwing silicon at the wall and having it fall down the machine.

One of the phrases that we used for the Alto in that period was that it was to be like Kleenex tissue. In fact, it was an explicit part of the plan, as I recall it, that the Alto was supposed to be completely replaced by 1975 with something that actually had more than a month's worth of design in it. There were things like a pathway back to the bus that Chuck wanted to put in, and a barrel shifter that he wanted to put in, that they explicitly left out in order to get it done. The memory size was perfectly adequate as long as the machine was replaced immediately.

Well, it wasn't replaced. I told George Pake then that whatever you're going to spend for the Alto, you'd better put that much plus 50 percent again in the bank to replace them. I think the biggest single change at PARC, from my perspective, was the one that happened in 1975, 1976, and 1977, when the Altos weren't replaced. All of the sudden everybody went into systems programming mode to try and get more cycles out of the machine. One of the things I've noticed is, as Bob Barton said, systems programmers are high priests of a low cult. I believe that you cannot design sensibly when you're in systems programming mode. So that is the way I recall that things worked out. It's also probably true that if Chuck had longer to design the machine it wouldn't have worked out as well. I believe that is almost always the case in design.

*Lampson*          Actually, we did, after we got the first machines working, allocate three or four months to think it all over to see if we could make any improvements. I think we were fortunate that we failed to find any to make, with the exception of writable control store. That was a big deal because, at the time that writable control store was first designed by Ed, the RAMS were $90 each. So it cost thousands of dollars for writable control stores.

*Allen Newell*          I just have two final comments on that Wes Clark story. One of them is that historians should note that it was not just Wes Clark randomly wandering through that organization. He was, in fact, a consultant to that organization and had been for quite a while. So, in terms of histories in which we read about these connections related to who belongs to what organizations and, therefore, you assume that they know, Wes Clark was, in fact, wired in. The other one is (I can say this to Ed McCreight because he was a student at Carnegie-Mellon), the reason that Gordon Bell and I wrote that book about computer structures is so that you guys wouldn't make mistakes like that.

*Ed McCreight*          It was too late!

*Jim Horning*          I've spent the last day and a half pondering about idea transfer and why some things catch on more quickly than others. It seems like, from the perspective of those of us who were at PARC, that it took a long time for the Alto ideas to get out. Then, listening to Doug yesterday, it seems to have taken even longer for his ideas. I wonder why that is.

At least two reasons why the Alto ideas influenced Xerox and then the rest of the world somewhat more quickly, go under the label of ubiquity and uniformity. It's sort of been touched on, but not really stressed. The fact that, when I arrived at PARC in 1977, every desk on the second floor [computer research laboratories], and many of them on the third floor [administration], had an Alto on it, represented a very big change in the way the human organizational structures around the Alto evolved. I could stop anyone in the hall and ask for help, and they were glad to give it. If I wanted to communicate with someone, I knew I could do this through the mail system. If my machine failed, I could take my disk and walk down the hall and find an Alto that would also serve my purposes. So it increased my mobility. Finally, something that was very hard for me to get used to at PARC (probably there's a whole generation now that it doesn't bother) was to turn my back on a machine and let it idle. It took me at least six months to really internalize the fact that the machine was there to serve me rather than vice versa. You have to have a lot of high-performance computing around before you can internalize that.

*Gordon Bell*

One final one on the question of transfer and that is, What was the diffusion of the Altos? How many Altos were built? And how many nets were built? Because that's really the key mechanism by which technology gets diffused. Who got a look at it?

I was down at Apple one day and asked people about that, and they said, oh, yeah, indeed, Jobs and one of the other people had in fact gotten a one hour view of it, and Mac was the effect of that. So you really need to be able to trace back whether people could get views of Stars and things like that. I think it's important to get it in the paper. Those were the things. So, who was able to view the research artifacts? It's the number of Altos getting out where a lot of people can look at them and say, ''That's right.'' When you say that somebody was influenced by the Alto, you are asking whether that person had an early look at it. Or, in fact, will they admit that they looked at it? That's the key.

*Lampson*

It's interesting. Although 1500 Altos were built, and they were diffused fairly widely throughout Xerox and in a number of external organizations, I think most of the influence came from people who visited PARC, or in many cases, who came and spent time as summer students or visitors or whatever. The Bell Labs BLIT terminal was built by a guy who spent several summers at PARC as a student before he went to Bell Labs.

*Gordon Bell*

I'll disagree with that. I don't think that that particular terminal had any effect, and I'd submit that Steve Jobs visiting had a much more profound impact on it.

*Lampson*

Well, Nikolas Wirth, for example, spent a year at PARC during which time Modula 1 was revised to Modula 2; many of the ideas of Mesa are present in Modula 2.

*Alan Kay*

We gave a lot of demos, but I think it's important to realize that we had very few visitors who were multiple-hundred dollar millionaires, in their 20s, and heads of companies. So most of the people who visited were not able to simply go back and, by fiat, say this is what we want. That was the Apple case. But one of the things that happened was that the Xerox lawyers, after some fairly hilarious incidents which I don't have time to go into right now, but including a great article in *Rolling Stone Magazine* by Stuart Brand, severely curtailed publications, especially in my group. I was one of the perpetrators of this *Rolling Stone* article; we wound up, as a result, communicating largely by demo.

I think demos were sort of a way of life at PARC, particularly in my group, and we demoed a lot. I think Adele kept a record in 1975. In 1975 I think the record shows that there were somewhere in excess of 2000 people (not one at a time, but sometimes in groups of 50 and 100, sometimes in smaller groups), who had been through LRG (the Learning Research Group) to get our standard line demo. We decided that that was too much and we cut it down considerably, but many, many people saw that stuff over the years. Some people were able to go off and build something from it, and other people weren't.

I think that the most important thing that I got from Butler's and Chuck's talks today is that it's not enough to have an idea, and it's not enough to actually go out and build it. One of the things that Butler, especially, and Bob Taylor had decided was to be conservative. PARC was always talked about as a forefront of technology but, in fact, part of what was done at PARC reacted against the bubble gum kind of technology that we all used to build in the 1960s that would barely work for the single person who had designed and built it. Butler and Bob and Chuck did not want to have that happen again. So you have these two interesting streams at PARC. One was kind of a humbleness (I'm sure that no Xerox executive would ever recognize that word, as applied to us), in saying that we can't do everything, we have to hold some limits in order to be able to replicate these systems. Then this incredible arrogance on the other side saying, but we have to be able to build every piece of hardware and software in order to control our own destiny. So you have these two things: the conservative attitude, and then pulling out all the stops once the idea that you had to replicate the systems was made. I think that, to me, sums up why PARC worked.

# THE LINC WAS EARLY AND SMALL

## Wesley Clark
## Introduction by Bert Sutherland

**Bert Sutherland**

**M**y name is Bert Sutherland and I first met Wes in 1962. I had just come out of the Navy, back to grad school at MIT, and was lucky enough to program on the TX-2 that you have heard so much about. My story about it was that it took quite a while for me to realize that most computers were not shut down on Wednesday for rewiring. It was really quite a marvelous old machine.

To introduce Wes, I'd like to tell you a little bit about what he's been doing recently, because it goes very nicely with the title of his talk—''Early and Small.'' Wes is a real designer with a sense of cleanliness in the things he designs. In the last few years, Wes has been interested in Chinese input to computers. He has built and developed a very clever, efficient, and swift scheme for touch typing Chinese characters. I went to see this device for the first time a couple of years ago. I walked into his Manhattan apartment to see his computer and his input keyboard. He had the keyboard handmade and painted a fiery red with a nice gold dragon on it. It was a kind of descendent of Doug Engelbart's five-finger keyboard. You could touch it up and down with one hand a variety of ways. His computer to run this keyboard was the Sinclair Timex.

Let me introduce Wes Clark.

345

Wesley A. Clark happily left the environment of neutron beams at Hanford for the safer and sounder world of bit streams when he joined the MIT Digital Computer Laboratory in 1951 as a Whirlwind I programmer. Over the following twelve years at MIT as Lecturer in Electrical Engineering and Associate Group Leader of the Advanced Computer Development Group at Lincoln Laboratory, he was principal architect of the TX-0, TX-2, L-1, ARC-1 and LINC computers, an early investigator of neural networks with Dr. Belmont Farley, and a minor contributor to the MIT/IBM SAGE System.

With Dr. Charles Molnar, Wes led Washington University's ARPA/NIH project on macromodular systems from 1964 to 1972 as Research Professor of Computer Science and Director of the Computer Systems Laboratory. Since 1972 he has been a systems design consultant, joining Sutherland, Sproull, and Associates for work on the Chinese input problem in 1982 and subsequently forming the New York consulting firm of Clark, Rockoff and Associates in 1985.

He has been a member of the NAS/NRC Computer Science and Engineering Board and the NAS Committee on Scholarly Communication with the People's Republic of China, and was a 1977–78 Sherman Fairchild Distinguished Scholar at Caltech. He received the ACM/IEEE Eckert-Mauchly Award for Computer Architecture in 1981 and is a charter recipient of the IEEE Computer Pioneer Award. Wes holds an A.B. in Physics from the University of California, Berkeley, and a D.Sc. (Hon.) from Washington University, where he is presently Sever Institute Visiting Professor of Computer Design.

# The LINC was Early and Small

*Wesley A. Clark*
Clark, Rockoff and Associates

[*Editor's Note:* Wes Clark's edited opening remarks are provided in order to include a number of his interesting comments and historical slides.]

Thank you, Bert. Actually the Z80 in the Sinclair Timex machine was really quite a good engine; you just had to learn how to defeat the machine's operating system.

Did you know, by the way, that Bert and his brother Ivan were perhaps the first programmers of microcomputers? I'm referring to their experience with Edmund Berkeley's "Simon," the early relay system that some of you may remember. I first saw a picture of this wonderful little machine on a cover of *Scientific American* and I can tell you that, simple as it was, it influenced my life a great deal. Well, as I understand it, Bert and Ivan met at Berkeley, and after a bit of programming, re-wired the machine and put in a table look-up multiplier. How about that! This was back in 1951 or 1952.

It is, of course, a great pleasure and honor to be here. I'm also a charter member of the club of those who can't turn down Al Perlis. This is a very big club, one that includes 800 million Chinese. In 1972, Al and I traveled in China together as members of a group that had been organized by Severo Ornstein. The Chinese adored Al, as does everybody who knows him or has been treated to his great wit and charm. On one banquet occasion at the Great Hall of the People, he toasted our host, a Vice Premier of the People's Republic of China, with orange soda pop. The Vice Premier returned the toast with a chuckle.

Al told me that his main motivation in asking me to participate in the History of Personal Workstations Conference was to get on record a group photograph of a bunch of the old timers. I thought that was a really nifty idea. I certainly wanted to have my picture appearing with many good old friends, and so here I am. But it's quite a challenge to participate in a program with such giants.

This paper is a revision and expansion of the paper "The Origins of the LINC", *Proceedings of the IEEE Seventh Annual Conference of the Engineering in Medicine and Biology Society,* © IEEE 1985; additional figures and tables are taken from *Computers in Biomedical Research Vol 2,* R. W Stacy and B. D. Waxman (eds), © Academic Press 1965. Permission of the publishers is gratefully acknowledged.

Do you know about the unit of facial beauty? I learned this one from Ivan: It's the *milli-Helen,* the amount of beauty sufficient to launch one ship. After Butler's presentation, we can now appreciate that in spoken discourse the unit (considered by some to be a theoretical limit) is the *Lampson.* I don't have an exact definition, but it's the mathematical product of clarity and speed, and measures the real information transfer rate. Of course, the "Lampson" is much too big a unit, so we ordinarily use the *micro*-Lampson. Now, I can talk reasonably fast— Icansometimesputoutalotofwordsinquiteashorttime—and I can also say some things with great clarity, especially if they're other people's words, such as "It is insufficiently considered that men more often require to be reminded than informed," a famous quote of Samuel Johnson's that Bob Taylor likes to contemplate. But, unfortunately, my speed-clarity product is terrible, probably only about ten or twenty micro-Lampsons, particularly when I'm trying to launch thoughts of my own. So you'll have to bear with me.

Someone's earlier reference to rising with authority from bean bags brings to mind another Lampson story. I remember one occasion when, to his great chagrin, Butler had a bad case of laryngitis and his voice was completely gone; yet from a bean bag and speaking only in a whisper—it wasn't even a loud one—he nevertheless commanded and reproved clear across the room, all at his customary breathtaking speed and with compelling clarity and force. Some of you may recall the incident. We all seemed to tiptoe around for several days thereafter.

A few years ago I got a call from somebody representing an ACM/IEEE awards committee wondering if I would accept, if offered, the Eckert-Mauchly award for computer architecture in which the LINC would be cited along with a couple of other things. I really hadn't heard of this award, or rather, I hadn't been following it; I am only an associate member of the IEEE and, forgive me Adele and others, I dropped my membership in the ACM many years ago when the Association became a little too mathematical for me to understand. So I thought that somebody had made a mistake. I was apparently to be promoted therewith to the rank of Grand Old Man or something. The caller told me that the first award had gone to Maurice Wilkes and the second one to Robert Barton. Well, you always have to give a new award like this one to the award-winning Maurice Wilkes to season it properly; but Maurice Wilkes *and* the near-legendary Bob Barton? I said yes.

I accepted the award in a modest ceremony (Fig. 1). What I want to make clear, though, is that the engineering of the LINC is really the work of my colleague and friend of many years, Charles Molnar, whom you see in this picture taken in 1963 and about whom you will be reading a great deal more (Fig. 2). Incidentally, I didn't quite know

**FIGURE 1**
Photo by Doug Clark.

what I was going to say at the award ceremony. Since I was expected to give some kind of talk, I immediately set about writing my memoirs in the projected role of Grand Old Man and began to put various reprints and magazine clippings into very dignified boxes for my library shelves, that sort of thing. My workstation in those days consisted of

**FIGURE 2**
Charles Molnar with some of the LINC, 1963.

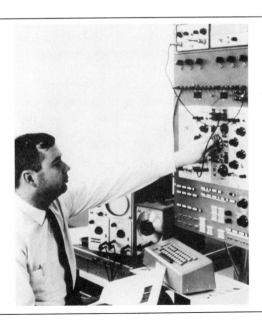

a desk and an IBM selectic typewriter—one thing IBM really does well—and a wastebasket. As it turned out, I mostly told anecdotes because I had very little else to say. My memoirs had only come to a page and a half, double-spaced. The wastebasket, of course, had done considerably better.

I have the same difficulty here. To say that the LINC was early and small almost says it all, since the LINC itself wasn't a very remarkable machine otherwise, except perhaps for its tape units. Anyway, Charlie and I have already presented a pretty good description of the LINC as a chapter of *Computers in Medicine and Biology* by Stacy and Waxman [1]. Fortunately Al had told me that what he wanted was anecdotes and old historical photos, so that's what I've put together for today's presentation.

Actually, I wouldn't be here today at all if it weren't for Howard Aiken. In 1949, while I was at Hanford out in the desert of Eastern Washington waiting for my security clearance, about the only unclassified stuff I had to read was a detailed description of Aiken's Mark II at Harvard. It fascinated me for some months and I learned a lot in studying it. I was then on leave of absence from the physics department at Berkeley, adjusting my perspective after a bruising experience in a seminar with Oppenheimer, and deciding for myself that I really wasn't all that interested in how the physical world works and how we understand it. This was about the time I had become very thoughtful about the Simon relay device, and had begun to think about more serious possibilities that were of a scale significantly smaller than that of the Mark II. A year or so later, I went to talk with Severo's now father-in-law, Laura Gould's father, the very famous numerical analyst and mathematician D. H. Lehmer, to see whether it would make sense for me to return to Berkeley to work on my ideas about small computers. But Professor Lehmer told me that the thing to do was forget all that small computer stuff, go with the big boys, that's where the action was. It was shortly after that, in fact, that I went off to MIT after answering an ad from the Digital Computer Laboratory that Jay Forrester and others had put out in a staffing drive. They were good enough to take me.

By the way, a story about Howard Aiken, whom I did not meet until many years later—here at Rickey's, as it happens, out in the lobby. I was here with Frank Heart, another old timer in the field and later Severo's boss when Severo built the IMP at BBN. Frank and I were on an assignment from Lincoln Laboratory for about a week or so, back in the days when there were still apricot trees around. And there, sitting in a corner of the lobby reading quietly, was this somewhat formidable looking gentleman. Frank said to me, ''I think that's Howard Aiken over there in the corner.'' ''Nonsense,'' I countered. ''What would an old frat like Howard Aiken be doing in a place like this?'' But Frank was adamant and insisted that we just go over and find out. So we marched over to this fellow, who looked up with amused interest as I announced, ''My friend here claims you're Howard Aiken.'' His response was energetic. ''I am!'' he said. ''I suppose you're wondering what an old frat like me is doing in a place like this!'' We then introduced ourselves and he explained that he was a regular guest at Rickey's during his frequent trips to California as a Lockheed consultant. Later, after we had all had a long, merry dinner together during which we became pretty good friends, he pointed out to me some of the many architectural innovations of the Rickey's buildings, which he greatly admired.

So to the subject at hand: The LINC was early and small; it was hard to build, given the technological and administrative climate of the early 1960s; and *it very nearly didn't happen*. That's what the following paper is about.

## Introduction

Twenty-two plus years ago, in September 1963, the last of about twelve freshly assembled LINCs was safely delivered by moving van from MIT to its new home in California. By itself, perhaps, this would not have been considered particularly noteworthy. But the event marked the successful completion of Phase I of a remarkable and unprecedented program. The twelve or so LINCs assembled during the very hot Cambridge summer of '63 had been put together by their new owners themselves. Each of these pioneers would take full responsibility for trial operation of the instrument as a workstation in his own biomedical research laboratory, and was expected to use it in the mode we have come to call, in Alan Kay's powerful paradigm, personal computing.

The participants in this innovative NIH/NASA–supported program had been selected on the basis of how suitable such a laboratory instrument would be in their ongoing or planned research activities. Each participant had agreed to assume individual responsibility for using and maintaining the machine throughout a subsequent 18-month period that defined Phase II of the program. The LINC Evaluation Program, as it was called, had been announced in *Science* and in descriptive brochures sent to academic and research institutions around the country. Candidates had been invited to submit proposals responsive to the scientific and technical objectives of the program. Computer programming or hardware experience was not required; the necessary fundamentals were to be learned in a 1-month intensive training and kit assembly program to be conducted at MIT by the LINC design team. Ultimate disposition of the assembled instruments was to be determined upon completion of Phase II.

More than seventy proposals had been received and studied by a specially created LINC Evaluation Board composed of distinguished scientists and engineers from research institutions across the country. After careful review, the Board had finally accepted just twelve. These represented the fields of psychology, physiology, genetics, pharmacology, biophysics, and neurology. The selected participants had been divided into two groups to be convened in July and August, respectively, with each principal investigator to be accompanied by one associate or colleague.

By mid-spring of 1963 all of the personal commitments had been made and much of the LINC hardware was in manufacture. But apart from one operating system/assembly program that had been developed and tested by simulation on a larger machine (the Lincoln Laboratory TX-2), the only LINC software in existence consisted of a few programs that had been written for an earlier demonstration prototype. With only two months to go, the final design of the LINC itself had not yet been completed.

How had all this come about? What was the LINC and what were its design objectives? Why did the field of biomedical research play such an important role in its development? I will try to recount something of the early history in answer to these questions. Like all such accounts of the introduction of a complex new instrument, the story is one of people, ideas, machines, and institutions and spans many years. As a principal instigator and designer of the LINC my perspective is limited to the events and circumstances that shaped only some of the scenes and acts. The full story must be left to others.

In what follows I will try to underscore and develop the title's assertion that the LINC, as personal workstations go, was early and small [1]. Early is evident; small, on the other hand, must be understood in the context of the memory capacity and the physical size of computers of the period. Since the machine's characteristics have been well documented (though not in the computer literature), I have indulged an urge to reminisce mostly about the people and events that really made the LINC experience such a rich and rewarding one. Some parts of the historical background may seem to be unnecessary embellishments, but I have included them in the hope that they will help in tracing the development of ideas and themes. The *dramatis personae* comprise extensive lists in both the computer and biomedical disciplines, and for the sake of simplicity I have kept professorial titles to a minimum and have arbitrarily ''Dr.'ed'' only those players who appear in character from the biomedical side of the stage. I hope that my friends will forgive me for this, as well as for any miscrediting of ideas and any errors or omissions of fact that may have settled into my own memory over the years.

# Background

### INTERACTING WITH WHIRLWIND AND MTC

Al Perlis and Doug Ross and I fondly remember the MIT Digital Computer Laboratory's Whirlwind computer, the machine on which I learned what little anyone knew about programming in 1952. One walked into it. What now sits comfortably on a small desktop, in those days required an entire room for the control consolery alone. Programming for its small electrostatic memory (1024 16-bit words on a good day) was a primitive affair carried out with the aid of heavily ruled coding forms on which to write out absolute-address instructions and octal numbers. Confronted by the prospect of having to program in such a manner, Al immediately designed a new, improved form that consisted of a large sheet of blank paper. But its early users did indeed walk into the control room and, for their assigned block of time, typically fifteen minutes or so depending on the time of day, the entire machine was theirs. In this regard the use of Whirlwind as a workstation of sorts was no different from that of many other early computers, especially in the universities. What makes the Whirlwind computer important in the history of the personal workstation is the fact that it was the first really high-speed machine with powerful interactive display capabilities [2].

But it was MTC that really drove the point home. MTC, the Memory Test Computer was designed and built by Harlan Andersen and Ken Olsen to provide a working computer system in which to try out the first ferrite core memory, a vacuum-tube driven 1K 16-bit unit engineered by Bill Papian, then a graduate student under Jay Forrester [3]. Blocks of time measured in hours were available and the entire machine, quite similar in architecture to Whirlwind, now occupied only a single large room. Bristling with toggle-switches, pushbuttons, and indicator lights, and provided with audio output as well as versatile CRT displays, it made interactive use a quite lively and memorable experience.

I suppose the idea of using even a very large computer such as the 1953 MTC just as one would use any laboratory tool was introduced to me by Belmont Farley, my teacher and collaborator in early computer simulation studies of neuron-like networks [4]. Belmont, a physicist by training and a man of considerable vision and strongly held convictions, joined the Digital Computer Laboratory shortly after my own move to MIT to learn computerology. I had almost become a physicist myself at one time, in what I now consider a close call; but that's another story.

Belmont and I spent enormous numbers of hours interacting with

MTC and with one another (he talked, I listened) as we tried out ideas, modified parameters, and studied displays of the simulated behavior of our strange little networks, grateful for such extensive access to such a powerful if not yet completely reliable machine. (A self-restarting test program was left running on MTC whenever the machine was otherwise unoccupied. In those pre-regulation days you could tune a radio to the frequencies being broadcast by MTC's long open-wire bus and hear the test program running, or trying to run, from several city blocks away. Sometimes when approaching by automobile for an extra-long simulation run in the dead of night the signal was clear enough for a decision to turn back home if things weren't going well.)

It was in these sessions that I began to learn from Belmont many of the basic attitudes toward computers that I hold firmly to this day: Computers are tools; convenience of use is the most important single design factor. Big computers are for big jobs; small computers, for small jobs. Separate personal files are safer than files held in a common shared space. Digital computers should handle analog signals as well. And so on. . . .

In what would become a very important liaison, Belmont and I began to attend the seminars of the Communications Biophysics Laboratory (CBL) under Prof. Walter Rosenblith, later Provost of MIT and presently Foreign Secretary of the National Academy of Sciences. Walter's group was concerned with the problem of quantifying neuroelectric phenomena. It was quite interdisciplinary in its approach and attracted students, post-doctoral fellows, and visiting scientists from many parts of the world. CBL had been developing various signal processing techniques. Much of CBL's work involved auto- and cross-correlation analyses based on data recorded on FM tape and then processed by analog devices. Work was just beginning on the analysis of the electrical signals from single neurons.

Our interaction with CBL started slowly. The Digital Computer Laboratory was absorbed into the recently established Lincoln Laboratory to become a component of Lincoln's massive program in air defense. Our base of operations shifted fifteen miles west to Lexington and we were assigned to a new group charged with advanced computer development, together with Ken Olsen, Bill Papian, Dick Best, Jim Forgie, John Francovich, Ben Gurley, and many other members of the former Digital Computer Laboratory staff. Belmont and I somehow managed to keep up our pilot studies in network simulation with much travel back and forth to CBL and to the MTC in Cambridge.

Bill Papian and others, bolstered by the immediate success of the 1K MTC memory (shortly thereafter replaced by a 4K unit), now began to build the largest core-memory array thought feasible, a 64K 36-bit unit. This array would be thirty-six times the storage capacity of the 4K MTC array and would certainly constitute a big step in computer memory technology. In my new capacity as leader of a small subgroup in logic design, I made sure that its potential for further simulation and modeling work was kept in mind.

## THE LINCOLN TX-0 COMPUTER

It was a time of transistors. Ken Olsen, in charge of the subgroup in advanced engineering development, joined me in proposing the construction of a very ambitious machine of considerable size, the TX-1, as a suitable vehicle for testing the large memory array [5]. When this idea was turned down by laboratory management (wisely enough), Ken and others began to develop new transistor circuits in earnest. I began the logic design of a new machine, the TX-2, which would have about the same architecture as that of the rejected machine but would take advantage of the new circuits. It is interesting to note that one of the main architectural features of the TX-1/TX-2 design—multiple program counters used in what I badly termed multi-sequence programming [6,7]—was later employed to great advantage by Chuck Thacker in the design of the Alto workstation [8].

I proposed that we first build a much smaller, primitively simple computer that I had designed and named the TX-0 [3,9]. (We had already used up ''1''; later Ken and I would say that we didn't build the TX-1 because we didn't like its color scheme). The 18-bit TX-0 would use only half of the large memory array and would be quite simple in logical structure, maximally RISCy, one might say today. When the second half of the array was completed the full array would then be installed in the TX-2, on which design and construction would have been proceeding. The TX-0 would then be retrofitted with a new memory unit of some kind and serve as a frontend processor to the TX-2, or perhaps simply be dismantled. In the meantime it would have served in early evaluation of the new memory and transistor circuits and would have been more than adequate to the task of network simulation as well as to other tasks more directly relevant to the Lincoln effort. Not a bad plan for an R&D program. It was adopted. The TX-0 was built and a three-year effort to design and build the TX-2 was begun [10]. In addition to powerful CRT display units designed by Ben Gurley, the consoles of both machines would ultimately bristle in the best MIT tradition.

The simulation work Belmont and I were carrying out had long had the interest and support of Bill Papian. Appointed leader of the Advanced Development Group, Bill actively encouraged further strengthening of the interaction with the CBL group. Students and scientists from Rosenblith's laboratory began to try their hand at digital processing of neuroelectric data on the TX-0 and later on the TX-2. One of these students was Charles Molnar (Figs. 3 and 4), who was to be-

**FIGURE 3**
**1963: The author and Mr. Charles E. Molnar with a LINC.** The photograph was taken in Cambridge following the first phase of LINC Evaluation Program activities in which groups of scientists were given special training at a one-month summer course at MIT.

come a primary catalytic agent in promoting sound relationships within and between the two groups. Charlie, I soon learned, was extraordinarily competent and talented both as an electrical engineer and as a student of biophysics. He shared the conviction that computer tools would play an important part in what was beginning to be called "the biomedical sciences" and proceeded to master the operational and technical details of both the TX-0 and the unfinished TX-2. Charlie

**FIGURE 4**
**1981: The author and Dr. Charles E. Molnar with a LINC in a recreation of the earlier picture following a Digital Museum Lecture (see wall poster).** Eighteen years grayed us both. Several of the original LINCs, also graying, were still in use in various parts of the world. (Photo courtesy of Digital Equipment Corporation.)

and I began to develop a basis of collaboration that would lead to the LINC and to many other developments over the years.

As the second half of the large memory array neared completion it became time to decide what to do with the TX-0. Bill Papian suggested replacing its memory with the group's new transistor-driven 4K memory unit (about the same capacity as that of the earlier vacuum-tube-driven MTC unit) and then moving the entire machine to the MIT campus. This would give a wider group of students and faculty an opportunity to experience the kind of hands-on interactive computer use that characterized our work at Lincoln Laboratory in the tradition we were carrying forward from Whirlwind and MTC.

By that time both of the Cambridge machines, Whirlwind and MTC, had been completely committed to the air defense effort and were no longer available for general use. The only surviving computing system paradigm seen by MIT students and faculty was that of a very large International Business Machine in a tightly sealed Computation Center: The computer not as *tool*, but as *demigod*. Although we were not happy about giving up the TX-0, it was clear that making this small part of Lincoln's advanced technology available to a larger MIT community would be an important corrective step. The machine was then being used in some very exciting work in interactive programming by Jack Gilmore (unfortunately never published) that anticipated much of what we do today; but Bill's argument that the group's attention would be shifting to the TX-2 prevailed. Arrangements were made to replace the memory, enrich the instruction repertoire, and move the modified TX-0 to the campus in Cambridge.

But where exactly should it go? The logical place, it seemed to me, was Walter Rosenblith's laboratory. After all, CBL was then using the TX-0 computer more actively than any other group of visitors from the campus, and expanded use by George Gerstein, Charlie, and other members of CBL was expected. To my surprise Walter declined to accept the responsibility. I therewith gained an important insight about what would work in a small laboratory setting and what would not. It seems in retrospect that the TX-0, small as it was for its time and demonstrably useful in CBL research, was still too much "the computer" and not sufficiently "an instrument." Its care and feeding and the constant need for justification might well have compromised CBL's research objectives. Walter's technical judgement, as usual, was correct.

The modified TX-0 eventually found a home under the larger umbrella of the Electrical Engineering Department, where it was used heavily by CBL and other groups and helped to train several generations of students in the interactive use of computers on-line. Somewhat later it was joined and largely upstaged by a PDP-1 computer (in some sense a production version of the modified TX-0) that had been donated to MIT by the Digital Equipment Corporation and would later be used in some of the earliest experiments in time-sharing [3].

Time-sharing had by then captured the imagination of much of the MIT computer science community (not yet a science, of course; it would not be so until a few years later, that Al Newell, Al Perlis, and Herb Simon said, "Let there be Computer Science," and there was). This seemed to me a bad idea and still does, the captive imagination aspect no less than the underlying premise itself. Improved access, yes; thrashing competition and waste, no. This is not to deny that time-sharing resulted in a huge and productive impetus to computer science at a critical time. Certainly it has given much gainful employment to computer scientists and manufacturers and salesmen over the past 20 years or so. But it seems to me that we could have done better than to divert so much of our attention and resources to trying to make good the promise of a patently unattainable "sensible simultaneity" for all. (I may not always be right, but at least I am consistent. When working out the multi-sequence programming idea some years earlier, I had considered and rejected the notion of competitive time-sharing by independent human users as grossly inefficient; much later at the dawn of the time-sharing era, I had no qualms about turning down a suggestion of Ed Fredkin's to set up such a system for the multi-sequence TX-2, much to his disappointment and, as I recall, disgust; in meetings of the MIT Long Range Study Committee in 1961 I objected, to no effect, that campus-wide time-sharing, so enthusiastically being rationalized as a panacea, would not be able to deal with real-time work such as CBL's and moreover would inhibit the development of any interactive computing that involved complex displays. The MIT Study Committee Chairman and I both declined to sign an otherwise unanimous final report. He thought it didn't promise nearly enough. Walter urged me to write a minority report, but I knew a steam roller when I saw one and went on to other matters.)

### THE ARC AND THE L-1

Not long after the decision to move TX-0 was made, Charlie and I met with Moise Goldstein and Robert Brown of CBL. The subject of discussion was the possibility of building a digital device to extract stimulus-evoked neuroelectric potentials from a background of unrelated electrical activity by means of a summation technique then being tried at CBL on analog equipment. Aha! A digital instrument for Walter! I immediately agreed to take on the design task.

The logic design of the instrument fell into place readily enough. I simply used many of the transistor-logic plug-in modules already designed by Ken Olsen and Dick Best for the TX-2, and my colleague Henry Zieman neatly solved the problem of memory by working out the details of a very small 256-word core array. An 18-bit structure seemed about right for the job and nicely matched that of the TX-0, with which the instrument might later be in communication. I designed two simple operating modes to provide response averaging and amplitude histogram compilation, both modes to be wired into the control circuits. With electronics, control switches, lights, CRT, plotter, and paper-tape punch, the whole thing—even without an analog-to-digital converter—required a cabinet about the size of two refrigerators turned on their sides. Today we would think it a machine of rare ugliness (as an unkind journalist once said of my automobile). We named it the ARC, an acronym for Average Response Computer [11].

The ARC was completed in early 1958. Though not all that much smaller than the TX-0, at least it was portable and rolled through doorways. I rode it in triumph into the Communications Biophysics Laboratory and it was almost immediately put into service. After about a year of operating experience the CBL staff decided that a third mode for compilation of time histograms of single neuron activity would be useful, and this was duly wired into the ARC control. Over the next several years the ARC served in a wide variety of studies, teaching researchers many new aspects of the neuroelectric behavior of the brain. It also confirmed my belief that there were indeed useful things that small digital computers could do in the laboratory.

But wouldn't it have been better to *program* these operating modes rather than wire them into the control circuits? I had since taken just that approach in designing an extremely simple stored-program computer of very limited capability, the 256 10-bit word L-1, for use in a special project [12]. There was no doubt in my mind that the far greater flexibility of the stored-program approach was of enormous value, even in computers small enough to be considered "instruments" for laboratory use.

At the first symposium of the Brain Research Institute held at UCLA in 1960, Belmont and I joined with Walter and several members of CBL and Dr. M. A. B. Brazier (of both CBL and the BRI) in discussing some of the viewpoints and accomplishments of the MIT work. In my presentation I contrasted the stored-program and wired-logic approaches [13]:

> The TX-0 is a relatively small but powerful stored-program computer. A rough comparison of the ARC and the TX-0 computers is illuminating. Both machines operate on 18-bit binary numbers, control analog-to-digital converters, have cathode ray tube displays, can be controlled by the experimenter, and hold about the same number of circuits derived from the same body of electronic technology. The TX-0, however, has about 8000 registers of digital storage and is organized as a general-purpose device.
>
> It is quite simple to program the TX-0 to act very much like the ARC;

in fact this has been done, requiring an investment of effort measured only in hours. The TX-0 can in addition generate quite varied displays of the data and of results of analysis, and can be programmed to carry out exceedingly lengthy and complex operations if desired. This flexibility of behavior is characteristic of the stored-program computer and is obviously of great value.

It is extremely important, of course, to provide for procedural flexibility and easy access to machines of this type in order to realize their full potential. Ideally the researcher would have the general-purpose computer in his laboratory for use ''on-line'', enabling him to observe and act on the basis of the calculated results while the experiment is in progress.

Stored-program computers like the TX-0 are beginning to appear in commercial form and there is reason to hope that these machines, or perhaps other general-purpose machines with a capability somewhere between that of the ARC and the TX-0, will find their way into the laboratory.

Well, there it was. Clearly, the thing to do was to go off and design a machine that would fill the niche I had just defined.

## Designing the LINC

It has been both pleasurable and dismaying to look over my design notebooks after a lapse of nearly 25 years. I can easily relive the exhilaration and sense of discovery in the pages detailing those rare ideas that ''worked'' and survived and were good. But there are other pages, too, some of them recording in distressing detail my false starts, muddled thinking, and irredeemably bad ideas. The design process is like that, of course; yet one always hopes that the overall record will reveal a higher order of thought and development. It is embarrassing to report, therefore, that the LINC design notebooks do not, on balance, document the workings of an orderly mind.

Following the October symposium at UCLA I increasingly began to sketch and doodle on various handy surfaces. It seemed to me that I now had most of the keys to the design process: a firm belief in the soundness of the goals and a good sense of the functional requirements; the general technology to be used; and the bounds of acceptable size, complexity, and cost. What I was trying to find was some gimmick, some architectural idea to start the process off in any promising direction. Taking the principal constraint to be the factor of acceptable cost, I arbitrarily set a target of $25,000. This figure, relatively small for computers as we then knew them, seemed about right. It was about the size of one staff salary, for example, or about what a department head could authorize for equipment without the approval of higher management, and so on. Remarkably enough it was little more than twice the cost of the a-to-d converter used with the ARC. Was there some architectural scheme that might yield a useful laboratory-size computer subject to this cost constraint, something that would propel me out of the back-of-an-envelope phase and into the discipline of the engineering notebook?

## FIRST ATTEMPTS

Volume I of my three LINC notebooks carries the dates May 24 to July 4, 1961—roughly Mother's Day to the Fourth of July. I had found a starting gimmick in the form of a serial-parallel scheme that appeared to reduce cost without seriously compromising speed (see Fig. 5). I would take advantage of a new family of plug-in-circuit modules then being produced by the Digital Equipment Corporation. Ken Olsen and Harlan Andersen had left Lincoln Laboratory to found DEC in 1957

**FIGURE 5**
**The 27 May (1961) page from the LINC design notebooks.** Early design was based on a serial-parallel logic using 4-bit shift register circuit modules made by DEC. Design progress was variably good.

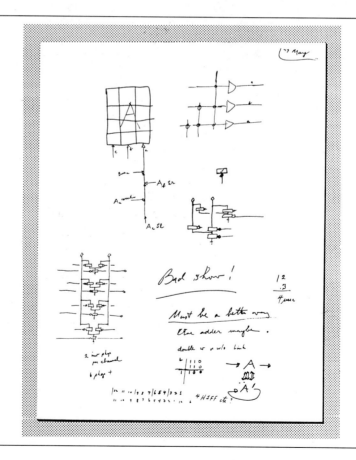

and were followed shortly thereafter by Dick Best, Ben Gurley (who later engineered the PDP-1), and others from the Lincoln group [3]. The circuit modules DEC was now manufacturing, forerunners of the integrated circuit chips that were not to appear for several more years, seemed quite suitable.

I knew that the machine would need two small tape units about the size of the "snapshot" unit I had proposed earlier for use with the TX-2 as a personal file input-output device and that my colleague Tom Stockebrand had tried to make. These units would have pocketably small reels for programs and data and would use block addressable magnetic tape like that of the TX-2's huge and frightening device for on-line files [14]. (The TX-2 tape unit used 14 inch reels of 3/4 inch tape, a very large inertial load. Its design was based on an observation of mine that the TX-2's multi-sequence capability made it possible to eliminate the usual requirement for finely controlled tape speeds, and I had further proposed that the positions of all bit-cells on the tape be fixed by prerecording timing and blockmark tracks. In programming use, the resulting unit's tape speed varied markedly with wrap diameters, as did inertias and vibrational resonances. At top speed in block searching mode the tape's linear velocity reached 60 miles per hour! The whole room shook!)

Most of the work over these first two months (see Fig. 6) went into thinking through the details of the serial-parallel architecture and an appropriate set of machine instructions. I knew that I had to build in a-to-d conversion channels and devote some of them to console potentiometers for convenient knob control of continuous variables (a good idea contributed by Belmont). I knew that CRT display would have to be inexpensive and would therefore use the same point-display technology that appeared in all of the MIT machines. A more difficult task, however, would be thinking through the control for the tape units and developing the right set of block transfer modes for their use. The 1K or 2K 12-bit words of memory that seemed feasible under the cost constraint would not permit lengthy program routines for tape operation. These routines would therefore have to be wired into the central control circuits (of course there were no ROM chips in those early days). Block addressability of the tapes would help in running useful programs in the very small memory, the sort of thing we now do with disk systems.

I worked at home. Early in the design work I returned to the laboratory briefly for an informal exposure of ideas to Charlie and Belmont and other members of the group, among whom were Severo Ornstein and a newcomer, Mary Allen Wilkes. There was lively interest in what I presented as a "Linc." (I had thought that a generic name for this kind of computer would be useful and had decided on one that sug-

**FIGURE 6**
**The 13 June (1961) page from the LINC design notebooks.** Timing diagrams still appeared to support the serial-parallel scheme and new ideas were still emerging.

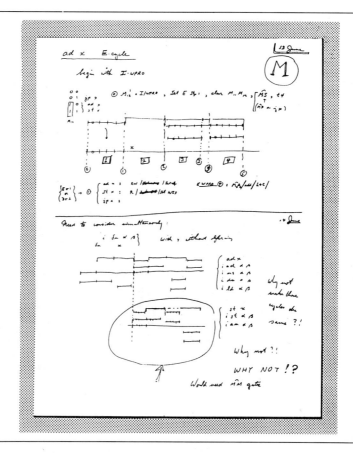

gested the instrument's Lincoln Laboratory origins; Linc would be promoted to LINC by later events.) Following the meeting, Severo and Mary Allen began to try programming with the proposed instruction set and I returned to the task of filling in design details. Charlie began to communicate his enthusiasm for the Linc scheme to CBL. Walter himself was later reported to be envisioning a relationship between a scientist and a computer similar to that between a scientist and a microscope. All was going well.

Alas, the serial-parallel approach turned out to be a false start. One month after its first exposure I had put enough of the design in place to establish the cost of the modules required by the central logic alone. Even without input-output devices or the core memory I had already used up my $25,000. Gad. The final entry in Volume I is the single line: "Crisis in River City!"

## THE PROTOTYPE LINC

For the next several months I concentrated on simplifying the design and detailing the tape unit and its control, the most complex part of the machine and the largest single unknown. Much of my earlier work translated readily enough into a more straightforward 12-bit parallel form. Somewhat to my surprise this yielded a substantially lower cost. So much for gimmicks. Notebooks II and III record a great deal of work over the remainder of the year in refining the instruction set and developing simple operating modes for the tape units (see Fig. 7). Sketches for the tape transport mechanism and console appear here and there.

The need to build up a project effort at Lincoln began to demand more and more of my time as other members of the group joined in. Tom Stockebrand and I built a working model of the new tape unit, with Charlie contributing helpful insights from his experience with its fearsome progenitor, the giant tape unit of the TX-2. Severo designed and built a special subsystem to pre-mark tapes with the required fixed backbone of block addresses, timing signals, and control code patterns. Hershel Loomis and I assembled a tape unit exerciser-tester, using DEC building block logic modules, and established that the Linc tape equipment would indeed function as I had hoped. We were on the right track.

By early September the instruction timing diagrams had been completed in enough detail to enable Mary Allen to write a Linc system simulation program for the TX-2 and begin to develop a compact machine-code assembler for the proposed machine. Bill Simon, another newcomer and a remarkably creative scientist and engineer, designed a dual-scope alternative to the single-scope unit we eventually settled on, and began to write a number of test and demonstration programs. Norm Kinch, my right arm in matters of making things happen, began to produce large working drawings of system logic based on my notebook sketches and placed orders for parts as they emerged from the design. Severo and others helped with details of package layout and wiring lists. Charlie reviewed the design of the proposed 1K 12-bit memory system and watched over general engineering specifications. The final entry in Volume III was dated Christmas, 1961. Construction of the prototype Linc was already underway.

**FIGURE 7**
**An abbreviated history of the LINC tape unit design.** *Upper left:* 28 June sketches of parts of the tape turn-around control, including a doodle of my foreboding of difficulties yet to come. *Upper right:* 6 August sketches of a possible arrangement of parts. *Lower left:* 15 August list of control logic expressions. *Lower right:* 27 October report of my realization that observed misbehavior of the prototype tape unit was caused by my design mistake. The unit worked well shortly thereafter. (From the 1961 LINC design notebooks.)

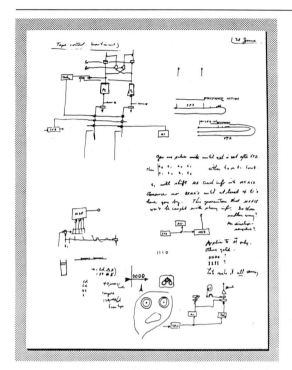

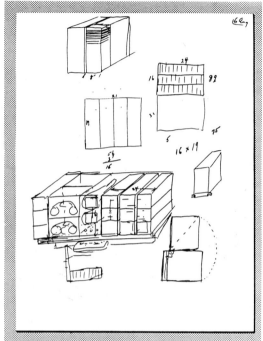

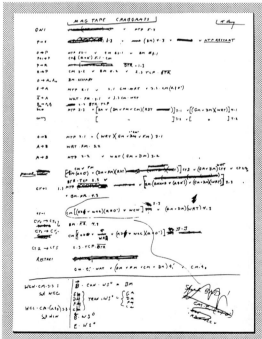

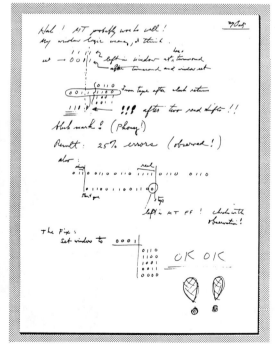

We hoped to complete the Linc prototype in time to take it to Washington for a demonstration in April at the forthcoming National Academy of Sciences Conference on Engineering and the Life Sciences. This had been urged by Walter and by Bill Papian as an excellent way to introduce the machine to a broad scientific and technical audience. Under this time schedule pressure, but with tireless support from an enthusiastic technical staff, the Linc began to take shape. Hand-wiring of the electronics cabinet took its toll in anxiety and time over the ensuing weeks, as did the slow accumulation of special equipment and parts. But Norm kept the construction pretty much on schedule and the machine was completed in late February. It was working well enough for a Laboratory-wide demonstration at the end of March 1962 (Fig. 8). The entire Linc group was justifiably proud of its accomplishment.

The demonstration prototype consisted of a set of four box-enclosed console modules, each connected by 20-ft long cables to a common electronics cabinet now the size of only *one* refrigerator; this general configuration would be used in all subsequent ''academic'' versions. One module, its box mostly empty, held a control panel that provided switches and register indicator lights (remember those?) together with speed and audio control knobs and so forth. A second module held a 5 inch CRT display adapted from a laboratory oscilloscope. A third module held the dual tape transport mechanics, while the fourth held a set of potentiometer knobs and jacks for analog input together with connectors for future input-output equipment. As an option for crowded laboratories, all modules could be removed from their boxes and mounted in standard equipment racks if desired. (Some-

**FIGURE 8**
**The Linc system demonstrated at the Lincoln Laboratory auditorium in March 1962.** Four console modules are connected by 20-foot cables to a cabinet holding the required digital electronics. The demonstration consisted of running a few simple programs toggled in by hand in advance.

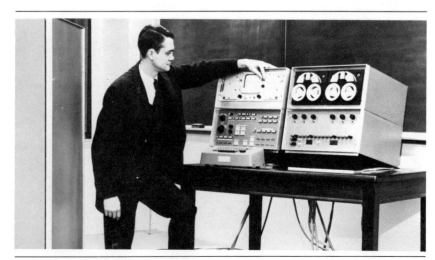

what embarrassed by the size of the electronics cabinet, we adopted the point of view that it was only the console modules, taken together, that constituted the instrument itself; the rest was merely the electronics that made it all go, and would be tucked out of sight in any convenient closet. We expected the electronics cabinet to disappear with advances in electronic packaging. It did, of course; but then so, eventually, did consoles.)

## THE NATIONAL ACADEMY OF SCIENCES DEMONSTRATION

Charlie, Norm, Bill Simon, and I took the Linc to Washington as planned and the National Academy demonstration was well if somewhat uncomprehendingly received [15]. Bill had arranged for closed circuit TV equipment and had set up several monitors about the meeting room. Charlie and I had spent the night before—*all* night—trying to fix some unexpected problem in the arithmetic element, crawling around the floor of our suite at the conference hotel with test equipment and soldering irons, discovering only by the dawn's early light that just outside our room there was a huge broadcast antenna tower that had been flooding everything with electromagnetic noise.

Norm commandeered one or two people from the hotel staff and moved the Linc to the meeting room for the presentation while Charlie and I dressed, Charlie in his Air Force uniform since at that time he was completing his military service with the Air Force Cambridge Research Laboratories and had to appear in official garb. I stepped to the podium not knowing whether the machine was going to work or not, Charlie still frantically toggling in program parameters and trying out the demos. But at the last possible moment he slipped me a scrap of paper that said, "The following programs have my confidence. . . . " The Linc performed perfectly. Whew! The only question asked, Charlie recalls, came from an older gentleman who seemed to be quite interested in the durability of the wiring insulation. He was from the Smithsonian.

## NIH INTEREST

After the Academy meeting Norm moved the Linc to one of the laboratories of Dr. Robert Livingston, Scientific Director of both the Institute of Neurological Diseases and Blindness and the Institute of Mental Health. There Charlie connected the analog-to-digital input channels to a multiple electrode array implanted in the brain of one of the lab's mascots, a cat whose name, I believe, was Jasper (Fig. 9). In short order he wrote a small program that displayed on the CRT the average neuroelectric responses of the behaving animal. The Linc was successfully performing its first scientific task.

**FIGURE 9**
**Jasper, one of several animals used in experimental work at a National Institutes of Health laboratory.** The other end of the cable leading from the cat's head was connected to the Linc in a 1962 trial, the Linc's first scientific assignment.

The writer Sam Rosenfeld, in a background paper prepared for a seminar held at NIH in celebration of the twentieth anniversary of the LINC, quotes Dr. Livingston's recollection of the event [16]:

> It was such a triumph that we danced a jig right there around the equipment. No human being had ever been able to see what we had just witnessed. It was as if we had an opportunity to ski down a virgin snow field of a previously undiscovered mountain.

(Jasper merely purred and looked pleased.)

It must be reported, however, that we did not have much success the next day when the Linc was moved to the laboratory of Dr. Mones Berman to see what it could do to isolate a very fast fluorescence transient produced in a particular biochemical reaction. Severo and Mary Allen answered an emergency call and came to Washington to help, but to no avail. Bill Simon would later write a superb program for the general problem of exponential decomposition, but the limits of Linc speed had been reached.

Nonetheless, the interest of NIH had clearly been engaged. The National Academy of Sciences had already made the suggestion to Dr. James Shannon, Director of NIH, that he set up a committee to monitor and encourage the development of computer technology relevant to biomedical research. In response, Dr. Shannon had established the Advisory Committee on Computers in Research. This committee, among whose members were both Dr. Brazier and Bill Papian, had been following the MIT activities closely. The Linc demonstrations at NIH had in fact been arranged by the committee's executive secretary,

Dr. Bruce Waxman, who would shortly take further initiatives leading to the funding of an evaluation program.

### Linc BECOMES LINC

The group at Lincoln had been joined by Dr. Thomas Sandel, a neuro-physiological psychologist who had been conducting auditory research at CBL. Tom had organized and hosted an NSF-sponsored workshop the previous summer in which some of the MIT computing techniques were shown to an invited group of biomedical researchers. He now proposed to use the Linc in a repeat of the workshop to be held in the summer of 1962. Plans were approved and a well-attended workshop was held, during which several new Linc programs were written and new applications were investigated. (An amusing side benefit was that in programming one of the data recording tasks, we discovered that we had neglected to wire in a pathway for the signal specifying the initial direction of tape motion. Since the tape units were designed to search for designated blocks in either direction [now at a sedate though still uncontrolled speed of about 3 miles per hour], the occasional misbehavior had been self-correcting and had largely gone unnoticed.)

We began to think in terms of expanding the work. Bill Papian had been given to believe that under the right circumstances funds for support of a larger program in biomedical computing would be forthcoming from NIH. Charlie and Bill Simon and I were already beginning to modify and improve the design of the Linc so that a number of soundly engineered replicas could be made, and Tom Sandel was proposing to set up a small lab in space adjacent to the TX-2 for relevant biologically oriented work. But it was not to be. Lincoln Laboratory management, sensing that there would be serious organizational difficulties in administering such a program within its established framework, firmly rejected both the expansion and "wet" lab proposals. Instead, we were invited to find a more suitable home for any further work. In reporting to a stunned Linc design team the management's decision and my own decision to leave, I announced that "Linc" had just become "LINC," an acronym for Laboratory INstrument Computer.

The principals subsequently spent the last several disheartening months of 1962 trying without success to find a "suitable home" for the continuation and extension of the work to which they were now deeply committed.

## The LINC Evaluation Program

Toward the end of 1962, Walter Rosenblith put forth an imaginative proposal: MIT would act as host institution in a multi-institutional, multi-disciplinary endeavor to be called the Center for Computer Technology and Research in the Biomedical Sciences; faculty and staff from several New England universities would join in providing the scientific and technical substance of a long-range program; a Center Development Office would immediately be set up to work out details, secure multi-institutional blessing, and formalize a proposal to NIH; and finally, to avoid loss of momentum the LINC team would immediately be taken in under the CDO wing to complete the redesign effort and mount a program for the dissemination of LINC technology.

This proposal was widely accepted almost at once. Funds for the establishment of the CDO, with Walter as Director and Bill Papian as Associate Director, magically appeared. Arrangements were made with Lincoln for the transfer of staff and equipment, and the entire biomedical research computer effort at Lincoln Laboratory, together with several members of CBL, moved to new quarters next to the campus in Cambridge in January 1963.

**REDESIGN OF THE LINC**

The next several months were ones of intense activity as we worked hard to complete the redesign in time for what was now formally known as the LINC Evaluation Program. Construction of 16 LINCs was authorized under the formal program. Twelve of these machines were to be assigned to biomedical research scientists selected by a nationally constituted LINC Evaluation Board for trial use in their own laboratories following a special Phase I training program at MIT. Four machines were to remain with the design team for coordination of Phase II evaluation activities and further refinement of the instrument itself. Given the new CDO framework, Dr. Waxman of the NIH Committee, in a dazzling display of civil service at its best, had been able to earmark about half of the needed funds from NIH and had persuaded Dr. Orr Reynolds of NASA to put up the remainder from NASA's recently established Bioscience Program. In parallel with this activity, NIH assembled the necessary committees to review the much larger proposal for the Center itself, and with amazing smoothness and speed authorized a huge MIT research grant of an unprecedented scale sufficient to warrant announcement on the front page of the *New York Times*.

The idea of providing replicas of the LINC to individual researchers seemed quite natural. Tom Sandel had outlined just such a plan following the summer workshop the previous year and the idea had taken hold immediately. Charlie had then suggested, only partly in jest, that the computers be put together by the workshop participants themselves, and I had promptly taken the idea quite seriously as an excellent way to teach the inner workings of the LINC. After all, it would be up to the participants to keep their machines running, wouldn't it? What better way to ease these good people into the discipline of digital systems? We would gather the parts and subassemblies together in the form of a kit and provide assembly instructions and any necessary documentation. This would not only keep the costs down but would also encourage later participation by other interested individuals.

Again the projected time schedule was extremely tight, especially for a development group in an academic setting. But morale was very high, as it always is under such circumstances, and every member of the now somewhat expanded design team proceeded to put in a magnificent performance. Charlie designed new circuits for the memory (now modularized in two 1K units, with only one to be included initially) and completely reworked the magnetic tape unit read-write amplifiers and motor control circuits. Bill Simon (Fig. 10) redesigned the a-to-d circuitry and worked out a new single-scope system for the display module. Severo expertly refined the tape control logic and incorporated the tape pre-marking subsystem. Mary Allen traveled back and forth to the TX-2 at Lincoln Laboratory to update the LINC simulator and complete the new LINC Assembly Program, LAP3. Don Malpass joined us temporarily from Lincoln and did an outstanding job of designing the power supply and the interconnection system, the high-speed computer's Achilles' heel if not very skillfully handled. Norm Kinch prepared and endlessly updated the necessary drawings and supervised our support staff as well as the beginning manufacture of subassemblies by local vendors. I concentrated on the surprisingly dif-

**FIGURE 10**
**William Simon with an interim version of the LINC.** The dual-display module provided both long- and short-persistence phosphor CRTs. Six potentiometer knobs supplied input parameters.

ficult job of working out the details of console control and the proper arrangement of indicators and switches, and generally tried to keep the overall program on target.

One month to go. Parts and subassemblies were continuing to arrive and the final LINC prototype neared completion (see Figs. 11 and 12). Mary Allen finished off the layout of the central control logic.

**FIGURE 11**
**Technicians assembling wired frames for the LINC electronics cabinet.** About twenty of these cabinets were required for the summer program.

**FIGURE 12**
**Charlie debugging a prototype of the final LINC system.** Modifications to the frame wiring were few but had to be made to all frames being assembled by a local vendor.

Mishell Stucki, a man without peer in attention to detail, organized the wiring lists in a form suitable for the electronics frame checkout so critical to the success of the kit concept. Mort Ruderman of DEC took personal responsibility for assuring that sets of DEC modules, about 90 percent of the required electronics, would arrive on time. Howard Lewis and Dan Calileo and others stepped up the pace of special parts assembly under Norm and Charlie's supervision (Fig. 13). Don O'Brien saw to it that the extensive and growing documentation was kept in good shape and had the assistance of Henry Littleboy of Massachusetts General Hospital. Severo was everywhere. One could not have hoped for a more dedicated and competent team.

One week to go. One or two frames had been completely wired but there was still difficulty in obtaining the necessary test equipment

**FIGURE 13**
*(Upper)* Norm Kinch *(left)* and Dan Calileo repairing a prototype power supply; *(lower)* Howard Lewis and Dan making "final" wiring changes to the electronics frames. Several additional modifications were later found to be necessary and were added, using white wires to avoid confusion with color-coded frame wiring already documented. (Phase I photographs taken by Bill Simon.)

to verify wiring accuracy. A last minute circuit problem that Charlie had discovered was overwhelmed with the help of Maynard Engebretson and Prof. Jerome R. Cox (a member of the Evaluation Board), who made a special trip from Washington University in St. Louis (Fig. 14). Tom Sandel, Chairman of the LINC Evaluation Board, monitored progress with increasing anxiety. Charlie and I maintained a facade of manifest confidence that masked serious concern.

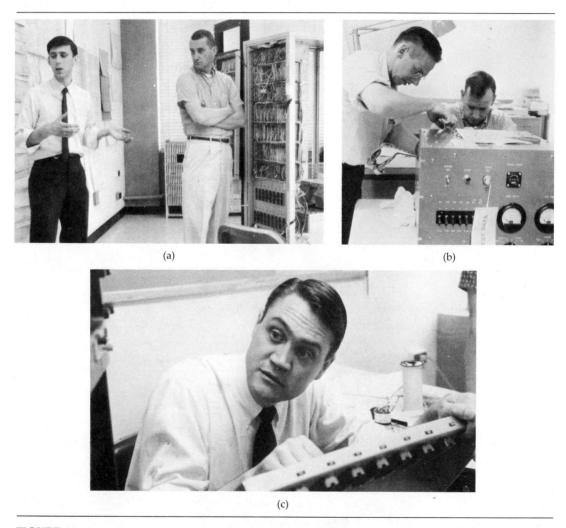

(a)

(b)

(c)

**FIGURE 14**
(a) Severo Ornstein *(left)* and Prof. Jerome R. Cox of Washington University review a last-minute problem; (b) Bob Brown *(left)* and Tom Sandel examine an incoming power-supply; (c) I check the wiring of a control panel module.

### PHASE I: THE LINC SUMMER OF '63

On July 1 the first group of visitors arrived, some of them with golf clubs they would never use. We immediately put them into a crash course on the theory and use of computers, a holding action managed by Mary Allen and Irving Thomae and Severo for the two more weeks it would be until the kits were ready (Figs. 15 and 16).

While classes were proceeding, the rest of us worked over the electronics frames and completed the job of checking out the wiring, using

**FIGURE 15**

*(Top to bottom)* Severo explains LINC logic to the first group of visiting scientists; Irving Thomae reviews timing diagrams; Mary Allen Wilkes shows LINC programming.

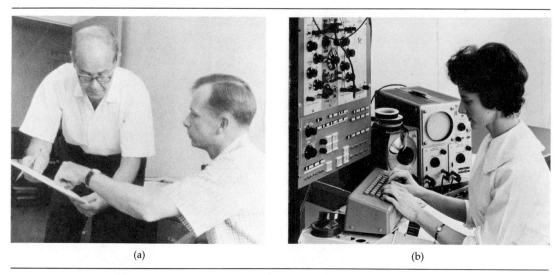

(a)                                    (b)

**FIGURE 16**
(a) Tom Sandel *(right)* in discussion with Dr. Gerhardt Werner of Johns
Hopkins University; (b) Mary Allen works on a program using rack-
mounted equipment.

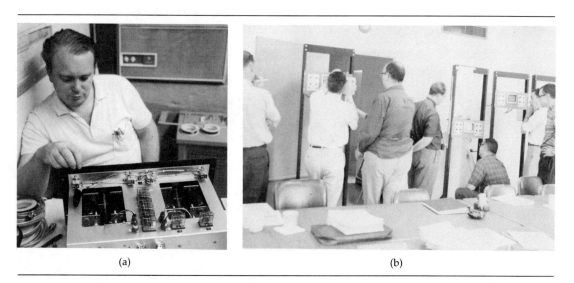

(a)                                    (b)

**FIGURE 17**
(a) Dr. A. J. Hance of Stanford University examines his tape unit module.
Tape unit modules were almost entirely electromechanical; one critical
component was a rubber-band. (b) A group of visiting scientists mount
displaying units in staging racks.

Mishell's well-organized lists. The only part of this miserable and boring task we found rewarding was the sparkling Christmas-tree light effect produced by the test equipment. We found only a few wiring errors and fixed them.

Finally the assembly process began. To our delight and relief all went smoothly, though many long days and nights of exhausting work were still required to make up the lost time and correct minor design mistakes as we found them. The visiting scientists energetically, and with much spirit and enormous dedication to the task, proceeded quite successfully to bring all six or so LINCs to life (Figs. 17 and 18).

(a)

(b)

(c)

**FIGURE 18**
(a) Dr. J. W. Woodbury of the University of Washington installs a plug-in unit; (b) Charlie discusses a point with Dr. K. Killam of Stanford *(right)* while Dr. Hance nods (it is 2 A.M.); (c) Drs. C. D. Geisler *(left)* and J. E. Hind of the University of Wisconsin examine wiring.

Each of the visiting teams was required to write and demonstrate a small program representative of the work of its home laboratory. With the completion of these final assignments, the machines were packed up for shipment. The entire group of hosts and visitors, now fast friends, celebrated with great exuberance at a farewell banquet.

(a)

(b)

(c)

**FIGURE 19**
(a) Dr. G. F. Poggio of Johns Hopkins contemplates the plug-in unit installation task; (b) Drs. N. Bell *(left)* and R. Stacy of North Carolina State College with staging rack; (c) Dr. J. C. Lilly of the Communication Research Institute installs a modification while Mishell Stucki *(rear right)* ponders a problem.

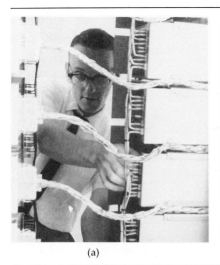
(a)

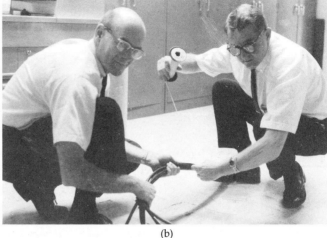
(b)

**FIGURE 20**
(a) Dr. C. A. Boneau of Duke University reaches into his cabinet to make an adjustment. (b) Drs. F. S. Grodins (*left*) and J. E. Randall of Northwestern University wrap interconnection cables.

The MIT hosts had only three days to recover before the second group of visitors arrived. This final session of Phase I went more smoothly than the first, with less pressured teaching and more time for thoughtful assembly (Figs. 19 and 20). Once again the visitors carried out all of their assignments with flair and great good humor, and again—on time—the LINCs were packed up for shipment (Fig. 21). Our

**FIGURE 21
A LINC for Wisconsin.**
Although some parts were crated for transportation, the electronics cabinets were simply taped up and carried in moving vans as furniture. Most of the machines were moved in this manner and all arrived safely at their new homes in laboratories across the country.

final banquet this time was an occasion for sober reflection on the magnitude and importance of what we had all achieved.

The LINC was now well and safely launched and in good hands. Charlie and I had little doubt of its ultimate success. For the most part the participants had all taken to the unfamiliar fairly well. For those few who had already worked with computers, the general acceptance of machine-level programming as the price of dealing with such a small memory had been cheerful enough. Productive software, however, would not begin to accumulate in the various laboratories until the following year; the first published version of the programming manual, the year after that; and the first edition of the final assembly program, LAP6, not until 1967.

We had had to formulate both teaching and assembly procedures as we went along, but this had resulted in only a few bruised knuckles and egos and a few inefficient hours (one of the visitors, a neurosurgeon, did have difficulty adjusting a tiny slotted-screwhead potentiometer deep within the recesses of the electronics frame, as I recall). Fixing design mistakes and modifying the circuits and wiring to reduce system noise meant repairing all machines in parallel. Each machine, by the way, had required a budget outlay of about $32,000, or so the accountants told us. Not too bad a miss.

Throughout it all we had been sustained in our endeavors, not only by our boundless energy and enthusiasm, our spirited sense of adventure, and our deep reserves of unshakeable conviction and commitment, but also by the Fox & Tishman Restaurant of Kendall Square, Cambridge. The F&T's sympathetic management and colorful staff fed and otherwise refreshed us at all hours of the day and night. (Following a suggestion of Charlie's, any member of the team who was responsible for a design goof agreed to buy one martini for every other member of the team at the end of the effort—one martini per goof, non-cancelling. On the day of reckoning we all repaired, of course, to the F&T. I don't remember how it all turned out.)

## THE MOVE TO WASHINGTON UNIVERSITY

The weeks immediately following our intensive summer effort did not go well. We were not only exhausted but were also confronted with an unanticipated organizational problem. The nascent MIT Center, prospectively multi-institutional and multi-disciplinary, turned out to be irremediably multi-problematical as well and de-materialized. The result was that once again the peripatetic LINC team found itself in need of a more suitable home for its work. We were . . . um . . . disappointed.

I suppose that these days it is natural to expect a group in such circumstances to form a commercial company. The LINC team, however, had always been more academically than entrepreneurially inclined. In many subsequent months of searching, the principals traveled about the country and met with many university presidents and trustees, examining several propositions quite seriously. But it was an unscheduled meeting in Cambridge with George Pake that convinced us that the best choice for the continuation of the program was Washington University in St. Louis, where Dr. Pake was Provost in the years before he left the academic world to set up Xerox PARC. He had heard about our situation from Professor Cox, he said, and had "just happened" to be visiting Cambridge on his way to Woods Hole (he never got there). He had stopped by so that we could, in his words, look him over. We were already well acquainted with Jerry Cox, an old friend even then, especially since those final hectic days before summer, and had a high regard for his innovative work in biomedical computing at Washington University. For many of us, then, this extraordinary meeting with George Pake made an already very promising possibility irresistible.

And so it was that the Washington University Computer Research Laboratory was established in 1964 under the direction of William N. Papian, Associate Dean of Engineering. CRL set up shop in newly renovated space made available by its new-found "sister laboratory," the Biomedical Computer Laboratory under Jerry Cox. Tom Sandel accepted an appointment as Professor of Psychology, and I became Research Professor of Computer Science and Associate Director of CRL. Many from the Cambridge team, including Severo, Mishell, Howard and Ken Lewis, and Constance and Joe Towler uprooted and moved to St. Louis, followed by others from MIT over the next few years. Charlie remained in Cambridge to complete both his military service and his doctorate at MIT and rejoined the group a year later as Associate Professor of Physiology and Biophysics. Norm Kinch rejoined us after an assignment at an experimental radar site operated by Lincoln Laboratory in the southwest. Mary Allen received her appointment letter from George Pake midway in a one-year trip around the world (she was then in Calcutta), but before coming to St. Louis spent another year as an extramural member of CRL working on a new assembly-program/operating system, LAP4, using a LINC set up in the living room of her family home in Baltimore—surely a first in personal computing. But the original team never entirely regrouped. To our great regret, George Gerstein and Belmont decided that their immediate scientific interests were better served by accepting appointments at the University of Pennsylvania in the Laboratory of Dr. Britton Chance, and Bill Simon elected to accept an appointment at the Harvard Medical School.

**PHASE II ACTIVITIES**

Four main tasks faced us in carrying out our Phase II responsibilities under the formal evaluation program.

1. We had to assure that the LINC equipment itself had been transplanted successfully into each of the participants' laboratories and was kept up-to-date.

2. We had to complete and distribute further documentation on the machine and its use.

3. We had to improve LINC software, starting with an enhanced version of the basic assembly program that provided automatic filing capabilities and improved editing and operational features.

4. Finally, we had to accumulate operating experience with the LINC in our own work in biomedical research and in other application areas.

Assuring ourselves and our sponsors that the LINC was taking root required considerable use of the telephone and post office as well as visits to each site. A few faulty switches and parts needed to be replaced, a few adjustments made, and a few circuit improvements installed as we verified their need. We adhered to the principle that any modification to one machine meant a modification to all machines. By and large, however, machine reliability was excellent, thanks to sound engineering by Charlie, Bill Simon, and Don Malpass, as well as to the robustness of DEC circuit packages when carefully used. (From one of the sites, the only call for hardware help we ever got dealt with what to do about the fact that the elapsed-time meter on the power supply had just jammed at 99999.)

Completing a set of finished documents on LINC hardware and operation was more difficult; the evaluation program participants had been able to take away from Cambridge only the roughest of descriptive material and operating notes. Among other things, it meant that a full production version of a LINC kit and its accompanying assembly and test procedure documentation had to be checked out and certified. Not long after CRL had been set up, Mort Ruderman brought the first complete DEC-produced kit to St. Louis (Fig. 22). Mishell and Severo then put it together and verified the accuracy of the documents and test procedures, making a few necessary corrections. Final documents were prepared with the help of newcomers Dave Stewart (who had worked with Charlie during his Air Force days), Gerald Johns, Robert Ellis, and Maurice Pepper. After printing and distributing revised final documents to all evaluation program participants, we sold document sets at cost to anyone who wanted them.

Building up a base of operating software was accelerated with the help of the Biomedical Computer Laboratory. A variety of utility pro-

(a)

(b)

(c)

**FIGURE 22**
(a) The LINC kit produced by DEC; (b) Mort Ruderman of DEC *(left)*,
Mishell *(rear)* and Severo assembling the kit; (c) Norm Kinch stacks console
modules.

grams were written by our BCL colleagues Jerry Cox, Mike Mac-
Donald, Sharon Davisson, and others. BCL incorporated these into
LAP4 (an interim modification of the LINC Assembly Program, LAP3),
and many of its operating features were later incorporated by Mary
Allen in the ultimate version, LAP6. Software was generally distrib-
uted on LINC tape reels via the mails. Since direct exchange of pro-

grams among the participants was rare, we did what we could to certify and distribute copies of application software that was submitted to CRL or written at CRL or its sister laboratory, BCL.

Use of the LINC in our own work was supplemented by work at BCL, where a few kits were assembled and used in connection with collaborative programs with the Washington University School of Medicine and its associated hospitals. Later we acquired several of the LINC variant machines made by DEC and others and began to use them in our developing research program in macromodular systems, which soon took over as the major focus of CRL activities. (BCL went on to design the Programmed Console, the result of a design seminar that Jerry and I taught in 1965 [17]. Known as the PC, it provided both autonomous and remote-connection modes of operation and thus was one of the earliest "smart terminals." It was subsequently produced in small numbers and made available to radiologists for radiation treatment planning under a national program modeled after the LINC Evaluation Program.)

### THE FINAL EVALUATION PROGRAM MEETING

The program participants began to use and then gradually depend on the LINC in their research. It had not seemed so, however, at our first regathering in June, 1964, when we all met for a show-and-tell at a distinguished old resort hotel in New Hampshire. Just short of a year since the Cambridge summer, there hadn't yet been enough experience gained in the use of the new tool, especially in view of the scarcity of software and the upsetting problem of relocating the LINC core group. No one was greatly surprised. But at the final LINC Evaluation Program meeting in St. Louis in March, 1965 (Fig. 23), the participants were well prepared and had by then accomplished a great deal of scientific work. The studies reported covered a wide range of topics [18]. Some of them were:

- Operant conditioning of pigeons and monkeys. (One series of experiments made use of a wonderful Lazy Susan holding a pigeon at each of four stations around its circumference, with indexing into data-collecting position, stimulus generation, and data analysis all provided by the LINC.)
- Spontaneous activity in thalamic and cortical neurons, behavior of single cochlear neurons, and somatosensory responses evoked in intracranial stimulation of cortex.
- Pulsatile blood flow, cardiac muscle behavior, hydrodynamics of the mammalian arterial system, and human finger tremor.
- Genetics at the bacterial and molecular level using mass spectrometers and other instruments.

**FIGURE 23**
**Preparation for the Final LINC Evaluation Program Meeting, March, 1965.**
(a) I talk with Joseph Foley of Spear, Inc. while a LINC is being set up on stage; (b) Prof. Harold Shipton *(left)* in discussion with Mort Ruderman and Winn Hindle of DEC; (c) Drs. L. Wienckowski *(left)* and Bruce Waxman of NIH.

□ Communication between man and dolphin. (An unanticipated equipment hazard: the dolphin, one Elvar by name, could accurately spit a stream of seawater a distance of twenty feet.)

In addition to their scientific accomplishments the participants reported several other technical and software development activities. These included the connection of the LINC to computation center machines, the development of a system for remote control of the LINC, the design of interface circuits for control of a blue-format tape transport and other laboratory equipment, and the development of several experimental operating system programs and floating-point routines.

By the end of Phase II the evaluation program participants had an accumulated experience of about 50,000 hours of LINC use with remarkably little trouble, and at least that many hours had also been accumulated at other LINC sites with similar results (Fig. 24). Nearly all of the original participants were awarded permanent custody of their machines following their reports of this strikingly successful operation in laboratories across the country.

## In Later Years

Although our formal responsibilities under the LINC Evaluation Program had been discharged, there was still work to be done that would take some of us a few more years.

### FINAL LINC MODIFICATIONS

Following the recommendation of the growing band of LINC users as reported at the final Evaluation Program meeting in St. Louis, a decision was made to undertake a number of hardware modifications. A new register and an arithmetic overflow circuit were provided to extend the range of arithmetic and to facilitate running a certified floating-point software package, for which a considerable consensus had developed among the mathematically inclined. These changes were seasoned, documented, and distributed (with a few installation visits) to all of the original LINC sites, as was the floating-point package itself.

**FIGURE 24**
Tom Sandel and a now bearded Severo in a visit to the laboratory of Dr. G. S. Malindzak of Bowman-Gray School of Medicine; visits were made by various members of the Washington University group to each of the participating Evaluation Program laboratories.

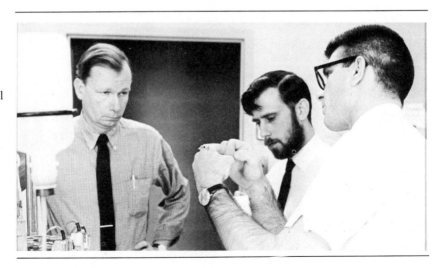

Similarly, data and program interrupt features were incorporated to improve performance in several high-rate applications. Altogether, six new instructions dealing with these added features were wired into all machines.

### THE FINAL LINC OPERATING SYSTEM

The final assembler-operating system, LAP6, was put together by Mary Allen with great care. Discussion of its specification had begun in early 1965 during her visits to several of the participating laboratories to develop a consensus of users' needs. A decision to double the initial memory size had already been made; but as Mary Allen put it, doubling a 1K memory produces another small memory. Despite this limitation she was able to design an extraordinarily efficient operating system based on a LINC tape scrolling algorithm developed by Mishell and Severo. LAP6 included a line-by-line editor, an assembler, automatic management of files, user-defined metacommands, and runtime debugging aids [19].

The achievement was remarkable. In a 1972 survey paper on operating systems, Brian Randell puts the compact scale of LAP6 in perspective [20]:

> This definition [of operating systems] is better appreciated when one realizes the extent of the spectrum of systems that it covers—from say, the LAP6 operating system . . . which contains less than 5000 instructions and took less than two man years to develop, to IBM's OS/360, which contains several million lines of code, and has taken several man-millenia of effort to develop.

LAP6 was thoroughly tested before being distributed in 1967, and the accompanying *LAP6 Handbook* still stands as a model of simplicity, accuracy, and usability [21]. A student of philosophy (today a lawyer in Massachusetts), Mary Allen quoted Kierkegaard in her foreword to the handbook:

> *To promise the System is a serious thing.*

The handbook and the second edition of its companion programming tutorial document published in 1969 [22] reflect the final form of what is now referred to as the "classic" LINC (Fig. 25).

### MANUFACTURE OF THE LINC AND LINC VARIANTS

DEC went on to manufacture about 50 or 60 classic LINCs, only a few of these in kit form—an idea whose time never quite came. (Some of the kits were assembled for others by Prof. Harold Shipton of the State University of Iowa, previously, a member of the LINC Evaluation

**FIGURE 25**
**The "classic" LINC.**
The author and
William Papian with
the final version of
LINC. (Photo: Saint
Louis *Post-Dispatch*.)

**FIGURE 25**
**The "classic" LINC.** The author and William Papian with the final version of LINC. (Photo: Saint Louis *Post-Dispatch*.)

Board. "Shippy," one of the most charming people ever to walk the face of the planet and well known to the biomedical community for his perceptive and imaginative engineering, later joined the faculty of Washington University.)

In 1965 I joined forces with Dick Clayton of DEC to design the LINC-8, a 32K dual-machine combination of the LINC and Gordon Bell's PDP-8, in which the complex LINC tape control logic was relegated to a concurrently executable program on the PDP-8 side using software written by Severo. While the nearly 150 LINC-8s were being made, Dick designed a new version of the machine, the PDP-12, of which about 1000 were manufactured [3].

In 1965 a new Massachusetts start-up company, Spear Inc., appeared. It began to manufacture a 4K integrated circuit version of the LINC, called the micro-LINC 1. Spear went on to produce the micro-LINC 300 (Fig. 26), a higher-performance 32K variant. (Spear, Inc., subsequently became a division of Becton Dickinson and Company. I have no doubt that the transaction helped Spear's former president further along toward his life-long goal of retiring to some small South Sea Island with an 18-hole golf course and a native monarch.)

## Denouement

With more than 1200 LINC or LINC variants at work around the world, research over the ensuing years began to result in very substantial contributions to the body of scientific literature. An effort was made to

**FIGURE 26**
A Spear Inc. micro-
LINC 300 *(left)*
providing operational
support to an
experimental
macromodular system
at Washington
University.

**FIGURE 26**
A Spear Inc. micro-LINC 300 *(left)* providing operational support to an experimental macromodular system at Washington University.

maintain a bibliography of LINC-related publications for the first few years, but the task soon got out of hand. The July 1969 edition lists more than 150 scientific papers, journal articles, and published books [23]. By then the volume of bibliographic references was already doubling each year, and the number of LINC programs and application notes alone soon became so large that responsibility for handling them had to be turned over to the DECUS Program Library.

The careers and lives of those associated with the LINC development continued to grow and change in many ways, as new academic appointments were assumed and new professional challenges undertaken. Many students of these early scientists and engineers, and their students in turn, went forth to seek their fortunes after training in the LINC and its ways.

Washington University's program in the medical and biological research uses of computer science and technology grew in prominence and soon came to be regarded among the foremost in the country. In the course of years Prof. Jerome R. Cox became Chairman of the Department of Computer Science, and Prof. Charles E. Molnar, Director of the Institute of Biomedical Computing. Dean William N. Papian retired from the University to private consulting practice, as did I. In a very saddening turn of the historical wheel Prof. Thomas T. Sandel, after many years as Chairman of the Washington University Department of Psychology, died just weeks before the LINC's twentieth anniversary gathering of old friends of the "Summer of '63" was to take place. He would have enjoyed looking back with us (Fig. 27).

The LINC design went on to influence the design of DEC machines that further reinforced the concept of the small computer as a

**FIGURE 27**
The birthday cake that made its appearance at the LINC Twentieth Anniversary Celebration held on November 30, 1983 at NIH.

tool for personal work and very soon took over center stage. Yet over the years the LINC and its variants continued to serve the needs of biomedical research. A few of them were still on the job productively in 1985, and one of these—perhaps the last of the "classics"—could be found at the Massachusetts General Hospital, not yet retired after more than two decades of continuous use.

## REFERENCES

[1] Clark, W. A., and C. E. Molnar: A Description of the LINC. In *Computers in Biomedical Research I.* R. W. Stacy and B. D. Waxman (eds), Academic Press, New York, 1965; ch. 2

[2] Redmond, K. C., and T. M. Smith: *Whirlwind—The History of a Pioneer Computer.* Digital Press, Bedford, Mass., 1980.

[3] Bell, C. G., J. C. Mudge, and J. E. McNamara: *Computer Engineering—A DEC View of Hardware Systems Design.* Digital Press, Bedford, Mass., 1978.

[4] Farley, B. G., and W. A. Clark: Simulation of Self-Organizing Systems by Digital Computer. *Trans. IRE,* vol. PGIT-4, 1954:76–84.

[5] Clark, W. A.: Design Considerations for an Experimental Computer. Linc. Lab. memo 6M-3536, April 1955.

[6] Clark, W. A.: The Multi-Sequence Concept. Linc. Lab. memo 6M-3144, November 1954.

[7] Forgie, J. W.: The Lincoln TX-2 Input-Output System. *Proc. 1957 WJCC*:156–160.

[8] Thacker, C. P. *et al.*: ALTO: A Personal Computer. In *Computer Systems: Principles and Examples.* Siewiorek, Bell, and Newell, (eds), McGraw Hill, 1982; ch. 33.

[9] Mitchell, J. L., and K. H. Olsen: TX-0, A Transistor Computer with a 256 by 256 Memory. *Proc. 1956 EJCC.* 10:93–101.

[10] Clark, W. A.: The Lincoln TX-2 Computer Development. *Proc. 1957 WJCC*:143–145.

[11] Clark, W. A., R. M. Brown, M. H. Goldstein, C. E. Molnar, D. F. O'Brien, and H. E. Zieman: The Average Response Computer (ARC): A Digital Device for Computing Averages and Amplitude and Time Histograms of Electrophysiological Responses. *IRE Trans. Biomed. Electronics,* 1961, BME-8:46–51.

[12] Clark, W. A.: A Functional Description of the L-1 Computer. Linc. Lab. Rept. 51G0012, ASTIA 236678, 1960.

[13] Clark, W. A.: Digital Techniques in Neuroelectric Data Processing. In *Computer Techniques in EEG Analysis,* M. A. B. Brazier (ed), EEG J. supp. 20, Elsevier, 1961.

[14] Best, R. L., and T. C. Stockebrand: A Computer-Integrated Rapid-Access Magnetic Tape System with Fixed Address. *Proc. 1958 WJCC.*

[15] Clark, W. A.: The General Purpose Computer in the Life Sciences Laboratory. In *Engineering and the Life Sciences.* NAS-NRC Rept., Wash. D.C., April 1962; 33ff.

[16] Rosenfeld, S.: LINC—The Genesis of a Technological Revolution. *LINC 20th Anniversary Seminar.* NIH Rept. November 30, 1983.

[17] Cox, J. R.: A Description of the Programmed Console. BCL Monograph #37, Wash. Univ., September 1966

[18] *Convocation on the Mississippi: Final Report of the LINC Evaluation Program.* Wash. Univ., 1965.

[19] Wilkes, M. A.: Conversational Access to a 2048 Word Machine. *Comm ACM.* 13:July 1970; 407–414.

[20] Randell, B.: Operating Systems: The Problems of Performance and Reliability. In *Information Processing 71.* C. V. Freiman (ed), J. E. Griffith and D. L. Rosenfeld (assoc. eds), North-Holland, 1972.

[21] Wilkes, M. A.: *LAP6 Handbook.* CRL Tech. Rept. #2, Wash. Univ., May 1967.

[22] Wilkes, M. A., and W. A. Clark: *Programming the LINC.* Wash. Univ., January 1969.

[23] Wilkes, M. A.: Bibliography of LINC-Related Publications. CSL Ref. Lib. LINC Doc. #14, Wash. Univ., January 1969.

# APPENDIX I.
# The LINC Evaluation Program Participants

Without any doubt whatsoever, as Tom Sandel would have said the success of the LINC is due in incalculably large part to the pioneering work of the evaluation program participants. Its formal members were: Drs. E. O. Attinger and A. Anne, Research Institute, Philadelphia Presbyterian Hospital; Dr. D. S. Blough, Dept. of Psychology, Brown University; Drs. S. Goldring and J. L. O'Leary, Dept. of Neurology, Washington University; Drs. F. S. Grodins and J. E. Randall, Dept. of Physiology, Northwestern University; Drs. J. E. Hind and C. D. Geisler, Laboratory of Neurophysiology, University of Wisconsin; Dr. J. Lederberg and Lee Hundley, Dept. of Genetics, Stanford University; Dr. C. A. Boneau, Dept. of Psychology, Duke University; Dr. J. C. Lilly, Communication Research Institute; Drs. G. S. Malindzak and F. S. Thurstone, Dept. of Physiology, Bowman-Gray School of Medicine; Drs. G. F. Poggio, G. Werner, and V. B. Mountcastle, Dept. of Physiology, and Dr. B. Weiss, Dept. of Pharmacology and Experimental Therapeutics, Johns Hopkins University; and Drs. J. W. Woodbury and A. M. Gordon, Dept. of Physiology, University of Washington.

The number of LINCs actually built in the summer of 1963 was about twenty. Several other investigators had been invited to participate on an informal basis. These informal participants assembled their computers alongside the others, using their own funds but taking advantage of whatever batch orders were placed for parts and subassemblies. They were: Drs. K. Killam and A. J. Hance, Dept. of Pharmacology, Stanford University; Dr. H. E. Tompkins and Mr. J. S. Bryan, National Institutes of Health; Dr. J. B. Lewis, M.I.T. Lincoln Laboratory; and Drs. R. Stacy and N. Bell, Institute of Statistics, North Carolina State College.

Under the chairmanship of Dr. T. T. Sandel of MIT, the LINC Evaluation Board included Dr. M. A. B. Brazier of the University of California at Los Angeles, Dr. J. R. Cox of Washington University, Dr. E. R. Dempster of the University of California, Dr. J. Macy, Jr., of the Albert Einstein School of Medicine, Dr. H. V. Pipberger of the Veterans Administration, Dr. M. D. Rosenberg of the Rockefeller Institute, and Prof. H. W. Shipton of the State University of Iowa.

# APPENDIX II.
# The Evaluation Program LINC Instruction Set

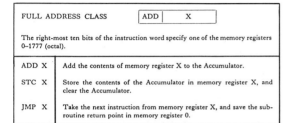

FULL ADDRESS CLASS | ADD | X

The right-most ten bits of the instruction word specify one of the memory registers 0–1777 (octal).

| | |
|---|---|
| ADD X | Add the contents of memory register X to the Accumulator. |
| STC X | Store the contents of the Accumulator in memory register X, and clear the Accumulator. |
| JMP X | Take the next instruction from memory register X, and save the sub-routine return point in memory register 0. |

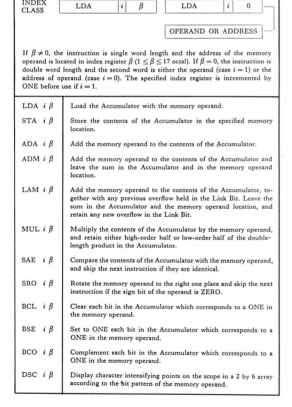

INDEX CLASS | LDA | i | β | LDA | i | 0

OPERAND OR ADDRESS

If $\beta \neq 0$, the instruction is single word length and the address of the memory operand is located in index register $\beta$ ($1 \leq \beta \leq 17$ octal). If $\beta = 0$, the instruction is double word length and the second word is either the operand (case $i = 1$) or the address of operand (case $i = 0$). The specified index register is incremented by ONE before use if $i = 1$.

| | |
|---|---|
| LDA $i$ $\beta$ | Load the Accumulator with the memory operand. |
| STA $i$ $\beta$ | Store the contents of the Accumulator in the specified memory location. |
| ADA $i$ $\beta$ | Add the memory operand to the contents of the Accumulator. |
| ADM $i$ $\beta$ | Add the memory operand to the contents of the Accumulator and leave the sum in the Accumulator and in the memory operand location. |
| LAM $i$ $\beta$ | Add the memory operand to the contents of the Accumulator, to-gether with any previous overflow held in the Link Bit. Leave the sum in the Accumulator and the memory operand location, and retain any new overflow in the Link Bit. |
| MUL $i$ $\beta$ | Multiply the contents of the Accumulator by the memory operand, and retain either high-order half or low-order half of the double-length product in the Accumulator. |
| SAE $i$ $\beta$ | Compare the contents of the Accumulator with the memory operand, and skip the next instruction if they are identical. |
| SRO $i$ $\beta$ | Rotate the memory operand to the right one place and skip the next instruction if the sign bit of the operand is ZERO. |
| BCL $i$ $\beta$ | Clear each bit in the Accumulator which corresponds to a ONE in the memory operand. |
| BSE $i$ $\beta$ | Set to ONE each bit in the Accumulator which corresponds to a ONE in the memory operand. |
| BCO $i$ $\beta$ | Complement each bit in the Accumulator which corresponds to a ONE in the memory operand. |
| DSC $i$ $\beta$ | Display character intensifying points on the scope in a 2 by 6 array according to the bit pattern of the memory operand. |

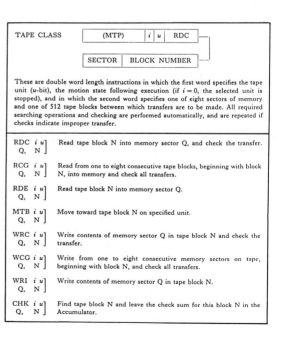

HALF-WORD CLASS | LDH | i | β | LDH | i | 0

OPERAND OR ADDRESS

Addressing is similar to that of the INDEX CLASS, except that the left-most bit of the address specifies which half of the memory operand is used. When $i = 1$ and $1 \leq \beta \leq 17$ (octal), the address word in index register $\beta$ is incremented before use, in such a way as to step through consecutive half-words, the address of the operand increasing by one on every second reference.

| | |
|---|---|
| LDH $i$ $\beta$ | Load the Accumulator with the specified half of the memory operand. |
| STH $i$ $\beta$ | Replace the specified half of the memory operand with the contents of the right half of the Accumulator. |
| SHD $i$ $\beta$ | If the contents of the right half of the Accumulator are not identical to the specified half of the memory operand, skip the following in-struction. |

TAPE CLASS | (MTP) | i | u | RDC

SECTOR | BLOCK NUMBER

These are double word length instructions in which the first word specifies the tape unit (u-bit), the motion state following execution (if $i = 0$, the selected unit is stopped), and in which the second word specifies one of eight sectors of memory and one of 512 tape blocks between which transfers are to be made. All required searching operations and checking are performed automatically, and are repeated if checks indicate improper transfer.

| | |
|---|---|
| RDC $i$ $u$ Q, N | Read tape block N into memory sector Q, and check the transfer. |
| RCG $i$ $u$ Q, N | Read from one to eight consecutive tape blocks, beginning with block N, into memory and check all transfers. |
| RDE $i$ $u$ Q, N | Read tape block N into memory sector Q. |
| MTB $i$ $u$ Q, N | Move toward tape block N on specified unit. |
| WRC $i$ $u$ Q, N | Write contents of memory sector Q in tape block N and check the transfer. |
| WCG $i$ $u$ Q, N | Write from one to eight consecutive memory sectors on tape, beginning with block N, and check all transfers. |
| WRI $i$ $u$ Q, N | Write contents of memory sector Q in tape block N. |
| CHK $i$ $u$ Q, N | Find tape block N and leave the check sum for this block N in the Accumulator. |

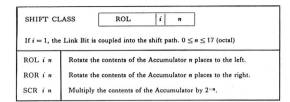

| SHIFT CLASS | ROL | $i$ | $n$ |
|---|---|---|---|

If $i = 1$, the Link Bit is coupled into the shift path. $0 \leq n \leq 17$ (octal)

| ROL $i$ $n$ | Rotate the contents of the Accumulator $n$ places to the left. |
|---|---|
| ROR $i$ $n$ | Rotate the contents of the Accumulator $n$ places to the right. |
| SCR $i$ $n$ | Multiply the contents of the Accumulator by $2^{-n}$. |

| MISCELLANEOUS | HLT | |
|---|---|---|
| HLT | Halt the computer and sound a gong. |
| CLR | Clear the Accumulator and Link Bit. |
| ATR | Load the six Relay flip flops from the right half of the Accumulator. |
| RTA | Load the Accumulator from the six Relay flip flops. |
| NOP | Do nothing for 8 microseconds. |
| COM | Complement the Accumulator. |

| SKIP CLASS | SNS | $i$ | $n$ |
|---|---|---|---|

Skip the next instruction if the specified conditions are met. If $i = 1$, the skip conditions are reversed.

| SNS $i$ $n$ | Check whether Sense Switch $n$ is up, $0 \leq n \leq 5$. |
|---|---|
| AZE $i$ | Check whether the Accumulator contains ZERO. |
| APO $i$ | Check whether the contents of the Accumulator are positive. |
| IBZ $i$ | Check whether either tape unit is reading an interblock zone mark. |
| SXL $i$ $n$ | Check whether External Level input line $n$ is negative, $0 \leq n \leq 14$ (octal). |
| KST $i$ | Check whether a key has been struck on the keyboard. |
| LZE $i$ | Check whether the Link Bit contains ZERO. |

| OPERATE CLASS | OPR | $i$ | $n$ |
|---|---|---|---|

These instructions form a general input-output command set whose execution is partially controlled by externally generated signals. Some functions of this instruction set are summarized below.

1. *Pausing*, with conditional restarting.
2. *Generating outputs* on any one of sixteen control output lines.
3. *Reading into the Accumulator* from either of two twelve-bit parallel sets of gates.
4. *Reading into the Memory Buffer* from either of two twelve-bit sets of gates.
5. *Clearing of A* conditional upon externally generated signals.
6. *Gating outputs* from the Accumulator to external equipment.
7. *Transferring information* from the Memory Buffer to the Accumulator under the control of external signals.
8. *Controlling high-rate inputs and outputs* between internal core memory and external equipment.
9. *Reading of keyboard.*
10. *Reading of console switches.*

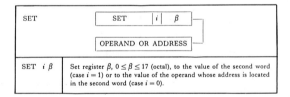

| SET | SET | $i$ | $\beta$ |
|---|---|---|---|
| | OPERAND OR ADDRESS | | |

| SET $i$ $\beta$ | Set register $\beta$, $0 \leq \beta \leq 17$ (octal), to the value of the second word (case $i = 1$) or to the value of the operand whose address is located in the second word (case $i = 0$). |
|---|---|

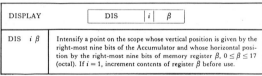

| DISPLAY | DIS | $i$ | $\beta$ |
|---|---|---|---|

| DIS $i$ $\beta$ | Intensify a point on the scope whose vertical position is given by the right-most nine bits of the Accumulator and whose horizontal position by the right-most nine bits of memory register $\beta$, $0 \leq \beta \leq 17$ (octal). If $i = 1$, increment contents of register $\beta$ before use. |
|---|---|

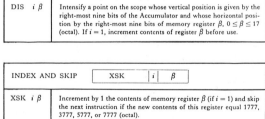

| INDEX AND SKIP | XSK | $i$ | $\beta$ |
|---|---|---|---|

| XSK $i$ $\beta$ | Increment by 1 the contents of memory register $\beta$ (if $i = 1$) and skip the next instruction if the new contents of this register equal 1777, 3777, 5777, or 7777 (octal). |
|---|---|

| SAMPLE | SAM | $i$ | $n$ |
|---|---|---|---|

| SAM $i$ $n$ | Convert the analog signal appearing on channel $n$, $0 \leq n \leq 17$ (octal), to an eight-bit binary number in the Accumulator. If $i = 0$, this instruction takes 24 microseconds; if $i = 1$, the instruction is completed in 8 microseconds although the conversion process continues for an additional 16 microseconds. |
|---|---|

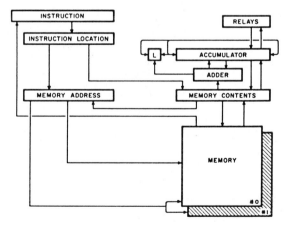

# Participant's Discussion

**Bob Taylor**

Tell us what prompted you to do two things with regard to the LINC. You put a knob on the LINC that could control the speed of the processor or of an accumulator. I was entranced by the notion that you could speed up or slow down the processor and consequently see a character, or whatever you were putting up on the display, gradually build itself up into a character or not. And so the reason that you put this speed-up, slow-down accelerater on the machine, I think, would be of interest. And why did you put a loud speaker on the LINC? I recall there being a loud speaker that allowed you to hear the machine process. In fact, as you cranked the speed knob up or down, you could hear the resulting sound through the loud speaker. What were your reasons for doing these two rather interesting things, things with which we could have a lot of fun today if machines were so instrumented.

**Clark**

Well, in fact that's the answer: I thought it would be fun.

I put audio channels on all of my machines, and slowing the LINC down put rapid bit-changes into the audio range. Any kind of feedback cues you get from complex systems are very useful, as has been observed here already. Naturally I'm speaking of systems that are complex at the time; the LINC, of course, is just a toy now, scarcely a bump in a cable (except for the tape units).

Speed control is also a useful thing in teaching people how the instruction cycle works and to help cement the perception of the great speed of the machine. You know, we live in such a narrow perceptual world; we can't see flowers bloom, except by using time-lapse cinephotography, and we can't see very fast things. We only have this little window from a tenth of a second to a few minutes. We're just not fast enough to capture high-speed phenomena, and we get bored with things that take too long. So anything we can do to make machine operation more understandable, especially when teaching people who have had no exposure to computing machinery before, the better.

**Alan Kay**

I'm sure everybody is reading between the lines of Wes's modest presentation, but I just have to react to the feelings of another user of that machine—me, when I started doing research at Xerox. You have to realize that the experience of using the LINC was like using a rather large microcomputer today. From it's description, it looked like it couldn't do anything; it only had 1K and these tape units. But, in fact, the integration of the software and hardware was so clever that you could go along and do all of the operations of editing your code and loading it and running it while the tape unit was going back and forth. The directory of the tape unit was located in the center of the tape. It had beautiful interleave code for going back and forth and finding things. There was essentially a virtual memory on this little machine. I think people would be hard pressed to do the same on 100K bytes today. After all, we live in an era in which it takes 20,000 transistors to make a flush toilet! I think that the thing that is really worthwhile in studying the LINC is to understand that this system was incredibly useful. It's, in some sense, a two-part invention of the computer field: It's the entire universe in its outline, and that's the best kind of universe you can ever have.

*Clark*          Well, Alan, would you like a few LINCs? There are still some around!

*Thelma Estrin*  One thing that's interesting is the concept that you had built a special purpose computer for the neurophysiologist. This machine ended up being too limiting, your decision to use a general purpose computer instead was a good concept and a breakthrough given that everybody was into special purpose digital computers business at the time. When you came to UCLA a couple of times in 1960 and 1961, I remember having the audacity to ask why didn't you make the machine IBM-compatible. I remember your answer, and the vehemence with which you wouldn't entertain that idea. So, today, when you said you had an IBM selectric typewriter, I was going to go up and say to you, "See, IBM does do something you like." But then, you did that punch line yourself.

*Allen Newell*   One of the questions I have wanted to ask you for a long time relates to Thelma's comment. I was not at all closely associated with your project, but I did show up occasionally as a member of site visit teams to see what was going on. I had this impression that there was an immense amount of anti-IBM rhetoric. It wasn't just Wes—it was throughout the whole team. There was a sense that IBM had the view that the only way you compute is through punch cards. I don't need to repeat the rhetoric, there were always some nice hints about it.

As you now reflect back on it some years afterwards, how important do you believe the sort of anti-IBM ideology was in driving the design of the LINC, and how much do you think that really wasn't important at all? How much do you think it was really the fact that you had immersed yourself deeply in the biologist's problems, the issue of the better instrument, and that you were using this problem to drive the whole effort? It seems to me that your focus on the better instrument computer is related to the question about IBM. It is also related to what Butler was saying about just not thinking of doing the spreadsheet because it was not the problem to be solved. That really represents some of the PARC ideology that has you pick up some things and not others.

One of the things that impressed me at the time with these groups (Wes's and PARC) was the extent to which they were trying to find another way of doing business with the computer that was more appropriate. They were not concerned with the core computations, but were concerned with the interface, with the style of interaction. They exuded a kind of a generalized unhappiness with the rest of the computer world that did not make the IBM world seem so far away.

My recollection was that there was certainly a lot of anti-IBM talk there all the time. One could react to the punch-card world, because it was the interface that counted then. One could react to the punch-card world and be looking for alternatives. We've had from Doug Engelbart a picture of the model of the world he built for himself, which was not satisfied anywhere, that he then drove himself to find a way of realizing. One could have seen that then. I thought, at the time, that such a notion of an alternative was one of the things that was really driving you guys. One could also take the view that that wasn't at all what was going on; it was really that you had decided that that instrumentation problem in the Life Sciences Laboratory was the real holy grail and you just didn't care about the rest of the situation. You probably saw it quite different than I did at the time, because I just sort of bounced against you guys every renewal period.

*Clark*                     First of all, Allen, I think we were too busy in that period to pay much attention to what IBM was doing commercially; and second, we were working in a different arena, that of real-time control systems. I'm speaking of the computer development group under Bill Papian and others. Our world and the business machine world of that period simply did not intersect.

You know, the magnetic core memory came out of MIT quite early, but it was not until several years later that IBM decided to replace the electrostatic storage of the 701 with core memory. It was only after Telemeter Magnetics (I think that was the company) began to make core memory units and sell them to IBM customers as replacements for electrostatic storage units that IBM picked up on it and decided they ought to market core memory themselves. I think I have those facts right.

One thing was clear: You could not do the kind of on-line, in-the-laboratory, hands-on experiments, where you could make mistakes and correct them on the spot, if all you had was machinery that was buffered from you by intermediate ranks of operators or by intermediating equipment with formats that were inappropriate to the real-time world of the laboratory.

I will admit to less than full enthusiasm for some of the activities that found their way into the commercial world—well, let's not say all of commerce, but rather, as the late Dan Slotnick once said, just into any company that had more than 50 percent of the business. In the LINC development, I think, things were simply moving in a different direction. What would one have done, how would one have encouraged more interaction between these two approaches? I don't know. I might say, by the way, that one of the early things done when LINCs were out in the field—not snuggled next to, but not all that far from computation centers with powerful machinery in blue tape format—was to put together the half-dozen plug-in units needed to provide an interface to IBM-compatible tape so that data could be taped off for more mathematical massaging and that sort of thing.

But consider the commercialization of cathode ray tube display, which is so central to what we do now. I remember a visit from some dignitaries from the International Business Machine Corporation who came to see the TX-2 at one point in the late 1950s. They said they had heard that we were using displays of various kinds and wanted to know what that was all about, since it wasn't something that IBM had at the time. I believe that subsequently a display monitor did appear on top of the Lincoln computation center's 709 cabinet. Just the one monitor; and of course, it atrophied shortly thereafter because it was of no use to anybody. You have to be oriented toward interactive use of machines before you realize that CRT display is the one essential thing that you must have for wide-band presentation of visual information, no matter what else you have.

I guess I can only say that I, for one, never paid much attention to what the limitations of existing commercial equipment were, except for the fact that you couldn't get your hands on the machinery, couldn't use it on your on terms, make your own mistakes with it without involving anybody else. I think that's what personal means, that you want to be able to ''blow it'' all by yourself, on your own terms. But then, I never learned to speak FORTRAN; I have just never been a part of that culture.

*Alan Kay*

I really believe in this idea that genre controls how you see things. I think it's by finding a genre that you get the degrees of freedom to actually do something within it. You can't look at everything in the world. My favorite example from the late 1960s was a machine put out by IBM called the 1130 which, in fact, looks like the personal workstation that we talk about today. It had a keyboard and the first one of those model 30 disk drives that we used on the Alto; it was, in fact, the machine that we did the prototyping of the FLEX machine on. I was astounded to discover that there's only one way, and one way only, of programming that machine, and it was by punch cards. The keyboard could not be connected. There's no piece of software that allowed you to ever type a piece of code, so what it was was actually a small operator console and you were expected to do your programs off line, put them on to the disk in binary form, and then some operator would invoke them to run. In fact, the genre was so strong in this machine that when you typed something on the keyboard, guess what was put into the A register of that machine? It was not a 6-bit number, not a 7-bit number, not an 8-bit number, but a 12-bit number! And I'll leave you to figure out what those 12 bits actually were.

*Severo Ornstein*     I think I'm the only person in the room who was fortunate enough to work for a number of years both for Wesley and for Bob Taylor and, in fact, also for Frank Heart in between. Sometimes I think that's all I've done. I wanted to respond, first of all, to your comment about Aiken, with a short story about my father-in-law, who we were picking up at the airport at one point. He seemed to be engaged in a conversation with a man in the airport, and we finally had to go in and pluck him away because, apparently, this man had gone up to Dick Lehmer and said, "Are you Mr. Brown?" And Dick had responded, "No, are you?" And then he fell into this conversation with this total stranger.

I wanted to say that I think when that picture of Wes looking very depressed was taken, I walked into his office one day, and he was looking very much like that, and I asked him why he was so unhappy. He stood there shaking his head, and I remember he said to me, "Charlie thinks I know what I'm doing."

I have two more short ones that I think are actually germain and important. I don't know whether Wesley remembers all these things. Once, when we were first building a LINC, I went into a very dark room one night. I didn't know Wesley was in there, and I discovered that the monitor for the machine was removed and was sitting down on the floor under a table. It was pitch black in the room, and Wesley was sitting in front of the monitor twiddling the dials and muttering to himself, "First you've got to get its attention."

The most important thing I learned, both from Wesley and then later from Bob, was a thing that Wes said, that most of what he does is for fun. That's really the key to success in all of these things, and I certainly learned that as hard as I could from Wes in the years I worked for him. So, thanks.

*Larry Roberts*     In terms of how many days or years a person has changed the field, Wes has to take the cake because, being at least a 15-year person and, because of all of the machines and all of the people affected by him. Certainly everything that I've done in my life has been profoundly affected by Wes. Similarly, I think all of us coming out of Lincoln Labs and MIT have been profoundly affected by the things that were done, including the early developments of the core memories. I'm sure the TX-0, the TX-2, and those machines, as well as the LINC and the later efforts, affected the momentum of history tremendously, even, in the long run, impacting IBM.

# HEWLETT-PACKARD AND PERSONAL COMPUTING SYSTEMS

## Chuck House
### Introduction by Warren Teitelman

**Warren Teitelman**

**M**y name is Warren Teitelman. I'm currently at Sun Microsystems, managing the Programming Environment Group. I was at Xerox PARC for much of the period that a lot of people have been reminiscing about. My job here is to introduce Chuck House, who's going to talk on the history of personal computing at Hewlett-Packard (HP). Chuck has been at HP since 1962 and is currently Corporate Engineering Director. Chuck's principal area of expertise is the reason why he's viewed as a contributor to the field. He is in the field of data domain test equipment and logic analyzers. In 1977, he was given the Electronics Award of Achievement and, in 1982, like Willey McCovey, he was inducted into the Computer Hall of Fame. He's currently IEEE Vice-President for Publications, and a contributor to Pinchot's book on Intrapreneuring, which is basically how entrepreneurs survive inside of corporate America.

I'm really interested in hearing what Chuck has to say. I remember when I first got to Xerox in the early 1970s, everybody was running out and spending $300 or $400 for these fancy little calculators with which you could do sines and cosines and trigs and logs. Wasn't this incredible? We all know now that we throw these things away when the batteries run down. So Chuck was at HP during this period; he is going to give us a perspective on what happened and why.

401

Charles (Chuck) House is Corporate Engineering Director for Hewlett-Packard, where he has been employed since 1962, primarily in research and development. He is responsible for coordination of engineering activities and productivity across Hewlett-Packard's twenty-five worldwide R&D sites, focusing upon strategic standards, tools, training and development, and communications. Chuck was the principal investigator, project manager, or laboratory manager, for Hewlett-Packard's first products in a number of areas including programmable oscilloscopes, computer graphics, space-video displays, medical surgery room monitors, logic-state analyzers, serial data and protocol analyzers, signature analyzers, and microprocessor software development systems.

Educated in Solid State Physics (B.S. California Institute of Technology, 1962) and Electrical Engineering (M.S. Stanford, 1964), Chuck also has a degree in the History of Science (M.A. University of Colorado, 1970). He has published widely on CAD/CAE tools, software development, data domain measurement, computer graphics, engineering careers, and engineering education. Active in professional societies, Chuck currently holds office as IEEE Vice-President, Publications, and is a member of the California Educational Foundation Board of Directors (since 1984) and the National Technological University Board of Directors (since 1983). He served on the IEEE Spectrum Board of Directors from 1981 to 1984, and as a member of the Colorado Air Pollution Control Commission from 1970 to 1972.

He co-authored *Logic Circuits and Microcomputer Systems* (1980, McGraw-Hill) and was editor of *Logic Analyzers for Microprocessors*, 1980.

# Hewlett-Packard and Personal Computing Systems

*Chuck House*
Hewlett-Packard

[*Editor's Note:* The following paper is an edited transcript of Chuck House's conference presentation.]

It is my privilege to be with you today. It's, I think, a little bit off beat for the conference, given the nature of the conference theme, because Hewlett-Packard (HP) is clearly a commercial enterprise. We value things at HP by how well they sell as opposed to how interesting they are in pioneering the field. So it's really kind of a different look at things, although it is true that we did both pioneer and sell personal computers.

The history of calculating goes back quite a ways. We used a picture of the first Marchant calculator (Fig. 1) in the HP journal that described the first HP calculator. The essential difference between the Marchant and our own is that we used electronics to do it.

Our first calculator was the 9100A (Fig. 2). This was the predecessor to the $400 calculator; it was priced at a hefty $4900. Introduced in 1968, it performed transcendental functions, log functions, all of the trignometric functions, and it did so in a powerful, interesting key-per-function way, in a very small package. It helped launch HP into

**FIGURE 1**
The first Marchant calculator.

**FIGURE 2**
The HP9100A
calculator, a first.

the computer business, certainly the personal computer business, somewhat to our astonishment. In 1960, the company was accurately described as an instrument company. By 1980, Paul Ely (currently president of Convergent Technology) could acclaim publicly that HP was now a "computer company," thanks in no small part to the 9100A and its progeny. Parenthetically, I might note that my keynote speech at the ACM conference in Colorado Springs in December 1979 opined that by the year 2000, the world will once again know Hewlett-Packard as an instrumentation company. It turns out that there are two possible routes to that answer. One is that you can default any business that you find yourself in, and the other is that the business itself can become intrinsically uninteresting. I suspect we could have both answers if we're not careful. The important point is that the computing business, per se, by the year 2000, will essentially be "big business" and to some degree "commodity business." Computers themselves will likely be intrinsically uninteresting components of the fascinating societal measurement systems that we will be defining and supplying. And once that's done, we'll focus once again on what happens for society as a result of having this incredible power. And that will be even more fun than our current excitements. We'll call that "instrumentation and measurement" of society's parameters.

Well, that's a little futuristic for a history paper, but I think it is germane to what happened at HP. To understand the personal computing history at HP probably requires some understanding of the history of the organization. Not only were we a leading supplier of electronic instrumentation, we were primarily good at frequency domain instrumentation. That is to say, we made measurements for the communications industry, almost exclusively. We built the test equipment for a generation of electronic communication system designers, in microwave, FM and AM radio, and television. It is almost apocryphal now that very early we tried projects such as tomato pickers and lettuce pickers. It is said that even Hewlett was unable to build a tomato picker that didn't make catsup in the field, and in 1940 there wasn't a big market for automated lettuce picking. HP soon concentrated on designing state-of-the-art instrumentation for people in the electronics industry. And, as a consequence of that, when digital circuits came into vogue in the late 1950s, we wound up involved in the new design issues. We also found ourselves in an interesting situation, vis-a-vis Tektronix and Beckman. Beckman Instruments was a leader in electronic counters and Tektronix developed a much-improved oscilloscope, both stemming from work at the MIT Radiation Labs during World War II. Hewlett had worked in those labs, as did Howard Vollum, who co-founded Tektronix in 1946. HP entered the counter business relatively directly, but refrained from the oscilloscope business since HP and Tektronix sold through the same sales force. (Coincidentally Dave Packard and Howard Vollum had both worked at GE in the early 1930s.) "All of a sudden," in 1955, Tektronix set up their own sales force and we felt obliged, essentially, to get into the oscilloscope business, which of course was the only instrument by which you could tell what AND-gates and OR-gates were doing in primitive computer circuits.

That led, I believe, to HP having to figure out how to make some unique measurements and find niche markets, because Tektronix was already well established. What that led to eventually was that we tended to have a few people, and really only a few people, who understood digital circuitry in some interesting ways. (I designed the first AND-gate/OR-gate trigger circuit for an HP oscilloscope, for example, in 1962.) As a consequence, when a couple of consultants showed up at HP in 1965 offering a clear way to do floating-point multiplication on the one hand and transcendental functions on the other, with what they called *algorithmic state machine* (ASM) design, replete with flow charting techniques, it looked interesting; the result after 2½ years was the machine pictured in Fig. 2.

And we sold it, as I said, for $4900. It was a fairly interesting little machine. The cover of the HP journal, September 1968, demonstrated that we had built some on a production line, which was interesting and novel in itself (Fig. 3) when one considers the extant unit volumes of computers at that time. Under the cover (Fig. 4) was an electrostatic cathode-ray tube, just as one might expect from an oscilloscope manufacturer. The memory system was a plated printed circuit board (Fig. 5) using the inductive connectivity between the crossings on the two sides of the board to accomplish storage of 32,000 bits of ROM. This

**FIGURE 3**
Production line for
the HP9100A.

In this Issue
The HP Model 9100A
Computing Calculator

machine was entirely discrete. Not a single integrated circuit. It had peripherals—an early floppy disk in "Master Card" format. It had other peripherals, including a digital plotter (one of the first commercially available digital plotters, and quite likely the first priced under $10,000). So it was a novel little set up. We sold just great car loads of them, at least by HP standards. Wang soon developed a similar product, and the two companies competed heavily in this business for awhile. And then Wang sidled sideways into office computation, and we moved in different directions.

Before leaving the 9100A, let me introduce its three chief scientists.

**FIGURE 4**
Inside view of the
assembled HP9100A.

**FIGURE 5**
HP9100A printed
circuit boards.

Tom Osborne was one of the consultants who came to us (Fig. 6). To me, he is most famous for his wry observations on the world. One was when we, four years later, got in the pocket calculator business, he wrote a small article that essentially said:

> When people get in the pocket calculator business these days, there are those expedient engineers at company A who pick LED's because

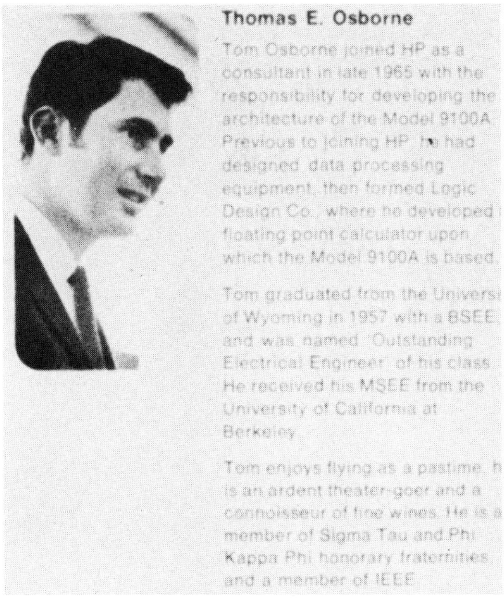

**FIGURE 6**
Tom Osborne, a
consultant on early
HP calculators.

**Thomas E. Osborne**

Tom Osborne joined HP as a consultant in late 1965 with the responsibility for developing the architecture of the Model 9100A. Previous to joining HP, he had designed data processing equipment, then formed Logic Design Co., where he developed a floating point calculator upon which the Model 9100A is based.

Tom graduated from the University of Wyoming in 1957 with a BSEE, and was named "Outstanding Electrical Engineer" of his class. He received his MSEE from the University of California at Berkeley.

Tom enjoys flying as a pastime, he is an ardent theater-goer and a connoisseur of fine wines. He is a member of Sigma Tau and Phi Kappa Phi honorary fraternities, and a member of IEEE.

they've never heard of any other display type; there's another company down the street, company B, who chose LCD's; and then, at a company like HP, we spend time evaluating which is the correct choice. The only true guarantee you can make is that the company that takes time to make the proper engineering choice will undoubtedly lose in the market.

This is to say we suddenly found ourselves in a business that did not have leisurely development times and long sales times. We were in a very faddish, a very competitive, a very exciting, dynamic business. And that's a fairly different ball game from the instrumentation business, as most of the valley and, I think, today most of the world knows. So Tom was an eclectic consultant who managed to ink a deal that got him a sizeable ($25) royalty for every machine sold with his algorithm.

Dave Cochran (Fig. 7) did the software for the 9100. This business is full of interesting people, and Dave is certainly right up at the head of the list. Dave was probably HP's first software engineer, although he was totally a hardware designer going in. Today Dave is involved primarily in custom VLSI device technologies.

Dick Monnier (Fig. 8) was the program manager. Dick is the only one of those first three people still with HP. He's been there now nearly 30 years. (He was my first manager.) Dick was chosen essentially because, at the time we started this project, he was one of a handful of project managers in the California labs of the corporation who had any

**FIGURE 7**
Dave Cochran, software engineer for the 9100.

**David S. Cochran**

Dave Cochran has been with HP since 1956. He received his BSEE from Stanford in 1958 and his MS from the same school in 1960. He has been responsible for the development of a broad range of instruments including the Model 3440A Digital Voltmeter and the 204B Oscillator. He has been working on development of electrostatic printing. Dave developed the internal programming for the Model 9100A Calculator.

He holds six patents in the instrumentation field and is the author of several published papers. Dave is a registered professional engineer, a member of IEEE and Tau Beta Pi.

**FIGURE 8**
Dick Monnier,
program manager for
the 9100.

**Richard E. Monnier**

Dick Monnier has a BSEE from
the University of California at
Berkeley, 1958, and an MSEE
from Stanford University, 1961.

Dick has been with HP since 1958
when he joined the group working
on sampling oscilloscopes. He has
been project leader on the Models
120B, 132A and 140A
oscilloscopes and the Model 191A
television waveform monitor prior
to the transfer of the project to
HP's Colorado Springs Division.
Since early 1966 he has been
Section Leader responsible for the
9100A Calculator project in
Palo Alto.

Dick holds several patents and is
a Member of IEEE.

background at all in digital technology. He had managed two projects
in our oscilloscope lab, and designed digital circuits for a third.

Now, let's move from the 9100A to its successors, including the
much more famous handheld calculators. Using Gordon Bell's way of
looking at life, we can place these machines on a price-time chart (Fig.
9). (We will re-examine this chart several times as the story of the prod-

**FIGURE 9**
Chart plotting price
versus time of the
development of each
HP calculator and
personal computer.

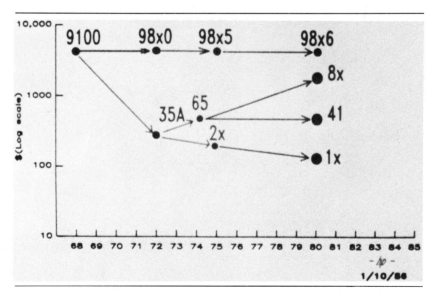

ucts identified is told.) The 9100A was given to a division in Colorado for business development. Dave Packard was born in Colorado, and so we had already opened some divisions there. The voltmeter division, not entirely an obvious choice, was given the chance to build the programmable desktop calculators. It took them four years to expand significantly on the product concept and to deal effectively with the Wang competition.

They introduced a program called the 98X0 series, X0 meaning models 10, 20, and 30. The title in our journal said "It's a series of three calculators, with lots of peripherals, and it's terrific." Physically, the machines were much more "industrial" in appearance than the sculpted 9100 (Fig. 10). The model 10 design team (Fig. 11) was large and had no continuity from the original team on the 9100. I could go through the names, but suffice to say most of those people are still with us, or else they've retired, and note also that none are especially famous outside of HP. Perhaps one would be—Bob Watson, the fellow standing, was for a time the group manager of personal products; today he manages a peripheral printing division in Vancouver, Washington.

The model 20 (Fig. 12) shifted to algebraic language instead of a key-per-function user interface; otherwise it looks the same. The model 30 (Fig. 13) offered BASIC programming. Now we begin using words such as "computer" and "terminal," and a big box appears on top of the machine so we could print. Chief designers and managers (Rex L. James and Francis J. Yockey) are names, again, that I suspect are not familiar to most of you.

**FIGURE 10**
HP9810 calculator.

**FIGURE 11**
Members of the
HP9810 design team,
including Bob
Watson (standing).

The point I want to establish is that at HP there have been essentially no individual stars on these products, other than maybe incidentally and accidentally for a period of time. There is no name or group of five names associated with the breakthroughs. It's a very rolling, project-oriented kind of thing, and people are generalists. They get good at it for a while and they move on to other areas. Whether that's right or wrong is immaterial, but that's how it is.

The 98X0 series machines were priced from about $3800 to $9000,

**FIGURE 12**
HP9820 had an
algebraic language
included.

**FIGURE 13**
HP9830 supported programming in Basic and thus qualified as a ''computer.''

and sold fairly well. They were built around an 8 MHZ proprietary processor designed and manufactured in our IC shops. This was in early 1972. These machines also used semiconductor memory. Now, bear in mind, this is coming at a time when you've had an entirely discrete machine available for the last four years. This line clearly established that HP understood electronic technology and how to use its power to construct computing machines. The base capability of the

**FIGURE 14**
98X0 series machines base capabilities.

| Comparing 9800 Series Calculators | | | | |
|---|---|---|---|---|
| | **9100A/B** | **9810A** | **9820A** | **9830A** |
| Language | Reverse Polish | Reverse Polish | Algebraic | BASIC |
| Keyboard | Key per function | Key per function | Key per function | Alpha-numeric |
| ROM size (bytes) | 4K | 5K to 11K | 8K to 14K | 15K to 31K |
| RWM size (bytes) Available to user | 128(A); 256(B) | 908 to 2924 | 1384 to 3432 | 3520 to 7616 |
| I/O structure | Special Purpose | General | General | General |
| User definable Keys or functions | None | Optional— single key subroutine | Optional— single key subroutine or function with pa- rameters | Standard— subroutine or function with one parameter |
| Recording device | Magnetic Card | Card with Cassette optional | Card with Cassette optional | Cassette standard |
| Display | 3 register numeric CRT | 3 register numeric LED | 16 character alphanu- meric LED | 32 character alphanumeric LED |
| Primary Printer | Optional 16 column numeric | Optional 16 column alpha- numeric | Standard 16 column alpha- numeric | Optional 80 column alpha numeric |

**FIGURE 15**
98X0 series machines
peripherals list.

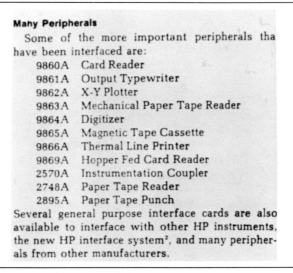

**Many Peripherals**

Some of the more important peripherals that have been interfaced are:

9860A    Card Reader
9861A    Output Typewriter
9862A    X-Y Plotter
9863A    Mechanical Paper Tape Reader
9864A    Digitizer
9865A    Magnetic Tape Cassette
9866A    Thermal Line Printer
9869A    Hopper Fed Card Reader
2570A    Instrumentation Coupler
2748A    Paper Tape Reader
2895A    Paper Tape Punch

Several general purpose interface cards are also available to interface with other HP instruments, the new HP interface system[2], and many peripherals from other manufacturers.

machines is shown in the table in Fig. 14. The extent of the peripherals listed in the table in Fig. 15 was also significant.

Given that you could get all of this system for less than $10,000, that was a fairly formidable lineup, especially when measured against the history of what was out there. One of the secrets was that these machines used a very standard block diagram (Fig. 16). One could un-

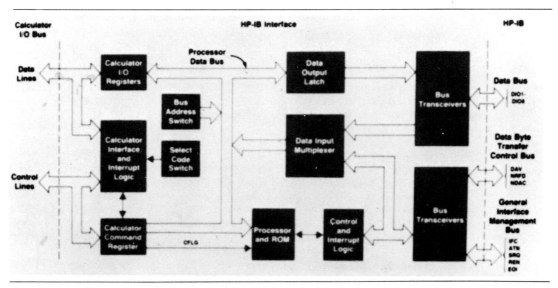

**FIGURE 16**
Block diagram of the design of the 98X0 series machines.

charitably say that we invented essentially nothing; we simply took all the ideas that were out there and figured out how to implement them cost-effectively in custom silicon, wrap them in plastic, and ship them. However, that is a most innovative activity in itself, so the accomplishment is noteworthy.

Then some people got very interested in Hewlett's favorite project. He wanted to know why he couldn't take his calculator home in his shirt pocket. No doubt one of the legendary ''What if . . .'' statements. The result on Gordon's chart was to go down the curve an order of magnitude and have it fit in a shirt pocket (note the position of the 35A on the chart in Fig. 9). The goals were: less than $500, less than 9 ounces, and fit in a shirt pocket. (We nearly had to build him a new shirt, but the basic products were there.) You undoubtedly all remember the famous results—the HP 35, 45, and 80 (Fig. 17). These machines were exciting; they were fun; and they changed a world. It wasn't just their size or cost or features. It was their ''personalness,'' their ''friendliness,'' their clear statement of the power of integrated electronics to do useful and powerful things very well and very inexpensively. They of course needed highly reliable and very dense electronics. Introduced in the autumn of 1971, they were based on a one-bit microprocessor chip (contracted both with Mostek and AMI). The units used a 56-bit serial shift register approach, which provided 14 4-bit nibbles. We had to invent logic analysis so we could watch what the nibbles did, and things like that, but the point was that all of a sudden we had a different beast on our hands, and it worked.

This was slightly ahead of Intel's introduction of the first commercial microprocessor, the four-bit 4004. Tom Whitney (Fig. 18) led this program. (Actually Bill Hewlett led this program, but he didn't get his name *in* the journal—he has it *on* the journal.) Tom became fairly well known in the industry. As you probably know, he later went to Apple

**FIGURE 17**
Pocket calculators—
HP 35, 45, and 80.

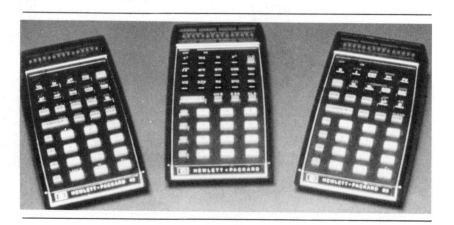

**FIGURE 18**
Tom Whitney led the pocket calculator design team.

**Thomas M. Whitney**
Tom Whitney holds BS, MS, and PhD degrees in electrical engineering, all from Iowa State University, received in 1961, 1962, and 1964, respectively. With HP Laboratories since 1967, he has served as digital systems section leader and as section manager for the HP-35 Pocket Calculator. He's also a lecturer at Santa Clara University, currently teaching a course in microprogramming. Away from electronics, Tom spends as much time as possible outdoors, with skiing, tennis, and camping the major activities.

and then into venture capital work. Probably, inside HP, his greatest contribution from my standpoint is he sold ASM design techniques to our corporation. Essentially he marketed the notion of incorporating ASM methodology using microprocessors throughout all of HP's product lines. It wasn't the calculator that was exciting, it was the conceptual thinking that allowed that clever design that was the generic gain. (Regretably Tom passed away in November 1986, a cancer victim, far too early in life.)

Chung Tung (Fig. 19) was a designer with Tom. Chung is today head of operations in Corvallis, Oregon where we still produce pocket calculators. Chung has a long history of contributions to the evolution of personal calculators at HP. And France Rodé (Fig. 20), hired the same day I joined, one of three college graduating engineers hired by HP into our California laboratories in summer 1962. To give you some idea, that was a lean time; but last year, when we had the hiring freeze and the 10 percent time off, we hired 850 college graduates, so that dimensions it a little bit. France says he left HP in 1969; it turns out he has left HP three times, the last in order to design home-security systems. Several weeks ago, he was around HP saying hello.

When the HP 35 came out, we had a market estimate of 1000 units a month. We exceeded that by 2500 percent within 2½ months—one of the worst marketing research studies in the history of our company, but certainly the kind you like! It did cause some agony for the microprocessor vendors, and as it turned out we had one notable reliability

**FIGURE 19**
Chung Tung, pocket
calculator designer.

**Chung C. Tung**
Chung Tung received his BS degree in electrical
engineering from National Taiwan University in 1961, and
his MSEE degree from the University of California at
Berkeley in 1965. Late in 1965 he joined HP Laboratories.
He was involved in the design of the 9100A Calculator and
was responsible for the design and development of two
of the MOS/LSI circuits in the HP-35 Pocket Calculator:
the control and timing chip and the read-only-memory
chips. Now working for his PhD at Stanford University,
Chung still manages to find time now and then to relax with
swimming or table tennis.

**FIGURE 20**
France Rodé, also a
member of the
pocket calculator
design team.

**France Rodé**
France Rodé came to HP in 1962, designed counter
circuits for two years, then headed the group that
developed the arithmetic unit of the 5360 Computing
Counter. He left HP in 1969 to join a small new company,
and in 1971 he came back to HP Laboratories. For the
HP-35, he designed the arithmetic and register circuit
and two of the special bipolar chips. France holds the
degree Diploma Engineer from Ljubljana University in
Yugoslavia. In 1962 he received the MSEE degree from
Northwestern University. When he isn't designing logic
circuits he likes to ski, play chess, or paint.

problem. That's not really the way to say it. You know about software bugs, right? Some of you do. We incorrectly computed the log of 2.02, but we did it reliably and repeatedly every time. So, consequently, once someone published this in one of those little journals, it could be replicated with every machine, and so we decided to replace that ROM in all machines (welcome to Manufacturer's Recall programs).

That's one of the fun things that happens in this business. Another is we had never really thought a lot about RFI and EMI. All of our products, of course, were tested for such concerns in industrial environments, but we didn't think especially about the problem of three or four people carrying these into the first class section on an airplane and jamming the electronics communications systems. Remember that? Then pretty soon, especially as lower-qualified competition proliferated, airlines began saying you can't use pocket calculators on airplanes. The point is, you get into business you don't really understand and, if nobody has really put them out there in quantity, you do your learning, your testing of your environment, on the world, and that's fascinating, sometimes. Another surprise we had, of course, was that the calculators were banned from many elementary schools. Texas banned them for a time, in general. Drexel University banned them for a long time. You couldn't use a HP pocket calculator on a final exam in the civil engineering department of Drexel University until the Fall of 1984!

So, sitting on a new technology, with a burgeoning marketplace, the question was, ''Now what?'' The choice we made at that point was to maximize the business by enhancing the features and keeping the price high (see Fig. 9). That was very successful until TI got in the business. But, meanwhile, what we built were different versions. You see the little yellow and the blue keys (Fig. 21). The point of that was to try and find a way, on essentially a shirt pocket device, to get 75 key caps. The way it was done was to shift into a second ''stack'' of keys via the yellow key and then into a third ''stack'' of keys with the blue key, and if you can keep track of all that while you're composing a multi-step algorithm, you can get the right answer. It was one of the more elegant engineering approaches one might have tried. These machines sold also in copious quantities. There was even a magnetic program storage mode in the top-of-the-line machine, the model 65, which we today might describe as a floppy disk with a stripline form factor (Fig. 22). Incidentally, these were used by the first United States astronauts who landed on the moon to compute their course corrections and many other spacecraft functions.

We finally got under the $100 mark with the 2X series. These units truly would fit in most shirt pockets. They were still in NMOS technology, but by now HP was investing heavily in CMOS as the breakthrough technology for low-power-consumption battery operation.

But the other thing being engineered was the mechanics of the system, rather than the electronics, which is where the costs are centered. So the journal article of that period focuses on the simplicity of the machine (Fig. 23). (There were 212 parts in that first HP 35. One time I was doing a TV show for somebody, and I lifted the cover off to show the machine inside, and I dropped it. There were parts everywhere. I've never since gotten that particular HP 35 to run again, but it was really an interesting pile of components.) The Corvallis designers achieved a very tight and very economical unit, and HP began to learn significantly about high-volume cost economics. Then, of course, this line was expanded into low-end desktops with printers and so forth.

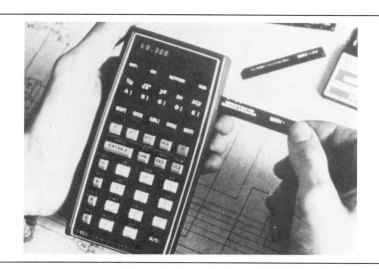

**FIGURE 23**
The HP2X series.

Let me catch you up on the upper side. Staying in the four to five thousand dollar range, we introduced another family, the 98X5 (as indicated in Fig. 9). This was about 1976. The first unit introduced was the 9825, which shifted the display concept from that original electrostatic CRT down to a little electroluminescent panel. It could do one line at a time (Fig. 24). As an instrument controller, that was fine, but for desktop computing it needed a CRT. This machine became known as the 9835. For the design team photo, the group opined that a really large CRT would be pretty good (Fig. 25). Interestingly, not a single member of the development team shown was on any previous team of any of the products I have already shown you. The top end of this line would be HP's first engineering workstations, the model 45 series (9845 family). The black and white display was $20,000 plus with peripherals, and you could buy a color graphics CAD engine for a modest $47,500 (Fig. 26).

The 98X5 family was all based upon a proprietary 16-bit microprocessor developed at Fort Collins in NMOS technology. Some 20,000 computers were shipped based upon these 16-bit micros before Intel provided any commercial sourcing of the 8086 chip set. This proprietary IC investment was then leveraged into 32-bit VLSI chip sets that would result in a chip having 450,000 devices by 1981. The good news is that we got the chip to work and the model 9000, series 500 workstations were introduced in early 1983. These machines presaged a virtual

**FIGURE 24**
HP9825 with
a one line
electroluminescent
display panel.

revolution in engineering workstations that today includes SUN, Apollo, and DEC MicroVAX as major contenders. We don't see these machines on Gordon's graph because I think the under $10,000 price is the significant story for this conference. Thus, while pursuing the 32-bit VLSI work, we reconfigured the 98X5 series using the Motorola 68000 family. It came out in 1980 in the $10,000 range as the model 9826 (Fig. 27). Notice what four generations of this kind of development can do. The designs get impressively cleaner, the boxes somewhat different looking, and the teams get slightly larger (Fig. 28). Once again, I believe there is not a single person in that picture who was shown previously.

**FIGURE 25**
The HP9835 design
team, highlighting
the inclusion of a
large CRT display!

**FIGURE 26**
HP's first
engineering
workstation, the
9845.

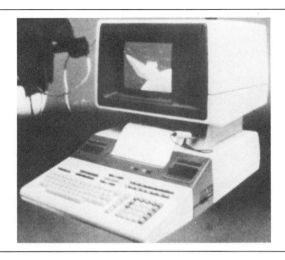

Just as with the 9835 enhancement, the 9836 was a reconfigured 9826 with a full 12″ display CRT on top (Fig. 29). This version became the most popular one; it was the most popular single piece of equipment shipped from the Hewlett-Packard Company in 1982 and 1983, measured in terms of dollars.

One point to note about the top line of Fig. 9 is what we did with the top end after we discovered the voltmeter division was hungry to have a new product line—we left it alone. We left it in Fort Collins, Colorado, and they basically stayed with that charter, building $5,000 to $10,000 equipment that became more and more impressive in capability. Today they have yet another machine, based on the Motorola

**FIGURE 27**
Model 9826, was
based on the
Motorola 68000.

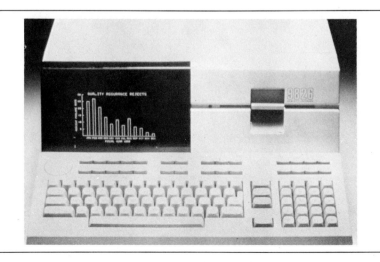

**FIGURE 28**
Again, the design
team—somewhat
larger but still made
up of the
traditionally
''unknown''
engineers.

68020 that features 8 megabytes of storage capability and stays essentially in the same price range. From 32K bits to 8 megabytes and 700 discrete transistors to a 175,000 device microprocessor is a fair move in that time span. For both memory and computing, that's a 250 times improvement, 38 percent per year for 17 years.

At the low end we were faced with three choices. Once you're down to one hundred bucks, it's hard to sell it through standard chan-

**FIGURE 29**
9836 had a full 12-
inch display CRT.

nels and make any money. So we lowered the price slightly with the 10 series. We tried to go into CMOS technology and do much more powerful machines. Then we got excited that there was a gap in the $2000 to $4800 range. Maybe the pocket calculator business people could become personal computer experts because the top end was concentrating on scientific uses. So we began the ill-fated, or the illustrious, depending on where you were in the scheme of things, 85 series. The calculators in this series tend to look pretty much the same; not much you can do with those, unless you're Casio. The 41C looks the same, but we charged five times as much for it; among other things, it allows you to save the program after you turn the power off. The model 85 looked for all the world like a little tiny personal computer (Fig. 30); this was spring, 1981. We built it as an instrument controller because we understood that business pretty well. We also built it, of course, as a machine for marketing people and people like us when we go home at night. Some of the design teams are shown in Figs. 31 and 32. These are familiar faces in Corvallis, but they are "new" to our story once again.

Going back to the chart in Fig. 9, we see that by now, this is spring 1981, the product line spawned from the HP 35 is now split into three divisions (Fig. 33). (I'm going to spare you the details of putting a calculator into a watch. It worked extremely well for people with fingers that have been sharpened in a pencil sharpener.) For any further details on these, I'll refer you to the IEEE's publication that includes a number of papers, including one on the evolution of the top end of this line (Gupta and Toong, "Insights into Personal Computers," *IEEE Trans. Ind. Electron.* USA, vol. IE-32, no. 3, 260–7, Aug. 1985).

**FIGURE 30**
HP Model 85, a personal computer built as an instrument controller.

**FIGURE 31**
Members of the design team for the Model 85.

What I'd like to turn my attention to now, very briefly, is what happened on the plotter side. We took the digital plotter (Fig. 34), continued the technology into the four-pen plotter (Fig. 35), and then into basically what became the personal computer plotter of America for a time, the 7470 (Fig. 36). That business has continued to flourish with technologies such as ink jet and laser print engines. Personal workstations have depended as much if not more on advances in price and performance from ''peripherals'' as from the computational engines through this period.

It might be interesting to look at the family sales for desktop computers, low-end calculators, and top-end calculators (Fig. 37a–c). These are linear plots of actual data. You see that each family essentially dou-

**FIGURE 32**
Members of the design team for the Model 85.

**FIGURE 33**
HP product line as of
Spring 1981.

bled in terms of total revenue. The market for desktop computers is
still increasing. The low-end calculator business, on the other hand,
did not grow after the initial surge. As a matter of fact, the second
product line was larger in units, but it was one-third the price; the
third was one-half the price of the second, and two-thirds the volume.
Naturally this had an effect upon enthusiasm in Corvallis. There's an
interesting message in these charts. By about 1980 we decided not to

**FIGURE 34**
An early digital
plotter.

**FIGURE 35**
Four pen HP plotter.

continue to roll over the product line at the same rate. That is to say, the competition is such and the market is such that there's no sense continually upgrading the product. But notice an interesting phenomenon: The sales have gone higher than any previous line and it took four years to do it. Unit sales were higher in 1985 than 1984 and, in fact, for any year in history. What happened? One possible answer is that we finally allowed, for the first time, the machine to stay on the market long enough that people could write books for the junior colleges, which is where this class of equipment really has its most widespread appeal. I mentioned the first machine selling 2500 percent of its original estimate. The successive machine was the model 80, marketed to insurance agents and bank note writers. It turned out they sold something like a whopping 8 percent of estimate—not a huge market

**FIGURE 36**
HP7470 personal computer plotter.

success. Simply put, it was too complex of a machine for the intended market. It just wasn't obvious at all to most insurance agents that they really needed to know the return on investment to four decimal places on a rolling monthly calculation. Thirteen years later, with a much more computer-conscious society, with much more money-market sophistication, and with a host of courses in real estate, banking, and other areas that teach computing skills using these tools, sales are indeed brisk.

**FIGURE 37**
Charts showing revenue per product during dates product was on the market.
(a) Desktop computers.
(b) Low end calculators.
(c) Top end calculators.

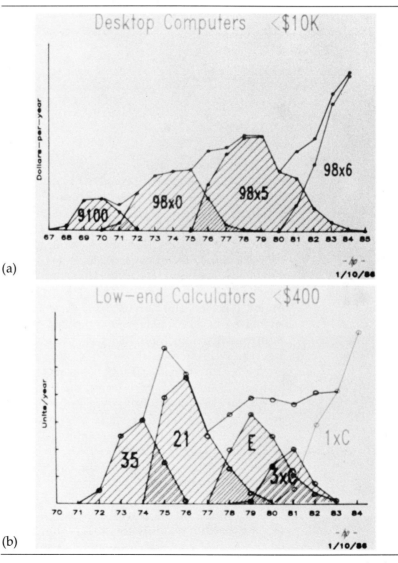

(a)

(b)

(Continued)

**FIGURE 37**
(*Continued*)

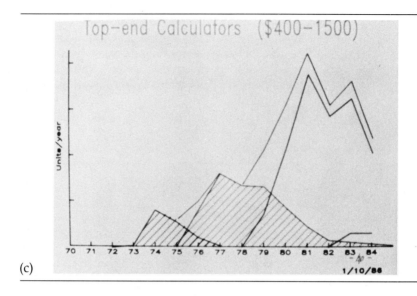

(c)

What happens in this business, of course, is that everyone is not equally skilled at using computers or calculators. So you need a cookbook that shows you the five steps or the twelve steps or whatever; and that book really has to be written, and followed or understood, in order to get value out of this equipment. If the books are written around a product that gets obsoleted around the time the books appear, it is difficult to maximize sales. The 21 series, of course, was obsoleted by competition, and E series merely tried to retain share. By the time of the 1XC family, competition and our own enthusiasm had waned. The top end is what kept the calculator business interesting and alive for many at HP. In the desktop end, of course, we sell more features. HP stands for higher performance, as well as higher price, in case you didn't know, and we have this algorithm that better mouse traps are going to command better wages. So HP tends to stay out of the high-volume, low-price sector. But these charts suggest something else to me. We, as an industry, cannot stay out of the high-volume, low-price arena. Whether we as a company can, remains yet to be seen, but we as an industry certainly cannot. This equipment, to be pervasive, *has* got to be really *available*. To be such, it needs to be used, hence trained upon, and hence standardized enough that the training can become established. It was an Achilles heel in personal calculators for HP, and I suspect it is a similar story for personal computing, circa 1986, for our entire industry.

It is hard to quantify the impact these products had on the company. The first year that the model 35 was available, pocket calculators alone accounted for 6 percent of our revenue. This happened to coincide with the end of the 1970–1971 recession, when the space program ended and engineers were in significant oversupply. More amazingly, the model 35 was 6 percent of our revenue, 25 percent of our unit shipments, and nearly 40 percent of our net profit. Another way of viewing the impact at HP can be seen from the chart on total patents (Fig. 38). Clearly these areas consumed a fair share of the leading thought at the company. Its ultimate impact, though, was to change our notions about design, manufacture, marketing, and even contribution for all areas of the company's programs.

One other thing that happened, I think, is more significant sociologically. The kinds of headlines on articles that got shipped to our PR department read like: "Calculated Clan Madmen" and "Ban the Calculator." I mentioned earlier the third-grade ban and the Texas State and the Drexel University bans in the use of calculators. It turns out there was a great hysteria about a year after this business started, when children started taking their dad's calculators to school. It seemed to be centered around three themes: One was that "rich" children shouldn't have calculators because it gives them an unfair advantage over the rest of the students, so we're not going to allow them. Of course, nobody ever seriously thought that engineers were rich, but there was this sort of implied richness if you carried around one of these little whizbangs. Another theme was that the "smart" kids will get privileged, and everybody else will get pushed to the side. Then somebody observed that actually it's going to work the reverse way. The "smart" kids are going to lose their math skills if they rely on this marvel and, if they go to some unethical "poor" place to buy gas, they will be at risk of being short-changed. I think it had more to do with the fact that many mathematics teachers were afraid of being displaced

**FIGURE 38**
Percent of patents related to personal computation and personal peripherals.

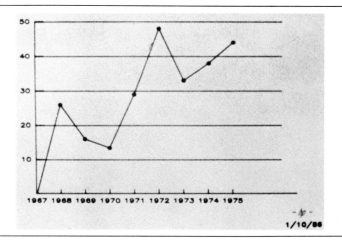

(i.e., more the kind of theme that Herb Simon mentions with AI, that the first people to go will be college professors, and that will be awkward).

Nonetheless, this all happened, and I've wondered from that day until this, and I guess I wonder more now than I did then. It is a known fact that the SAT scores in math have fallen for 20 years in this nation. And it is a known fact that that coincides with the calculator revolution and the point-of-sale terminal revolution. There's an interesting way to test that: You might go to a Wendy's or a Burger King on your way home, and just after the clerk has poked the cheeseburger key and the malt key, challenge the amount. Suppose it says $2.09. You say ''That's wrong,'' and see what happens. My bet is 99 out of 100 people running that cash register will poke the buttons again and say, ''No, see . . . ''

Trying to capture that sentiment and concern in a little broader way might be an effective place to close. It seems to me that what happened in electronic suppliers in the world over the first century, more or less, can be captured in the chart of Fig. 39. Until the pocket calculator, HP was outside the mainstream of electronics suppliers to the world. We were supplying tools for the electronics industry, which in turn spawned the computing industry. And then, all of a sudden with the HP 35, we found ourselves thrust into a situation where our products were the subject of political and social debate, much to our amazement. But in this respect too, we may be simply a bellwether, and that is the challenge I'd like you to ponder.

If you consider electronics in the 1980s, we've got a quite interesting situation in the world. I tried in Fig. 40 to draw circles that repre-

**FIGURE 39**
Ways in which electronics has been used in the world.

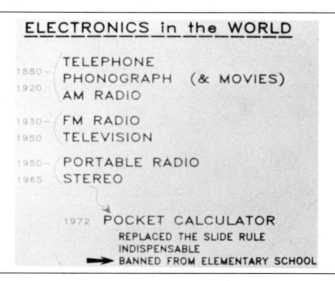

**FIGURE 40**
A view of electronics that groups electronics as toys for kids (upper left), adults (right), and industry (lower left).

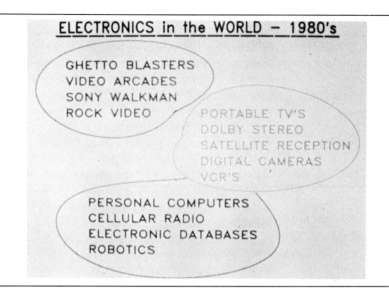

sent the situation as I see it. The upper left-hand corner are examples of electronics toys for the kids of the world from our industry. The circle on the right includes toys for adults, and the one on the lower left lists special toys, toys for the industry, *us*, with our employers' money. In the same way that I am asking, rhetorically, "What was the net effect of pocket calculators?" I would ask, "What will be the impact of the net of these 'toys' 25 years from now?" I think it comes down essentially to this: Electronics is the largest manufacturing industry on the face of the globe today, and computing is its most sophisticated element. That fact, coupled with the communications improvements and the enhanced communications available via database networking and graphical literacy, means it absolutely will have sociological impact upon virtually all peoples of the earth, relatively soon. For the first time, it's going to be subjected to more legal and political constraints than we ever dreamed possible. For example, when it gets "known" publicly, as it has been reported in small audiences in most nations of the world, that the Sony Walkman was the single most important element of the overthrow of the Shah of Iran, it's fascinating to think about what might happen. I've tried to assess these ideas in terms of the car revolution and to think about other people who build a product that would affect the future dramatically. Henry Ford took a "products" view, not unlike HP product designs today. The intended user is a systems thinker, though, rather than a product thinker. If they couldn't get paved roads, cheap gas, and effective carburetors, it would probably not be worth buying a car to get to Grandma's on Thanksgiving. Very analogous to marketing HP 80s to real estate agents? And then the buyer brought the new car home and the kids had an entirely different idea of how to use the new tool, which I think is the way kids always are. Remember the control system of rural America? People knew everybody for miles around. It turned out that in a car on a paved road you could get away from where anybody knew you in 30 minutes, which is pretty terrific. I've taken advantage of that myself a couple of times. And, of course, that "naturally and logically" led to the breakdown of Victorian mores, and suburbs, nuclear families, and the kind of lifestyle that we have today. It would be probably incorrect to conclude that Henry invented the car because he was not socially adept, and it's probably equally ludicrous to expect us in the industry inventing these tools to expect that we can extrapolate what the impact on the world might be. But I think it's a fascinating question.

What will be the major points remembered about the personal computing revolution in 50 years? Apple II, Visicalc, CP/M, and Space Invaders—these four elements are more recent than anything being honored at this meeting, but I'm going to suggest that this is where the computer revolution really began in the sense that the world knows it. Consider that there are today roughly 7 million or so Apple II's and perhaps 1.5 million legal copies of Visicalc. CP/M represents the first "generic" operating system, and there's only about 400,000 copies of that. And Space Invaders—the first year it was out, it was estimated to have been played by 45 million Americans, none of whom read an instruction manual and few of whom knew which microprocessor drove it. Essentially none of them knew the clock-rate or the bit-width of the micro. I suggest that until that kind of pervasive, easy use happens, this industry is still experts talking to experts, and the opportunity for real estate agents and their counterparts in our society to be helped by computing with the HP 80A to HP12C product shift will go begging.

# Participant's Discussion

*John Sechrest*        I did some work on the 41, so I have some inside knowledge. It's a long story but one of the things that purveys the HP culture (you didn't talk so much about the culture as the PARC folks did) was the "next bench" syndrome. I thought I'd like to hear you comment about that. I would also like to hear you comment about the fact that HP was the first one to put out a 68000 machine. It was the first in a lot of areas, and yet it certainly wasn't, from my point of view, successful. There's a lot of machines out there that had a lot of capability, and yet did not become all that pervasive. I'd like to hear you comment on that too.

*House*        Let me take them in inverse order. The book that I showed, *Insights into Personal Computers,* is fascinating because of the choices. It seems to me that practically every machine they listed failed. Every machine of consequence, in other words, as a pioneer, essentially did not sell well. One conclusion one might draw from that, although I think it's too jarring, is that we probably weren't trying to be successful in the business that I think is your topic for this meeting. I think that's important to note. We didn't have the benefit of hindsight to know what we should have tried to do. I don't want to be quoted on that, but HP is usually a niche-market player and, in the niche that we tried to serve with the 68000-based machine that you described, we actually had an enormous market share. We got all of a little bit, and that's just great with us. When you try to do broad-brush serving and large market share, it changes the instincts and the perception of what you're trying to accomplish. So it's a little bit in the eye of the beholder. Whether we were successful or a failure is measured, at least in part by, say, a division whose charter is and business goal is to sell equipment to be used on physics and chemistry workbenches. In comparison to a company aimed at supplying products through ComputerLand or BusinessLand, such a strategy would be easily described as failing abjectly and miserably.

The "next bench" syndrome, I think is part of the story. We are essentially best at solving problems that we know a lot about and that we find intrinsically interesting. In that sense, I think we're more like some of the research environments: We like to solve problems for ourselves, not necessarily for the rest of the world. The theory of the next bench syndrome is that probably there's somebody in the rest of the world like us, and if we can solve the problems for ourselves, and they're really big problems for us, chances are good we'll sell a few to

433

folks like us if we can locate them. We tend to think those people are other engineers and people like that. I don't mean to sound either arrogant or naive about that, but that sort of describes the culture. So what you see is a lot of people working on something fairly tough and someone else saying, "What are you really trying to do? Maybe I can contribute something that will help solve that."

*John Sechrest*     And what that led to is that there was a perception, like PARC where they never thought of doing a spreadsheet, that it was impossible to get people to move out of their idea of the world. So when you say to somebody that the 85 would be good at some other thing that they would even like to do, they do not see it. So a lot of products were not utilized, even though the power was there; they were not utilized in what other products have been done to do simply because it was impossible to get HP out of the niche of "I'm solving my problem."

*House*     That's been true, I think, in many companies and many environments, but we certainly share some of that heritage.

*Mark Rosenstein*     From like 1971 to 1976, I used an HP personal workstation, the 2114B. I may be the only person in the country to have done so. Where did that machine come from in the HP world?

*House*     Well, there's a prehistory to the machines I described and the prehistory included the 2114. If you were to trace the specific history, and the specific history basically started at the scope lab, here, actually in the old building, when we split from the "real company" and they sent us into exile down at 395 Page Mill, the original building. We were building a sampling scope for IBM after Tektronix said that it couldn't be done, and IBM got very interested in what the scope could show. We, in turn, got interested in their problems. A fellow named Kay Magleby was working on that. He introduced me to the problems. I built a Boolean trigger so they could watch, so they could synch on digital logic signals. When we moved the scope division to Colorado Springs a year later, Kay didn't want to go. He'd lived in the Rockies as a youth, and preferred to stay in California. So he went to Stanford to finish a Ph.D. with HP support and he developed the 2114A concept while there, as an instrument controller. That became the genesis of our first line. When I went to Colorado Springs then, I did the display graphics system that went with the 2114, the 1300 system. Then we married those two to make the 9100 when Osborne came in, and then I slanted sideways and built the test tools, which became the 1600 series logic analyzers, to try and understand what these things did. Monnier was project manager for both programs.

*Mark Rosenstein*     Did many of them make it out into the world?

*House*     The 2114? Oh, yes, we sold them in sizable quantities. In fact, that's the basis of today's 1000 line and is still one of the better known RTE systems around.

*Tom Osborne*     There are a couple of corrections, some things that I think are important that some of the people should know. You referenced an ASM machine. Most people here probably don't know what that means, but it's a turbo finite state machine. It does some pretty marvelous stuff, and it still works well. It hasn't been accepted too well, but I think that's because people haven't taken the time to learn about it.

Earlier in the day, we heard somebody talking about the word "just." You said that the 9100 was just a 32K machine. The 9100 was a programmable machine, and it did some pretty exotic things. You mentioned that it had a 32K byte read only memory in it. Well, it was 32,000 *bits* not bytes, and having been involved with a lot of those bits, I wish it did have the factor of 8.

One other thing that I thought was terribly interesting was the hate mail that we got on the log of 2.02. It has to do with the creativity of people that, given a piece of computing gear, how they'll use it. It wasn't the log of 2.02 that was bad, it was the inverse log of 2.02. That's a rather strange one because it has about 14 decimal places hooked on to it, and so it would not give the log of 2.02 and the inverse log. Of course, the person found it by just plunking numbers, in log inverse, log inverse, and so on.

Also, another interesting thing is, we had no static at all on how we did transcendentals for at least two years until someone else had a computer that would do transcendental functions. All of a sudden, two people with different products would get together and find out they got different answers and just think the end of the world had happened. The only reason that the large computers didn't experience that is that they couldn't get them in the same room together. I don't think that it made any difference anyway.

There are a couple of people I think that played some key roles and that did carry over from one project to the next. None of this would have happened, I think, without Bob Watson, Chuck Mear, and Lou Dose. HP does have a marvelous way of rotating people in, and I think you get incredible creativity that way.

Another thing, and the last thing I do want to say, is about two of the products. They were quite elegant internally: the 9820 and the 9830 both were interpretive, they both had compilers that generated close to almost purely compiled code, and we could reverse compile so we could give you back what you wanted. I think that was a significant advance at the time; people simply weren't doing that, but our customers didn't know that it couldn't be done that way, so nobody ever made a big fanfare out of it. But I think it was a contribution. I do have, if anybody wants to see it, one of those layers of the original ROM around.

*House*    Well, I appreciate that addendum, Tom. Tom has really been revered around HP for all of his contributions and he stayed six years on a consulting basis.

*Tom Osborne*    Well, I try to hide as much as I can, but I still go down. HP has been very active in their licensing campaigns and I spent most of the time that I do now going down to see if somebody hasn't infringed a patent. I really would like to see people pay more attention to patents. We engineers totally underestimate the career field of the attorneys. I think that we don't know what they do, so we figure that they do it poorly. My first introduction to one went like this: "Tom," he said, "you don't understand what our business is about, because you're not interpreting when I'm reading a patent correctly." He said, "I'm going to claim that a tripod is a device having one leg, and you're not going to agree with that." And then he said, "And I'm going to hold a tripod up, and I'm going to say, is that a leg? And you're going to say yes." And that's where I rest my case. And they're right. And you think they're not, but they're as good at their profession as we are at ours, perhaps better in some ways. They've had a lot longer history. So don't underestimate, don't shove them aside; get in and listen to what they say. Maybe they'll get you a $25 calculator some time.

Anyway, I have an example of 4000 bits of read only memory, and it's an inductive memory. Each bit is a transformer going one way or the other. It turned out to give a few pico-joules of countable electrons that came out every time we got a bit. It was a 64-bit wide word. ASM machines operate in a different way than computers. We do a branch every state, and we give many instructions simultaneously. We gave up, oh, on the average of seven, and we could give up to eleven micro-coded instructions simultaneously. So there were a lot of buses in the machines, but, boy, did they go fast—and they still do.

*Bill Spencer*    There used to be a rule that you couldn't be a division manager within Hewlett-Packard until you got to be a millionaire. Hewlett-Packard had a very lucrative plan of returning stock options to people who were participating in various projects. I believe that's no longer the case. Was that a tool for getting ideas off the engineering bench and into the market, and has it been stopped?

*House*

Well, it was a tool, and it is a tool. I think that it's really only been slowed. A company our size doesn't have the upwardly mobile stock prices that you find in smaller organizations with higher growth risks, but by traditional business standards we have a very large plan in which one engineer in eight participates over any five-year interval.

*Wes Clark*

I'm sure we all remember the impact we felt personally when we first had in our hand the pocket calculator. It was just unlike anything we had ever seen before. I would like to recount my own experience with that.

Tom and I were both at a conference just a few miles south of here in Los Gatos. In fact, as I recall, it was put on by the mythological Bob Barton; it dealt with education kits, a very interesting topic, and it was about 10 or 15 years ago. Tom had brought with him what must have been practically the first release of the HP 35. He passed it around for people to see, to fondle and finger. It went to Bob Barton, and he was amazed. He poked the buttons, and calculated the various things that were manifest on the compact keyboard. It went to Chuck Seitz who was there, and to Eliott Organick, who was among them, and it made the rounds, and it finally got to me, and I put it in my hand. I was just stunned. I studied that thing. I didn't touch it. I just looked at it and I studied, for what must have been several minutes, looking at the functions. And my old designer's mind was going around furiously, trying to figure out how anybody could put that much stuff in that little box. Finally, I just took it back and gave it to Tom, and shook his hand. It was an astonishing thing.

*House*

I think we all shared that experience to some degree, and it was certainly fun to be close to it, but I wasn't close like Tom. Thanks.

# A HISTORY OF THE PROMIS TECHNOLOGY: AN EFFECTIVE HUMAN INTERFACE

## Jan Schultz
Introduction by Peter Denning

**Peter Denning**

**H**i, I'm Peter Denning. I've been asked to be the discussant for this session. Let me open by relaying some of Jan Schultz's background. Because I have a strong interest in wine, I tend to use vintages as memory aids. Jan Schultz's career is marked by many fine vintages. Jan entered undergraduate school in Illinois in the vintage year of 1959. At that time, he majored in mathematics and didn't care much about computers. However, by the completion of his undergraduate degree, he was beginning to get interested in computers. By the time he got his master's degree in 1966, another vintage year, he had come in contact with the Socrates project and had really gotten turned on by interactive computing. At that point, he went off to graduate school at Case, but quickly decided that a Ph.D. program was not for him. He met Dr. Weed there and they conceived PROMIS, which stands for Problem Oriented Medical Information System. They wound up at the University of Vermont in 1969 to begin work on it. Finally, in 1981, still another vintage year, they struck out on their own and formed a company.

Jan R. Schultz has lived in Burlington, Vermont for the past 17 years. He was associated with the University of Vermont from 1969 until 1981 as a Research Associate in the Department of Medicine. He coordinated computer related activities at PROMIS Laboratory during that period and did research in programming languages and database management systems. In 1981 he left the University and started PROMIS Information Systems, Inc.

Jan grew up in Chicago, Illinois, and went to the University of Illinois. He majored in Mathematics and Philosophy, and has a Master's degree in Mathematics. While working on his master's degree he helped develop a very early computer-based teaching machine called Socrates. Enjoying his computer work, he combined computers and mathematics, studied automata theory, and began work on a Ph.D. at Case Western Reserve University. While at Case, he met Larry Weed and decided to devote his full energies to what became the PROMIS project.

# A History of the PROMIS Technology

*Jan R. Schultz*

PROMIS Information Systems, Inc.

[*Editor's Note:* Jan's preliminary comments are included as a preface to his paper.]

Coming late in the program gives me the advantage of seeing what spaces in computing have already been covered. The dimensions of the space that we, in fact, worked in are very different from a lot of the things that we've seen and discussed earlier in the program. One of the things we felt very strongly about early on was keeping data in an electronic form. And so, unlike Xerox PARC, we didn't have the influence, or perhaps the pressure, of having to get things out on Xerox machines.

We're really looking not at automating offices, but at automating companies. In our case, the company was a hospital. But it was a large organization, and we were trying to build tools that could match the variety of the organization. The tool had to have enough complexity in it to be able to control the organization, so it had to be able to maintain the variety of the organization within it. This really defined a fairly complex sort of a computer system that had to be able to do that. Like Butler Lampson, we were interested in interaction rather than programming for the users of our system. In trying to come up with a title for the paper, the notion of an effective human interface was as far as I could go. To try to put a touch-screen in it was just too limiting because it isn't just the touch-screen that makes the system effective, it's a touch-screen with a large database in a very interactive environment. It's a combination of all those three things that makes the thing work.

## Introduction

It is perhaps unusual for a computer technology to grow out of a social movement, but that is what this story is about. A small group of medical and computer people worked together for 15 years developing a computer technology to support a medical philosophy. The grant proposal of 1967 that provided our original funding set forth the goals that were to guide us:

> We propose that: (1) the medical record, utilizing a "problem oriented" approach, be the instrument whereby the following objectives can be

441

implemented, and that (2) the technique of record keeping described in previous publications (Weed, 1964, 1968) be the basis for the beginning realization of these goals, and that (3) a real-time computer system be used to overcome the data distribution and time barriers that are insurmountable on a manual basis using conventional hospital and clinical medical records.

Objectives: To develop a system that will:

1) Facilitate *good patient care* by making immediately available (in minutes) to the individual physician a complete, updated list of problems on any patient and by providing simultaneously, as a unit, all the data in sequence (narrative, laboratory, etc.) pertinent to any of these problems.

2) Make possible *epidemiological studies* and other research endeavors in terms of problems, having all the data on any given problem immediately available.

3) Make possible a *medical audit* whereby the standards of care being provided for a given entity (e.g. hypertension) can be rapidly assessed because of the specific orientation of all the data.

4) Make possible a *business audit* to assess the physical, financial and time resources that go into the solution and management of a given problem. The need for a more organized, efficient and economical approach to the management of common medical and surgical disorders may then be documented.

These remained the objectives of the project throughout its history.

I met Lawrence L. Weed, M.D., in November of 1966. Weed had published his initial paper on a new organization of the medical record, ''Medical Records, Patient Care and Medical Education'' (Weed 1964). He was interested in exploring the implications of automating the new organization of the medical record. We decided to work together for six months and see if during that time a longer-term plan of collaboration could be worked out.

When we began our work, other medical record research groups took the dictated or written words of physicians and other medical personnel and manually entered them into a computer. We decided from the very beginning to interface the information originator directly to the computer and develop techniques and tools to facilitate this direct interface. We decided on this direction for a number of reasons: first, the time lag between the dictation and the entry of the medical information could have a negative impact on the patient care delivered; second, the use of the computer as a recall and structuring mechanism for medical knowledge and medical records could allow the medical personnel to operate from a universe that potentially could be much larger than what they could remember; and third, the data gathered in a specific section of the record could be consistent among all health practitioners entering it. The decision to directly interface the information originator brought us directly to the major areas of our research:

the *form of the human interface* and the *representation of medical knowledge* within the computer.

Using computer technology to store and retrieve a medical record required that the medical knowledge entered into the computer have a rigorous structure. The medical community considered the notion of structuring a present illness, a medical history, or a physical examination tampering with the art of medicine. Developing outlines of the structure of the various elements of the medical record was only the beginning of the effort. We had to find internists, nurses, pharmacists, laboratory technicians, radiologists, and other medical personnel who were capable of externalizing the medical logic they had acquired and were willing to expend enormous mental effort to fill in the outlines with medical knowledge to make the system usable. The medical group in the Problem Oriented Medical Information Systems (PROMIS) Laboratory was such a group of people.

The structure of the problem-oriented medical record (POMR) served as our guide in defining the organization of all the data in the patient's medical record. The structure corresponds to four medical actions. The first is collection of a *database*; from this the *problem list* is formulated; for each active problem *initial plans* are written; and each problem is followed in *progress notes*. Without this structuring mechanism, our job would have been much more difficult because the traditional medical record has no logical structure but organizes data by its "source." For example, in the traditional record, all nursing notes are kept in one section of the record and laboratory reports are kept in another section.

The logical POMR structure requires that the same data be retrievable in many different ways. It is necessary, within a patient's record, to look at all progress notes for a single problem or all progress notes for the last 24 hours or a tabular array of specific physiologic parameters (a *flowsheet*). The requirements of the POMR were beyond typical database management systems of 20 years ago (and are beyond most of them today).

The medical record contains both *narrative* and *numeric* data. The narrative data of the medical record is variable in length and the numeric data has many forms. It was impossible to define a fixed length container or set of containers that could encompass all the data in the medical record. It was necessary to manage variable length text strings that could be retrieved in different orderings to different output devices. The numeric data contained in the medical record had hundreds of forms and had to be retrieved as part of a narrative note as well as part of a flowsheet. Both narrative and numeric data needed encoded information associated with it to facilitate the various retrievals and to make the data a legal medical record.

The initial decisions to interface the information originator directly to the computer system and to use the POMR to structure the record and provide an outline for the guidance within the computer system carried the medical and computer groups far into computer technology research and into advanced exploration of knowledge base development for the representation of medical knowledge.

# A Search for the Correct Form for the Human-Computer Interface

### INITIAL TOOLS FOR THE HUMAN-COMPUTER INTERFACE

The initial plan for the entry of medical record information was to use *optical scan sheets* and the IBM 1092-1093 *programmed keyboards* with an attached typewriter keyboard. Optical scan sheets were designed for the past medical history and systems review as well as for the physical examination. The programmed keyboards plus the attached typewriter keyboard were to be used for entry of all other information. The programmed keyboards accepted opaque plastic overlays or keymats placed over an array of 26 columns of 10 keys each, for a total of 260 labeled key locations. Each keymat could be removed and the programmed keyboard could sense the particular keymat being used, thereby identifying the type of entry into the system. Keymats were designed for each major medical subspecialty and were organized, minimizing the changing of keymats and maximizing the amount of information that could be entered from the keymat without having to use the typewriter keyboard. All information entered using the programmed keyboard was printed on the attached printer so that it could be verified before being stored in the computer.

During the first six months of 1967, several thousand past medical histories and systems reviews were processed, using two trained interviewers to fill out the optical scan sheets for entry into an IBM 1440 computer. The house staff at the Cleveland Metropolitan General Hospital was trained to fill out the physical examination scan sheets, and several hundred physical examinations were done. Great care had to be exercised in filling out the sheets or the optical scanner would reject them. The house staff had difficulty filling them out, and because of the large number of rejections, the use of the scan sheets was discontinued.

During the summer of 1967, Charles Burger, M.D., the designer of the keymats, tested the feasibility of using the programmed keyboards to enter a complete medical record. Burger's work was conclusive; the programmed keyboard presented the user with too much information, and the subsequent search time to find the proper key was excessive. The search time combined with mat changing time resulted in slow operation. A sample record took six hours to enter, at least double or triple the time required to write the original record. Scan sheets and programmed keyboards didn't solve the problem of effective entry of narrative data.

## EXPANDED SEARCH FOR APPROPRIATE TECHNOLOGY

Because readily available off-the-shelf hardware was inadequate, we decided to investigate hardware and software approaches that could solve the difficult problem of an effective, facile human-computer interface whether or not the technology was commercially available or economically justifiable at that time.

We had a number of options open to us: We could develop the necessary hardware and software ourselves or we could find a group with experience in the relevant areas to leverage our own development efforts. I felt strongly that we should take advantage of whatever work other groups had done, so we began a search. IBM was promoting the use of the programmed keyboard that we already knew was not appropriate for us. Lee Stein was the first full-time computer person to join me at the Cleveland Metropolitan General Hospital. She had just come from the Hospital Computer Project, a joint Bolt, Beranek, and Newman, Inc. (BBN) and Massachusetts General Hospital research project to study, develop, and evaluate computer techniques to serve hospitals in their information handling. Stein and I visited BBN and spent a day with Paul Castleman. I decided that a time-shared teletype terminal operating at 10 characters per second could not support the type of interface we needed. During this same period, Weed and I traveled to System Development Corporation and spent a number of days studying their efforts in the areas of database management, time-sharing and graphics, and light-pen terminals. Again the technology did not fit my perception of what we needed. The massive graphics terminals seemed inappropriate for the hospital setting and the teletype terminals were too noisy and slow.

During our expanded search for an appropriate technology, we met Robert Masters and Harlan Fretheim of the Research Division of Control Data Corporation. They jointly developed a cathode ray tube (CRT) terminal with a touch-sensitive screen, the *Digiscribe*, with software to support it. The software consisted of three interrelated programs: the *Human Interface Program* (HIP) managed user touch-screen selections, the *Selection Element Translator* (SETRAN) managed the entry of new frames of information into the frame dictionary, and the *SHORT operating system* managed the execution of programs called from selections.

## INITIAL USE OF A TOUCH-SCREEN TERMINAL

From August of 1967 through February of 1968, we used a Digiscribe terminal connected over phone lines to a Control Data Corporation 160-A computer in Lansing, Michigan, at the St. Lawrence Hospital (Fig. 1). Initial versions of the Human Interface Program and the Selection Element Translator were available, and the new software tools required that the programmed keyboard keymats be restructured. This was to be the first of many conversions of the medical content to fit it into an expanded and more capable technology designed to enhance its use. In April of 1968, we installed a Control Data Corporation 1700 computer at Cleveland Metropolitan General Hospital.

The Human Interface Program and the Digiscribe touch-screen terminal allowed medical personnel to be directly interfaced to the computer system. An array of choices was displayed on the screen and users selected one by touching their finger to the screen over the selection. For each of the twenty selection areas, the Digiscribe generated a different character that the Human Interface Program could interpret. Based upon information in the frame, a branch to another frame could take place and new information could be displayed to the user (see Fig. 2). During normal selection processing, the keyboard was used for special functions such as erasing the last selection, aborting the current message, and quickly exiting the system. Selection processing used an internal stack of frames waiting to be displayed as well as user written programs that extended the normal selection processing. The result of a user's selections was a message displayed on the top three lines of the screen as well as other informaton not seen by the user but used by programs to interpret the selections. This unseen information included the frame number, the choice number within the frame, and

**FIGURE 1**
Jan Schultz at a Digiscribe showing a visitor the system.

**FIGURE 2**
**Message generation frame.** The ''F'' parameter associated with ''Onset'' defines the output format for the title ''Onset.''

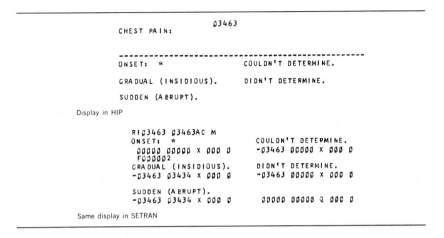

internal parameters included with the selection on the frame. The internal parameters were used to code selections so that programs interpreted compact codes rather than alpha-numeric data. The internal parameters were the coupling mechanism between the users making selections on the screen and the programs to store, manipulate, and retrieve the medical data.

The Selection Element Translator was a program to edit frames. It was used to enter new frames and alter existing ones. The branching among the frames was also defined by the Selection Element Translator. The frames were organized into three types and contained selections that could fit on a single screen. A frame was a physical unit defined by the screen size. The frame types were defined by the function they were to perform, and it was not possible to mix these functions among other frame types. The three functions were: the starting of new messages (and the termination of old ones), the generation of a message, and the display of textual information. The first type displayed an array of 7 × 2 choices, the second an array of 6 × 2 choices with the top three lines for the display of the generated message, and the third consisted of between 1 and 19 text lines.

We trained physicians and other personnel to use the Selection Element Translator so that the medical knowledge could be entered into the computer without a computer person acting as an intermediary. This ability was fundamental during the development of the system because of the massive number of displays that had to be entered.

The *SHORT operating system* supported multiple terminals as well as application programs operating in a multi-programming environment. The frames, application programs, and all medical data were mass-memory resident. Most selections made by a user required four disk accesses, and the station state data were resident in central memory only while the selections for that station were being processed. SHORT supported four classes of application programs: the first two allowed extensions to the Human Interface Program, one class allowed keyboard input (e.g., the Selection Element Translator), whereas the other did not; the next application program class ran in parallel with the user at the terminal and could communicate with the terminal (e.g., a retrieval program to display information to the CRT); the final class executed in the background after the user signed off the terminal. The data generated by the user could be passed to each program class.

The *hardware base* consisted of a Control Data Corporation 1700 computer and associated peripherals. The CDC 1700 had 32k 16 bit words of central memory with 1.1 micro-second cycle time, and the CPU executed most instructions in 2.2 microseconds. The mass-memory was CDC 854 disk drives, each holding 7.2 million bytes of storage and each with an average seek time of 70 milliseconds. The Digiscribes were connected to the CPU through a display controller with a delay-line for each terminal. The maximum distance between the display controller and a terminal was 1000 feet. The transfer rate between the CPU and the display controller was *50,000* characters per second. The CRT screen had 20 lines of 50 characters each. The Digi-scribe consisted of transparent, conductive pads on the CRT screen and the associated electronics sensed which of the 20 pads were touched. Each pad covered the left or right 25 characters of every other line.

## INITIAL MEDICAL CONTENT DEVELOPMENT

Developing a system that enabled a physician, nurse, or other medical personnel to enter narrative medical information using a touch-screen as the primary interface was a major challenge. Stephen V. Cantrill (Fig. 3), an IBM Fellow during the summer of 1967 (before starting Case Western Reserve Medical School), analyzed a large number of manu-ally recorded cardiovascular problems and defined 90 frames that to-gether could be used to enter most cardiovascular problems. Also, during the same time period, the frames defining present illnesses for GI and liver problems were written.

Because of the limitations of using the optical scan sheets for pa-tient questionnaires (which included no branching capabilities, inter-viewer administration, and a high rejection rate), we investigated the feasibility of having the patients use the touch-screen for eliciting his-torical information. Werner Slack, M.D., a medical researcher at the University of Wisconsin using a LINC computer, had demonstrated that directly interfacing the patient with a CRT terminal for data collec-tion was feasible for a selected patient population. We questioned whether we could do it routinely for all patients. We developed two

**FIGURE 3**
Steve Cantrill,
showing off the
Terminet printer.
Photo by Jim
Wanner.

short questionnaires for self-administration and found that except for people with poor eyesight, with poor reading skills, or with limited ability to read English, the questionnaires could be used easily. Children down to the age of 10 years could also use the touch-screen terminals to answer the history questions.

### INITIAL ELECTRONIC RECORD DEVELOPMENT

The programs to store and retrieve all types of medical data were evolving in parallel with the experimental entry of the narrative medical data using frames. All medical data that we thought could be effectively stored in an electronic record were classified as either narrative or numeric. Narrative data was further classified as resulting directly from selections or resulting from self-administered patient questionnaires (translated data). There were three types of data stored in the medical record: direct narrative, translated narrative, and numeric data. Keith G. Morgan, a Ph.D. student in the Engineering Program at Case Western Reserve University, joined us at Cleveland Metropolitan General Hospital. Morgan developed a program to store numeric data and wrote retrieval programs to display the numeric data in flowsheet form. Cantrill developed a program to translate a questionnaire's responses into narrative text for storage into the patient's record. He also developed a program similar to the Selection Element Translator for the entry and modification of dictionary elements used in the translation process. Lee Stein developed a program to transform the user's selections into narrative text for storage into the patient's record. I developed routines to assist in the display of the stored data. One routine, called FORMAT, interpreted codes stored with the narrative data so that the internal form of the record data was output device independent.

The ability of the Human Interface Program to couple narrative selections with internal parameters stored in the frame allowed the frame developer to enter the parameters needed to encode the data and to define the data's output format at the same time the content in the frame was entered.

### INITIAL PHASE OF DEVELOPMENT

The initial phase of the development focused on the correct form for the human interface. Other options were tried, but very early on we settled on a CRT with a touch-screen as the ideal interface for both medical personnel and the patient. At the time we did not fully realize that the interface was effective not only because of the touch-screen, but because of the high data rate of 50,000 characters per second between the CPU and the terminal and the system's ability to process most selections in under 0.5 of a second.

## In Search of the Right Development Environment, We Move to Vermont

In July of 1969, a group of five families moved from Cleveland, Ohio, to Burlington, Vermont, and PROMIS Laboratory was formed. One of the original goals for the automation of the POMR was the integration of the patient's bill with the clinical medical record. The hospital in Cleveland was a county hospital, and while we were moving from the initial phase of our research to a phase requiring access to more of the hospital, the hospital's data processing department was shifted to the county data processing department. This meant that there would be no opportunity to integrate the electronic medical record with the patient's bill and the hospital's administrative operation. We began looking for an appropriate site to continue our research.

The University of Vermont's Medical School and Medical Center Hospital offered us the opportunity we were looking for: a teaching hospital closely associated with a University through which our funding could continue and an assurance that the data processing department at the hospital was progressive and willing to work with us.

## The Medical Knowledge Database in the Early 1970s

The medical database consisted of two large bodies of knowledge: knowledge that traditionally resided in medical libraries, journals, and textbooks and knowledge concerning the individual patient. The generic medical knowledge was housed in frames; patient-specific knowledge resided in electronic patient records. This section will describe the frame-based generic medical knowledge.

Getting the initial PROMIS system operational on a medical ward in 1970 required a massive amount of medical content to be available on the frames for selection by the medical users. Drs. Larry Weed and his wife Laura B. Weed worked together translating medical content into a form that could be displayed for a medical user. The first step was to create a skeleton structure, as a first approximation, that was a synthesis of remembered experience, a review of classical textbook descriptions of disease, and a review of the appropriate current literature. This process was completed in a year. Once the initial framework was complete, consultants in various subspecialties were used to help continue the building process.

## DRUG INFORMATION FRAMES

The *drug information frames* were constructed by George Nelson, M.D., Genevieve Gilroy, registered pharmacist (Fig. 4), and Brian Ellinoy, Pharm. D. The drug information frames provided the medical user using the system with the basic facts about commonly used drugs. The guide for entry of the initial information was focused on the common drugs, since most adverse reactions occurred with them. One hundred and thirty of the most commonly used drugs at the Medical Center Hospital of Vermont were compiled, and by 1972 over 180 separate drugs were represented in the system. The information was largely abstracted from standard textbooks and articles in pharmacology, with supplementation from the current literature. The drug data was organized in displays entitled "Check Problem List for," "Side Effects to Watch for," "Drug and Test Interactions," "Usual Dosage," "Mecha-

**FIGURE 4**
Genevieve Gilroy and George Nelson discussing drug information at a CDC 211 terminal attached to the CDC 1700 system. Note the touch strips on the CRT screen and the antenna in front of the keyboard. Photo by Jim Wanner.

nism of Action,'' and ''Metabolism and Excretion.'' All information was reviewed by other physicians interested in clinical therapeutics.

## DIAGNOSTIC PROCESS

The initial system was used as an aid not only in making therapeutic decisions, but also in arriving at diagnostic plans. George Nelson did the initial work on the diagnostic plans. This was not diagnosis by computer, but it used the computer's recall ability and the electronic medical records to assist the physician in the diagnostic process. The first step in the process was the creation of problem formulation sequences for most medical problems and the association of each problem with a unique number, called the *problem plan number.* Plans were broken up into *get more information* and *treatment.* The *get more information* section was further broken up into *for more data base, diagnostic process,* and *for management. The diagnostic process* was further subdivided into three sections. A single problem plan number could have information about six or seven aspects of the plan.

By August of 1973, there were problem-specific diagnostic and therapeutic plans for over 600 problems covering a wide range of medical problems. The plans were audited by outside medical authorities to assure the safety and appropriateness of the decision pathways. Most of the frames were documented by reference citations and the citations were available in the Medical School Library. We did not have enough mass-memory space available to keep the citations on-line. By this time the drug displays had been expanded to include over 300 individual agents.

## RADIOLOGY REPORTING

The initial system also included frame-based medical knowledge for use in support of the radiology department. Peter Dietrich, M.D., a radiologist, developed the medical content in this area. The x-ray plans for many problems formulated in the computer were built. A structured reporting format specific to both problem and radiologic procedure was developed. Reporting sequences for over 150 problem-procedure pairs were built by October of 1972.

## PROBLEM PLAN NUMBERS AND TABLES

In order to accommodate the problem-specific information in the system, a new container for medical knowledge was necessary. The information in the container was never seen directly by the user, but was needed to collect together all the frames that related to one problem plan number. The new container was called the *branching information table*, and it had *slots* for each type of problem-specific information. Each slot contained a frame number that could be put into the branch stack that the Human Interface Program used, so that if a specific selection were made on a frame and the patient's problem were known, then the problem plan number could be used to look up the correct branching information table slot for the selected problem. The branching information table was the first of many tables that would come to exist as part of the medical knowledge database.

The *table* was the container for all machine-readable data related to a medically defined problem or procedure or other entity such as a system user or terminal. Each table had a unique address or code. Most of the data in a table was not visible to the medical user, but was used by programs to perform actions or do special display branching.

# An Operational PROMIS on Medical and Gynecological Wards

The PROMIS system replaced paper records with a problem-oriented electronic computer record for six months on a general medical ward and nearly four years on a gynecology ward in the Medical Center Hospital of Vermont. More than 3000 patients were followed using this system during its operation, from July of 1970 through November of 1974. More than 500 individuals (internists, nurses, medical students, house staff, radiologists, pharmacists, social workers, ward secretaries, dieticians, and laboratory technicians) used PROMIS as the sole mechanism to add to and retrieve information in patient records. The prototype PROMIS system demonstrated solutions to many general problems seen in other computer applications. Through redundant hardware, careful maintenance, and good diagnostic tools, the system was made available to users more than 99.6 percent of the time, within a scheduled 24-hour, seven-day week operation. The system was designed for fast response to facilitate use, and would respond to a user's selection by presenting another screen within 600 milliseconds for over 50 percent of the selections. Response was both rapid and comprehensive as the terminal made available the patients' complete records as well as more than 30,000 displays of medical information for guidance.

Eligible personnel throughout the institution were allowed access to the electronic record. Terminals on the ward, in the operating suite, in the pharmacy, in the clinical laboratory, and in the department of radiology demonstrated the synergism possible using an electronic record.

The overall goal during this time period was getting PROMIS operational on a single hospital ward and analyzing the operational hardware and software system in enough detail to allow realistic estimates for the size, cost, and system structure necessary to implement PRO-MIS throughout a hospital.

### THE SOFTWARE TO SUPPORT AN OPERATIONAL PROMIS

The software developed to support the operational PROMIS (Fig. 5) included the SHORT operating system, the Human Interface Program, and the Selection Element Translator, supplied by CDC. The Store program transformed the data generated by the Human Interface Program into patient record and other system files. The Retrieve program abstracted information from the patient's record or other system files and displayed the abstracted data in the form of a narrative report or a flowsheet. When all of the application programs were written for the

**FIGURE 5**
The elements of the application software.

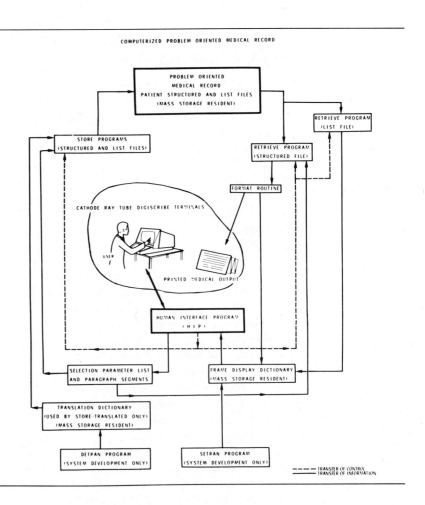

CDC 1700 system, there were over 250,000 lines of assembly language code (Schultz, Cantrill, Morgan 1971).

## THE FORM OF THE DATA WITHIN THE ELECTRONIC RECORD

An individual patient's electronic record was mass-memory resident and required a structure that facilitated its manipulation while minimizing the number of mass-memory accesses required to perform the manipulation. An individual record consisted of one fixed length index block and a variable number of fixed length data blocks. The index block was an index to all the data in the data blocks and was accessible using the patient's system identification number. The index block contained a variable length list of pointers to the data blocks along with other information to identify the type of data in the data block. To access data in the patient's record, a search was performed through the index's data block pointers looking for those pointers that satisfied the retrieval request. For any single data item retrieval, two mass-memory accesses were required.

The internal form for a data item within the electronic record depended upon whether the item was narrative or numeric. For narrative data, the internal parameters associated with the selections were interpreted as format codes to be used to define the retrieval format. For numeric data, the internal parameters associated with the selections were interpreted as data types and each data type was stored in a separate fixed length field. Consider the following example: a temperature's internal parameters were an internal code number, a time (10:23), a date (February 23, 1970), a title (Temperature), a numeric value (38) and a numeric qualifier (degrees Centigrade).

## THE SELECTABLE LIST FILES

To facilitate access to rapidly changing patient record information, it was necessary to present the patient information on displays for selection. A list of patients on a ward or the list of current medications for a patient are examples. Displaying the lists for selection required that the data to be displayed be readily available so that it could be retrieved quickly. The *selectable list files* were an abstraction of data stored in the patient's record to facilitate the rapid retrieval of selectable lists.

## THE MEDICAL GUIDANCE TO SUPPORT AN OPERATIONAL PROMIS

When health care providers sat down to use the terminal, they first chose the name of a patient presented on their terminal screen and then selected one of the sections of the medical record—the database, problem formulation, plans, and progress notes—in order to add to or retrieve from that part of the patient's record.

### Database

The nurse entered the patient's chief complaint, patient profile, and the general appearance and vital sign components of the physical examination. The patients, after only two to four minutes of instruction, entered their own review-of-systems by answering a series of up to 275 yes/no and multiple choice questions. Only the positive responses were stored in the record. The review-of-systems was then retrieved and reviewed by medical students and house officers. Positive responses were developed into present illnesses by touching selections specific for each symptom. The physical examination would then be entered using up to 1410 frames, the number actually used being a variable related to the patient's physical status.

### Problem Formulation

After completion of the database, the physician formulated the patient's problems by making a series of display selections. Each problem would be stated at its level of definition, ranging from a symptom to a firm diagnosis. The displays facilitated further description of problems by guiding the user—frequently providing them with criteria to help use consistently precise language. These criteria or definitions were taken from the literature with a library reference citation noted on the display. The system facilitated easy updating of any problem when new information gave added insight. Problems could be added or their status changed (e.g., from active to inactive) at any time.

### Plans

For many problems in the system, each component of the plan was individualized. The system contained displays based on the current literature detailing how to evaluate, treat, and follow the problem. These displays removed reliance on memory and aimed toward providing a new intern the ability to evaluate the problem with a degree of accuracy and completeness comparable to a subspecialist. The displays did not constrain the users; they were free to order whatever they pleased, but the displays served to guide them. More than 600 specific disease entities had some degree of problem-specific information in the system.

### Progress Notes

Progress notes are all notes written about a problem after the initial plans and include those written by physicians, nurses, social workers, chaplains, and others. All progress notes were entered by first selecting the appropriate problem on the terminal screen from the patient's list of problems. The symptomatic and objective sections took the user to frames specific for the body system of the problem. The nurses were encouraged to enter progress notes according to the severity and rate of change of each problem of each patient under their care. They used the same displays as the physicians, although some displays were used more by nurses than by physicians. Operative notes, radiology reports, clinical laboratory reports, social service consultations, and specialist's consultations were also entered as progress notes under the problem they addressed.

In September of 1974 there were approximately 30,000 frames in the system. A breakdown showed that 6000 of these were database frames, 4000 were problem list frames, 7000 were plans frames, 8000 were progress notes frames, superstructure and others made up the remaining 5000 frames.

### DATA RETRIEVAL

The above four sections comprise the basic patient record. This data was kept in electronic form in the computer system during a patient's hospitalization. There were no written records maintained in parallel. The updates to the record were printed each day and were available on the ward. Patient information could be retrieved at any time at any terminal by an appropriately identified medical user. Since the record was in electronic form, data could be retrieved in many ways. Information could be retrieved on a specific problem, on all problems chronologically, or in flowsheet format. Current outstanding drug orders, investigations, and accumulated charges were also available by problem. The problem of absent or lost records was nonexistent. The records were all legible. Any number of users could simultaneously retrieve from or add to a record.

### PROBLEM-ORIENTED LIST OF CHARGES

One of our initial goals, the creation of a *problem-oriented list of charges,* was accomplished. We compared a hospital bill with a list of charges calculated from the chargeable items in the electronic record. We also presented a patient's problem list with the charges associated with each problem so that medical users and administrators could see the cost of treating each problem. We discovered that the problem-oriented list of charges created from the electronic record was different from the hospital's bill since it represented everything that was recorded in the record that could be charged, and not just those things that had a charge slip written for them.

## THE HARDWARE TO SUPPORT AN OPERATIONAL PROMIS

The hardware base consisted of two Control Data Corporation 1700 computers and associated peripherals (Fig. 6). Each central processing unit had 32k words of central memory and had seven disk drives with 7.2 million bytes capacity each. There were 22 local terminals and 8 remote terminals. Remote terminals operated at 4800 bits per second and contained their own delay line refresh memory. The remote terminal multiplexor communicated full duplex at 4800 bits per second. A modem at each end of a C2 conditioned, leased 4-wire phone line was used to connect the remote terminals to the terminal multiplexor. The 4800 bps modems cost over $10,000 each and had to be manually equalized to the telephone line.

## INFORMATION UTILITY

The continuous operation of the system required the development of a reliable, backed-up hardware base that the users considered to be an information utility. One of the major elements that contributed to keeping the system in continuous operation was our ability to see patterns in the occurrence of various system problems. Whenever a problem occurred that affected the operation of the system or more information on the problem was available, we described the problem in problem-oriented fashion and posted it so that periodically we could discuss the current operational problems. We kept paper logs of all operational problems since there was not enough mass-memory space available to keep the data on-line (Fig. 7). Eventually, when more mass-memory was available, we kept the problem statements on-line. There were four major problem categories, divided into hardware, software, architectural relationships, and undefined. Each category

**FIGURE 6**
Ernie Preiss working on the CDC 1700.

**FIGURE 7**
This is 50 megabytes of mass-storage in 1970.

was divided into maintenance, operation, environment, financing, personnel, development, and education. Problems in the hardware, central processor, and peripherals operation category ranged from "core parity errors" to "idle time low for unknown reasons." Problems in the hardware environment category included "Ernie's tools disappearing" and "CPU room floor dirty and place a mess." The total log for this time period included over 500 active problems. One of our mottos for the period was to "let the problem lead us," and we had enough problems; the only question was where they were to lead us and which problem would be the leader.

## The National Library of Displays

The medical group within PROMIS Laboratory was formed to create and maintain the thousands of computer displays. The *medical content* was viewed as a textbook or encyclopedia organized and available according to the patient's problems. As Dr. Weed wrote (Weed 1972):

> The opportunity now exists in modern medicine for making available to health care personnel tools which will permit them to perform with excellence without depending on an encyclopedic memory. . . . It is therefore an appropriate goal to seek to make available to all health care personnel a tool which amplifies to a uniformly excellent level their initiative, memory, and ability to create and to execute reasoned and disciplined plans. . . . The goal can be accomplished in large part if the tool has built into it the parameters of guidance and currency of information required by health care personnel as they perform and record their work. Then, individual human memory and initiative will cease to be the critical link between all we know and all that must be done.

## THE PROCESS OF MEDICAL CONTENT DEVELOPMENT

The process of creating the medical content involved much more than just entering the medical knowledge onto the frames. Prior to the release of the medical content for on-line use, a rigorous in-house audit was completed. Outside experts in the relevant medical subspecialties were invited to Burlington for a three to five day period, to audit each frame sequence for safety, accuracy, currency, and completeness. The audit comments were then reviewed by the author of the frame sequence, and appropriate changes were made. Each step of the process was documented. Finally a check of the branching was done to verify that the sequence worked as planned.

## PRELIMINARY STUDY BY NATIONAL BUREAU OF STANDARDS

The process outlined above was limited by the resources of the medical group of PROMIS Laboratory. It became clear that prior to the widespread distribution of systems with the characteristics of PROMIS, a national body should be created to assume the responsibility for the review and distribution process. This would ensure that the systems represented accepted standards in medical care as well as computer performance. The National Bureau of Standards in conjunction with the Health Services and Mental Health Administration sponsored a study directed at identifying actions appropriate for facilitating the widespread use and maintenance of PROMIS. Melvin Conway, Ph.D., was hired by the National Bureau of Standards to do a preliminary study.

The report from the study was available in October of 1972 and was an initial planning document. It raised many issues: display library accreditation, standardization, distribution, quality control, the administrative tools required by the library, certification in the field of the record-maintenance systems that are using the displays, and controlled evolution of the entire process. The report defined terminology and concepts that we incorporated into our thinking and ultimately into our evolving system. It defined *generic system specifications* that set forth criteria for initial certification for record-maintenance systems so that system vendors could design to the specification. It defined under this a *system line,* which is a definition of a class of concrete record-maintenance systems, and under this a *system instance,* which is an individual medical record-maintenance system.

A parallel, three-level hierarchy of definitions existed for the collection of displays. The *generic library* is the primary standard resident in the national repository from which all specific display collections residing in system instances are drawn. A *sublibrary* is a subset of the generic library to allow distribution of nonidentical display libraries. A *library instance* is a machine-readable data set of a sublibrary intended to reside in one system instance. And finally, a *library instance update* is a portion of a library instance that is sent out to a system instance when only part of its display collection needs to be changed.

### RELEASE OF FRAME AND TABLE LIBRARY

PROMIS Laboratory was committed to the formation of a *National Library of Displays*. John M. Nelson, M.D., coordinated this activity. We resisted efforts by the government and private industry to get early releases of the display library; we feared if multiple copies were released, it would become impossible to provide updates since the mechanisms for creating sublibraries and library instances had yet to be worked out. The merging of already released library instances with a library instance update was a difficult problem. The tools to perform the library instance update were not in place until 1979.

Our National Center for Health Services Research contract in 1976 required that a *data description language* be developed to externalize the frame and table library in a form that was machine independent. We made available on magnetic tape, yearly, the complete library as well as a copy of all of the computer software from 1976 until the last contract expired in September of 1981.

## Expandable and Exportable Architecture Is Defined

Besides the continued operation of PROMIS in the hospital and the entry of new medical knowledge, a major effort was undertaken starting in the spring of 1973 to define an architecture that could serve a full hospital as well as be exported to other medical settings and different size institutions. Wesley Clark and Mel Conway were hired by the National Center for Health Services Research to assist us in this task. The operational CDC 1700 served as a resource for defining the subsystems for a new architecture. The CDC 1700 system consisted of three subsystems: The *human interface manager* had both hardware and software elements. The station hardware included the cathode ray tube terminal, the Digiscribe unit to make the screen touch sensitive, the hardware logic to make the terminal behave in the expected way, and the display controller or multiplexor that interfaced the terminal and the CPU. The software to control the human interface interpreted the frames, concatenated the selections together to generate English narrative, determined the next frame and presented it to the user for selection, and then reinitiated the cycle. The *patient record manager* included the mass-memory to store the patient's record as well as the software to update, retrieve, and take patient data on and off-line. The *frame manager* included the mass-memory to store the frames and tables, and the software to create and modify them.

## SUBSYSTEMS CHARACTERISTICS

Each of the subsystems had characteristics that were used to help us determine the means of instrumentation. These characteristics were determined by the way the system was implemented and by the way it was used within the hospital. The major characteristics of each subsystem are described below.

### Human Interface Manager

This subsystem had to be extremely responsive. We defined extremely responsive to mean that the time from user selection to complete display of the next screen's data was less than 0.25 of a second, 70 percent of the time. This responsiveness was necessary to facilitate the effective interface of professional non–computer trained people to a functionally complex computer system. The human engineering of the touchscreen is essential for the interface to work well. The data rate between the frame manager, the human interface manager, and the station must be high. Only 50 milliseconds was allocated for the transfer time between the frame manager and the station. The displays used to generate data were sparse, with an average of 6 choices used out of a maximum of 14. The combination of the highly responsive system with sparse displays facilitates pattern recognition and rapid interaction by the user. Unlike other computer systems where the function of the human interface was to get to a computation, in our case the interface was the computation.

### Patient Record Manager

This subsystem must be extremely reliable so that patient data is never lost and so the many types of retrieval requests for individual patient records as well as for groups of records are handled rapidly. Individual records ranged in size from 10,000 to 100,000 characters (or more) with an average of 6000 characters of data added daily. The access time to one element of a patient's record was 65 milliseconds, and it took from 2 to 200 accesses for most retrievals. An average storage into a single patient record required 6 accesses to the record file and 20 to 100 accesses to the input data generated by the human interface program.

### Frame Manager

This subsystem contained 30,000 frames and potentially could contain two to three times that number. Over 18 million characters of storage were required, and the average number of characters per frame was 600. The 600 characters included not only data to be displayed to the user, but other branching and internal parameters. The internal form was not densely packaged; groups of fixed length fields were present whether filled or not. Two mass-memory accesses were required to retrieve one frame. Twenty percent of all accesses were to two percent of the frames, so that a faster access time storage media for a small number of frames could have an impact on the throughput of this subsystem.

## POTENTIAL EXPANSION OF THE CDC 1700 SYSTEM

The CDC 1700 system could not be expanded to operate the total hospital, not only because it was technologically disadvantaged, but because the system software had many limitations that could only be changed with a major software restructuring. It is valuable to consider the types of walls present in that system. They became the guide to a redevelopment effort. Each wall was a design decision in the Human Interface Program or the patient record structure. The Human Interface Program's design restricted the maximum number of selections that could be made within one generated unit so that frame sequences had to be changed to keep the generated unit from overflowing; the frame library could contain a maximum of only 32,000 frames, and we were very close to overflowing it. The structure of the patient record restricted the size of the patient record index to a single mass-memory block so that some very long patient stays would overflow the block requiring the starting of a new record; the numeric information for one data item in the record had a fixed maximum size; a maximum of 144 patient records could be on-line at one time; the patient's problem and order lists had a maximum size so they had to be monitored and cleaned up as some of them reached maximum size; the numeric and narrative data were stored in separate parts of the record and retrieval functions that operated on narrative data couldn't be applied to numeric data and conversely. This made it impossible to retrieve a flowsheet of narrative data.

## INCORPORATE EXPANDED FUNCTIONS

It was also necessary to incorporate expanded functions into the system's operation. We wanted to be able to fully exploit the electronic record by allowing its full access in all the supporting areas of the hospital; by performing data compression of the electronic record; by making available at all times the patient's problem list and current medications for all patients in our population; by developing a patient record that could span multiple admissions and serve for the patient's lifetime; and finally, by linking the medical data in the record with the patient's financial data.

## SCALE TO SUPPORT TOTAL HOSPITAL

The new system had to be able to support the total hospital. The size of the system was determined by the number of active patients in the system at one time and the total served by the hospital, by the size of an individual patient's record, and by the number of terminals active at one time.

The Medical Center Hospital of Vermont in 1973 handled 20,000 admissions and 120,000 outpatient visits per year. There were between 25 and 85 admissions per day and 10,000 outpatient visits per month.

The size of a single patient admission was determined by looking at a "typical" six-day period of system operation and extrapolating. We used figures for the number of admissions per year and outpatient visits per year to arrive at the amount of patient record growth expected in one year. It was 1.24 billion characters or the equivalent of 4 double density IBM 3330s (the measuring stick of that era).

The number of terminals for the hospital was calculated based upon 4 terminals per 20 bed ward and 7 terminals per 34 bed ward and terminals in all the supporting areas. The total number was 200.

## ARCHITECTURAL CHARACTERISTICS ARE DEFINED

Given the functional characteristics of the CDC 1700 system and the characteristics of the site for installation, an architecture for a PROMIS system was defined. The major elements of the PROMIS architecture were redundancy of hardware elements for reliable service, guaranteed responsiveness with minimal sensitivity to load, and access to any patient's record from any terminal within the system. The architecture had to support the locational diversity of the health care system since health care is not practiced in one geographical site, yet it was important to allow communication among the sites.

## TWO REMAINING ISSUES

Besides the elements for the architecture listed above, there were two issues that had to be explored before a final decision on an architecture could be made: first, should the subsystems be functionally partitioned into separate hardware elements, and second, should the patient record files be centralized or distributed?

One potential architecture was a *network of minicomputers*. Each node of the network was to be one minicomputer that would handle between 10 and 30 terminals. The number of terminals per node would be determined by requiring a system response of less than 0.25 of a second 70 percent of the time. The nodes would each contain the three subsystems. A communications medium would allow the nodes in the network to communicate. The patient records that were normally accessed by the terminals connected to one node would be contained in that node. Other nodes' access to a patient record would be on-demand and would require a transfer across the network. For storage into a record, packets of data would be shipped to the node that contained the patient's record.

Another proposed architecture was a *functional partitioning of each subsystem into separate hardware elements.* There would be frame engines containing the frames in a read-only form. Each frame engine would be a small minicomputer with mass-memory to contain the frame library and communication ports so that the human interface subsystems could communicate with it. The human interface subsystems would contain no mass-memory and would multiplex many terminals. Each human interface subsystem would have communication ports for connections to both a frame engine as well as a record processor. The record processor would be fully duplexed minicomputers with communication ports for connection to the human interface subsystems and to remotely located printers.

The issue of whether the patient record file should be centralized or distributed was posed in the following way: Can we build a system that can serve New York City as easily as it serves the City of Burlington and the State of Vermont? Ultimately there would have to be a medical record network serving a very large region; the question was, Shall we learn the problems of building such a network while it is small or wait and solve the problems posed by such a network only when it is no longer feasible to keep the data files centralized?

A paper simulation was done of the system data traffic among the subsystems, assuming the architectural model of a network of six minicomputers with each minicomputer managing 50 terminals and with intranode traffic for a distributed patient record file being 25 percent of all accesses. The average total data rate was 42,000 characters per second; assuming a burst rate of ten times that rate and assuming maximum intranode traffic for the patient record files, the data flow would require only 25 percent of a million word per second I/O bus. The remaining bus capacity would be available for instruction execution, data pool swapping, and program loading. Given the system data traffic requirements and the type of hardware available at the time, there was no need to segment the functions into separate hardware units.

**FINAL DECISION**

Our decision was to define an architecture consisting of a network of minicomputer nodes with each node containing the three subsystems. The patient record files would be distributed across the network. To reduce network traffic associated with access to these files, a medical record placement scheme was used to maximize the probability that the patient's record and the provider's terminal were local to one another on a network node.

## Specify Technology to Support the New Architecture

With the architecture defined by the end of 1973, our next year's jobs were set out before us. A minicomputer, terminal, inter- and intranode communications bus as well as a programming language had to be specified and selected for the new PROMIS system. We had been looking for a hardware person to round out the PROMIS computer group when James Wanner (Fig. 8), an astronomer and mechanical engineer with digital electronics experience, walked through the door. His first task was the writing of a terminal specification. We decided to use MOS technology where it could be applied. MOS was "mostly off the shelf," and those items we could not find on the shelf we tried to put on the shelf. Detailed specifications were written for all of the items and we set things in motion to begin the procurement process.

### MINICOMPUTER SPECIFICATIONS

The *minicomputer* had the following specifications: central memory of at least 128k, 16 bit or greater words with a cycle time of one microsecond or less, and direct memory access to peripherals; the environment protection had to include power failure restart circuitry and error checking on all data paths in the system; multi-level interrupts; memory protection consistent with any memory mapping or multi-

**FIGURE 8**
Jim Wanner and Ernie Preiss discuss the Megadata terminal specification. Note the prototype Megadata terminal on the table in the right rear.

programming executive; mean time between failure of less than one processor failure per year. Mass-memory was divided into 10 millisecond fast access for 2 million characters and 65 millisecond access for 200 million characters. Communications subsystem (four wire or phone) must support printers and intercomputer communications at 50,000 bits per second or faster. Up to 50 local touch-screen terminals operating at 16,000 characters per second or faster had to be able to be connected to the system. Other standard peripherals had to be available.

## TOUCH-SCREEN SPECIFICATIONS

The *touch-screen terminal* had the following specifications: 8½ inches high by 11 inches wide screen; two display modes (the first having 24 lines by 80 characters each, with 12 lines aligned under the touch-pads on the screen, and the second having 36 lines by 100 characters each with the bottom line aligned with the bottom line of touch-pads on the screen); alphabetic characters shall appear in at least three distinct ways; if a cathode ray tube is used, the display shall be flicker-free for all users; the touch pad screen shall have an array of transparent touch pads each covering a fixed block of characters in a displayed page of text. The pads shall respond to the operator's finger touch, independent of body position. When a pad is touched, the text lying under the pad shall be emphasized. This emphasis will continue until a new display is received by the terminal. The bottom line of screen display text shall have 10 touch pads, each pad covering 7 characters, with a one-character-wide space between the pads. Eleven additional lines of text, on approximately ⅝-inch centers, shall have four touch-pads each covering 19 characters of text. Parallax errors between text and touch-pad positions shall be minimized by mounting the pads as close as possible to the text. Data flow into each terminal shall be at the rate of 15,000 characters per second, or faster. Data flow from each terminal shall proceed at a rate of at least 15,000 characters per second, or less if appropriate to the terminal controller subsystem. The terminal interface subsystem shall support at least 24 terminals in apparent concurrent active use. Each terminal shall have access to more than one central processor unit, for use as back-up on CPU failure. Portable terminals shall be provided by means of terminals mounted on wheeled carts with single plug interface to the system and taps at various locations.

## COMMUNICATIONS SUBSYSTEM SPECIFICATIONS

The *communications subsystem* had to be able to support up to 50 touch-screen terminals operating at 15,000 characters per second full duplex, up to 20 printers operating at 9600 characters per second, and at least one intercomputer connection operating at 50,000 bits per second.

## PROGRAMMING LANGUAGE SPECIFICATION

The *programming language* specification included the following description. A high level language is desirable, but not at the expense of execution speed or mass-memory access efficiency. The language includes character manipulation instructions. It is *machine independent* so that the application programs do not have to be rewritten when the machine is changed and so that the same programs can run on multiple machines. The language must be transparent to the operating system. The language must incorporate the ideas of structured programming. There can be separate languages for application programming and systems programming. The original assembly language programs were very efficient, very difficult to change, and had very little documentation as part of the program; we must do better this time around!

# The Architectural Elements

### MINICOMPUTER PROCUREMENT

Request for proposals was sent to eight computer manufacturers. Four offered no bid. IBM said they had a "hole" in their product line and that a network of their computers would be too expensive. Digital recommended an 11/45, which met the hardware requirements, but would not make information available on their software. Although they offered to sell us hardware, they made no bid on our request for a proposal. PRIME and INTERDATA made no bid.

We received four proposals. The Modcomp, Inc., proposal met the hardware specifications, but the system they proposed, the ModComp IV, was not yet available for testing. Control Data Corporation sent an extensive proposal; William Norris, the CDC President, delivered it and spent the day at PROMIS Laboratory discussing the continuation of our long-term relationship. CDC proposed the most interesting system. It was a system composed of 10 peripheral processors from a CDC 7600 with a large shared central memory. However, the system was not a standard product, and a simulation showed that for our type of architecture the multi-processor system got in the way of responsiveness. The DataGeneral proposal met the hardware specifications, but the software could only address 96k of the 128k address space so it did not fit the software specifications. Edson DeCastro, President of Data General, visited PROMIS Laboratory to discuss their proposal.

Varian Data Machines submitted the winning proposal with their V77-400 computer system (Fig. 9). It fit both the hardware and software

**FIGURE 9**
The V77-400 in the temporary computer room. Photo by Jim Wanner.

specifications and the company was interested in working with us on the joint development of a communications subsystem to support the high-speed touch-screen terminals.

### TOUCH-SCREEN TERMINAL PROCUREMENT

There were three departures from the mainstream in our terminal specification: the touch-screen interface, the dual display modes (24 lines by 80 characters for selection and 36 lines by 100 characters for text retrieval), and the high-speed data transfer. After discussions with over 30 potential suppliers, we decided to drop the dual display modes as an essential requirement. We received eight responses to our specifications, and MEGADATA Corporation was selected to build the new high-speed, touch-screen terminals. The terminal was a random-logic PDP 8 so that it could be programmed to perform our specialized functions. It had expansion slots for the two special boards to be built by MEGADATA, one for the touch screen and the other for the high-speed line interface. The touch-screen did not have set pad locations on the screen, but was an $x-y$ digitalizer that had a resolution of 0.25 of an inch. It sensed a finger touch via echoing of surface waves. The first group of 20 terminals cost $8500 each.

### COMMUNICATION SYSTEM PROCUREMENT

The terminal-to-computer communications remained largely undefined until a computer system was selected in early March 1974. Soon thereafter a suggested communications system was formulated, using the standard Varian Data Communications Multiplexor and VTAM software as a starting point. A research contract was signed with

MITRE Corporation in July 1974, to assist us in designing and implementing a communications system that would support digital traffic on a CATV-type distribution sytem for the PROMIS architecture. The resultant system was to provide highly reliable, low error rate and flexible reconfiguration capabilities for the PROMIS digital signals among the many terminals and several computer nodes. The data rate was to be at least 15,000 characters per second. Of secondary importance was the ability of the system to simultaneously support the communication of other services such as entertainment and educational television. MITRE was selected for this work because of their pioneering efforts with the MITRIX system, which used CATV technology to build a time-division multiplexing scheme on a CATV bus for internode data transfer. They had developed CATV modems as part of the MITRIX system.

## PROGRAMMING LANGUAGE DEVELOPMENT

The only high level language available on the V77-400 was FORTRAN. Its code was not re-entrant, and it had an extensive run-time environment that was not appropriate for our tasks. We had done extensive programming language research. I wanted a language with syntax that would support structured programming; a semantics that would support the manipulation of logical records of variable type and length; and a pragmatics that would support frames, records, and indexes to both. We wanted to be able to manipulate strings that could grow to be very long (up to 32k characters) and to be able to access mass-memory resident data logically. Facile control of the touch-screen terminal was also a requirement, as was network access to the logical data structure and network access to multiple communicating processes.

I designed a programming language based upon our CDC 1700 assembly language experience and a study of other languages. Morgan and I wrote an interpreted version of the language on the CDC 1700 with semantics as defined above. The interpreted version accessed the data using a structure similar to a list processing languages' ''property lists.'' Extensive searching through the data structures was required for any operand access, and consequently it executed very slowly. It would ''run like the wind'' and could take more than 30 seconds to process one selection.

We decided to develop a compiler language, the PROMIS Programming Language (PPL). PPL was a combination of a high-level procedural language with a very powerful embedded database management system. It included procedures to manipulate the touch-screen, schedule and sprout processes throughout a network, transfer data across the network, and manipulate strings effectively. It was efficient in terms of CPU cycles because it was not an interpreter; all data access to 16 bit numerics was in-line code and the internal form of the data required no searching. Each data element was accessed either with an absolute address or with a pointer variable and a relative address that was bound at run-time. Cantrill wrote the code generator, and I wrote the scanner and parser for the compiler. It compiled source code at 2000 to 6000 lines per minute.

The syntax of PPL was a major departure from "ALGOL-like" languages of that era. PPL's assignment operation was from left to right, the way one reads English. PPL had no explicit statement delimiters, that is, no ";" after each statement. PPL's comments could appear after implicit statement delimiters, and except for an * at the start of a new line, there were no explicit comment delimiters. Control statements all had explicit statement terminators. For example, an IF statement was terminated by an ENDIF or FI. Lists of statements could replace a single statement without requiring a BEGIN and END for the block. The syntax of a control statement required it to be spread across multiple lines, and no more than one statement could be put on a single source line. The PPL syntax supported our ideas of what "structured" code should look like.

PPL was designed for the programming of applications. We could not afford to wait until the compiler was done before we began programming its run-time support routines. We were also concerned about the efficiency of PPL for systems programming tasks; since PPL code was to be machine independent, we were also concerned about distorting PPL to fit various systems programming tasks. For these reasons, Cantrill developed a structured preprocessor to the Varian supplied macro-assembler. Called STRAP, it allowed all assembly language code to pass through. Statements recognized as STRAP commands caused output of the appropriate macro-assembler instructions. The preprocessor was originally written in STAGE2, a machine independent macro-processor, but it processed code too slowly. When written in STRAP itself, it could process up to 5000 lines of code per minute.

## Software and Hardware Specification

Our funding agency was devoting a large percentage of their budget to our development efforts and wanted to be assured that we were up to the task. An advisory committee was put together to oversee our development. The committee included Ivan Sutherland, Allen Newell, George Robertson, Herbert Sherman, and Jack Hall, M.D. Newell and Robertson had previously developed a menu selection system called ZOG, which sensitized them to our work. They applied the PROMIS interface ideas of a rapid response, large network system to ZOG.

The implication of the new architecture involved coordinating efforts of multiple hardware vendors and the PROMIS Laboratory computer group. We had limited time and money. We followed D. L. Parnas's advice. The implementation used

> specifications sufficiently precise and complete that other pieces of software can be written to interact with the piece specified without additional information. . . . The specification must be sufficiently formal that it can conceivably be machine tested for consistency [and] completeness [in the sense of defining the outcome of all possible uses]. . . . By this requirement we intend to rule out all natural language specification. (Parnas 1972)

We had been using decision tables for program development for a few years. Henry Beitz, a CDC consultant, convinced us that an unlimited entry decision table could be used as the basis for demonstrating an understanding of a problem and also as the fundamental design document. Decision tables were used to design and test the interface among hardware and software modules.

The run-time environment developed to support PPL (described in the next section) was defined in 17 decision tables and 78 rules. The definition of the polled multidrop protocol to connect the high-speed terminals to the CPU was a set of 12 decision tables with a total of 77 rules. The protocol was used by Varian Data Machines, by MEGA-DATA, and by PROMIS Laboratory. When the hardware was delivered and the terminals were connected, the system operated correctly the first time it was tried. One problem was discovered in an error pathway in the hardware, and six problems requiring software modification were discovered. We also used "thin-wire" protocols to define our run-time environment. We sent messages among three separate tasks: the PPL code environment to manage the resources of the CPU, terminal input/output to manage the terminal and printers, and block input/output to manage mass-memory.

## Run-time Environment Supporting PPL

The PPL run-time environment consisted of facilities to support the work requirement modularized into processes, to support the internal form of the PPL logical data type (the paragraph) and to minimize the number of mass-memory accesses.

### PROCESS SUPPORT

A process required access to three types of resources: the CPU for execution of PPL code, the mass-memory devices for access to the PPL paragraphs, and the terminals and printers. Each of these three types of resources was accessed using a task in the Varian Data Machines VORTEX II operating system. Based upon the resource required by the PPL code being executed, messages dispatched the PPL process among the different tasks.

### SUPPORT FOR THE PPL LOGICAL DATA TYPE

Files and individual blocks were manipulated by the file system. The PPL logical data type was broken up into paragraphs, sentences, and sentence elements and were manipulated by sentence input/output routines. The file system, developed by Henry Stambler, used the VORTEX II software as a foundation, and provided the following enhancements:

1. A file was configured as a set of discontiguous components spanning several VORTEX file areas or disk packs. Up to 64 components were allowed for each file.
2. New components could be added as needed.
3. A file could be as large as 2048K blocks. In VORTEX the maximum was 32K sectors. A block could be up to 2K bytes long.
4. The table defining the files resided in central memory so that any block could be obtained in a single disk access.
5. Software checksumming and read-after-write validation were provided.

The sentence I/O routines, developed by Morgan, performed the mapping between the PPL operands and words within the file system blocks by maintaining state variables and a map-in area for each environment, making possible all the logical and string operations in PPL.

### MASS-MEMORY ACCESS

PPL programs required rapid access to large amounts of data. It was impossible to keep even a small fraction of this data in central memory, and it was undesirable to access mass-memory every time a piece of data was needed. A *memory buffer pool*, developed by James LeMay, housed all data accessed via PPL instructions. The data in the pool ages, and because a PPL program normally accessed the same information many times during its execution, the pool frequently still contained the information. The pool was a resource used by the resource management tasks; it was transparent to the PPL programmer. The ratio of block to disk accesses was typically between 2:1 and 25:1, based upon the type of program and the amount of data it needed.

# The Library System: Management of the Medical Knowledge

Medical knowledge entry was controlled in a manner similar to patient record data entry and retrieval. The *library builder* made selections at a touch-screen terminal. By answering questions and selecting the next step in a series of actions, the builder was guided through the steps required to add new information to the database or update previously entered knowledge. The *library system* was developed to manage the *frame* and *table library*, in the same way that PROMIS was developed to manage the patient care functions. PPL was used to implement the library system on the same hardware base that the PROMIS system was implemented. The library system managed *frames* and *tables*.

### TABLES

Tables were developed for many uses. The information in a *procedure table* was used, for example, to

1. determine branching to a subroutine of frames at certain points in the frame sequence;
2. define information that is specific to a site (such as drug prices and inventory levels);
3. define lists of logical actions that should take place when this procedure is stored in a patient's record;
4. specify lists of synonyms for the procedure to make it accessible on various alphabetic lists;
5. classify the procedure for all uses;
6. point to other data structures that are related to this procedure; and
7. list all frames and tables that access this table.

### FRAMES

The frames were interrelated in a network; each choice on each frame pointed to a frame to be displayed when that choice was selected by a user. The network was a *guidance system* in which every frame was simultaneously medical content and structure for the next finer level of content. The most general frames, *superstructure* frames, served as high-level indices to other frames in the network, establishing the context (such as the current section of the medical record) the user would be working in. As the user progressed through the network, the frames became more specific, containing, for example, drug information or lists of diagnostic procedures, and enabling procedure ordering and reporting (see Fig. 10 for a frame sequence).

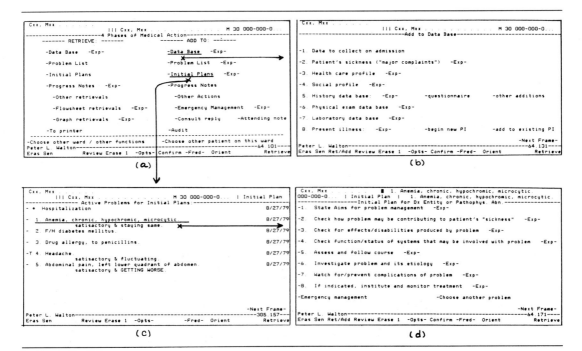

**FIGURE 10**

**Example of guidance frames.** Frame (*a*) is the initial frame that was
presented after a patient was selected from the list of patients whose records
the user was allowed to access. From this frame, all additions to and
retrievals from a single patient record can be performed. (Note the titles
RETRIEVE and ADD TO near the top of the frame.) Selecting *Data Base*
branches to the add to Data Base frame (*b*). Selecting *Initial Plans,* on the
add side of (*a*), brings up a list of the patient's active problems. All patient
care actions are taken in the context of a specific problem. If *Anemia* were
selected, as in the example, the appropriate planning structure frame (*d*) is
presented. The displays contain frame content as well as context information
for the user. The context changes as the user makes selections. The user's
name is displayed in the lower left corner. Once a patient has been selected,
the name is shown in the upper left-hand corner. The selected problem is
on the top line in the center.

## SIZE AND MAINTENANCE OF THE FRAME AND TABLE LIBRARY

By 1979 more than 10,000 tables and 37,000 frames comprised the library. These frames and tables contained information on about 2700
medically defined problems, 640 drugs, 800 clinical laboratory procedures, 200 radiologic procedures, 700 diets, activities, physical thera-
pies and ward procedures, a comprehensive physical examination,
patient history questionnaire, and problem-oriented superstructure.

Content was built in frames and tables from accepted texts and from articles in medical journals that satisfied selection criteria. More than 60 journals were regularly reviewed by medical librarians. Source, date, and builder of each piece of content was recorded in a reference. Auditing of existing content was performed continuously.

The frame and table library was maintained via an interactive frame and table editor (FRED—originally for FRame EDiting only), a syntax checker, a pathfinder, and other tools. The syntax checker reported violations of the rules used to build the frames and tables. The pathfinder found all frames and tables that access a given frame or table. FRED manipulated the content in frames and tables. FRED was table driven: the type and form of each data element manipulated by FRED were specified in a set of tables accessed by FRED. FRED initiated backpointing and indexing among the frames and tables.

The frames and tables referenced each other in order to define display branching or to use an entity. It was necessary to know how and where each paragraph was referenced to effectively manage the frame and table library. All backpointing was performed by a routine scheduled by FRED.

## CAPTURING MEDICAL KNOWLEDGE

The medical content form and structure evolved from emphasis on providing guidance to capturing the information needed to build the guidance capability. From 1976 to 1979 Drs. Peter Walton, Robert Holland, and Stuart Graves worked with the assistance of Larry Wolf, a software specialist, on the means of capturing and codifying the medical knowledge. What evolved was the idea of capturing the basic units of medical knowledge, the *facts* (Walton, Holland, and Wolf 1979). A fact can simply state a relationship among entities or qualify a relationship in greater detail:

> By stating relationships, facts provide a means for structuring medical knowledge. The structure can be viewed as a network of relationships. In qualifying relationships, facts capture the content of medical knowledge.
>
> Facts are the fundamental data base of medical knowledge and are structured in ways that facilitate access to the data base. For example, the fact in . . . [Fig. 11] is a "cause fact." Cause facts state an etiologic relationship between a *predecessor* (iron deficiency) and a *successor* (transferrin saturation) when the predecessor is considered sufficient to explain the successor (i.e. iron deficiency "causes" a transferrin saturation of less than 16 percent). . . . Predecessors and successors are used to define links which the system traverses to access the knowledge pertaining to a particular entity.
>
> The ingredients needed to offer computer-based health-care guidance are now all in place. Knowledge is captured in atomic form in

**FIGURE 11**
Fact in expanded text form.

```
Fact 135.00303
    Dx: iron deficiency
    Mf: transferrin saturation
    Value: below 16 % (average 7%)
    P[Mf|Dx] = 1

    Fact audited.
    Pr (coded): iron deficiency
    Su (coded): transferrin saturation

    Flags: p[Su|Pr] = 1;

    Refs:
       Clinical Hematology
       Wintrobe MM, et al., Eds.
       Philadelphia: Lea and Febiger, 7th ed., 1974
          Ch 16: Anemias characterized by deficient hemoglobin synthesis and
                 impaired iron metabolism
          pp 621-634
    Process: 134.1 Dependence fact from authority source
    By: RR Holland MD-SP    1/17/79
    Documentation audited.

    Refs:
       Clinical Hematology
       Wintrobe MM, et al., Eds.
       Philadelphia: Lea and Febiger, 7th ed., 1974
          Ch 17: Iron deficiency and iron-deficiency anemia
          pp 635-670
             Laboratory findings
             pp 656-660
    Process: 134.1 Dependence fact from authority source
    By: GW Gilroy RPh-SP    1/22/79
    Documentation not audited.
```

the facts. Facts are organized using a directed network. The network facilitates understanding and use of the facts to offer guidance. Building of this guidance capability is done in an explicit and rigorous fashion. Each step in the process of transforming knowledge to facts to guidance is documented and connected in electronic form to make both guidance and knowledge maintainable and adaptable.

## The Master Library and Instances

The library system incorporated ideas outlined in the Conway report on the National Library of Displays. There were three classes of information in the generic library:

1. generic information that applied to all instances;

2. local information that applied to only one instance; and

3. protocol information that may apply to several instances, but is designed and built with a specific set of values in mind.

Generic and protocol information were integrated into PROMIS by the library system. The generic library was responsible for maintaining all generic information and some protocol information. All other information was to be maintained locally by the instance that built and used it. All instance-specific data was identified in the PROMIS frame and table library, and procedures were implemented to allow the updating of only the generic information.

## PROMIS Returns to a General Medical Ward

In December of 1976, the newly implemented PROMIS became operational on a 20 bed general medical ward (Brown III) in the Medical Center Hospital. The Brown III site was linked to the pharmacy, clinical laboratory, and the radiology departments.

Functionally the new PROMIS was a major improvement over the CDC system. It was easier to use and to maintain (Fig. 12). It had expanded functions and was more responsive and reliable (Fig. 13). Until September of 1981 when PROMIS Laboratory left the University of Vermont and became PROMIS Information Systems, Inc., there was a steady stream of improvements and new functions. Some of the features of the 1980 PROMIS system are described in the following material.

### ADDITION OF ADMINISTRATIVE FUNCTIONS

The administrative functions that are the basis for most computer based medical systems were not initially integrated into PROMIS. LeMay, along with other members of the PROMIS computer group, rewrote an existing administrative package to operate in conjunction with the electronic patient record. The resulting administrative system included patient billing, accounts receivable, accounts payable, and general ledger functions. All manual input was entered at a terminal. Admission, discharge, transfer, and charge data were generated automatically as a byproduct of use of the electronic record. Input to the general ledger from patient billing, accounts receivable, and accounts payable was generated automatically.

**FIGURE 12**
Larry Weed using the
Megadata Terminal.

**FIGURE 13**
Megdata Screen with
inverse video
function pads.

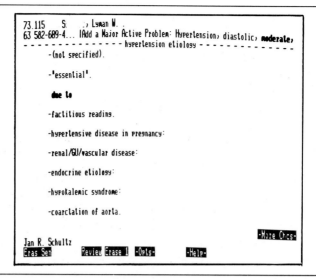

## NETWORKING WAS MADE ROUTINE

A two-node configuration was used routinely for PROMIS and system development; additionally, heavy simulated loads were applied to three nodes in order to validate the effects of contention for the basic network resources. Experiments were performed placing all terminals on one node and all medical records on another; this forced internode activity for each storage and retrieval operation. Under these conditions the user perceived little if any performance degradation due to the network.

## POPULATION STUDIES WERE ADDED TO PROMIS

The ability to interrogate the electronic patient records as a group for patient care or clinical research was provided by the population study system, developed by Stephen Reynolds. Population studies attempted to answer questions a clinical investigator might ask of the patient records. The population study system enabled three types of interrogation:

1. Type of question:    Who has a specified combination of attributes?

     Form of result:      List of patients

     Example:      Who is receiving gentamicin?

2. Type of question:    What are the results of a set of specified procedures?

| | |
|---|---|
| Form of result: | Array of values |
| Example: | What is the standard deviation of BUN in patient group Y? |
| 3. Type of question: | What problems appear on the problem lists of patients in a specified group? |
| Form of result: | Ordered list of problems |
| Example: | What is the incidence of all problems identified in patients in group Z who have diabetes? |

Peer Standards Review Organization personnel at the hospital performed audits using the population study tools, the results of which were submitted to the hospital administration and medical board. Questions were similar to:

IF (date of serum creatinine) MINUS (date of digoxin) GREATER THAN 2 OR (date of digoxin) MINUS (date of serum creatinine) GREATER THAN 2
  THEN "Serum creatinine not ordered in time"

The result of this query would be a list of patients for whom the assessment "Serum creatinine not ordered in time" (as defined by the Boolean expression) was correct.

The processing and display of a patient set based upon the simple presence or absence of attributes was done while the user waited—usually within ten seconds or less; a patient set based on attributes qualified by time or other variables took longer depending on the complexity of the question and the number of patient records processed.

It was also possible to pass data from the electronic patient records to the MINITAB II statistical package (developed by the National Bureau of Standards and modified at the University of Pennsylvania) for statistical analysis. MINITAB was implemented with the commands as choices on frames, allowing easy, rapid, controlled, and structured access.

All *patient attributes* (see, for example, Fig. 14) within the electronic records that were used for population studies had to be coded. Complex relationships within one *procedure report* could not be captured. A coding mechanism was needed to parallel the text string seen by the user. The development of the code string, a tree-structured, frame-driven encoding mechanism, would have to wait for the next application design iteration.

### PATIENT LIFETIME RECORDS WERE DEVELOPED

The structure of the electronic record was expanded to allow multiple inpatient admissions and outpatient visits within one record. The *encounter* was the structuring mechanism for the patient's *lifetime record*.

**FIGURE 14**
Example of vital
signs flowsheet for a
single day.

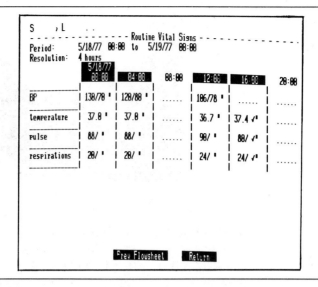

Each inpatient admission or outpatient visit was a new encounter. The user could specify any encounter (or all encounters) from which to retrieve patient data.

## COMMUNICATIONS SYSTEM USE

The MEGADATA touch-screen terminals, as well as printers and other peripherals, were connected to the CPU with a high speed communications bus. The data communications lines could be extended up to 20 miles (32 km) by cable and further extended with microwave links. A very high frequency (VHF) 2-way coaxial bus was employed to provide many inexpensive interconnect ports. Full-duplex modems operated at 307,200 bits per second. Programmable controllers managed peripheral devices and operated at the remote interconnect ports. The line control protocol was a simple polling protocol. Each remote device was assigned a unique poll address. Because of the line protocol and the nature of the bus, users were free to move terminals and other peripherals from one location to another and continue without any access (sign-on) requirements (Wanner 1978). The bus was extended with a microwave link to the Grand Isle Medical Clinic (Fig. 15) 17 miles from the Hospital.

## ALTERNATE POINTING DEVICE INVESTIGATED

From the early 1970s on, we received questions about the utility of the touch-screen as our primary input device. We decided to investigate other commercially available pointing devices as part of the new

**FIGURE 15**
**The Grand Isle**
**Clinic.** Find the
microwave dish?

PROMIS technology. Our investigations revealed that the only other commercially available pointing device was the light-pen. We purchased an 8080 based terminal from Zentec, Inc. It accepted a light-pen as a peripheral. Jim Wanner developed a special high-speed interface board to allow the terminal to connect to the CATV bus. He programmed the Zentec terminal for the CATV bus protocol and for emulation of a Megadata terminal with a light-pen instead of a touch-screen. The light-pen was cylindrically shaped with a button on the side. A cursor would appear on the CRT screen if the light-pen were pointed at a selection. When the button was pressed, the selection was made.

The Zentec light-pen terminal was available in PROMIS Laboratory from April of 1976 until September of 1981. It was used by most computer and medical personnel associated with PROMIS Laboratory. On a number of occasions we presented it to our medical users outside of PROMIS Laboratory. There was a general consensus that it was not as usable as the touch-screen. There were a number of problems with its use: First, the light-pen had to be picked up, thus interfering with either typing or writing. Second, when the button on the side of the light-pen was pressed to make a selection, often the pen's aim was disturbed, resulting in wrong selections.

## Conclusion

### HUMAN INTERFACE

The combination of a response rate of less than 0.25 of a second and the large database of frames allows users to navigate through the network of frames very rapidly, accomplishing their tasks without using the keyboard. The interaction rate is very high since a single selection results in the presentation of a full screen of new text. A complete thought can be communicated in a single touch. The database available to a user is a combination of electronic records generated from past selections and of frame and table knowledge. The user can operate from a universe larger than what can be remembered and has only to recognize the correct selection (and not recall it). These features provide for a unique and very effective human-computer interface.

The building of the database of frame and table knowledge has been time-consuming and intellectually challenging. The PROMIS frame and table library took over 200 person-years of effort to build. This type of interface can be successful if the cost of developing and maintaining the knowledge base used by the interface can be spread across many users.

In order for such an interface to work, both an extensive knowledge base and a different relationship to the computing resources it uses are required. For PROMIS, the interface is the computation and not a means to get to a computation. As computing power gets less expensive, this interface becomes more cost effective.

Robertson, Newell, and Ramakrishna discuss the PROMIS/ZOG type of interface and claim that this

> type of interface is a preferred mode of man-machine interaction, even over the use of natural language dialogue with the computer in the role of intelligent agent.
>
> There are two polar views about how to structure man-machine interaction. One is the computer as tool. . . . Control remains with the user. The other view is the computer as intelligent assistant. In this view one wishes to make the computer more intelligent and communication with it more natural. . . . Precisely what an intelligent assistant is supposed to provide is freedom (of the user) from the effort of understanding. Put one other way, delegation requires an act of faith.
>
> ZOG is an evolution in the tool direction. It seeks to produce a transparent device which, in itself, has no intelligence at all, but is immensely responsive to the user. It seeks to do this in the arena where we normally expect to use natural language, namely, dealing with large bodies of knowledge. Indeed ZOG uses natural language for its output (though arranged in a sort of spatial dialogue), for the user has good devices for assimilating it. However, its own internal structure, which governs what it says and when it chooses to say it, is completely open to examination by the user. (Robertson 1977)

## APPLICATION DEVELOPMENT

In October of 1981, PROMIS Laboratory left the University of Vermont and formed PROMIS Information Systems, Inc. We realized that the potential for the PROMIS technology was broader than medicine alone and that work was needed on the application development software. From the very beginning of our development in 1967, the Human Interface Program interpreted the frame in the process of bringing up the next display. It was *table-driven* since the frame (the programs table) defined how the program was to operate. Other parts of the system were not table-driven. The frame editor has been table-driven since 1978, but the storage and retrieval programs had embedded within them the logic of the problem-oriented medical record and could handle only one type of record structure. We have rewritten the application subsystems so that they are all table-driven. This allows the development of systems as large and complex as the PROMIS medical application without writing PPL programs.

Application development without writing programs makes programmers more efficient by a factor of between 10 and 100. What we have developed is not a programmer-less system, but a set of tools that makes programmers more effective. The tool kit uses the concepts of programming to accomplish the tasks of programming, but the writing of procedural programs is not required.

## CONTROL OF INFORMATION

The PROMIS development coupled medical knowledge with electronic medical records and increased access to both for all personnel who used PROMIS. The medical knowledge captured in frames and tables was available to all users. Since PROMIS was the medium through which users performed many medical tasks, the presence of the medical knowledge at the time they performed their work facilitated excellent performance without the reliance on an encyclopedic memory.

The electronic medical records were available to all properly identified health care personnel. The boundaries of space, availability of only a single copy, and legibility were gone. Users could access a patient's medical record from anywhere a terminal was located. Once accessed, the information was legible and presented in either narrative or flowsheet form.

Electronic medical knowledge and electronic records moved the control of the information from the physicians to other users. In other words, PROMIS shifted the source of power away from physicians. Examples of the shift for nursing and supporting areas (pharmacy, radiology) follow.

The role of nursing was enhanced by PROMIS in a number of ways: First, all orders written for a patient were immediately available. Second, all information added to a patient's record could be reviewed at any terminal; there was no queuing behind the single copy of the paper record. Third, medical knowledge was available at the terminal, and not as in the past only in text books or the user's memory. Fourth, the patient-administered questionnaire resulted in a complete medical history, which nursing used to help define the patient's problems list.

At times this resulted in physicians demanding of the nurses: ''Why did you give my patient all those problems?''

The role of the supporting areas (e.g., pharmacy and radiology) was enhanced. Each supporting area had access to the patient's record along with the requisition for service. The order could be checked for appropriateness using the full record to provide a context. New reports could be compared with older ones to see if significant changes had occurred. Results reported using the terminal would be immediately available on the ward. For narrative reports, there was no time lag because there is no need to type the dictated report.

## THE FUTURE

When we began our work, a touch-screen terminal operating over telephone lines at 2400 bits per second cost over $20,000. Today, a similar terminal can be purchased off-the-shelf for under $3000. The personal computer I'm using to write this paper has more central memory in it than the CDC 1700 system used for the initial development and the personal computer's central memory cost 200 times less. The technology is available now to make the type of interface and systems described in this paper cost effective and widely available.

The PROMIS system has been installed at the Baycrest Geriatric Hospital in Toronto, Canada. It is still the most advanced medical information system in existence and the only one to manage a fully electronic medical record. It has yet to be used as the information system for a total hospital, but its time is coming.

## ACKNOWLEDGMENTS

This paper represents the efforts of many individuals in medicine and in computer science, both within and outside the past PROMIS Laboratory. I would like to acknowledge the group from PROMIS Laboratory who have stayed together to keep these ideas alive. This work was funded primarily by the National Center for Health Services Research, Department of Health, Education, and Welfare. I would like to thank Adele Goldberg, Tony Stern, and Sue Burton for suggested additions and editorial comments.

## REFERENCES

(Hertzberg, Schultz, Wanner 1980) Hertzberg, R. Y., Schultz, J. R., Wanner, J. F., ''The PROMIS Network,'' *Computer Networks* 4, 1980, pp. 215–228.

(Parnas 1972) Parnas, D. L., ''A Technique for Software Module Specification with Examples,'' *Comm. ACM* 15(5):330–336 (May 1972).

PROMIS Laboratory Staff, ''The Representation of Medical Knowledge,'' *Proc. Second Annual Symposium on Computer Applications in Medical Care*, Washington, D.C., November 1978, pp. 368–400.

(Robertson 1977) Robertson, G., Newell, A., Ramakrishna, K., *ZOG: A Man-Machine Communication Philosophy,* Department of Computer Science, Carnegie-Mellon University, August 4, 1977.

(Schultz, Davis 1979) Schultz, J. R., Davis, L., "The Technology of PROMIS," *Proc. of IEEE 67:9,* September 1979.

(Schutlz, Cantrill, Morgan 1971) Schultz, J. R., Cantrill, S. V., Morgan, K. G., "An Initial Operational Problem Oriented Medical Record System—For Storage, Manipulation and Retrieval of Medical Data," *AFIPS—Conference Proceedings,* Vol. 38, 1971.

(Walton, Holland, Wolf 1979) Walton, P. L., Holland, R. R., Wolf, L. L., "Medical Guidance and PROMIS," *IEEE, Computer,* November 1979, pp. 19–27.

(Wanner 1978) Wanner, J. F., "Wideband Communication System Improves Response Time," *Computer Design,* December 1978, pp. 85–91.

(Weed 1964) Weed, Lawrence L., M.D., "Medical Records, Patient Care and Medical Education," *Ir. J. Med. Sc.,* June 1964, pp. 271–282.

(Weed 1968) Weed, Lawrence L., M.D., "Medical Records that Guide and Teach," *New England Journal of Medicine,* 278:593–600, 652–657 (March 14, 21), 1968.

(Weed 1969) Weed, Lawrence L., M.D., *Medical Records, Medical Education and Patient Care,* Case Western Reserve Press, Cleveland, Ohio, 1969.

(Weed 1972) Weed, Lawrence L., M.D., *Problem Oriented System,* chap. 29, "Background Paper for Concept of National Library Displays," J. Willis Hurst and H. Kenneth Walker (eds), Medcom Press, 1972.

# Participants Discussion

*Allen Newell*

One of the things we got the feeling for, both in Jan's talk and in the one that House gave about Hewlett-Packard, is the notion of quite separate developments. But I wanted to at least put on record some rather interesting connections in which, in the technological society we deal with, things get tied together. A key person here is Bruce Waxman, who was a man associated with the Life Sciences effort at the NIH. He used to come around and bug me about how they've got this big AI program that's got 32,000 frames on it up in Vermont some place, and how I really ought to go and see it because they've sort of done what you guys are trying to do. I ignored him for the first couple of years. Finally, I went up there and saw the PROMIS system and, with a colleague of mine, George Robertson, ended up on a technical committee to review some of their work for a couple of years. We ended up building a system called ZOG at Carnegie-Mellon, which was a direct follow-on and copy of PROMIS. So, even in a conference like this, there are connections that seem really quite separate. In fact, the influences have moved back and forth.

*John Sechrest*

I'm curious about how you see the PARC user interface affecting the interface that you have for PROMIS. I'm also curious how you got an overview of a patient's data; not how you looked down a road, but how you looked at the road map from an overview point of view.

*Schultz*

The interface we used has been around a lot longer than the PARC interfaces. Ours is a talking narrative interface; pictures and graphics could certainly change it. I would imagine that over time the two approaches will merge and we'll have a slightly different sort of interface.

As to the second question, there are many different ways you can look at a patient's record. There is no single overview. Depending upon who you are and what your interests are, you want to basically look at it in different ways; our tool facilitated multiple views. There are problem-oriented records, and source-oriented records; you could retrieve all of the data, all the laboratory data, all the radiology data. There are time-oriented records; you could just retrieve the data chronologically; you could retrieve it by problem. Basically, you could take any view you wanted of this data, unlike most other record systems. We had placed eight different indexes on a single record, and you could traverse those indexes in different ways.

*J. C. R. Licklider*    I was on one occasion one of the visitors, and I will attest that the taxi driver did indeed know how to get there. I was very much impressed with the rapid touch-screen action. I believe it was true that most of the people in the hospital who used the system liked it very much. They all gave it very high marks. On the other hand, I noticed that in the marketplace such screens don't seem to be going very well. My impression is that Hewlett-Packard ceased to emphasize touch-screens as a selling point. Maybe that's wrong, but what's your perception of the touch-screen as a contender in this mouse/light-pen sweepstakes?

*Schultz*    You can't look at just the touch-screen. Our company is now supporting all pointing devices. If someone wants to use a mouse, they can use a mouse. As long as the system is responsive, you don't need a "gorilla arm" to use a touch-screen; a light touch will do. My right arm is the same size as my left one, and I've been using a touch-screen for over 20 years. You can't just say, touch-screens, light-pens, mice—you have to say, "What is the whole system?" I think ultimately people are going to want to use a touch-screen more than a mouse; what's more natural than pointing? The parent has to tell the kid, "don't point." Well, we all want to point.

I used to go up on the wards. We had probably five thousand patients take their own history using the system. We would just sit them down and say, "Read what's on the screen and point at the thing, you know, just touch the yes or no." The patients would do it. And after a while, I would ask, "Well, do you realize what you were doing? In fact, it's branching when you touched the screen." And they said, "No, I'm just answering the questions." That's the kind of interface that you want. The computer is completely transparent, and what becomes important is the knowledge behind it.

# USER TECHNOLOGY:
# FROM POINTING TO PONDERING

## Stu Card and Tom Moran
## Introduction by Allen Newell

**Allen Newell**

**W**e've arrived at the last session of this conference. It's going to be my pleasure to introduce Stu Card and Tom Moran. You know there are many ingredients to the workstation; we've been talking about them. Several people here have mentioned the different dimensions: the process and memory, graphics, networking—lots of different dimensions, all of which add up to this notion of a personal workstation. The people that pushed these areas were fundamentally technologists, and the story we've got here is really the story of a technology development. Sometimes, as in the work that Jan Schultz described, but also the work of Wes Clark and even the Culler-Fried effort, an area of application is very strong. A particular medical concern or a neurosciences problem or a physicist's need—there's an area of application that's driving the development, as well as just the technology.

However, there is also a person in the interface, as you are all aware. As one looks at the workstation area, the issue of the psychology of the human and what we know about the psychology has not played a very large role. It's played a fairly muted role. Now, a muted role doesn't mean no role at all. In fact, you can see in the things we've had in this conference, the ways in which it has been included. For instance, you can look at Doug Engelbart's work. Doug has presented to us a notion that focused on what the human was doing. The key element for me in that is that the limiting channel is really the motor

489

channel. As Doug does so effectively, and I can't do so, if we could just get it all going all at the same time, then we'd really allow the human to really communicate with the machine. There is a model of the human involved there. You can see it in some of Alan Kay's work. You can also see it in Licklider. I don't know if most of you know, but Licklider is a psychologist; he cut his teeth on psychoacoustics. In Lick's talk, he kept dropping back to little pieces of data about human behavior in the situations that come out of the human factors world that he knew about, and that most of you probably don't know about. One of the things I got out of that part of his talk was that very often he was disappointed in terms of what actually resulted. It didn't quite turn out the way he thought it was going to, and he couldn't understand when everyone would realize what the data said. That's what you get for being a psychologist in this field, I guess.

Although the nature of the human in the interface and what we know about it, has certainly not been the central driver in the development of the workstation, telling some of the parts of that story is also part of the history. And this brings in the part of the PARC story that relates to Tom and Stu. I thought that I might just take one half second, since I was involved in that a little bit, to set the context. I will tell the very early part of that historical story, because I was introduced to PARC very early. It was actually in December of 1970 when I went to Palo Alto to talk to George Pake and Bob Taylor. I spent three months here—not at PARC, but sitting up at Stinson Beach on a mini-sabbatical.

Out of that mini-sabbatical came the notion, just in talking during those three months, that maybe one could start down a path to learn about how humans actually interacted with these machines, and to build some serious models. We talked about it as the time being right to apply cognitive psychology to this sort of an applied field, but it still required a lot of research. Then, we'll start down the path and do more research to make an applied cognitive psychology. Now one of the things that hasn't been strong at this conference, is that there is a long history of work in human factors. It has not been much in evidence, except for Lick's comments, in this whole development that we've been seeing. But the idea took root at that time, between PARC and myself, of doing something halfway between cognitive psychology and human factors. However, nothing happened for a couple of years, until two students showed up, all of a sudden. Of course, graduate students never just show up all of a sudden, they hang around for years. Nonetheless, two graduate students at CMU matured at the same time: Stu Card in psychology, actually in an interdisciplinary program between psychology and computers, called the the Systems and Communications Sciences Program; and Tom Moran, in computer science. Both of those students had an interest in artificial intelligence, cognitive psychology, and the nature of human interaction.

The opportunity provided by Stu and Tom caused a negotiation with Xerox PARC about whether we ought to go down that path. One of the beautiful things about the PARC environment at that time was that, although cognitive psychology clearly wasn't in the main line of their path, the organization was very flexible. They simply included the new topic in. We set up an agreement that we would do the research to set up what we called an *applied information processing psychology* that would focus on the nature of human behavior and the computer. Then one of those peculiar things happened where one does the right thing for the wrong reason. It was in response to some minor internal matters, which make no difference now. We planned to study how humans program; and we would have done that if we'd located in the Computer Systems Laboratory. Instead we moved into the Systems Sciences Laboratory, because that's where the POLOS system was being developed. (POLOS was an experimental office system underway at PARC.) As a result, we shifted our attention to how people interacted with editing systems. That set the scientific problem that we then focused on for the next several years.

Stuart Card has an A.B. in Physics from Oberlin College and a Ph.D. in Psychology from Carnegie-Mellon University (1978). Since 1974 he has been a member of the research staff at the Xerox Palo Alto Research Center, where he is now a Principal Scientist and Manager of the User Interface Research Group. He is an affiliate associate professor in the Department of Psychology, Stanford University. With Thomas Moran and Allen Newell, he is co-author of the book, *The Psychology of Human-Computer Interaction*.

Tom Moran is a Principal Scientist and Director of the Rank Xerox Cambridge EuroPARC laboratory for the study of human-computer interaction in Cambridge, England. Tom is educated as an architect, with a bachelor's in architecture from the University of Detroit (1965) and graduate studies in Architectural Science and Operations Research, Cornell University, from 1965–1967. His Ph.D. is in Computer Science from Carnegie-Mellon University, 1973.

Interested in general problems of human-computer interaction, Tom is a Research Affiliate of the Cognitive Science Program at Carnegie-Mellon, and an affiliate associate professor in the Department of Psychology, Stanford University. He is founder and has been editor of the journal *Human-Computer Interaction* since 1982.

Tom has worked with Allen Newell and Stu Card for several years on basic psychological research formulating cognitive models and theories of computer user performance. This work culminated in the book, *The Psychology of Human-Computer Interaction*, which provides the first major scientific framework in this field.

# User Technology: From Pointing to Pondering

*Stuart K. Card and Thomas P. Moran*
Xerox Palo Alto Research Center

From its beginning, the technology of personal workstations has been driven by visions of a future in which people would work in intimate partnership with computer systems on significant intellectual tasks. These visions have been expressed in various forms: Memex (Bush, 1945), Man-Machine Symbiosis (Licklider, 1960), NLS (Engelbart, 1963), Dynabook (Kay, 1977), and others.

The tight coupling between human and computer required by these visions necessitated advances in the ways humans and computers interact. These advances have slowly begun to accumulate into what might be called a *user technology*. This user technology includes hardware and software techniques for building effective user interfaces: bitmapped displays, menus, pointing devices, "modeless" command languages, animation, and interface metaphors. But it must also include a technical understanding of the user himself and of the nature of human-computer interaction. This latter part, the scientific base of user technology, is necessary in order to understand why interaction techniques are (or are not) successful, to help us invent new techniques, and to pave the way for machines that aid humans in performing significant intellectual tasks.

In this paper, we trace some of the history of our understanding of users and their interaction with workstations—the personal part of personal workstations. In keeping with the spirit of other papers at this conference, we have centered this review around our own experiences, perspectives, and work and have not attempted a complete history of the field. In concentrating on our own work, we do not wish to minimize the importance of others' work; we simply want to tell our own story. Our focus is on what we have learned about users in our years of studying them and how we see our findings relating to the original visions of the personal workstation.

## The Vision of an Applied User Psychology

The opportunity to tackle a science of the user brought us to PARC in 1974 (collaborating with Allen Newell, as consultant). As other PARC researchers were beginning to pursue the vision of highly graphic, interactive, network-based personal workstations, we were following a

493

vision of our own. The idea was to draw concepts from cognitive psychology and artificial intelligence to create an applied cognitive science of the user. We called our project the Applied Information-processing Psychology Project (AIP). A 1971 memo by Allen Newell proposing this project to PARC stated the basic argument this way:

(1) There is emerging a psychology of cognitive behavior that will permit calculation of behavior in new situations and with new humans. . . .
(2) Several of the tasks that are central to the activities of computing—programming, debugging, etc.—are tasks that appear to be within the early scope of this emerging theory.
(3) Computer science in general is extremely one-sided (for understandable reasons) in the treatment of its phenomena: almost no effort goes into understanding the nature of the human user. . . .
(4) There is a substantial payoff (in dollars) to be had by really designing systems with detailed understanding of the way the human must process the information attendant thereto.

In 1974, we were in the position of having to create a new field. Psychological theories and methodologies held the promise of being able to represent and manage complex cognitive tasks, but the only body of research pertaining to human-computer interaction was in the field of human factors, where studies were largely empirical and evaluative, concentrating mostly on sensory-motor questions like the best shape for a switch. Human-computer interaction, involving two active agents each capable of initiating an exchange of information, inherently involves human cognitive processing. Our vision was to create a science of the user rooted in cognitive theory. But we also wanted the science to be practical, providing the system designer with the conceptual tools to think about the key characteristics of the user and the calculational tools to take account of the user's behavior.

To simplify a rather complex history for the purposes of this paper, we will narrate just a few strands of what unfolded. Each strand is organized around a particular aspect of the interface between the user, the system, and the task. The strands are organized into a sequence of ever-broader interfaces, from the physical interaction of the user with devices and displays to the symbiotic interaction of the user with the system while grappling with complex intellectual tasks—that is, from pointing to pondering:

1. *The physical interface:* The user interacts with a system by means of physical input devices, such as a keyboard and a mouse, and output devices, such as a high-quality graphical display.

2. *The cognitive interface:* The user has certain characteristics as an information processor, such as a limited working memory, that together with the goals he is trying to achieve determine his behavior.

3. *The conceptual interface:* The computer system is also a complex information processing mechanism, and the user needs to have some kind of mental model of it in order to effectively interact with it.

4. *The task interface:* Systems are designed to help their users do tasks, not only small, routine tasks, but also larger, difficult intellectual tasks that are the object of the grand visions of personal workstations.

The story within each strand of our work is chronological; but the first three strands, representing our previous work, overlap in time. The last strand represents our current work.

## The Physical Interface: Pointing

Bill English, who had among other things engineered and built the mouse for Doug Engelbart (English, Engelbart, and Berman, 1967), was one of the people who migrated to PARC when it was founded. We worked for English when we first came to PARC. Engelbart and English had always considered the mouse to be an interim device, and English wanted to see if it was possible to invent other devices that would improve on its speed. In particular, he was interested in whether one could put a key on the keyboard that would sense force and direction without requiring the user to remove his hands from the keyboard. He had a number of devices built, and we helped design an experiment to test them. The results (Fig. 1) showed that none of the devices tested improved on the mouse either for speed or for error rate (Card, English, and Burr, 1978).

| Device | Trials N | Movement Time for Non-Error Trials | | | | | | Error Rate | |
|---|---|---|---|---|---|---|---|---|---|
| | | Homing Time | | Positioning Time | | Total Time | | | |
| | | M (sec) | SD (sec) | M (sec) | SD (sec) | M (sec) | SD (sec) | M | SD |
| Mouse | 1973 | .36 | .13 | 1.29 | .42 | 1.66 | .48 | 5% | 22% |
| Joystick | 1869 | .26 | .11 | 1.57 | .54 | 1.83 | .57 | 11% | 31% |
| Step Keys | 1813 | .21 | .30 | 2.31 | 1.52 | 2.51 | 1.64 | 13% | 33% |
| Text Keys | 1877 | .32 | .61 | 1.95 | 1.30 | 2.26 | 1.70 | 9% | 28% |

**FIGURE 1**
**Overall pointing times for all devices.** Homing time is the time to move the hand from the keyboard to the device, positioning time is the time to move the cursor to the target. Times are based on a standardized set of distances and target widths. Averages are computed on the basis of four users × 600 trials/users. Reprinted from Card, Moran, and Newell (1983, Fig. 7.4) with the permission of Lawrence Erlbaum Associates, Inc.

This was a typical human factors experiment: We compared a set of systems to determine which one performed best. But this direct empirical comparison between devices was just the sort of methodology of human factors testing that we wanted to improve: We wanted to understand the reasons why the results came out the way they did. We therefore made mathematical models of each device and tested them against the data until we found models that fit. The model for the mouse was particularly instructive. The mouse was best modeled by a version of Fitts's law:

*Movement Time = Constant* + .1 $\log_2(D/S$ + .05)sec,

where $D$ is the distance the hand moves to the target and $S$ is the target width (see Fig. 2). The significance of this result is that this is the same law that describes movement time for the hand alone, with about the same constant of proportionality. The limiting factor in moving the mouse, therefore, is not in the mouse, but in the eye-hand coordinate system itself. That, in turn, means the mouse is nearly optimal, at least with respect to the set of muscles used. Therefore, designing a device that is faster than the mouse would be difficult.

Here was a prototypical example of the kind of theory we wanted

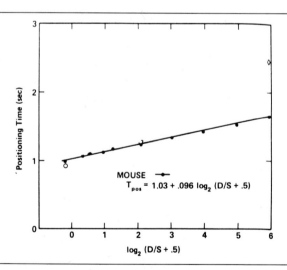

**FIGURE 2**
**Positioning time for the mouse as a function of Fitts's Index of Difficulty.**
The fit of positioning time data to the straight line in the figure shows that time for the mouse is governed by Fitts's law (is proportional to Fitts's Index of Difficulty). The constant of proportionality, 0.096 sec/bit (= 10.4 bits/sec), is approximately the same value as for pointing with the hand alone.
Reprinted from Card, Moran, and Newell (1983, Fig. 7.8) with the permission of Lawrence Erlbaum Associates, Inc.

to build—a model precise enough to enable designers to perform back-of-the-envelope calculations, a model that identified key constraints in the design space for pointing devices. With this model we could be sure that the data giving comparisons among devices would probably generalize to new situations, because we knew the main factors that governed the results. Furthermore, the model provided guidance for interface designers: make distant buttons large, for example. These studies were heavily used in the debate within Xerox that led to the decision to depart from tradition by including a mouse with the new Star product.

## The Cognitive Interface: Cognitive Skill

### THE MODEL HUMAN PROCESSOR

An interesting result of the mouse study was the way an evaluation of pointing devices led to a consideration of human information processing characteristics. This experience pointed to the need for an engineering model of users that would summarize such characteristics. We knew of many phenomena scattered in the literature of psychology, such as Fitts's law, that would be helpful for system design.

To someone who is not a specialist, such as a designer, this literature appears disorganized and contradictory. Psychologists love to split hairs and find small contradictions in published models. The robust but approximate generalizations that might be made to work for engineering tend to get trampled in the debates. Although we had the notion of such a model from about 1974, it wasn't until 1982, when we were nearing the completion of our book, that we were able to formulate it. The model, called the *Model Human Processor,* was inspired by the processors, memories, and switches (PMS) notation of Bell and Newell (1971) for describing the architecture of computing systems. It was a simplified architecture of the user, described in terms of three processors, four memories, 19 parameters of these, and 10 principles of operation (Fig. 3).

As an example of the sort of calculation that can be done with the Model Human Processor, consider the case where a programmer is programming a video game version of billiards. He needs to know how long he has after the collision of two balls to compute the balls new trajectory before the illusion of causality breaks down. The Model Human Processor tells us that every event that occurs within 100 msec will be perceived as a single event, so a rough estimate is 100 msec. But it also recognizes that second-order phenomena can change this number, so it also supplies a range of uncertainty for this number (in this instance, 50 to 200 msec).

In this case, we can say that if the programmer can make the balls

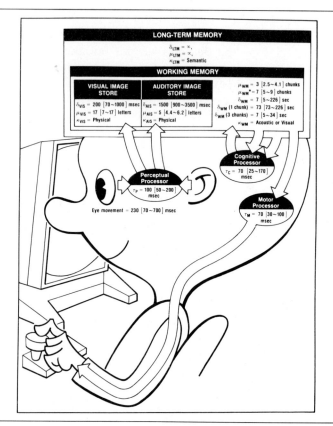

**FIGURE 3**
**The Model Human Processor memories and processors.** Depicted
schematically in the figure are the memories, processors, and constants used
for making simple computations. The basic architecture of the model can be
summarized thus: Sensory information flows into working memory through
the perceptual processor. Working memory consists of activated chunks in
long-term memory. The basic principle of operation of the Model Human
Processor is the recognize-act cycle of the cognitive processor: On each cycle
of the cognitive processor, the contents of working memory initiate actions
associatively linked to them in long-term memory; these actions in turn
modify the contents of working memory. The motor processor is set in
motion through activation of chunks in working memory.

Predictions are made using time constants from the figure and a set of
associated principles of operation: (P0) The recognize-act cycle of the
cognitive processor; (P1) the variable perceptual processor rate principle;
(P2) the encoding specificity principle; (P3) the discrimination-principle; (P4)
the variable cognitive processor rate principle; (P5) Fitts's law; (P6) the
power law of practice; (P7) the psychological uncertainty principle; (P8) the
rationality principle; and (P9) the problem space principle. Reprinted from
Card, Moran, and Newell (1983, Fig. 2.1.) with the permission of Lawrence
Erlbaum Associates, Inc.

move within the 50 msec lower bound for this parameter, then it is pretty certain that users will perceive the collision as the cause of the balls change in direction, regardless of secondary effects such as brightness or contrast ratio of the screen.

The Model Human Processor can be used to compute predictions about human performance: how fast people can read, how fast they can scribble, the effect of different abbreviation schemes on memory error, and so on. Derivations based on the Model Human Processor were used to set the maximum velocity of the mouse on the workstation for the Xerox Star.

### TEXT EDITING AND COGNITIVE SKILL

The Model Human Processor also contains, as one of its principles of operation, Herbert Simon's bounded rationality principle. Our version of this principle may be stated:

> A person acts so as to attain his goals through rational action, given the structure of the task, his inputs of information, and bounded by limitations upon his knowledge and processing ability. (Card, Moran, and Newell, 1983)

That is, in order to predict a person's behavior, one needs to analyze the task he is trying to do, because the person will simply do what is rational to accomplish the task, constrained by limitations in his knowledge and ability to process information. Studies of how people solve problems had shown (Newell and Simon, 1972) that their behavior could be modeled as a search through a space of states of the problem, a *problem space*. We expected that in studies of human-computer interaction we would find users searching through problem spaces to accomplish goals, trying various solutions, backing off and taking other tacks when they ran into trouble.

Two early decisions we made led us to results that were contrary to our expectations. Although we had come to PARC initially with the intention of studying computer programming, we decided once we arrived that there were strategic advantages to studying text editing. A second, tactical, decision was to work with expert subjects rather than novices, in order to have more stable behavior to analyze. Further, to make sure that all our subjects had the same goals in mind, we presented them with a fairly explicit task—the "manuscript editing task"—which required them to work from a marked-up manuscript, making the changes explicitly indicated.

When we analyzed videotaped protocols of our subjects doing this task, we were surprised to find little of the search behavior of problem solving that we had expected. Subjects simply looked at the tasks and did them. The tasks were not problematic. The subjects had done similar tasks many times before, and had built up a large repertoire of methods that could be applied to the tasks. This wasn't problem solving; we came to call it *cognitive skill* and set out to build models to characterize and predict this mode of behavior.

We applied our theories of human information processing to the kind of specific skills necessary for the text-editing task. The result was a class of models in which the user's cognitive structure consists of four components: (1) a set of familiar goals that the user would recognize when faced with a specific task; (2) a set of primitive operators (actions) that the user was skilled at performing and could deploy whenever necessary; (3) a set of methods, consisting of ''compiled'' sequences of subgoals and operators, that the user could use to attain his goals; and (4) a set of selection rules that enable the user to choose among competing methods for goals. We call a model specified by these components a *GOMS model* (Fig. 4 shows an example of one).

**FIGURE 4**
**GOMS Model K2 for the text editor POET.** This model has a grain of about 0.5 sec/operator. The user is using a line-oriented editor to make changes to a computer file previously marked on a paper manuscript. Reprinted from Card, Moran, and Newell (1983, Fig. 5.12) with the permission of Lawrence Erlbaum Associates, publishers.

```
                                 KEYSTROKE LEVEL
        Model K2:
         GOAL: EDIT-MANUSCRIPT
          . GOAL: EDIT-UNIT-TASK                   . repeat until no more unit tasks
          . . GOAL: ACQUIRE-UNIT-TASK              . . if task not remembered
          . . . GOAL: TURN-PAGE* (see below)       . . . if at end of manuscript page
          . . . GOAL: GET-FROM-MANUSCRIPT*
          . . GOAL: EXECUTE-UNIT-TASK              . . if an edit task was found
          . . . GOAL: LOCATE-LINE                  . . . if task not on current line
          . . . . CHOOSE-COMMAND
          . . . . [select  GOAL: USE-QS-METHOD
          . . . .              GOAL: SPECIFY-COMMAND*
          . . . .              . GOAL: SPECIFY-ARG*
          . . . .          GOAL: USE-LF-METHOD
          . . . .              GOAL: SPECIFY-COMMAND*]    . . . . . repeat until at line
          . . . GOAL: VERIFY-LOC*
          . . . GOAL: MODIFY-TEXT
          . . . . CHOOSE-COMMAND
          . . . . [select  GOAL: USE-S-COMMAND
          . . . .              GOAL: SPECIFY-COMMAND*
          . . . .              GOAL: SPECIFY-ARG*
          . . . .              GOAL: SPECIFY-ARG*
          . . . .          GOAL: USE-M-COMMAND
          . . . .              GOAL: SPECIFY-COMMAND*
          . . . .              GOAL: SPECIFY-COMMAND*    . . . . . repeat until at text
          . . . .              GOAL: SPECIFY-ARG*
          . . . .              GOAL: SPECIFY-COMMAND*]
          . . . GOAL: VERIFY-EDIT*


        * Expansion of goals appearing several times:

              GOAL: TURN-PAGE
               . LOOK-AT-MANUSCRIPT                . repeat twice
               . ACTION
               . MOVE-HAND                         . repeat twice
               . TURN-PAGE
              GOAL: GET-FROM-MANUSCRIPT
               . LOOK-AT-MANUSCRIPT
               . SEARCH-FOR
               . LOOK-AT-DISPLAY                   . optional
              GOAL: SPECIFY-COMMAND
               . GOAL: GET-FROM-MANUSCRIPT*        . if not already selected
               . CHOOSE-COMMAND                    . if not already selected
               . GOAL: TYPE-STRING*
              GOAL: SPECIFY-ARG
               . GOAL: GET-FROM-MANUSCRIPT*        . optional
               . CHOOSE-ARG
               . GOAL: TYPE-STRING*
              GOAL: VERIFY
               . LOOK-AT-DISPLAY
               . GOAL: GET-FROM-MANUSCRIPT*        . optional
               . COMPARE
              GOAL: TYPE-STRING
               . HOME                              . optional
               . LOOK-AT-KEYBOARD                  . optional
               . LOOK-AT-DISPLAY                   . optional
               . TYPE-STRING
```

Together, these components constitute the user's cognitive skills for performing tasks. If a user has enough knowledge of this kind, it isn't necessary to use problem-solving strategies. All that is needed is to examine the task, characterize it in terms of a specific goal, select the appropriate method, and then execute it.

In order to test our GOMS models, we ran a set of experiments to determine whether we could explicitly specify this kind of GOMS knowledge and thus predict what users would actually do. We also wanted to learn how the degree of resolution—the grain of specified detail of such a model—affects the degree of accuracy of predictions based on the model. We expected fine-grained models to yield increased accuracy. Knowing that it takes a lot more work to develop a fine-grained model, a practical question related to the applicability of our models was whether the additional work of constructing a fine-grained model was worth the effort.

To find out, we built a family of models in the GOMS framework that characterized the behavior of users of a specific computer text-editing system and ran experiments to test our predictions from these models. We were surprised to discover that fine-grained models did not yield a worthwhile or even a significant increase in prediction accuracy (Card, Moran, and Newell, 1976, 1980a). More felicitous, practically speaking, was our discovery that even the crude models seemed to capture and predict behavior fairly well. These properties suggested that the GOMS model could be turned into the kind of engineering tool that a designer could use to model and predict skilled user behavior in computer-mediated tasks. That was what we proceeded to try next.

### THE KEYSTROKE-LEVEL MODEL

In simplifying the GOMS models into an engineering model that we could hand to a designer, we constructed an idealized prediction problem:

> Given a task (possibly involving several subtasks), the command language of a system, the motor skill parameters of the user, the response time parameters of the system, and the method used for the task, predict how long an expert user will take to execute the task using the system, providing he uses the method without error. (Card, Moran, and Newell, 1980b)

The Keystroke-Level Model enables a system designer to make such predictions with a "back-of-the-envelope" style of calculation.

To do the calculation, the designer codes the method a user employs to do a task in terms of a set of operations derived from one of the fine grain GOMS models (Fig. 5). In this simplified model, all

FIGURE 5
**The operators of the Keystroke-Level Model.** The figure lists the operators needed to analyze user interface methods and to make calculations of user performance with these methods. Reprinted from Card, Moran, and Newell, (1983, Fig. 8.1) with the permission of Lawrence Erlbaum Associates, Inc.

| Operator | Description and Remarks | Time (sec) |
|---|---|---|
| K | **PRESS KEY OR BUTTON.** Pressing the SHIFT or CONTROL key counts as a separate K operation. Time varies with the typing skill of the user; the following shows the range of typical values: | |
| | Best typist (135 wpm) | .08 |
| | Good typist (90 wpm) | .12 |
| | Average skilled typist (55 wpm) | .20 |
| | Average non-secretary typist (40 wpm) | .28 |
| | Typing random letters | .50 |
| | Typing complex codes | .75 |
| | Worst typist (unfamiliar with keyboard) | 1.20 |
| P | **POINT WITH MOUSE TO TARGET ON A DISPLAY.** The time to point varies with distance and target size according to Fitts's Law, ranging from .8 to 1.5 sec, with 1.1 being an average. This operator does *not* include the (.2 sec) button press that often follows. Mouse pointing time is also a good estimate for other efficient analogue pointing devices, such as joysticks (see Chapter 7). | 1.10 |
| H | **HOME HAND(S) ON KEYBOARD OR OTHER DEVICE.** | .40 |
| $D(n_D, l_D)$ | **DRAW $n_D$ STRAIGHT-LINE SEGMENTS OF TOTAL LENGTH $l_D$ CM.** This is a very restricted operator; it assumes that drawing is done with the mouse on a system that constrains all lines to fall on a square .56 cm grid. Users vary in their drawing skill; the time given is an average value. | $.9n_D + .16l_D$ |
| M | **MENTALLY PREPARE.** | 1.35 |
| R(t) | **RESPONSE BY SYSTEM.** Different commands require different response times. The response time is counted only if it causes the user to wait. | t |

keystrokes are assumed to take a constant amount of time; and pointing with the mouse is also assumed to take a constant amount of time. Mental activity by the user is reduced to a single generic mental preparation operation, and rules governing when it will occur are provided.

A typical use of the model to analyze a method is given in Fig. 6. This method is one way in which a hypothetical text-editor could be used to replace a word recently typed by the user. Each action of the method is described in terms of the operators of the model, then a time for the method is computed. In this case, the method is expected to take the same amount of time regardless of how many words back the word to be replaced is located. Figure 7 shows the expected time for performing this method and two other methods available in the editor as a function of the number of words back the to-be-changed word is located. It can be seen that the time profiles of the three methods are quite different and that each is fastest at different times.

Even though our GOMS study suggested that simple models could be effective, and even though the Keystroke-Level Model was a careful simplification of one of the GOMS models, we felt that it was necessary to rigorously test the explicit performance assumptions of the model. To validate the Keystroke-Level Model, we ran a large set of experiments in which people performed tasks with text editors,

**Method R (Replace):**

| | |
|---|---|
| Terminate type-in mode | **MK**[ESC] |
| Point to target word and select it | **H**[mouse] **P**[word] **K**[YELLOW] |
| Call Replace command | **H**[keyboard] **MK**[R] |
| Type new word | 4.5**K**[word] |
| Terminate Replace command | **MK**[ESC] |
| Point to last input word and select it | **H**[mouse] **P**[word] **K**[YELLOW] |
| Re-enter type-in mode | **H**[keyboard] **MK**[I] |

$$T_{execute} = 4t_M + 10.5t_K + 4t_H + 2t_P$$
$$= 12.1 \text{ sec}.$$

### FIGURE 6

**Encoding of Method R.** Use of the Keystroke-Level Model to describe one possible method in a mouse-based display editor for replacing a word previously mistyped. It is assumed the word is still visible on the screen. Reprinted from Card, Moran, and Newell (1983, p. 289) with the permission of Lawrence Erlbaum Associates, Inc.

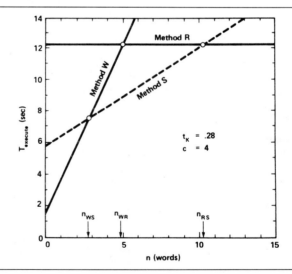

### FIGURE 7

**Execution time of three methods for the misspelled-word task as a function of n.** This figure shows the use of the Keystroke-Level Model for the parametric comparison of three different methods for accomplishing the same goal. In this case each method appears to be superior in a certain range of $n$. Reprinted from Card, Moran, and Newell (1983, Fig. 8.12a) with the permission of Lawrence Erlbaum Associates, Inc.

graphics editors, and executive subsystems. The results (Fig. 8) showed a good fit between predictions derived from the model and observed times required for the tasks. Therefore, our simple approximative model would be of some use in making practical time estimates.

The Keystroke-Level Model has actually proved useful in real system design. One application was the determination of the number of buttons on the mouse for the Xerox Star product. Several schemes for selecting text in the Star text editor were proposed. These schemes required different numbers of buttons. The goal was to make a mouse with the smallest number of buttons possible, so that it was easy to learn to operate. Experiments to test the schemes were reasonably easy to run with novice subjects. Everyone is a novice subject on a new system, and being a novice doesn't require training. But understanding how well the schemes would work for expert users (which most users would be for most of their time on the system) was expensive, because a long time would have to be spent training the users. The solution was to run experiments for novices and to use the Keystroke-Level model for predicting expert performance.

The Keystroke-Level Model allowed us to carry through, at least in regard to a very specific kind of behavior, part of our original vision of packaging psychological knowledge into a model that designers can use to calculate user performance with a variety of interactive computer systems.

## THE UNIT TASK

Not all skill characteristics can be reduced to simple counting, however. In studying text editing, we observed a characteristic of cognitive

**FIGURE 8**
**Predicted versus observed execution times in tests of the Keystroke-Level Model.** Predicted execution times were calculated from the Keystroke-Level Model. Observed execution times come from empirical observation. Reprinted from Card, Moran, and Newell (1983, Fig. 8.6) with the permission of Lawrence Erlbaum Associates, Inc.

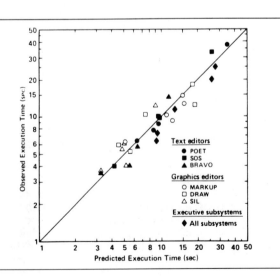

skill that is fundamentally cognitive, namely the organization of user behavior into short, quasi-independent tasks, which we call *unit-tasks*. Figure 9 shows a typical timeline of user behavior, in this case from a protocol of an electrical engineer using a graphic CAD system to design a VLSI circuit. The figure shows that the behavior is divided into chunks, each consisting of a few seconds of pause (to formulate a task to do) followed by a few seconds of activity (to execute the task). Each think-execute chunk of behavior is a unit task.

The unit task structure of cognitive skill is interesting because the performance limitations of the user show through the purely rational organization of his behavior. The most significant reason why the unit task breakdown of behavior arises is because of limitations in the user's working memory. If the user can manage input and output streams in his working memory, then the user's behavior will have a continuous structure, as in touch typing from a manuscript. But, when conditions on the inputs and outputs do not allow this, then behavior must be structured into a series of unit tasks.

Figure 10 portrays a trace of the working memory load of the user, based on logical considerations of when information must be available in memory in order to do a task. As we can see, memory requirements build from a low point at the start of a unit task to a high within the

**FIGURE 9**
**Time line representing the user's behavior sequence in a VLSI design session.** Each single-character symbol represents one second of behavior. The symbol sequence begins on a new line at the beginning of each unit task, and the clock time is the time at the beginning of the unit task. Reprinted from Card, Moran, and Newell (1983, Fig. 10.7) with the permission of Lawrence Erlbaum Associates, Inc.

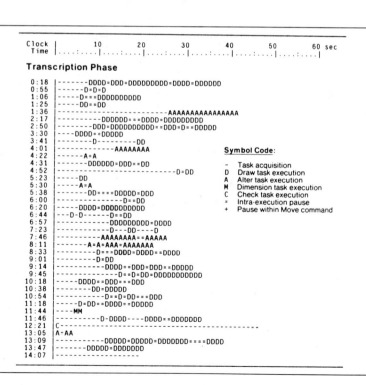

**FIGURE 10**
**Data in working memory during a unit task.** This figure is an hypothetical trace of the performance of one unit task. Time runs to the right on the horizontal axis. The bars indicate the time during which each piece of information about the task is needed. The arrows indicate the initial time data is available and the subsequent times it is needed. The histogram on the top plots the total working memory load over time, showing how the load peaks within a unit task and dips between unit tasks. Reprinted from Card, Moran, and Newell (1983, Fig. 11.12) with the permission of Lawrence Erlbaum Associates, Inc.

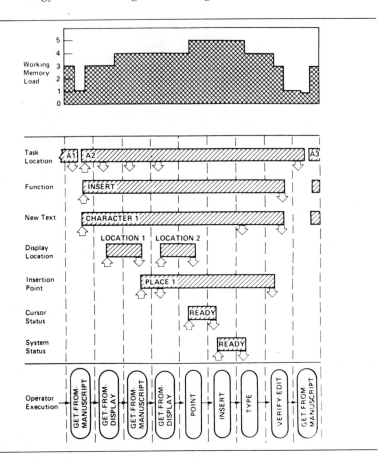

unit task, where information for the task has been assembled, and back to a low point at the end of the unit task, where the information is no longer needed. If the information in working memory should reach a level higher than the working memory capacity, then user performance will suffer, usually manifested by the user committing errors. To avoid these errors, the user must break down the overall task into smaller (unit) units, each of which can be managed in the available working memory.

Unit-task behavior is at present a theoretical notion based on empirical observation (see Card, Moran, and Newell, 1983, for further discussion). But it represents an important feature of user behavior—a sort of "cognitive rhythm"—that should be taken into account in designing user-computer interfaces that are sensitively tuned to the user's capabilities.

**THE PSYCHOLOGY OF HUMAN-COMPUTER INTERACTION**

In 1978, one of us had completed a doctoral thesis (Card, 1978) that consolidated much of the work we had been doing. The thesis helped convince us that the time was appropriate for writing a book presenting our vision of an applied science of the user. Work on the book gave us the opportunity to focus on the larger vision instead of just the pieces, and we became aware of some missing unifying theoretical work that we felt we had to do.

Although we had several calculational models (Fitts's law for the mouse, GOMS models, the Keystroke-Level Model, plus other minor models), there were questions of relating these to the classical literature in cognitive psychology and human factors. We had long sought a unifying framework for tying together the relevant psychological knowledge about users (one of our 1974 working papers called this conception the "Handbook of Cognitive Man"), but had made little progress. In preparing the book, we revived this goal and came to a much more satisfying conception, the Model Human Processor, that captured the relevant psychological literature in the terms of a unified, approximate model. This model also provided a foundation for our other models.

The other big missing piece for us was to understand the relationship between the cognitive skill we had discovered and the classical notion of problem solving in cognitive psychology. Here we built a theory of the behavioral continuum between problem solving and cognitive skill and showed how practice on a task would gradually change problem-solving behavior into skilled behavior. This is an active area of research in cognitive psychology today (e.g., Anderson, 1981).

The result of these efforts was the book, *The Psychology of Human Computer Interaction* (Card, Moran, and Newell, 1983). However, the book represented only the main line of our research efforts that fit together into a tightly knit view. There were many other areas of our work that we decided not to put into the book, such as the issues of learning and of users' mental models.

# The Conceptual Interface: Mental Models

The early effort of the AIP Project was focused on understanding expert user performance. As we explained in the previous section, skilled performance is characterized by methods that users know and quickly execute to accomplish tasks. That is, we were focused on what is typically called procedural knowledge ("how-to-do-it" knowledge). However, from the beginning, we were aware that methods are not sequences of meaningless actions, but that expert users also have an understanding of what the procedures cause the machine to do. That is, the expert users have some sort of *mental model* of what is happening inside the computer (''how-it-works'' knowledge).

The first AIP memo in 1974 proposed the notion of the ''user's model,'' which refers to the conceptual model that the user can have of the system. A user's conceptual model is distinct from (but related to) the designer's implementation model. It is an abstraction of the system's architecture and software structures—the conceptual entities that the architecture and software implements—that is simple enough for nontechnical users to grasp. (For example, a user might not know how the mechanism of the delete buffer of a text-editor works, but would simply know that the deleted text goes into a ''clipboard.'') A user's model would typically include knowledge of where information is stored (core memory, local disk files, remote file servers). It is important for the user to have an understanding of these kinds of features, for they are often not visible to the user.

The user's model provides an integrated package of knowledge that allows the user to predict what the system will do if certain commands are executed, to predict the state of the system after the commands have been executed, to plan methods for novel tasks, and to deal with odd error situations (by characterizing the system's state according to the model, then choosing operations necessary to leave that state).

## EARLY ENCOUNTERS WITH CONCEPTUAL MODELS

Early in our research we tried to write down rudimentary descriptions of the elements of conceptual models, which included the conceptual objects, their properties, how they related to each other (the characters in a text editor, for example, including the notion of a blank space as a character), and the conceptual operations that could be performed on those objects (inserting, moving, or deleting characters, including blank spaces).

Given the obvious importance of this kind of knowledge for the user, we were surprised to find that almost no system documentation ever clearly laid out a conceptual model of the system for the user. We were also surprised to discover what a difficult inductive task it is to specify such a model, even for a seemingly simple text editor. It was a detective game in which we were forced to hypothesize and test elements of possible models in order to find a succinct conceptual characterization of how the system worked. It was a game that took us days (not minutes) to do, hence not a game in which busy users were likely to engage.

It is clear that users attempt to make sense—by building mental models—of the behavior of a system as they use it. If a simple model is not explicitly or implicitly provided, users formulate their own myths about how the system works. These user-invented models may be inaccurate or misleading outside the very limited situation from which they emerged. Therefore, we believed that if the user is to understand the system, the system has to be designed with an *explicit* conceptual model that is easy enough for the user to learn. We call this the *intended user's model,* because it is the model the designer intends the user to learn. Just what mental model the user actually forms is another issue, which depends on how clearly the intended user's model is designed, how well it is implemented, and how well it is documented.

Although we were very concerned about the mental model issue, we didn't pursue explicit studies for several reasons: We didn't have a satisfactory methodology for studying it, we didn't have satisfactory representations of it, and we were busy pursuing the performance issues we have discussed. Still, we felt that the intended user's model was an important consideration in the user-interface design process.

## USER-INTERFACE DESIGN METHODOLOGY

The practical application of our concerns came when Xerox began arranging the technology transfer between PARC and the Systems Development Division (SDD), which was created to develop office system products based on the research at PARC. In the spring of 1976, a joint PARC/SDD committee (which included one of us) was formed to advise SDD on the design of the user interface of the office systems.

The committee decided not to try to design an actual interface, but to propose a methodology for SDD designers to follow in designing their interfaces. The methodology (Irby et al., 1977) included four parts: (1) analyze what tasks the user will want to do and the steps they go through to accomplish the tasks; (2) design an intended user's model in terms of which the tasks may be cast; (3) design a command language to make that model work; and (4) design an information display to reflect the operations of the system in terms of the conceptual model.

Thus, we recommended that the designer should lay out an intended user's model before designing the command language and the information display. The whole design effort should be oriented toward keeping this model "under control" (i.e., keeping it simple, consistent, and clear enough for users to grasp).

The original designers of the Xerox Star interface, the workstation product SDD built, used this methodology. The conceptual model was clearly laid out in the system's functional specifications, and the designers worked hard to keep the model consistent. Although this model was represented informally, the fact that the designers focused on it contributed heavily to the widely recognized success of Star's user interface. The conceptual model is an under-appreciated aspect of Star's interface, but Star's more widely-touted icons and desktop metaphor only make sense with respect to its underlying conceptual model.

William Newman, another member of the committee, presented this methodology in the second edition of his book with Bob Sproull (Newman and Sproull, 1979).

### EMPIRICAL STUDIES

By 1979, we were ready to tackle some empirical studies in order to understand the role of the user's model. The first study was an attempt to elicit the knowledge that real users of real systems have about the systems they use every day. The system we chose to study was the Alto Executive, a system that was in wide use at PARC for several years by nontechnical support people as well as programmers.

We wanted to find out what Alto users knew about the Executive. The goal was to see whether we could find some kind of mental models buried in the user's knowledge. The methodology we used was to transcribe interviews with several users into logical propositions and then classify them into categories.

The surprising result was that many nontechnical expert users (e.g., secretaries who used the system effectively every day) gave no evidence of having anything but very shallow models of how the system worked. (Perhaps we shouldn't have been surprised, because no conceptual model was documented and training was informal.) This led us to consider more carefully the role of the user's model.

In order to characterize the role a user's mental model would play in the use of a system, we performed experiments with the simplest kind of system we could devise, a simple stack-based calculator (Halasz and Moran, 1983; Halasz, 1984). We thought that a model of a stack might well be useful to help rationalize what for many users is a nonintuitive postfix command language. The formal experiment compared one group of users who were taught an explicit conceptual model of the stack, and a group of users who were carefully shielded from the stack model. The model group was trained in relation to a specific model and were told how that model related to the methods for solving arithmetic problems. The no-model group was only taught specific methods for performing the same tasks. Then we gave the two groups sets of problems that were categorized as simple routine tasks, slightly more complex tasks, and very difficult "invention tasks" (which required the user to invent new methods to solve).

The results (see Fig. 11) revealed no difference between the two groups in both the routine and complex problems, but the model

| Problem Type | No-Model Users | Model Users |
|---|---|---|
| Routine | 98 | 95 |
| Complex | 87 | 88 |
| Invention | 25 | 67 |

**FIGURE 11**
**Percentage of problems correctly done in the calculator experiments.** There were two groups of users; one was taught an explicit conceptual model of the calculator's stack and the other group was prevented from having such a model. There were three types of problems, each of a different difficulty relative to what the users were taught.

group performed much better on the invention tasks. The most surprising result was that even some of the no-model group were able to perform some of the invention tasks. We wanted to account for these results according to the cognitive theories we understood, so we analyzed the protocols gathered from the users as they performed the tasks.

We divided the users' behavior into skilled method execution, as we had modeled in our earlier studies, and problem-solving. We found (see Fig. 12) that in the routine and complex problems, the behavior was almost all skilled method execution: The subjects had been taught what to do, and they did it; even for the complex problems it wasn't difficult to knit together the methods they had learned for solving the problems.

| | No-Model Users | | | | Model Users | | | |
|---|---|---|---|---|---|---|---|---|
| | | Problem Solving | | | | Problem Solving | | |
| Problem Type | Skilled Method Execution | Model Space | Methods Space | Task Space | Skilled Method Execution | Model Space | Methods Space | Task Space |
| Routine | 90 | 0 | 8 | 2 | 89 | 11 | 0 | 0 |
| Complex | 94 | 0 | 6 | 0 | 91 | 7 | 0 | 2 |
| Invention | 2 | 0 | 84 | 14 | 7 | 71 | 19 | 3 |

**FIGURE 12**
**Partitioning of the users' behavior in the calculator experiments.** The users' behavior was divided into four behavioral modes: skilled method execution plus three problem solving modes, which are distinguished according to which problem space they were working in. The partitioning is based on an analysis of verbal protocol records; each line of protocol was categorized into the mode it manifested. The numbers in the table are the percentages of lines of protocol in each behavior mode. We believe that this measure underestimates the amount of work in the task space.

Our hypothesis going into the study was that the conceptual model we taught the model group of users would provide them with a problem space through which they could search in order to find solutions. According to this theory, the user would characterize a difficult "invention" task in terms of this problem space: the state of the system when they started, the state of the system they would like to achieve, and a set of operations to move them through that space; they would solve the problem using generic problem-solving strategies.

However, when we analyzed the users protocols, we found two other kinds of problem spaces in which the users worked when they were problem solving. One was a *task space* within which they manipulated the given arithmetic task in various ways, such as dividing it into subtasks that could be solved by known methods. Another space in which they worked was a *methods space*, where they took known solution methods as strings of steps, manipulated those steps in various ways to produce new methods, and tried them to see how they worked.

We found that the most critical (although not very time consuming) problem solving was in the task space, where the user analyzed the given task into subtasks and delegated them to the model space or the methods space. The main difference between the users who had a model and those who didn't was that they had different problem spaces in which to work (see Fig. 12). The model space was an effective problem space, within which the solution to the invention problems could be found; the method space was not particularly effective, but it was sufficient to allow some no-model users to stumble onto solutions to some of the invention problems (often, much to their surprise).

We concluded that mental models can be useful for novel task situations, but we found that users only use their models in specific subtasks; there was a lot of switching between the task space and other problem spaces. Users were cautious about going into a mode of behavior that involved thinking through a mental model. Model-based problem solving appears to be very mentally intensive, so users avoid it if they can apply cognitive skills. But, if users don't have appropriate methods available, they will retreat to some kind of problem solving. In these cases, a good conceptual model provides an effective problem space in which to work.

Thus, system designers should think of a conceptual model of a system as not just a simple view of a complex system, but as a problem space through which users can search for solutions to a variety of novel problems. The conceptual entities and operators in the intended user's model should be closely related to the kinds of tasks the users are likely to do, and the users should be provided with heuristics for moving through the model space.

## THEORETICAL STUDIES: TASK MAPPING

We also worked on a theoretical analysis of conceptual models to show where they fit into the overall structure of the user interface. The Command Language Grammar formalism (Moran, 1978, 1981) shows how models related to the task domain, the command language, and the detailed user-computer interactions. According to this theory, the conceptual model provides the user with a link between his task domain and the syntax of the interactive dialogue. That is, on the one hand the conceptual model serves as the semantics of the dialogue actions, while on the other hand it serves as a base into which the task can be mapped into the system.

Richard Young called this kind of mechanistic conceptual model a *surrogate model* (Young, 1983). Interactions on these issues with Young, who was exploring the domain of simple calculators, led to the discovery of a new kind of mental model—*task-action mappings* (Young, 1981). The properties of radically different calculator designs, such as algebraic versus stack calculators, could be best understood by an analysis of how well calculation tasks could be directly mapped into the actions available on the calculators. Surrogate models were completely bypassed in this analysis, which helps explain why people sometimes seem to get along with systems without having surrogate models of them.

In further work along this line, we have proposed a calculus, called *ETIT analysis,* for task mapping (Moran, 1983). The "fit" of a system to a task domain can be assessed by enumerating rules for reformulating system-independent task descriptions ("external tasks") into system-specific task descriptions ("internal tasks"). Rule-based system description techniques, such as this or Payne's (1984) *task-action grammar,* are beginning to provide a way to help us formalize the fuzzy notion of the *consistency* of a system (both internal consistency and consistency with respect to a task domain). Such techniques look promising as a way to provide system designers with calculational techniques for predicting the learnability and "guessability" of systems.

# The Task Interface: Pondering Ideas

Let us now turn to the role of a science of the user in the future development of the personal workstation. For us, the real challenges for user technology are now at the larger task level in which users are grappling with complex intellectual tasks. This is, of course, a return to working directly on a modern version of the original vision of augmentation workstations.

We now have workstations powerful enough to give each user a personal system equivalent to one that only a decade ago would have been shared with a hundred other users, and we are on the verge of major upgrades to even greater computing and communication power. We now have a much more developed base for user technology—not only techniques for designing user interfaces, but also models for understanding users. Thus, we are now in a better position than ever before to explore systems that can really augment human intellectual endeavors.

The challenge is to create systems that, through intimate cognitive interaction with users, aid them in structuring and manipulating their ideas. With such systems to help them, people will then be able to cope with more and more complex intellectual tasks of all sorts—authoring books and multi-media presentations, designing products and programs, composing music, analyzing experiments, the arguing points of law and policy, reasoning about scientific and social issues, and on and on.

The key to building such systems is to find ways by which a user can act on his ideas as objects, just as current text editors allow him to act on words as objects. This is difficult, since ideas are often tacit and ill-formed. A means is needed to *externalize* the ideas, to get them out of the user's head and into a form that can be organized and shaped. Two problems require solution:

1. The user needs new ways to *represent* his ideas—to get the user's mind around the ideas, as it were. For this we can exploit advances in artificial intelligence and cognitive science.

2. The user needs new ways to *manipulate* his ideas—to get the user's hands on the ideas. For this we can exploit advances in interactive computer graphics.

These problems are part of our current research agenda. In this endeavor we must not only build on our current base of understanding of the user, but also advance that understanding. For one thing, we have to launch studies into the nature of the complex intellectual tasks we wish to augment. This calls for a shift in our research strategy from studying users of existing systems to studying users of new systems that we ourselves build, which enables us to understand the nature of the tasks and the limits of users and systems for dealing with them. We give illustrations of this strategy from some of our own current projects.

**REPRESENTATION: IDEA STRUCTURING**

Word processors and text editors, even powerful ones, are tailored for the final stages of writing a paper—crafting the text and graphics of the final product. Outline processors help with the previous stage of outlining. Although the latter are sometimes called ''idea processors,'' it is clear that idea processing begins well before the stage of outlining. A genuine idea processor should allow the user to deal with ideas that are vague and ill-structured and help him gradually add structure as it is discovered.

We use the term *authoring* to refer to the larger intellectual task of gathering information, extracting and discovering ideas, structuring them, and finally composing them into a readable product. Authoring in this sense is a highly general task composed of generic subtasks, as illustrated in Fig. 13. One begins by collecting sources of information; from these a set of notes (idea-sized units) are created to represent potentially relevant facts and ideas. As notes accumulate, they need to be filed in a structure suitable for retrieval, such as a topic hierarchy. But these notes also need structures that organize the ideas into meaningful, coherent themes. Such structures must be discovered, elaborated, supported by evidence in the notes and other sources. One then communicates these ideas by composing them into an interpretable product—a document, a slide presentation, or a browsable network of ideas.

The key research issue here is to help the users develop explicit mental models of idea structures, so they can see them, play with them, and evaluate them. This requires the invention of representations for *externalizing* ideas and idea structures. Cognitively, these

**FIGURE 13**
**Schematic diagram of the generic authoring task.** The boxes are the types of information to be managed in the authoring process, and the arrows are some of the processors for generating and transforming the information.

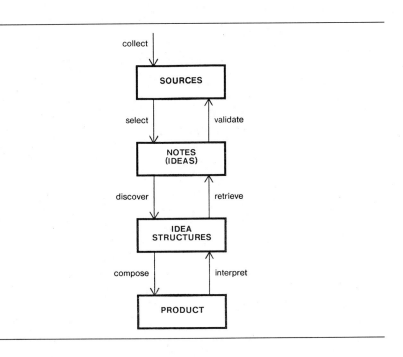

representations serve the users as problem spaces; and new representations can fundamentally alter the way they are able to deal with ideas. Some representations should be "weak" in the sense that they can easily capture a large variety of even vague ideas; other representations should be "strong" in the sense that they can precisely capture and process particular classes of idea structures; and facilities must be provided to help users transform weak representations into strong ones.

We are developing a system, called *NoteCards*, to explore the broad nature of the authoring task. NoteCards supports the orienting metaphor of the notecard as a medium for capturing an idea. Notecards can be stored in fileboxes and linked into complex structures, which can then be viewed in graphic representations (such as the one shown in Fig. 14). NoteCards is designed to be an open, flexible environment, so that we can use it as a "laboratory" to explore new representations and tools to support authoring tasks. Because it is an open system, NoteCards users are faced with the problem of devising appropriate ways to use the system, that is, mapping their particular tasks onto the basic elements of the system. This leads to a further interface issue of making the environment tailorable by users themselves to the wide variety of situations that we encourage them to bring to NoteCards (paper and documentation writing, scientific and legal argumentation, instruction authoring, design analysis). Thus, in contrast to our earlier methodology of observing a controlled, skilled user population, we are now observing a population of idiosyncratic, exploratory users.

## MANIPULATION: IDEA BROWSING

The representations in an idea-structuring environment must be assimilated and manipulated with facility and speed. Idea-processing tasks are difficult for users, because they involve the retrieval, tracking, and manipulation of a large number of ideas (as is being attempted in Fig. 14). Authoring a paper, for example, may require hundreds of notes and scores of references; programming may require hundreds of routines. But, as the Model Human Processor shows, only limited amounts of information can be handled in the user's working memory. These limitations lead the user to structure his behavior into unit-task bursts.

These considerations lead us to ask how a computer system can compensate for human cognitive limitations. The display can be used as an external memory to augment the user's internal working memory. This partly explains what has made the "desk-top" metaphor successful: Users can use windows and icons to keep track of more documents, notes, and messages from other users than with the previous style of command language interfaces. By having these things visi-

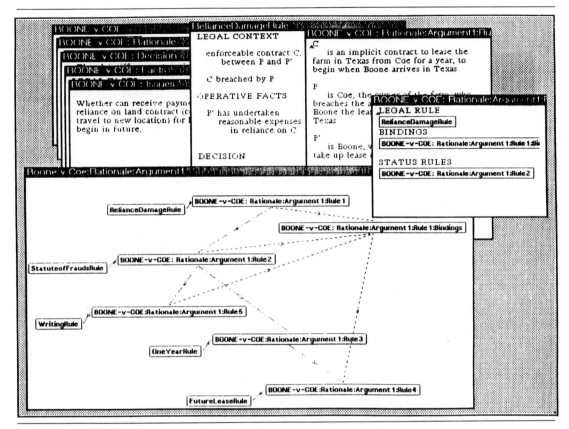

**FIGURE 14**
**A screen image of the NoteCards system.** The application shown is the
analysis of a legal argument. A variety of legal rules must be brought to
bear in arguing a particular case. The graph shows how the rules are related
by applicability conditions and by bindings to the particulars of the case.

ble as reminders, the user's effective working memory is increased,
enabling him to do more complex tasks.

But the problem is that these techniques, which work well with a
few dozen objects, do not scale well up to the several hundred or even
thousands of objects necessary for the idea-processing tasks we wish
to do. Here, it helps to begin with a better understanding of the nature
of the problem. Again, our method for gaining that understanding is
through approximative models of user behavior. In this case, we have
sketched a model called the Window Working Set Model (Card, Pavel,
and Farrell, 1984) that analyzes access to screen objects in a manner
analogous to the analysis of virtual memory operating systems. Informally, this model suggests that screen space itself is the key constraint

and that at some point as the number of, say, overlapped windows required increases, user performance will decrease in a sudden and nonlinear way, sending the user into the window version of thrashing.

Thus there are limitations on the uses of current graphical interface techniques for browsing large sets of ideas. Advanced graphics systems, however, open up a new set of possibilities. Figure 15 shows a fragment of an organization chart from an experimental browsing system we are implementing (the DandeIris, combining a Xerox DandeTiger Lisp machine and a Silicon Graphics Iris graphics processor). The node that is the user's focus is largest and is readable in the most detail. Nodes become smaller with distance from the focus. The user can fly around this chart to see it from different points of view and change his direction of gaze; if he points at a node, indicating a new focus of attention, it grows larger. The transitions are all animated in real-time, color, three-dimensional representations to help the user keep track of the transformed identities of various objects.

Such a display is designed to help the user navigate among a large number of objects; only a few of these objects would be visible in detail

**FIGURE 15**
**Experimental DandeIris browser for organization charts.** The photograph shows a view of a fragment of an organization chart as seen by a user flying around this chart. The chart is laid out on a simulated two-dimensional whiteboard. The user can change his location in simulated three-dimensional space, his direction of gaze, and by pointing with the mouse to indicate focus, the relative sizes of different organization chart boxes. (The experimental program was written by S. Card, A. Henderson, L. Lovstrand, and B. Verner.)

at any time, but many more would be visible as orienting cues and retrieval keys. The visual movement technique is coupled with other retrieval techniques for allowing the user to focus on a limited number of items at a time (as required by our understanding of user's processing capacity) while retaining rapid access to a large number of items (as required by our understanding of the requirements of complex intellectual tasks). By coupling experimental programming with the analysis of user behavior, we hope to find theory-based techniques to aid the user in keeping track of and maintaining effective browsing and retrieval capability for large information structures.

## Conclusions

What has been learned about users and how does this relate to the original visions of personal workstations? The short answer is that, unlike the early 1970s when little was known scientifically about computer users, we now have a vision of the form of an applied science of the user and a few areas of knowledge where that vision has been realized. In this paper we have narrated some of our efforts at building this applied science.

At the physical interface level, we have discovered that user performance with pointing devices is constrained by the information-processing capacity of the user. We have learned the quantitative law describing this constraint and have determined that certain devices, such as the mouse, are at the performance limits allowed by this law.

At the cognitive level, we have learned that routine human-computer interaction, such as text-editing, does not involve problem solving, but rather cognitive skills based on the execution of known methods. We can see the information-processing constraints of the user show through this skilled performance in the unit task of users. We have characterized cognitive skill to the extent of developing an engineering model for use by user-interface designers.

At the conceptual level, we have learned that users often have mental models of the systems they use, and that such models enable performance of novel tasks. System conceputal models provide the basis for users to acquire mental models, and thus are an important basis for system design. But mental models are cognitively intensive, and users will avoid them by attempting to map directly from their tasks to the actions required in a system. Theories of task mapping are just beginning to emerge.

At each of the above levels, it has been possible to base an applied science on a theory of the cognitive mechanisms underlying user behavior. At each level, the applied science was shown to be practical, in particular by being influential in the design of the Xerox Star.

The challenge for us today is to use our understanding of users to discover new ways to augment users to complex intellectual endeavors. Thus, we are concentrating our efforts in those areas where users' cognitive limitations need to be overcome and where users' cognitive abilities can be aided with computer-based tools. We believe that the most interesting problems are at the task level: understanding the nature of complex intellectual tasks and finding ways to build idea-structuring tools, both representation tools for structuring ideas and display tools for browsing ideas.

Whereas we once studied users empirically using existing systems in order to understand the nature of human-computer interaction, we now use what we have learned about users to help drive the creation of new experimental systems.

## REFERENCES

Anderson, J. R. (1981). *Cognitive skills and their acquisition.* Hillsdale, N.J.: Lawrence Erlbaum Associates.

Bell, C. G., and Newell, A. (1971). *Computer structures: Readings and examples.* New York: McGraw-Hill.

Bush, V. (1945). As we may think. *The Atlantic Monthly,* August.

Card, S. K. (1978). Studies in the psychology of computer text editing systems. Unpublished doctoral dissertation, Carnegie-Mellon University, Department of Psychology.

Card, S. K., English, W. K., and Burr, B. J. (1978). Evaluation of mouse, rate-controlled isometric joystick, step keys, and text keys for text selection on a CRT. *Ergonomics, 21,* 601–613.

Card, S. K., Moran, T. P., and Newell, A. (1976). *The manuscript editing task: A routine cognitive skill* (Technical Report SSL-76-8). Palo Alto, Calif.: Xerox Palo Alto Research Center.

Card, S. K., Moran, T. P., and Newell, A. (1980a). Computer text-editing: An information-processing analysis of a routine cognitive skill. *Cognitive Psychology, 12,* 32–74.

Card, S. K., Moran, T. P., and Newell, A. (1980b). The keystroke-level model for user performance time with interactive systems. *Communications of the ACM 23,* 396–410.

Card, S. K., Moran, T. P., and Newell, A. (1983). *The psychology of human-computer interaction.* Hillsdale, N.J.: Lawrence Erlbaum Associates.

Card, S. K., Pavel, M., and Farrell, J. E. (1984). Window-based computer dialogues. *Proceedings of IFIP Interact '84,* 355–359. London: IFIP.

Engelbart, D. (1963). A conceptual framework for the augmentation of man's intellect. In P. W. Howerton and D. C. Weeks (Eds.), *Vistas in information handling,* Vol. 1. Washington, D.C.: Spartan Books.

English, W. K., Engelbart, D. C., and Berman, M. A. (1967). Display-selection techniques for text manipulation. *IEEE Transactions on Human Factors in Electronics, HFE-8,* 5–15.

Halasz, F. G. (1984). Mental models and problem solving in using a calculator. Unpublished doctoral dissertation. Stanford, Calif.: Stanford University.

Halasz, F. G., and Moran, T. P. (1983). Mental models and problem solving in using a calculator. *Proceedings of the CHI '83 Conference on Human Factors in Computing Systems.* New York: ACM.

Irby, C., Bergsteinsson, L., Moran, T. P., Newman, W., and Tesler, L. (1977). *A methodology for user interface design.* Palo Alto, Calif.: Xerox Palo Alto Research Center.

Kay, A. (1977). Microelectronics and the personal computer. *Scientific American,* September, 230–244.

Licklider, J. C. R. (1960). Man-computer symbiosis. *IRE Transactions on Human Factors in Electronics, HFE-1* (March), 4–11.

Moran, T. P. (1978). *Introduction to the command language grammar* (Technical Report SSL-78-3). Palo Alto, Calif.: Xerox Palo Alto Research Center.

Moran, T. P. (1981). The command language grammar: A representation for the user interface of interactive computer systems. *International Journal of Man-Machine Studies, 15,* 3–50.

Moran, T. P. (1983). Getting into a system: External-internal task mapping analysis. *Proceedings of the CHI '83 Conference on Human Factors in Computing Systems.* New York: ACM.

Newell, A., and Simon, H. A. (1972). *Human problem solving.* Englewood Cliffs, NJ: Prentice-Hall.

Newman, W., and Sproull, R. (1979). *Principles of interactive computer graphics,* 2nd ed. New York: McGraw-Hill.

Payne, S. J. (1984). Task-action grammars. *Proceedings of Interact '84: First IFIP Conference on Human-Computer Interaction,* London. Amsterdam: Elsevier.

Young, R. M. (1981). The machine inside the machine: Users' models of pocket calculators. *International Journal of Man-Machine Studies, 15,* 51–86.

Young, R. M. (1983). Surrogates and mappings: Two kinds of conceptual models for interactive devices. In D. Gentner and A. L. Stevens (Eds.), *Mental models.* Hillsdale, N.J.: Lawrence Erlbaum Associates.

# Participants Discussion

**Allen Newell**    I know the following is something Tom wanted to say, because we talked about it beforehand. I want to observe that there is a connection between the NoteCards system that he was describing, the ZOG system that I made a remark about earlier, and the PROMIS system.

Are there any comments or questions that anyone would like to put to Stu or Tom?

**Doug Engelbart**    I'm really thrilled. That's just marvelous, and my only question is to the rest of the world, Why aren't there just about 20 times, or 100 times that many people working on this side of the issue? You know, it's weighted so heavily on the technology, the hardware and software side. This side that has to grow to make it work; it's long overdue and good for you. And then, while you're at it, answer for Jan and me, How long does it take a person to learn to use a mouse? To go from rhapsody to something small and practical?

**Allen Newell**    While Stu is coming up, I'll answer the first half; then he can answer the second half. The first half is an analog of Butler's comment that building interfaces is hard. Doing science about interfaces is even harder, especially if you want to do good science and if that is to include the user. The kind of thing that Tom was talking about, which begins by being very qualitative, is a momentary extrapolation from a fair amount of effort down at the level we've talked about, where some kind of models exist. One can only go so far in such extrapolations; one has to keep building that science base. The base grows very slowly and is very hard to do. Furthermore, there are lots of people in psychology who don't quite have the vision that psychology ought to be an engineering science.

**Card**    I can't give you real data to answer your question, but it turns out that the important thing to look at is the distribution of time it takes people to learn to use the mouse. There are a lot of people who learn it in a minute, but when you take this thing into the real world of offices, you find there is a small percentage of people, 2 or 3 percent, who never really do quite get the hang of the mouse, or who otherwise have some fairly strange characteristics. One person, who is in charge of customer training for Xerox, came over and was trying to show me how to do something. It turns out that she holds her mouse upside down. Somebody who worked with me recently made another mouse especially for women with long fingernails that has "fenders" on it so you don't scrape your fingernails. So there is a residual of people. We found another application in which people didn't like the mouse at all. BBN was doing a study for the social security administration, and the social security representatives have a fair number of hard luck customers who come in. It turned out that they didn't like the mouse at all because the mouse has a cord that one of their patients could wrap around their neck. So, for most people, five minutes will do it, but there's this residual.

*Sig Treu*

I'd like to identify what I consider to be really the most significant contribution that this particular group has made—Stu Card and Tom Moran and Allen Newell. I am doing this from my personal vantage point and based on my experiences in having tried to look at this sort of interdisciplinary area of computer science and psychology for quite a few years. The fact of the matter is, and this is partly in response to what Doug was just commenting on, in many computer science departments over the years there was a certain aversion, indeed, you might almost call it a "looking down upon" someone who was willing to engage in something as subjective and vague as user psychology. There were much more exciting deterministic and precise kinds of things to attend to in the area of hardware and software. I feel that this group at PARC, with a very supportive and respected kind of environment that they have been able to enjoy, have put this research area on the map. I can assure you, as a result, in my own department, and I'm speaking from personal experience again, I can see a recognition that, sure enough, there must be something to that and it's not as though computer scientists are somehow diluting themselves by looking at the user psychology side of things. So I think it's a very welcome kind of trend and I think, for the historical record, that it should be viewed as an important contribution. Thanks.

*Charles Irby*

I'd just like to add a few comments about the work at Xerox SDD and the design of Star. I was charged by Xerox with the responsibility of overseeing the design of the functionality and the user interface for Star. What we basically did, following this interdisciplinary group that was set up that Tom described, is we took our design group out into the field. We got our product planning people to identify target office environments. I took the designers out there, and had them sit for about a two-day period with these people to understand the tasks that they did. That was the task part of the model that Tom described. We then came back and put a very large emphasis on the whole notion of a conceptual model—the objects that are dealt with in these tasks and the operations you can apply to those objects when doing the tasks.

We had about half of my group doing design prototypes; they were doing software implementations, working right along with the designers on a day-to-day basis, and trying things all along.

We set up a laboratory down in Los Angeles, staffed by a variety of people, some of whom were psychology people, some of whom were engineering people. We brought subjects in and tested various aspects of the interfaces, tested parts of the conceptual model to make sure that our understanding was correct, and we changed quite a bit of the design as a result of that work. Then finally, we produced a rather substantial document called the *Star Functional Specification* that described the entire user interface in great detail. It was entirely organized on the basis of this conceptual model—the objects that were dealt with, and the actions that could be applied to those objects, with a great deal of illustration showing exact pictures of the user interface as it should look all through the course of these operations. So I just want to substantiate what Stu and Tom have been talking about. This work has been very important inside Xerox. The discipline was applied quite sternly within the design group and I think the payoff was very large.

**Doug Ross**      With regard to the last part of your presentation, and how we can have mental models and express them in ways that are suitable to these display techniques that are now available, I would like to call to your attention my own structured analysis and design technique, which is now about a dozen years old. It has been very heavily used and is very successful for those who do use it. Most recent descriptions of it have appeared in the *IEEE Computer* magazine, both an article and an interview with me in a later issue. I'm very much hopeful, although it's had a history of lacking the graphic tools to go with the mental discipline and the paper and pencil, that it will start to serve some of these functions. Like many of our things, it seems to have been a few years before its time, and we think that the time is about right now for it to start fulfilling this role of being, if you will, a more disciplined and rigorous and structured way of doing the same sorts of things as your NoteCards are intended to do.

**Bruce Tagliazini**      I'm from Apple Computers. We're the ones who perfected the mouse by getting rid of those extra buttons.

Because of the parade of people through my office I keep your book open on my desk all the time showing the chart that shows that the mouse is superior to function keys and cursor keys. These people are always attempting to add function keys and cursor keys.

There seems to be a difference between the subjective time of the person using the computer and the objective time shown by a videotape, wherein the mouse is proven superior. How do you deal with people who decide, because of the subjective time, that the mouse is the inferior device. How do you convince these people? It's one thing to prove it through cognitive psychology, but how do you motivate, through motivational psychology, that in fact the mouse is the superior device?

*Card*   Well, whether the mouse is superior or not depends heavily on how it's used. I'm always astonished at how you can take a very good interface technique and completely botch up an interface by using it too much, or the wrong way. The mouse is certainly one of those. In fact, for many interfaces we run on right now, there's such a love affair with the mouse that it's used for both the argument that you're selecting and the command, say on a pop-up window, that you're doing. So you end up having to go back and forth and back and forth with the mouse. There's one of these interfaces, a calendar system, I once did an analysis of, and I discovered that by using a mouse they managed to make it take four times as long as it would have taken had you used keys alone. You actually have to do a much broader analysis.

The reason that the mouse worked for Doug's system is that they had the other hand doing the functional keys, and so they could keep from overloading any one thing. You know, interfaces really take four hands to operate. It's unfortunate that people don't come with four hands, otherwise it would just be wonderful. It takes one hand for doing the functional thing, one hand for doing the mouse, and then two hands for typing in on the keyboard. You can look at various interfaces as ways of compromising and getting the number of hands down. Bravo (text editor), for example, used modes, so you were either in insertion mode or command mode, and that made the interface only take three hands. So you got rid of the function keys. There are other ones that compromise in various ways.

I don't know if that answered your questions directly, but I think that when you try and tell people, "Oh, the mouse is better than this in the abstract," that's now as powerful as if you look at the particular ecological circumstances. The mouse is better in this particular circumstance because this hand isn't doing anything, and it's overloaded, and there aren't very many of these, and that sort of thing.

*Bruce Tagliazini*   I do have one other very quick question since I think we have the right people in the room, I'd really like to know what is the plural of mouse.

*Card*   There aren't any systems that have more than one mouse.

*Mark Richer*   Can I make a quick comment? I think that it's not just the context that's important, but the person. I hope that the computer companies will support all the input devices. I'll give you an example. I know a disabled programmer who's a Macintosh programmer. He can't use the mouse, but he can use a head device. So I think if you keep that in mind, maybe we'll stop having religious arguments about these devices.

*Card*

The people who are mouse afficionados, like Engelbart and English, and me to a certain extent, are probably the least religious people about the mouse. Along with them, I see it as a provisional device that you might be able to do better with in some circumstances. You're not going to beat the speed with those muscles, but there are other ways. So, for a person with a particular handicap, for example, there are obviously going to be better ways. For a particular kind of interface, like for PROMIS, there are particular things that might make the touch technology better.

*Allen Newell*

I see, I really lost control. At an historical conference, I let a mice conversation get going. So let's try and wrap it up. I'll just make one or two remarks, and then hand it over to Alan.

It was a really great idea to have this conference and it was a great idea to put it on record. I like the view that says that the job in these ACM conferences is, as participants in the history, to try and lay out enough of it for the real historians to be critical about it later. We had a number of good illustrations in addition to the main line that we've been talking mostly about, namely that goes back to MIT and Whirlwind. You can see the workstation start there. But two or three streams of work clearly got represented here: the Hewlett-Packard work and the PROMIS work. This is what we really ought to be doing—putting on the record the kind of information about how each of these fields has developed. We're talking here about the personal workstation, but there will be other conferences on other parts of the field.

# Closing Remarks from the Conference Chairman

There was a song in the show *Oklahoma* about the girl who couldn't say no. Well, I'm the guy the speakers couldn't say no to. When a history about Napoleon was written, a critic said the history is quite incomplete, having written about Napoleon, but not the people around him, for example, his tailor. We've been fortunate: The Napoleons who spoke here were quite happy to speak about their Taylor and well they should, because he suited them very well, as he suited the rest of us.

This conference has proceeded as smoothly as it has because of the unremitting work of John White and the people associated with him at PARC and the local ACM area chapters. We certainly owe them a round of thanks. I totaled up the cost to Xerox for my long distance calls to get this meeting arranged, and it cost all of $36.55, so it was rather cheap to arrange. One last remark that I was reminded of when Jan Schultz spoke. It is a canard that IBM wedded together a color display and touch-screen technology to produce a system for the display and use of colored sense cards on a CRT.

This meeting has been a great success, and we're going to have to hold another one, not next year perhaps, but in about 20 years. If, at that meeting, the same people who were speakers here today speak then, it will either be because the field is a failure or else we're witnessing a miracle. Some of the people who have developed personal workstations have said that the workstation will disappear, and certainly that part of it that deals with work will disappear. It'll disappear into the innards of various kinds of devices. But please note that when Alan Kay was talking last night, he was not talking about workstations, he was talking about imagination stations. Until we get hardware and software that coupled together have more imagination than we do, which may be a long time coming, the game will be the same, albeit with different tools and different people, 20 years from now as it is today: To force out of the devices available to us what our feverish imaginations think we ought to have.

Another reason why 20 years from now the cast of characters will be different is that we are unfortunately constrained by success. There are other things coming along now like 64000 processor computers. Even though Gordon Bell draws graphs with appreciative slopes, he's graphing the enabling time to get things into the marketplace. It is the

527

nonlinearity in the availability of devices and the nonlinearity of the imagination jumps that our successors will take that really determine what we'll be listening to 20 years from now and not the extrapolation of Gordon's otherwise accurate curves.

In any event, I want to thank you all for attending. In particular, I think we owe a big vote of thanks to the speakers, the discussants, and the admirable staff of people that, together, put on this conference. I personally thank them all.

Alan Perlis

# Index